D1358457

THE PORTABLE PEDIATRICIAN'S GUIDE TO KIDS

THE PORTABLE
PEDIATRICIAN'S
GUIDE TO KIDS

LAURA WALTHER NATHANSON, M.D., F.A.A.P.

HarperPerennial
A Division of HarperCollinsPublishers

HarperCollins books may be purchased for educational, business, or sales promotional use. For information, please write to: Special Markets Department, HarperCollins Publishers, Inc., 10 East 53rd Street, New York, New York 10022.

FIRST EDITION

Designed by Nina Gaskin

ISBN 0–06–273347–8

96 97 98 99 00 ❖/RRD 10 9 8 7 6 5 4 3 2 1

To Sara and to dear friend Megan Callan,
for having been such great Kids;
to all the Kids and their parents who have let me be part of their lives;
and in memory of one special Kid, Jose Luis (Joey) Llamas.

▲

CONTENTS

Acknowledgments   ix
Introduction   xi

CHAPTER 1:   FIVE AND SIX   1
CHAPTER 2:   SEVEN AND EIGHT   99
CHAPTER 3:   NINE, TEN, AND ELEVEN   167

Appendix A: Deciphering the Growth Charts   255
Appendix B: Safety   263
Appendix C: Immunization Schedule   271
     Glossary   273
     Partial Bibliography   311
     Index   315

ACKNOWLEDGMENTS

●■▲■○

Thank you to my partners Fred Frumin, Rosalind Dockweiler, Gary Gross, Nick Levy, Chris Wood, and Sangita Bhasin (all M.D., F.A.A.P.'s) at El Camino Pediatrics for their professional skills, constant encouragement, and good humor. Thanks to our office therapists Sandra Blumberg and Candace Fagan for taking such good care of the Kids I send their way. Thanks to our office manager Denise Jennings for going far beyond the call of duty in her devotion to patients, doctors, and staff. Thanks to all the staff for taking such good care of our patients and for coping with my frequent organizational crises.

Thank you to my colleagues at UCSD Medical Center, Children's Hospital, Scripps Memorial Hospital, Scripps Encinitas, and Sharp Hospital for their fellowship and wisdom.

Thank you to Scripps Memorial librarians Janis Emmert and Esther Pusich, for putting up with a lot of requests so gracefully, and to the hospital's "Official Grandmother," Lanie Carter, for her support.

Thank you to all my friends at *Parents* magazine and at Channel 8 in San Diego, for their dependable good sense and good humor.

Thank you to my agent, Sandra Dijkstra, and her superb crew, for their enthusiasm and skills. Thank you to Rob Kaplan, who makes each book fun, and to Aileen Boyle, for all her hard publicity work. Thank you to Linda Weber, copy editor, who saved me from dozens of aesthetic embarrassments.

Thank you to Lois and Marshall Harrington, for their incredible talents at photographing a camera-shy pediatrician and a crew of Kids again, and again, and again, until we got it right. Thank you to the patient parents of those wonderful Kids: Christian Cummins, Elizabeth Deponte, Bethany and Rachel Gilstrop, and Amber and Adam Jarrah. Thank you to Joe Sweeney, personal trainer, for all these huge muscles.

Thank you most of all to Chuck, for hanging in there, taking the brunt of it all, for three books in three years; and to Marian and Ben Nathanson, for putting up with a very busy set of offspring.

INTRODUCTION

"Kids," I can hear my mother saying, "are little goats. Little human beings are children."

She had a point. But I prefer "Kids." "Child" is a tender, sentimental term. "Kid" has an aura of liveliness and spunk. Children are vulnerable, but Kids are sturdy. Children ought not to have problems, and when they do, it's dreadful and you can't focus on anything else. Kids are supposed to have problems—who doesn't? But they are not defined by them. Life goes on. Children feel like a different species to adults. Kids are like we used to be when we were younger.

This is a book about Kids. It's about how they develop in the last half of childhood, from ages five to twelve. I wrote it partly because it is such fun to be with Kids (I've known plenty of them in twenty-plus years of pediatric practice).

But I wrote it mostly because I think that as a society we are in danger of losing a sense of what it means to be a normal Kid. When we lose that sense, parents have a tough time feeling in charge and an even tougher time taking pleasure in their parenting role.

The very parents who felt so competent, so expert, and had so much fun when their children were little often start to feel fed up, put down, and done in during the second half of their Kids' childhoods.

For one thing, Kids this age increasingly belong to a larger world of friends, school, activities, sports, and the media. It's easy to feel that you're taking a back seat to all these other involvements, thrust into the role of chauffeur, bank, alarm clock, appointment book, concierge, chef, and vacuum cleaner.

At the same time that parents are demoted to these impersonal tasks, they are assailed by worries about whether their Kids are doing all right. There's so much to protect them from, to beware of, to monitor, and to try to control. It can feel as if most of the time you're staving off problems, from a missed orthodontic appointment to mood disorders and school failure.

The overwhelmed, underrewarded parent syndrome is partly a reflection of the child-care literature about children this age. There is a huge quantity of information in parenting books and magazines about the normal development of children up to age five, but almost nothing about normal development from ages five to twelve.

What literature there is focuses mostly on potential ways of tripping up. Helpful, well-written books they may be, but amassed on the shelves they communicate mostly worry. If you're the parent of a Kid, they whisper, "Be on guard for a bunch of troubles": depression, hyperactivity, lying, stealing, defiance, aggression, learning disabilities, obesity. (Yes, I confess: I've got a book—*No More Babyfat!* (HarperCollins, 1995)—on those shelves.) In fact, almost any behavior or trait, from being shy to being gifted to being an only or second child, can be seen as a problem.

Of course, there are more general books for parents but, by and large, they emphasize early childhood. Here is one with 480 pages on children from birth to age three and only 24 pages on those from ages six to eleven. Here's another that devotes a page of text and another of illustrations to describing how an infant learns to pull up to a standing position but only three paragraphs to how friendships change between the ages of seven and eleven.

In fact, this is a wonderful, fascinating age, filled with discoveries and achievements. Moreover, it's an age during which parents are enormously important to Kids.

Some of the milestones Kids attain are pretty obvious. Kids go from counting objects they can see and touch to manipulating symbols in their heads: from adding apples and dividing pizzas to performing long division and making charts. They go from decoding phonics to reading automatically. That is, if there is print in their field of vision, they comprehend its meaning without making a decision to do so. Once this happens, the world of print is as much a part of Kids' lives as their socks are—they take it for granted. But reading without stopping to think shouldn't be taken lightly: this is the sine qua non of true literacy.

They go from training wheels to fully geared mountain bikes, from peewee soccer—in which the rule is to kick the ball and run away—to team sports with leagues. By age twelve, most girls and some boys will show signs of puberty, and many of the girls will be as tall as their mothers and will have started menstrual periods.

It's easier to catch Kids in the act of growing up mentally and physically than it is to watch them mature morally, but they are working vigorously on their ideas about equality, justice, and fairness. These ideas are molded through working out dilemmas in daily life and through mulling over and talking about their conclusions. You may think they're squabbling over a hockey puck or whose turn it is to ride in the back with the dog; but it's quite likely they're working out a crucial philosophical principle.

But the most important milestone of this age is subtle, even invisible. This is the one that causes most of the behavior that can leave a parent downright flummoxed. What to make of the Five who talks your ear off and bores you to tears, the Six who breaks your heart by yelling "I hate you! You aren't my friend any more!", the Seven who goes upstairs to get a book and is discovered twenty minutes later staring in the mirror and muttering, the Eight who thinks the sun rises and sets by the cattiest little clique in the entire third grade, the Eleven who rolls his eyes and pretends not to be related to you in public. This is supposed to be fun? Yes. This is supposed to be important? Yes, indeed.

These are all signs that a Kid is developing the trait that defines us as human: self-consciousness.

Self-consciousness means that you have a public life and an intimate life, a core of self that is truly off-limits to your parents. You are no longer transparent to them. You are something of a mystery. This can be very discombobulating to both Kids and parents. It's at the root of an enormous amount of hurt feelings, anger, broken rules, unmet promises, and general distress. Parents feel that their Kid is growing away from them, rejecting them; Kids feel as if parents are talking to them from the moon.

No wonder. After all, when adults recall their own growing up, they don't remember, "Gee, that was the year I developed self-consciousness." Instead, they remember all the things that went well or badly from the point of view of their younger selves. And kids are hardly likely to say, "Mom, Dad, you've got to put up with this behavior; I'm working out the Meaning of Life."

During ages five through eleven, Kids learn to become their own audience. They start to narrate their lives to themselves and realize that they have secret, inner lives that are their own private preserve. One of the main functions of that inner life is to constantly monitor how a Kid measures up to an ideal self. That stretch to reach a little farther, do a little better, is the keynote of healthy development at this age—and it's brand new. Kids need to have self-images that are just a little bit superior to their present selves.

Parents are the guardians of that precious ideal self. The job of parents during this age is not a menial one nor an onerous one. It is to provide the stretch and support that Kids need to grow up to be competent, self-confident adults. This may sound like a concept of the Parent as Undergarment, but, in fact, that's not a bad analogy. A really good foundation garment doesn't constrict—it allows growth and activity, merely molding the wearer so that he or she presents a competent, confident self to the public.

When I see parents having a great time with their Kids, it's because they recognize with miraculous intuition what's going on. They seem able to sense where the Kid is right now and to judge how much challenge and stretch that Kid can handle. Then they apply that stretch in a way that (usually) doesn't send the Kid stomping out of the room, slamming the door in the parents' face. They are able to figure out how to change along with their youngster. How they listen, how they talk, how they set limits and negotiate and praise, what they laugh at together—it all moves right along.

Sometimes I think that these parents take their good fortune for granted, but I don't. I see other parents who love their Kids and who felt competent and authoritative when their children were younger. They want to go right on feeling competent as parents and having fun as a family, but they have trouble keeping up with the changes, because nobody warned them ahead of time. Parents in this situation get their feelings hurt, feel inadequate and overwhelmed, and don't have a good time. No wonder they often just opt out. When that happens, adolescence can be very, very tough.

In this *Portable Pediatrician's Guide to Kids,* I've merely followed the same format for the Fives to Twelves that childcare experts have done previously for babies, toddlers, and preschoolers. I've described how Kids evolve in their capacities to think, feel, learn, and behave. I talk about how they mature in their ideas about justice and equality. I look at the challenges they may face at school and at home, and how they grow in their ability to face those challenges. I've discussed how they grow and develop physically, both in their bodies' shapes and sizes and in what they can perform on the playground and playing field. I talk about illness and injury, and how Kids of different ages handle these traumas.

But most of all, I try to give parents a picture of how the changes in Kids' behavior reflect their progress through the intricate pathways to emotional, social, intellectual, and physical maturity. I talk about how the skills of parenting can grow as the Kid does, just the way these skills did when their Kids were much younger.

Here, then, is a different way of looking at Kids from age five to adolescence. I believe that parents will recognize their own Kids in each chapter, because Kids have to solve the same problems with the same basic tools no matter how enormous may be their differences in temperament, talents, interests, and styles.

I hope that parents will come away feeling more what they felt during their Kids' earliest years: confident, expert, in charge. Most of all, I hope that parents will find this guide to

Kids fun to read, and that reading it will make it more fun to be a parent.

The Portable Pediatrician's Guide To Kids

MAIN BOOK

There are three long chapters: Five and Six; Seven and Eight; and Nine, Ten, and Eleven. Each chapter is divided into ten sections.

OVERVIEW OF THE AGE

Each chapter starts with a peek at a child and parent interacting and a discussion of the way in which that interaction sort of sums up what that age is all about.

GROWTH OF THE SOUL

Here are the main conceptual tasks of this age and how Kids are equipped to think and feel about them. How do Kids learn to be patient, assertive, compassionate, honest? How do they learn to make friends, cope with the popularity bugaboo, deal with cliques? Parents can help the maturing process along in many effective ways.

RESPONSIBILITY, DISCIPLINE, AND LIFE AT HOME

Home is where you practice being civilized, which means something different to Kids of different ages/ —and to their parents and siblings. Home is where you learn not to be bratty, how (and why) to do chores, what to do with an allowance, and—as Rodney King says—how to all get along.

SCHOOL

It can be very tricky. School is a lot more complicated than it used to be, whether you're deciding if Taylor is ready for kindergarten or how important it is for Jordan to have a home computer or what to do about the peculiar fifth grade teacher or the new curriculum that focuses on something the brochure calls psychosexual whole world neo-ecology. Even without all that, it's tricky, and the trickiness changes a lot between kindergarten and sixth grade. Whether a Kid is precocious, right on track, or finds school a burden and a bore, parents are called upon to monitor what's going on. Also, it's fun just to know what the classroom ambience is likely to be in first or fourth grade.

EXERCISE AND SPORTS

If your Kid is a true jock, it's nice to know that he or she isn't being pushed too hard or underchallenged. If your Kid has average abilities, it's a good idea to know how and why to build self-confidence and skill. And if your Kid would prefer to be elsewhere when the whistle blows, you might want to consider whether and how to intervene. Boy, does this change with each age.

GROWTH AND NUTRITION

How much does a girl or boy grow at each age? What does a normal body shape look like at each age? What if you think your Kid is too tall, too short, too fat, too thin? When is puberty likely to occur, and what if it starts too soon? How do you explain puberty to Kids? Even harder, how do you get them to bond to their vegetables, instead of regarding them as The Enemy?

BEHAVIOR PROBLEMS

No Kid behaves perfectly all the time. Often the behaviors that bother parents most, like thumb-sucking or bed-wetting, are innocent and insignificant but annoying. How can you help without turning a minor problem into a Major Deal? Once in a while, it's obvious that something is very, very wrong. Maybe you're worried that your Kid is depressed, angry, withdrawn, too aggressive, or hyperactive. How can you tell for sure, and what can you do about it?

HEALTH AND ILLNESS

As Kids mature, they change in their ideas of what illness is, how medicine works, what doctors do and why, and what it means to let somebody else judge your body. It can be very delicate. And once puberty begins, which is often earlier than you'd think, it's a whole different ball game.

WINDOW OF OPPORTUNITY

Sometimes it's best to strike when the iron is hot, whether it's teaching somebody how to ride a two-wheeler or encouraging overnights at a friend's house or picking up keyboarding skills. My mother would say that striking a window of opportunity with a hot iron is a dreadfully mixed metaphor, and she would be correct.

WHAT IF?

No life is free from untoward experiences. Kids in each developmental age react differently, whether the stress they're exposed to is positive, like traveling, or mixed, like moving or adjusting to a new sibling, or traumatic, like hospitalization or divorce, or disastrous, like the death of parents or sexual molestation.

APPENDICES

APPENDIX A

The first appendix consists of growth charts with an explanation of how to use them—and how NOT to.

APPENDIX B

The second appendix lists sports and activities that present specific safety concerns.

APPENDIX C

This contains the immunization schedule for Kids of all ages.

GLOSSARY

The third section contains an informal glossary of medical terms (with pronunciations) that includes thumbnail sketches of symptoms and illnesses most likely to be useful to Kids' parents.

BIBLIOGRAPHY

The fourth section is a list of books and articles of interest to readers.

This book contains advice and information relating to health care for children. It is not intended to replace medical advice and should be used to supplement rather than replace regular care by your child's pediatrician. Since every child is different, you should consult your child's pediatrician on questions specific to your child.

While certain sections of this book contain advice for dealing with emergencies when a doctor is not available, it is recommended that you seek your child's pediatrician's advice whenever possible and that you consult with him or her before embarking on any medical program or treatment.

THE PORTABLE
PEDIATRICIAN'S
GUIDE TO KIDS

1

⬤■▲■⬤

FIVE AND SIX

Overview of the Age

Megan is spilling over with excitement and socks.

"Megan! You've got your Pocahontas bathing suit on again. I've told you that's not appropriate. That's just for dress up. Please get into your party dress. Your guests will be here any minute."

Her father is running out of tact. What he wants to do is to pick Megan up and march her to her room and remove that bathing suit. It is a two-piece fuchsia number with strips cut to make lots of fringe. Megan has modified it, pulling the right-hand strap off the shoulder and tucking it into the top to achieve a sarong effect just like Pocahontas in the movie. To make the resemblance even more accurate, she has stuffed in socks, creating a décolletage.

"And guess what!" Megan dances in front of him as he manoeuvres her down the hall. "My friends are all going to bring me a present, and then, and then, and then, guess what! We will have lunch and ice cream and play

games and have fun and sing and guess what!"

As they reach the door to her room, Megan twirls around and dashes to her toy box. She searches for a few moments and pulls out a stuffed tarantula.

"And guess what! I can sing the spider song." She thrusts the tarantula at her father, then twists her fingers into spiders and stares at them, entranced. "Listen to me sing the spider song. This is the spider song. Here is the first verse. 'The itsy bitsy spider went up the walker scout. And the rain came down. And spider washed out. And the itsy bitsy spider went up the walker scout again.'"

"Megan, it's time to change your clothes. Here's your party dress."

"And guess what! Look what I can do!" Megan hops and flaps her arms and then lies down on the floor and performs a peculiar squirm. She catches sight of a favorite stuffed animal. "And guess what! My roody old rooster hides under the covers and—"

▲ 1

The doorbell rings. "Oh oh oh! Here is my party!" Megan leaps to her feet and, to her father's shocked horror, poses in front of the mirror adjusting her décolletage. "Here is my happy birthday to you party!" She wiggles round her obstructing father and dashes down the hall.

Her father leans against the wall. He still can't stop jumping a bit every time Megan lobs over a "guess what!"—he's conditioned to expect a surprise. It's quite wearing. To say nothing of all the party preparations, tracing the etymology of walker scout (A form of jeep? A reference to the wilderness badge her 16–year-old cousin recently earned?), and that décolletage. Only gradually does it dawn on him that he has been the dupe of a master of the art of distraction. He finds himself staring into his own eyes in Megan's door mirror, her demure blue party dress still hanging from one finger, a green tarantula from another.

Bamboozled again.

Fives pretty much have parents wrapped around their little fingers. It's easy for them, because they really do think that parents are wonderful. They would do anything, anything to please their parents—anything, that is, but something that they really don't want to do, like take the socks out or put on the party dress.

Fives are into sex and bathrooms. "Poophead!" they call each other. Sometimes, out of the blue, they just say "Peepee!" and fall on the ground giggling. They are interested in breasts. Megan is not the only Five to stuff socks into her customized Pocahontas bathing suit. And who plays with Barbie dolls, solemnly changing outfit after outfit? Fives. Flat-chested dolls just don't pack the same wallop. If you catch two little Kids playing "doctor" with their clothes off, they're probably Five.

Tact is not a strong point in Fives.

"Why does that lady smell so bad? Why is that man so fat?" they query loudly, without apparent concern about wounding feelings. This is not on purpose. Fives are still learning that what they say can make another person happy or sad. They are just learning to see the world from somebody else's point of view. Fives blurting out something tactless can be distressing, but this trait also gives Fives their quality of guilelessness. Five has no ulterior motives.

Megan genuinely doesn't see why her father should be upset by her tacky outfit. In her mind, seeing herself from his point of view means looking in the mirror: and what she sees is beautiful Indian maiden Megan in her gorgeous filled out bathing suit. She doesn't then ask herself, "Why is Daddy upset?" She doesn't ask herself anything. She merely charges ahead to the task at hand: diverting Daddy from his strange attempt to make her change her clothes.

This guilelessness and transparency can be charming and frustrating. When parents start a rebuke, "Stop that! Can't you see that I'm . . ." Five is genuinely bewildered. No, Five can't really see that Mommy is exhausted from being up all night with the baby or that Daddy is changing a tire and can't play. Mommy or Daddy's anger seems to Five to be coming out of the blue. Five is crushed.

Sometimes you can catch a Five trying to puzzle out just what kind of behavior a parent wants. I see it in the office. A parent and I are discussing something serious and perhaps a little anxiety-producing. Five hears the tones of voice and immediately decides that the grown-ups are straying into dangerous territory and need distraction. Like Megan, most Fives are expert at this. "Look at me! See what I can do!" Five carols, spinning around and hopping on one foot.

That kind of unselfconscious pirouetting is one of the delights of Five. Five doesn't yet hold dear the concept of competence, of getting better at something. When Five executes a somersault, it doesn't matter if Five sprawls to the side or goes perfectly straight and ends with a leap to the feet. One is as good as another: somersault, Gertrude Stein pointed out, is a somersault is a somersault. Fives are always flapping their arms or drawing a red squiggle or making a funny face and calling, "Look at me! Guess what! See what I can do!"

Another charming facet of Fives is their take on the world.

Fives are crossing out of the magic years, when the real and the pretend blur. But if they can tell real and pretend apart, why is talking with a Five so much like talking with someone from another planet? It's because Fives assume that they understand what they've picked up from adults. They don't know what they don't know. When Fives hear something that doesn't quite make sense, they don't puzzle over it and ask about the incongruity. Instead, Fives force the information into place the way you would a recalcitrant jigsaw puzzle piece that almost but doesn't quite fit. Adults don't realize Five's misconception until it comes out in conversation.

That's why Five may believe that changing planes involves trooping across the wings in midflight, or that the Christmas carol describes a scene in which "angels washed their socks by night." When the spider goes up the walker scout, no doubt Megan has quite a vivid mental image of this arachnoid adventure.

Much of Five's energy is focused on getting his or her own way from a parent whom Five regards as the Ultimate Boss. When you adore somebody and want to get your own way, you use charm: flirtation, presents, displays. If you can't get your own way through charm, you turn up the heat and whine. If you continue to be at odds with that person, however, your heart breaks. How could such a beloved person deny you what you want? When that happens, you don't question your parents' authority, but you do let them know that your adoration has been injured. "I hate you!" Five screams. "You're not my friend!"

When Fives go to kindergarten, they focus on the teacher. Love the teacher, please the teacher. Everybody in the class is more focused on the teacher than on each other. Kindergarten starts out by feeling like an extension of home, of preschool. The other children are there to play with, your job is to play with them, and you may even make a true friend or two. But the real meaning of day-to-day life is embodied in how teacher feels about you.

A beloved adult in the presence of a Five can feel like a god. There's no doubt about it: bamboozlement or not, Five is a hard act to follow.

Turning the corner towards the age of six brings changes. Six discovers that when you do something or say something there is an audience that judges you. No longer can you say "Look at me!" and take for granted that people will drop what they're doing to watch you flap your arms. No longer can you assume that if they don't react the way you want them to, it's because you haven't insisted hard enough. Six suspects that when you want people to look, you'd better have something worth watching.

In discovering this, Six takes the first step in being aware of a public world. One of the most striking aspects of a public world is that it works by rules. This makes it different from home. Oh, parents may think that home runs by rules: that it's a rule not to draw on the walls or to hit the baby or whatever. Uh uh. Those aren't rules. Those are what Mommy and Daddy say you mustn't do. That's different.

Rules are what keep the public audience respecting you. Six wants very much to be respected. Being respected means that people don't laugh at you unless you are trying to be funny. They don't take your things or say mean stuff that makes you cry. Obeying rules gets you the approval of grown-ups in power. Understanding rules and following them makes you feel good about yourself.

This getting clear about rules and audiences is a big part of Six. To Six, rules can't be changed or modified; they must not be complicated in any way. This makes Six pretty tyrannical. You should never, ever lie: so it is wrong to say you like the sweater Aunt Ruth knitted when it is purple and itches. You should never, ever break a promise, so the doctor who has to do a blood test when Mom promised "no pokes" has forever violated your trust. (Yes, even though it was not the doctor who promised.)

For Six, parents are no longer the only bosses. More and more, rules are the boss. Adults are the sources, interpreters, and deciders of rules. When an adult changes a rule, or gives a command or request that isn't based on a rule, Six is likely to yell, "No fair!"

This preoccupation with rules and judgments keeps Six's eyes open wide all the time, looking about at the big world and all the people in it. This is strenuous and frightening. No wonder Six feels a strong pull back to the land of home, security, parental adoration—the world of Five. The land where there weren't really rules, but only What Mommy or Daddy Says.

The cozier the relationship with parents, the more attached the child and the harder it can be to forge on into the world of Six. Some Sixes can only do so by trying to erase that cozy attachment. It's as if they have to stomp on their younger homebound selves in order to assuage the panic of leaving home.

"All of a sudden, she's unbearable! The mouth on her!" "He won't do a thing I say! And he used to be the sweetest child!" "Stamping her foot! She glares at me as if she hates me!" It's easy to feel shocked, rejected, and betrayed. Six is

trickier and requires even more sophisticated parenting than did Five.

Nature conspires to let parents know that Six is a whole different ball game. Compared to Five, Six is not as cute. Five is still a bit round, with a babyish face. Six is pretty much elbows and knees and angles. Dennis the Menace is supposed to be Five; Calvin of Calvin and Hobbes is supposed to be Six.

Six is more of a challenge, clearly. Parents can feel dethroned from their roles as gods. What they get in exchange is a more complicated, savvy, sophisticated person. Six wants very much to be competent and cute. When Six thinks well of himself or herself, there's nobody more fun to be with.

As Christopher Robin says, "Now I am Six, and I am so clever, I think I will stay Six forever and ever."

Growth of the Soul

Fives want to be Good. Sixes want to be Right.

It may not seem like a big difference, but it is. What is good is decided by your parents. What is right is decided by—well, at first, it's decided by rules from outside. Rules from parents, teachers, coaches. At first, those rules seem clear, simple, and inflexible. Only as you grow do you start seeing rules as complex, having to take into account this situation or that exception. Then you start making your own interpretations of those rules, which makes it feel as if those rules come from inside.

Fives worry about what parents think of them. Sixes are discovering that their behavior determines how people in the Big World treat them. That's a huge difference. Fives rely on their parents' unconditional love. Bad behavior doesn't get tallied against them permanently; they get a clean slate each time. Sixes begin to realize that their behavior adds up in other people's minds. In the world of school, friends, and activities, other people might treat them well or poorly depending on their reputation—not just on how they behave at that particular moment. This is a difficult concept that takes a long time to develop. But it starts at this age.

If Fives aren't stretched a little bit, morally speaking, they can get stuck in the land of good and bad, of pleasing or not pleasing parents. If Sixes aren't stretched, they can get stuck regarding rules as inflexible—inflexible rules that aren't really fair at all because they don't take people's situations into account.

If Fives are protected against moving out into the big world, they're also denied the opportunity to develop a reputation on the basis of their behavior. If Sixes aren't held accountable for their reputations, they can't make them more and more creditable. Parents get to do the stretching and the letting go.

The trick to stretching Fives and Sixes is to catch what coaches and teachers call "the teachable moment." That's the moment in which the lesson to be taught is right before the child's eyes. How can I remember which loop comes first when I tie my shoes? How can I hold the scissors and paper so the cut is where I want it? How can I put my head under without the water coming up my nose? With a little help from an adult, Fives and Sixes can see for themselves how to do something. Without that help, the lesson may go unlearned. With too much help, the child tunes out. It doesn't feel as if he or she really owns the insight.

It's the same thing with moral lessons. What did I say that made Jimmy cry? If I really want Max's truck, can I just take it?

The prime moral lessons of Five and Six are honesty and compassion. (These pave the way to the prime social lesson, which is fairness.) Of course, you've been teaching Five/Six about these concepts since birth, by the way you yourself behave and by what kind of behavior you reward.

But things are different now. Honesty takes on a whole different complexion once you can tell the difference between real and pretend. Compassion becomes a real possibility as you learn to see things from somebody else's point of view.

HONESTY: THIS DOESN'T JUST MEAN PUNISHING LYING, IT MEANS ENCOURAGING HONESTY

It's natural to expect honest behavior and to be outraged when you don't get it. But that's not really teaching honesty. Teaching honesty means making many opportunities for Five and Six to practice and be rewarded for telling the truth, and telling them explicitly when they've been honest.

Fives

Fives' main concern is having their parents think of them as good. Moreover, Five is still just a step away from the magical thinking of preschool, where you could make something true just by saying it. In Fives' attempts to be thought well of by parents, they certainly might want to invent scenarios in which they are heroes. "Today, we went to the fire station and the firemen let us slide down the pole. And then they took us on the big truck and they had a house on fire and they let us put it out."

Five recounts this in his most believable voice, staring right into your eyes, excited and proud. For a moment, just a moment, you believe him. Then you catch yourself: no permission slip from school; not soaking wet. And then it hits you: This is a totally incredible tale. They never left the kindergarten classroom.

Fives can also be tempted to exaggerate a little about achievements. Especially if they've been working very hard for a long time and suspect that their parents are getting a trifle impatient. "Daddy! Daddy! I can ride my bike with the training wheels off!"

Hmm. This time, Five is excited and proud, but there's something fishy in his voice and the way he isn't making eye contact. Also, he doesn't rush to demonstrate his new skill.

These are teachable moments. In both cases,

telling a lie is clearly just wishful thinking. On one hand, it may be tempting to let such little falsehoods sneak by as part of the charm of Five. After all, the lie doesn't hurt anybody.

On the other hand, these are easy lies to confront in a gentle, kind, good-humored fashion. Correcting the lie isn't going to require a major loss of face, with subsequent tears and arguing. Calling Five on this kind of thing is good practice. (A good book: Dr. Seuss's very first one, called *And To Think That I Saw It on Mulberry Street*.)

"That's a super pretend story. Let's write it down and you can illustrate it. My, what an imagination you have! It's a good idea when you tell a pretend story to say that it's pretend."

"Someday soon those training wheels will come off. Then you can really surprise us! This was just a practice surprise. It's a good idea to say when you're practicing a surprise. You could say, 'When my training wheels come off, I'll run and shout to you!'"

Moreover, confronting Fives in such exaggerations confirms their suspicions that parents can read their minds and tell exactly what's going on there. This is a misconception that they will outgrow soon enough: make the most of it while it lasts.

Thus when Fives tell bold and brazen lies, ones that are designed to remove the blame from Fives and place it squarely on somebody or something else, they assume that you will see right through them. "I didn't squeeze that baby. She was sitting right there in her car seat and Brandy Rufus came up and sat on her and made her cry."

Right. Sure. Five, clenching fists and blinking back tears, red of face and now grabbing her crotch, doesn't even care that Brandy Rufus can be heard howling in the backyard, where he's been all morning. In Five's mind, this isn't really a lie because Five doesn't really expect it to be believed. It is a confession of the unbearable truth disguised as a plea that Five still be seen as perfect.

Correcting this kind of lie is tricky. The impulse is to punish the lie and to let the misbehavior wait to be dealt with later. This is too complicated for Five to deal with. It doesn't take into account Five's still limited mental capacity.

Fives need to believe that telling the truth will make them feel good and that telling a lie will not. So they must never be made to feel afraid of telling the truth. They need to know that if they tell the truth about having done something bad, the truth-telling will be recognized as commendable, but it won't get them off the hook for misbehavior. Fives need to have a parent recognize and deal firmly with lies that take the blame off them, but not in a scary fashion that threatens withholding of love.

Here are some techniques.
• When you catch Five lying, don't let it go unnoticed, even if the lie is unimportant.
• Don't explain how you know that it was a lie. This is likely to turn into an argument and deflect attention from the issue of honesty. Some Fives show disconcerting skill—you may be tempted to sign them up for the law SAT's.
• If you know Five did something naughty, don't ask for a confession. Address the misbehavior directly.

You come upon disorder in your handbag and Nellie is wearing a lot of gooey red. If you ask, "Did you take my lipstick out of my handbag and play with it?" you are likely to evoke a lie. Instead:

"My lipstick is gone from my bag and it's smeared all over your face! I get angry when someone takes my things without asking. And then makes a big mess. Now we have to take time to clean up this mess right now. That means no story time or playing Candyland or snack."

• Congratulate Five every time he or she tells the truth when you think it might have been tempting to lie.

"I'm so glad you told me about the tennis ball in the toilet. Now we can get it out before we flush the toilet and make a flood. Next time, I know you will remember not to play ball in the bathroom."

• Talk about when other people tell the truth or lie. Let Five know that you get very upset when someone you trust lies.

"The man who fixed my car told me that part cost much more money than it really did. He wanted to get extra money, so he lied to me. I will report that man so that other people know he is not honest. I sure won't go back there to have my car fixed!"

"Cassie told me that she was going to the library, but she went to the movies instead. I am very upset. She didn't tell me the truth. She can't go out in the evening again until she can prove to me that she will not lie about where she is going."

• If you catch Five in a serious lie, the lie must be punished, but in a way that does not encourage future lying. The corrections must be made in a firm, nonsympathetic voice. However, too much anger will scare Five and the lesson may well be lost—or backfire. After Five is taken to task in a serious way, forgiveness must follow. This can be very difficult when you are furious, but it's important.

"I know that it is easy to hug Baby Lucia too hard. That can happen when you feel angry at her. When she gets hurt from being squeezed, she cries and you feel bad. But you must tell me the truth. If you don't I don't know when to believe you. I can't trust you."

"I am upset that you hugged Baby Lucia too hard. From now on, no touching Baby Lucia unless I am right there. But I am more upset that you didn't tell me the truth. I want you to lie down on your bed and think about that until the timer goes off in five minutes."

"Now the five minutes is up. I know you thought and thought about telling the truth, even when it is hard. You are my good thinker. Let's take Baby Lucia and go to the park. She wants to see her big sister pump high on the swings."

• If you ask Five to keep a secret, make it seem a whole lot different from lying.

Fives can be confused about whether keeping a secret is the same thing as telling a lie. Indeed, sometimes it is. So when Five has a secret, or is asked to keep one, it's good for adults to keep the whole thing light. The secret-sharers get to whisper loudly and openly and giggle a lot.

• Go over "white lies" ahead of time or very soon after.

"Daddy is going to tell Aunt Dill that he loves the tie she gave him even though he doesn't. He doesn't want to hurt her feelings."

"I told Mommy I like her haircut even though we all know it's too short. To me she always looks beautiful. I want her to know that."

Sixes

Sixes lie in a whole different manner.

For one thing, they have more at stake. Six is starting to understand the meaning of having a reputation. Surely, reasons Six, if you recount that you have done strong, brave, exciting things, people will treat you better because they think you are strong and brave. It only occurs gradually to Six that when these escapades are shown as imaginary, you are seen not as strong and brave but as someone who doesn't tell the truth. Sixes may also lie to get something they want or to get someone else into trouble.

For another thing, lying is more complicated for Six. Keeping a secret, telling a white lie—these are praised. Moreover, telling the truth can get you into trouble: "Tattletale, tattletale!" the other Kids taunt, and your parents look at you disapprovingly. Well, but, Ginny did say she was going to eat the dog food, and if she did, that would be wrong, wouldn't it?

It's all very confusing. Some strategies can help Six figure it all out.

• Conspicuously model truth-telling behavior.

It helps Six to know that even adults can have trouble confessing to mistakes.

> "I put Mommy's white shirts in the wash with your red socks and now all her shirts are pink. She will be so upset. I wish I didn't have to tell her I made such a bad mistake. She'll be really mad at me. But if I don't tell her the truth, she will not trust me anymore."

• Demonstrate how one can tell the truth without hurting somebody's feelings.

> "I really can't stand the perfume Aunt Marty sent. But I don't want to hurt her feelings. Maybe I can say, 'My, that is SUCH a fragrant perfume!' That way I don't really tell a lie."

• When a Six achieves a white lie, whether in words or by behavior, it's helpful to recognize that achievement.

> "When you opened your present I know you were disappointed. You wanted a Gameboy and Papa Frank gave you a game of dominos instead. But you smiled and said thank you. It was more important to make him feel good than to tell him you were disappointed. I think you did the right thing. It was kind of a lie, but it was a good lie."

• Whenever possible, don't put Six in a position of being tempted to lie.

If you know who committed the mischief, don't ask. See **Fives,** earlier in this section.

• If you are asking for a confession, let Six know what the penalty will be—both for the "crime" and for a lie—before Six decides whether to tell the truth or to lie. The penalties should not be so severe or humiliating that Six feels like an unredeemably bad person.

> "I need to know who broke the glass plate. Whoever broke the plate will have to earn some money to buy a new one. And the new plate will have to stay right in the cupboard and not be used for cookies. If nobody tells me who broke the plate, I will be very upset. I won't know whether I can trust my family. I probably won't be able to smile or laugh for a while. If the person who did it tells the truth, I will be happy again."

• Try to make clear what tattling is. There's a difference between tattling and alerting a grown up.

"Yes, I hear you: Cassie is on the phone instead of doing her homework. But it is not your job to tell me if Cassie does something naughty like that. It is your job to tell me if you think somebody could get hurt doing something naughty. I am not going to rush up to Cassie. I will give her a chance to tell me the truth herself."

"I'm glad you told me when Lucy and Paul were trying to climb out the window. They could have been hurt."

• If Six willfully sticks to a lie, take it seriously. The lie needs to be condemned, but Six still needs to feel like a cherished person.

"I know how hard it is to change from a lie to telling the truth. The reason I am being so firm about it is that I know how hard it is. But if we don't tell each other the truth, we cannot trust each other. I can't be my happy self until I can trust you. I want you to go and lie down in your room, without a book or a toy or TV or music, until you can tell me the truth. Then we will talk about what to do about (whatever the lie is about)."

If this doesn't work and you are sure Six is lying, something is amiss in Six's life. Sixes who stick to a lie in the face of serious parental disapproval are too angry or too scared to tell the truth. That means that they are very, very angry or very, very scared.

Find out what is going on. If you can't figure it out, discuss the problem with your pediatrician.

• Praise Six when he or she tells the truth in a difficult situation, but do so carefully. You don't want Six to think that bad behavior will be excused and forgotten if the truth is told.

"That was hard to tell me that Miss Waters had to talk to you about throwing the books in class. I am very glad you told me the truth. It is wrong to throw books. Books are special things. They take hard work to write and make. If you wrote a book, you wouldn't want to think people were throwing it around. I think this is such an important thing to learn that I want you to find two of your own really good books that we can give to the Salvation Army for children who don't have enough money to buy books."

• If Six continues to lie on a fairly regular basis, something is up. Find out what it is. But continue to discipline the lying.

Such repeated lying is an attempt at communication. Often, what Six is trying to say is that he or she needs more attention at home. A "cure" may involve simplifying life so that there is room for one-to-one time with each parent, time spent focused on and enjoying Six.

In fact, frequent lying may be due to a vicious cycle. Six gets attention for lying, but it's negative, critical attention. That makes Six feel bad about himself or herself, which leads to anger at parents, which leads to more lying. The cure: Catch Six being good. Notice and talk about achievements. Don't let every conversation and comment be judgmental—about whether Six is behaving or not. Be sure you're giving Six lots of physical affection.

Six might also be striving for notice at school. A Six whose social skills are immature may be lost in a first-grade classroom. Lying about possessions, achievements, and so on may seem like a short and easy path to acceptance.

A Six having academic trouble in school can become panicky and depressed and lie out of a deep feeling of terror. Make sure that Six is progressing well and is not at sea when it comes to reading and math.

COMPASSION: LEARNING TO PUT YOUR-SELF IN THE OTHER GUY'S SHOES

Fives and Sixes have made a lot of progress in compassion compared to their younger selves. When an older infant sees another one crying, the onlooker often will cry in sympathy. A toddler may try to comfort an upset little friend by giving him her *own* teddy bear to hold. A preschooler may give that weeping friend the friend's own bear: Four has put himself into the friend's shoes to a degree and given the friend what Four himself would want in similar circumstances.

Fives and Sixes make giant strides in the art of compassion. They start to realize that what *they* would want in a sticky situation isn't necessarily what *somebody else* wants. At the same time, it gradually dawns on Fives and Sixes that when someone else is praised, this doesn't mean that they themselves have been left out or criticized. At some point, Kids at these ages even start to think before doing or saying something that is likely to hurt another's feelings.

Of course, parents have been pointing this stuff out all along. Finally, at this age the lessons start to take. They can take even more effectively when parents talk about compassion as a difficult and worthwhile attainment.

"You worked so hard on your picture, even though you couldn't find the colors you wanted. You were so frustrated. Then Mr. Hamilton chose Nicki's picture to go up on the wall. That made you so jealous and angry. It's hard to remember that Mr. Hamilton chose your clay vase to show on his desk. And it's hard to remember that you like Nicki and it's nice to see Nicki be happy."

"The lady can overhear you ask why she smells bad. I know you are curious, but your voice is louder than you think, and she can see you staring at her. She is turning away and looking upset. I'm afraid her feelings are very hurt."

"That little girl on TV is crying because somebody stole all her toys. What could we do to help?"

"George is having trouble learning how to read. It makes him feel bad. We don't want to remind him that he is having trouble. That might make him think that we are bragging about how easy it is for you. When he comes over to play, what would be some good things that you don't have to be able to read to do?"

"Remember when you lost your red Power Ranger down the gutter? That's how Joey feels about losing his Octopus Man."

"The big Kids laughed when you started to cry when Mark got hit by the swing. They called you a baby. But you knew Mark was hurt and you felt bad for him. That's very grown up. Those big Kids weren't acting grown up when they laughed. I am proud of you."

Rewarding caring actions with a tangible goody is likely to backfire. "Poppy dear, if you'll stop building your model and play with little Tyler for a few minutes so he stops crying, I'll give you two of these cookies."

Poppy is likely to amuse Tyler in return for this small bribe, but the next time Tyler cries, she will be even more reluctant than usual to tend to him without the prospect of a reward. She may even hold out for three cookies and a glass of chocolate milk to boot.

Instead, continue to appeal to compassion.

"Oh, Tyler is so unhappy! He is frustrated and his fingers still hurt and he's too little to amuse himself. Poppy, can you think of anything to make him feel better?"

EMOTIONAL DEVELOPMENT

As Fives and Sixes venture out into the larger world, they need more emotional tools: patience; resilience in the face of teasing, correction, and criticism; and tolerance of being less than perfect.

PATIENCE

One of the great gifts parents can give a Five/Six is the ability to withstand waiting.

A very few Fives and Sixes never get bored, often because they have a passion. They carry fanny packs filled with superheroes, dinosaurs, planes, trucks, Barbies, whatever. Sara, at Six, was utterly engrossed in model horses. When we arrived in our new home before the van with the precious boxes did, she invaded her father's sock drawer and named each rolled-up pair. "This is Eclipse, and this is White Arrow, and this is Land of Sunshine," she chanted, making them canter and jump.

But most of the time Fives and Sixes need to be helped. They need to be provided with ideas of what they could do with materials on hand or how they could use their imaginations.

"The doctor is going to be a little late. Let's see if you can draw a mural on the paper that is on the exam table."

"We have to wait in the airport while the plane gets cleaned up. My, look at the pictures on the wall! All those skiers and skaters! Can you make up a story about some of the pictures? Then come and tell me the best ones."

"The fluoride needs to stay on your teeth until the timer goes off. I know it tastes yucky. Why don't you pretend in your mind that you are in charge of the Wild Animal Park and that you are going to feed and pet all the animals?"

"This will be a long car trip. Be sure to take along some tapes and some toys for playing quietly. No books or Gameboys, though, because using those could make you carsick."

RESILIENCE

Sometimes a Five/Six will burst into tears at the smallest sign of criticism, rejection, or teasing. It's easy just to say that such a child is very sensitive. But this doesn't help the Kid to become a little more able to cope. Something is going on.

Inexperienced Kids

A Five/Six who hasn't had much experience with other Kids may find the rough-and-tumble of the classroom and playyard overwhelming. His or her only recourse may seem to be to cry or to get an adult to come to the rescue. The passage of time usually helps. So do the techniques that teach assertiveness (see **Social Development,** page 13).

Over-conscientious Kids

Sometimes a young child will feel as if he or she has to be perfect or love will be withdrawn. Such a child will turn pale and tremble or cry when corrected even kindly and gently. What helps here is a conversation with an experienced teacher, pediatrician, or counselor, and a rethinking of how the child is being disciplined. The techniques that help with perfectionism also help here (see **Tolerance of Imperfection and Frustration,** below).

Feeling fragile

Sometimes parents can't help thinking of a child as specially vulnerable. This is especially likely to happen if the youngster was very ill in infancy or if a previous child has died.

Regarding a child as specially vulnerable can happen even when the child was never really sick. An abnormal result of a prenatal test, later proved to be an error, can produce these feelings in parents. Even the recommendation of a change of formula or a blood test to rule out infection in a newborn can lead parents to see a child as particularly fragile. New babies seem so mysterious and delicate that human beings are designed to worry over them intensely.

These feelings can persist even after the medical concern is long past and the child is clearly normal and healthy. Parents may express their worry directly or may reveal their concern indirectly by body language and tones of voice. Counselling in such cases is extremely valuable. Very often, both the parents and the "vulnerable" child benefit from such counselling. Pediatricians can help parents both to recognize what's happening and to obtain assistance.

Five and Six are the ages in which this kind of worry is likely to become intense as Kids leave the home nest. It's a good time to tackle it head-on.

Manipulative Kids

A few Fives/Sixes will exaggerate how sensitive they are to avoid discipline. Such Five or Sixes are usually social, even rowdy children with adoring parents.

Parents of such a child soon learn that the merest hint of disapproval brings an avalanche of apparent self-hate: "I'm no good! I can't do anything right! You hate me!" This make parents, at least, collapse in guilt. However, onlookers can detect indications that the child is putting on an act. The child watches the adult with an assessing eye, has a false note in the voice, and can be

completely distracted from the outburst, only to resume again.

The cure is to good-humoredly but firmly state the correction or criticism and not reward the apparent anguish with hugs and cuddles and apologies.

TOLERANCE OF IMPERFECTION AND FRUSTRATION

"It's terrible! I'm so stupid! I can't do anything!"

Hear that? It's probably a Six. Fives are usually spared attacks of perfectionism. They think they're just fine the way they are. It's Sixes, newly aware of being performers with an audience, who collapse in self-criticism.

One normal parental response is to leap in with reassurance. "It's a wonderful picture! That dog looks just like the Reichers' Great Dane! You're a terrific artist!"

Whoops!

"It's not a dog! It's a horse! I told you it was terrible!"

Stomp. Rip. Tears.

Another normal reaction is to argue.

"How can you say you're stupid? Look how well you can read. You're in the top of the group!"

Whoops!

"I'm not the top! Francesca is the best reader! She can read chapter books! I'm so stupid dumb!"

The hard truth is that perfectionism feeds on parental distress. Children often take such comments by parents as a secret wish that the child should indeed be perfect or that parents can't trust the child to feel good about himself or herself on the basis of merit and so have to make up extreme praise. The more parents bolster, contradict, and argue, the worse the perfectionism gets. Six is a spin artist, perversely twisting parental reassurance into criticism.

Tears and tantrums ensue. At this point, a

well-meaning parent generally either becomes exasperated and escalates arguments or concerned and escalates reassurances. Six takes either response as a challenge and just goes wild.

"I hate myself! I am so dumb!" and even "I wish I was dead!"

Most of the time, this kind of reaction does not indicate depression or devastatingly low self-esteem. On the rare occasions that it does, there are other signs: general sadness; inability to take pleasure in life; trouble eating, sleeping, and playing; and withdrawal from friends and family. A depressed child's complaints ("I'm so stupid, I'm so dumb, I hate myself!") sound bitter and sad rather than frustrated and angry. A depressed child is more likely not to make an effort than to be dissatisfied with the result. Of course, if you see these signs of depression, get help!

However, when statements of self-disregard are not accompanied by other such serious signs, the question is how to deal with a little Kid in the throes of perfectionism. Here are some strategies.

• Call an end to the enterprise when you see ominous signs developing. "Enough painting for today! Time to clean up and go outside and dig holes." This is briskly stated, accompanied by the parent's getting in there and picking up the paint water. No asking if Six is ready to stop painting. No arguments. No apologies. No explanations, either: "I can see you are getting frustrated" is likely to bring on an explosion of temper.

• Once the display of perfectionism begins, underreact a bit. Behave as though being discontented with one's performance is a normal and expected part of being a human being. Do not make suggestions about how to improve performance. Do not argue. Do not reassure.

• Sixes in a twit are very sensitive to tones of voice. An "I've been there myself" inflection gets a better response than sympathy, exasperation, or brisk cheerfulness.

• The most reassuring thing a parent can do is to name Six's feelings and say that they are normal, not scary, and not something that parents get all worked up about.

"Boy, drawing can be frustrating."

• Sixes absorb how parents react to frustration and mistakes. If they see self-forgiveness, humor, and resilience, they're likely to imitate.

"Oh gee, I can't get these egg whites to whip up. I forgot to get the cream of tartar at the store. Sometimes I just forget things. Oh flibbertigibbet! I think I'll go kick a can!"

SOCIAL DEVELOPMENT

They've got a lot on their plates, these Fives and Sixes. They need to find a way to join a group of children, make friends, stand up for themselves, be clear on what is fair, and deal with their own and other people's sexual curiosity.

MAKING FRIENDS

Shyness means not making overtures to other children and not responding to overtures from them. It means retreating from contacts with adults who aren't intimately known. Many Fives and some Sixes are shy by this definition. Often, it just means that right now, as they take the big plunge into public life, they need some time to warm up.

Most Fives and Sixes warm up on their own. After a few weeks of kindergarten, they comfortably join groups, seek out other children, and make friends. What these Kids need from adults is permission to go at their own pace, without being labeled shy, or being hovered over, coaxed, nagged, or bullied into social activity.

Some shy Fives, though, need a little help. Children whose temperaments are not very outgoing and spontaneous may need extra incentive.

When that's the case, there are two avenues to assistance. One is to help even such a young Kid find a best friend. This is usually not easy. Best friends at this age tend to play with each other for extended periods. They are nice to each other in the way older Kids can be. Such a best friend is a rare bird and to find one takes a lot of searching or luck. Best bet: Look for a Kid with an even temper, a happy disposition, and a sustained attention span.

The second avenue is to help a shy little Kid learn techniques that will make him or her comfortable in groups and to communicate your own cheerful confidence that friends will come in time.

Convey confidence

• Be sympathetic but optimistic.

> "I felt funny around other children too when I was your age. But after I learned how to practice being with them and playing, I started having fun."

• Be careful not to unwittingly feed into the shyness. If your child clings to you and refuses even to look at another child or an adult, let the child own the behavior. Don't panic or apologize or hug the child closer as if to protect him or her. Don't keep trying to lure or command your child to enter into the action. Make casual, cheerful comments about the activities:

> "Why, that Bongo is just like yours at home." "I guess they like to jump, too. I wonder what it feels like to land on that moon strip."

• Don't label or let others label your child as shy. Name the behavior in a calm and matter-of-fact manner.

"Terry likes to watch awhile before he joins in." "Isabelle likes to think things over before she tries something new."

Facilitate friendship

• Find a child who shares Five/Six's current interests. This should be an unaggressive, non-boisterous child. Ask the child to come to play at your home. But don't just leave them alone together with some toys. Instead, involve them in something riveting so that they can talk about the activity. Baking something, planting and digging, going to an interactive museum or a very involving play area are all good choices.

• If your child clings to you even in this only-one-visitor situation, try to engineer a minor crisis in which everybody has to help. The KoolAid spills or the bag of groceries rips.

• Whatever you do, don't embarrass your child by ordering him or her to interact. Don't let your child think you believe he or she is a failure because of the shyness.

• If, and only if, all else fails, have a thrilling children's video and a good snack ready. After one or two afternoons just sitting together, a shy child may feel comfortable enough to play.

Make manners a requirement

Inform a shy Five/Six that shyness with grownups is not good manners. Most adults in this country regard good manners in a child as including eye contact, a smile, and a few words of greeting. Rehearse these with your child at home, and remind him or her before going out. A shy child may need incentives to achieve this: a star chart or a small reward.

Practicing unshy behaviors with stuffed animals is also helpful. The parent can be the shy one, and Five can practice being the scary group that the shy one is trying to enter. Here is a scenario for joining a group.

• Watch from the sidelines for a bit.

• Spot a same-sex child who looks nice and who isn't a ringleader, in the center of activity.

- Approach with a smile.
- Say "Hi, my name is Kevin."
- Have an opening gambit: "How do you play that game?" or "I like your dinosaur shirt" or "I've got one of those."
- Listen to the answer and then say something in response.

Then practice in real life, at the playground or the park. Praise each step Five or Six accomplishes, even if progress takes days.

"Every time we go to the park, Christian holds my hand tightly and watches. He grabs my head down and whispers in my ear, 'That looks like a nice boy. I like that boy.' It's the same boy each time. The boy's name is Bubba; I hear the other children calling him. But Bubba's mother isn't at the park, and I can't just go up to a strange child and invite him over to play."

No, but she could write a note to Bubba's parents with Christian's phone number and an explanation, and send it with Bubba's accompanying adult.

Rarely, a child will be severely shy and withdrawn. Sometimes this is actually inherited. There is usually nothing abnormal going on, but such withdrawn behavior can keep a Kid from exploring all the opportunities open to him or her. Such a Kid often benefits from the special skills of a counselor trained in helping shyness.

ASSERTIVENESS

Being nonassertive is not the same thing as being shy.

A nonassertive Five/Six can be outgoing, pleasant, and have many friends. He or she just doesn't stand up for himself or herself when conflict arises. (A shy Five/Six, on the other hand, may have trouble entering a group, but may very well object loudly when somebody behaves offensively.) An nonassertive Five/Six can get along very well if the surroundings fit his or her style. But the usual social life of Kids this age requires a certain amount of assertiveness.

Boys can be more isolated than girls by a lack of assertiveness. Boys tend to communicate by actions rather than through conversation. By second grade, most boys find little to talk about with each other, even with best friends. So nonassertive boys lose out on two counts: they get no action-oriented contact and no conversations, either. Both sexes need to be able to take turns being leader and follower and to express both positive and negative feelings.

Adults usually focus on telling young children what *not* to do when conflict arises: "No hitting! No mean teasing!" When adults tell Kids what *to* do, it is often something wimpy: "Go find the teacher!" "Just walk away!" Or something vague: "Use your words!" These directives often don't work in real-life situations, and they may keep a naturally nonassertive child from learning to stand up for himself or herself.

Here are some specific suggestions:
- Make it clear that parents approve of being assertive. Being assertive doesn't mean being aggressive and trying to make somebody feel bad. There's no need to condone mean teasing, hitting, pinching, pushing. Being assertive just means standing up for yourself when you need to.
- Don't overly encourage going to the teacher when conflicts arise or when another child is mean. Let Five/Six know what are appropriate other options. When these fail, or if Five/Six is honestly scared of a bully or a big Kid, then going to the teacher is appropriate.
- Be specific and act things out, using dolls or stuffed animals. It often helps if the child gets to be the attacker and the adult acts out the assertive strategies first and then reverse roles.

"When I was little, I didn't know what to do when my friend Cash tried to push me around. Let's use the stuffed bear and the stuffed frog. Cash is the bear and I'm the frog. One day I got a beautiful fire truck. I wanted Cash and me to play firefighters. But Cash said in a big voice, 'You give me that truck right now! I want to play with that truck.' So I didn't know what to do. Usually I would give Cash what he wanted, but it was my own beautiful fire truck!"

What could a Kid do to contend with a Cash?

• Say an I statement of intent. "I want to play with my own truck." That's more effective and less contentious than "You can't have my truck." It makes the speaker feel bigger and stronger, too.

• Say an I statement of feeling. "I don't like it when you grab my truck away from me." That's much more effective and less demeaning than, "You always grab! What's the matter with you !"

• If those statements don't work, make a demand, delivered in a loud voice, with a stamp of the foot and a jutting of the chin: "You give me back my truck right now!" That's much more dignified than, "You give it back or I'll tell on you!"

• If that doesn't work, make a face, using your fingers and eyes and tongue.

• It's okay to call names if they're not hurtful. "You Phenotype! You Blitherskate!" Hurtful teasing, like calling somebody "retard" or a racial epithet, is forbidden.

Putting this into action takes guts and practice. Parents can help by noticing and appreciating even small steps.

> "I heard you tell Noah that you didn't want to play pirates again. That was terrific." "I liked your big voice when you told Jasmine to put down your can of bugs. I bet next time you'll stamp your foot, too."

ALL ABOUT SEX

All Fives and Sixes get sex education, many of them engage in sex play together, and some of them masturbate when in the presence of others. So sex is a big topic.

The facts of life

Some sex education may not look like sex education, but it is:

> "We don't like Marcie. She's adopted. We aren't going to play with her." "Barbie and Ken can't have a baby because they aren't married." "My little brother went to the doctor and the doctor broke his penis because he cried." (Circumcision)

Some of it is all too obviously sex education:

> "Kari and Mark were having sex in the coatroom!" (The 6-year-olds were holding hands and kissing.)

> "What's French kissing?" (Variations: What's gay? What's sixty-nine? What's...? Fill in the blank.)

> "I'm glad I'm little, so I don't have to have sex and get AIDS." (The child who said this was actually a Four.)

> "We don't let Denny play. He plays with girls. He's a fairy." (And this child was a Three.)

Most experts advise parents to wait for children to ask questions and to answer those questions simply and honestly. They expect young children to ask things like, "Where do babies come from?" or "How does God make the people?"

Sometimes children do ask these things, but when they do it's usually long before Five and Six. Many children never ask. Sometimes that's because they assume that they know the answers.

> "Dr. Nathanson makes the baby at the hospital."

"The mother swallows a seed the father gives her when they kiss and the baby grows in her stomach."

"The mother feeds the baby through her belly button." (Which is why this young lady had carefully snipped a little hole in all her own clothes, right over her belly button.)

Sometimes the reason Kids don't ask is that they've received so many signals that parents are uncomfortable with the topic.

In any event, the problem is not so much that Fives and Sixes get the facts wrong when they get them from other Kids. That can be corrected later. The problem is that the underlying attitudes about sex are contagious. The innocence of Five/Six is in jeopardy when parents leave sex education to casual information. Children this age are vulnerable to everything they hear and see and to everything their friends and classmates hear and see, too. That means TV at home or anywhere, news reports, commercials, billboards, songs, overheard conversations, movies they glimpse when their parents think they are sleeping, and on and on.

Parents who feel that the biggest favor they can do for their Kids is to keep silent are losing an opportunity. Very often, children get the idea that by their silence parents are expecting them, ordering them, or pleading with them not to ask. When they suspect this is the case, most Kids will do anything to avoid bringing up the subject. Not only will they not ask their questions, they will reject information when it is offered, reflecting what they perceive as their parents' reluctance.

When a child is put into the position of protecting a parent, the whole relationship gets out of kilter. Children grow and learn best when they feel confident that their parents are fully adults, in charge and able to deal with the world of other grown-ups. In America, the world of grown-ups is practically synonymous with the world of sex. When parents give the impression that they are frightened of or unable to deal with the realm of sex, it can make a Kid feel as if parents might not be able to cope with other things, as well.

Silence can even be dangerous. A child who is molested may feel absolutely unable to confide in a parent who, in the child's mind, might react in a way the child thinks is not grown up: frightened, shocked, panicked, angry. Even a young child may take on the whole burden himself or herself, dealing with the molester and shielding the parent.

When parents talk with Kids about sex, youngsters get the comfortable feeling that parents are "askable" and "tellable." Being askable and tellable means that parents treat sex the same way they treat other important issues in a Kid's life. This helps to establish a basis for conversation that will stand you in good stead in the years later on.

In fact, talking about sex between parent and child is a way of "immunizing" a Kid from some of the fallout of our oversexualized culture. If sex is something that Mom or Dad can talk about without fuss, the mystique of the forbidden doesn't gain much hold. By without fuss, I mean without sitting down at the table for a somber, embarrassed birds and bees conversation. This kind of conversation usually doesn't work. The child is too self-conscious, because of the parent's discomfort, to take away anything but a desire to avoid further talks in the future.

For some parents, talking about sexual matters means just continuing the conversation started when their child was a toddler or preschooler. Others are starting from scratch. In either case, here are some suggestions that may make it easier to deal with the topic.

• Talk about it when there is a cue: a pregnant friend, an advertisement, a picture book.

"Janie's mother is going to have a baby. That baby is inside its special place in her belly. If you watch, maybe you will see her shirt bounce when the baby kicks!"

• If there isn't a cue, invent one:

"My, look at that field of wheat. When I was a little girl, I thought that spaghetti grew like that. I thought people would come and cut down the noodles and put them in boxes! I thought a lot of things that weren't true. I even used to think that if I saw a little boy naked, I would get pregnant and have a baby."

• Listen to the ideas of Five/Six, and see if the Kid can reason around to the correct interpretation.

"But Janie's mother doesn't have a hole in her shirt. How does the food get through her belly button to the baby?

• Keep the explanations brief and simple.

"The father makes a seed that comes out his penis. The mother makes an egg in a special part of her body deep inside. The father puts his penis into the entrance to that special part, and when the seed and the egg meet, they start a baby."

Don't be surprised if the information doesn't seem to take. Many well-taught Fives and Sixes still tell me that babies come from K-Mart, even if they've felt the baby kick. They really do know the facts; they just don't think the facts are as good an explanation as K-Mart. Or maybe they think that K-mart is the polite, grown up, public explanation.

More important than facts, parents communicate feelings and values. They do this best when they keep the emotional tone reasonably calm. Yelling and cursing immobilize Kids; they literally don't hear what's being said.

"Yes, those teenagers on TV are going to have a baby. Isn't that too bad. Those teenagers like to go to parties and surf. They don't have any money. They haven't finished school, so they won't be able to get good jobs. They will have to stop going to school and parties and surfing and work hard all day. They won't even be able to be at home with their baby. They will have to work hard all day and then come home and wash the baby's dirty diapers. The poor baby. His mother and daddy won't have fun with that baby. They won't have time to play."

The following is a good guide to what Fives and Sixes need to know (that is, what they'll hear first from somebody else if they don't hear it from you pretty soon).
• How the baby gets started (see explanation suggested earlier in this section).
• Where the baby grows (not in the stomach where the food goes).
• How the baby exits (not from the same place the poop exits).
• What a cesarean section is (if they don't hear it from a friend, they'll see it on TV).
• What adoption means (most families openly discuss this with adopted children; it's the non-adopted ones who need to hear a straight, kind explanation).
• What happens during menstruation (where is there a Five who hasn't seen a feminine protection ad on TV?).
• What masturbation is (Kids need to know what it is to fully understand that it is okay, but private).

What if a Kid encounters much more sophisticated concepts—homosexuality, prostitution, AIDS? For the sake of continuing conversation, it's important not to react in an intense, shocked, angry manner. Many parents will be able to give a simple explanation along with their own judgment on the matter. If your feelings allow you to do so, separate your condemnation of behavior from your attitude toward those who engage in it.

If a topic comes up that you feel strongly is not appropriate to discuss, don't just ignore it. Instead, say

> "That's very grown-up stuff. It's not secret, but it's really for older people. I promise we'll talk about it when you are older."

Be careful, though; your Kid may already have been exposed to a great deal of information, true and false, about that topic. A cautious response is to ask the Kid, "What do you think?"

Masturbation

> "Only Mommy and Daddy and the Doctor are allowed to touch you down there. Did anybody else ever touch you there?"

> "Yes!" Secret smile.

> "WHO?" Heart in mouth.

> "Me!"

Girls and boys both masturbate, and especially below the age of Six, many do so without much self-consciousness in the presence of family or friends. Usually a tactful whispered comment reminds the young person that this behavior is not socially acceptable.

When should parents be concerned about masturbation? When it is done from anxiety or boredom or as a response to genital irritation or because of too intense a preoccupation with sex. You can tell that it's not "ordinary" mastur-

bation when a child appears driven to masturbate and is unable to stop when asked or when offered a different, tempting activity. Sometimes the timing of such masturbation tells you what's driving the child: perhaps it occurs only when getting ready for school or watching an adult TV program or when the new baby is being nursed.

Excess masturbation will not hurt a child physically in the long run, though it may produce irritation and discomfort in the short run. Nor will it cause mental or emotional problems in and of itself. But some of the reasons underlying excessive masturbation—anxiety, inappropriate encounters with adult sexuality, the rare case of sexual molestation—can themselves produce such difficulties. The Kid who masturbates in school may be indicating that he or she is not ready for this particular grade at this particular time or that there is something in the classroom situation that is upsetting, or he or she may be expressing separation anxiety.

Punishing a Kid for masturbating in public or excessively is self-defeating. The punished child is likely to feel even worse about life and seek comfort by masturbating even more. What does pay off is to find the reason for the behavior.

Anxiety

As with any nervous habit, masturbation can be self-soothing. Sometimes the source of the anxiety is pretty obvious: parental hostilities, a new sibling, a move. Sometimes it's not. Many Fives and Sixes find "children's" movies and videos very anxiety-producing. Most popular ones, such as *The Lion King* or *The Little Mermaid*, depend on a plot that revolves around the death or threatened death of a parent because of some action or inaction on the part of a child. Fives and Sixes can find this idea terrifying.

At any rate, the key is to find the cause of the anxiety and to address it. That may mean turning off the TV or making sure that despite the arrival of the new baby each parent is spending attentive one-to-one time with Five/Six. Adults may also need to recognize that bitter words and silences between parents affect a child as much as do physical blows.

Boredom

Many Fives and Sixes have such vivid imaginations that you'd think they'd never get bored. But they do. When a Five/Six masturbates as a reaction to boredom, there's usually something else going on as well. Perhaps the adults in the vicinity are arguing. Perhaps parents are or have been preoccupied, and the Kid is feeling deprived of attention. Perhaps Five/Six is waiting to perform: either formally, as in playing a piano tune, or socially, as in "being nice" to people. Perhaps something nerve-racking is on the agenda, like a doctor's visit with pokes.

It helps to anticipate such periods of boredom and to supply the Kid ahead of time with something concrete to do: crayons and paper, a knapsack with dolls and action figures, a quiet computer game. And to be sure Five/Six is getting sufficient, focused one-on-one attention on a regular basis.

Genital irritation or infection

This is usually a condition of little girls. Most vaginal irritation starts from hygiene problems. Once in awhile, there is an infection, especially with the bacterium called strept. Chubby little girls are more likely to be prone to this, as the vagina, sealed off by chubby thighs, is harder to keep clean. (There may be an odor present even after baths.) An irritated vagina itches. Masturbating temporarily stops the itching, but increases the irritation and the subsequent itch.

Treatment starts with a visit to the pediatrician to see if antibiotics are needed. At home, stop the bubble baths for little girls prone to these irritations, except for a rare treat—that also means no sitting in shampoo water or keeping the bar of soap in the tub so the water gets cloudy. Five/Six girls should be wiping from front to back, so as not to carry germs from the rectum up to the vagina. Substitute loose-fitting clothing for tights and leotards as often as possible, both for treatment and for prevention. It often helps to cleanse the vagina daily with a special lotion for the purpose, such as the nonprescription one called Balneol, and to put a quarter-cup of baking soda into the bath water.

Sexual stimulation

The biggest worry of parents, and the rarest cause of excess or public masturbation, is molestation. Almost always there will be some other indication that the child has been traumatized: clinging behavior, mood swings, withdrawal from activities, a diminishing in the joy of life, a fearful rejection of a previously trusted adult. A talk with the pediatrician and an examination and culture is the place to start.

At the same time, don't discount other sources of inappropriate sexual stimulation: movies and videos and even real-life encounters. The occasional incident of a Five/Six walking in on family members engaged in intercourse is not likely to trigger unusual sex play or masturbation unless there is something else going on: an unexpected pairing, for instance, or repeated exposures, or the child witnessing a couple having sex for a prolonged period. This is a good reason to have Five/Six sleeping in a room not shared by sexually active adults, for single parents not to bring home sleep-over dates, and for all parents to beware the power of TV.

Sex play

"We got caught red-handed!" That was a Six talking.

Fives are preoccupied with anything having to do with bathrooms, whether the endlessly hilarious peepee and poopoo or sex. Many Fives will be found on occasion "playing doctor" with a friend or friends of the same or opposite sex. Six is much less likely to be so discovered. That's because of Six's newfound preoccupation with rules of social and gender behavior. Six is more determined not to be "caught red-handed."

When sex play is a result of normal curiosity and titillation, these features listed are almost always present.

• The children are no more than three years apart in age.
• All the players are pretty willing participants. Nobody complains of being coerced except when defending oneself from adult accusations.
• The play includes looking at, touching, and talking about the genitals. Acting out intercourse, with one child lying on top of another and rubbing, is not rare, nor is playing intercourse with dolls like Barbie and Ken.
• The play does not include inserting fingers or objects into vagina or rectum or taking genitals into the mouth or any kind of aggression—that is, intent to harm. These behaviors are strong signs that the child acting them out has himself or herself been abused or is otherwise having emotional problems that need addressing.
• The play is not the sole purpose of being together. Other activities are enjoyed and usually preferred.
• When discovered, the children are embarrassed but not devastated, unless the adult response is devastating. Nor are they "smart-alecky" or insolent.
• Nobody complains to a parent about the play.

If sex play fits this picture, it is most unlikely that a participating child has been traumatized by the play, or that the play has been prompted by an episode of molestation or abuse that has caused a child to act out sexually.

Given that the play is normal, what is an appropriate response? Most parents want to teach Kids "caught red-handed" several things about sex. First, that sex is an adult activity and that children have other things to play. Second, that sex is private and personal, and not an activity to be shared with casual acquaintances. Third, that sex is a powerful and important force, and should be given respect. (How intense each of these feelings is, based upon religion, culture, or personal conviction, varies considerably.)

Communicating these concepts to Kids is difficult if parents react with intense emotion. For many parents, the shock of finding one's innocent-seeming Five or Six engaged in giggling naked games overwhelms the teaching instinct. The urge is strong to scream recriminations and accusations, get everybody dressed, send the other children home after emotional phone calls to their parents, and then to have a solemn reproachful talk with one's own Kid. Variations include giving the Kid a spanking or a time out, removing a privilege, or calling the other parent or a grandparent and telling all about it while Five/Six stands by pale and weeping.

This kind of overwhelming parental response can devastate one's own Kid, frighten his or her friends, and anger the friends' parents. True, many Kids will never again be caught engaging in sex play. But those same Kids often take this intense reaction to mean that sex is completely off-limits as a topic of calm discussion with parents. This is hardly the outcome that is desirable in today's world. Moreover, some of those Kids will become fascinated and preoccupied by that sex play that so upset parents and may seek it out surreptitiously.

A more effective response is to try to underreact. What you want to communicate is that you are an adult and that children are little Kids. Therefore, nothing they can do will shock you or scare you. However, you don't want them playing sex games for the reasons above. And since you are their Boss, you are telling them not to play those games. You are telling them to get dressed and to come out of the bedroom and play dress up with old pillow cases and hats. NOW. By the way, it's a good idea to name for them what they are doing.

"I see you are playing games about sex and the private parts of your body."

Naming the activity takes away the secret and the mystery and puts the power back in the hands of the parent.

It's safest to notify the parents of the other children, because if you don't some will be angry, if they hear about it from another source, and think you are hiding something. When you do so, it's a very good idea to describe the play in a way that doesn't label one or another child as the instigator. This kind of play is usually a community effort, no matter what your own Kid said in his or her defense and no matter what was going on at the moment you interceded. Children do best when their parents can discuss this kind of thing sanely and agree on a strategy for all the families.

Depending on your level of emotion about the topic, it may be a good idea to rehearse your response in your head every so often. By all means, discuss the whole issue with the other parents or with friends, religious advisors, and your pediatrician before you encounter it in the flesh.

Atypical sex play; worrisome sex play

If you come upon sex play that does not fit the profile of normal play, it still makes a lot of sense to react calmly and in a controlled manner. That's partly because of all the reasons mentioned earlier in this section, but mostly because with abnormal sex play, the Kids may already be frightened and confused. Moreover, it's a good bet that one of them, at least, has been traumatized sexually by an adult. Nobody needs an angry, out-of-control parent in this situation. Moreover, your calm attitude will allow you to be clear about what you are seeing and hearing.

Once you have stopped the play and redirected the children, write down the aspects that concern you. You will want to discuss the implications of this kind of play for your own child with your pediatrician and may need his or her help in discussing the situation with the other parents.

It is rare, but not impossible, for a child to be traumatized both emotionally and physically by abnormal sex play with another child. The more likely worrisome scenario is that the abnormal play itself was triggered by an incident involving an adult.

Life at Home

RESPONSIBILITY

Home is the pony slope for teaching responsibility. Doing chores—not for pay, not to "help" somebody else, but because chores are necessary for civilized family life—is what you learn at home. That's the first step toward higher peaks of commitment.

Five is a good age for learning the nature of responsibility. Five just loves to do a good job. Waiting until a Kid is Six can make learning about responsibility tougher for everyone.

Yes, Six loves rules and regards them as sacrosanct. Unfortunately, Six may very well have already made up a rule about chores, which is: "I am the person around here who doesn't have to do chores." If this has occurred, it will take a united front of all loving adults, persistence, and insistence to change Six's mind, but boy is that worth it.

Opportunities to learn responsibility at Five and Six are pretty much restricted to chores and schoolwork.

If schoolwork is the only forum for responsibility, no one else is dependent on Five/Six to perform well. Five/Six may well do schoolwork responsibly, but if not, he or she is not in the position of letting down the team.

Even if the household runs smoothly without the Kid doing chores, parents may want to find some for the child for teaching purposes. For this to work, though, everybody in the household needs to be responsible for a few chores. The lesson, after all, is that chores are the work family members do to make home life good.

Appropriate chores for Fives and Sixes:

• Are safe. Using toxic cleaning chemicals, cleaning up pets' litter, doing anything from atop a ladder or chair, running errands that require crossing a street with cars on it, and working with anything hot or sharp are tasks that are all too perilous for Five or Six.

• Lend themselves to being performed the same way each time. Examples are setting the table and making the bed. Teach the method step by step; don't expect instant and consistent success without a learning period.

• Have a definite end point. The table is set when there are plates, utensils, glasses or cups, condiments, etc. The end points of chores like dusting or sweeping are pretty vague and unsatisfying.

• Are performed on a daily basis at the same time. Fives and Sixes have only a vague idea of the functions of the calendar and the clock.

• Are very visible when not performed. Who is going to be upset if Six has not retrieved all the toys from under the bed?

• Aren't gender bound. Boys and girls can and should do the same tasks.

• Aren't fatal if neglected. Fives and Sixes should not be entrusted with feeding, watering, or any other life-dependent task for a pet or a person.

Fives can usually make their beds, even if it means emerging like a letter from an envelope, pulling the covers up neatly. They can fold their clothes and hang them up if they can reach the hangers. They can put away toys and set the table. Sixes can do all this plus help with cooking: they can wash and dry the salad, stir anything that isn't hot, pour glasses of milk or water.

The key in reinforcing chore-doing is to recognize and appreciate how well Five/Six performed a task this particular time, but at the same time to take for granted that the task itself is to be performed every day.

> "After you made your bed today, you made a little story on top with Barbie and Ken and that tiger. I wonder what they will do with that tiger!"

This approach works better than "Thank you so much for making your bed! You are mommy's big helper!"

Being Mommy's big helper means that when you *don't* make your bed you aren't skipping your own responsibility; you are merely not helping Mommy with hers.

Six is more likely to object to having to do chores than Five. Six may give a number of reasons: "It's not fair," "I'm too little to do that," "It's not my job; it's your job," "Rennie doesn't have to set the table at her house," "That's a girl job. I'm a boy!" "That's a boy job. I'm a girl!"

If Six is being recalcitrant, several ploys can work.

• Make a chart showing each chore, and let Six put up a sticker when each chore is accomplished. A full chart—perhaps three chores a day for seven days—might get an extra privilege: something modest, not something spectacular. Gradually chores become habitual and the chart can be dropped. If you start out rewarding a filled chart with extra-special treats, though, the chart will backfire. Studies actually show that when children perform tasks for rewards, they are less likely to do the tasks on a long-term basis.

• Let consequences be the natural discipline rather than nagging. If the bed isn't made before leaving for school, it must be made before playing after school. If the clothes are left on the floor, they must go into the Floor Clothes box and not be worn for a day or a week. Toys have a similar Floor Toys box.

Here's what won't work:
• Talking about the work you had to do as a child
• Calling Six lazy, sloppy, forgetful. These labels tend to be adopted by Six and lived up to.
• Doing the work for Six

DISCIPLINE

"How much bratty behavior is normal? I want to know how much I have to put up with and how much I can stamp out."

Bratty behaviors are those that are defiant, aggressive (intended to cause harm to others), untruthful, self-centered, and manipulative.

From the child development point of view, behavior is considered normal if most healthy children engage in it on occasion. Therefore, normal children can and do behave in a bratty manner on occasion. However, they are not *obliged* to behave in a bratty manner in order to be normal. Consistently avoiding bratty behavior does not make a child a wimp, a goody-goody, or a too-good-to-be-true little angel. Preventing bratty behavior does free up a lot of the child's, and the parent's, time and energy for adventures of all sorts.

Of course, some children find it much easier to behave well than others. A perfectly lovely little Kid may have a temperament that makes it difficult for him or her to control impulses, make transitions, or use words instead of actions. Such a child needs enormous amounts of adult patience, consistence, and affection, as well as effective discipline.

More often, however, a child whom others label as a brat has merely gotten into a whole lot of bad habits of behavior. Unwittingly, parents reinforce those bad habits, not only by not disciplining effectively but by not praising effectively.

Since standards of behavior vary, however, how can you tell if your child is behaving in a bratty manner or not? You can tell there's a problem if parents don't enjoy the Kid's company, if siblings can't enjoy each other, or if other Kids regard a Kid as somebody to stay away from, placate, or watch out for. There's a problem if other adults—coaches, teachers, pediatricians, medical personnel—express by words or actions that they are surprised and unhappy about the Kid's behavior.

Such a child exhibits a low-level, constant obnoxiousness. Life with such a child is wearing and just isn't much fun for anybody, including the child. Usually, such a child responds beautifully to a change in parental expectations and a more sophisticated approach to praise and discipline.*

Here is a guide to bratty behavior. No doubt some bratty behaviors have been omitted. No doubt parents have allowed some of these behaviors in the past. And no doubt most of these behaviors seem normal, childish, and age-appropriate: that's correct, they are. They are still bratty and need effective discipline.

DEFIANCE

• Refuses to obey requests until begged and coaxed, but obeys all true commands or demands
• Interrupts other people

---

*A small number of kids show a much greater investment in those bratty characteristics. They escalate their obnoxious behavior so that no one wants to trust, play with, teach, coach, or even be in the same room with them. Life with such Kids is a constant challenge and worry. Most often, a family with such a Kid needs professional help: everyone is too unhappy and involved in the behavior problem to see how to change it. In some rare cases, a young child shows bratty behavior that is not in any way ordinary—performing acts of outright cruelty and aggression, not appearing to care about others' feelings, or engaging in dangerous defiance. A child with such characteristics has a serious disturbance; the family **must** have professional guidance.

- Is stubborn about changing activities
- Obeys with bad grace—making a face, stomping a foot, growling, and so on
- Regularly mouths off to adults: "You look dumb" "You aren't the boss of me!" "That's stupid!" "I hate you!"

AGGRESSION

- Gets into a screaming match but draws the line at hurtful teasing and physical aggression
- Taunts, makes faces, stamps foot, talks loudly
- Uses forbidden language: swearing, profanity, dirty talk
- Says hurtful things—for example, "retard!"
- Nags, teases, and bickers
- Bosses other people around

UNTRUTHFULNESS

- Makes naughtiness out to be "not my fault"
- Takes others' possessions with the excuse, "I'm just borrowing it"
- Tells on other people so as to place the blame on someone else

SELF-CENTEREDNESS

- Refuses to share or shares unequally
- Complains about not being treated fairly when it is not the case
- Shows off competitively when someone else gets attention
- Refuses to show ordinary politeness by using such expressions as "please" and "thank you"
- Makes a mess on purpose, not as the byproduct of a game or a project
- Intrudes when someone else is being praised

MANIPULATION

- Pits one adult against the other
- Tattles on others to make himself or herself look good

- Whines to complain or to demand
- Responds to correction with "You don't love me anymore" instead of "I'm sorry"
- Sets up a friend or sibling to be in the wrong, inviting attack or aggression
- Spies on siblings in order to tattle

EFFECTIVE PARENTING

When Kids indulge in bratty behavior, there's a risk that the behavior will escalate. This happens when a vicious cycle gets started—the kind of unpleasant interaction between child and parents that just runs by itself, increasing in energy as it goes: The worse a child behaves, the less a parent likes to be with him or her. The more a parent indicates that a Kid is not fun to be with, the less likable the Kid feels. The more unlikable a Kid feels, the worse he or she behaves.

Five and Six are the ages to get in there and stop this cycle. If it continues on and on, everybody's behavior can become a habit and seem normal. Then you're sunk.

Kids are unable to break out of this vicious cycle on their own. There is no way that a Kid who feels unliked can change behavior, shedding all the bratty habits and blossoming into a joy and a delight. What such Kids need are areas in which they feel liked, virtuous, and proud of themselves. It's up to parents to make the Kid feel liked.

The normal human impulse when faced with bratty behavior is definitely not to seek ways of making a Kid feel liked. The normal impulse is to seek a punishment for bad behavior, a wonderful, effective, soul-satisfying punishment guaranteed to produce apologies and reform. Well, no such punishment exists.

The problem is that any kind of punishment is likely to make the Kid feel even less cute, virtuous, and enjoyed. So punishment may be very appropriate and justified, and it may indeed work for the occasional descent into brattiness, but it won't do as a constant, day-to-day means of molding your Kid's behavior.

EFFECTIVE PRAISE

A guideline frequently cited in parenting literature is that the ratio of praise to criticism should be at least 3 to 1. Interestingly, the ratio of positive to negative encounters that seems to make a happy marriage appears to be higher: 5 to 1. Hmmm. At any rate, the ratio ought to be so high that a Kid feels surrounded by a positive, loving atmosphere.

What we usually think of as praise is not likely to create that type of atmosphere. It feels condescending and awkward to keep up a constant barrage of "Good! Wonderful! Terrific! Marvelous! Splendid!" "I feel like a Thesaurus," one weary mother confessed. Such praise creates an atmosphere that isn't so much positive and loving as it is a sticky-sweet coating over hidden anger.

What does work is a way to give recognition to good, or to merely appropriate, behavior in a way that:

• Shows that you're really paying attention

When parents use the same old words every time they praise, Kids feel as if they are a little preoccupied, a little in a rut. One way to jolt a parent out of a rut is to indulge in a little bratty behavior.

• Lets the child keep hold of the behavior

When parents consistently label a child's achievement as "brilliant" or behavior as "wonderful," a Kid sometimes feels as if that achievement or behavior only matters if somebody is watching and praising. Kids need praise that encourages autonomy.

• Rings true to the child

When parents praise in a way that sounds false to the child, the child may well reject the behavior that called forth the praise.

• Feels natural to the parent

Nothing is more wearing than going about with a fixed smile of appreciation, generating a constant flow of "Good! Terrific! Way to go!" Spending much time at this labor tends to make people want to bite.

• Encourages mature behavior

One of the tricky things about Five and Six is that the definition of good behavior becomes more complicated. For instance, a Five who has been extremely docile and obedient and "good" may need encouragement to take risks, be assertive, and think for himself or herself. A Six who is oppositional and stubborn may need help in feeling more self-confident and independent, not just in knuckling under to orders.

What works well and covers all the bases is merely to describe what is going on in tones that are interested and approving, adding a comment that moves the conversation along, preferably a comment that makes the child feel grown up. That additional comment keeps the youngster from feeling as if you are giving a knee-jerk response.

"You washed your hair in the shower and you remembered to use the conditioner! What do you think: you like that better than the gardenia stuff?"

"Baby Louie just laughs and laughs when you make that frog face and croak! He could watch you all day long! We should make a video of you and sell it to mothers who need their babies entertained."

"You ran all the way home when you heard me call. I need somebody to taste this gravy, and you have the best too-much-salt detector."

Kids also respond when they overhear themselves being talked about.

"Robby put all his toys on the shelves. Not one was left on the floor."

"Judy is working on learning how to tie her shoes. She kept at it for a long time. I'm sure she'll get the hang of it soon."

"Connor used his words instead of hitting Jordan. He said, 'That's my truck. I need it now. You can have it after I'm done.' I didn't remind him at all; he did it all by himself."

Even very special achievements can be more effectively praised if the tired adjectives are replaced with careful, enthusiastic observation.

"Nicole did a great job at her skating finals. She landed perfectly, even after the hard jump, and even though the ice was rough. She was a little nervous beforehand because of the crowd, but she got right out there and gave us her very best. We have it on tape."

"Dionn remembered the way here, even with all the detours around the flood. I can't believe it. I never would have got here without him. He really can keep his head in a crisis. Dionn, you remember how to get home?"

Dionn's mother eyes the six year old anxiously. Dionn, who does not shine in school nor on the playing field, seems to have grown two and a half feet taller. "No problem," he states graciously.

"Tara is learning to imagine how other people feel. We passed a homeless person on the way to the bus. Tara saw that he was dirty and dressed in odd clothes and that he smelled bad,

but she didn't even mention that. She wanted to know how a person could be homeless and how we could help. She decided that we should buy some hot food from the vending machine and give it to the man. I'm very proud she thought of that by herself and knew it was important to do it, even though we were late to her dance class."

To Five and especially to Six (and to older Kids), this kind of praise pays the highest compliment: I am being observed and appreciated in detail. It is a constant proof that parents find Five/Six engrossing and enjoyable. A Kid who feels engrossing and enjoyable is far more likely to set high standards and work for them than a Kid who feels: "I only get noticed when I do something wrong" or "No matter what I do, I get praised, so why should I bother to do anything special" or "They praise me just to get me to do what they want."

In particular, Kids are sensitive to praise that is:

Untrue

Joshua is making a half-hearted scribble of a house. "Josh, that's a wonderful picture," his father says after a cursory glance, with a wink at me. "Josh is a real artist." Josh takes the black crayon and slashes it all over his scribble.

Automatic

I ask Paul to take off his shoes and socks, which he does. "That's wonderful, Paul. That's wonderful cooperation," Carol says. The words wash right over Paul. I can see why; any action that isn't outright obnoxious brings the same praise. What would she say, I wonder (and I bet Paul does, too) if he really did do something wonderful?

Manipulative

"Jenny is such a good little mother, she doesn't mind sitting on the floor quietly with her doll while the baby gets examined." It may sound like a compliment, but Jenny's mother is giving a "do what I say" glare at Jenny, who is actually engaged in seeing whether she can rock the rocking chair hard enough to catapult it into the wall. Jenny stops rocking, stalks over to the doll, and stomps on it.

Overblown

Belinda leaps onto the exam table. "She's the most graceful child in the world. She's poetry in motion," her mother says dotingly. Belinda looks distressed and embarrassed. Her movements immediately become awkward and self-conscious.

Criticism and self-applause disguised as praise

"Guess what, at long last we've got a real grown-up Kid here! Monty finally learned how to ride his two-wheeler without the training wheels, thanks to good old Dad. Poor old Dad's back really got sore there, bending over and running along behind." Monty stares at his shoes. Did his father expect him to glow with pride?

Everybody drops into some of these kinds of praise now and then. But when these styles become the habitual, main form of encouraging a Five or Six, "praise" no longer shapes good behavior. In fact, it may produce exactly the opposite.

Besides praise, there are incentives, rewards, and bribes.

Incentives

Once in a while an incentive for achieving a specific goal can be very helpful. Suppose Five/Six is shy to the point of tears about playing *Little Pony Trot* on the piano for relatives. If a few M&M's pave the way the first few times, applause and pleasure should soon make them unnecessary.

Incentives become a problem when they are "payment" for what should be normal civilized behavior. Giving candy for sitting still while the doctor examines you or for not hitting your sister or for making your bed—that's going right down the primrose path toward spoiled and bratty behavior.

Rewards

Rewards are for behavior beyond the call of duty.

> "Shauna knew I'd been up all night with the baby, and she brought me breakfast she made herself!"

Sometimes a tearful amazed hug and smile are the best rewards.

There are a couple of traps lurking even in the realm of appropriately given rewards. First, it's easy for the reward always to be food. Does anybody else associate hot fudge sundaes with piano recitals? For many children that's fine, but for children who have a chubbiness tendency, the reward food can assume immense importance and desirability and become a little bit of a craving. It's a good idea then to give nonfood rewards: a postponed bedtime, a toy, extra time for reading aloud or games.

Second, sometimes it pays to call the reward something else. Take the kindergarten "shots." These are harrowing for most Fives. Children who never even talk back may wind up kicking and shrieking, "I hate the doctor!"

You certainly don't want to reward such behavior. Nor do you want Five to construe the reward as an apology. The "shots" were important and necessary and for Five's own good. On the other hand, Five certainly needs a cheerer-up.

Rather than calling the ice-cream cone or visit to the toy store a "reward," then, call it something else: a "feel better," maybe. Don't apologize to Five about the shots. Instead, explain why they are necessary, and tell the truth why they hurt.

> "No one has been smart enough to figure out how to give those medicines without using a needle. Maybe when you grow up you will be a scientist and find a way."

Third, some rewards are really apologies. "I'm so sorry we couldn't see Pocahontas. I thought it was playing at that theater, but it wasn't. I know you are very upset. Here is a new Barbie outfit for being so understanding." But the present is not for being understanding. Five/Six in fact does not understand one bit.

Five/Six may be confused when you label it that way, when she doesn't feel understanding and forgiving at all. It's an apology present.

> "Here's a Barbie outfit because I feel so bad I didn't check carefully first. I knew you were so excited about the movie."

Bribes

Sometimes the only possible response to a desperate situation is a bribe. What's a desperate situation? It's when you are asking for behavior that is *unfairly* good. This should be rare. Most difficult good behavior—for instance, behaving well in public or being nice to much younger children—doesn't qualify. These are necessary, growing-up challenges. What works better than a bribe in these situations is a clear explanation of what's expected and why, an expression of confidence that Five/Six can do it, and an appeal to compassion.

> "When your little cousins are here, it's important to share your toys and not start fights. I know you can be good to them. If you were visiting cousins who were older than you, you would want them to be nice."

But there are bribable situations. They occur when you know the child has a track record of not being able to do what you are going to ask; and when the reason for doing what is required is hard to explain convincingly. They stand out.

> "If you will pee into the little cup I will get you a chocolate bar."

> "If you will play *Happy Farmer* for Aunt Bea even though she always talks while you play, I will play three games of Chutes and Ladders with you at bedtime."

EFFECTIVE DISCIPLINE

When you discipline Five/Six, you aren't just correcting a behavior; you are laying the foundation of how you will deal with problems throughout childhood and into adolescence. But it's a tricky age. Fives seem still like babies and are so anxious and eager to please that calling them on their misbehavior may seem painful. Sixes, on the other hand, can seem out to get your goat, and that's often accurate. It can be all too tempting to sink right down to Six's level and call names right back.

The fact of the matter is that starting at age five, children need to learn to be responsible for their bad behavior. To be responsible, they need to understand the effect of what they have done and to feel as if that behavior is something they don't want to repeat *because* of its effect on other people. As children mature, this wish to avoid harming or annoying others changes into a concept that such behavior is wrong because it violates the moral rules by which we live.

Stopping behavior because it affects others is quite different from stopping behavior because you are afraid of punishment—that comes from the authoritarian style of discipline, in which parents lay down the law without explaining the law's reasoning and impose discipline that is harsh and makes the child feel like a bad person.

It's also quite different from having nothing much happen when you do something wrong and being assured that you can do no wrong no matter how you behave. That's permissiveness. Children raised in either manner tend to have problems with self-reliance, assertiveness, and responsibility. They don't have lots of practice in initiating behavior, reaping the consequences, and thinking about what happened. Instead, they rely only on parental response in gauging how to behave. Their boundaries are blurred, and they aren't sure where they end and their parents begin.

Discipline that helps Kids mature pays positive attention to good behavior; labels and assigns responsibility and imposes a penalty for bad behavior; and gives Kids skills so that they can be assertive and self-confident without behaving in a bratty manner.

WHAT WORKS

• Set your standards high.

When you set a limit, set it before things really get out of hand. If 5-year-old Kate gets into her older sister's things just to fondle them and make her sister mad, you address it right then and there—not after Kate has broken or taken something. If Brandy calls Max "a stupid little brat" even once, you nip that in the bud. You don't wait until there's slapping and sniping and tears.

• Adjust your response to the seriousness of the offense.

Annoying behavior that isn't mean-spirited doesn't deserve the large, serious response you'd give to behavior that violates moral codes, such as stealing, lying to put the blame on someone else, or purposely devastating someone with mean teasing or physical violence. A sigh, exasperated glare, reprimand, and request to change activities will do.

• Explain the limit clearly.

Define hurtful teasing: making fun of how someone looks or smells or the way his or her body, including the brain, works. This explains why such terms as "retard" are off-limits. Define a lie, as opposed to a secret or a "white lie." Define aggression: hurtful teasing and name calling, hitting, pinching, punching, kicking, biting. Define stealing: taking somebody else's

possessions without permission, no matter what the excuse.
• When the rule is broken, use your Parenting Presence.

Make your voice swell and deepen with disapproval. Use your "I am displeased" body language. Define exactly what happened and how it violated a rule of the home.

> "I heard Jeffy call Max stupid! Stupid is a nasty word for not being smart. Nobody can help it if they are very smart or a little smart or not smart. We don't call people stupid."

Suggest what Five/Six could say or do instead.

> "If you are mad at Max, tell him why you are mad. If he took your truck, tell him you want it back."

• Have the consequences be a natural effect of the misbehavior.

If children can't share a toy, nobody can play with it. If teasing gets out of hand, the children must separate and not play together. If Five/Six is whining with unbelievable intensity, he or she needs to take a three- to five-minute silence break. If Five/Six didn't get the room tidied or the bed made before school, it must be done after school before play, snack, TV, or whatever.
• If the offense is a major one, it warrants a serious talk and either a withdrawn privilege, a penance to be performed, or a period of time out.

For this to work with Fives and Sixes, you have to be *consistent, firm, and act immediately.*

When CJ got upset at the arrival of a new baby brother, he took all his mother's makeup and perfumes, dumped them on his bed, and smeared them on the walls.

"I was tempted to tell him that he would have to stay inside all weekend and not go to the party he was looking forward to. But it was only Monday. I didn't know if he'd remember by the weekend. Instead, that day after school, I had him sit quietly without any book or TV while I cleaned up his room. I talked about how I knew he was mad that Connor is getting so much attention, but that he is getting lots of attention too. I told him that this was stealing things and destroying them. I could see he was miserable, but I wanted him to know that this kind of behavior is inexcusable."

CJ's mother had to struggle not just with her anger at CJ but with her own guilt at having imposed a sibling on him. She was torn between overreacting—imposing a very severe punishment, a weekend of time out—and between scooping CJ up in her arms and apologizing and weeping and telling him she still loved him best. Either choice would have been bad for CJ, of course.

> "When I caught Mandy in her sister's room coloring on all her sister's stationery, I told her that this was like stealing—she'd taken her sister's things and ruined them. I told her that to make up for what she'd done, she had to think of something she could do for her sister, something big and important. We decided that she would do extra chores for me at fifty cents a pop and give her sister five dollars to buy new stationery."

Mandy's first idea of a penance was that she would play six games of Candyland with her 14-year-old sister. Her next idea was that she would go with her father to the store and pick out new stationery and maybe a little something for herself. Mandy's father had trouble keeping a straight face at these concepts of repentance. He made sure that the extra chores really were chores and required some sacrifice: setting the table instead of watching TV, getting up fifteen minutes early to wash the grapes for the lunch-boxes, and so on.

• Once the discipline has been applied, leave the incident alone. Don't bring it up with the child or let the child hear you talking about it to someone else.

To bring up the incident again takes the action and the blame away from the child. It blurs the boundaries between parent and child in the child's mind. The child comes to feel as if the whole story belongs to the parent and that he or she was merely a character in it. He or she may even start to feel as if this "character" is something to live up to by continuing to misbehave in the same fashion.

• Don't label the child. Label the behavior.

> "When you take someone else's things, that's stealing. What if somebody took your trucks and you could never play with them?"

Instead of:

> "You're a little thief."

> "When you don't tell the truth, that is a lie, and it makes me not able to trust you."

Instead of :

> "You little liar! I can see right through you!"

Try it on yourself. Which statement makes you want to repent?

THE TROUBLE WITH SPANKING

When you spank, you give a child a whole bunch of messages. Here are some of them.

• People who love you are entitled to hurt you physically. In fact, if they don't hurt you, they don't love you.

• The only time you will feel bad about misbehaving is if you get caught.

• Spanking is the punishment for misbehaving. Once you have been spanked, you have been punished and you don't need to feel bad for misbehaving. It's over until you misbehave and then get spanked again.

• The only reason to behave well is not to get spanked. Since other adults—like teachers—aren't allowed to spank, you don't need to behave for them.

• You only get my fully focused attention when you do something bad and I spank you.

• As a parent, I feel unable to influence your behavior except by hurting you.

• As a parent, I expect to be able to influence your behavior only until you are too big and too old to spank.

• The only way to get people to behave is by catching them being naughty and then hurting them.

What will you do if spanking doesn't work? Spank harder?

SHARING, ESPECIALLY WITH SIBLINGS

Fours understand that to live in a social world you've got to share. It just hasn't sunk in yet that sharing means sharing *fairly*. When Four shares, it's pretty likely that Four will get a lot more than everybody else. Four doesn't understand equality.

Fives and Sixes decide that equality means that everybody must get exactly and precisely the same thing. When Fives and especially Sixes are together, they make a big hullabaloo about it. Dividing a pizza among 6-year-olds may require a measuring tape and a pepperoni count.

Even while Five and Six work out the nature of absolutely equal portions, parents can stretch them and their concept of fairness a little further. Shouldn't someone who worked harder—someone, say, who set the party table—get an extra good piece of cake? Shouldn't somebody who has had a bad thing happen—someone, say,

who fell down in the sack race and scraped her knees—get a candied flower for recompense?

The biggest opportunity probably comes during sibling battles about fairness. When parents give things to siblings—whether it's love, toys, or privileges—the Five/Six insistence that fairness means absolute equality can't be the rule. Buying each sibling identical toys, measuring out desserts with a gram scale and tape measure, using a chart to make sure everybody's getting equal praise: this is the road to a nervous breakdown, massive unhappiness with all gifts, an overdrawn credit card, and sibling brattiness.

Here are some things that help.

• Be sure in your heart that you are treating each child fairly. It's so common that one child "fits" a parent more than another does, and it's so tempting to enjoy that child to the hilt. This may not seem unfair, but it is in the eyes of the other child. Try to find ways to enjoy each to the hilt.

• Once you are sure in your heart, don't get into quarrels about which child you love more.

> "Love and bedtimes don't have anything to do with each other."
>
> "Love and cleaning up the toys don't have anything to do with each other."
>
> "Love and who got more candy corn don't have anything to do with each other."

No apologies, no arguments, no anxiety-producing explanations. If you radiate calm certainty, you can make the discussion end right there.

On the practical side

• Have everybody help to decide who does which chores. Draw chores as lots from a jar—one jar for little Kids, one for big Kids, one for each parent. Allow trades.

• When choosing a gift, take the other sibling(s) along. The picker-outer tends to bond to the act of giving, which adds value in the eyes of the receiver and keeps the picker-outer from being jealous.

Fives and Sixes learn a lot about fairness from friends, at school, and on the playground. Adults in those situations can make a huge impact. A teacher who makes the rule that "nobody can tell anybody else 'you can't play'" is worth his or her weight in gold.

So is a coach who allows everybody to play and focuses on having a good time rather than on beating the other team. Winning, to Fives and Sixes, is something you do as an individual; they don't really "get" what a team win is. Since the team concept doesn't mean much to them, what they do is decide that the other team is bad. This is not a useful lesson in sportsmanship.

School

"All of a sudden, I had this flashback to the patent leather shoes I wore to kindergarten the first day, thirty years ago. I could smell them."

"My first grade teacher always wore purple and smelled like cinnamon. She wore a furry hat. One day she sent me in from the playground to get her hat. I stuck my hand into her desk drawer and felt the fur and thought it was a live animal!"

"I walked Lila to kindergarten the first day and my heart just sank. Her teacher was a ringer for Miss Post, my old kindergarten teacher. Miss Post wouldn't let me pat the rabbit because I pulled Dodo's pigtails."

Isn't it hard to believe that the Five or Six you're sending off to school will have similar memories in a generation? These first two years determine a great deal about how school will go from now on. Fives and Sixes need to be placed in the right grade at the right time. They need to find school a comfortable and challenging place. Their parents need to feel as if they've gotten Five/Six off to a good start.

Here are some of the most frequent parental concerns:

A. Is Five ready for kindergarten's demands? If not, what's the best course?

B. Is Six ready for first grade's demands?

C. If Six isn't ready for first grade, what's the best course?

D. If there is a choice of schools or of classes, which is likely to be the best fit?

E. What if Five or Six is physically different—shorter, taller, from a different racial background, or bearing an obvious "difference" like a birthmark?

F. What if Five or Six seems to have skills that are more advanced than the curriculum?

G. What if parents are worried or shocked by some aspect of the school program?

H. What if Five or Six doesn't like school? What if Five/Six refuses to go? What's going on and what should parents do?

DECIDING WHETHER FIVE IS READY FOR KINDERGARTEN

Parents have three jobs when it comes to kindergarten.

• First, make sure the child is ready for the specific kindergarten you have chosen.

That means casing the joint (see section beginning on p. 45).

• Second, make sure Five is ready physically, emotionally, and mentally.

Get the kindergarten checkup: a complete physical and developmental exam, including hearing and vision tests, routine tests such as the blood test for hemoglobin and the skin test for exposure to TB, and immunizations (see **Appendix C**). Solicit the opinions of your pediatrician and of Five's preschool teacher or an adult at your child's daycare see box titled **Kindergarten Readiness,** page 35).

• Third, make home a good place to leave and a good place to come home to.

If Five is used to a pleasant home, with consistent and nonpunitive discipline; parents who are sane, reliable, and fun; and conversation and reading, this is a lucky Five indeed and one whose kindergarten experience is likely to go well.

If Five is worried that something dreadful will happen if he turns his eyes away from the home front—that parents will divorce or that Mommy will elope with the new baby—Five is going to reject kindergarten and make everyone miserable.

If Five suspects that Mommy or Daddy will pine away without Five, that separation is going to be unbearable for Mommy or Daddy, Five will develop a great repertoire of ways to stay home from school.

Once you've ensured that the child is ready on all fronts and that issues at home are in order, clear up a few things with Five. Fives often believe things that aren't true. When disillusioned, they become very angry. So make sure that Five understands two big issues: the facts of life and the facts of reading.

Fives who haven't yet asked about the facts of life may be silent on the subject either because they have received the unspoken message that they shouldn't ask or because they have developed their own theories. Either way, when a highly sophisticated classmate educates his or her friends during recess, such an uninformed Five may be frightened or angry. This isn't ideal sex education. It's better to instruct Five yourself, if you haven't started earlier (see the section on sex education for Fives/Sixes under **Social Development,** page 16).

Fives usually know that they will learn to read in kindergarten. Many believe that they will return home on the very first day magically possessed of this key to the universe. Are they ever furious when this falls through. I always make a point of telling Fives that learning to read *takes the whole year, and you learn it a little bit at a time.* Some have turned pale and started to cry. But better to face facts earlier than later.

Knowing when a Five is ready for Kindergarten is as much an art as it is a science. Often, an immature Five will shape right up as older classmates serve as examples and inspiration. On the other hand, a Five who isn't quite ready yet may flounder. Kindergarten requires some skills, and Fives who don't have them in place or who don't acquire them rapidly may be much happier postponing school entry for another year. Here are some of the most important of those skills.

READINESS TO PAY ATTENTION

Kindergartners need to be able to pay attention for at least twenty-five minutes at a time. During that twenty-five minutes, they need to decide what in particular they will concentrate on: which parts of the story being read to really get into or whose Show and Tell to get excited about. At the end of that twenty-five minutes, the Fives have to suddenly switch gears and pay attention to something entirely different.

So there are three parts to being able to pay attention: focusing, choosing what to concentrate on, and switching gears.

Fives who have trouble paying attention may simply be immature. Such immature Fives can concentrate for fifteen minutes, but sitting still longer than that just doesn't work. While they are concentrating for those fifteen minutes, they don't fidget, they aren't distractable, and they can tell you what they were absorbing.

They have good social skills, they don't have frequent tantrums or aggressive outbursts, and their pediatricians have passed them as normal in development, hearing, and vision. And they

KINDERGARTEN READINESS

As far as general characteristics go, a child who usually takes kindergarten in stride:

- Has no significant medical problems that require prolonged absences
- Has normal hearing and vision, corrected if needed by hearing aid or glasses
- Speaks the language of the classroom
- Is five-and-a-half or older at the start of the school year
- Is at or above the twenty-fifth percentile of height for his age, if a boy
- Separates easily, no matter how attached the parents are
- Can pay attention for at least twenty-five minutes
- Has had some successful experience in groups of children his or her own age
- Knows how to use adults as a resource and does so after having figured out that a task is too difficult to do without help; can get the attention of adults in a variety of appropriate ways, rather than by whining or throwing a tantrum
- Can take turns, share a toy, and take the role of both leader and follower when playing
- Can express feelings, both positive and negative, to adults and to other children
- Knows what "a good job" is, is proud of accomplishing a "good job," and is competitive in wanting to do so
- Has no overwhelming reason to worry about how things are going on the home front: no seriously ill parent (mentally or physically); no severe parental fighting; no abuse, drugs, or neighborhood violence

Many children who do not possess all of these characteristics still will do well in kindergarten, but will need support and understanding from parents and teachers.

As far as specific skills go, the successful entering kindergartner usually possesses the following:

Language

- Talks routinely in sentences of five or more words, clearly enough for strangers to understand (yes, a mixed blessing, I agree)
- Can recall parts of a story and tell them to you
- Can follow a three-part command (if he feels like it): "Please take your frogmen to your room, put them in your toychest, and bring me your empty cereal bowl"
- Uses the future tense
- No longer stutters or stammers very much

Math

- Understands number concepts: "I have three blocks and you have four"
- Can count to at least ten

Knowledge

- Can name the primary colors
- Can be taught address, phone number, and where parents work

Thinking

Can answer the following questions:

- Why do we have houses, books, clocks, eyes, ears?
- What is a chair made of? A dress?
- Can complete the phrase: "A hat goes on your head, shoes on your ... "

KINDERGARTEN READINESS (cont.)

- Can repeat four digits given out of order. For example, "Six, nine, three, seven."

Hand Skills
- Can draw from a model (without seeing a demonstration) a circle, a cross, and a square, holding the pencil or crayon in the "adult" manner
- Can cut with scissors

Self-Care Skills
- Can dress himself or herself, except for tying shoelaces and buttoning buttons in back
- Can pee and poop in the toilet, flush, redress, and wash and dry hands

Motor Skills
- Can hop, walk heel-toe, pedal a trike or bike, throw a ball, kick a ball, and catch easy balls

can pay attention in a variety of settings, not just in front of the TV or when actively engaged one-to-one with an adult. These Fives just need a little marinating.

If the kindergarten is relaxed and not very academic, with a warm teacher who likes active children, Five can do the marinating in kindergarten. If the kindergarten doesn't fit this profile, or if Five would be one of the youngest in the class, it may well be better to wait a year.

A Five who can't concentrate for even fifteen minutes or can only do so under certain highly gratifying circumstances, though, has something else going on.

- You have to see and hear well if you're going to pay attention. Vision or hearing difficulties can be impossible to detect without formal testing. Fives assume that their abilities are normal and universal, even when they have severe problems.

> "I used to think that the trees were big green blocks," says a Six in recently acquired glasses, "and that the leaves were chips that the birds pecked off."

> "Mommy," says a glowing Five whose chronic ear infections finally have resolved, "the children have started talking to me!"

- An uncomfortable Five is a restless Five. Some causes of discomfort, like allergy, are obvious:

drippy nose, watery eyes, constantly smearing the hand up the nostrils (the "allergic salute.")

Others are invisible, and the greatest of these is constipation. Just as Fives don't know when they can't see or hear normally, they also aren't aware when constipation is a problem. And most parents have no suspicion that their Five is constipated. I know. I ask, as I encounter an incredible poop-distended abdomen, "How do you feel?" "Fine," says Five cheerfully, as she jitters and wiggles on the table. "Do the poops ever come out hard like a rock?" Five's mother is shaking her head no, but Five says, again cheerfully, "All the time."

Modern diets are heavily constipating. Most cereals are not high-fiber (which means five grams of water-soluble fiber per serving): they can constipate. Children love low-fiber starches: white bread, rice, bananas; they eat processed cheese by the package. I believe that the kindergarten population avoids universal constipation only because of its widespread addiction to apple juice.*

* Beware apple juice. Check the label: unless it's added artificially, you won't find more than insignificant amounts of iron or vitamins. It's all sugar and potassium. And just because the sugar is "natural" doesn't mean it's good. Apple juice has the uncanny ability to spoil the appetites of thin children and increase them in fat ones. Its sugar contributes to tooth decay. Given a choice between nonfat milk and apple juice, most children choose the juice, which, because of the sugar, inspires thirst, so that they then drink more juice. Beware, beware.

• An anxious Five can't pay attention. What makes Five anxious? Parents fighting, custody battles, a new sibling, a parent's illness … the list goes on and on. It is safe to say that if parents are constantly, frequently, or intensely anxious, so is Five. Fixing the problem is the ideal solution but not always possible. Talk with your pediatrician about how to help your Five. (And see **What If?** in this chapter, beginning on page 91, on talking with Fives/Sixes about illness, death, and family secrets.)

• A sleep-deprived Five is a restless Five. Fives need an average of eleven hours of good sleep. If Five is getting nine or fewer hours of sleep a night, or if sleep isn't high quality, don't expect good attention. Interrupted sleep can be caused by an obstructed upper airway (from enlarged adenoids, tonsils, allergies.) If Five snores loudly, seems to gasp or pause for breath between or during snores, suspect sleep apnea—periods of not breathing when the brain is deprived of oxygen. If you notice sleeping problems, see your pediatrician.

• A Five who gets mixed signals from family about what is "cute" behavior may try the same tricks at school. Interrupting, roving the classroom, acting up, nosing into other children's work, demanding to be center stage: these may work fine with Mommy and Daddy and Nana and Poppa, but are trouble in kindergarten. It's not delightful to recognize that one's doting has backfired, but the sooner it is recognized and Five is redirected, the better.

Choosing what to concentrate on is a learned skill. To perform that skill, you must be able to pay attention and get some feedback about what you've learned. Fives who don't get much adult attention or "debriefing" about their experiences are at a disadvantage.

READINESS TO MAKE TRANSITIONS

This is hard for many young children. These are the Fives who won't come to sit when it's circle time or won't come in from the playground. In fact, they have a hard time getting to school in the morning and coming home in the afternoon. If they have packed schedules with after-school care or activities, these Fives are a mess.

Practice and maturity often help a lot, but sometimes a child has shown a reluctance to make transitions practically from birth. If a Five shows this pattern, there are several things that can help.

• Talk to the teacher about giving the class a signal five minutes ahead of time that the present activity is drawing to a close.

• Ask if the transition can be done in stages, rather than all at once. Instead of dashing in from outside play for lunch, the children get into a quieted-down group on the playground, talk about going in for lunch, then walk in. Most kindergarten teachers do this anyway.

• Play school with your Five, with him or her being the teacher. Being the person in control of making a transition and in charge of warning somebody else about it helps one feel more mastery.

Once in a while, you may suspect a Five who is very distractable, impulsive, fidgety, or unable to pay attention for a sustained period of having Attention Deficit Hyperactivity Syndrome (ADHD). This is definitely a matter to take up with your pediatrician. (See Hyperactivity under **Behavior Problems**, page 75, in this chapter.)

DECIDING WHETHER SIX IS READY FOR FIRST GRADE

A Six who loved kindergarten is probably going to love first grade. But some checking up is well worth while. After all, kindergarten, with its coziness and naps, may seem like an extension of home. First grade is the big, wide world.

For first grade to go well, all that needs to happen is for Six to feel like a big success. To Six, this means keeping up with the rest of the class in reading and math, feeling as if the teacher likes you, and that the other children *especially those of your sex* like and respect you. It means not being frightened: of a teacher's too-harsh criticism; of a bully; of a school environment that is violent or dirty; of the rules about bathroom visits or of the bathroom itself; of the chaos of lunch and playground; of getting to and from school; or of after-school care.

It pays off hugely to make sure first grade goes well because after first grade it's very hard to reverse course. Having to repeat a year of school in the upper elementary grades not only may not solve the problems that led to the repetition, children dread it. One study showed that children rank repeating a grade harder than the death of a close friend, perhaps because it feels a bit like "losing themselves," or their ideal selves.

In many areas, children are not permitted to repeat a grade except for truly extraordinary reasons. Partly this is because of schools' reluctance to damage self-esteem; partly it is because of already-overcrowded classrooms.

The first grade experience can determine how schooling goes for the rest of a child's life. If first grade starts well, but after a few weeks or months Six seems to flounder, waste no time in finding out why and fixing it.

First grade is sounding out new words and reading with expression; it's thinking through math problems, rather than just counting and adding; it's printing words and then sentences, not just the alphabet and one's own name. First grade means using the bigger Kids' playground, bathroom, and lunchroom. It is teams instead of circle time. It is making friends on the basis of how they behave toward you, not just because you're sharing toys, space, and the teacher's attention. Kindergarten means artwork brought home to show off on the refrigerator. First grade also means homework.

We know that what creates self-esteem in children is succeeding in achievements and feeling as if their achievements are based in great measure on their own abilities and efforts. Fostering achievement implies an accepting attitude toward mistakes. Not only are they accepted; better yet, mis-

takes are *expected.* If people didn't make mistakes, they wouldn't learn anything.

During the first year of grade school, Six may seem to push parents away. But this is only an illusion. Six is really pushing *off*, not away— off into more independence. Parents may need to rearrange their attitudes to maintain closeness then, but the effort is worth it.

FIRST GRADE CHALLENGES

PAYING ATTENTION

First graders will be asked to pay attention for up to an hour at a time! And not only pay attention, but sit at a desk without talking much to neighbors. You can't just get up and wander around the room. If Six is *very* jittery and distractable after the nervousness and excitement of the first few weeks have subsided, talk with the teacher and with your pediatrician.

REALLY READING

First graders need to be able to read by sounding out (not just recognizing from memory) simple words. A Six who doesn't seem to grasp this concept needs help.

But sometimes Six doesn't let you know that this is the case. Even a devoted teacher can miss a non-reading Six. I've known many a child who is the apple of the teacher's eye, charming, well-behaved, responsive, but who, when passed on to second grade, has terrible difficulties because he or she is unable to read. Such a child has developed admirably complex techniques for "passing."

Such a Six may memorize a book after hearing it read out loud several times. (If you've memorized *The Cat in the Hat* from frequent reading, you know how easy it is.) She may discover that her teacher unconsciously, or for encouragement, mouths the words Six is supposed to be reading out loud and she become an expert lipreader. She may hear her friends and neighbors whispering the answers.

Six is not really cheating when she does this. Often, a Six who can't understand phonetics has no idea that other people really can. She thinks everybody else is memorizing and guessing, too, but just doing a better job of it. Even after it dawns on her that she can't do something her classmates can, it take an enormous amount of bravery to admit it—even to herself.

The kindest and most effective way to make sure Six is truly reading on schedule is also the most fun: Read out loud at home. Together. Six could read one page, you the next, or each of you could read one story.

To make sure Six hasn't merely memorized the beloved books she seems to read so well, get new ones. If Six refuses to read new books, she could be hiding her problem—or she could just be strongly attached to the old books. To find out what is going on, read a new book out loud to her, one of the same difficulty as her old ones. Then pause when you are reading your part of the book, and ask Six to help you out. "What's that word? My old eyes see only a blur."

If Six sounds the word out and even kindly finishes the sentence for poor old Dad, you're reassured. If Six looks stumped and then guesses a word—say you are reading one of the Frog and Toad books and she guesses that the word "pond" is the word "frog"—this is suspicious. If she is usually compliant and helpful but now refuses to help at all, or giggles and flirts (or acts rowdy) with you to change the subject, I'd be concerned.

By the end of first grade, Six ought to be able to read out loud with expression, then talk about the story afterward.

TROUBLE READING

A Six lagging behind in reading may do so because of mere immaturity or may have an underlying problem that will cause trouble with reading later on as well. How parents deal with Six's difficulties depends on their child's particular learning profile, first grade teacher, and school.

If Six is a young Six, and the school is very relaxed and tactful about repeating grades, one tactic is moving Six back to kindergarten. Forging ahead with first grade despite major problems can make things worse. Increasingly, Six begins to feel left out and incompetent.

If Six is *at least six-and-a-half years old* and still struggling, the problem is much less likely to just be one of immaturity. In this case, parents are well advised to seek help. If there's a family history for reading problems, find help earlier.

A Six-and-a-half with reading problems needs a physical examination that includes vision and hearing tests and testing by an expert for learning disabilities. Reading is an incredibly complicated task involving more skills than just "decoding" a word. It requires recognizing the sounds in words, understanding that letters make those sounds, learning which letters make which sounds, putting letters together to make words, putting the words into sentences, and judging whether the sentences make sense. And each of those steps is made up of many smaller steps, each dependent on complicated neural connections.

What helps

Identifying exactly where the problem is. This means a physical exam, vision and hearing testing, and a complete evaluation by a psychologist specializing in learning disabilities.

Tutoring by a qualified person who is warm and encouraging. Such a tutor breaks down learning to read into small steps and rewards each small advance. Make sure that the tutor is using phonics, not methods that depend on word recognition by shape. Ideal tutoring is one to one: the closer to that goal, the better.

Consistent daily practice reading, at school and with a tutor. The more time spent practicing, the better—as long as the learning doesn't feel punitive to Six.

Controlling parental anxiety. The more a Six

feels as if parents are hovering overhead, propellers anxiously buzzing, the less Six is able to concentrate. Antidotes to anxiety include stressing Six's strengths, praising his efforts to concentrate and learn, and reading out loud to Six without being asked, just for pleasure. Find the kind of books that Six likes and enjoy them together.

Making sure that Six is never embarrassed or humiliated because of being unable to read. Request that the teacher not call on Six to read out loud in class and that he or she protect Six's graded papers from being seen by the other children.

Consciously striving not to compare Six's reading ability with that of other children—friends, classmates, or siblings. Reading ability and virtue, like reading ability and intelligence, are two different things.

Orchestrate having the TV "break." Get rid of it. Give it away. Not having a TV or not having one in working order is the very best way to avoid the fatal attraction of the screen. Next best: no watching at all, for anybody, on school nights, including Sunday night. Third best: give Six not more than ten tokens (poker chips are fine) each week. Each token "buys" a half-hour of TV. When all tokens are gone, no more TV that week.

Let Six see you enjoying the act of reading your grown-up books.

What doesn't help

Eye exercises. There do seem to be subtle, complicated visual problems in children with severe reading problems but they are too "fine-grained" to be fixed with vision exercises. If your child is referred to someone for such treatment, get a second opinion before spending big bucks, raising what may be false hopes, and perhaps wasting a great deal of time. Ask your pediatrician to review the plan to correct visual problems or to refer you to a qualified psychologist specializing in learning disabilities.

Teasing, nagging, shaming—by anybody, including siblings.

Colored transparencies placed over the printed page. (These were in fashion a few years ago, but studies showed them to be ineffective.)

Special glasses for children with normal vision.

Enforced practice crawling. This may seem a loony idea, and indeed it is. However, some quasi-medical groups have advocated this bizarre "therapy." It is based on faulty reasoning: that a child who never went through a crawling phase missed out on important brain development that can be helped by making her crawl later.

First, many excellent readers never have crawled, and many with severe reading disabilities were magnificent crawlers. Second, the true believers in this method never get around to publishing results and are somehow reluctant to allow others to check on their "successes." Third, it is demeaning to Six to be forced to crawl. Fourth, it raises false hopes and cruelly deprives Six and Six's parents of focusing efforts where they are likely to work.

Ignoring the problem, hoping that Six-and-a-half will "grow out of it." In the very unlikely event that Six-and-a-half will grow out of it, it will be just as likely to happen while being tutored.

Repeating first grade in the same classroom without special help. Since reading delay is sometimes maturational, you'd think that just taking an extra year would make a big difference. Once in a while, it does; but staying in the same classroom rarely works. The memories of frustration and loss of self-confidence get in the way of learning. A child who needs to repeat first grade for reading problems needs special assistance and benefits from a fresh start in a new classroom.

REAL MATH

First grade means the beginning of math. Sixes need to be able to solve basic problems, not just to add and subtract. They need mathematical logic skills: Are these shapes the same or different? Why? "If" I do this, "then" what will happen? They need to store facts in their memories and visualize shapes mentally, not just recognize them on paper.

Keeping tabs on what kind of math Six is doing at school and echoing it with interesting practical problems at home is great support.

> "You found money in the crease of the chair! You can have the two coins that are worth the most. Which are they?"

> "I guess we should pour the leftover soup into a storage container. Which one is big enough but not too big?"

> "We have two dollars to spend on the presents for Danny and Boo. Let's see what that will buy."

When parents try to *teach* as opposed to practice specific math skills, their good intentions can backfire. More than any other subject, math is taught by whatever method is currently in vogue. Some schools teach beginning binary math and even algebra concepts in first grade. If you confuse Six, heaven help you. "Mr. Hopper," the note that came home written on a Six's homework paper warned, "if you would like to join the class, I would be happy to explain these problems to you." And each problem was marked with a rather stern, unhappy face.

MATH TROUBLE

Considering how many math concepts Kids need to absorb in first grade, it's surprising that only about six or seven children out of a hundred have major problems with basic math.

But a problem with math is just as significant as a problem with reading, and maybe even more so. Math is a series of steps, with each depending on the previous one. Missing a step means falling off the staircase.

As with reading, a Six may camouflage math misery. If Six brings home incomplete math papers or papers with sad faces on them, make an early appointment to talk with the teacher. If Six brings home wonderful happy-face papers, but you are astonished because Six can't do the same problems at home, also see the teacher.

I'd be very alert to signs that math makes Six angry or embarrassed. "He gets mad if I even try to help," says David's father, sadly. If Six becomes stranded in the early stages of math, anger and embarrassment tends to paralyze the child in the later stages. It's crucial that Six not come to think of math as The Enemy.

What helps
• Positive encouragement and praise that focuses on effort as well as on achievement.

> "You figured out exactly how many forks to bring to set the table." "You gave me the exact right number of pennies for my nickel." "You concentrated so hard on that problem! My, what a strong mind muscle you have."

If Six seems truly lost, testing by a psychologist specializing in learning disabilities to see where Six's strengths and weaknesses lie.
• Letting Six in on the diagnosis.

> "You are very smart in lots of ways. You read with so much expression, you figured out how to make Chloe a new cage, and you are an authority on dinosaurs. But math is different. You have the same problem with math that I do. We have trouble seeing numbers and shapes in our minds. We don't have problems when we put them on paper, but it is hard for us to see numbers and shapes with our eyes closed. This makes math hard for us."

• Tutoring, if the psychologist advises. Make sure Six likes the tutor and the tutoring session.

Part of the work of a good tutor is to make Six feel good about learning.
- Games. Visit a toy store. Dice games and Junior Monopoly can be helpful.
- Rewards, especially those built into the math challenge.

> "If you fish out all that change in the crack of the big chair and tell me the names of all the coins, you can have the one that is worth the most pennies."

- Making math "real" by using it in practical tasks at home:

> "We have five apples but two of them look as if a worm lives in them. If I don't serve these, will everybody in our family be able to have one?" "How many socks do you guess are in Daddy's drawer? Let's see how many pairs we can make from these sixteen socks."

(The answer is not necessarily eight.)

- Making sure that what goes on in the classroom doesn't humiliate Six. Make sure Six isn't called on unless Six is madly volunteering and the teacher is pretty sure he's got the right answer. Other children shouldn't grade Six's papers or see the marks on his work.

What doesn't work and makes things worse
- Trying to tutor Six yourself. A child who is having trouble with math concepts is frustrating to teach. The ensuing clashes are likely to monsterize the whole subject.
- Repeating a grade only because of math trouble. This is a terrible idea. It won't solve the child's problems with math and is guaranteed to be seen as punishment. Difficulty with math does not usually stem from immaturity. Tutoring, parental support, and summer school are much more likely to help Six develop the math skills he needs than holding a Kid back a year.

- Teasing, nagging, shaming, by anybody—including siblings.

PRINTING AND WRITING

First graders need to be able to print and spell simple words and to copy from the board.

Fortunately, there are lots of ways for parents to help Sixes practice these skills at home. There are placecards, thank-you notes, Welcome Home and Happy Birthday signs, and there are postcards to grandparents, party invitations, and Keep Out signs for bedrooms.

Printing some letters backward once in a while is usually perfectly normal. Printing whole words backward or most letters backward all the time can mean a problem. A conference with the teacher is in order.

The mid-Six who tries to copy a simple sentence but gets it all scrambled up sometimes has a problem. If you see this happening, talk it over with Six's teacher. Such a problem is rarely visual, though vision should be checked. More often it's one of "central processing," in which the brain has trouble taking visual information (the sentence the teacher wrote on the board) and transferring it into writing. Exercises can help a child improve this skill greatly.

HAND SKILLS

Cutting with scissors, crayoning in the lines, painting with a brush, drawing a diamond (as well as a square and a circle), creating a person with a head, body, face, and arms and legs coming out of the body: A Six who has real trouble with these and other hand tasks, such as buttoning, screwing on tops, and so on, may need to have a few sessions of occupational therapy; your pediatrician can help. But for most Sixes, the key is practice and fun. Projects at home—cutting out collages, helping in household tasks such as folding napkins, making placecards, snipping flowers, peeling vegetables with a peeler, cutting up old sheets into dust cloths—can be very valuable.

PHYSICAL SKILLS

On the playground, Sixes can be expected to run fast, throw a ball, catch it sometimes, hit a "T-ball" with a bat, understand the rules of games such as dodgeball, and not disrupt a game. This combination of mental and physical skills is pretty sophisticated. A Six who is active and well-coordinated may just need ripening to be able to hold her own on the playground. But a Six who is having trouble with the basic skills of running, throwing, catching, kicking, hopping, skipping, and climbing should have a pediatric visit. Sometimes there's a problem with vision, strength, balance, or coordination that needs addressing. When the problem is simple nonathleticism, a parental coaching and cheering section (not a nagging section) can work wonders.

BATHROOM COURAGE AND CONTROL

Then there's the bathroom issue. This is a hot topic among Sixes. Of course, an "accident" is the thing that must not happen, even more so than in kindergarten. For some Sixes, raising one's hand is easy, natural, and nothing to get upset about. For many, it's fraught with problems. What if the teacher says "No"? (And yes, this can happen.) What if Nancy and Marty giggle every time somebody gets up to go? What if the bathroom is dirty or there aren't doors on the toilets and you're a private person? What if the big Kids are there and might tease you or beat you up?

Scout out the premises. Talk with the teacher. Visit the bathroom yourself, during school hours: ask yourself if you would consider using it.

You may also have to help Six change a few habits. Waiting until the last minute to go, and unzipping and depantsing damply in a rush, may be fine at home and may not have been a problem in kindergarten, but it clearly won't do here.

The Six who is used to having a bowel movement during the day, rather than in the morning (or evening), is all too likely to not stool at all

once her only option is the school bathroom. The seats sometimes are so high Six's legs dangle, so it's hard to push; the seat is cold/warm/wet/nonexistent/not private. The tension of the classroom discourages performance. Not stooling at all is a big problem (see Constipation and Encopresis [soiling] in the **Glossary**).

On weekends, give a Six who may be holding back bowel movements at school a loosening diet, with perhaps a dose (a tablespoon once or twice a day) of mineral oil in juice, and offer rewards for developing a morning habit. Maybe the timing will carry over into the school week. At the very least, you can be sure that Six is emptying out at least once a week.

IF SIX ISN'T READY FOR FIRST GRADE, WHAT'S THE BEST COURSE?

Sometimes it's obvious to parents and teacher that Six isn't ready to take on the challenges of first grade. Perhaps Six has trouble sustaining an attention span of more than twenty minutes or is still working on the concept of phonetics or is overwhelmed by the social challenges of kindergarten and doesn't play with the other children. The best course for Six depends on what is going on with the child and what the school is willing and able to do in order to help.

REPEATING KINDERGARTEN

Repeating kindergarten is different from repeating any other year. It's much easier, for a number of reasons.

First, it's easier socially. Friends in kindergarten are not as bonded as friends later. Kindergartners generally define "friends" as "who I play with," and "who I play with" is defined as "whoever wants to play what I am playing."

Beginning in first grade, friends are more clearly defined. First, most Sixes make friends of their own sex. Second, friends are more and more seen as "someone who does things for me and whom I do things for."

Second, it's easier on parents. Adults define kindergarten differently, more sentimentally, than they do first grade. Repeating kindergarten has little adult stigma, and this feeling of comfort is passed down to Fives and Sixes.

Third, kindergarten teachers are often pleased to have a slightly older child, one who knows the ropes, back in the class the next year. Such a child can pass out materials, find the hamster food, and motivate people to sit in a circle.

Finally, the other children are unlikely to tease a repeater. They are more likely to be respectful and intimidated, which doesn't hurt anybody.

If Five is socially immature and/or attentionally immature, repeating kindergarten can be terrific. This is particularly true if Five can meet and play with children who will be in her new kindergarten class ahead of time and if the teacher is kind and enthusiastic.

Some schools have strict rules against repeating any grade, including kindergarten. Parents who strongly suspect that Five is having problems that will keep him or her from being ready for first grade when the time comes would do well to check the school's policy on repeating kindergarten. In many cases, the way around the policy is to pull Five out of kindergarten before the year is complete and reenroll her the next year.

SPECIAL HELP

If Five is socially and attentionally mature, and the single, only reason for keeping the youngster in kindergarten is that he or she is struggling with prereading skills, it pays to be sure that repeating kindergarten and not doing anything further will really help in this regard.

How do you tell if there is a reading problem?

Suspect a problem if:

• Five's kindergarten teacher is concerned about Five going into first grade because "he didn't seem to catch on to the work in the classroom."
• Either parent has a reading or math disability.
• Five doesn't seem to recognize what rhyming

is. Trouble rhyming may mean difficulty with phonics.
• Five seems angry at books and wants to avoid any reading activities.
• Five has trouble with reading and math thinking skills: sorting objects and shapes, telling back a story read or told, recounting an experience in sequence, telling why two things are the same or different, thinking in "if ... then" concepts.

If testing shows that Five has a problem in one or more of the complex skills necessary for reading, discuss special help for Five. Most of the time, the right person to talk with first is Five's kindergarten teacher. If he or she feels that Five had more difficulty than the rest of the class, my suggestion is to pay close attention.

Testing for reading disabilities is a complicated enterprise. It's done by developmental psychologists. The one Five goes to should be experienced, kind, and tactful.

What do you tell Five about such testing?

It depends. If Five has let you know through words or behavior that she is upset about trouble learning to read, by all means tell her that many children have such problems and that you are taking her to a special teacher who helps such children. She is likely to be relieved.

If Five seems happily oblivious, I would suggest that you merely say that this is another kindergarten checkup for the "second part of kindergarten."

A developmental psychologist is usually able to tell with some accuracy why Five is having problems, suggest special areas on which to focus, and give parents suggestions on how to do so. I believe this is well worth the time and money. (The school will not pay for this exam for kindergartners. Once in a while, medical insurance will pay for at least part, if the reading problem might be due to a health problem such as extreme prematurity.)

Kindergarten a second time is likely to be a much more peaceful and comfortable place than first grade. Most children don't dread repeating kindergarten in the same way that they dread repeating levels in grade school.

For many parents, too, repeating kindergarten feels more comfortable. It doesn't feel like failure. It feels "like having my baby still a baby for one more year."

IF THERE IS A CHOICE OF SCHOOLS AND CLASSROOMS, WHICH ONE IS LIKELY TO BE THE BEST FIT?

Of course, if you have a choice you are most likely to choose a school with a good reputation for safety, and educational achievement and one that meets your philosophical, cultural, and aesthetic standards. You are most likely to choose a classroom in which the teacher seems kind and competent and the room itself child-friendly.

Studies on what makes for a good learning environment mostly indicate just what you'd expect. Children do best when the school is clean and safe, when the principal is a sane, effective leader whose policies are clear and reasonable, when parents are closely involved with the school and its extracurricular activities, when children are motivated by praise and rewards rather than by punishment, and when teachers are enthusiastic, proud, and happy with their career choice. All other things being equal, one study found that learning was most effective in schools with about 160 students, rather than smaller or larger schools, and when the class size was no larger than twenty-four children. Classes of more than twenty-seven children became significantly less effective.

I know from experience, however, that there are some aspects of schooling that parents often don't know to take into account. Here are a few.

YEAR-ROUND SCHOOL

Some schools are on a year-round track, with school in session for a few weeks, then recessed for a couple of weeks, then back again. It is very tempting to choose the track that has the schedule most convenient for the family vacations or the schedule that all the other children in the neighborhood are locked into. All other things being equal, those are very valid ways to choose.

However, in many schools one or two tracks are coveted, either because the teachers on those tracks are considered superior or because those tracks have special enrichments built in or because there has been a tradition of more parental involvement.

Once a child starts on a given track, it is often very difficult to change that track, not only in the middle of a school year but when a Kid starts a new grade. So it's very wise to go to the school and observe the classes in the tracks you are considering. Talk with each teacher. Talk to other parents, especially those who have children in upper grades. If they rave about or condemn a specific track, investigate for yourself.

Bear three things in mind. First, if a specific teacher is the reason for a track's being considered superior, make sure that teacher is planning to stick around for the duration of your child's tenure in his or her class. Second, what is considered a drawback that makes a track less attractive may in fact be an advantage. You may well be grateful that your child picked up a foreign language from the children who were bussed in to his classroom or that your child had the opportunity to be with children of different racial or cultural backgrounds. Third, the quality of a given track is very dependent on how much input the parents give. A track with high parent participation is likely to be an excellent one. If you are a natural leader, you can turn your child's track into a superior one.

MAGNET SCHOOLS

Some schools in your district may receive extra funding to support special programs. There are magnet schools for gifted children, for arts and music, for science, for languages. Here are a few things to know about magnet schools:

• Some of the very best magnet schools are kept something of a secret. They tend to be over-applied to and don't need to advertise. It pays to call the superintendent's office and ask specifically for a list of magnet schools in your area.

• The quality of magnet schools varies enormously. Some are magnet schools in name only, with little funding or expertise in the area in which they are supposed to excel. Don't take for granted that just because your child's school is a magnet school that the education is one that really should draw people to it.

• In some magnet schools, only certain classrooms really perform the magnet function. For instance, a magnet school for the gifted may have only one classroom for each grade that is geared for accelerated learning. The competition for that classroom may be fierce. Moreover, some of the special magnet programs may not start until the later grades. If this is the case, you may want to find out if admission to that later-grade magnet program is on a competitive basis, and if so, whether attending the school from early on gives a child an advantage.

• Magnet schools, like all schools, are at the mercy of federal, state, and local funding. Their quality is dependent on the guidance of the principal and the competence of the teachers. Find out if any big changes are about to occur.

BILINGUAL SCHOOLS

What a great gift for a child to learn a second language by listening and talking at the age—before puberty—when picking up such a language is not only easy and accentless, but paves the way for learning more languages later on.

But check out bilingual schools and classes. It's not uncommon that all the children whose first language is not English are channeled into one classroom rather than integrated into the school. In such a classroom, English is taught as a foreign language. An English-speaking child in that environment is likely to be confused and may have trouble establishing friendships.

Rather than merely choosing a different track or classroom, parents can do their own children a giant favor by working to make each classroom truly bilingual, with English-speaking children learning a second language just as the other children learn English.

WHAT IF FIVE/SIX IS PHYSICALLY DIFFERENT FROM THE OTHER CHILDREN?

SHORTER

The most frequent parental concern about physical appearance is the child—especially the boy—who is shorter than average. This is a tricky topic. Does "shorter than average" mean shorter than 25 percent of boys his age? Shorter than 5 percent? Shorter than 50 percent? What if Henry is of average height for his age, but shorter than 90 percent of the boys who will be in the kindergarten class—because Henry just turned Five and most of the other boys are nearly Six?

There are a few solid pegs on which to hang your hat.

What's average?

The height for age chart tells you how tall your child is compared to other children of the same age and sex (see **Appendix A,** page 258). Find your child's age along the bottom and height along the side. Draw straight lines from each point and see where they intersect. That point of intersection will be somewhere in relation to the curved percentile lines. If it is at the 50-percent line, that means a child is exactly average. If you lined up your child with 100 other children of the same age and sex, fifty would be taller and fifty would be shorter.

Children at or above the 25-percent line for their age are not short by anybody's standards. They are in the average range. If a child is in the twenty-fifth percentile for height, that means that if you lined that child up with 100 other children of the same sex and age, twenty-five would be shorter and seventy-five would be taller.

Unusually short

Children below the fifth percentile for height, whether boys or girls, are unusually short. Most often, this is normal shortness, inherited from a parent or grandparent. Sometimes, too, it is a temporary shortness, and at puberty the child shoots up to average or above-average height. Rarely, though, such unusual shortness can be the sign of a hormonal or other medical problem: a child this short should always have a thorough checkup with the pediatrician, focusing on height.

A child this short will be seen as different by classmates and teacher. Because the interactions of boys are mostly based on physical encounters and action, a very short boy is likely to have a harder time making friends and standing up for himself than a little girl. This is not automatically a reason to hold a child back, however.

Waiting a year for growth makes some but not a great difference. Say you hold back a boy who is shorter than 95 percent of other 5-year-old boys so that he grows for an extra year. When he is six, he will be shorter than 75 percent of 5-year-old boys.

For all such unusually short children, the main temptation for adults to avoid is overprotection and infantilization. Teachers and parents alike need to consciously bear in mind that a boy or girl really is five not three. It's very important to help a very short child to be assertive, to make friends, to gain all the physical and intellectual skills that are age-appropriate.

Ordinary short

Relatively short girls (between the fifth and twenty-fifth percentiles) do fine in both the short run and the long run. Even if they are relatively young, and thus will have puberty later than other girls, this does not seem to damage self-esteem or cause behavioral or academic difficulties.

Relatively short boys, however, may have some problems of self-esteem and trouble with competition. This is especially true if the youngster also is young (younger than five-and-a-half) and is relatively immature socially and intellectually. Such a boy is likely to have difficulties not only in kindergarten, but in first grade and thereafter. Because boys' social success depends so much on physical contact, the short boy may be at a disadvantage. He is also somewhat more likely to have puberty later than average, which is associated with self-esteem problems in boys, though not in girls.

Of course, whether these problems occur depends on the Five, as well. My friend Stevie had turned five only a week before kindergarten started and was in the fifteenth percentile for height. His parents, however, had no doubts about Stevie's readiness, nor did I. Stevie was already reading *The Cat in the Hat* and riding a two-wheeler without training wheels. Given ten minutes in our waiting room, he once marshaled those assembled into a parade over and under the chairs, which made the other children loath to come into the exam rooms. He was known to have persuaded me to let him look in my ears with the otoscope, a favor not granted lightly. He is now in eighth grade and is thriving. He has not, as his father feared, taken on the role of class clown or mascot because of his height.

RACIALLY OR CULTURALLY DIFFERENT

Kindergartners' behavior is so cued by that of adults that a great deal of what a racially or culturally different Five experiences depends on the teacher's attitude. A visit to feel out that attitude is mandatory.

If the teacher shows prejudice, I would make every effort to prevent Five from being in such a class. (To say nothing of taking up the problem with the administration.) Given that the teacher is kind, sensitive, and unbiased, consider rewarding the special attention and efforts that he or she is going to be making. Certainly, this is expected professional behavior. But then, so is answering midnight phone calls for pediatricians—and I've never been known to object to a little zucchini bread.

Parents can help a Five be proud of his or her background. Every child should be taught the name of his race and its history and heroes of both sexes. A Five with information to share generally finds listeners. A Five with fascinating objects to show is even more certain of an audience.

Sharing cultural information and objects can also help a Five to make friends. Making friends in kindergarten has more to do with sharing activities than with having any sort of personal affinity. Given the opportunity, a Five is likely to make a friend, unless the other child seems *very* different. Since Fives are so gender-conscious, it probably is a good idea to make an effort at dressing Five as much like the other children of the same sex as seems reasonable, within the bonds of one's culture. It's also kind to make sure that Five knows the basic playground skills. These vary, so visit the playground well ahead of time and take notes.

As to racial or ethnic name-calling: Fives want to do the right thing, to win approval. So the teacher's role is crucial. If Five uses an offensive name in ordinary conversation, with no apparent consciousness that it is insulting, Five should be corrected firmly but casually. You don't want to make it fascinating by getting upset and excited. But if such an epithet is used as a taunt, time out is appropriate.

Sixes are more group-conscious. They hold the teacher in awe because the teacher is judge and rule-giver. A first grade teacher can talk a little about the evils of prejudice, set up classroom rules, and enforce them. One of those rules can be: "Nobody can tell anybody else they can't play."

Sixes base friendship increasingly on how good a friend makes them feel. Since a child from another culture may have different social rules—about eye contact, sharing, gender-appropriate behavior, demeanor toward authority, privacy, and so on—making friends can be difficult. Parents can help by getting to know other parents in the class, by finding opportunities for children to get to know each other in smaller groups than in the classroom, and by thinking through their commitment to cultural traditions that may get in the way of their children's friendships.

Parents of mainstream children, of course, can help hugely by encouraging positive curiosity, open-mindedness, and a spirit of friendliness and by not putting up with any prejudiced, insulting talk or behavior.

COSMETICALLY DIFFERENT; DIFFERENT PHYSICAL ABILITIES

Attending kindergarten is a crucial experience for a child with a cosmetic deformity or a physical handicap. The key is to get the kindergartners and the teacher on your child's side.

• Demystify the problem. Name the disorder. Tell what the doctors say about it and what is or will be done to help it. Sometimes a medical person can come to school and talk to the class. Teachers usually welcome this.

• Think like a Five. Fives will want to try out and talk about the wheelchair and crutches, hearing aid, glasses. They will want to touch the birthmark, examine the fingers or the prosthesis. If they are allowed to do so, they will feel a kind of pride of ownership that makes them act in a friendly manner. Tell your cosmetically or physically different Five that this is likely to happen.

Of course, she can let them or not, depending on how she feels. But put a good light on their curiosity. Your Five should be able to say the name of her problem and to explain it to other children and adults—when he wants to. "I have spina bifida. My back grew wrong before I was born, so my legs don't work," Martin explains. "This is how my wheelchair works. I can go in little tiny circles when I want, like this."

When she doesn't want to, she should be able to say that, too. "My hands are different," says Jessie stoutly. "But I'm like everybody else." End of conversation.

A Five who starts out the first day with a great desire to teach about his braces or her hearing aid or feeding tube is likely to make out very well indeed.

Freely use favors. This needs a teacher's cooperation. Persuade the school to break the no cupcakes in school rule. Invite a few children to go to the circus with your Five and you.

Talking with parents of children with similar problems can be very useful. Your pediatrician might very well be able to steer you to support groups, either local or national.

Sixes are curious too, but have usually learned the rule that you aren't allowed to barge up and ask what's on your mind. This drives curiosity underground, where it all too often surfaces as taunts and teasing. Left to their own devices, Sixes can be pretty nasty to other children who are different—as well as to other children who aren't.

Sixes have a very basic idea of what is "fair." They generally think that being fair means dividing up the goodies equally. The concept of giving somebody extra attention, time, treats, or of letting somebody have a head start or an easier test because that person has a disability is much too advanced for most Sixes. They aren't being mean; they are merely acting their age. This doesn't mean that you leave them there, stuck in their primitive idea of fairness. Of course you educate and monitor behavior. But when Six is mean to a child with a disability, it helps to try not to take this personally. Anger and contempt are not helpful emotions when it comes to teaching fairness and compassion.

Parents in this situation recommend some of the following ploys.

• It's crucial to meet with the teacher and principal before your child enters school. You can brief them about any special logistical problems, such as bathroom use or need for extra help. Just as important, you can establish a pleasant, mutually appreciative relationship. Offer to help, as well as asking for help. If you ask for assistance that isn't funded, it's important to appeal that decision. When doing so, make clear that you are not criticizing the teacher or the school. Address your complaint to the person or body who allocates funds.

• Ask one of your child's doctors to address the class before your child enters, explaining exactly what the problem is and how doctors are fixing it. The teacher can then pick up on this, outlining for the children how to behave appropriately.

• Ask the teacher for the names of a couple of children of the same sex he or she thinks might be good "introducers" for your child. If possible, have them over for a fun couple of hours and enlist them as buddies to go into the classroom with your child on the first day. That first visit or two goes best if the time is structured, with something for the children to make or do or experience together. It also needs adult supervision so that nobody gets ganged up on.

FAMILY SECRETS—THEY'RE NOT NECESSARILY SHAMEFUL

Some kindergartners and first graders have single parents, male or female; some are raised by grandparents; some have two parents of the same sex. Some children are adopted. Some families are interracial. If the family constellation is one that parents of the other children in the class are likely to regard with disapproval, several considerations apply.

Children this young always believe that their own family structure is normal and that everybody lives the way they do. Any variation, even one that adults would find insignificant, will catch their attention. This attention is not critical, merely incredulous.

> "Gina's grandmother lives upstairs in a little room," says Troy, eyes wide. You can just see his vision of Grandma and that room—maybe three feet square, with little tiny furniture."

When Fives and Sixes quiz or tease other children about their families, it's almost always because they've picked up such manners from adults. If a given family constellation is unusual, but not controversial, Fives and Sixes are not likely to be made unhappy in any way by their classmates.

If parents do anticipate teasing or worse, they may make an attempt to have the family difference be kept a secret and tell Five/Six not to talk about it, not to tell anybody. This is likely to backfire and cause confusion and unhealthy distress in the minds of Five and Six. For one thing, they are terrible at keeping secrets—any secrets. Much more importantly, it violates the strong instinct of Fives and Sixes that their homelife is perfectly normal.

This is a very important instinct for Five and Six. It provides a deep sense of continuity between homelife and the big, public world of school. When this sense is disrupted, Five and Six can become preoccupied, withdrawn, and sad. So merely telling Five or Six to keep family a secret is disruptive.

Parents really have just three choices.

• They can keep the family situation a secret from the child. Of course, you can't keep it a secret from Heather, as the picture book says, if she has two mommies. But you can teach Heather to call one mommy auntie. You can't keep it a secret from Carl that his father is terribly sick, but you can keep from him the fact that the disease is AIDS. You can't keep it a secret from Brad that Daddy works downtown, but you can keep from him the fact that he manages the factory that just laid off most of the parents at his school. You can't keep it from Isobel that her mother is an attorney, but you can make sure she doesn't know that her mother prosecutes pro-life activists or that she defends pro-life activists, either one.

Would anybody willingly advocate keeping a child in the dark about important family matters? No. But it may be the appropriate recourse for families who truly fear repercussions.

• They can tell Five/Six the whole truth and try to prepare him or her for any consequences

To be honest, this is tough. It is very hard for Five/Six to keep straight a coherent explanation of the potential problem, much less to understand strategies to deal with harassment. It is much more likely that Five/Six will be so worried and fascinated and preoccupied by the situation that the child precipitates an unnecessary encounter. This strategy is a dandy one, though, for most children by age nine and for a few as young as seven.

• They can try to prepare the way, educating and making friends with the teacher and other parents.

Theoretically, morally, aesthetically, this is ideal. Parents who take this tough and honest route in an effort to protect their child and create a more tolerant world have all my respect. My only advice, humbly given, is to make sure that their cause does not override their personal, intimate, one-to-one relationship with their child.

WHAT IF FIVE OR SIX POSSESSES MUCH MORE ADVANCED SKILLS THAN THOSE OF THE CURRICULUM?

When Five knows how to read but the kindergarten spends the first three months learning the alphabet, it's easy to foresee problems. Or suppose Six is reading chapter books while the rest of the class is laboring over *Green Eggs and Ham*. Will Five or Six be bored, become an unbearable intellectual snob, or get teased as an egghead?

Most parents are aware that being intellectually accelerated has nothing to do with social maturity. They are loath to move a Five or Six out of the world of kindergarten or first grade merely because of increased academic advancement. But they are also aware that in today's competitive world, getting a jump educationally can be an enormous advantage—unless it's at the cost of a warped psyche.

When confronted with such a bittersweet dilemma, the first thing to do is not jump to conclusions. The ability to read early can be taught to most children if it's gone about with determination, kindness, and method; many preschools, such as some Montessori schools, consistently graduate Fives and even Fours who can read.

So even 5-year-old "bookworms" who love to read may not actually grasp the point of what they are reading or be able to tell back the story when asked. Success in the academic aspects of school requires a whole lot more than reading: the ability to manipulate concepts and numbers, to analyze, to think logically, to arrange items in categories and sequences. Even children who are intellectually quick and retentive need to mature into these skills.

However, now and then it is clear to everyone, not just to parents, that a Five or Six is functioning well beyond the usual academic abilities. Such a child may indeed find school boring and studies show that very advanced children in a regular school class may come to regard classmates with a degree of contempt. This is not because they think of the other children as less bright, but because they think they aren't trying. Bear in mind that this study was done on older children, however. Kindergarten and first grade are so socially engrossing that Fives and Sixes may have no awareness that they are being taught something they already know or that they are quicker to understand new material than their classmates.

When you have a feeling that your child is accelerated enough that the local school is not appropriate, it's best to get a more objective opinion. Preschool teachers are often good judges of a child's degree of intellectual acceleration. Sometimes, though, they are swayed by affection for the child and parents. If you are considering dramatic action regarding schooling—an expensive private school or a long commute to a different public one or skipping a grade—it's a very good idea to have your Kid formally tested first. Your pediatrician should be able to give you some names of psychologists skilled in this field.

Skipping a grade at this age is very hard socially. Children change remarkably in the early childhood years in how they think of and make friends, in their ability to contend on the playground, and in their relationships with authority. Skipping also means being a grade younger when all one's classmates enter puberty, obtain drivers' licenses, and are exposed to the dangers of drugs, alcohol, tobacco, and sex. Children who skip a grade take the SAT's a year sooner, with less preparation and maturity, and compete for honors courses or to make the hockey team a year earlier than their classmates. You have one fewer year to save and one fewer year for the child to work for college tuition. And you have one fewer year with your child at home.

Before you leap into a major life-altering decision, schedule a visit with your child's kindergarten teacher. Take with you some samples of your child's abilities: a book she has read and understood and enjoyed, samples of drawings, of stories written, of arithmetic skills. Since you will be discussing your child, don't take him or her along. It is most likely to be a successful visit if you make clear that you are not soliciting awe and praise but asking for assistance and advice.

> "Would it fit into the class if Bobby could read quietly by himself during reading period if he wants? He usually has a book he's engrossed in." "What can I do to make it possible for Bobby to learn at his own rate and still be a part of the classroom activities?"

Here are some other alternatives.

• Some areas have magnet schools, whose programs are designed to draw and teach children with various strengths (see **School,** earlier in this chapter).

• Some school systems have one or two levels of (unfortunately named) "gifted and talented" programs. Many are so overapplied for and underfunded that they come close to being secret. To find out about them you must ask explicitly:

• Is there a gifted and talented, honors, or accelerated program in this school district or one nearby?

• Is there just one level or are there several? What are the requirements for each level? (There may be two or even more levels, often based on IQ testing. You may have to ask this question several times to get a straight answer.)

• At what grade does the program start? (Many don't start until third to fifth grade.)

• What kind of program is it? (Time out of the regular classroom; a separate classroom; and even a separate "magnet" school are all possibilities.)

• How does a child get tested for such a program? (Must a teacher recommend a child for testing? Will the school accept private test results? If so, which testers and what test(s) qualify?)

• Is there a waiting list?

• Where can I pick up printed information on the program?

• Is there a teacher in the program I could talk to (not just for information, but also because sometimes teachers have a say in who gets accepted).

WHAT IF PARENTS ARE WORRIED OR SHOCKED BY ASPECTS OF THE SCHOOL CURRICULUM?

School today can be a lot different from what you remember. If you are lucky, it's different in wonderful ways: better trained, inspired, child-friendly teachers of both sexes; brighter classrooms with seating that fits children better than rows of desks; projects rather than workbooks. Most parents welcome these changes.

But what about some of the others? First graders using calculators for math and CD-ROMs for reading. First graders teaching kindergartners. Children with disabilities, mental and physical, mainstreamed into the regular classroom. Classrooms integrated racially and culturally. Bilingual classrooms. Class discussion about different kinds of families, including lesbian and gay families. Multicultural units that don't focus on what we grew up thinking was important. Sex education. Self-esteem education. Some of these features may throw parents for a loop.

Part of the force of reacting to such innovations has nothing to do with the innovation itself: it's realizing that one is responsible for the academic success of one's child. A brand new role.

Time and again, I've seen parents act effectively on their child's behalf. But time and again, I've seen the whole thing blow up: parent angry, teacher angry, principal in the middle, supervisor unreachable, child more and more anxious and phobic and learning less and less.

The parents I know who are effective, who feel proud of themselves and pleased with their children's education, have followed some guidelines.

• They ignore rumors and the ranting of the media. They go to the classroom and talk with the teacher and examine the materials.

• They do all this in a friendly and open way, without baring their teeth and growling or howling. They don't just barge in without an appointment. They book a special time and start the conversation with a compliment. Even when they are secretly raging, or frightened, or aghast.

• They make clear what educational goals they have for their child and why they worry that whatever they're concerned about might keep their child from attaining them.

"If she uses a calculator, how will she ever learn the multiplication tables?"
"If she's in a first/second grade class,

won't the older children get all the attention and bully her?" "She can't speak a word of Spanish. How will she learn?" "How can you give someone self-esteem? Don't they have to earn it?" "What is this whole language program? Won't she wind up not learning phonetics or spelling?"

• Then they listen. They take notes, but not in a hostile manner. "Those are good points for me to think about. I just want to jot them down."

• They find a way to check their own perceptions. They visit the classroom as volunteer aides—and then visit a classroom that contrasts, to get perspective. They ask the teacher for studies on whatever features they are concerned about. "The sex education unit turns out to be mostly about plants," Margot admits rather shamefacedly. "At the end of the year, they graduate to eggs."

• They stay cool in front of their child. A Five or Six who hears mommy or daddy screaming or crying about something or someone in the classroom is a candidate for a giant case of school phobia.

• If they decide to fight whatever it is, they marshal their facts and present them through the hierarchy, starting with the teacher.

• They don't call names or use profanity. They make sure to behave the way they keep trying to make their Five or Six behave: with decency and intelligence. "So no matter what goes on in the classroom, I figure he's getting a good education just watching what I'm doing."

Alas, there are other classroom problems that are not at all controversial. To start school in a classroom that is downright dirty or dangerous is an outrage. If filth, disrepair, or violence are features of your child's school, my heart goes out to you. I hope you can gather together other parents, overwhelm schoolboards and politicians, do whatever it takes to repair matters.

But what if the problem is more personal? A teacher who seems to your child and you to be acting inappropriately, or a child or children in the class who are bullies or so disruptive that no one can learn?

The parents who act effectively on these concerns also maintain civility. They also are careful to make their own observations, taking others' remarks with a pinch of salt.

• They try to discuss the problem directly with the teacher. Sometimes the teacher agrees that there is a problem. "I'll always respect Mr. Hogan," Tammy says. "He told me he had no idea he was calling on the boys all the time and not the girls." "Cory's teacher said that there are two boys in the class who are almost impossible to control. She said she thought it was her fault, because she's a new teacher. But I told her that all the mothers know these Kids. She said she'd talk to the principal about splitting them up into different classes and making playground rules."

• If the teacher is clearly making an effort to solve the problem, effective parents make sure to give positive feedback—and not just to the teacher. They write a letter of praise to the principal and the supervisor.

• Sometimes the teacher is unresponsive. "You know what she said, when I told her the children were afraid of her? She said, 'I can't help it. It's just the way I am.' I told her that calling them 'a bunch of idiots' was terrible. What a role model." If the teacher reacts this way, the parents try to find other parents willing to make a group effort: signing a letter to the teacher, first; if that doesn't work, sending a copy to the principal or the supervisor.

• If nothing appears to be changing, they move their child to a different class

If a pediatrician is asked to write a note to change a child's class for a medical reason, most will need to know what the child's symptoms of anxiety or stress might be and how severe they are. Most will also insist that parents try other means of remedying the situation before resorting to a change of classroom.

WHAT IF FIVE/SIX DIGS IN HIS OR HER HEELS AND REFUSES TO GO TO SCHOOL?

It's hard to go to school sometimes. Occasional wishes to stay home are normal; everybody likes a little variety, a little time away from the usual chores. But kindergarten and first grade are supposed to be so involving and so full of masterable challenges that children should be eager to go to school most of the time. The occasional attempt to stay at home is usually ambivalent enough that the merest encouragement to go to school wins the day.

Sometimes the trouble is what awaits a Kid at school and sometimes the trouble is leaving home. Once in a great while, the trouble is getting to school: the glare of a harassed school bus driver, the rowdiness of older Kids in a car pool. In any case, Fives/Sixes rarely give the real reason for wanting to stay home. Instead, they say "My stomach hurts," "My head aches," "My body feels sick." But they have no fever nor do they throw up nor do they cough or limp or even lie around in bed. Once they have irrevocably missed the opening bell at school, they are as happy as clams.

Rarely is there a real illness in the absence of objective symptoms, especially given that the child perks up and plays energetically when relieved of the burden of going to school. If you have doubts, a visit to your pediatrician will clarify matters and is well worth the effort, no matter what the findings.

When a Five or Six shows a really intense wish not to go to school, sticks to his or her guns, and does so more than one day, something is up. The normal parental response, especially when life is chaotic and demanding enough, thank you very much, is to override the child's protests and contradict his or her complaints. "You're not sick! You don't even have a fever! You look fine!"

This can backfire. The child gets to school in such an upset frame of mind that you get a call a few hours later: there's been throwing up or lying around palely or weeping.

Instead, try to slow down the morning rush and take a few minutes to listen. Try not to intrude your own diagnoses. A good ploy is simply to repeat the child's own complaints in a sympathetic manner. "Your tummy hurts?" "You don't want to go to Miss Galt's classroom?" You are pretty likely to get to the reason behind the refusal. Perhaps somebody wet their pants yesterday and Six is terrified it will happen to her. Perhaps Miss Galt had to discipline Five's good buddy, who cried. Perhaps there was a substitute for Miss Galt who smelled funny and didn't smile.

If that doesn't elucidate matters, you need to do some detective work.

Most advice-givers tell parents that a child with school phobia must be made to go back to school. That's true. For one thing, it's the law. For another, if school refusal is the product of a mild case of separation anxiety, insisting on school attendance will almost always produce a cure as the child becomes more and more comfortable and involved with the classroom. However, if Five/Six is refusing school because there is a major problem that is not addressed, things will get worse.

Real trouble at school, such as violence, overcrowded or impoverished classrooms, dirty or gang-occupied bathrooms—is beyond the scope of this book. But if the child has problems with the teacher, classmates, or schoolwork, that's different. Individual parents can and should make a difference.

FIVES

Trouble at school

• Stage Fright

If Five has had no preschool experience, the whole ambience of the classroom can be overwhelming: being surrounded by unfamiliar children, following orders addressed to a group, having a strange adult give those orders, being asked to take care of his or her own personal needs, using a strange bathroom with perhaps no privacy, being disciplined in front of the other children.

It is easier to prevent this than to fix it. Taking the child on repeated and cheerful visits to the school, playground, and classroom before the school year begins and to visit the teacher ahead of time; practicing school skills at home; and making a friend who will be in the class— so the Kid will have a ready-made buddy the first day—will make a big difference.

If it's too late for this, just pretend it isn't. Start over. Take a few days off if you possibly can to go with Five after school, to explore and chat with the teacher when the children aren't there. Take Polaroid pictures of the nap corner and the cubbies and so on to look at home. Make sure Five has a gift to take the teacher the first "real" day. Try to find a "buddy" for the child to get to know on home turf before that first day occurs.

• Teasing and Bullies

A gently reared Five may interpret and report even friendly teasing and ordinary grabbing of a toy as being "beat up." But sometimes there is a real mini-bully in kindergarten. A chat with the teacher ought to reveal which of these two scenarios is going on. If the problem is getting a Kid used to casual rough-and-tumble and to being assertive, see the section on assertiveness under Social Development earlier in this chapter. If there is a real bully, the teacher needs to take special action to isolate and investigate that child's behavior.

Bullying behavior is frequent (an average of two Kids in each classroom are victims) and dangerous for both bully and victim: the former have a high risk of growing up into violent criminals; the latter, for depression and poor self-esteem. Kids can't deal with the behavior on their own. I urge parents and teachers to send for and establish the program **Bully-Proofing Your School.** *Write to Sopris*

West Publishing at 1140 Boston Avenue, Long-mont, CO 80501, or call 800-547-6747.

• Bathroom Terror

A Five whose training has emphasized cleanliness and privacy may find the casual public bathrooms of kindergarten dreadful. The situation may become acute if another child has an accident. Five may feel that this is a fate worse than death, no matter how understanding and kind the teacher and how unperturbed the other children. The only solution here is reassurance, the passage of time, and Five's continued attendance, even over his or her objections.

Trouble at home

For Fives to leave home happily, they need to be sure that parents want them to leave. They need to feel sure that nothing terrible is going to happen, such as parents fighting or a parent disappearing, when they walk out the door. They need to know that Mommy is not relieved to be rid of them so that she can play with the new or younger sibling.

But even if Fives' worries are based on a truly less than perfect homelife, Five needs to go to school even as these problems work themselves out. The larger world of school, with its own plots and melodramas, helps to diffuse the worry about home and also gives Five the kind of confidence that comes with mastering challenges.

Fives are so sensitive and so attached to home that they can have quite fierce separation anxiety, even when all is well at home. A loving parent who delights in being with Five has every right to shed a few tears as Five goes off to kindergarten. Unfortunately Five may interpret this poignant parental response as meaning that Parent will be devastated by the separation. The cure is a cheerful insistence that kindergarten is Five's appropriate destiny in life.

As thousands of teachers, pediatricians, and

psychologists have said, the cure for separation anxiety is separation.

SIXES

Trouble at school

Leaving the safe nurturing world of kindergarten for first grade can be a shock. You can't run to the teacher every time somebody hurts your feelings. You have to pay attention for twenty-five minutes—sometimes for an hour. You have to learn to read and write and manipulate numbers. Classmates are more choosy and excluding. The boys chase the girls and the girls chase the boys and you are no longer the littlest Kids in the school, who are protected. No wonder Six can feel overwhelmed.

- Trouble Learning

Some Sixes who are floundering in reading and math will go to enormous lengths to hide their difficulty. The chances that this is the cause of school phobia are greater if you or Six's other parent had trouble in first grade, if Six manages to get out of reading out loud at home, and if Six has no problem making friends in the neighborhood and getting along on the playground. If you believe learning problems might be the cause, make an appointment with your child's teacher.

- Friend Trouble

Classmates can make life tough for a six. Sixes tend to be pretty materialistic, which influences the way they choose friends and making someone feel popular: it's often on the basis of who has great toys or lunches or spending money. Also, friends can be very fickle, playing with you one day and pushing you away the next, or being your best friend at lunch and somebody else's best friend on the bus home.

What helps is an understanding parent who can sympathize with the pain but not overreact or panic or take it personally. What helps even more is having a friend who isn't a school friend, someone a Kid can see regularly in a context in which she isn't competing with other children. Talking with the parents of the pain-inflicting child or children only helps when the talk addresses ways of getting the children together happily—not when it focuses on complaints of fickleness. What helps most is the child's growing up.

- Gender Trouble

In many first grades, it's the boys against the girls, chasing each other at recess, excluding each other from activities. A child whose good friends used to be children of the opposite sex can be torn and tormented. Recognizing the problem and finding ways to maintain the old friends and to gradually make new friendships does help. Trying to enlist the teacher in maintaining a non-sexist atmosphere is worth a try, but it is battling big odds.

Trouble at home

As with Five, if Six is worried that things at home will disintegrate in his or her absence, refusal to go to school is a likely consequence. And as with Five, it is vital that Six continue to attend school even as the problems at home get worked out. A Six permitted to stay home under these circumstances is more likely than Five to become persuaded that he or she is the only force holding home together. Such a burdened Six is unfortunately more likely to contribute to any anxiety at home.

The Six whose homelife is relatively tranquil but who still can't stand to leave home to go to school may be suffering from guilt about growing up. The child at age six takes a big step toward independence and responsibility. When homelife has been very cozy and self-contained, striding away into the world can feel like betrayal. The cure is encouragement to take on new risks and adventures—playing at a friend's house all one Saturday; taking up a team sport; learning a skill like diving or roller skating—and calm parental insistence on going to school.

Sports and Exercise

It's easy to think that Fives and Sixes get plenty of exercise in their daily lives, just because they are energetic little Kids, but this may not be the case. Many are bused or driven to school. Only 36 percent of American public schools have daily physical education. Even then, the P.E. class may only be half an hour long, with a good ten minutes spent getting outdoors or to the gym and getting back again.

Physical education class itself may not be very active. Kindergarten and first grade lend themselves to games like dodgeball and red rover and duck duck goose, in which you spend most of your time standing around and screaming, with a little jumping up and down and brief spurts of running thrown in.

Recess and lunch can be pretty active, if there's room and time to play and the weather is reasonable. However, as Five turns into Six, the division of the sexes often means that—except for games of chase the boys or get the girls— girls may spend most of recess in very inactive pursuits, with Barbies or playing other quiet games like hopscotch and jump rope. Great for the person jumping, not much exercise for the rope-twirlers or those waiting in line for a turn. Boys may be very much into superheroes and weapons, but even such aggressive play may be lacking in true exercise. Much of that play consists of making the superheroes do things and emit loud noises. Finally, some children just prefer to play quietly rather than to dash about.

After school and on the weekend, there's the lure of TV, Barbie dolls, computer games, and other nonactive enterprises.

The moral of the story is that parents can't count on their children getting a lot of exercise automatically. For many children, exercise has to be purposely incorporated into the daily and weekly schedule. That means finding the time, the place, and the incentive for the child to get active and sweaty.

Fives are not likely to engage in spontaneous group activities. They don't yet generate group games like chase the boys or War or Pirates. Left to their own devices, they tend to just roam around, encountering each other. If they are with older children, though, they're usually eager participants in games the older Kids direct. Sixes are usually pretty good at starting games, such as chase and so on, with the rules changing all the time. They don't need any special equipment, just large, interesting, reasonably safe space.

Fives and Sixes can learn to ride two-wheelers, with most of the training wheels off by age seven. Many can master roller skates, safe in-line skates, skateboards, and ice skates. (Of course, all this equipment comes with two parts: the bike or skates PLUS the helmet, and in the case of skates and skateboards, knee-, elbow-, and wrist-pads.)

Fives generally can be taught to swim, though they're six by the time many can coordinate breathing and strokes. Most Fives can learn to pump a swing, cross the monkey bars hand-over-hand, and throw and catch a softball-sized ball. By age five, most children can hop, skip, and walk heel to toe on a curb, for instance. By age six, they can skip in time to music and walk a balance beam. Most Fives and Sixes can turn somersaults, and most Sixes can hang by their knees from a bar and turn somersaults over a bar.

Karate and judo are possibilities for Sixes and for some Fives of both sexes, if the teacher is experienced with children. Dance of all varieties is also likely to work up a sweat. Gymnastics may or may not give much aerobic exercise, depending on how much time is spent standing in line. One aerobic gymnastic activity, the trampoline, has been the subject of a statement by the American Academy of Pediatrics. Trampoline use, even with spotters, and no matter what size the trampoline, is disproportionately associated with serious injuries—especially spinal cord disasters.

Skiing is huge fun for Fives and Sixes, with their low center of gravity that makes it easy to balance and accelerate. But they are more vulnerable to injury than older children. Most injuries stem from cold and from accidents. Collisions account for 75 percent of children's ski injuries and falls for 20 percent. Kids this young can be demolished by an adult traveling at 30 to 45 miles an hour; they should be on their own part of the mountain (and so should the demon skiers be on theirs!). Bindings need careful checking: in injured children, they fail to release 50 percent to 75 percent of the time. Children are top-heavy, which increases their chances of serious head injuries: they need helmets.

NON-ATHLETIC CHILDREN

Some perfectly normal, bright Fives and Sixes are quite clumsy. They can't hop on one foot, nor can they skip; they kind of pretend to do each, never quite getting it. They protest taking the training wheels off the bike. They are always tripping or bumping into or dropping things. How will they improve? You can't even get them to practice! They say that the playground is boring or that they are scared of falling off the bike or that the skates make their toes tingle, or that it's too cold out. Or too hot or wet or bright or noisy or quiet.

Well, of course. The klutzier you are at something the less fun it is to do it. Nonetheless, the only way to become more graceful and agile is through practice. Parents can help a lot. They can tutor Five/Six themselves or hire a cheerful, kind older Kid to do so.

• Analyze the skill. For instance: When you pump a swing, you stick your feet out and lean back when going forward; you stick your feet back and lean forward when going back.

• Break down the skill the child is trying to learn: for instance, pumping the swing. Take it one step at a time: "When you are going forward, stick your feet out. Let's try that with you just sitting in the swing. Now I'll push you and every time you go forward, stick your feet out. Like that. Now at the same time you stick your feet forward, lean back. There you go! Super! We'll practice again tomorrow."

• Help the child to practice.

• Find a practice location where Five/Six won't be in danger or teased. The world of exercise can seem like an untrustworthy place to a nonagile child, and getting hurt physically or emotionally can make that child want to have nothing to do with it. Never ever let Five/Six hear adults calling him or her clumsy or think you are disappointed in him or her. A good thing to say, if there is a grain of truth in it, is that when you were a Kid, you found all these skills terribly hard, and you were much older before you caught on to the things he or she can do now.

• Make sure Five/Six understands the small step that you are focusing on as a goal for that lesson. Practice each step of the skill until it is easy and automatic before going on to the next. When you come to the next skill, keep practicing the previous ones in sequence.

• Keep practice lessons short, fun, and give

THE VIRTUES OF EXERCISE FOR FIVES AND SIXES

• To have fun
• To learn how to rough-and-tumble with other children
• To burn up extra energy that otherwise could inspire less lovely activities
• To burn up extra calories to prevent becoming overweight
• To learn and practice skills
• To use imagination and intellect
• To get used to minor injuries and discomforts without making an undue fuss
• To start to get the idea of games and sports with rules

them regularly, preferably daily. Call a halt to the lesson before Five/Six whines to stop.

• Keep practice sessions supervised. If a nonagile Five/Six keeps trying a skill without help, he or she is likely to keep reinforcing bad habits.

• If Five/Six seems to be having a terribly hard time with physical activities, discuss this with the pediatrician. Make sure Five/Six has had a vision test and a hearing test and full exam, including a neurological exam for balance, strength, and cerebellar function. Once in a while, a Five/Six benefits from formal physical therapy or (occupational therapy for fine motor activities).

What doesn't work: putting Five/Six in a class in which he or she can't keep up.

TYPICALLY ATHLETIC KIDS

In the middle of the agility spectrum are the great numbers of Fives and Sixes who need some practice to perform skills, but who don't have to agonize over them. It can be tempting to praise and encourage *only* the child who can run really fast, actually catch the ball, get it into the basket, and so on. Of course, this actively discourages the unpraised players.

The natural athletes themselves also may suffer. They may come to believe that they are good at sports because they are good, period, and confuse ability with worth. Moreover, since they don't understand rules and winning yet, they may get it into their heads that any time they perform well their team *should win*. This leads to the idea that if their team did not win, the other team "wasn't fair." If this idea gets entrenched stubbornly enough, it can stand in the way of the child's enjoyment of team sports in the next few years.

Many experts have condemned team sports for young children. Pushing children to win at all costs, breaking hearts and spirits by letting only the most skilled athletes play, inciting rage and contempt for the other or losing team—these are evil activities. No parent should tolerate such an atmosphere in any activity.

But little Kids have always played rudimentary team sports: dodgeball, red rover, tug-of-war. These games, though, are different in two important ways from other team games. First, the skills involved are pretty basic. Have you ever heard a Kid described as a real demon at dodgeball or a "natural" at red rover? Since it's so rare that a player stands out as really good or really awful, feelings don't get hurt.

Second, these traditional team sports for little Kids don't really have rules; they have consequences. Who wins? The last Kid in the center of the dodgeball ring. The last pair with unbroken hand-grasp in red rover. The team tugged by the other in tug-of-war. It's visually self-evident.

Trying to involve Fives and Sixes in team games with rules is another story. Everybody can learn a lot and have a great time as long as adults understand that they may need to completely rearrange their ideas of a team sport.

TEAM SPORTS

Parents involved with teams sports for Fives and Sixes spend a lot of time gawking with their mouths open, scratching their heads, and making statements that start out, "Well, uh...."

True, Fives and Sixes have had some experience with games that have rules. Many play Candyland and Chutes and Ladders and other board games. But there is a difference between these and team sports with rules. Board games are ritualized, and you repeat the same actions over and over. Team sports are unpredictable, with something new happening every minute. In a board game, you take turns: I have the dice, you have the dice. In a team game, either you have to get the ball by force or complicated rules determine who gets it next. In a board game, when you lose, you play another round and maybe you win. In a team game, once the game is over somebody won and somebody lost and that's it.

I guess that's what they mean by the saying: "It's a whole different ball game."

That's why an adult version and a Five version, say, of how to play soccer are so different. Here's a Five version of the game.

HOW TO PLAY SOCCER

• Kick the ball whenever you can. Kick it real hard. Kick it in any direction.

• If you had a bat you could bat the ball. You bat the ball in tetherball, so you could bat it in soccer if you had a bat.*

• If you try to kick the ball and miss, sit down on it so nobody else can kick it.

• If you have to go to the bathroom, tell the coach.

• Run to wherever the ball is. Run after the person who is kicking the ball.

• Yell a lot when anybody kicks the ball.

• Keep your shirt tucked in.

• If somebody finds something interesting on the playing field, go and look at it. If somebody makes a goal while everybody else is looking, that goal doesn't count.

• When the whistle blows, ask a grown-up who won.

In Five's set of rules, there is nothing about the point of the game or about penalties or even about the sequence of play. No one rule is more important than any other rule. There is nothing about teams, the duty of a player to the team, or about strategies for one team to gain the advantage over the other team. This is why conversations about sports with this age group can be pretty bizarre.

In even more complicated games, like baseball, or even tetherball, it is pretty obvious that the Kids haven't a clue, at least at first. Fives and Sixes are still working on understanding symbols. First, second, third, and home are symbols; the foul lines are symbols; an out or a strike or a ball is a symbol. It just seems so much more likely to Five or Six that the point of the game must be to whack that ball and then run around a lot.

Because their understanding is at such a rudimentary level, Fives and young Sixes need a special approach from adults. What they are learning as they play a team sport are:

• Specific skills, like kicking or throwing or catching the ball

• The very beginning of the idea that each game has a set of rules

• The idea that you can have two groups of players—two teams—trying to do the same thing, and that one team tries to keep the other team from doing it

• The concept that even though winning is the object of the game, the team that doesn't win isn't bad or naughty

Kids have to learn these lessons before they can get hold of the rules of an individual sport. Parents and coaches who try to teach more sophisticated concepts at this age are likely to burn out quickly. Fives and young Sixes whose coaches try to teach them more sophisticated concepts are more likely to burn out and to do so even more quickly.

To introduce Fives and just-turned Sixes to team sports, it works well to:

• Focus on lots of praise for anything, no matter how small, that shows bravery or skill or a concept of fairness and sportsmanship: falling down and getting a little hurt but getting right up again; giving the ball to the person who had it first; kicking the ball in any goal; holding the bat correctly; praising somebody else's good kick or throw.

• Bend the rules a whole lot. Fives and Sixes don't get three strikes and four balls or even six strikes and eight balls: they get to swing until they get a hit and a hit is never a foul ball. If a grown-up is playing outfielder, that adult moves slowly and doesn't tag somebody out; if playing basketball, the grown-up doesn't make all or even most of the baskets (even though

---

*It is not a good idea to bat a soccer ball. I have had to admit one Six with a concussion from doing so. The eyewitnesses weren't sure what happened; I suspect he hit himself with the bat.

you've lowered the net by several feet).

• Keep the emphasis on playing, not on winning. Don't audibly keep score. Don't announce who won unless somebody asks.

It is remarkable how much growth in understanding rules can take place over the year a Kid is six. By the beginning of age seven, most children understand the basic rules of the games they play regularly and some are authorities on the fine points.

But here's a funny thing. It may seem as if mastering rules gets in the way of sportsmanship. Show me a game played by Sixes and I'll show you a lot of squabbling and myriad versions of the statements, "I had it first!" and "It's not fair!" The abstract rule may be very well understood, but if enforcing it means that Six "loses," the rule is seen as the enemy.

This is just an apparently necessary phase in mastering the whole idea of rules, though. With adult help and kindness and firmness, Seven and Eight can work through this phase to real sportsmanship.

Growth and Nutrition

GROWTH

Five and six are key ages when it comes to growing. For many parents, this is when they first see their child in a largish class of children (theoretically) his or her own age. Comparing one's own Five or Six to the others is inevitable. Is Five or Six the right size? Too fat, too thin? Too tall, too short? Misconceptions can lead to regrettable actions: placing Five or Six in a class by size rather than by readiness; judging Five or Six to be too thin or too fat without a basis other than how the other children look.

HEIGHT

Fives

The average boy of five is about 43 1/2" tall, but the range of normal is considerable: from 40" to 46". Of course, there will be a few perfectly healthy Fives beyond this range. Five percent will be shorter than 40" and 5 percent taller than 46".

The average girl of five is 42" tall. Ninety percent of girls will fall within the height range of 39¾ and 45½". Five percent will be shorter than 39¾" and five percent will be taller than 45½".

Six

The average 6-year-old boy is 45¾" tall. Ninety percent of 6-year-old boys will be between 42½" and 48½" tall.

The average 6-year-old girl is 45¼" tall. Ninety percent of 6-year-old girls will be between 42" and 48" tall.

Most children who are outside these ranges for height are perfectly normal, following inherited genetic trends. Rarely, however, diminished growth in height is due to a medical problem, so your pediatrician will want to investigate a bit, usually with a complete history, physical examination, and sometimes with lab tests or x-rays. This is particularly important if Five used to be in the taller range on the chart, and his or her growth rate has slowed down. Very tall Fives also usually come by their height through heredity. Once in a blue moon, extreme tallness can also result from a hormone disturbance, so the yearly physical is a good idea.

You can't really predict adult height very well from the growth charts. We all know girls and boys who were tiny all through school then shot up in high school, as well as some who towered over everybody in fifth grade and then stopped growing, to wind up in the very front row of short people in the senior yearbook. Knowing the parents' growth curves, including when the same-sex parent had puberty, can make the guess more informed.

WEIGHT

Most Fives and Sixes gain about 6 to 7 pounds a year, though a very short, slender female Five may gain as little as 3 pounds. Also, a chubby child may appropriately gain practically nothing, and a very thin one may appropriately gain more than 7 pounds.

How much a child should weigh depends on height, gender, and body build—the thickness of bones and frame, which follows family, gender, and racial tendencies. Some variation, but not much at this age, can be due to differences in muscle development.

To determine the range of normal for a child of a given height and gender—a range that takes into account variations in body build—it's usual to use a growth chart. This is the "weight for height" chart shown in Appendix A. To do so, first make sure you have the chart for the appropriate sex of the child. Find the child's height along the scale at the bottom, and make a dot. Find the child's weight along the scale at the side, and make a dot. (Make sure not to confuse inches and centimeters, pounds and grams!) Then draw lines at right angles from each dot and see where they intersect. Call this place the point of intersection.

That point of intersection will fall somewhere in relation to the curved lines on the graph that are called percentile lines. They're marked 5 percent, 10 percent, 25 percent, 50 percent, 75 percent, 90 percent, and 95 percent. These lines tell you what percentage of children of your child's gender and height weigh more or less than your child.

For instance, if your child's point of intersection falls on the 50-percent line, half of children of the same sex and height weigh more and half weigh less than your child. If it falls on the 90-percent line, then ninety percent weigh less and only 10 percent weigh more. If it falls on the 10-percent line, only 10 percent weigh less and 90 percent weigh more than your child.

There is a normal *range* of weight for every child of a given height and gender. That range for most children lies under the 75-percent line. That is, if a child's weight for height falls

above the seventy-fifth percentile, it is likely that the extra weight is due to extra fat and that the child is plump. If the weight is over the ninetieth percentile, it's just about certain that the extra weight is due to extra fat. Such a child is almost always too chubby. If the weight for height is over the ninety-fifth percentile, the child is almost always obese.

What about thin children? Most children will weigh above the twenty-fifth percentile for height. But of those below the twenty-fifth percentile, only a few will be worrisomely thin. A healthy child with a normal physical examination who is active and developing normally might very well be growing appropriately, even though his or her weight falls at the fifth or tenth percentile. There are some cases of thinness, though, that need the pediatrician's evaluation:

• If the thin child is sickly or not developing well
• If the child has lost weight
• If the child's weight for height "falls down the percentiles," say from the fiftieth to the twenty-fifth to the tenth over a period of time
• If the weight for height is below the fifth percentile
• If the height is below the fifth percentile for the child's age

Fat children

Over and over, I've seen children who were of normal weight all the way through the infancy, toddler, and preschool years suddenly become chubby during this period. Statistics back me up. Most children who go into adolescence overweight start becoming chubby between ages six and nine. If there is a family history of obesity, this is the age to be alert!

HOW CAN YOU TELL IF YOUR CHILD IS TOO THIN, TOO FAT, OR JUST RIGHT?

You can get a ballpark figure from the growth charts

Make sure you are using the correct chart Make sure you have the girl chart or the boy chart, depending on your child's sex. Then make sure you have the weight *for height* chart. You don't want the chart that is labeled weight *for age*. At this point, you're not concerned with what your child weighs compared to others of the same age. At any age, some children will be tall and are supposed to weigh more, and others will be short and supposed to weigh less.

So you want the weight for height chart (see Appendix A). This chart has a scale for height running along the bottom and the scale for weight running up the sides. Plot your child's weight for height as described above.

If your Five or Six has previously been in the fiftieth percentile or below in weight for height but now has gone up to the seventy-fifth percentile, this could be the start of a trend you want to nip in the bud. If your child weighs between 75 percent and 95 percent more than other children of the same height and sex, suspect chubbiness that needs attention. If Five or Six weighs more than 95 percent of children of the same height and sex, suspect chubbiness that is tending into obesity.

Some children will be gaining extra weight as muscle, but to gain that much as muscle rather than as fat is most unusual, even for athletic children. In any event, it's always best to confirm your opinion with a visit to the pediatrician. Rarely is there a hormonal or other concern.

You can look at the child

Looking can be deceiving. A child may look bony to a parent but padded to a pediatrician or vice versa. I'd hate to see a too-thin child mistakenly thought to be normal, or a normal one to be chubby. Even though this rarely happens in my experience, it is a real danger.

It's much more common that a chubby child is seen as normal weight or even as skinny. Most normal-weight Fives and Sixes of both sexes look bony, with knees and elbows that stick out.

A chubby Five or Six often doesn't look padded but just cute, because you don't see any bones. When a chubby Five or Six stands up, you may not even see much of a belly. But when he or she is sitting, you'll spy a tummy sticking out and "love handles."

When a Five or Six is truly obese, weighing more than 20 percent over the normal weight, you can see it. There is jiggly fat, a double chin, and "cellulite." Often the child waddles as he walks. He or she may be short of breath when running and extra-sweaty. Little girls may be prone to vaginal irritations and infections because of chubby thighs. The penises of little boys may be hidden in fat and seem to disappear. Even so, sometimes parents have become so used to their child's body that they don't see the child's extra weight; or if they do, they regard it as "baby fat."

WHY DO SO MANY CHILDREN START GAINING TOO MUCH WEIGHT AT THIS AGE?

In America, a perfectly normal and wholesome lifestyle can lead to gaining too much weight. Often, it is only an inherited metabolism that burns extra calories instead of turning them into fat that *keeps* a child from gaining too much weight. An extra 50 calories a day taken in over what is burned adds an extra 5 pounds of weight in a year. That can move a child into the realm of chubbiness. An extra 100 calories a day adds 10 pounds. That can move a child into obesity.

Parents who have a personal or family history of problems with being overweight do well to be extra vigilant of children at this age. Several traps can make it easy for weight to accrue.

"My child is too thin!"

I can't tell you how often I've shocked a parent by suggesting that Six has gained more in the last year than is desirable. I can't tell you how often a parent or grandparent has dumbfounded me by worrying that a plump Five or Six is "so skinny."

Worse, I am regarded with disbelief and suspicion when I show parents the growth chart. "Eric weighs exactly the right amount—he's exactly average for a 6-year-old boy of his height," I say.

"Then how come his knees and elbows stick out? And his backbone?"

"Well," I say, "they're supposed to."

You see chubby children at school, in the park, on the playground; in photos in newspapers; in parenting magazines; on TV. No wonder the Erics look skinny.

"My child doesn't eat enough!"

It's hard to believe that a young child shouldn't eat three good meals a day. Many parents don't realize, or can't believe, that for many healthy prepubertal children a normal eating pattern is to eat a good breakfast, a fair lunch, and practically no dinner. Even if they don't enforce a "clean plate" rule, they may cajole and lure a child into eating a big first helping or a second helping that isn't really desired. They may make an effort to serve high calorie foods or to prepare food with "extra nutrition."

"When it comes to exercise, my child says, 'That stuff is for boys. I like to play with my dolls.'"

Fives and Sixes are great sexists. They are far more rigid than younger or older children on the topic of what boys do and what girls do. In my experience, girls are more at risk for gaining weight without parents noticing than are boys at this age. This may be because the friends of a little girl who is gaining extra weight are likely to be gaining extra weight also, so nobody stands out.

Most girls who are five and six like to play with each other. Over the preschool years, boys are subtly encouraged to adopt a more aggressive play style. By kindergarten, the difference is pronounced enough that even active little girls may prefer not to play with boys. Since the games become further sex-restricted, the differences in play style become even more exaggerated and the lack of activity for girls becomes a self-fulfilling spiral.

Little girls who like to play quietly with dolls, books, and crafts are often left to their own preferences. Because they don't play actively, they aren't skilled at playing actively, and what starts out as a preference for one kind of play becomes a deliberate, strong avoidance of the other kind of play. Even little girls who enjoy active games can feel a great deal of pressure from their classmates to join them in the dollhouse corner.

Often, the little girls who start to become chubby at ages five and six were merely slightly above average on the weight for height chart during preschool: not over the seventy-fifth percentile. But when they come in for their 6-year-old's checkup, they plot out above the ninety-fifth percentile. It's not that they are eating more or eating the wrong things: they simply aren't getting any exercise. They ride to kindergarten. They find ways to do little running during P. E. During recess, they play with similarly-inclined friends. After school, they play with their dolls and books.

In first grade, this style can become self-reinforcing. Increasingly, children choose friends based on shared interests, and they choose teammates based on athletic interest and ability. It gets harder and harder to persuade these sedentary little girls into other activities. Such a child is often unhappy about being overweight, but can't make the connection between her beloved activities—after all, they are "good" interests—and what seems like the punishment of excess weight.

"He/she gets plenty of exercise."

Childhood is full of action: running and jumping, dashing here, rolling around there—isn't it? For many children, it's not. Only 36 percent of our public schools offer daily physical education, and even when they do, the class may not be very active for very long. Recess can mean sitting around in groups, giggling. After school activities may consist of TV, homework, or classes in crafts or music. Weekends may be spent watching things: movies, sports, TV. Many children don't even walk to school, they are carpooled or bused. Some of the classes that children love—like gymnastics or ballet or horseback riding—involve learning skills more than expending energy.

My child comes home from school and says, "I think I'll watch cartoons and have another bowl of Chocolate Crispies."

Another group with weight problems is children of both sexes whose inactivity is enforced. They have nothing to do after school or on weekends but watch TV and snack. Very often, parents themselves feel immobilized: there's not enough time, money, and energy to find alternatives. A chubby little boy or girl doesn't seem like a big problem. But a chubby preteen may feel so bad about himself or herself that a big problem does result.

Television is only one, but a powerful one, among many food cues—that is, activities so associated with eating that it's hard to imagine the one without the other.

CAN PARENTS HELP KIDS STAY IN THE RIGHT RANGE OF WEIGHT?

You bet. But it means fighting the whole culture. For children with an inherited predisposition to chubbiness and obesity, a normal, wholesome lifestyle can produce excess weight-gain. You have to make a special effort to keep this from happening.

Of course you don't want to make a little girl or boy feel bad about being chubby. You don't want to engender a neurotic preoccupation with good foods and bad foods and calories. But you don't have to. What parents do need to do is:

• Analyze where all the extra food cues are coming from and get rid of them.
• Analyze what kind of exercise their child is getting and find ways for him or her to get more of it in daily life.
• Use nonfat or 1-percent milk, cheese, and yogurt.

• Supply water instead of fruit juices and sodas as a beverage.
• Keep a healthy eating style at home—regularly scheduled meals and snacks, emphasis on grains and vegetables, very little if any red meat, and modest amounts of low-fat fish, chicken, and turkey.

NUTRITION

Most Fives and Sixes need about 1,600 to 1,800 calories per day, depending on their size and activity level. About 30 percent, that's about 500 to 600 of those daily calories, should be fat—much of it unsaturated fat, like vegetable and olive oil. Those 500 calories can go pretty fast: about 70 in a slice of bologna, a glass of whole milk, or an ounce of cream cheese. A quarter-pounder with cheese has 270 fat calories.

Fives and Sixes need a diet that is rich in grains, veggies, and fruit. They need about 12 to 16 ounces of milk, preferably nonfat or 1-percent milk, for calcium. It's hard to get enough calcium without dairy products, though some breads and orange juice are calcium-fortified. Kids who are five and six need iron from meats, fish, poultry, dark green leafy veggies, and iron-supplemented cereals.

MEALS AND SNACKS

Fives and Sixes are teachable. Five will believe anything you say, and Six likes to know about rules to follow. Make the most of it. Talk a lot about healthy foods and healthy eating. No matter how much you talk, you will not talk more than the ads on TV for items like chocolate-covered sugar bombs. Try to get Five and Six interested in planning menus, choosing foods at the store, and cooking.

Fives and Sixes who are not at risk for extra chubbiness can have some leeway in choosing snacks and lunches. Some misguided experts even advocate a carte blanche approach, keeping on hand a wide variety of snacks including fat-rich cookies, cakes, and candies, soda for breakfast, and frequent desserts, on the theory that this encourages children to make free autonomous choices about what and when to eat. Alas, such choices are not truly autonomous. They are highly influenced by ads, especially TV ads. To say nothing of the fact that many parents feel those Ding Dongs calling to them, too.

Children don't resent it when their parents stock healthier choices; in fact, they are relieved. It helps them feel cared for and safe.

When it comes to actually sitting down (or standing up or lying around) and eating, however, children do best when they are in charge of choosing how much to eat of whatever is offered. That means not nagging or coaxing them to finish something or withholding dessert as a reward for eating the rest of the meal or denying them a third helping of whatever (a good reason to have healthy desserts like fruit, and when there is a rich item on the menu, to have only enough for one helping apiece).

All children do best when parents mandate a healthy eating atmosphere without grabbing and gobbling, without moaning and complaining about the food, without squabbles, whining, and teasing.

Fives and Sixes generally eat one good meal a day—often breakfast or lunch—and the rest of the time just pick. Thus, they may want and need to be excused from dinner sooner than everybody else or be allowed to sit and continue the conversation but not be asked to eat.

Health, Illness, Injuries

Hospitalization is discussed in the **What If?** section at the end of this chapter. Specific illnesses, injuries, and sports safety are discussed in **Appendix B.**

HEALTH

Five and six are pretty healthy ages compared to the toddler and preschool years.

Fives' and Sixes' immune systems have matured, so when they do get sick they are better than they used to be at fighting off symptoms. Fives and Sixes usually have outgrown the frequent illnesses—colds, ear infections, sore throats—that plague toddlers and preschoolers. At this age, they reap the rewards of having built up all that immunity. The average number of colds for a 5- or 6-year-old child is about six a year, but they are usually mild, without much pain or more than three days of fever. Because Five's and Six's anatomies have matured, most colds don't turn into middle ear infections any more, thank heavens.

It is unusual for a Five to have a fever convulsion or croup and rare for Six to do so. Breath-holding spells and night terrors also are pretty much restricted to the under-Fives. Isn't that nice.

When they do get sick, Fives and Sixes are still likely to take illness personally. The germ theory doesn't grab them: they suspect instead that somehow somebody was out to get them. Or that they did something wrong and are being punished. Taking a throat culture or blood test and giving bad-tasting medicine or an injection are seen by Fives and Sixes as a personal assault—not as a necessary means of diagnosis and treatment. They are very dubious that something good—feeling better—can come from something bad, such as a needle poke.

Even after they do feel better, they tend not to make the connection and to be suspicious if you point it out to them. A warm and trusting relationship with the pediatrician is invaluable: Five and Six may not believe that the procedures and medicine help, but they are very kind about forgiving a person whom they like.

When sick they regress, just like everybody else. Cheerful and eager-to-please Fives may whine and cling. The feeling of closeness from being at home and being taken care of in intimate ways may make Five tempted to prolong this return to babyhood after the illness is all over. Try to take this as a compliment, even as you firmly return Five to the world of kindergarten, chores, and friends.

Sixes may drop their cloaks of independence and superiority and settle back into being eager to please and adoring. That's if you're lucky. Some Sixes become very demanding and histrionic when ill. They focus in on a symptom with enormous intensity and "need" drinks of water, cushions, the remote, and so on. Most often, the degree of intensity is inversely proportional to the seriousness of the illness.

Either way, once Six is well, be prepared for a bit of a rebound as Six launches again into the vortex of friends, school, and activities. Six may need to go through a period of sassiness and hoity-toityness in order to get up enough momentum to assert his or her independence. Don't put up with it, but don't take it personally, either.

Both Fives and Sixes who are homebound with an illness may have trouble returning to school afterward; school phobia can start this way. If it does, the best remedy is to gently but firmly insist on school attendance. It helps to be brisk, cheerful, and casual. This means not worrying in any perceptible way about whether Five/Six is really all better; it means not making even a joking reference about "What will I do all day without you?" or complaining that now that Five/Six is well you have to go back to work yourself.

Other separation problems, like sleeping alone after having spent a few feverish nights in parents' beds, can appear, too. Certainly, preventing this ought not be your first thought when caring for a sick child. Coddling and cuddling are important therapeutic treatments. However, when Five or Six is clearly on the mend, it's a good idea to start encouraging a little self-reliance: returning to one's own bed, amusing oneself, getting one's own glass of water, and so on.

MEDICATION

Fives and Sixes must be supervised when given medication. Since they don't really think the medicine helps, they have no compunction about pretending to take it and then getting rid of it, hiding chewable tablets under the sofa cushions, or spitting the liquid into the toilet. A trick that often works is to give the child a few sips of ice water to dull the taste buds, then the offending medication, then something cold and sweet to get rid of the aftertaste.

Learning to swallow tablets like an adult is still dicey at this age; choking is a real possibility. An older Six who simply must take a tablet for some reason (perhaps the medication doesn't come in a liquid or chewable form; perhaps the insurance only pays for the adult form) often can learn by practicing on hard-coated candies, starting with small Tic Tacs, then moving to M & M's.

Fives and Sixes tend to do better with medications like eyedrops, nose sprays, and inhalers, if they can be in charge as much as possible.

Eyedrops: Let Five/Six examine the bottle and squeeze a drop on a clean finger. He can sniff it, taste it, touch it to his eye to check that the drops don't sting or sting only for a second. (If they really do hurt, check with your pediatrician.) It's easiest to put them in if you have the child stand up with something in the mouth like a lollipop. This helps relax the eyelids. Have the child stare at an upward angle at something. While Five/Six is staring, pull down the lower lid and drop in a couple of drops.

Nose spray: The big objection to nose spray is the smell and taste. Before you give the spray, hold a very aromatic substance under the nose: vanilla extract is good. After the spray, have a sip of tangy beverage like lemonade ready.

Inhalers: Hand-held inhalers for asthma need a spacing device for Kids in this age group to be able to use them effectively. Otherwise, Fives/Sixes wind up swallowing a good amount of the medicine instead of inhaling it into the lungs. This can be a particular problem if the child is on long-term treatment with a cortisone inhaler. The swallowed cortisone can produce decreased growth, suppress the immune system, and cause other serious side effects.

Nebulizers: A nebulizer is a machine that turns liquid medicine into a mist. It's noisy and the mist may not smell or taste very good. Nebulizers are most often used for asthma attacks. Most Fives and Sixes will rebel initially, but soon discover that the machine treatment makes them feel much better. Some young children need to take the mist through a mask held up to the face; others can use a mouthpiece to inhale the mist. Either way, it's most tactful to allow Five/Six to get fully acquainted with the mask or mouthpiece, tubing, and machine before foisting a treatment on him or her. Let your Kid turn the machine on and off a few times to get used to the weird effect of loud noise and wizardlike clouds of steam.

TRYING NOT TO CATCH KIDS' GERMS

Fives and Sixes can learn not to pass along infections. They can learn not to cough, sneeze, or blow into the faces of other people—not even their parents, siblings, or pediatrician!—and to wash their hands when they're done. They can blow their noses into tissue, throw it away, and wash their hands afterward.

Your best protection against catching whatever your child has is to wash your hands and dry them carefully before you touch your own eyes or nose.

WHAT'S NORMAL AND WHAT'S NOT

• Fives/Sixes' tonsils and adenoids are supposed to be large. Being large shouldn't cause trouble, however. If Five/Six always breathes through the mouth instead of the nose or has multiple recurrent ear infections, it's a good idea to ask your pediatrician about assessing the adenoids. If Five/Six is a very loud snorer,

check for sleep apnea: pauses of breathing followed by momentarily waking up and gasping for breath or two snores on the same inhale; very restless sleep; trouble waking up in the morning and sleepiness in the daytime.

• About 15 percent of Fives and nearly that many Sixes, have never been dry for more than a couple of nights in a row. This is called primary nocturnal enuresis and is usually normal and inherited. It's worth bringing up with your pediatrician, however, to be sure that there is no chance of an underlying problem and to discuss how to handle the wetting tactfully. It is not normal for a previously dry child to start wetting the bed (an occasional lapse from fatigue or stress doesn't count). Renewed bedwetting can indicate a urinary tract infection or other disorder, and calls for a visit to the pediatrician.

• Children without underlying medical problems rarely wet their pants at ages five and six. A child who does so needs a pediatric evaluation, performed with lots of reassurance that this problem is not his or her fault and that the doctor sees many children with this difficulty.

• A Five or Six who has poops in his or her pants has a condition called encopresis. Most often this isn't caused by emotional problems or medical pathology; it's a result of long-term constipation (see the Glossary).

• No sign of puberty, such as breast development, pubic hair, or body odor is normally present in Fives/Sixes. Any such sign warrants a visit to the pediatrician.

• At this age, the sounds of a child's speech ought to be completely understandable, including pronunciation of the "s," "th," "l," "r," and "y." Stammering may still occur when a child is excited or stressed. Normal stammering usually consists of repeating the same word or beginning letter of a word two or three times: "Where where where did the boat go?" The child doesn't grimace or close the eyes or show other signs of tension. The treatment of such stammering consists of ignoring it and "gentling down" the situation that's causing the tension. If stammering is more severe and doesn't fit these guidelines, see the discussion of stuttering in the glossary.

• Voice quality ought to be smooth and effortless. A chronically hoarse voice may be a sign of nodules on the vocal cords, often a sign of voice overuse: your pediatrician can help you find diagnosis and treatment. A "peanut butter on the roof of the mouth" voice can indicate obstructing adenoids or a chronically stuffed nose, often from allergies.

THE 5-YEAR-OLD'S KINDERGARTEN CHECKUP

(See **Appendix C**, page 271, for schedule of immunizations.)

What a tricky visit this is!

What's on the minds of parents? Not ear infections anymore or frequent viruses. For most Fives, those are pretty much all in the past. Instead, parents want to know about bed-wetting and thumb-sucking, about kindergarten versus another year of preschool. Plus: Why are Fives so bossy, so perfectionistic, so shy? What about sex play and sibling squabbles?

What's on the minds of the Fives themselves? Pleasing their beloved adults, feeling good about themselves, doing what they regard as their jobs and doing those jobs better than anybody else. Plus: Will there be any pokes? Will it be scary? Will the doctor like me?

What's on the mind of the pediatrician and the office staff? Height, weight, blood pressure, hearing test, vision test, complete physical examination, developmental evaluation, blood test for hemoglobin and cholesterol, skin test for exposure to tuberculosis, urinalysis, and—the grand finale—immunizations: the oral polio drink and two shots, the booster of the diphtheria, pertussis, tetanus vaccine (DPT) and the measles, mumps, and rubella shot (MMR). Plus: How can we help Five's ego stay bolstered through this ordeal? Will there be time to go into all those parental questions? If we answer during the visit, how do we do so tactfully with Five listening to every word? If *not* during the visit, when?

By the end of the visit, everybody can usually use a lollipop and a hug. If Fives are to come out of this demanding visit thinking well of themselves, they need a loving parent undistracted by tagalong siblings. They need to be prepared for the exam by parents reading them a book about going to the doctor or by practicing with their own doctor kits. Fives need to be told ahead of time that it's the doctor's job to look at all the parts of the body, even the private parts; a confusing concept, because Fives have been told again and again that it is their job to keep private parts private.

Fives need tactful language. Not "I need to take your blood pressure now" (Take my blood? With THAT?) but "Now this squeezer will give your arm a tight hug so we can see how strong your heart is working." Not "It's time now for the seeing test and the hearing test" but "Let's go find the special picture machines and noise machines and make sure they are working okay."

Once in a while, Fives will be so fearful of "failing a test" that they will do anything to "pass." For instance, a Five with poor vision in one eye might peek around the patch covering the strong eye. If that happens, a vision problem can go undetected for a long time. Most pediatricians have "peek-proof" devices, but it pays to ask.

If they know that there will be needle pokes that day, many Fives will be so spooked that they simply won't be able to cooperate with any aspect of the visit. Some parents and pediatricians agree to have all the "scary stuff" of labs and immunizations done during a separate visit, so that a promise can be made of "no pokes today!"

If this isn't feasible, it's usually best to tell Five about shots just beforehand. "You did such a good job at this visit! But we are not quite done. At this special visit when you are Five, we finish with some pokes. These are special medicines to keep you from catching bad sicknesses. And the doctor needs a drop of blood to make sure you are eating all the good things to make your blood healthy. Everybody who is Five must have these pokes. The president made that a rule. If the pokes hurt, it is okay to cry. We will have a treat afterward."

Fives aren't the only ones who need to feel liked and understood by the pediatrician. Parents need to feel the same way when it comes to talking about their concerns. Pediatricians are trained to deal with behavioral and developmental puzzles of all kinds. It's worth taking the time and effort to seek out a pediatrician who likes this role and who has developed ways to help parents take advantage of the doctor's advice in these areas.

Some pediatricians offer special appointments—sometimes as phone consultations—to address behavior questions adult to adult. Another option is to have a second adult sit with Five in the waiting room while the parent and pediatrician confer, but there may not be enough time scheduled during the routine visit. It's best to call ahead and ask if either of these choices is available.

If you haven't been able to find out beforehand if there will be time to address your questions, give the pediatrician a note with your questions before the exam. If the questions can't be addressed at that visit, your doctor will be able to tell you how to arrange for a consultation.

ILLNESS

See the glossary for specific symptoms, illnesses, and terms.

Most of the illnesses that attack Fives and Sixes are viruses and most remain anonymous—they come and go without being named. Unless a virus causes an illness with a very distinctive picture, it usually goes unidentified. That's because laboratory tests to identify viruses are generally lengthy and expensive. Most of the time, by the time you get the test back, the child is well and you don't care anymore.

Today, children are vaccinated against many of the famous, distinctive viruses of childhood—measles, mumps, rubella (three-day measles) and chicken pox. Moreover, viruses that often give a typical picture in teenagers and adults give quite a different and milder one in children this age. A Five or Six may catch, and make immunity to, influenza, infectious mono, or even hepatitis A, even though the illness is very mild and without any of the usual symptoms suffered by older people.

FEVER

Most Fives and Sixes can hold a glass thermometer under the tongue for at least a minute. Ear thermometers are more reliable than they are for younger children, because it is easier to position them correctly. (The probe must be in a straight line with the ear drum; it shouldn't face the side of the ear canal.) Pull the outer ear up and forward.

But you probably won't need to take the temperature that often. At this age, the degree of fever is a very unreliable guide as to whether an infectious illness is serious or not. Many mild viruses will give temperatures of 104°. On the other hand, once in a while a serious infection like pneumonia may produce a low-grade fever of less than 102°. A better indicator of how much to worry is to look at the child's behavior and at any other symptoms.

INJURIES AND SAFETY

See Appendix B for safety concerns about specific sports and activities.

INJURIES

Injuries to Fives tend to occur when the Kids are put into situations that they can't handle. They aren't great risk-takers themselves; Fives usually have a pretty good idea of what they can and can't do. Injuries to Sixes tend to occur because they put *themselves* into risky situations.

Parents have a delicate line to tread, encouraging Fives and Sixes to take up new challenges that may involve some risk, and protecting them from enterprises in which the risk is unacceptably high. The list below does not include the huge array of activities children this age may engage in these days. It does include some special age-related considerations when these apply to a particular activity.

Traffic

At ages five and six it is time to be very consistent and picky about traffic rules. Pointing out traffic signs and talking about how to be safe is a great way to pass the time when you're driving with a sharp-eyed Five or Six. It's lovely to hear them outraged and moralizing about people not using seat belts or helmets, jaywalking, or running stop signs.

Even though they can recite the rules, Fives and Sixes are not to be trusted. They aren't old enough to cross or even to walk along busy fast-moving streets without an adult. A Five is likely to just get confused or to misjudge how fast a car is going; a Six may be overly confident that she can get across the street fast enough that she won't be hit.

Fives and Sixes tend to trust adults too much, to think that a grown-up in charge of a car is in complete control. Moreover, they are just not experienced enough to pick up traffic cues and anticipate traffic behavior: the car about to back out or turn, the response of cars to an oncoming siren, and so on.

Fives and Sixes might safely ride their bikes along the safe neighborhood street they live on. However, they are not mature enough to ride along or to cross busy streets on their own. They certainly aren't grown up enough to ride their bikes along the side of a road with cars passing unless you are riding right along in front of them and are sure that they won't impulsively sprint ahead or across the lanes.

They're absolutely not old enough to bike out of the neighborhood by themselves onto roads with cars, even if you have supervised them for months and now feel that they've gotten the idea and will be safe on their own. Five/Six just cannot be trusted not to dash out between parked cars or wobble right into incoming traffic or take a tumble into an oncoming car while trying to do a wheelie off a curb.

Cars

Five and Six need to be safely restrained while riding in cars. Children over 40 pounds can use lap seat belts fastened low, below the belly button. Adult shoulder belts shouldn't be used on a child under 4½' tall, because of the possibility of neck injuries: tuck the belt behind the child. Putting Five/Six in charge of making sure everyone's belted up before the car starts is a good idea.

Car-related hazards:

• Five/Six should keep fingers off the buttons that control car door locks and windows. A Five/Six who sticks an arm or head through the open window (from either inside or outside the car) and then touches the window-closing button may panic and not get extricated as the window inexorably closes

• Just as dangerous: trying to run out from under the garage door after triggering it to close

• Riding motorcycles is a problem, even when the Five/Six rides safely and with a helmet. If I had a nickel for every Five/Six I've seen with exhaust burns on the leg, I could buy a motorcycle myself.

Guns

I remember being shocked when the mother of one of Sara's 6-year-old playmates asked about our gun policy: I thought she was being paranoid. Today, though, I ask just about every Six if he or she knows a person who owns a gun: most do. Then I ask if the child has ever touched or played with a gun: about half the boys have done so, frequently to the horrified astonishment of their parents.

The mixture of a gun and a young child is always a potentially tragic one. Fives and Sixes are at particular risk because they still may not be quite sure that TV and real life are not the same thing and because they trust adults to keep them safe—it doesn't occur to them that they need to be careful themselves.

Guns should be locked up, unloaded, separate from the ammunition, which should be locked up separately. Teaching gun safety to a child this young does not mean instructing in how to handle a gun properly: it means telling the child:

• Never touch a gun, even if somebody says it's not loaded and can't hurt you.
• If you are with another child who touches or says he or she is going to touch a gun, say "No! Don't do that!" and get an adult right away. That is not tattling!
• If you are at another home and a grown-up handles a gun in any way, tell your parents.

You have a right to know if your child has been in any danger or if another adult has given instructions different from your own.

Household equipment

Bathroom: Fives and Sixes are certainly old enough to take unsupervised baths and showers, *as long as an adult is within hearing distance*. Before you leave them to it, though, make sure that you have taken some precautions.

• Keep using the no tears type of shampoo.
• Turn the hot water heater down to 120°F— hot enough for all purposes but not likely to produce bad burns from a sudden splash.
• Remove those hair dryers, non-water safe radios, and other small electric appliances! Five/-Six is very unlikely to remember that taking them into the bathtub can cause fatal electrocution.
• Realize that any chemical in the bathroom is fair game for Five/Six to pour into the tub to make bubbles. Get caustic ones out.
• Mouthwash usually has a very high alcohol content and sometimes a high fluoride content and is very tempting to drink. In quantity, it's poison. Be explicit about telling children not to touch it. Better yet, move it elsewhere.
• Put nonslipping adhesive-backed stickers on the floor of tub and shower.
• Beware curling irons. Not only can they electrocute in the bath, they can burn when left on the counter.

Kitchen

Fives and Sixes can pour, stir, measure, make sandwiches, use an old-fashioned egg-beater, toss salads, and of course cut out and decorate cookies. They can stand on a stool and wash dishes in warm water or dry them. (Remember to turn the water heater to 120°F.) Make sure nothing sharp gets into the dish-water.

They are not to be trusted with knife-work, stoves, ovens, or hot food or liquid. Beware the garbage disposal.

Exercise area

Treadmills, step machines, weights—they're all fascinating to Fives/Sixes and letting Kids near them is just asking for trouble. Fives and Sixes drop free weights on their toes and fingers; they get distracted on the treadmill and fall and break their ankles; they catch body parts in a machine's moving parts.

Hot tub

Really hot water, hot enough to have to get into it slowly, is dangerous for children this young and can produce hyperthermia or heatstroke. There is also concern that heat of this degree may damage the ova or eggs already present in the ovaries of little girls.

The hot-tub drain may also be a danger when the jets are on, when it sucks water down. A mermaid or merman can be sucked down too: not just by the hair, but by the bottom. Underwater hot-tub swimming is not a safe enterprise. The rule for the hot tub should be the same as for a pool: never go in by yourself, always with a grown-up! Everybody needs to know how to turn off the jets RIGHT AWAY.

Miscellaneous

• Check out the school bus. If the driver can't maintain discipline in the Kids and calm in herself or himself, or if there's a clearly dangerous aspect to the route, find an alternative way to school for your child while you complain about the situation.

• When you fly, keep Five/Six buckled into the seat belt all the time, even when the sign is off. Turbulence can send somebody who only weighs 40 pounds crashing right into the ceiling.

• **Believe** those signs at amusement parks that say "If you can fit through here, you can't ride." Believe them even if the nice attendant says it's okay to make an exception.

Behavioral Problems

Every Kid will behave at times in ways that upset parents. This section looks at problem behaviors that are upsetting beyond what is ordinary. Either they are minor but annoying, like thumbsucking and bedwetting, or they are scary or angrymaking, like aggression. I have not included hard and fast guidelines about when to seek professional help in this section because there aren't any such guidelines. It is true that there are formal guidelines that list the behaviors that constitute a psychiatric diagnosis, such as "conduct disorder" or "oppositional disorder." However, these guidelines are used only to assist mental health professionals in recordkeeping and billing. To use such lists as a guide for "when to really worry" is inappropriate. Pediatricians are usually able to help parents to decide at what point they need professional assistance for a troubled Kid.

One kind of behavior that worries parents is not included in this section. That is behavior that suggests a Kid is unhappy with his or her sexual identity. Such feelings on the part of a Kid do not, in my opinion, constitute a behavior problem, but rather a condition of the spirit that we as a society don't understand or handle very well. It is more like a difficult situation than a behavior problem. So I've placed discussion of this conundrum in the **What If?** section of this chapter.

PHYSICAL AGGRESSION

Aggression means acting with the intent to do harm. It doesn't mean fighting to defend yourself, to get what you want, or to gain attention. Physical aggression usually begins to phase out after the age of four and is replaced by mean teasing, nagging, bossiness, and other kinds of verbal aggression (see **Responsibility, Discipline, and Life at Home,** earlier in this chapter).

A Five or Six who is in the habit of pushing, punching, hitting, biting, kicking, or displaying other kinds of physical aggression usually has a problem of some kind and also sees aggression being modeled by other people. Because this is not developmentally appropriate—the way shyness and lack of assertiveness and bratty behavior are appropriate—such behavior needs investigation and treatment.

Sometimes the cure is as simple as 1, 2, 3:

1. More positive focused attention, one on one, by parents
2. A firm stance against aggression, that doesn't tolerate even a slap or a pinch
3. Turning off the TV

Sometimes it's much more difficult, especially if parents use physical aggression or bitter words and hostile silence as weapons against each other or other family members. If physical aggression continues to be a "reaction of choice" for Five/Six, don't wait for your child to outgrow it: discuss the issue with your pediatrician!

CHILD IS DEMANDING, BOSSY; PARENTS CAN'T DO ANYTHING RIGHT

"I don't want juice; I want KoolAid."

"OK, here's some nice cherry KoolAid."

"I don't like cherry! I like orange-vanilla!"

"Well, okay, here, here's a glass of orange-vanilla."

"But I wanted it in my bunny cup, not in that old glass!"

"There. I've poured it into the bunny cup."

"But there isn't any ice cube!"

Clink.

"But there isn't any straw!"

Rip. Plunk.

Slurp: One sip. "Here. That's enough. I'm not thirsty any more. I want some animal crackers!"

Both Fives and Sixes are vulnerable to this pattern of behavior. This is usually a classical case of a vicious cycle, which works like this:
• Five/Six pushes people—friends, siblings, parents—around in an exasperating manner. This often begins during times of family stress, when nobody has a lot of time or energy to devote to Five/Six.
• People get annoyed and complain at being pushed around. They become worn out and give in or they dread the possibility of a tantrum. They soon start dreading having to spend any time with Five/Six.
• Little Kids sense when they are not liked and enjoyed. This feeling makes Five/Six feel desperate for more attention. But it's hard to act likable and cute when you feel as if people are avoiding you. Thus: more pushing and demanding!

Sometimes there are complications to the vicious cycle. Parents may feel guilty about their parenting. Perhaps they are over-extended at work or preoccupied by problems. They may well feel as if they are guilty of liking another sibling more than pushy old Five/Six. They may feel that Five/Six is suffering from low self-esteem, for any number of reasons. So they try to make it up by to Five/Six by knuckling under more.

When faced with a vicious cycle of behavior, the most effective thing to do is to intervene on all fronts at the same time. This means that parents need to increase Five/Six's self esteem and simultaneously eliminate any rewards for pushing people around.

The following is a blitz method of intervening.
• Spend at least half an hour a day in one-to-one time focused on Five/Six. That means no interruptions. It also means sharing some activity other than watching TV together. It doesn't mean expensive exotic enterprises. A walk with conversation, a few games of Chutes and Ladders (for variation, try going up the chutes and down the ladders), making cookies, reading a book and discussing the story are all good choices.
• See **Effective Praise** in this section. Use the techniques listed in that section frequently. Reward all nondemanding behavior with your attention.
• When Five/Six makes a first request, pay attention. Don't regard it as just another nag. Express an interest in the request and state the alternatives. If there are no alternatives, and you have to say "No," be sure that you recognize Five/Six's desire, validate it, and express sympathy that it can't be fulfilled. But stand firm.
• When Five/Six starts to push, underreact. Don't apologize. Don't let Five/Six believe you are scared of a possible tantrum. If the pushing escalates to tantrums, however, state the rule about tantrums and enforce it.

The interchange above could be rewritten:

"I want a drink." (What I really want is attention. Am I the cutest thing in the world or not?)

"Are you thirsty for water or do you want something for the taste?"

(Ah. Maybe she really cares! She's listening to me!) "Taste."

"I usually like juice for taste."

(I see that she's interested in my wishes, but maybe she's trying to push her ideas on me. I won't be bossed around.) "I want KoolAid."

"We have cherry or orange-vanilla."

(I'm still not sure she has my interests at heart. Maybe she's just saying what's easy. At any rate, I need even more attention!) "I don't like cherry or orange-vanilla! I want grape!"

"All we have is cherry or orange vanilla."

"I want grape! I want grape! I want grape!" (Now we'll see whether she really likes me or not. If she gets really mad and shouts, I'll know she doesn't really like me.)

"Next time we go to the store, be sure to tell me to get grape."

(I'll bet if I get furious, she'll confess that she really can't stand me. She'll shout at me and tell me she's fed up and I'm a brat. I've got to see for sure.) "I want it now! Grape grape grape!" Kicking and screaming.

"A tantrum means going into your room until it is over. When you are all done, come back and tell me if you still want cherry or orange-vanilla KoolAid."

(I'm going to finish this tantrum, but at least I found out something. She doesn't think I'm horrible. She's not fed up with little me. And I guess my tantrums aren't really as powerful and important as they feel to me. Maybe I really could give them up. Besides, she gave me a chance to make up without losing face.)

In a surprisingly short time, most interchanges won't get anywhere near the tantrum stage.

HYPERACTIVITY— ATTENTION DEFICIT/ HYPERACTIVITY DISORDER (ADHD)

Fives and Sixes can have a lot of energy. But you're hearing about hyperactivity all the time. How can you tell if your small whirlwind is just normally rambunctious or fits the category of ADHD?

ADHD is not a disease; it is a description of a set of behaviors. A child can be hyperactive and not have ADHD. A child can have ADD and not be hyperactive but rather inattentive.

There's no specific test—no blood test, no psychological test, no try-the-medicine-and-if-it-works-he's-got-it test—for hyperactivity or ADHD. The diagnosis is based on the history, family history, physical examination, and assessment of questionnaires from parents and teachers. Sometimes pediatricians need to order blood tests or x-rays to exclude other problems.

Many Fives and Sixes who don't have ADHD are plenty impulsive, inattentive, and active. It goes with the territory. If you are concerned that your Five or Six is way beyond the usual in these ways, a visit to the pediatrician and a conversation with the preschool or kindergarten teacher is a very good idea.

To make the diagnosis of ADHD, a particular child must fulfill the criteria in the box below.

Do notice that these requirements spell out that the behaviors must have lasted for six months or more to a degree that is causing impairment in learning, making friends, and being at school and that the symptoms must show up in at least two different settings. If Kiddo is "hyperactive" only at preschool or only at home, it's more likely that there is something hyperactive about the setting, not the child.

When pediatricians investigate the question of ADHD, they always gather information from adults at school and at home about the child's behavior. This is in the form of questionnaires. There are several different ones, but they all cover the same kinds of behaviors: fidgetiness, impulsivity, and distractibility.

The focus of the physical exam and any lab work (lab work is not routine) is to make sure that fidgetiness, impulsivity, and distractibility aren't caused by something that should be fixed. That "something" could be medical, emotional, intellectual, or environmental. For instance:

Medical problems: Decreased hearing; poor vision; sleep apnea with ensuing fatigue; constant low-level discomfort from constipation,

MEDICAL CAUSES OF ATTENTION PROBLEMS

This is only a partial list!

Medication side effects: Antihistamines; anticonvulsants (for seizure disorders); asthma medications—albuteral, theophylline, cortisone.

Diminished hearing: Kids don't know that their hearing is off; they think that their present state is normal.

Diminished vision: Kids also don't know when they can't see well. "Before my glasses, I used to think that trees were big, green blocks and the birds chipped them and made leaves."

Learning problems: A child who is lost academically will have many behavioral problems. Sometimes it's just a matter of grade placement; sometimes there's a specific learning disability or mild mental retardation.

Emotional problems: Anxiety and depression are enemies of attentional skills.

Chronic constipation (especially with soiling): See "encopresis" in the Glossary.

Chronic sinusitis: See "sinusitis" in the Glossary.

Allergies: See "allergic rhinitis" in the Glossary.

Sleep apnea: A Kid who has large, obstructing tonsils and/or adenoids may stop breathing for half a minute or longer many times a night. So may a Kid who is very much overweight. Lack of sleep and brief, frequent deprivations of oxygen can produce a lot of trouble behaviorally.

Lead poisoning: Whether you suspect there's been opportunity for lead exposure or not, have the child tested with a blood test.

Thyroid problems: Very rarely, a Kid may have a resistance to his or her own thyroid hormone and not be getting enough.

Absence seizures (petit mal): Rarely, a youngster may be having brief but frequent interruptions in consciousness. A brain wave test (EEG) diagnoses the condition, which is treatable with medications.

ATTENTION DEFICIT/HYPERACTIVITY DISORDER

To meet the diagnostic criteria, at least eight of the following must be present for more than six months, and they must have begun before the age of seven.

1. Often squirms in seat or fidgets, pulling fingers, twiddling hair, and so on
2. Has trouble staying put in his or her seat
3. Is easily distracted
4. Has difficulty taking turns
5. Often blurts out an answer before a question is finished
6. Has difficulty following instructions, even when trying to do so
7. Has a hard time paying attention to tasks or play
8. Goes from one unfinished project to another
9. Has a hard time playing quietly
10. Talks too much, without perceiving that this is bothering others
11. Interrupts a lot, can't mind his or her own business
12. Doesn't seem to listen much of the time
13. Loses things and has a hard time being organized
14. Takes risks without thinking; acts impulsively

sinusitis, or allergies; the side effects of medication—especially allergy medication; thyroid problems; rare, inherited metabolism problems; Tourette syndrome; lead poisoning;

Emotional problems: Chronic anxiety or depression;

Intellectual problems: Learning disabilities, language disabilities, including not speaking the language of the classroom fluently;

Environmental problems: Trouble at home, including neglect or abuse; inappropriate school placement—either bored or frustrated; distracting classroom; crowded classroom; or inappropriate discipline or teaching methods.

Many schools and pediatric offices are affiliated with pediatricians, neurologists, or psychiatrists and psychologists specializing in ADHD. Their help is especially useful in making sure that there aren't any emotional problems or subtle learning difficulties contributing to or causing the behavior.

Treatment for ADHD in Fives and Sixes may or may not include stimulant medication such as ritalin (methylphenidate) and dextroamphet-amine. It always includes advice about helping parents design an environment in which a child can be successful and feel in control.

With help, many children with ADHD can really love school, do extremely well in their studies, make and keep friends, and in general be a pleasure to themselves and others. The chances are great if parents keep alert and informed.

TICS AND NERVOUS HABITS

Five is pretty calm. When Five engages in nervous behaviors, he or she usually does so out of habit rather than from excess tension. Habits often start either with minor physical disturbances (nail-biting from a hangnail, for instance) or by imitation (a beloved uncle sucks his teeth).

Six is a pretty tense age, so it's not surprising that Six is jumpy. Sixes may bite their fingernails and have twitchy tics—blinking, sniffing, throat-clearing—as a way to express tension. They can take very seriously such compulsions as not stepping on sidewalk cracks: superstitions are merely another set of rules they think should be observed. Usually this is a normal part of being Six, not a sign of Tourette Syndrome or any other disorder.

Often the nervous habits and compulsions of Five and Six will go away by themselves if nobody gets too upset by them. Nagging and reminding never help: in fact, they usually make the behaviors seem irresistible and important. Here's what does help.

• See if there's something that is unnecessarily producing anxiety such as marital fighting, feeling displaced by a sibling's need, trouble at school either in the classroom or on the playground. If so, the habits and compulsions are not likely to decrease until the anxiety and its causes are addressed.

• Most often, nervous habits and compulsions increase with boredom. They may really accelerate while the child is watching TV. Make sure Five/Six has mind and body occupied happily much of the day.

• Excessive fatigue is another source of fuel for nervous habits. Most Fives/Sixes need at least nine hours of sleep at night.

• Make sure that any little physical inducements are addressed. Keep nails short and filed and take care of hangnails. Make sure itchy scalps don't inspire hair-twiddling.

• Instead of telling Fives/Sixes to stop the behavior, give them something to do instead, something that is incompatible with the behavior. Often the time before dinner is a high tension time, combining hunger, fatigue, and boredom: helping with preparation of the meal can solve all the problems. Many little nail-biters, male or female, can be taught to knit or crochet. Computer games can help, but may also increase tension so that the habits resume as soon as the game stops.

Tics and nervous habits range from being mild to being severe. Most of the time, the tics of this age group are mild and fade out as time goes on, unless circumstances of tension increase.

However, most parents have heard about the tic disorder called Tourette Syndrome (T.S.), and many fear that their child has the syndrome and will be ostracized for life. There are two things to remember here. First, Tourette Syndrome is comparatively rare. Second, a diagnosis of Tourette Syndrome does not automatically doom a child to social and academic problems.

TOURETTE SYNDROME

T. S. occurs in only one out of a thousand people, with boys four times more likely than girls to have the disorder. The average age of onset is the year between ages six and seven, but it can appear any time before the age of twenty-one. The thought of T.S. is very scary for parents. But remember that treatment is now much more sophisticated for all the aspects of Tourette's than it used to be. Many people with Tourette's have made important contributions to their world and have lived very satisfying lives. (See the discussion in Chapter 2.)

THUMB-SUCKING

It has to be the right thumb; the left won't do. You have to have your blue blanket with the silky edging to stroke your ear with. You get a glazed look on your face. If the sky suddenly lit up with fireworks, you'd cast your eyes up, and maybe you'd suck a little more slowly for a minute.

Why do they do it? Are they emotionally disturbed? Traumatized? Not usually. Most confirmed kindergarten and first grade thumb-suckers suck from simple habit. But that doesn't mean that it's a harmless pastime. The problems that result can be dental and/or mental.

DENTAL

Frequent, chronic thumb-sucking not only can push out the upper front teeth. It can change the entire look of the face, with the lower jaw and chin receding. By no later than age five, the confirmed thumb-sucker needs to have an assessment by a dentist skilled in pediatrics. If the verdict is that Five is in orthodontic trouble, ideally the next visit should be with a pediatric orthodontist. Sometimes early orthodontic help to preserve teeth spacing and jaw development is needed. Sometimes, with the active consent of Five, the dentist will insert a gizmo (prosthesis) that will physically prevent further thumb-sucking and additional pressure on the teeth. Always, a kind, child-friendly trained dentist can talk with Five about the problems of thumb-sucking and with you about ways to approach it.

MENTAL

Emotional distress, insecurity, and anxiety are not usually the cause of thumb-sucking. The cause is usually persistence of a habit that was found pleasing when the child was an infant. But when school-age children persist in thumb-sucking, the habit itself can make for emotional distress. Studies show that when other children see a youngster sucking his or her thumb, they tend to ignore and isolate that youngster.

Perhaps they are concluding that the thumb-sucking is a kind of Garboesque statement: "I vant to be alone." Perhaps the thumb-sucker is sending a signal that the thumb is a far more satisfying comrade than another human being. Perhaps the other children are threatened because thumb-sucking looks babyish and Fives and Sixes want to be seen as grown-up. Perhaps they are merely, like adults, repelled on hygienic grounds, though I doubt it.

Whatever the reason, they do tend to ostracize thumb-suckers. Because the thumb-sucker needs to make much more effort than normal in order to participate and meet other children, the thumb-sucker can become shy and self-conscious. All of which can lead to a considerable amount of distress.

What not to do

Jerking the thumb out of the mouth; yelling; commanding; rolling your eyes; sighing; making exasperated and sarcastic comments; imitating with your own thumb in rude exaggeration. These methods won't work. They merely make the thumb-sucker unhappy or defiant, and thus more likely to suck.

What to do

• Visit the dentist and enlist his or her help in explaining to Five/Six the reasons for making an effort to stop.

• At home, make it a rule that,

> "When you suck your thumb, I know you are tired. You may go and lie down in your bed when you need to suck your thumb. But that is rest time, not play time."

No TV, books, toys, music, and so on.

• Also, make it a rule that any blankets, cloths, silky items, or other "lovies" stay in the bed. Very often, thumb-sucking is triggered by the stroking of the "lovie."

• Find the excellent paperback book *David Decides: No More Thumbsucking* by Susan Heitler (Avon Books, New York, 1993). With the help of his family, David, age six, beats the habit. There's text for both the thumb-sucking child and the fed-up parent.

BED-WETTING

Like thumb-sucking, wetting the bed can upset children and parents alike because it seems babyish. How tempting to feel that if the child would just grow up, have a little consideration, and put his or her mind to it, the sheets would stay dry! At least, you'd think, he or she could get up and go to the bathroom!

Not so. Most children who wet the bed generally do so involuntarily, in such a deep stage of sleep that you couldn't wake them up to get to the toilet if you tried.

Bedwetters come in two varieties: those who wet the bed because of a normal delay in the maturing of their central nervous system, and those who wet the bed because of an underlying medical or emotional problem.

Most kids with an underlying problem show this because they start to wet again after they have previously been dry at night. This wetting isn't just once in a while, after too much excitement, liquid refreshment, caffeine, or stress, but just about every night. Such a pattern may indicate emotional trauma, a urinary tract infection, or even diabetes. Rarely, a Kid who who has never been dry will be found to have a medical problem, but usually there will be other indications: very slow growth or weight gain, excessive thirst, frequent large volumes of urine, or a weak dribbling stream. Any such pattern or sign requires a prompt visit to the pediatrician.

When Kids don't have an underlying problem but have never been able to get through the night dry, it's not because they don't try or do it on purpose to annoy. The reason that they wet is that the bladder automatically relaxes while the Kid is in a deep sleep. In fact, for some of them wetting the bed appears to be inherited as a genetic trait that governs this bladder-relaxing tendency. This tendency persists as long as the gene tells it to. The Kid with such "inherited" bedwetting tends to outgrow the trait at the same age as did the relative from whom he or she inherited the gene.

About 20 percent of Fives and 10 percent of Sixes have never been dry at night, so it's more a variation of normal than a behavior problem. Moreover, most Fives and Sixes aren't yet ready to spend the night at a friend's house, so the question of embarrassment in front of buddies doesn't arise.

Efforts to help a Kid this age stop bedwetting generally don't work and can make matters worse when the cause is an immature nervous system. Even methods that seem "innocent" can backfire.
• Using rewards (such as a star chart) for dry nights is likely to be frustrating for everybody. Such rewards are based on the theory that a child can control the bedwetting, perhaps by giving himself or herself a strong subconscious suggestion at bedtime. There's very little evidence that this works. (For older Kids, true hypnosis by a professional can produce improvement, however.) Most often, however, the child winds up frantically trying to stay awake so as not to wet the bed.
• Depriving a child of fluids after dinner hardly ever works because it doesn't address the cause of the bedwetting: bladder-emptying that is automatic and unconscious. Of course, if the bladder is less full, the flooding will be less; but when you come right down to it a wet sheet is a wet sheet, whether puddled or soaked. Fluid deprivation feels to the child like punishment for something he or she can't help.
• Trying to wake and "potty" the child when parents go to bed, or at some other time of the night, merely deprives the parents of sleep. Most children who wet the bed can't be roused from deep sleep. Even if they do empty their bladders at, say, 11 P.M., they will still have a refilled bladder later on, and will let loose during sleep in the wee hours. For the same reason, trying to teach the child to wake up on his or her own every three or four hours to go to the bathroom is likely only to disturb the Kid's sleep. (Bedwetting alarms, used for older Kids, do work, but do so on a different principle.)
• Bladder stretching or stengthening exercises suffer from the same problem: they don't address the underlying cause of the bedwetting for most Kids.
• Asking a Five or Six to strip and change the bed each morning is likely to be perceived by a Kid this young as punishment; it's not a chore that is likely to be assigned to friends or siblings. It doesn't serve as a deterrent to the bedwetting, but only as a critical reminder of something the youngster can't help.
• Using medication or a bedwetting alarm (see Chapter 2) for such young Kids is also usually

considered inappropriate, since most are not socially handicapped by the bedwetting and since many will outgrow the tendency by the time they are ready for overnights.

The best thing that parents can do for such young bedwetters is to try to make it a non-problem for everybody as far as is possible. This may mean shelling out $150 a year for disposable pull-ups, or it may mean a plastic coating for the mattress and a daily laundering and change of sheets, performed with businesslike cheerfulness by a parent. It certainly means not teasing Five/Six or allowing anybody else to do so.

Your pediatrician can help you to be absolutely certain that the bedwetting has no underlying medical or emotional cause, and can help your Kid understand that he or she is not to blame and will eventually outgrow the tendency. The biggest gift parents can give a five- or six-year-old bedwetter is their cheerful acceptance of the situation. After all, as Molly's mother points out, one wet blanket in the house is more than enough.

SOILING

As with thumb-sucking and bed-wetting, this unpleasant problem doesn't usually arise from emotional problems; rather, it tends to cause them. That's understandable. Most of the time, a Five/Six who poops other than in the toilet is chagrined and ashamed. In fact, many try to hide the evidence—for example, the underpants—in the back of the closet or buried in the trash or whatever. The wrath of the discovering parent and the ensuing recriminations can be devastating.

Most children who soil in their pants don't do it out of revenge or the desire for attention or to manipulate and terrify their parents or because they have a pathological involvement with poop. They do it because they are constipated.

When a child becomes well and truly constipated, the enormous bulk of the stool stretches the muscles of the large intestine and rectum. This weakens the muscles and diminishes sensation. Alas, the outcome is that the stool doesn't move along normally and the child doesn't sense that it is time to poop.

Little dribbles of softer or even liquid stool sneak around the hard masses of poop and stain the underwear. Or you may find just smears as the large mass of poop moves, with glacierlike slowness, out of the body. As far as toilet findings go, you will see either no poop, little pebblelike turds, or the infrequent humungous one that requires breaking up to flush and the occasional visit by the plumber.

Definitely not fun.

The upside is that most cases of soiling in such young children respond to a combination of enemas and laxatives, a regimen of diet and stool softeners, and rewards when the child poops in the toilet.

Do not wait to see if the problem will solve itself! The sooner you get started, the better, and the happier everyone will be. Waiting until age seven or older can cause real emotional problems for the child and for the whole family.

Window Of Opportunity

VALUES, RITUAL, AND RELIGION

For a number or reasons, this is a key age for nurturing a child's spiritual education, whether or not you are a member of a religious faith. Here are some considerations:

• Fives and Sixes are just starting to be able to think in symbols and they come to this new ability with eagerness. For the first time, a child understands that a picture (a star of David, a cross, a figure of a holy person) can stand for a story, and that the feelings inspired by the story can be evoked by the picture.

• Children at ages five and six do not doubt that adults have a grip on the truth, with a capital T. They believe that their loving adults' idea of the universe is unchallengeable.

When Fives and Sixes look at the world, sights that a jaded adult takes for granted astonish them. Moreover, they have not yet had enough experience to put their own interpretation on events. For instance, if an adult and a Five/Six encounter a person who is homeless, the child will be full of questions: What happened to his house? His family? Is he sick? Does he care? Should we give him money? And on and on. How the adult answers every question is likely to be engraved deeply in the brain of Five/Six.

There is a danger at this age: If parents don't consciously take on spiritual education, Fives and especially Sixes may well patch one together of their own and it may be one that you don't intend.

• Fives and Sixes enjoy ritual if they can be participants. Performing the same actions in a set sequence gives them a feeling of power and control.

WEIGHT CONTROL

If Five/Six tends to be chubby, this is the time to make sure that weight does not become a problem. The lives of Fives and Sixes are still pretty much designed by parents: you determine what kind and how much exercise they get and have some control over meals and snacks.

At Five or Six, there are still several years for parents to help a child to shed extra baby fat, merely by slowing down the rate of gain—a far easier process than having to lose weight once adult height is reached. Waiting until ages seven or eight or older means that the child has fewer years of growth left to gradually lose baby fat. Moreover, extra weight brings about early puberty, which limits the time to lose weight even more. For girls, the hormones of puberty encourage even more chubbiness; once puberty has begun, slowing weight gain is exceedingly difficult.

So if Five/Six has shown an upward swing on the weight for height chart; if Five/Six has a jiggly belly and looks chubby next to his or her classmates, it's a good idea to consult the pediatrician.

MANNERS

Five and six are good ages to teach Kids:
• How to greet an adult: Make eye contact, smile, say hello and the person's name, hold out your right hand (some Fives and most Sixes know which it is) and give a firm handshake. Rehearse a lot, remind the child just ahead of time, and reward afterward. Praise every aspect that went well, even if it was just the smile or the eye contact. Criticism backfires.
• To say please, thank you, you're welcome, excuse me, I'm sorry
• To stay seated at the table until they ask to leave, rather than to dash away
• Write thank-you notes promptly. Sixes and most Fives can usually manage: "Thanks. Love, Dmitri." They like to make their own stationery.
• To respond to a gift with a smile and a statement of appreciation, even if it wasn't just what you wanted
• Chores! See **Responsibility** in the section on behavior earlier in this chapter.
• Start discussing TV critically. Watch with Five or Six. Talk about your views of how the TV characters behave.
• Point out that advertising says things that aren't true.

> "On TV, this toy looked much bigger and shinier. They made that up." "This ad makes it seem as if eating that cereal will make you grow big overnight. Do you think that could happen?"

SPECIFIC SKILLS

• Learning a foreign language by immersion is very successful at this age. Children are less wary of differences between people than they are later on and less self-conscious and more adept in imitating accents. Learning a foreign language at age five or six—any foreign language—makes it easier to learn additional ones later on. It is as if the brain gets rewired, so that the pathways for processing new languages are already in place.

• Sports skills: Five and six is a good age for learning to: ride a two-wheeler, ice skate, roller-skate, turn a somersault, skip, and walk a balance beam. Fives and Sixes take instruction well in how to swim with coordinated breathing, ice skate, bat a ball, catch a ball, hit a golf ball, hit a tennis ball, downhill ski, and sometimes practice karate or judo.

• Music and dance: Moving to music comes naturally to children this age. Formal dance programs are often fun, but most get just as much out of twirling around the living room to some rousing beat. As for performing music, some programs (Suzuki, Yamaha) start very young children on musical instruments. These programs generally require not only significant parent participation, but a focus on achievement and performance rather than "just" appreciation.

What If?

Events that disrupt the tranquillity of everyday life occur to every child. Fives/Sixes react to these events in their own, inimitable ways. Parents can help young children cope more effectively if they understanding what's going through Kids' minds at the time.

MOVING

From the point of view of Fives and Sixes, a move is a very big deal. They have just achieved enough maturity to really make sense of their world: home, neighborhood, school, activities. Since that achievement is unique in their memory, they have no real confidence they can start over again in a new environment. Anything

you can do to help is a good idea. Here are some suggestions:

• Get as much visual information as you can about where you are moving to. Even if Five/Six goes with you for pre-move visits, take pictures and videos. Make a scrapbook.

• If Five or Six is to start a new school year after the move to the new home, try very hard to allow time for your child to visit the new school before classes begin. Try to find a "buddy" for the child to stick with when going into school the first day.

• If Five/Six is going to enter school in the middle of the school year, try to make friends with the teacher ahead of time. Send a packet about Five/Six: nice color photograph, letter about interests. Many teachers welcome the idea of a school project, having the class write letters about themselves to their new classmate. See if you can get permission for Five/Six to bring a treat of cookies or the like the first day.

• Explore the library for books about children (or animals) who undergo a move. Talk and listen as you read. Otherwise, Five or Six may assume that his or her experience will exactly duplicate the story and be mad when it doesn't.

• On the day you move out and the day you move in, arrange for Five/Six to be closely supervised by someone not engaged in the move. Children younger than five should be "absolutely elsewhere" because of the high risk of accidents on moving day, often weird ones, like trying to fly out of the upstairs window or stowing away in the moving truck. However, Five/Six often does better emotionally watching the process. Being presented with a fait accompli may cause great upset.

• Try to have the movers set up the younger children's rooms first, and have them arrange the furniture in the same way as in the old home.

• Pack Fives/Sixes a special knapsack with precious stuff in it: "action figures," dolls, whatever toys or security objects they sleep with, and whatever else they hold dear. BUT DO NOT TRUST FIVE/SIX NOT TO LOSE THE KNAPSACK! It should be the first thing on your checklist as you travel from spot to spot. Beware of leaving it on the roof of the car and so on.

• Don't be surprised if, once moved, Five/Six seems to have no memory of or attachment to once beloved friends. This does not indicate a shallow or callous nature; it's developmentally appropriate.

TRAVEL

If you are traveling out of the country, check with your pediatrician about the immunization for hepatitis A, and with your travel advisory or the Center for Disease Control (404–332–4555) about other travel precautions. Make sure you have any medications you need. Do not pack injectable insulin in baggage checked with the airline! It will freeze and lose its potency.

Fives and Sixes are eager but unreliable travelers. First, they have only just so much capacity for newness before they collapse. Second, Fives are usually reluctant to venture into realms in which they do not feel competent, and Sixes tend to take on rash, risky endeavors and then get angry at YOU when they don't work. But it can be lots of fun traveling with Five and Six if you bear in mind that:

• They tire easily and suddenly. Fives and Sixes can walk at least a mile, but the mile needs to be worth walking. Look at your surroundings from their eyes. Choose the toy museum over the Louvre, the park over the art gallery.

• The constant stimulation of traveling saps their energy. It's usually not a good idea to dole out little bits of food all day long, but it may be necessary on a long trip. It's better to opt for taking rest stops for the child to exercise or have the child take a nap, but food is sometimes all that's available to ward off fussiness.

• Fives/Sixes are not entranced by newness. This is because they are still finding just about *everything* new. After all, they are just beginning to make coherent sense of the world. They may regard newness as a terrible thing ("But why DON'T they have peanut butter here?") or as a normal part of everybody's world ("When we get home, I will have a snake just like that one on the man's head") or as a breech of conduct ("That lady should take off that thing on her face").

• For a feeling of security and competence, they rely heavily on things that they already know. This gives rise to misunderstandings. "Tasha, put down that Barbie doll and look at the waterfall!"

• They need constant, age-appropriate adult interpretation. This works best when the description is as vivid as possible.

> "That was a very, very bad king. He was so bad the people cut off his head." "Here is a big, old house that was very, very fancy. But in this whole big house, there wasn't … one … single … bathroom! So they had to make peepee and poopoo in little bowls they kept under the bed!"

• The biggest challenge of all is likely to be bathrooms. Give your child practice using bathrooms outside your home in the area where you live before you travel. And don't restrict yourself to bathrooms: have him or her practice "going" behind a bush or tree, as well. Trust me.

• If you are in a very "foreign" place from the child's point of view and emotional disintegration seems imminent, allow the child to *regress*. Spend a whole day playing Chutes and Ladders (I hope you brought it along; if not, draw your own board) and eating comfort food like imported, creamy peanut butter.

• Remember that every physical sensation is exaggerated at this age. If you are cold, Five/Six is colder; if hot, hotter; if tired, exhausted; if needing a bathroom… well.

NEW SIBLING

This is usually a wonderful age for a child to have a new sibling. Most often, Five/Six takes on the role of big brother or sister with affection and just enough detachment. What helps in this sibling relationship:

• Include the child as soon as you know you are pregnant or about to adopt. Fives and Sixes are so sharp that they'll figure out something is up and may fantasize unbelievable scenarios unless they are let in on the coming event. Encourage participation in all the action leading up to the birth or adoption. Regard the questions of Five/Six as serious and important and make sure to answer each and every one.

• Do not over-reassure. Especially, don't say, "We'll love you just the same after the new baby comes" or "You'll always be our first, favorite little boy (or girl)." When you reassure, you raise the possibility that another course of action is possible. The best reassurance is to show by your manner that there is no doubt in anybody's mind: Five/Six is securely adored and that's that.

• Make a regular time to spend alone with Five/Six every day and keep it as a first-priority commitment after the new baby comes.

• Don't promise that the new baby will be a boy or a girl. Once in a blue moon the tests are wrong. Even the ultrasound. Even the amnio. You may understand this, but Five/Six will be completely thrown for a loop.

• Most Fives/Sixes don't do well being in the room for the delivery. They aren't yet mature enough to have visualized and understood the whole thing ahead of time, even though they've been coached and instructed. It will all be new and scary to see adults displaying unusual emotions, like crying or moaning or cursing.

• When the older child first meets the new baby, don't be holding the new one in your arms. Those arms belong to you know who. Greet the older one with a hug first and then introduce the new baby.

• Don't display guilt at loving the new baby. Fives and Sixes are so dependent on adults being "in charge" that they will believe you. They will agree that you did the wrong thing by having another one.

• Make sure the older child hears you say, many times,

> "You will have to be patient a minute, new baby, while I listen to what Five/Six is trying to tell me."

After all, you'll be saying it the other way round often enough.

• Let Five/Six glory in the importance of having a new sibling. A nice ritual: allow Five/Six to carry a Polaroid snapshot to school of the new one, cradled in his or her arms and wrapped in a receiving blanket, plus a treat to pass out to classmates.

• Create ways for Five/Six to help with the new baby that are not onerous but get a great deal of thanks and applause. NEVER should Five/Six be in charge of the newborn or of any crucial and tricky activity, such as warming the bottle or pinning the diaper. Fives and Sixes are not old enough to carry the baby; they will let the head flop and wobble—dangerous! Enforce the rule that the holder must sit in a big chair under close supervision.

• If Five/Six is not yet reading, put a reminder sign on the door for visitors: "Please make a fuss over the older child before you ask to see the new baby."

Jealousy

Once in awhile, a Five/Six is very jealous and resentful of the new baby. Almost always, this is an indication that Five/Six is not feeling like a success in life. This can happen even when parents are making every effort to give Five/Six lots of attention and praise and special treats. In fact, such attention and praise and treats may seem to make matters worse.

WHAT HELPS

• Make a regular time just to hang out and play with Five/Six. Half an hour a day is usually about right. Board games, playing catch, going to the playground, reading books, cooking something fun are all good bets. Watching TV together doesn't count.

• Take complaints and statements like, "I hate the new baby. He has ruined my life" calmly and without anger, apology, or expressions of regret or guilt. Such statements are often experimental, designed to see what kind of response ensues. Acting devastated or angry or apologetic tends to make Five/Six feel justified and encourages an escalation in negative words and behavior. Over-reassurance does so even more strongly.

Instead, it often works to say something like,

"I can remember feeling upset when Uncle Theo was born. It takes time to get to know a brand new baby."

Or,

"Babies cry a lot and need a lot of attention at first."

End of discussion. Then direct Five/Six to a new activity. The goal is not to be unsympathetic. It's to communicate that such feelings are normal, though not pleasant, and that nobody is upset by them because they will pass in time.

• Make sure that Five/Six has at least two areas of life in which he or she feels successful and no areas in which he or she feels completely at sea, incompetent, and alone. Trouble making friends or difficulty with schoolwork needs to be addressed.

• Fives and Sixes need to feel cute. With a cute new baby around, they need to feel really, really cute. Make a point of laughing at their jokes, listening to their point of view, asking their opinion. Let them overhear you telling other people what a cute thing they said or did. Don't let on that you know they are listening.

• Set limits and enforce them. Temper tantrums and aggressive behavior require firm, unambivalent responses. Changing your discipline tactics in the face of Five/Six's jealous behavior is a bad idea. Most especially, if you haven't spanked before, don't start now. If you have, consider using more controlled and authoritative responses to bad behavior. Physical punishment may make Five/Six feel as if the boundary between parent and child has become blurred; after all, hitting is just what children do. At the time that a new baby arrives, Fives/Sixes need to have that boundary very clear and secure.

• Hiring a nice, trustworthy, cheerful older youngster of the same sex to play with Five/Six on a one-to-one basis every day can work wonders. Five/Six loves hero worship and usually adores big Kids ages nine to fifteen. It's as if this gives Five/Six new dignity and maturity, almost by osmosis.

WHAT DOESN'T WORK

• Apologizing for having the new baby or for needing to spend time or give attention to the newcomer will fuel the fire of jealousy amazingly.

• Trying to reason with Five/Six, pointing out all the good things in his or her life, will backfire. The child tends to take this as "arguing." This is pretty much guaranteed to end in anger and tears.

• "Being extra nice," by being more lenient about behavior, chores, and so on, pushes Five/Six to escalate misbehavior.

YOUR CHILD SAYS: "I WISH I WERE A GIRL." "I WISH I WERE A BOY."

Most children have moments when they wish to be the opposite sex, either just to try it on or because the opposite sex seems to be getting all the perqs. I remember my grandmother telling me, at age seven, that if I achieved the ability to kiss the tip of my own elbow I could turn into a boy. I nearly dislocated my shoulder in the attempt.

The kind of cross-sex behavior that concerns parents and pediatricians is much more pervasive than the sort that springs from such transient impulses as curiosity and envy. It means that a Kid almost always prefers friends of the opposite sex and avoids children of the same sex. It means that a boy yearns for, or a girl shuns, typical feminine dress, accessories, and playthings. (Most male dress, accessories, and playthings are actually unisex.) It means that when a Kid daydreams, dresses up, or makes up imaginative games, he or she almost always chooses an opposite-sex role. A Kid may state firmly that he is "really" a girl or that she is "really" a boy.

Parents of such a Kid usually have three questions. Is my Kid's behavior in the normal range for age? If not, does it predict that he or she will be homosexual as an adult? Do parents "make" their Kids homosexual?

Answering these questions is tough.

Studies of cross-sex behavior in childhood look at the question, "Do Kids of a certain age ever show a particular behavior?" They give a statistical answer about a certain population. They rely on questionnaires filled out by parents, whose answers may be based on incomplete observations or influenced by their own ideas of what is "okay" to report. I will give these statistics in each chapter of this book, but they should be interpreted with caution.

Studies that look at whether cross-sex behavior in childhood is linked to adult sexual orientation come in two varieties.

1. There are studies that look at children (almost always boys) referred to psychiatric clinics because of cross-sex behavior and follow these children to adulthood. In one such study,

73 percent of the boys turned out to be homosexual as adults. In a second study, 43 percent of the boys described themselves in adulthood as exclusively homosexual and an additional 25 percent described themselves as bisexual. The problem is that for every child troubled enough to be referred to a psychiatric clinic, there may be a dozen whose cross-sex behavior is not regarded as needing professional help. Their outcome is unknown.

2. There are studies in which adults answer questions about their memories of childhood. These are fraught with technical problems. Selective memory is the biggest. People whose adult life is shaped by homosexuality may remember cross-gender activities in childhood with more intensity than those who are heterosexual and vice versa. A homosexual man might remember hating physical sports for their aggressive components and forget completely having loved a whole summer of gentle sandlot baseball. Or a lesbian woman might remember hating playing with dolls and completely forget beloved Belinda, who accompanied her everywhere. Similarly, an adult heterosexual may selectively remember episodes of gender-traditional play and repress cross-sex behavior.

3. Studies that look at whether or not a Kid became homosexual because the parents behaved in a certain way are also problematic. Many of the early studies were based on evaluations of homosexual male adults receiving psychiatric care. These studies showed a very high proportion of abnormal parenting—mostly over-dominating and intimate mothers and distant or hostile fathers. However, the studies were unable to distinguish among the following: did this parenting style cause the homosexuality or did it just cause the distress that led to the psychiatric care or did it cause both?

When such studies are repeated using adults who are not in psychiatric care, the results are mixed. In at least one large well-controlled study, no difference was found in the way homosexual adult males versus heterosexual adult males had been parented.

So my suggestion is that parents try to reframe their worries. Here are four more useful questions to ask.

1. Is my Kid's cross-sex behavior appropriate for his or her age? I address age-appropriate cross-sex behavior in the **What If?** section of each chapter.

2. If the behavior is not age-appropriate, is it caused by something gone astray in his or her daily experience of the world?

• Perhaps there are familial signals that one sex is valued much more highly than the other.

• Perhaps one or both parents very much hoped for a child of the other sex, and actively, though often unconsciously, visit this wish or their disappointment on the child.

• Perhaps the Kid's talents, temperaments, and strengths blossom only when he or she engages in activities that other people associate with the opposite sex, such as contact sports or ballet.

• Perhaps a narrow version of the same-sex role makes that role seem dreadful. Maybe a boy is expected to swagger and fight and is kept from showing vulnerability or gentleness. Nasty! Maybe a girl is made to feel as if looks and dress are the most important of her features and that she isn't supposed to take risks or accept challenges. Boring!

3. Is my Kid likely to suffer, because of his or her cross-sex behavior, with diminished self-esteem and restricted opportunities—or even with a chance of being in physical danger from bullies? If this is the case, parents have an obligation to try to help.

4. If I decide to step in and try to change this behavior, what are the age-appropriate ways to do so?

• Parents can let a Kid know that he or she isn't alone. They can tell even a young child that other people have similar feelings. Most of all, they can let their Kid know that they are behind him or her, every step of the way. They won't allow siblings or other relatives to tease meanly or to talk about the Kid's behavior outside the family.

• They can help a Kid develop a firm sense of self, a self that incorporates features of both sexes. This means making sure that the Kid has many choices of activities and role-playing and many choices of potential friends of both sexes. It means nurturing feelings and behaviors that may seem gender-limited but really aren't: bravery, empathy, assertiveness, gentleness, a sense of adventure.

• They can teach their Kid explicitly that certain statements, mannerisms, and behaviors are not socially acceptable.

• They can avoid labeling their Kid. Referring to a prepubertal child as gay or homosexual or lesbian is to prematurely introduce the idea of sexual orientation. This sexualizes a Kid's experience inappropriately and constricts his or her self-image. After all, you wouldn't go out of your way to label a Kid heterosexual.

As parents intervene in their Kid's gender-atypical behavior, it's important to keep in mind that there is no evidence for or against the proposition that changing childhood behavior changes adult sexual orientation. Many people who are homosexual state that they knew they were different very early in childhood and that no amount of behavior modification or inner resolve could change the matter. A parent's job is not to change a child's inner core, but to help make his or her public life a source of pride and pleasure.

Your pediatrician may well suggest counseling to help the whole family rise to the challenge. It's a good idea to make sure of the counselor's attitude and credentials in this area, however. It is not the counselor's job to confirm a Kid's (or parent's) feeling that he or she is bad, sick, dirty, or just plain "wrong." It's the counselor's job to help strengthen self-regard and family ties.

CROSS-SEX BEHAVIOR IN FIVES AND SIXES

No wonder many Fives show a great deal of what seems to be cross-sex behavior. They aren't yet concerned with their public identities and act pretty much in the way that feels most comfortable, without regard to what the rest of the world expects. There is much more room for and acceptance of cross-sex behavior in Fives than there is for Sixes.

Gentle, sensitive, verbal 5-year-old boys may avoid rough-and-tumble play. They can't stand it that the other kindergarten boys won't take turns and would rather give orders than agree on a plan. They may prefer playing house or with Barbie dolls to batting, throwing, and catching balls. They may cry easily, be frightened of anything from big dogs to amusement-park rides, and be reluctant to engage in risky physical feats. They may like to dress up in female garb or be enticed by female fantasy figures like Cinderella or Snow White.

A lot of energetic, assertive, action-loving little girls are bored or confused by the "mitigating" style of little girls, with all the taking turns, words instead of action, and emphasis on getting along together. They prefer a style in which the strongest, loudest, or fastest rules the day. They love action heroes and want a cape (to fly in) or toy guns. They may reject feminine dress and refuse to play with dolls. They like to roughhouse and talk loud.

Sometimes parents see behavior in their Kids that seems worrisome but is really typical of the age. At other times, parents are quite right to be concerned. How do you know which? Studies in child development can be helpful. But you have to be careful.

For instance, one large study[1] showed that 22.8 percent of boys and 38.6 percent of girls show 10 or more different "gender atypical behaviors." This seems like a large number, and may paint a picture of Five/Six as not having much commitment to masculinity or femininity.

However, many behaviors the study described as "gender atypical" aren't regarded as such by many parents: boys playing with girls or girls playing with boys; children doing things with relatives of the opposite sex; girls being interested in automobiles; boys liking fairy tales and girls liking books about dinosaurs and space; girls dressing sloppily or liking to roughhouse. Moreover, a Kid was counted as engaging in an activity even if that activity occurred only rarely—once in three months or less. Nevertheless, the statistics are reassuring for parents who might expect very rigid compliance with "masculine" or "feminine" behavior and are alarmed at any deviation.

This study also showed that some behaviors are very unusual indeed. Fewer than 3 percent of boys experimented with cosmetics and fewer than 2 percent dressed up in feminine clothing more than once in a six-month period. Fewer than 5 percent of girls ever played dress-up in men's clothing, and fewer than 3 percent said out loud that they wanted to be male any more often than once in a three-month period.

Another study[2] showed that before age seven, about 7 percent of both boys and girls indicate in some way a desire to be the opposite sex, and that 6 percent of boys and 9.5 percent of girls dress (as opposed to "dressing up" for fantasy games) like the opposite sex. Before age seven, 16.9 percent of boys and 20.6 percent of girls choose roles of the opposite sex in their imaginative play. Before age seven, 63.3 percent of boys and 71.4 percent of girls play with toys

[1]The Prevalence of Gender-Atypical Behavior in Elementary School Children, by David E. Sandberg, Ph.D.; Heino F. L. Meyer-Bahlburg, Dr. Rer. Nat.; Anke A. Erhardt, Ph.D., and Thomas J. Yager, Ph.D., *J. Am Acad. Child Adolesc. Psychiatry*, 32.2, March 1993, pp. 306–314.

[2]Normative Sexual Behavior in Children, by William N. Friedrich, Ph.D.; Patricia Grambsch, Ph.D.; Daniel Broughton, M.D.; James Kuiper, and Robert L. Beilke, Ph.D., *Pediatrics*, Vol. 88, No. 3, September 1991, pp. 456–464.

traditionally associated with the opposite sex.

The second study also looked at explicit sexual behavior, behavior that imitates adult sexual activity. This behavior, whether cross-sex or same sex, is rare. Fewer than 1 percent of children under age seven masturbate with an object. No boy under seven, and only 2.8 percent of girls, inserted an object into their genitals or anus.

Both studies show us that Kids under age seven engage at least occasionally in some cross-sex behavior. After age seven, all these behaviors become much less frequent.

The moral of the story is this. Precociously sexual behaviors that are statistically rare, whether cross-sex or same-sex, call for an evaluation of the child. They may indicate inappropriate exposure to adult sexuality, even molestation. Cross-sex behaviors that are rare, such as boys dressing up as girls or using cosmetics or girls dressing up as male fantasy figurs, or any Kid stating a wish to be of the other sex, may be within the typical range if they are few and far between. However, if a Five/Six shows more than a couple of these rare behaviors or engages in them more often than once every few months, parents would do well to talk over the situation with the pediatrician.

These studies don't give us a full picture of why cross-sex behavior diminishes as Kids grow older. No doubt, some Kids discover that they actually prefer same-sex activities as they grow and change. Others discover that their preferences are not socially acceptable and get them into trouble. They learn to modify their style of play and friendship to some degree and to camouflage their real preferences. If they are lucky, they find same-sex friends with tastes similar to theirs and activities that are socially acceptable, but that also satisfy their interests and temperaments.

However, it is likely that this change doesn't start suddenly at age seven, but comes about as Kids discover the importance of the public world and the existence of their own public selves—usually in first grade. This is crucial, because if they have not started to hone a socially acceptable public role in first grade, they're likely to find second grade miserable. That's when Kids become exclusionary. They tease and bully Kids who are different.

The more intense and preoccupied a Kid is with cross-sex wishes and behavior, the earlier parents should be concerned about how that Kid will fare in the years after first grade.

A Five who *can* play happily with same-sex playmates at traditional same-sex games is probably going to do fine, even if he or she prefers opposite sex companions and activities when given a choice. A Five who avoids same-sex playmates, who can't join in their games, who seems unhappy and depressed when in their company, who frequently wishes that he or she were of the opposite sex or who insists that "I'm really a boy" or "I'm really a girl" is likely to have trouble. Whatever a parent's attitude toward homosexuality, such a Kid needs professional help: help in the form of acquiring the skills to negotiate public life in second grade and beyond.

What if a Kid isn't that intense about cross-sex preferences but hasn't started to change behavior by mid-first grade? Such a Kid, too, needs help, but often parents can do this on their own.

• Look for activities in which your Kid will shine and in which the participants are same-sex children. If your Kid does turn out to enjoy the activity, make every effort to nurture a friendship between your Kid and a same-sex participant.

• Don't forbid an activity your Kid loves, but do impose some rules. For instance, a boy who loves dressing up in frills or playing with Barbie dolls may do so at home when there are no visitors. A girl whose style is rough-and-tumble must learn to take turns and negotiate.

• Almost any cross-sex activity has aspects to

it that are present in a same-sex activity. For instance, a girl may like gymnastics, horseback riding, or any number of skating-type activities. A boy may enjoy arts and crafts classes, a children's theater, a coed dance class, or karate.

• See the sections in this chapter about encouraging assertiveness as opposed to passivity, shyness, or aggression.

• Make a friend of your Kid's teacher at school, in religious education, or in other studies and of your Kid's coaches. Encourage these adults to pair up your Kid with a same-sex kindred soul. Ask them to let you know if your Kid is being teased or excluded.

Your pediatrician will be able to talk with you about your concerns and to refer you to another professional for help if you think it is needed.

SERIOUS ILLNESS IN A PARENT OR SIBLING

Five/Six is a difficult age to experience a serious illness of an immediate-family member. They are so sharp that they overhear everything, but they are so inexperienced that they can't organize the information. They don't even know what to ask. Moreover, they are so egocentric in their thinking that they believe everything that happens is because of something they themselves said or did or didn't do. Here are some things that can help.

• Have a quiet, serious one-to-one talk with Five/Six. It is okay to cry, to be upset. However, it is best to try to hide fear or anger: Five/Six is likely to think these emotions are directed at himself or herself.

• Be honest. Say that the disease is a bad disease. Say the name, even if you know the child won't remember it; he'll recognize it when he overhears it and won't think it's being kept secret.

• Tell what is being done to help. Make it simple. "The doctors are giving strong medicine" is fine.

Reassure specifically on the following points:

• Nothing that Five/Six did or said or thought could have caused the illness or kept the person from getting sick.

• The person did not get sick because he or she was bad.

• Five/Six is not in any danger of getting sick.

• You (or someone the child knows and loves) will be constantly there for Five/Six if he or she has questions or worries.

• Five/Six may ask very upsetting questions or make very upsetting comments. Be prepared for this. This is because of the inexperience of a child this age; it's not a sign of a corrupt, cruel, or uncaring nature. You may hear, "She got sick because you had a fight." "I hope he dies." "Can I have his bear if he dies?" The response to this kind of question has to be measured and calm, not angry or dismissive or shocked.

• Five/Six may not show much emotion after this conversation or even in the light of all the commotion of the illness. Instead, expect mood changes and tantrums, trouble with eating and sleeping, and regressive behavior: thumb-sucking, clinging, whining, wanting a bottle. A lifesaver: a relatively unaffected but loving adult who can give Five/Six a great deal of low-key attention and physical affection.

• Try to keep the child's schedule regular and as normal as possible.

• Fives and Sixes may believe that if only they can distract the adults from worrying everything will be all right. Don't be shocked if they indulge in showing-off behavior at the most distressing times. The kind response is to give a small smile and a hug and tell the child that it's okay, that it's not his or her job to make everything all right.

DEATH OF A PARENT, SIBLING, ADULT OR PET THE CHILD LOVES

Children aged Five and Six don't seem to be able to organize or hold onto the concept of death. They tend to ask the same questions over and over: questions about burial and cremation, and about heaven and what you can do there. They may seem to understand all the complexities of illness or accident that lead up to the death. But at the time of the death, they often don't weep or scream or dissolve. Instead, they react to each new thing that happens: adults upset, change in where they live or sleep, new person in charge or helping out at home, funeral, the attention of adults they know or strangers—and they react with caution, withdrawal, regression, or acting out.

They roam around watching and listening. They seek out physical affection from everybody, even people they don't know very well. They have short fuses: temper tantrums, hitting, even biting may occur for the first time in ages, and sulking, whining, and tattling blossom. They show off and clown around, trying to distract the grown-ups from their grief.

This is all normal and very painful.

WHAT WILL HELP

• As much cuddling and physical affection as Five/Six wants

• The presence of a loving adult who is not disabled by grief

• Any discussion of plans for the child's future should not be done when he or she can overhear. If there will be big changes in living arrangements, make sure that these are firm before announcing them. Children this age often need to be told many times before they understand. They require a good deal of reassurance about practical detail: where they will sleep, who they will play with, what possessions they will have.

• A clear explanation of why the beloved person (or pet) died, with special attention to these details:

  • The person who died will not be able to be seen or heard or touched any more.

• The person who died did not die on purpose. He or she did not leave Five/Six behind because he or she was angry or upset at or tired of the child.

• Usually only very old people die, but sometimes somebody dies when they are not old. They get very sick or very hurt. Five or Six does not understand terms like "sometimes" very well, however. Make sure to say that all the other people Five or Six knows are not going to die until they are very old.

• Never try to draw a moral from the death. Do not say that a person died because he drank too much or because she took drugs or because he was homosexual. In the years to come, you can talk about this kind of thing, but not at this stage.

• Nothing anybody else did caused the death. Thinking angry thoughts or saying angry words doesn't kill people.

• Dying is not like going to sleep. Sleep is a completely different thing, even though dead people have their eyes closed.

• Even if you have no religious beliefs, try to talk about the person's soul as opposed to the body. This is a hard concept for everybody, including Five/Six. But children this age are much more worried about all the details: the act of burial or cremation and how it must be scary or hurt. It is not an act of betrayal to talk to a child who is five or six about a heaven you don't believe in. You can pick up the conversation a few years later if you need to.

• Books about death for children this age do exist, but they never substitute for repeated conversation.

• Five/Six needs to know what a funeral or memorial service is. If there is to be an open casket, this needs to be discussed carefully with the child. Five/Six should have a choice about attending the funeral; he or she needs to know that adults may be very upset and cry. Five/Six should be seated with a relatively calm adult and should be allowed to leave with that adult at any point in the service or afterward. If the service is one in which emotion is actually repressed and people do not cry, it is a good idea to talk about this with the child as well.

> "People were trying hard not to cry. Many grown-ups don't feel right crying in public. This does not mean that they weren't very, very sad."

• Expect it to take a long time before the death sinks in and becomes real. Children may let you know months later that they are still waiting for the person or pet to return.

HOSPITALIZATION

A parent or other guardian should try to be with a hospitalized child at all times, unless the hospitalization is very prolonged and this becomes completely impractical. There is no reason for any hospital to exclude parents from a child's bedside, though it may be necessary for parents to wait outside during certain procedures.

Not only does the presence of a parent or guardian calm and reassure the child, such an adult also can keep an eye on medical procedures and intervene in the case of a mistake. We like to think that mistakes in hospitals are rare; they are not rare, though usually there aren't any serious repercussions.

If you're with your child at all times, you can make sure that the pain medication is given promptly, that the infiltrated IV is noted and changed before there's a lot of swelling; that the oxygen or the monitor that is turned off for a test is indeed switched on again. Be there and be alert.

Yet you do not want the staff to consider you an enemy or a spy. Your child's stay will be much more pleasant if you can find time to thank people, to write a note to the nursing supervisor or hospital administrator in praise of any special (or even ordinary) kindness or competence, and to bring in a treat to eat.

For Five/Six, the worst things about being in the hospital are: separation from parents, lack of control over what happens, pain, exposure to strangers of the private parts of the body. Fortunately, the child can be helped to handle each terrible thing.

SEPARATION FROM PARENTS

Most hospitals and all children's hospitals make an enormous effort to allow parents to stay with children. If you are not invited or asked to stay during a procedure or overnight, ask to do so. If your request is denied, persist; ask if there is anything you can do to make it possible. If your child is having an elective, scheduled procedure, make togetherness a priority in choosing the hospital.

If you have time to get them together, take along a sleeping bag, pillow, sleep mask, and earplugs, as well as your personal toothbrush kit. It's a great idea to bring a couple of big bottles of bottled water. Hospitals are very dehydrating places and often surprisingly devoid of water sources.

LACK OF CONTROL

When Fives and Sixes are in a powerless position, they tend to collapse altogether, regress to babyhood, and refuse to make any effort to cooperate or rely on themselves. When they give up control, it requires those caring for them to be even more controlling, which results in even greater feelings of powerlessness. This kind of vicious cycle can be annoying and upsetting and even get in the way of recovery.

Ahead of time

If the hospital stay is a scheduled one, it's worthwhile to prepare Five/Six. Going to the hospital isn't like just getting a shot at the pediatrician's, which is unpleasant but brief; in that situation, preparation isn't worth the cost in apprehension. A hospital stay is a big deal, and Fives and Sixes do better when they know the ropes.

Reading aloud a picture book about going to the hospital can be very helpful, if the procedure is a scheduled one. It's especially useful if you have an idea of which aspects your own child is likely to face and how his or her experience is likely to match or be different from the one in the story.

Make a preadmission visit with a Polaroid camera, so that you can review what the hospital is like at home several times.

Don't go into detail about painful procedures, but don't promise that there will be nothing unpleasant or painful. Stress that going to the hospital is necessary and important and that many, many children need to do this.

During the stay

It's a good idea to try to involve the child at every juncture, unless urgency or the child's condition make this impossible.

> "Would you like to bring Teddy or Elephant with you?" "Here are the buttons that make the bed go up or down. You can push them and see what they do." "Here is some magic air [anesthetic] so that you won't know when the operation happens. It could smell like mint or like pine trees. Which would you like?"

During early convalescence, be alert to every little indication that Five/Six is ready and able to take control.

> "You hold the cup while I get another pillow." "Here's the remote for the TV. Pick out what you want to watch." "Let's go see what's going on in the playroom."

Let Five/Six overhear you making pleased, positive statements.

> "I knew he could stand up and take steps. He's a very strong Kid." "She's already asking for crayons and paper. I tell you, she's got talent and spunk."

At home, start to incorporate productivity into convalescence.

> "You sit in the big chair here and shell peas while I make the soup." "Our refrigerator needs four new pictures." "Here's a job that needs doing: all these recipes need to be cut out of the magazine."

PAIN

Pain from the disease or injury may be inevitable; it may need to be monitored to give clues to the medical staff until diagnosis and plan of treatment are established. But once it serves no useful purpose, pain should be managed aggressively. Children's specialists are increasingly able to give pain medication that the child controls, pushing a button when more is needed. If this technology is not available, medication should be given promptly "by the clock" without waiting for symptoms to recur. If your child isn't getting pain medication that truly makes him or her comfortable, be aggressive yourself in finding out why and what can be done.

Some Fives and many Sixes are able to use their imaginations to help control pain. Biofeedback techniques used with adults are even more effective with children. A good reference for you or your child's doctor: "Imagination Training: A Tool with Many Uses" by Jeffrey L. Brown, M.D. (see **Partial Bibliography**).

PRIVACY

Fives and Sixes are acutely modest. The whole issue of potty control is a recent and intense one in their minds, and they are frequently reminded about good touch/bad touch.

They are also fascinated with gender differences and with the job of creating a private self versus a public self. Many Fives and Sixes will become more panicked and outraged at having to take off their underpants than at having a needle poke.

Everybody ought to respect Kids' modesty, but in the hustle bustle of the hospital it may be forgotten. It may help to keep reminding Five/Six that the examination is important, that you, the parent are right there, and that you have given the doctors and nurses permission to examine Five/Six's whole entire body.

Here's a great big suggestion: Take along to the hospital a smallish blanket. When Five/Six is accidentally, carelessly, or unnecessarily left exposed, cover him or her up quickly with the blanket.

Of course, you want to be sure yourself that no one takes advantage of Five/Six. Hospitals are big places, with many staff members. It is rare that an adult with pedophilic impulses gets through the screening process, but it's still a good idea to try to stay with your child, ensuring that there is appropriate supervision during the entire visit.

DIVORCE

It's just about impossible for Fives and Sixes to understand divorce, because they don't really understand marriage. Home is their universe: they believe that whatever goes on at home is normal and appropriate and pleasant, even when parents quarrel, fight physically, or abuse drugs or alcohol. When parents separate, Fives and Sixes are at a complete loss. To make sense of what has occurred, they will come up with their own egocentric explanations, based on their own feelings and what they have overheard. They do this even when parents believe that they have explained the situation clearly.

This doesn't mean that explanations are wasted, but it does mean that a parent's actions speak much louder than words. Alas, in many divorces, parents are so depleted of energy and calm, so agitated and bitter, so preoccupied, that it feels as if actions, such as those described in the next paragraph, are impossible. If this is the case, professional help and the support of family and friends are crucial. Patterns established right after the divorce are very hard to break and can set the tone of the new family arrangements for years to come.

For instance, in the most usual divorce, in which children stay with the mother and the father moves out: Five/Six often believes that daddy left because of anger at the child, "because he doesn't like me any more." Parents explain carefully that Daddy's love for the child is unchanged; that the divorce was between parents, not child and parents.

What Five/Six needs, though, are regular phone calls and visits with the father. Visits that make Five/Six feel liked and loved emphasize physical affection, conversation that features Daddy doing a lot of listening and giving focused attention. Giving many gifts and then going to watch some form of passive entertainment, like a movie, won't do the trick. Moreover, a father who is reluctant to set limits or impose discipline worries Five/Six, who knows very well that fathers "are supposed to" do these things.

If Five/Six, unreassured by parental actions, persists in the belief that he or she is responsible for driving away the parent who left, behavior is likely to deteriorate. Some children become increasingly defiant, untruthful, and aggressive; others become withdrawn and depressed. Physical symptoms like constipation, weight-gain or weight-loss, and nervous tics often develop.

Five/Six often believes that Mommy prefers the child to the absent father. Indeed, Five/Six may work very hard to take the place of the absent parent. Parents need to explain carefully that it was the relationship between the parents that caused the divorce and that "nothing has changed" in the relationship each has with the child.

What Five/Six needs, though, is demonstration that he or she is still a child, not a replacement mate. This means that neither parent uses Five/Six as a go-between, confidante, or spy. Each parent pays focused attention to Five/Six and sets limits and enforces discipline. Parents ensure that Five/Six is unable to manipulate them, playing one against the other. Neither parent relies on Five/Six for physical, sexual, or emotional nurturing—there is no sharing of beds or baths; no weeping with Five/Six giving the comforting.

If Five/Six does not receive this reassuring message, the child is likely to assume more and more of a pseudo-parenting role at some times and to regress and act out at others. This can result in a parent's feeling helpless, belittled, and confused. Professional counseling is usually very helpful. In any case, Five/Six always does best with a regular schedule and a loving, supportive adult relative or friend on hand who has not been severely shaken by the divorce.

The practical aspects of custody arrangements should take into consideration that Fives/Sixes need to attend the same school on a regular basis and to establish neighborhood and community bonds. What's most important about custody, however, is that Five/Six is not put in the position of having to choose one parent over the other or to take sides in a battle. Parents who avoid bitterness and fighting during changes of custody do children and themselves a big favor.

Keep in mind that Fives and Sixes are skilled, fascinated eavesdroppers. Discussing the faults and foibles of the ex-spouse, recounting court battles, custody disputes, and child support failures within hearing range of Five/Six imposes an enormous burden on the child. While Five/Six may appear to take sides at the time with the parent who is so upset, in the long run the child is more likely to resent the parent who does the complaining than the parent who is being complained about.

SEXUAL MOLESTATION

Fives and Sixes are not too young to keep a secret, but they keep it poorly. Their behavior gives them away. A child who has been sexually molested may not tell you, but is likely to undergo a sudden change in behavior: clinging, depressed, aggressive. A child thus traumatized usually loses the ability to play contentedly alone; he or she is too preoccupied with the burden.

Sometimes there is a big clue: increased masturbation or panicky avoidance of the adult or older youngster who perpetrated the molesting. A child who has been molested may show a change when drawing a person, by putting in the genitals. He or she may be driven to acting out the molestation in sex play with other children.

If you suspect your child could have been molested, there are a few crucial rules to protect both the child and any police or protective service investigation.

• When you talk with your child, avoid planting any suggestions yourself. Children this age are very suggestible. For instance, you might say "I see that you are touching yourself in your private place a lot. I wonder why?" instead of "Did Mommy's boyfriend touch you there?"

• If the child tells you that an incident has taken place, focus on the child's feelings first, rather than on outrage against the adult. Listen, listen, listen. Rather than ask questions, try to reflect back what the child has already said. "And so he pulled down your panties?"

• Reassure the child that you will protect him or her and see that it never happens again. Tell the child that everything that happened was the grown-up's fault and that you are very angry at the grown-up.

• If you are sure that abuse took place, call the Child Protective Services abuse hotline in your area and make a report.

• If you are unsure about whether abuse took

place, consult with your pediatrician over the phone. Sometimes your own pediatrician should be the person who interviews and examines the child; sometimes the nature of the suspected abuse suggests that a specialist be consulted.

• For your legal protection, start taking notes immediately. Write down what your child said, what you asked or said, and any other details. Save any clothing, unwashed, that the child was wearing during the incident. Document your encounters with any medical, legal, or protective agencies: write down everybody's name.

Every now and then, a Five or Six may cheerfully say something that sets off all kinds of alarm bells in a parent's mind: for instance, "And in the night Daddy came in and pulled my jammies down and looked and poked!" This was what a Five told his kindergarten teacher a few years ago. Daddy, on my instructions, was looking for pinworms, which exit the rectum at night! When Five/Six tells you something along these lines in a cheerful, confident, "listen what happened to me today" manner, try to underreact and get more information. Hearts and lives have been irretrievably broken from false accusations.

2

SEVEN AND EIGHT

"STAY HERE WITH ME!"

Overview of the Age

"I don't mind *knowing* about bears. I don't mind *writing* about bears. I just don't want to *talk out loud* about them." Kyle rolls onto his back. He glares at his mother and then covers his face with a splayed-open book. "Nobody wants to hear about bears. Everybody is sick of bears."

Kyle's mother experiences a pang of guilt: she herself is a little sick of bears. "That's not true, Kyle. Bears are fascinating. Aren't you going to talk about all that stuff on hibernating?"

"I can't talk about going to the bathroom! In front of the whole class! That's all there is to say about hibernating. How they don't pee or poop. Everybody'll think I'm a dork, talking about peeing." He picks up one of a thousand scrawled-on papers and peers at her through an eraser hole. "Mrs. Fogle doesn't like me anyhow. I'll bet she gives me an F. You should tell her that giving a report in front of the whole class is too hard for third grade."

"Well, what about strategies to use when you meet a bear? Should you stand still or run or climb a tree? You could act it out. You could get one of your friends to be the bear."

"Yeah, a bear on roller skates, that'd be neat!" Kyle leaps to his feet and becomes a roller-skating bear, then collapses back into a gloomy lump on the floor. "Mrs. Fogle'd have a cow. Roller-skating in school. She'd give me another yellow slip. Why can't I just write this stupid thing? Why do I have to give a report to the whole class? Boy is she mean."

"But Kyle, Mrs. Fogle says that in class you're always wanting to talk. In fact, that's why you get so many yellow slips. I should think you'd have a good time talking to the class."

"*I* don't talk to people! *They* talk to *me!* What am I supposed to do, not answer them?"

"Well, anyway, you don't have to have the bear on roller skates. It's rare, I believe, to encounter a bear in the wild on inline skates." From the look on Kyle's face, this gentle joke was ill-advised. "Don't you think the class would like to know how to escape an attacking bear?"

"If the bear tears your head off, do you think for a second afterward before you die? What do you think you'd think about? Like, 'Where's my body?' Or would your eyes be looking at the bear's insides? And you'd be thinking, 'Ooh, yuck, there's undigested squirrel in here?'"

"I don't think that's quite the right tack for a class report. Okay, if you don't want to do hibernating or what to do if a bear attacks you, what *do* you want to talk about?"

Kyle sighs exasperatedly. "I'm going to just make a big picture of a bear and tell all the parts of the body and how big he is. That's all. That's all anybody wants to know."

You'd think that being the parent of Seven and Eight would be a breeze. Middle-age Kids can take care of themselves pretty much. They're so busy, what with school, friends, sports, lessons, TV, video games, books, collecting things, and making things that it's hard to see where they fit in homelife.

When you add up all the things that Kids learn during these middle years, the list is impressive. They go from sounding out words to reading for entertainment to reading for information. They go from printing capital letters to writing cursive script. They go from counting objects to adding, subtracting, multiplying, dividing, and comprehending fractions. They go from a confused understanding of what a rule is to playing little league baseball and soccer. Many go from friendships based on willing-ness to play to friendships based on intimacy.

Surely this is enough to occupy them.

So how come Seven and Eight are such parent-intensive years?

"They need you for everything," a mother of a Seven reports. "She wants me to watch her put away her toys. She has to show me every article of clothing before she puts it on and I have to smell it to be sure it smells clean. She needs me to stand outside the bathroom door while she has a bowel movement. I tell her she can wipe herself, but she wants me outside the door while she does it."

Why? Because one of the most important things Seven and Eight are struggling with is consciousness of self. For the first time, Kids discover an inner voice: an I that can think about a me. Once a child discovers that inner voice, it's the end of a certain kind of innocence and the beginning of a certain kind of sophistication.

What is at stake here is the creation of a public self—a self that can perform with ease in public. If you are to have a life—much less a career— outside the home, you need to foster in yourself a public self. This is a complicated undertaking. The problem is that the successful public self isn't self-conscious. The successful public self is confident of itself because that inner audience, the I judging the me, is "silent with approval." There's no self-doubt, no little voice saying, "That's stupid" "You sound like a dork" "Who's going to be interested in that" "And besides, your hair looks dumb."

But when you are just starting out with that inner voice, you don't know how to tame it and educate it and shut it up. Sevens and Eights are pretty much at the mercy of whatever that inner voice comes up with. What they need is something that overrides that inner voice and teaches it to behave. That something is a parent. The mere presence of a parent seems to give Seven and Eight confidence to deal with the murmurings and hesitations and doubts of that inner voice.

So they want you to be there, watching them

every second, as they throw the ball against the garage a million times, play a video game, or examine their collections of "action figures" or model horses or rocks or pogs. They don't want you to instruct, or help; all they want is your comforting presence. This does not, however, mean that you can sit there and read a book or listen to your walkman: you have to pay attention. "Don't go!" they cry, as you sidle away, limp with boredom. "Stay here with ME!"

A parent who can just be there for Seven or Eight is fulfilling a major part of the job description. However, just being there can be a very wearing occupation: ask Kyle's mother. As a matter of fact, she is going well beyond the call of duty—she is actually trying to help Kyle with what she believes to be his problem: thinking of a topic for an oral report on bears.

However, this is not really what Kyle's problem is. Kyle's problem is how to shut up his critical inner voice so that he can construct an oral report on bears that he is clearly capable of delivering. If an adult were in Kyle's shoes, we'd say he had writer's block. (Kyle doesn't mind just writing a report on bears, because he doesn't yet see the act of writing as a public act: he doesn't visualize a reader as an audience.)

It's tricky to be the parent of a Seven and Eight. Kyle's mother thought afterward that she could have handled the situation better. Perhaps she shouldn't have made any suggestions at all. Perhaps she should have just sat there with a smile and reflected back to Kyle his own statements so that he could lead himself to a conclusion. Perhaps she should have asked him questions about bears as if she herself didn't know anything about bears.

With Seven and Eight, you never know. Any of these strategies probably would have gotten very much the same response from Kyle. He was in a little fit of self-consciousness, and what he needed was just her presence: a loving parent with a strong track record of thinking Kyle is wonderful. A calm, adult presence to let him know that no matter what happens about the bear report, his reputation as a terrific Kid is safe. Most importantly, Kyle's mother didn't criticize him for worrying; she didn't judge him as a slacker; and she didn't take over the job and write the report on bears herself (though she certainly was an authority on the subject by that time).

As it happened, Kyle stuck with his exceedingly basic report on bear body parts and size, but then the class burst out with questions and he fielded them all: "Only a thimbleful of pee during the whole winter and it's so concentrated it's solid!" "Never turn and run from a bear!" "Two cubs in a litter!" Mrs. Fogle was very impressed and gave him an A.

This new consciousness of self explains a lot of things about Sevens and Eights that can perplex parents and drive them bonkers.

• Sevens and Eights marvel at and test and worry about being their own unique selves. This leads them to think about deep questions, which they sometimes will voice. "Why am I me? If you hadn't had me, who would I be?" "Will I be the same me when I grow up?"

• For the first time, they understand that death means the ceasing of that self-consciousness. Many then become preoccupied with this, asking questions, and stating worries. Anything having to do with death is instantly fascinating: what happens after the bear bites off your head is more interesting than how to keep the decapitation from occurring in the first place.

• They feel their souls as separate from their bodies, and at times this makes them feel insecure about those bodies. They worry about subtle physical sensations: "When I bend my hand real far back like this and go sprong sprong sprong on my fingers, it hurts *here!*" Their pants rub, their waistband feels funny, they can't wear anything with a chin strap: bicycle helmets become a struggle. That old 2-year-old problem about pooping (Is the poop part of my body or outside it?) resurfaces, but in a new form. Seven, especially, may need moral support, the comforting mere presence outside the bathroom door.

• They worry about everything: money, politics, parents' fighting, the environment, what will happen at school, what their teachers think of them, who likes them and who doesn't, what to have for lunch, whether they will have time to do their homework, and what to do if they don't.

• They are absent minded. It's as if they start to do something—fetch their hats from the bedroom, say. But on the way that little inner voice distracts them, perhaps with a new worry or perhaps simply by observing: "I am going into the bedroom to get my hat. I, me, myself. Kyle. This is my bedroom. My hat. Me. What does it all mean?" They will then need to spend some time staring into space or muttering to themselves or just gazing into the mirror.

• They need a lot of what one parent calls "idiot time"—time spent in a semi-vegetative state, a state in which it is clear that the little inner voice is lulled to sleep. They may repeatedly play very simple games they've outgrown or dig holes or make large lumps of sand. ("No, I don't want to make a castle. I just want to make a sand lump.") They collect things, objects which are barely able to be distinguished from each other: stones, drinking straws, bottle caps. The point of collecting is going into a trance.

Sometimes all this peaks at Seven; sometimes at Eight. The timing and intensity will be different with every child. But it is safe to say that during these two years, you'll see some of it. Most of the behavior, the concerns, and the problems of this age have their root in this new awareness of self. Keeping that in mind may not make this age easier to deal with, but it may help to put the weirder aspects in an understandable context.

Growth of the Soul

You can't overestimate how much Sevens and Eights learn from each other—for better or worse—about morality, compassion, and justice. Let this sustain you as you accompany Seven/Eight through these years of best friends and worst enemies, of clubs and cliques, of sleepovers and—it had to come sometime—slumber parties.

Up until about Seven, children look to adults to determine whether an action is good or bad: they tend to regard those two categories as inflexible and determined by somebody other than themselves. If Fives or Sixes do something good, they believe that it was good because a parent would be proud of them; if they do something bad, a parent, they fear, would be disappointed. A Good is always Good (don't break things) and a bad is always bad (even if what you break is a window, because you're locked out and Grandma is sick inside).

Starting at age seven, Kids are left more and more to their own devices, out of reach of adult authority. Once you start spending a lot of time with people who have no real objective authority over you, you have to work out a whole new way of thinking about the world.

MORAL AND ETHICAL DILEMMAS

Sevens and Eights have only a rudimentary idea of fairness. Like Sixes, they basically believe that fairness means that everybody gets the same thing. They are beginning to have a suspicion that there are exceptions to this, however: that somebody might deserve more because of virtue or that it might be fair for somebody to get a special deal for having an extra challenge to contend with.

The moral dilemmas encountered by children this age can be very complex.

• When you and your buddies adopt a turtle and you have to decide who gets to keep it and for how long, you have to take into account who saw it first, who created a terrarium out of a Tupperware tub, and that Timmy has to go to the hospital for a tonsillectomy on Wednesday.

• When you and your clique decide that Georgianne smells bad and dresses funny, and you tag her, then chase the other children, smearing them and yelling, "You've got Georgianne on you" so that they shriek and run away, you have to decide if this is cruel or if this is a good way to punish someone who is different.

• When you and your buddies find a wallet with eight dollars in it, you have to decide what to do with it. And when the wallet goes unclaimed and the eight dollars belong to the three of you, you have to decide how to split it up.

In the absence of adult authority, Kids themselves have to decide what is good or bad. As they do so, they start to form ideas—as individuals and in groups—of what is right or wrong, fair or unfair.

They may do well in this regard. "Frankie gets to have six strikes instead of three because he's so little." "Sydney gets the frosting because it's her birthday." "Orrie gets first choice because he found all the stuff in the first place." They may, on the other hand, do terribly. Just ask Georgianne, if you can find her and if she will talk to anybody at all in a trusting and coherent fashion.

To these encounters, Kids bring their whole selves: what they've learned at home and at preschool and in kindergarten and first grade about how to treat other people; they bring kindness and loyalty and generosity. "Gordie's teacher in second grade never complimented anybody, but Gordie was always telling other Kids when they did a good job." "When Todd had to have chemo, Chelsea decided to have her head shaved. Those long red curls. How I wept."

They also bring anger, prejudice, and the knowledge of evil. Many children smoke their first commercial cigarette, in a group, at age eight. Another significant portion encounter marijuana or begin to drink alcohol. "A Kid named Hojo took all the third grade boys aside and told them about fellatio, cunnilingus, and sodomy." "The second grade teacher sent a letter home about the white Kids calling the black ones nigger and the black ones calling the white

ones pork." "Somebody named Hootch told all the boys that they had to carry a knife to school."

Older gangs recruit children this age because they are so group-focused. This can happen in schools where you would not dream it could. For the degree of pathology on the playground some of these scenarios suggest, the only solution is concerted parental action. When things go this wrong, they are far beyond the scope of this book. But that doesn't mean that they are far beyond the reach of solutions.

The moral of the story, however, is that parents do well to keep close tabs on how friendships are going during this period. When children actually consult adults on these matters, it's easy to pontificate on justice and fairness. But the Kids often don't ask for advice. More often than not, it's up to parents to start the conversation about moral dilemmas. A good way to do this is to talk about examples in your own life or in the news. Be sure to give highly positive comments when your child shows moral maturity and constructive criticism when he or she falls short.

"I saw Bernie looking really sad this morning. He was all by himself. Wasn't he good friends with Paul—the boy who moved away last week?"

"We made out our work schedules today so that everybody can celebrate their own religious holidays. I'm working Christmas so that we can observe Yom Kippur and Hanukkah."

"Your teacher told me how you made the new girl feel comfortable. It's hard to be new in a class, especially when you have a mark on your face that makes you look different. But, you know, it can be hard to go up to that person and make friends, too. Sometimes the other children think it's cool to tease her. So you have to be brave. I'm honored to know such a brave, kind person as you."

SOCIAL

BEST FRIENDS

Being a Kid in a group is only half of what friendship is about at this age. For the first time in a child's life, having a best friend resembles the adult definition of having a best friend. Of course, younger children have best friends: somebody to play with and hug and defend and push down and yell at and laugh with and be loyal to. But up until now, children didn't have a public self, as opposed to a private self. Now they do, and the person you share that private self with is your best friend.

Your best friend knows that you still sit on your mom's lap sometimes, that you hate the action movies that other Kids love and keep your eyes closed in the scary parts, that your Mom lost her job. Your best friend and you aren't embarrassed to be naked in each other's company. You can sleep over at your best friend's home and even wear your pull-ups. When you're with other Kids, your best friend and you go right along with them, but you have your secret jokes and gestures. You can fight hard with your best friend, and stay mad only a little while, and then make up.

A best friend is a buffer against the world. If you're lucky, your best friend helps you fit into a group and, at the same time, helps you feel good about your innermost self.

If you're unlucky in your choice of a best friend, you are at risk. Your best friend may take on so much importance that you are uncomfortable without him or her, unable to make your way in the group. Or your best friend may make you feel disloyal if you go with the group.

If you are really unlucky, your best friend may even betray you. A fickle best friend can break your heart: "You're not my friend any more. I'm best friends with Janet now." A disloyal one can turn the group against you: "Jason stinks! His mom puts garlic in everything she makes! Ewww, yuck! I smell Jason, I smell Jason!" Worst of all, a best friend may have so many problems at home that you "catch" them and take them on as your own. "Tammy's stepfather molested her and got sent to jail, and now Becky won't go anywhere by herself, not even to the bathroom."

So it's risky to have a best friend and it takes a lot of energy and effort. No wonder many Sevens and Eights seem not to need or want such a friend. They seem perfectly happy to play in a group of children or to attach to one chum today and another tomorrow. This is a perfectly valid choice, and many who opt out now are ready to establish a close friendship later on.

For those who do establish close friendships at ages Seven or Eight, this is often a bumpy ride. After all, a friend is supposed to be somebody you trust, somebody who expects favors and ill turns to balance out, somebody who makes you feel good, most of the time. A friend has to weather the ups and downs of how the group thinks of you. A friend has to put up with your parents and your family life and be prepared to keep secrets about what happens at home.

In a sense, you are performing when you are with a friend. You think about what you are going to do to enhance that friendship and make your friend think well of you. And for the first time, Seven and Eight can foresee what would make a friend feel good and plot their behavior so that they can accomplish this.

But in another sense, you are not your public, performing self with your friend. Best friends function for each other the way the presence of a loving parent does: they soothe that critical inner voice and give a person permission to "just be." With a best friend, you can talk about things you'd never discuss in a group: confide a secret, share a fear, make fun of a powerful classmate.

Trouble in the name of friendship

With all this complexity and intensity going on, it's not surprising that a Seven or Eight would resort at times to unseemly tactics to establish a close, intimate friendship.

If I act just like my friend, it will make him feel good and he will like me

Why is it that to "act just like my friend" usually means acquiring some distressing mannerism? Why can't it ever be something endearing, like practicing the piano or taking thorough baths or getting homework done right after school?

> "He's gotten in the habit of punching the wall just like Buster, he has to drink everything with a straw and blow bubbles and make a disgusting snorking noise with the dregs, and he even talks like Buster, who can't say his R's. He sounds as if he's got a Harvard accent."

> "She'll spend the afternoon with Dody, and come home sort of a Dody clone. She squinches up her nose and rolls her eyes, and every time you ask her something, she says, "I don't know," in this little wispy singsong voice. She wants her hair to curl like Dody's and she wants cowboy boots with taps and a cap pistol."

When parents "actively ignore" (that is, pay absolutely no attention, studiously avoiding smiles and eye contact) such acquired habits, they usually fade by themselves and don't do any harm. However, if Seven/Eight picks up truly undesirable traits, the most effective cure is to provide alternative activities and to dilute the friendship.

> "Gregory's friend Bill is a really unhappy child from a terribly dysfunctional fam-

ily. Bill seems full of anger, and his language is so racist, sexist, and hateful it scares me. When I heard Gregory calling a woman on TV a dirty bitch, I said to myself, that's it for Bill. We just got so busy there wasn't time for Bill. Greg had a fit for a day or two, and then, you know, he seemed relieved and a lot happier."

If my friend thinks I am important, she will like me

> "Why you must be Samantha's father! She's told us so much about you. How excited we all are about your new talk show! And congratulations on your Presidential medal! When do you leave for New York?"

Sevens and Eights know when they are telling a lie; they don't confuse a lie with a truth (though they may think that something is true that is not). What they don't know is that telling a certain kind of lie is wrong. They are clear that you should never lie to cover up wrongdoing or to put the blame on somebody else. They aren't so clear that it is wrong to lie in order to increase one's prestige.

When caught telling such a lie, Seven/Eight is more likely to be embarrassed than ashamed. The trick is to get across the point without making the lesson shaming and devastating; such lessons tend to do more harm than good. There are many good children's books that have this as a theme: a good one is *Sam, Bangs and Moonshine* by Evaline Ness (Henry Holt, 1966).

If I give my friend something, he will like me

Giving away one's own or stolen treasures is very tempting; an easy way to purchase regard. Sevens and Eights may try this once or twice, but when parents react with serious concern and disapproval, they usually can stop easily and find other ways to make friends. A Seven or Eight who continues to steal things to give away or who gives away precious possessions is pleading for help in making friends.

Sometimes giving things away is an indication that Seven or Eight really should be playing with younger children and that perhaps he or she should have grade placement reconsidered. Sometimes it results when the child's class has been allowed to form really nasty cliques and to ostracize one or two unfortunate classmates. And sometimes a Seven or Eight who is constantly bearing gifts has problems with social interactions that make it very hard to win friends in the usual way: perhaps Seven/Eight is bossy and aggressive, or pseudo-mature and adultlike, or whiny and easily upset.

Certainly, a discussion with the teacher and your pediatrician, and perhaps with a child therapist, is in order.

Broken hearts

Besides committing these foibles in the name of friendship, Sevens and Eights tend to suffer from the occasional broken heart.

This isn't surprising. While Sevens and Eights do tend to clump together, the composition of each clump tends to change from one day or week to the next. Sometimes one child will be the target of this reclumping over and over again, bounced out of one clique and then another, for a few weeks; then, for mysterious reasons, the group changes its collective mind and targets somebody else. Moreover, it's not unusual for someone that Seven or Eight thought was a "best friend" to switch alliances overnight.

The brokenhearted target of such a fickle friend tends to be a sweet and sensitive youngster. The normal parental reaction to such an episode is thus to be very sympathetic toward the child and angry at the feckless friend. Repairing a broken heart may seem to take a long time and to involve special treats, privileges, extra understanding when chores go undone, and so on.

This parental reaction can cause more trouble than it cures, however. One of the tasks of Seven and Eight is to define a self, and when parents take on a Kid's personal burdens, the boundaries of that Self can become blurred. When a parent seems to be as brokenhearted as a Kid, this is blurring the boundaries.

What works better in the long run and what helps Seven/Eight mature is adult perspective. "I remember back when I was in second grade—gee, that was back before there were computer games or anything—my dearest friend Belinda all of a sudden went crazy over this new girl in the class, Bonnie. I felt so terrible. It took me a while to feel better. But after a few weeks, I found a new friend and I liked her even better than I had liked Belinda. In fact, we stayed friends right through junior high!"

Other things that help:
• Invite over a new potential friend, one that hasn't been active in the jilting. Make sure that the activities are engrossing and special.
• Avoid involving Seven/Eight in groups of three. If the Kids are going through a cliquey phase, two will gang up on the third.
• Make sure that Seven/Eight doesn't have to rely on just one group, like the class at school, from which to choose and court a friend. Consider religious school, Cub Scouts and Brownies, sports teams, and classes in areas of interest as fertile friend-making ground.

The inappropriate best friend

Parents' hearts don't get broken by their Kid's best friends, but they often do sink right down to shoe level.

"Annie's best friend Loolie is the most hyper little girl I've ever met. She just can't keep still, and as her energy winds up she inevitably gets the two of them into trouble. Big trouble. Last Saturday they decided they'd wash the cars in the neighborhood, but what they wound up doing was lathering all the windshields." "I know you like Beau a whole lot, Randy, but his language is terrible. I won't have those words used in our home." "Jake, how can you put up with Jackson? He bosses you around all the time! I think if he told you to jump off a cliff, you'd jump!" (Jake grins; you can see him getting ready to leap.)

The solution to the inappropriate friend is to use parental authority to cut down contact and parental ingenuity to find opportunities for your child to make new friends. These two strategies must go hand in hand. Fortunately, the appeal of an inappropriate friend often lies solely in the inappropriateness, so most of the time Seven/Eight is fairly willing to be distracted away.

CASUAL FRIENDS, PEERS, AND CLIQUES

Sevens and Eights are just starting to work out a complicated idea of friendship. You can be a public friend and a member of the group, and you can be a private friend and share your heart.

Statistics show that boys work harder at the public role and girls work harder at the private one. When girls are together, they talk a lot with each other about what is going on in their lives at home or at school. Boys, even two boys who are best friends, don't talk about their private lives. They play actively and discuss what they are playing.

In fact, boys and girls tend to have such different styles of friendship that not many of them are able to be friends with the opposite sex. This may be something to consider when deciding between classes at school: a class that is overwhelmingly composed of children of one sex may make friendship a challenge for those in the minority.

At ages seven and eight, Kids discover the power of groups to win power over and approval from the rest of the class, club, team, or whatever. Often Kids this age will refer to their own and other groups as "gangs." It sounds tough,

but it usually, in most areas, still means just a group of Kids who call each other friends.

Whatever they call themselves, Kids in a group define themselves by a whole bunch of behaviors. They may all wear red on Wednesday, drink the same soft drink, spend their allowances the same way. They tend to meet on special turf: this corner of the boys or girls bathroom; this area of the playground; this lunch table. They scorn and adore as a group: a teacher adored by the power clique will be pampered; one who is scorned will reap whines and exasperated sighs.

A clique seems to offer a Kid a safe way to survive in a big group. It serves to protect not only from enemies—the ordinary kind, as well as bullies—but also from the need to have a close friend (a boon for children not yet ready for such an intimate buddy).

Perhaps this is why second and third graders tend to be so cliquey and to be so suspicious of newcomers. Cliques exist primarily to exclude people. If there are several cliques in a class, every child may belong to one. But on occasion a child may be truly ostracized. Children who are physically or culturally or even sartorially different from the group tend to have a tough row to hoe. Usually the "victim" of this kind of social nastiness is a sweet, kind, sensitive boy or girl who is very upset about the experience. Of course: otherwise, where's the excitement and gratification for the other children?

Adults should not underestimate how cruel young children can be in this situation nor the excellent effect that a kind, strong teacher or classroom aide can have on the situation.

If parents are aware that their Seven or Eight is doing the ostracizing, a serious talk about kindness and fairness can go a long way toward squelching the meanness. On the other hand, silence may reinforce the cliquishness and lead to an even more intense version in the older grades. This is a very good reason for parents to step in now, even if their own Kid is not the one being ostracized. The tables can turn at any moment.

When parents and other adults have the attitude that "Kids will be Kids" and "let them work it out themselves," they are avoiding one of the duties and pleasures of parenthood. Sure, Kids will learn from each other about taking turns, sharing, fairness, and kindness. But what they learn won't necessarily reflect what parents want them to learn. After all, when they are with their peers, they only learn what the group knows.

Some teachers and schools have experimented with outlawing cliques. The rule is "nobody can say that somebody can't play." Generally, children this age are not yet tempted to regard adults as adversaries. They may object to such a rule and test it, but when convinced that the adults mean what they say, the cliques dissolve.

One ploy that I've seen work, but that requires truly devoted parents, is to have Seven or Eight start a club—a club that includes all the same-sex children in the class. Sevens and Eights just love clubs, with a motto, an identifying badge or hat, and refreshments. The fine thing about such a club, if it is mounted with enough adult enthusiasm and direction, is that it overwhelms for the moment *all* the cliques. Of course, the club rarely lasts for very long. But when it dissolves, very often the cliques have lost a great deal of their power and appeal.

What should parents of an ostracized child do?

• Communicate sympathy, but calmly. For a child this age, almost anything is easier to bear than parents who seem unable to handle a situation. A good tack to take is: "Children your age are known for doing things like this. But we won't let it continue. Of course, it's not your fault. They had to find somebody to pick on and it was you."

• Analyze what might be contributing to the ostracism, but without discussing this with the child. If Seven/Eight has body odor or bad breath, consult your pediatrician: there certainly

could be a medical/dental cause. If Seven/Eight tends to whine or try to bully other children, you would need to help the child get over these traits even if there were no ostracism. If the suspected cause is something intrinsic to the child, such as a physical disability, a cosmetic problem, or cultural, religious, racial, or language differences, the job is to change the class's behavior not to change the child.

• Make an appointment to talk with the teacher. Try to make this a friendly visit, in which you start with a compliment about the classroom and his or her teaching style. State the problem and ask for advice. Have some suggestions of your own: perhaps one of the other children is known to be kind, strong, and outgoing—it might be possible to invite that child to spend an afternoon with yours, and thus gain a buddy for your youngster. Perhaps you or your spouse could split the job of class parent with another family. (Before taking this on, feel pretty sure that you'll find the job fun and that the children will come to respect and like you! Otherwise, your presence may increase the hard time your Kid is having.)

If the teacher shrugs off the problem or communicates an impression that the child is "asking for it," end the discussion and seek help from the school psychologist or the principal.

Changing classes or schools may not work. Joining a new class during second and third grade often means confronting the same cliquishness and suspicion you left behind in the old one. An exception: a school or class in which these traits are explicitly discouraged—one with strong adult leadership. Religious schools are more likely to offer this environment.

One final word about friends and gender.

When groups of girls are together, they tend to be excessively "girly." Parents may be very startled to observe their competent, independent, risk-taking daughter suddenly talking about boys and having babies. They may be worried that all the little girls seem to dote on a female teacher, worshipping her almost to a degree that may seem to border on the sexual: "I just love Miss Cooper! She is so beautiful! I love how her ankles go down into her shoes!" What are they doing when they go on like this? I suspect that they are once again working on their public, performing selves, trying on what it would be like to be a grown-up woman. Solution: Try to involve Seven/Eight in organized activities—sports, classes, scouts—that counteract this trend.

When groups of boys are together, they tend to be at a loss unless they can talk about what they are doing right that second. If they aren't actually doing anything right that second, the talk will tend to veer toward sex and/or violence.

> "Ben invited four of his friends, all boys, over for his eighth birthday. It was fine when they were actually doing something, like eating the cake or throwing water balloons, but in the car on the way to the movie all they talked about was kissing girls! That's ALL they talked about! How you do it and what it tastes like and who had done it and a lot of stuff about tongues and teeth and braces and that little thing that hangs down the back of your throat. I was just shocked."

This time it was sex talk; next time it could be talking about violent scenes witnessed on the VCR.

Solution: keep boys in groups active, active, active all the time, even in transit.

ENEMIES

When a Seven/Eight says he or she has an enemy, that usually means Seven/Eight is being picked on. Often this is not true bullying—no physical threats or even mean teasing. The degree of emotion can be alarming: "I hate him! He beats me up all the time! Every day he beats me up!" A parent's heart can sink.

Before drawing conclusions, however, it's a good idea to investigate further. To Seven/Eight, being beat up doesn't have to mean fisticuffs. It's more a feeling that one's precious self is being made mock of or taken lightly: "She stares at me all the time. She touches me." "He pokes me in line and he kicks my seat and he breathes on me. He told Missy that I wanted to be her boy friend." "He just bothers me. He bothers me and bothers me. I don't like the way he looks and how his eyebrows grow like that."

This is another area in which parents can expect to be mightily bored by the lengthy complaints of Seven/Eight. A person can generate just so much sympathy before wearing out. Sevens and Eights usually work out their own ways of dealing with enemies. If parents are called on for suggestions, here's what has been known to work:

• Go everywhere with a buddy. If the enemy still "attacks," start conversing with your buddy in a convincing sounding nonsense language. Practice this. If you persist, the enemy is likely to be torn apart with curiosity and a feeling of being excluded.

• Stare hard at a particular body part of the enemy, like his or her right ear. Get up close and stare at it. Don't say a word. Look very concerned and offended. The enemy will almost always become self-conscious and put off his or her stride.

• Whisper, as softly as you can, your opinion: "You are really a jerk. Why do you keep staring at me. I can't stand you." This is spooky and intimidating.

Bullies

A true bully is a very troubled, difficult child who actively torments others. Bullies of seven or eight attack repeatedly with intent to hurt and may even threaten with or use weapons, such as knives or rocks. Bullies tackle "loners," smaller or weaker Kids, and those with disabilities. They may extort or steal money, jewelry, or clothing, and may coerce children to steal for them.

> *Bullying behavior is frequent (an average of two Kids in each classroom are victims) and dangerous for both bully and victim: the former have a high risk of growing up into violent criminals; the latter, for depression and poor self-esteem. Kids can't deal with the behavior on their own. I urge parents and teachers to send for and establish the program Bully-Proofing Your School. Write to Sopris West Publishing at 1140 Boston Avenue, Longmont, CO 80501, or call 800-547-6747.*

At Seven and Eight, bullies may already be experimenting with alcohol, drugs, or tobacco (see Glossary). They may be trying to "medicate" their own bad feelings with these substances.

The solution to stopping a true bully is medical and psychiatric. A child who fits this description is a child at high risk for future delinquency. Many children with this profile have been abused in one or more manners. Parents of a child who is truly being bullied need to take this seriously. Most often, bullies attack more than one child: parents of victims can band together to petition the school to take action.

School personnel need to intervene on behalf both of the bullied and the bullies, and call in the bully's parents for a serious discussion and referral to professional help.

In the meantime, parents of bullied children can counsel them.
• Try to stick together with at least one other buddy whenever the bully is likely to be present.
• Give the bully what he (or, rarely, she) demands. Standing up to a true bully can be dangerous.
• Never pack a weapon to defend against a bully. If Seven/Eight is tempted to do so, you

have a very serious problem that needs immediate action.

SLEEPOVERS AND SLUMBER PARTIES

Most Kids seven and older enjoy spending the night at each others' homes. If a child is reluctant, there are several possibilities.
• Just not ready: Some Kids are just perfectly happy to stay home and have a great fondness for their own "stuff." If a youngster has a group of friends with whom he or she can play comfortably, takes appropriate risks and challenges, and has no problem with daytime separations from home, there's nothing at all wrong with this style.
• Separation anxiety: If Seven/Eight senses that his or her presence keeps parents from arguing or that one or both parents depend on him or her for comfort, spending a night away from home feels very scary. Sometimes a loving parent just hates to think that the little Kid is growing up so fast and sends out signals that inhibit forays from the nest.
• Worries: You would not believe what worries Seven/Eight about spending the night. "What if I have to go to the bathroom in the night? What if I get lost finding it? What if the light wakes people up? What if flushing the toilet wakes people up? What if I get lost coming back and get into the wrong bed with Mr. and Mrs. Hochschild? What if I don't like what they have for breakfast? What if I get sick over there? What if their dog barks and I can't sleep? What if you forget to pick me up in the morning and I have to stay with them all day or they leave me alone in the house?" If your Kid is a worrier, a reality check and a promise to come and fetch him or her right away if you receive a desperate call should do the trick.
• Bed-wetting: With the advent of camouflaging pull-ups, this is less of a problem. But some Sevens and Eights can't bear the thought of even unlikely detection. A visit to the pediatrician is needed, both to rule out any medical cause of

bedwetting and to address remedies (See **Health** section, later in this chapter.)

• Rational fears: Sometimes the child doing the inviting is not trustworthy—known to spill secrets or be mean. Sometimes the parents of that child are known to be difficult or scary. Sometimes the inviter has "promised" something that the potential guest secretly dreads: food or entertainment that the guest just can't tolerate, for instance. Or perhaps the guest list includes some of Seven/Eight's "enemies."

Parents' reluctance to allow a Seven/Eight to attend a sleepover or slumber party parallels that of Kids.

• Just not ready: Parents, like Kids, need time to come to terms with developmental changes. If it seems to be taking unduly long—if you are having trouble allowing Eight-and-a-half to spend the night elsewhere—you might want to peruse the other categories to see if one of them might apply, as well.

• Separation anxiety: If the presence of Seven/Eight is truly required for marital or parental well-being, some investigation and perhaps some counseling is in order.

• Worries: What if Seven/Eight does something tactless? "He was trying to be polite and he asked Doug's mother when the baby was due and she's not pregnant." What if he doesn't understand the customs of the home? "She saw everybody else cross themselves and she didn't know what to do so she tried to imitate them and got it all wrong." What if she gives away a family secret? "Did you have to tell everybody about Grandpa and the Ferrari?" What if Seven/Eight feels very uncomfortable but is afraid to say something? It is certainly worthwhile to list rational fears and to check them out. It's vital to know that the family of the inviting child is sane, relatively wholesome, and responsible and that the home itself is safe. In particular, you are justified in being concerned about:

• Guns: It is quite appropriate to ask the other parents: Do you own guns? If you do, what are the safety rules? (Guns should be locked up, unloaded, with ammunition locked up in a different area.)

• Supervision: Are the parents going to be home all evening and all night? If not, what are the arrangements? Even if you know the family and the other child well, you may not want a stranger babysitting your child. Whoever is supervising should be able to maintain some order, administer first aid, and summon help in English.

• Food: If your Kid has a serious food requirement, fit your behavior to the degree of concern. For instance, a severe food allergy means going over the menu and all off-menu food that may be offered with the host family. Also make sure that the adults have your Kid's allergy kit and know how and when to give adrenalin.

• Entertainment: My friend Greg went to a birthday/slumber party for 8-year-olds; the entertainment was an R-rated horror movie video. Greg took quite a while to recover. You can't really ask ahead of time whether the entertainment will be appropriate without being judged as intrusive, but you can have a way out.

Make up a code word. For instance, if Seven/Eight calls and says, "You forgot to pack my other micro-machines!" you know to say, "That's our code word. Do you need to come home right away?" If Seven/Eight says, "Yes," parents can come up with a not-quite-lie to explain to the host family: "We forgot we have an early appointment tomorrow morning!" and come and fetch the distressed youngster.

SEX PLAY

Sex play in the sense of girls and boys "playing doctor" diminishes at ages seven and eight (or at least they don't get caught as often), but not because children that age are not interested in sex. Indeed, Seven and Eight are much more aware of the power of sexuality. They talk about sex and worry about it more. Perhaps that undermines their desire to play sex games. Also, of course, boys and girls play separately pretty much. And Kids of this age are more self-conscious about how they behave in a group, shy about undressing or otherwise revealing their private selves.

Within groups of boys and groups of girls, sex is alive and well as a topic. Both groups huddle together and tell dirty jokes that they may or may not understand. Girls and boys both are hyperalert to overheard conversation or to any depiction of sex in the media.

When Seven/Eights are found together playing sex games, either with same-sex Kids or children of the other sex, the main concern of pediatricians and mental health professionals is motivation. Are they playing out of curiosity and pleasure? Or are they being driven to play sex games because they have sustained a sexual trauma, or are highly anxious about something, or are being coerced to play?

The same questions arise when a Seven or Eight initiates sex play with younger children. This can be upsetting for everybody when the children are discovered in flagrante delicto, and the parents of the younger children may be panicked. Sometimes such play is merely the bored response to a rainy afternoon with no other entertainment available, plus an impulse on the part of the older child to show off. But sometimes something else is going on.

No matter who is playing with whom, it's a good idea to consider possible motivations.
• If an older child has initiated such play with children five or under, this can mean that Seven/Eight is socially more comfortable with younger children in all ways. If a child consistently seeks out as companions children three or more years younger, this is unusual. A child with this preference should be evaluated for intellectual and emotional problems.
• Seven/Eight may be exposed to a highly charged sexual situation and find no other ways to express his or her feelings. One Eight had a

handicapped older sister who had to be given daily enemas, which were not performed in private. A Seven had been an upset onlooker when her younger sister was found to have been molested by a relative. Another Eight's father had a strong interest in pornography and had strewn magazines all over the house. A child in such a situation needs counseling and protection from further exposure.

Alas, such acting out may even reflect the fact that Seven/Eight has been sexually molested. Suspicion would be increased:
• If the play included inserting fingers or objects into vagina, rectum, or the opening of the penis
• If the play has a frantic or compelled quality to it or occurs repetitively
• If there is a ritual aspect to the play: props, a certain setting, each child with a certain role
• If the other participants have been coerced and/or are upset by the play
• If Seven/Eight shows other worrisome signs, such as mood swings, nervous habits or tics, separation anxiety, public or excessive masturbation, constipation or urinary tract infections that don't respond to treatment, avoidance or fear of a previously trusted friend or relative

Most parents are to some degree upset, shocked, angered, worried, and disappointed when they find their children playing sex games. They fear that one or more of the children might have been injured physically or warped emotionally by such games and may be haunted by the thought that sexual abuse might have inspired the play. It's important to remember that it's unlikely for a child to be either physically or emotionally damaged by play with a youngster the same developmental age and that a history of sexual abuse is only one factor of several that can encourage such play.

They may also be shocked simply by evidence that their children have picked up more than parents realized about sexuality. Yet parents cannot control a child's whole world. Television and videos have brought the world of R- and X-ratings into the home—maybe not yours, but perhaps that of your child's friends.

Once in a while, parents aren't at all shocked. They may remember their own escapades at that age—escapades that may well outdo the behavior they've encountered in the present generation.

In either event, it is better for Sevens and Eights if parents take a stand against playing sex games and that they do so calmly.

• Taking a stand against sex games—even if you have fond memories yourself—tells children something important: that you regard sex as an important, serious, very private topic. When parents condone, indulge, or encourage sex play it can feel to a child as if the parent is deriving some satisfaction from the play. This blurs an important boundary between child and parent. When parents don't allow or respect that boundary, especially in matters sexual, children can become confused, even frightened.

• A calm but firm manner achieves several things. First, it reinforces that boundary: By your manner you are saying that of course you're not shocked or frightened by this behavior, that it is childhood stuff and doesn't threaten you. Second, if the play is normal sex play inspired by pleasure and curiosity, your calm firm response will take a lot of the pizzazz out of the act of discovery. An excited, outraged parent is such a spectacle that Kids are often tempted to repeat the play, half-hoping to get another reaction. Third, if the play is worrisome, the last thing you want to do is frighten the participants into silence.

A strategy to consider might be:

Name the game.

"I see you are playing sex games."

This establishes your authority and robs the whole thing of its mystification.

Stop the game.

"This is not an appropriate game to play. I want you to stop now."

Postpone discussion.

"I am upset to find you playing this game, and I will want to talk with you later, before dinner."

Redirect.

"Now I want you to go outside and pick up all those branches and tin cans and fishnet you were working with before."

SOCIAL DANGERS

You might think that children are protected from "teenage" problems at the ages of seven and eight. Would that they were! The fact is, we mustn't wait until adolescence to talk with Kids about alcohol, smoking, and illegal drugs. It's not just that a small but growing number of children as young as this experiment with each of them. The problem is that other people *are* talking to them and very persuasively.

The ads for cigarettes and chewing tobacco, beer, wine, and hard liquor are bad enough. Joe Camel has come in for a lot of flak as a "role model" of the cool sophisticate urging teens to smoke. But for younger children, Joe looks like—a Dad. There he is: bald, heavy-featured, a calm strong welcoming grin on his face, broad shouldered—utterly reliable and endearing. And dressed in a suit. When I asked every Eight I saw for two weeks who Joe reminded them of, guess what they said.

But there are also rock stars, sports heroes, TV stars for Kid-popular shows drinking, chewing, smoking, talking and singing about their favorite vices. A soft drink company (Royal Crown) even put out a soft drink in an amber, long-neck bottle and labeled it "Draft."

With this barrage of propaganda going on, parents must talk about the downside of these dangerous habits. When you do, remember that Kids this age do not comprehend fine distinctions about possibilities. If you say that something is "probably" going to happen, they may assume that the chance of it happening is maybe one in four, not three in four. They have the same trouble with terms such as "likely," "might," and "usually."

Instead of saying something like "Cigarette smoking might give you lung cancer and it's pretty certain to stain your teeth" try "Cigarette smoking damages your lung tissue. Lots of people who smoke get lung cancer. Smoking always makes your teeth dirty and it even gives you wrinkles in your face while you are still young. Yuck!"

Children this age also pick up parents' attitudes toward sexual activity. It's not enough just to make comments: "That girl on the talk show is much too young to take care of a baby! She doesn't even know who the father is!" though that certainly doesn't hurt. Children are hyper-alert to behavior cues. How parents lead their own lives, what they say when they gossip, what they laugh at on TV or at the movies, what kinds of magazines they look at, and how they talk about people at work shape children's attitudes about tolerance, virtue, and what they believe they can aspire to achieve.

Responsibility, Discipline, and Life at Home

RESPONSIBILITY

Sevens and Eights thrive when their increasing competence is recognized. They also have an important lesson to learn about "Who takes care of me?" and "Who takes care of us?", meaning the family. It's good for Seven/Eight to learn that the answer to the first question is "I do" and the answer to the second one is "We do."

The two big areas that require parental decisions here are allowances and chores, including the chore of taking care of oneself.

AN ALLOWANCE

Kids today understand money at an early age. "The tooth fairy brought me a dollar fifty," John, just seven, tells me. "Now I have ten dollars and sixty-five cents saved up, and when I get another four dollars and thirty-five cents, I'm going to buy a rocket ship that soars 300 feet in the air."

Parents who don't have much discretionary money may feel that giving an allowance is an unaffordable extra. Parents who have a lot of discretionary money may feel that an allowance is unnecessary; their Kids get just about anything they ask for—as well as gifts from relatives and friends—because why not?

There are lots of opinions about allowances and each faction has good points. Getting paid for chores you do and not paid for those you don't fosters accountability. Getting a regular sum each week (regardless of work done) helps Kids learn how to manage money—the virtue of saving up, rather than spending it all. Not getting an allowance at all, just asking for things as needed, gives parents control over what kind of junk Kids buy.

If you start an allowance, Seven/Eight is an appropriate time. Kids this age lust after inexpensive items, so a very small allowance, even ten or twenty-five cents a week, actually can mean something to them: they can save up for four or five weeks and buy something good. Kids also regard having money as status at this age. Moreover, they're into collecting things, and money is a great thing to collect.

Here is the way I think about allowances.

• Consider giving a basic allowance not based on chores or good behavior. (For a discussion of chores in general, see page 115.)

Kids do need to learn to manage money: to spend, to save, to give, to borrow or lend, and to invest. At this age, they can learn about at least the first three—and probably the fourth, as well. One way to do this is to give a weekly allowance, but with the proviso that on a monthly basis at least a certain amount must be saved and a certain amount must be given. The child decides what it is saved for and to whom or what it is given. Parents can use this as an opportunity to expound on everything from true vs. false advertising to worthy vs. unworthy objects of charity.

• Consider making some special nondaily chores available for earning extra money. Polishing the silver, washing windows (safely), some outdoor tasks are all good candidates.

• Consider defining what you will and will not buy for your Seven/Eight so that the allowance has some meaning.

If Seven/Eight has every acquisitive whim fulfilled, the allowance will have no point. But if Seven/Eight has to save up for every item no matter how high-priced, it's all too easy to become jaded, disillusioned, and angry. Being required to save up for the two-wheeler the child yearns for, if parents can readily afford just to spring for it, could nip a young capitalist's eagerness in the bud.

• Consider talking with Seven/Eight about all the functions of money and its complexities.

Seven and Eight love to know that adulthood is a demanding occupation, one that has its secrets and difficulties. Don't just let your Kid see you writing checks. Explain how they work, and that you pay for the privilege of lending the bank your money. When you pop your card in the automatic teller, make clear what the transaction really means. Talk about interest rates. Your child has probably seen movies involving investment bankers, accountants, and commodity brokers. Try relating these occupations to real life.

Kids who are eight and older might get a kick out of, and learn from, a subscription to *Zillions:*

Consumer Reports for Kids. Besides reporting on all the appurtenances of Kidhood, the magazine advises on money matters. P.O. Box 5481, Boulder, CO 80322–4861, (800–288–7898).

CHORES

Sevens and Eights suddenly seem so competent. They can do just about everything for themselves, from flossing their teeth to inserting their pierced earrings (see box titled **Taking Care of Themselves,** page 116). They are capable of performing practically any household chore—with some exceptions owing to safety and lack of strength—if they are taught how and if they feel like it.

It can be maddening, therefore, when Sevens and Eights collapse into a bundle of incompetence, reluctance, and rebellion and refuse to so much as put on their own boots. "I can't do the *heel!*" they whine.

Chores, especially, tend to bring out their histrionic talents: "I am the Cinderella of this whole family. Nothing but work, work, work. I bet I'm really adopted and you got me to do all the work" (or "You adopted me so that you could make me do all the work"). "You expect me to do everything perfect. How can I do everything as perfect as you. You are thirty-two and I am only eight. You are four times me." "I am always working in the house and never get to see the beautiful, blue sky."

There are several pitfalls parents of Kids this age group do well to avoid when it comes to self-care and chores.

The good helper syndrome

Sevens and Eights are very sharp when it comes to figuring out whose job something is. (No wonder: performing a job well is a key factor in creating a comfortable public self.) Younger children would often glow with pride at the idea of being grown-up enough to be big helpers. Sevens and Eights have a different approach. When they hear praise like "You're such a good helper!" they deduce that.

TAKING CARE OF THEMSELVES

**Most Sevens and Eights can learn to take care of themselves in the following respects. Compli-
cated tasks can be broken down into steps and learned a piece at a time.**

BATHING

*Be sure all electric appliances are completely inaccessible. Seven/Eight should be warned about the
danger of electrocution if an appliance is in contact with water, but the temptation to put an appliance in
water should never exist. Antislip devices should be placed in tubs and showers. Turn the hot water
heater down to 120°F. to avoid accidental serious burns.*

Take bath or shower, including washing face and genitals.
Little girls should avoid bubble baths and baths in soapy or shampoo water due to risk of
vaginitis; uncircumcised little boys need to be reminded always to pull the foreskin back
up after washing the glans of the penis.
Sevens and Eights often forget to wash their faces, not because they can't stand to but
because the face somehow seems to them exempt from getting dirty.
No Q-tips in the ears! This is a big source of ear canal and eardrum injuries in this age group.

HAIR

Sevens and Eights may campaign for extreme haircuts or do's. A couple of caveats:

• Make sure there is no danger of a "look" being mistaken for a gang signal.
• Make sure the cut does not violate any school rule.
• Tight braids, traction on hair, and excessive use of oils or lotions may predispose Kids to fungus
infections, which look like dandruff and itch.

Wash and condition hair unless it is very long or tangle prone.
A Seven/Eight may be able to blow-dry hair. NEVER trust him or her with a curling iron,
however.
Brush hair if the hairdo is uncomplicated.

TEETH AND NAILS

The Pediatric Dental Association recommends that parents give a final brush to Kids' teeth
up to age eight. Children over five, the Association advises, also ought to floss (with assistance), because once the permanent teeth come in their surfaces touch.
Sevens and Eights are great at applying nailpolish, often quite neatly, but are almost never
able to manage filing or cutting nails.

TOILETING

Go, wipe, and flush.
Wash and dry hands afterward.

DRESSING

Pick out appropriate clothing.
Dress self, including buttoning buttons, zipping zippers, tying shoes, buckling belts, putting
on pierced earrings.
Get into and out of outer-clothing, including snowsuits, boots, hats, mittens, or gloves. (It's a
good idea to make sure mittens or gloves are attached somehow.)

TAKING CARE OF THEMSELVES (cont.)

Beware clothes or jewelry that are inappropriate, especially those that are too precocious, seductive, or dangerous, expensive items that invite theft, or clothing that suggests a gang affiliation.

Caution Seven/Eight not to trade pierced earrings, due to the tiny risk of transmission of blood-borne diseases.

Caution Seven/Eight not to trade hats, especially if he or she has long hair or a complicated hairdo. This is a big age for head lice, a condition that, though not dangerous, is exhausting (see **Glossary**).

UNUSUAL TASKS

At seven, many children with diabetes can learn to give themselves their own insulin injections. Similarly, children who require bladder catheterization can often learn to perform this at seven. Direct adult supervision is vital throughout these years, however. Don't count on Seven/Eight to remember to do the task nor to tell the exact truth about whether it got done.

Most children are unable to manage contact lenses on their own until ages ten or twelve, at the earliest.

Most Sevens/Eights can handle replaceable orthodontic devices without assistance.

• Housework is entirely the responsibility of the grown-up(s) who made the comment.

• No other grown-ups or children are obliged to participate in housework.

• If they do perform household tasks, they are going beyond the call of duty and are owed something by the grown-up whose work they are doing.

This can lead to undesirable behavior, like whining and complaining and refusal to pick up one's socks. More longlastingly, it can lead to a very pervasive attitude toward housekeeping and chores: that such work is demeaning, that the person who performs it is inferior, and that people who are not required to perform housework are smarter, better-looking, richer, and in general more worthy than those who are.

In fact, this is the main problem with making an allowance dependent on the child's performing household chores: it puts the child in a special, duty-exempt position. You'd think that they would figure out: "If I want an allowance, I must

live up to my responsibilities." Nope. Instead, they think: "I'm not going to do their work for them. It's not my job. Maybe next week I'll want some money bad enough. We'll see."

To get away from the good helper syndrome, it's necessary to communicate the idea that taking care of the home is the job of everybody who lives there. This means avoiding power struggles as much as possible. Power struggles merely indicate to Seven/Eight that parents have a need to dominate children and make them do what they want them to do. Power struggles don't really teach much, besides being unpleasant and fatiguing.

What works: as much as possible, have chores built into everyday life so that NOT performing a chore has a natural and less than delightful consequence. Here is an approach:

• Define the daily chores expected of Seven/Eight (see box titled **Chores for Sevens and Eights**, page 119).

Self-care, like bathing and brushing teeth, is

HOW TO PERFORM A CHORE

- Make the chore possible to do without excessive frustration. For instance: closets with bars and hooks low enough for Seven/Eight to hang up clothes; enough drawer or box space for clothes and toys; a clothes hamper for dirty laundry; fitted sheets and a bedding arrangement that doesn't require a decorator's license and a haberdasher's coordination to get straight.
- Introduce the chore as "something everyone should know how to do that is your job from now on." Don't ask whether he or she would like to do it or is old enough to do it.
- Don't apologize for assigning a chore.
- Start by telling the child when the chore is to be done. "Every day after you have brushed your teeth, it is time to make your bed."
- Break down the chore into several sections, if necessary.

  "First pull all the bedclothes back. Then straighten the bottom sheet. Then pull up the top sheet and smooth it. Here is how you make the corners neat. Then pull up all the blankets and smooth them. Finally, replace the pillows and your stuffed toucan."

- Supervise the first couple of times, giving only praise if Seven/Eight is putting in a good effort. If Seven/Eight is not trying hard, however, try not to get into a power struggle. Merely say, "That sheet has lots of wrinkles." "The bed is made, but it looks pretty lumpy."
- Don't forget the chart of chores, to be filled in with checkmarks or stars or stickers.

not included. All the chores put together might take about half an hour, if performed without dawdling. This is enough time for them to make an impact without being truly onerous. A typical list: make bed, put away clothes and toys, set the dinner table, clean the kitty litter box.

- Make a chart with a picture and label of each chore, and a place to check off or place a sticker when each is done.
- If a chore doesn't get performed at its appointed time, have a well-understood consequence. If the bed doesn't get made before leaving for school, it has to be done after school before the child does anything else. If toys or clothes are still strewn about by the time they were supposed to be tidied, they have to go in the "No Using" box and no one can play with them or wear them for a day. To get them back into use, they have to be first put away and stay put away for a day. If the table doesn't get set, then the person who was supposed to do it has to clear the table: that person can't do anything

after dinner until the table is cleared. If the kitty litter doesn't get changed and someone else has to do it, the kitty can't be played with until the box is due to be changed again and gets changed without reminding.

The key with this method is not to argue, coax, or fuss in any way. When a chore doesn't get done, the consequence is automatic and low-keyed. If you need to, just keep restating the rule: "The bed didn't get made before school. Nothing gets done now (after school) until the bed gets made." No "If you'd only done it then" or "I told you this morning that" or "When will you ever learn that." Try to stay detached and only mildly interested in something that is, after all, none of your business.

The substitute parent temptation

When you're overwhelmed as a parent, a sympathetic, competent, loving Seven/Eight can seem like a godsend. Seven/Eight can do all the usual chores and even the toughies: scrub a floor, make a simple meal, watch the baby.

CHORES FOR SEVENS AND EIGHTS

Sevens and Eights do best when chores take up a total of about half an hour each weekday and half an hour to one hour on a weekend day

SAFE AND APPROPRIATE

Make his or her bed.

Tidy the bedroom: put away toys, hang up clothing.

Set the table.

Clear the table.

Dry the dishes.

Carry out trash.

Dust furniture.

Vacuum a room (not stairs).

Polish silverware or other unbreakable items.

Dig weeds (be sure he or she knows what a weed is).

Sweep with a broom.

Rake leaves.

Shovel light snow.

Sort and fold laundry and match socks.

Make a sandwich; fix juice and cereal.

Dress and toss a salad.

Shop for and cook a meal, with constant adult supervision.

Feed, water, exercise, OR groom a cat or dog (Only one task). Adult supervision absolutely required.

Complete daily care for a reptile, fish, or some birds—but only when an adult does a daily checkup. Pets should not have to pay the price for a child's absentmindedness.

TOO MUCH RESPONSIBILITY

Watch a baby or toddler without an adult in the same or a nearby room (even with an adult nearby, more than fifteen minutes of babysitting is asking for trouble).

Fix a bottle for or feed a baby or toddler.

Carry a baby or toddler.

Care totally for a demanding pet: feed, water, exercise, groom.

Sort clothes for washing; manipulate the washing machine (likely outcome for everything: very small and very pink).

Take care of an adult: cook for, clean up after, awaken, help get dressed or take over the usual duties of an adult: care of the entire house, shopping, laundry, and so on.

The problem with the abovementioned tasks is not that Seven/Eight is incapable or irresponsible; it is that being responsible for these chores puts Seven/Eight into the position of being an adult—a confusing and frightening situation.

UNSAFE

Handle guns in any way (the problem is not that Seven/Eight is not capable or competent when supervised, it is that he or she may become so used to guns that he or she handles them without supervision).

Cook on the stove or microwave without an adult in constant attendance.

Use a garbage disposal.

Use a food processor.

Run or be near a power mower, leaf-blower, electric saw, or other power tools.

Do anything on a ladder.

Do anything using toxic chemicals, such as ammonia. Spray bottles are particularly dangerous.

Use real kitchen knives.

Iron.

Moreover, Seven/Eight often can talk and listen in a way that mimics another adult.

It's easy, then, for parents in distress to be tempted to call on Seven/Eight to "co-parent" with them. When Sara was seven, her father took a visiting position in California, leaving the two of us in Amherst, Massachusetts: and it was the year of the great gypsy moth invasion. Our home was surrounded by about fifty trees, each under attack from innumerable furry caterpillars. Every dawn and dusk, Sara and I could be found manning the defenses: wrapping each tree trunk with aluminum foil smeared with a special caterpillar-trapping grease and scraping the little fuzzy corpses into buckets of soapy water.

All around us, caterpillar droppings fell to earth, the pitter patter putting one in mind of a rain forest—or of very distant gunfire. I was so focused on the enemy that I barely noticed the joy going out of Sara's smile and the paranoia developing in her eyes. "Mommy," she asked one day, "is this what it's like in a war zone?"

I hadn't just enlisted her in the good fight. I'd cast her in a real-life Alfred Hitchcock film. Worse, I'd treated her as if she were, well, her father.

It's easy to let this temptation to treat the child as an adult creep up on you, especially if you're a single parent— either permanently or temporarily, when your co-parent is geographically, physically, emotionally, or mentally unavailable. If Seven/Eight is performing an hour or more of chores a day or if some of those chores are clearly out of the usual ballpark of responsibility or difficulty, suspect that you are getting into the war zone area.

Substituting for an absent parent can be very confusing to a Seven/Eight who is working on developing a public self. It may make him or her act in a pseudo-mature fashion that can put off other children or even call up their teasing and ridicule. It may take the joy and energy from Seven/Eight's life and push him or her into "relaxing" the way adults do, with mindless TV and junk food. It can even push parent and child into dangerous areas where boundaries break down into behaviors that border on incest.

The "wait until he or she is a little older and more responsible" daydream

Sevens and Eights can fall into trances, dawdle, and forget what they were doing even in the middle of doing it. They can stand there with a sad, helpless look on their faces, staring hopelessly at the unmade bed or the rising tide of toys and rumpled clothes as if they were middle-aged accountants on April 14.

Naturally, it may occur to a parent that the solution is to get the job done oneself, so that everyone can move on to something more fun, educational, meaningful, important, whatever. This will backfire. If you wait until age nine to try to make chores part of normal daily life, you will be contending with overpowering forces. Nine has a very firm concept of his or her role in the family, and if chores are not part of the concept already they are unlikely to be easily assimilated. Nine will look at his or her schedule of school, homework, lessons, group activities, sports, "necessary" stuff like regular TV programs, play dates, important projects, and computer addictions, and will ask you, "Where is the time for chores?"

Nine will mount sophisticated arguments: "By the time I grow up, this'll all be done by robots. Don't you want me to spend my time learning something *useful?* " "If I didn't have to spend all this time polishing the silver, I could be *learning* about *Egypt* on the computer." "Are you glad that your mom and dad made you learn how to shell peas? Don't you wish that they'd made you learn how to change a tire instead? I bet I could change a tire." Nine's capacity for self-pity will be far greater and his or her repertoire of smart-alecky, cute, hilarious, incisive, and heart-shattering comments far larger than they are now.

SIBLING RELATIONS

Sevens and Eights are working so hard to grow up and are so distracted in their efforts that their relationships with siblings can be a little rocky. To siblings, Seven/Eight is something of a mystery. Is he or she a little Kid or a big Kid? Somebody to push around, somebody to confide in, somebody to trust? It can seem as if someone who is Seven/Eight is a different age from one day to the next.

Similarly, one of the things Seven/Eight is trying extremely hard to work out is his or her position in the family. Who can I boss and who is the boss of me? What is my claim to fame in this family group? What scares me most, what makes me proud, what can I get away with, how can I be hurt in my soul?

The trick for parents in all these issues is to nurture Seven/Eight's growing sense of self and responsibility while maintaining boundaries in the family. If Seven/Eight begins to confuse his or her role with that of the parent, family relationships deteriorate. Yet it can be very tempting to elevate the status of Seven/Eight: Kids this age are often able to reason and to express themselves with what can seem to be extraordinary maturity.

DISCIPLINE

Bratty behavior usually is much less of an issue at ages seven and eight if parents have previously taken measures to prevent or control it. (If not, see the section on brattiness in the previous chapter.) Instead, many discipline concerns now focus on sibling relationships.

NAGGING AND BOSSINESS

Why do Sevens and Eights engage in these behaviors so much? Partly, I think, it is because they are such control freaks—searching for certainty in a world they are just starting to figure out. Partly, however, it is because nagging and bossiness can easily become habits.

Eights, especially, are great naggers. They nag parents, siblings, friends, even pets—usually about things that are absolutely none of their business.

"Greg, you shouldn't wear that hat. I told you and told you that hat is too big. It squashes your ears and you can't even see out from under it when you look up. That hat looks so silly I could just laugh. If I had a hat like that, I would hide it in my drawer and never look at it or I would give it away to somebody who didn't care how they looked. Mommy, look at that hat Greg is wearing. Oh, my goodness. What a terrible hat. At least they could have made it not that yucky maroon, and then they put that awful green logo on it, and there isn't even a band on so you could make it tighter so it doesn't even fit, and besides...."

What do you do—if you're a sibling—with a nagger? If you argue, you just get embroiled in fine points, like hat hair and forehead creases. If you give in, they nag you about how you always give in. If you tell them to stop it, they know they've got you but good and they redouble their efforts. If you run away, they'll lurk in wait for you, and find you right when you're with your friends and trying to look cool or when you're really involved in something. Oy.

Siblings of naggers really *can't* defend themselves. That's one reason for parents to intervene. Here are two more:

• Naggers don't just nag siblings and friends; they nag parents. A nagged parent is a demoralized, unhappy parent, with diminished credibility and authority.

• Nagging is in large part done from habit, not really from need. It is surprisingly easy to root out. When you do, the nagger, as well as all the naggees, are much happier.

Denagging a nagger

• Make sure that the nagger has a full, rich life and plenty of opportunities for thinking well of himself or herself.

• Make a special time to sit down with the nagger and present the problem. Define nagging: it is going on and on to someone about something that is none of your business. A tactful way is to say that nagging is a habit, just like biting your fingernails or whatever (perhaps you can think of someone the nagger knows who has an annoying habit) and that it is your duty as a parent to help the nagger to stop.

• If the nagger says he or she doesn't nag, don't argue. Say that perhaps this means that there will be no more nagging, and that's fine. But if the nagging happens again, you will come and place a hand on the nagger's shoulder and say a special, secret word or phrase, such as, "There's a great big bee in the backyard." This is a signal that the nagger should become quiet immediately and go with the parent to a different part of the home. That's it. There will be no punishment, no discussion, no reward for not nagging.

• However, if the nagger does not obey the signal, there will be a significant discipline: a loss of privilege or a chore imposed.

• Then stick to the penalty. Do not allow yourself to become entangled in a discussion of whether the nagger was really nagging. Announce yourself as the authority: "If I say it is nagging, it is nagging."

FIGHTS

Sevens and Eights are constantly engaged in figuring out their ranking in the pecking order of siblings. Naturally, this makes for a certain amount of bickering and jockeying for position.

Many of these battles between siblings aren't really about anything. Kids bicker and snarl and tease and poke and wrestle just as a way to be together. If they are enjoying it, as is clear from their expressions and tones of voice, they are best left to their own devices. If someone is viciously angry or if someone is clearly being injured by blows or by words, it's time to intervene with seriousness and firmness and to impose a penalty either on both or on the attacker.

Such bitter fights usually aren't over an issue, either. Bitter fights usually occur because one or both of the participants is feeling absolutely awful for some reason. Sometimes the fight instigator is suffering from a terrible self-image due to trouble at school or with friends; or from heartbreak due to the loss of a friend or a pet; or from worry about parental health or stability; or from jealousy due to real or perceived parental preference for another child. After the bitter fight has been broken up and discipline applied, it's crucial to try to sort out where the bitterness originated.

Bitter fights are not to be confused with big fights. Big fights are over an issue: two people want the same thing and only one can have it— so who does it belong to? That "thing" can be a toy, a piece of equipment, a block of time with a person, TV, or computer, a certain space, an identity as winner… or whatever.

Winning such a fight doesn't necessarily mean getting the "thing," but it does mean being able to express your point of view, listen to the other person's, propose solutions, and end with some kind of agreed-on outcome.

This is a great age for siblings to learn how to conduct a "big fight" with each other. This is an important skill, very valuable throughout life. Parents who want to endow their Kids with this gift do a great service to them by teaching this skill, rather than just squelching battles— or abandoning Kids to their own means of settling arguments.

Teaching Sevens and Eights how to fight fairly and effectively means teaching them the rules of fighting, modeling those rules when you yourself fight, and intervening and leading Seven/Eight to use them when a fight is in its early stages.

The rules of a big fight

• Each person gets to say what he or she thinks the fight is about. They can argue about what the fight is about, but no calling names or inflicting blows.

• The adult clarifies the position of each contender until both can agree what the fight is about.

• When the fighters agree on what the fight is about, they both have to think of some solutions that will give each one what he or she wants. There usually have to be compromises and trade-offs.

• The grown-up helps the Kids think through the possibilities.

• The goal: find a compromise that both fighting parties can agree on.

• The grown-up praises both fighters for coming to terms and offers a "reward time," which could be a game with the adult participating, a drive, a walk, a bike ride, or a good snack.

• The grown-up lets it be known that he or she expects the siblings to learn to follow the rules without adult intervention and that praise and rewards will be bestowed when that happy day occurs.

This doesn't sound like much fun and it's

not. In fact, most parents wind up weary, badgered, and bored by the exercise. Here's the good part: Kids wind up weary, badgered, and bored also. After a few experiences with it, they will try to avoid the exercise at all costs. The result: they will try to avoid having a big fight in your hearing. If a big fight does occur and you appear at once on the scene, negotiating expression on your face, they will insist that they can work it out on their own. Take them at their word!

So the trick is to enforce the exercise very diligently when you first start out. You may need to do so two or three times or more in a two-day period. Once the Kids begin to avoid fights or settle them themselves, you may need to administer a "booster dose" when you see them slipping back into big fights, no longer respecting your zero tolerance of these outbreaks.

Will they engage in big fights in your absence? Probably. Make that assuredly. But merely knowing that there is a civilized standard for resolving disagreements in the adult world will make an enormous difference in their behavior as time goes on.

TATTLING

Sevens and Eights can develop tattling to a fine art. Fives and Sixes tattled without subtlety: "Misha's doing it again. He's on the phone. He's talking to Leah. He's sitting on the floor in his closet. I listened. You'd better go stop him right now!" All out in one breath with a red face and eyes wide with horror.

Not so with Seven and Eight. "Excuse me, Mom, I need to tell you something private. Misha isn't supposed to be talking on the phone with Leah after eight o'clock. It's 9:23 and he's sitting in the closet with the phone. I bet he's talking to her." Blink. Blink. Blink. Stare.

A dilemma. You may be grateful for the info. You may be duped into believing that Eight's motives are pure and guileless. But even when the tattling seems to be altruistic and helpful, in the long run it's destructive.

• The Seven or Eight who is not discouraged from even "appropriate" tattling easily branches out into active spying. This can lead to a pre-occupation with discovering siblings' foibles—leading to lurking behind doors and peaking through keyholes and laying traps.

• If the tattler is not foiled in these attempts, he or she is likely to be tempted to make up or exaggerate tales of misbehavior. It may become impossible to know if or when the tattler is telling the truth.

• A Seven/Eight who is allowed to feel that his or her information is received with gratitude and approval temporarily is elevated to the status of co-parent. Every time this happens, the authority of the parent suffers, and the boundary between parent and child is blurred.

Of course, you want to know if something physically dangerous is imminent. What to do? Many parents find it useful to make a series of inflexible rules and stick to them:

Rules for tattling

If someone is likely to be seriously hurt, telling is not tattling. This means that the information being given needs to be announced or shouted, not confided or whispered.

But what if the information that Seven/Eight picks up is very serious, and this rule keeps Seven/Eight guiltily silent? For instance, what if Misha was sniffing coke or Leah is pregnant? What if both are in gang trouble?

If parents suspect that something of such a serious nature is going on, and that Seven/Eight is privy to important information, ASK.

The first corollary to the tattling rule is: If a parent asks for the truth, telling is not tattling.

But what if parents do not suspect that something unusual is going on? What if Seven/Eight is the lone observer? What if Seven/Eight has clues to seriously worrying behavior of a sibling?

The third rule is for the parent: Once a child tells a parent about a sibling's behavior, the child has no further involvement in the situation.

It is all too tempting, especially for single or "functioning-as-single" parents, to discuss the implications of what has been heard or seen with the informing child. From there, it is a short, easy step to encouraging Seven/Eight in further spying and tattling and even to asking the advice of Seven/Eight on how to handle the situation. "Do you think I should talk with Misha about his feelings for Leah, or do you think he'd just yell at me and stalk out of the house?" Once this occurs, it will be a tough fight to regain full parenting status in the eyes of Seven/Eight.

Tattling to one parent about another

Sometimes a Seven/Eight, carried away with a vision of how people should behave, will incorporate into a one-Kid vigilante committee. "Mom told Grandma all about the money you guys lost at the casino," he announces to Dad in a man-to-man voice. "She said it was your fault that you kept not doing what she said." "Dad went off his diet and he had a praline ice cream cone and a Mounds bar," she whispers, thin-lipped and disapproving, to Mom.

It's particularly important that Seven/Eight not get away with this type of tattling. Sevens and Eights really need parents to be parents, not confused with siblings or companions. A Seven/Eight who is allowed to turn a parent into a nonparent may seem to assume a self-satisfied, superior air, but is really upset and angry that this is allowed to happen. He or she will find a way to obtain revenge. "I don't have to do what you say. You don't do what you're supposed to do. Why should I?"

When Seven/Eight tattles on an adult's minor foibles, the response needs to be the equivalent of raising one's shields: show no interest in the information, pay no attention to the content of the tattling, immediately condemn the tattling behavior, make no follow-up reference to the information conveyed (at least, in the hearing of Seven/Eight).

Unfortunately, once in a while, Seven/Eight tells on a parent who has committed a serious offense. This is quite a different situation. The child is already frightened by the act he or she has witnessed—frightened about losing the guilty parent. The parent on the receiving end has as a first duty reestablishing that the child is a child: the youngster's responsibility has been thoroughly discharged by giving the information. It mustn't be the child's job to console, advise, or soothe the listening parent or to gather further information.

When a child is put in the position of tattling about serious parental problems more than once, this should be a strong indication that the family and both parents need professional help.

TELEVISION

Isn't it remarkable that a single entity can produce both violent behavior and obesity due to inactivity in Kids?

Here are some ideas.

• Discuss your TV philosophy with your Kids. Go over a TV schedule and highlight the programs you approve of or at least tolerate. Explain why you are making the choices you make, and ask for their input.

• Give a TV allowance. Several families I know use poker chips. A typical rationing is 21 chips a week: each chip is worth a half-hour of television-watching. When the chips are gone, that's it; no more TV.

• Make a sibling rule: siblings must decide together which program gets watched. If there is fighting and batting back and forth of the remote with subsequent tattling and chaos, the TV set just gets turned off.

• Purchase and have a computer-adept teenager install the chip that filters out programs flagged as violent by network and cable companies. This will probably be available and cheap (perhaps only five dollars) by the time you read this.

• Enlist your Kids in helping to change programming. If you can't allow them to watch a program on, say, Wednesdays, and they're mad about it, collect the names of advertisers of the program they can't watch, and let Eight type out a form letter in his or her own words to be mailed to all of them.

School

In second and third grades, children learn to take reading and basic math skills for granted. This is so important, and such a powerful tool for later learning, that parents need to monitor that it's really happening.

ACADEMICS

"Millie had a terrible time with spelling. Just terrible. The tests were awful. She'd miss four or five out of every list of fifteen words—not enough to fail, but way below her own standards. Then all of a sudden in the middle of second grade something clicked. Now she doesn't have to go over the words; she just looks at them. It's as if she learned how to learn."

Millie's dad has summed it up. This is what Seven and Eight are about: learning to learn. You can't take for granted that this will come automatically, though.

What clicked with Millie? Perhaps the part of her brain that recognizes words by sight suddenly turned on. Or perhaps she suddenly realized that she wasn't being asked to *memorize* mysterious, meaningless, and unpredictable patterns of letters, but to *recall* familiar words that she read every day. Making that kind of connection is one of the remarkable everyday miracles that happens to Sevens and Eights. Parents can help.

"We started out by just going over the spelling lists over and over again until we were both bored to tears. Then we made flashcards and used M&M's for rewards. It was awful. Then we invented a game: we'd try to make a story using all the words in the list. The stories were pretty hysterical. I don't know what finally worked, but she finally just, well, clicked."

For something to click, a Kid needs to encounter a concept in many forms and to think about it from many different points of view. You can't make the click happen by just pointing it out: "Look. The spelling words are exactly the same words in your reader. It's just that they are in a list" or "When we talk about the ones place and the tens place and the hundreds place, it's just like money: pennies, dimes, and dollars" or "The point of reading is not to sound out every word correctly, it's to understand what the author is saying."

Waiting for something to click can make parents fidgety. Of course, venting fidgetiness on Seven and Eight will backfire. Learning is a risky business, and if you are feeling hounded or as if you are a disappointment or as if you must be perfect, you are not going to feel up to taking chances. You'll be keeping an eagle eye out for the word you don't know, and by golly, you'll find one and trip. You'll be so worried about getting the right answer that you won't be able to remember whether Jane had six apples or five apples. You'll be so concentrated on forming your lowercase letters that you lose track of what you were going to write.

Sevens and Eights on the verge of clicking need lots of comfortable parental silence while they try to figure things out, lots of pleased parental attention when they contribute an idea—even if it's off-base, and lots of invitations to think. They need to be asked questions to which there are many right answers, not just one.

On the other hand, parents need to make sure that Seven/Eight is gaining the most basic skills, the ones that make all the other "clicks" possible. The key skill is reading. By Second Grade, Kids are assumed to be able to read for meaning as opposed to merely "decoding" print. A Kid who is still having a problem here needs extra help (see box, **Is Your Kid Reading or Merely Decoding Print?**, page 127).

But reading for meaning is just the beginning. During these two years, Kids need to make three basic, enormous learning leaps.

THEY NEED TO LEARN THAT READING IS FOR TELLING THEM SOMETHING THEY DIDN'T ALREADY KNOW

Beginning readers use books to reinforce concepts that are already very familiar. For instance, a young Seven may have had a lot of story experience with familiar plots: the little baby animal gets cozily taken care of by the mommy; the youngest child in a family of three outshines the older two and gets rewarded; the timid child takes a risk and becomes stronger. Any book that follows one of these nice, familiar plots will be devoured, but Seven won't remember much else about the book. The unfamiliar parts fall away like discarded fabric from a pattern.

When a reader in this age group picks up a children's book about armadillos, say, he may "learn" that even these bizarre creatures take care of their babies. An Eight reading the same book can look beyond the familiar parts of the story, to the new stuff: Armadillos can cross a river by walking along the water's floor. They give birth to identical quadruplets. They can roll up to become like an armored tank.

Sevens and Eights can be drawn into this more adventurous approach to reading in a number of ways. Poems and verses are designed to be surprising: so are comic books. (Beware the presence of adult-only comics, of course.) CD-ROMs are spectacular assists. Do not dis-

IS YOUR KID READING OR MERELY DECODING PRINT?

Learning to read is an enormous achievement, one that can take a Kid's breath away—decoding print into words! It can actually come as a shock that *that's not all there is to it.*

Good reading programs concentrate on teaching meaning and on language skills at the same time that they teach word recognition and phonetics, but each child gets the idea in his or her own particular way. Some Kids seem to "know it from the beginning." Others make the discovery gradually, often in the course of being read to by a parent or teacher. For others, there's that sudden click. A few don't make the discovery on their own at all: they need very special assistance. However the click gets clicked, Kids need to have made this discovery to enjoy second and third grade.

To see if your Seven or Eight has made this discovery, listen to her as she reads out loud.

• A decoder reads or sounds out each word, sometimes easily and sometimes laboriously, but there's no feeling or no sense of punctuation in the child's voice—he performs in a monotone. A reader gets in the commas and the periods and grins when he's reading something funny.

• A decoder can misread a word, so that it changes or destroys the whole meaning of a sentence, and not notice. "The mother duck took the grace in her beak." A reader will misread a word, look puzzled or annoyed, and try to figure out the right word or ask for help.

• A decoder can't spell. She's used to deciphering words, not regarding them as units of meaning, so they're as hard to remember as any code. A reader may not be a great speller, but she'll take a cheerful stab and make understandable errors. You could ask a decoder to spell a word she's just read correctly, and she'll stare at you appalled.

• A decoder doesn't enjoy reading and often looks tense or self-conscious when faced with the task.

• A decoder doesn't know what he or she just read—doesn't spontaneously comment on the story and can't answer questions about the material. The Kid isn't likely to tell you that he doesn't understand what he read, however. This is not because he's lying or covering up. It's because the concept "understand what you read" has no meaning to him.

If your child is still decoding rather than reading for meaning, don't panic. Some Kids don't click with this until they are over seven. A child in this position does need extra help and consideration, however. If he or she is made to feel inadequate, reading will come to seem a form of torture.

Here are some ways to help a decoder.

• Read out loud. The more a decoder simply gets to know his or her way around books, the more ready he or she will be for the click to click. Reading out loud helps a decoder to grasp the idea, for instance, that most stories have a beginning, middle, and end and that they have a main character; that verses rhyme; that instructions come in a sequence.

• Make reading a pleasure, with affectionate contact, mutual enjoyment of the story, and even a snack. Every pleasant contact with a book is a plus.

• Make reading interactive, but not as if you were conducting a quiz. Invite comments by making your own:

"Oh, dear. MaryAnn [the steam shovel] looks just exhausted. Look at her tired eyes."

Ask questions as if the answer matters—not as if you are checking on comprehension:

"What on earth is that horse thinking of!"

• Make the learning environment rich and stimulating. To read for meaning is much easier when you have a big store of experience: it's much easier for the words and ideas to catch hold in your mind.
• Avoid being perfectionistic or rigid. A person who reads for meaning makes mistakes, skips over words, and invents pronunciations for words he or she doesn't know.
• Talk with the teacher about special help. The best reading programs for a decoder are those that reward every behavior that characterizes a good reader.

dain the humble cereal box, the fast-food placemat, the collection of riddles or jokes (see box, **Learning to Love to Read,** page 129).

One of the most rewarding features of preserving reading aloud time with Sevens and Eights, is that, even though they can read by themselves, adults can pick stories that stretch them just the right amount, presenting them with something other than the familiar characters and plots.

WRITING NEEDS TO BECOME AUTOMATIC, SO THAT IT CAN BE USED TO EXPRESS THOUGHTS IN ORDERLY SEQUENCE

Fives and Sixes write as if they are drawing, making each letter and word lovingly. They look at the finished product as something to maybe hang on the refrigerator. Sevens and Eights need to learn to regard writing as a way to communicate a feeling or an idea. If they concentrate on every letter or word, the feeling or idea is likely to disappear in mid-sentence.

The more writing for communication that Seven and Eight can do, the better.

"Leave me a note about what you want in your lunchbox." "Before you can wear your new sweater, you need to write Aunt Lou a really good thank you note. It can't just say 'Thanks. Love.' It has to name the present, and

tell what you think of it and how you will use it." "See what you would like to add to the shopping list." "Put a note on the door to tell the plumber to come round to the back where the leak is."

Of course, a good writing program at school means that very few worksheets are true/false or involve checkmarks or crossing out answers. A daily journal, read and appreciated by the teacher, is a fine thing; so are pen pals or email buddies, or interchanges, carefully supervised, via the internet.

THEY NEED TO LEARN HOW TO USE NUMBERS TO SOLVE PROBLEMS

Fives and Sixes learn to count and add and subtract. Sevens and Eights need to think about how to use these skills to get around in the world. Using adding and subtracting to solve problems makes the rest of math fall into place: if you can figure out how many micromachines there will be if Branden, Rain, and Sophie pool their collections of six each, it will be easier to get the idea of multiplying six times three and of dividing eighteen by six.

Of course, there aren't all that many occasions in real life that provide the kind of problems found in second- and third-grade classrooms. Making up such problems artificially usually doesn't work; Seven and Eight detect the artifice and rebel. Happily, there are lots of daily occasions for simply thinking in a mathematical way: thinking that involves logic, number manipulation, categorization, and memory (see box, **Memory Builders**, page 131).

One of the main lessons for Seven and Eight to learn is that you believe them competent to solve problems, that you trust them to do so, and that you are appropriately grateful for their help (see box, **Helping Math Click**, page 130).

> "Buster figured out where we'd parked in that dreadful thing. He remembered that there was a beer ad on the wall and that the place where we parked looked down on that little church. If

he hadn't, I'd still be walking up and down the ramps, weeping."

> "Do you think we have the right number of potatoes for the salad? I hate having too much leftover potato salad. I hate when it turns green."

> "If you sort out the junk drawer, you can have whatever is in it that you want. Unless it's dangerous."

LIFE IN THE CLASSROOM

These aren't easy grades. Teachers have to put up with Sevens' and Eights' performance anxiety,

LEARNING TO LOVE TO READ

• Let your Kid know that *you* love to read for fun. Talk about what you read and how eager you are to find out what happens in your current book. Let your Kid hear you laughing in the bathtub as you read.

• But don't let your Kid have to compete too much with books. He can wait until you've come to a good stopping place, but then really stop and really pay attention to the Kid.

• Have books around the house, especially where people tend to come to rest: the bathroom, the kitchen table, the family area. Books in the TV room can even seduce a Kid away from a boring rerun.

• Find books for your Kid that you like, too. Borrow a book from your Kid occasionally, just to read for fun.

• Make comfortable reading places in your home. A bed with a good light is great.

• If you have money to fulfill whims, let your Kid know that you will buy any books that she wants: toy purchases, on the other hand, need to be negotiated and planned.

• Set a ten-hour-a-week maximum on TV-watching. See the section on television in **Responsibility, Discipline, and Life at Home**, earlier in this chapter.

• Allow a half hour for reading in bed after the official bedtime. If Seven/Eight is in the midst of a gripping story at the end of the half hour, pretend to ignore the fact that he is reading under the covers with a flashlight. Secret reading is a special pleasure.

• Ask your Kid to read aloud directions when you are cooking or assembling something: a very direct way to appreciate the meaning (or lack thereof) of words. Have you ever carefully assembled a casserole and then been assaulted by the words: "dribble honey over each layer as you go"?

• Encourage writing. Have the materials around. Thank you notes, love notes, angry notes, silly notes, computer productions, diaries with locks, lists of model horses, door signs warning people to stay out, memory joggers.

absentmindedness, perfectionism, and self-consciousness. They have to teach kindness and tolerance in the face of the cliquishness of this age. They have to get used to being adored one minute and being regarded as the ogre the next.

Studies have shown that teachers tend to call on boys more than girls and to foster boys' sense of success disproportionately. This can happen to the most vigilant and well-meaning teacher. When children are in a classroom where the gender lines are very rigid, the boys will often have attention-getting behaviors down pat: They'll call out and reach that hand high and jiggle; they'll fall out of their chairs and bounce back up still reaching for the ceiling. When they give a wrong answer, it feels just terrible to have to rain on their parade. It's a lot easier to give them a second, third, fourth chance, or to twist that wrong answer into a right one.

Meanwhile, the girls sit and watch. The boys' behavior makes them uncomfortable; they don't interact that way. All that energy can be distracting, and the girls may lose track of what the subject is, so that when they are actually called on they have nothing to say. This either brings down the disapproval of the girls in the class, which effectively discourages other girls from raising their hands, or the other girls may in fact regard the lack of performance as sex-appropriate and subtly reward it.

Of course, this all tends to become a vicious cycle, with the boys being rewarded for monopolizing the teacher's attention and the girls being ever more disinclined to seek it.

HELPING MATH CLICK

- Use car journeys.

"We're supposed to go seven miles down this road. The speedometer says 44,823 miles right now. So how will we know when we've gone another 7 miles?" "We're driving at 60-miles-an-hour, so that's 1 mile a minute. How long will it take us to get home at this rate?" "We have only enough gas to go about 30 miles. Can we get to the zoo and back without stopping at the gas station?"

- Play games.

Sevens and Eights can learn the rules of grown-up games like gin rummy and poker. Using poker chips requires an understanding of ones, tens, and hundreds and packs a lot of incentive. Checkers, chinese checkers, Connect Four, chess, Othello, Yahtzee: Any game involving strategy helps with problem solving in general.

- Give an allowance (see section on **Responsibility, Discipline, and Life at Home,** earlier in this chapter).

- Enlist the help of Seven/Eight with real life math tasks.

"How many ears of corn should we get?" "We've got three dollars each for dinner at McDonalds. How are you going to spend yours?" "Could you please measure out the milk for this recipe and pour it into the batter."

- Make the most of dividing things equally.

"We need to divide this pizza into six slices. How should I do it?"

- Help chant the multiplication tables while you and Eight are standing in line. With luck, other people in the line will join in. Chanting is also good when you are driving or walking someplace.

MEMORY BUILDERS

• The Kim game: Everybody gets to look at a tray of assorted items for 60 seconds, and then gets to say back what was there.

• Concentration: Spread out two identical decks of cards face down on the floor. Each person takes a turn choosing two cards, one from each deck, to turn over and display. If they're identical, that person keeps the pair. If not, flip each one back over *in the same spot.* The player with the most pairs at the end wins.

• Memory word games like: "I packed my grandmother's trunk." The first person "packs" an item beginning with A. The second packs an item with B, but has to repeat item A. The third adds item C, and repeats B and A. The crazier the items the better.

• Piano lessons: in which Kids memorize Trot Pony Trot and so on.

• Verses and limericks, riddles and jokes, songs. Try long, long songs like "The Twelve Days of Christmas," or "Whitticomb Fair" or "Clementine."

• Teach Seven/Eight your own favorite memory devices: tying a string around your finger; putting an umbrella in the hall to remember to water the plants; leaving your car windows open so that you know to get gas the next day.

"Port is left because they both have four letters. Starboard is right."

• Reminisce about past events and ask Seven/Eight to help you out. "Remember when Daddy ran off into the fog and left you and Marly and me on the beach, and I could find you in the mist because you were wearing yellow? But, what was Marly wearing? Gee, did we ever get to the merry-go-round?" Go through photo albums now and then.

• Brag about Seven/Eight's memory in his or her hearing. Don't make up anything, though.

Most experienced teachers have lots of ways of getting around this. They limit how much time is spent competing to answer questions; they get children working in groups; they try to keep the classroom busy and quiet for long periods. It's worth making a visit to see what a typical day in your child's classroom is like, just from this point of view.

But parents play a big role here. Encouraging girls to speak up in class means encouraging their self-confidence at home. Parents who solicit girls' opinions help enormously. This is especially true when parents bring up topics that are unexpectedly nonhomebound, nonfeminine, and nonchildish:

"These floods are terrible. Do you think the government should tell people they can't live in places that flood so often?"
"I wonder if this country will ever have a woman president. What do you think?"

Of course, soliciting opinions is only part of the task. The other part is listening and continuing the conversation in the same vein that you would with another adult.

HOMEWORK

Many schools start homework in second grade or earlier, as a preparation for the years to come. For children aged seven and eight, the daily dose generally is work that would take about fifteen minutes to do in the classroom. This does not mean that Seven/Eight will take fifteen minutes to do it at home. Sevens and Eights are so proud to have homework, it's quite touching: "Here's my math assignment," says Toby, sighing heavily. "What I need is a calculator." But being proud and getting the stuff done promptly are two different things.

• There is a one best time for each child. Find that time and stick to it. Maybe she has to get outside and run around a lot first, and then can get it done right before dinner. Maybe he can't do homework on an empty stomach and can fit it in just before bedtime. Maybe she is so worn out by the school day that she just can't stomach the sight of it and has to get up half an hour early to do it before going to school.

• If Seven/Eight doesn't get the work done, don't try to enforce it. When parents take over the job of policing homework, they take away Seven/Eight's own incentive to see the job as his or her own. If the homework doesn't get done, Seven/Eight will have to face the disappointment of the teacher and the disapproval of the class.

• Give homework dignity. A special desk with a good light, a place to hold pencils and erasers, and a little snack make Seven/Eight feel like a professional.

• Honor the worker. It never hurts to tell other adults, in the child's hearing, how proud you are of the way the homework gets done promptly every night. A pat or hug to the worker who's just uttered a deep sigh is a good reward. Comments about the neatness, thoroughness, or creativity of the work let you give praise without being the teacher who grades the actual answers.

When there's trouble with homework, it usually springs from either or both of the following:

IT TAKES FOREVER

"One page of arithmetic! It should take you fifteen minutes!" But here it is an hour after Blake started and he's on problem six out of twelve. How come? There are a number of possibilities.

• The timing is wrong. Blake is hungry, tired, weary of schoolwork, antsy for exercise, or strongly feels he ought to be doing something else, like watching "Rescue 911." Try a different approach: before dinner with a snack rather than after; early in the morning; just after coming home.

• There are too many distractions. The TV is on, something is sizzling on the stove, siblings are fighting in one room, and the dog is yapping in the other.

• The child didn't understand the work this morning at school and he knows he's not going to understand it now. He doesn't want you to try to teach it to him, either.

• He is feeling unappreciated and needs some parental one-to-one time.

• He is worried about something: something at home or at school or about a friend or that he saw on TV or heard on the news.

• He is physically uncomfortable, even though nothing really hurts: constipated, full sinuses, a mild asthmatic attack, whatever.

• He has the impression that parents or siblings think that homework in second grade is inappropriate, or so easy that it's just pretend homework, or cute and babyish, and he's rebelling.

• He doesn't want to go to bed, for any of a number of reasons, and is dawdling to postpone that exile.

• He can't get organized. Where is his homework? In his knapsack? Where is the knapsack? And his special pencil?

• He has features of Attention Deficit Disorder, with trouble concentrating (see box, **Medical Causes of Attention Problems**, page 76).

IT GETS DONE, BUT IT'S TORTURE

"She erases so hard, she's gone right through the paper and erased most of the varnish on the dining room table."

"He gets the whole sheet done and then he writes his name at the top but he didn't leave enough room so that his last name is all cramped, so he throws a fit and tears the whole thing up."

"She just puts her head down and cries. Then I have to come and she sits on my lap and finally she gets it done."

"He can't get started. He can't find the paper, can't find the book, can't find the page. He worries that he's got the wrong assignment. He worries that Peter is going to do better than he does."

There are several possibilities here.
• Perhaps all this perfectionism means that Seven/Eight is constantly feeling judged and needs more room to manoeuvre. A Seven/Eight who is engaging in several performance enterprises—say, soccer, piano lessons, and tap dancing—may feel as if homework is the straw that broke the camel's back.
• Perhaps the perfectionistic child is crying for more one-to-one parental attention. Here is Mark, the third of five bright competent children, who discovered one day that a yell for help with his math got his father up and away from shooting baskets with the older kids.
• Perhaps perfectionism is "allowed regression" in somebody who is having to make grown-up efforts in other parts of life. Here is Mindy, who is expected to help her career parents by watching her 3-year-old twin brothers; who is expected not to tell anyone outside the family about her grandmother's alcoholism; and who is counted on to behave beautifully on every occasion. But Mindy knows that her mother had a hard time at school and that she is full of sympathy at homework time.
• Perhaps the perfectionistic tendencies are an expression of worry about how things are going socially at school. If there weren't homework, you could forget about how nasty Gretta and her pals are to you during recess. But homework reminds you how much you hate that part of school and you just go to pieces.

• Perhaps the work really is too hard, and a conference with the teacher and some special testing is in order.

AFTER-SCHOOL LESSONS

Seven and Eight's task is to get an idea of what is out there to become competent in and to taste some of those things. What will I like? What will I be good at? Is there anything out there that I hate or just can't get the hang of?

This is such an exciting question that it's not surprising it rings all kinds of parental bells.

"I always wanted to learn how to tap dance like my friend Dodo, with a little yellow tutu and shiny black mary janes, but my mother said it was tacky and I had to take ballet."

"If they'd had karate classes back then, and if I'd learned a little self-confidence about my body, I'd be a different person today."

"I thought everybody threw up before a piano recital. I thought it was part of the whole deal."

"I was just like every other little girl: I thought that paradise contained just girls and horses."

"No way is Caleb going to get rushed around the way I was, from one lesson to another. He's going to have time to daydream and just play."

"My parents couldn't have cared less if I ever learned anything. Andreas is going to have all the opportunities I missed!"

Well.
When it comes to lessons, there are lots of

opinions but no real studies. Here is what I have learned from parents and children after more than two decades in practice.

• If you are absolutely determined to avoid repeating a childhood experience, you are still very likely to repeat it anyway. I think it's a little like learning to ride a two-wheeler: You see an obstacle you are set upon avoiding, and for some reason you steer right at it. The only cure: confide in your spouse, friends, pediatrician, whomever. Ask them to watch over you, so you don't make the same mistake with your child.

• Everybody's idea of paradise is different. For me, it is a yellow tutu and tap shoes; for her, a pony; for him, karate. And for a particular child—who knows? A sketch pad? A computer? The violin? Chess?

• The greatest gift, and the biggest protection from going astray, that you can give to a Kid is this: a passionate interest in and success at a subject, skill, hobby, sport, or artistic endeavor that can be cultivated right through to adulthood. Passion and success at something, it matters little what, is the foundation for a sense of self that can withstand the hormonal and social upheavals of the teenage years. It is also a neutral or positive turf on which parents and youngster can interact, no matter what else is going on in their lives. This is the age for exploring the options and for letting a Kid seek out what that area in life might be.

Activities such as Scouts, day camps, and religious groups bring four great benefits to this age:

• They shuffle the deck. A Kid who is excluded from a clique in the classroom may become a buddy of the clique high command in Brownies.

• They offer new opportunities for finding a best friend to a child who wants one but hasn't found one in his or her other contacts.

• They encourage teamwork and team spirit. Seven and Eight thrive when their group is working toward a goal.

• They allow the acting out of different roles

safely, since the group is going to stay together no matter what you do. When you are a member of a group, your reputation is what you make it: you can ask for or give help, you can "not care," you can be the clown or the eccentric.

Therefore, it's a good idea to select a group that really does fulfill these expectations.

Here are some questions to ask.

• Is the leader experienced?

• Is the leader committed to staying for the whole session of the activity?

• Is the leader likely to be in a conflict-of-interest situation—for instance, is he the father of the local bully?

• Does the group really allow your Kid to meet new children with whom he or she is likely to have something in common?

• Is the group itself clique-ridden? Even in a Sunday School class of six children, it's possible to have two cliques and one outsider.

• Is the group engaged in stimulating, fun activities? Friends are most easily made when everyone is occupied and the conversation takes care of itself. A Brownie group that never goes anywhere or does anything is not a good investment of time.

If you ARE the leader, be warned: starting now, you can embarrass your Kid in a way you couldn't before. Dress nice. Don't wear weird stuff. Don't spit on your handkerchief and clean your Kid's face in front of everybody or call him your special nickname or tell stories about him. Be nice to everybody. Don't let any of the Kids or their parents intimidate you. Be fair. Give out treats. Don't use bad language. Laugh at everybody's jokes.

Exercise and Sports

The two years during which Kids are seven and eight are crucial ones for determining how children feel about physical activity. Here is my public self on the playground. Can I keep up?

Will the captains choose me fairly willingly for their team, or will I always be chosen reluctantly and last—or, even worse, used as a bargaining chip? "No fair! Why do we got to have Blake? Huh? If we got to have Blake, then we get to bat first and we get extra outs."

Do I run after the ball or actively avoid it? Do I look good when I dance or turn a cartwheel or skate? Kids six and younger never think about that kind of thing. They might be "shy" about being watched—not about living up to an ideal. For the first time, performance anxiety can happen not just on stage, but in every day life.

Ideally, Sevens and Eights will emerge as Nines feeling good about how their bodies perform, no matter what their individual endowment of coordination, speed, and strength. Parents and grandparents can help a lot. For one thing, they can make sure that their favorite Kid really is moving around as much as they think. The recommended minimum amount of activity for Kids in the school years is a half hour a day of sweaty, out-of-breath stuff.

EXERCISE

It's tempting to assume that Kids get a lot of exercise just from being Kids. Aren't they always running and jumping and twirling about? Answer: not necessarily.

FOR KIDS OF BOTH SEXES, THERE MAY BE NO OPPORTUNITY, ENCOURAGEMENT, OR INCENTIVE TO BE ACTIVE

Only 36 percent of American public schools offer daily physical education classes and these may not be very vigorous. You can spend a lot of time waiting in line or learning the rules or just getting dressed and redressed. Many Kids are driven or bused to school; when they get home, they may not be able to go outside to play, for any of a number of reasons. Weekends may be spent cooped up because of weather or safety or lack of nearby play space or playmates.

SOMETIMES A CHILD OF EITHER SEX SHIES AWAY FROM EXERCISE BECAUSE IT SEEMS TO BE AVAILABLE ONLY IN THE FORM OF COMPETITION

"Andy can't stand either winning or losing. It really upsets him."

"Peggy won't go to horse shows because it makes her sad that some horses have to lose. She doesn't mind about the riders, but she thinks it breaks the horses' hearts."

"He used to get so wrought up before a game he'd have diarrhea. When his team won, he felt sorry for the other team and when they lost he felt as if it was his fault."

SOMETIMES TRADITIONALLY GENDER-APPROPRIATE GAMES DISCOURAGE ACTIVITY

"They play with their Barbies, and they make stuff like clay jewelry or weave potholders."

"Recess? Well, me and Kayla and Ashley go up in the giant hammock and play. Play? Oh, we have these books where we write our dolls' names and stuff, and then we decide what they're going to do today."

"Play with the *BOYS!* You've got to be Kidding (giggle giggle giggle)!"

This kind of little girl play is so engrossing, wholesome, and adult-friendly that it can be hard to find the heart to steer—or entice—little girls into something more active. There are good reasons to do so, however:

• In our food-rich culture, Kids need exercise to maintain their appropriate weight. This is a special issue for girls this age. This is the age at which chubby little girls have their last real chance to slim down before puberty—that is, to grow in height while slowing down weight gain. (See **Growth and Nutrition,** later in this chapter.) An extra 50 calories a day that don't get burned off in growth, activity, or as waste add an extra five pounds a year—that's the number of calories in a half-tablespoon of mayonnaise. A Seven who gains an extra five pounds a year will be fifteen pounds overweight by age ten: depending on height and body build, that's likely to put her in the obese range.

• Exercise doesn't just help burn up extra calories. It gives Kids a comfortable sense of their bodies; it acts as a natural spirit-booster; and it helps keep skills developing so that Kids' activity options stay open. It changes metabolism so that extra calories are more likely to burn than to be added as fat.

• When girls play only with girls at traditional girl pastimes, they become increasingly uncomfortable with the rougher, noisier, more active world of the mixed-sex playground and thus tend to cling to the traditional girl pastimes. Preparation for life in the real world in our culture includes some rough-and-tumble and contact with both sexes.

• Many girl pastimes don't have an end point—like a run scored or a pass caught—that gives girls a sense of "Yes, I did that!" Who is to say when Barbie is dressed perfectly? When the necklace is strung "correctly"? At what point the woven basket is "done"? These are wonderful activities, and everybody needs open-ended pastimes like these. However, a solid feeling of self-confidence needs to be nurtured by experience that includes lots of "Yes, I did that!"

• The combination of a lack of body awareness, chubbiness, and shaky self-confidence may help

to predispose Kids toward eating disorders later on.

When a Kid of either sex leads a primarily sedentary life at this age, for any reason, this is incorporated into the public self that Kid is starting to carve out. That's going to be hard to change or modify later on. Possible, but not easy. It's worth a lot of effort to find vigorous exercise for your Kid, no matter what the obstacles (see box, **Enticing Exercise,** page 137).

If your child has been sedentary for a long time, consider a period of warm up and tutorial first. Nobody wants to be thrust into the middle of anything, even jump rope, where everybody else knows the rules and has their own special style and there you are, tangled up and turning red and wishing you were home with a book. Don't assume that your Seven and Eight already knows how or will easily pick up any of the usual skills for this age: throwing, catching, batting a ball; swinging across the monkey bars hand over hand; twirling and jumping over a jump rope; kicking a soccer ball; hopping/skipping/jumping at hopscotch; roller-skating, much less inline skating.

Perhaps you do not fancy yourself much of a coach or teacher. On the other hand, you don't have to be able to actually perform any of these things in order to teach the rudiments. If you just can't see yourself in a coaching role, consider hiring a high school student to tutor Seven or Eight.

Successful tutoring requires tact. It's useful to:

• Break down a complicated feat into its component parts.

• Teach one step at a time, and at each lesson start right at the beginning again.

• Never look or act bored or displeased.

• Recognize each small advance.

• Start each lesson by recalling the small successes of the last one.

• Encourage lots of repetition before proceeding to the next step.

• Before and after the lesson, discuss unrelated topics. Be interested in the Kid, not just the skill.

PLAYING THE GAME

Left to their own devices, Kids this age play war, cops and robbers, and a million variations of imaginary situations, from space attackers to medieval tournaments. They enact horse shows, circuses, and imitate nearly anything they've seen on TV or in the movies. They play street hockey, softball, volleyball, handball, basketball, whatever. They ride bikes with gears, inline skates, skateboards, and surfboards.

Kids this age *need* to play together without adult structure some of the time. For one thing, they need the experience of making their own rules and of deciding who was right without the intervention of some grown-up with a whistle. If your Kid is only engaged in organized, adult-coached teams, he or she may be shocked and appalled when thrust into a Kid-run play-ground. "They don't have any rules!" Meredith tells me, outraged. "They just make them up! I tried to tell them, but they wouldn't listen! Boy, I'm not going to play with them again!" The "them" are her neighbors. Meredith is missing out on an important part of childhood.

When Kids negotiate and invent and haggle over rules, without adults, they're engaged in a very important task. Kids six and younger get much of their ideas about morality from adults: they think of actions as being good or bad, depending on whether parents would approve or not. This is called heteronomous morality: it comes from outside.

Kids seven and older start to work out their own ideas and start calling actions right and wrong instead of good and bad. Their ideas of morality are internal; this kind of morality is called autonomous morality. They are also more flexible. Kids six and younger believe that a rule is a rule and that breaking it for any reason is bad. Sevens and older come to understand that the spirit of the law can be different from the letter of the law: Sure, it's a rule that you only get three strikes. But here's Natalie with her arm in a splint: let's give her five swings. Sure, it's wrong to go on somebody else's property, but there's our ball right in the middle of Mrs. Jarit's petunias.

ENTICING EXERCISE

• Dance doesn't just mean tap, jazz, ballet. Look around your neighborhood for classes in all kinds of ethnic dance: Greek, Irish, Hawaiian, or old-fashioned square dancing. You may be surprised and delighted.
• Running is the best exercise for most Kids, and even the reluctant ones can be persuaded to run for a cause. Training for and running in a 3 or 4 kilometer run that benefits a school, church, or a cause such as cerebral palsy can start a long-term habit.
• Karate is a noncompetitive exercise that can be aerobic and that is designed to promote self-confidence and body awareness. A requirement: a coach who likes and understands children.
• Hula hoops, jump ropes, and hopscotch may have been passed over for more modern games, but they're still very appealing, cheap, and great exercise. A book of jump rope rhymes helps do the trick.
• Performances, with family audiences, can generate a lot of exercise, not just practicing the feats but setting up the event.
• Pretending you are show horses jumping over jumps can give a good workout to pony-struck Sevens and Eights.

Fascinatingly, the more Kids assume the responsibility of deciding what is just and right, the more closely they stick to the rules that reflect the spirit of the law and the more strongly they feel about doing so. Power has given them a sense of ownership, responsibility, and loyalty.

Unsupervised play raises two other concerns, however: morals and safety.

TOY GUNS

What about gun and weapon play? There are studies that show that when Kids play with store-bought weapons, their play is more aggressive and violent than when they have to create their own. Certainly, Kids grew up playing with make-do weapons for eons before the toy companies took over.

On the other hand, play with guns and weapons is very difficult to forbid. It may mean effectively removing your Kid from neighborhood play—not just the gun play, but the play that naturally evolves after the guns get boring. Also, a Kid who is not as fast or as agile as his peers in other games may be far more equal in games where weapons and pretending substitute for speed and coordination.

Kids of seven and eight are much more sophisticated in their weapon play than those six and younger, and parents may be shocked and upset at some of the scenarios acted out. However, it may be that they are actually performing important work in this play. If making up your own rules for games is an important step toward mature morality, maybe Kids need to work through issues that have to do with violence, heroism, and death. If there are studies on this aspect of gun and weapon play, I have not been able to find them.

If parents decide to permit gun play, they can still make some rules to keep the play within bounds of safety.

• No real-looking guns. Not only do they move the game too far from pretend, they can be dan-

gerous if an armed adult believes them to be real.

• No body contact with weapons. Guns can "shoot" from afar; they can't be used as clubs. Sword-fighting and spear-throwing are not allowed.

• The game stops when it's over. No carrying over the "war" sides into real life, where they can be mistaken by the participants for gang behavior.

Safety can be just as tricky, but here parents have a very clear-cut obligation. Kids who are engaged in risky activities need to wear their protective gear or they don't play. The place where they play must be reasonably safe: Parents may need to campaign, find transportation, and sacrifice some time, energy, and money to make sure that it is.

For specific activities, see **Appendix B**, page 263.

ORGANIZED SPORTS

Organized sports for Kids this age can be great if the adults running them keep clear about whose ego is on the line. This includes parents of the participants as well as the coaches. A Kid who is made to feel as if he or she wears a badge that says "Lost the Game by Fumbling" suffers in his or her soul. A Kid who is labeled, "Star Soccer Player and Savior of the Blue Blazes" may feel that there is nothing left in life to accomplish; the pinnacle has been reached. What makes the difference is how maturely the coaching and onlooking adults behave.

Coaching for Kids this age needs to be positive, with the good stuff pointed out generously and with enthusiasm. "You almost got it! Good running! Keep the ball in front as you run to get it; that way you can see its trajectory" instead of "I don't care how fast you are, you never catch the ball. Keep your eye on it, dummy!"

One of the troubling questions for good coaches is what to do about crucial games. You want the team to do well, but you want to let everybody play. This dilemma becomes easier to handle when Kids are older and more likely to have their own opinions about who should play in special games. At this age, tournaments that build up a great deal of tension over winning a title can cause a great deal of distress. On the whole, it's better to let the gifted players take over the field for the critical times and at the same time to try to counteract some of the hysteria which can boil around a play-off game.

MY MOM, THE COACH

Kids whose parents coach their team can have double the pleasure or double the performance anxiety. Happily, children this age are not terminally embarrassed by the mere proximity of a parent. A Kid certainly gains status with teammates when Mom or Dad is a great coach: one who is positive, cheerful, and competent. It really is a good idea to prepare a bit before taking on a coaching position: Kids have radar that detects uncertainty and fakery. When your mom or dad coaches your team, you still need to feel that he or she is paying special attention to you: a wink, a high-five, a hug after a special play or a bad fall. "Ralph is such a great coach. He really sparks them up, win or lose. The Kids adore him and Jeffrey's so proud."

A parent coach who gets too ego-involved, swearing at bad plays, stomping around and spitting, yelling, speaking brusquely, taking everything much too seriously, embarrasses and confuses a Kid. Ask such a Kid, "Isn't it great to have your Mom (or Dad) as your coach?" and he or she'll glance darkly at the parent and then shrug. Bad moment.

Onlookers, too, need to behave. Nobody, and I mean nobody, this age should get booed or hissed or yelled at insultingly. Everybody should get at least an affectionate yell and cheering should be rife. Criticizing the coach for allowing a less-than-proficient player in the game should disqualify a parent from the stands.

Safety is an issue for organized sports, just as it is for unsupervised activities (see Appendix B for information about individual sports).

Growth and Nutrition

GROWTH

These are the prepubertal years. Wow. I know. Most parents think that ages nine to twelve are the prepubertal years. *Au contraire.* Puberty is a process—the start of hormonal changes, with breast buds and pubic hair for girls and growth of the penis and changes in the scrotum for boys, and hormonal tides for both.

Puberty begins in girls at the average age of ten: by twelve, 95 percent of girls will show some signs of puberty. The average age to start menstruating is twelve-and-a-half. Boys tend to start puberty later—at about eleven or twelve—but some will start as early as nine. See the section on growth under **Nutrition and Growth** in Chapter 3 for a full discussion of pubertal changes in both sexes.

During these prepubertal years, some kids will start to look a little chunky. Is this a normal laying down of fat stores before the pubertal growth spurt or is it something that should be addressed? Less commonly, a Kid this age will look truly abnormally skinny. Does this mean something is wrong?

Chubby

A good way to find out if a child is overweight is to "put your child on the growth chart." But be careful to use the correct chart. You don't want to use the weight-for-age chart. This is the one that is often used during office visits, but can be very misleading.

For instance, suppose your 8-year-old girl, let's call her Mollie, is average height, 50", and weighs 70 pounds (see growth charts in Appendix A). If you plot this weight on the weight-for-age chart, you would find that Mollie weighs more than 90 percent of girls her age. Many pediatricians and experts would find this to be an appropriate weight, as it is only two big percentile lines higher than the 50% height curve.

However, if you use the weight-for-height chart, you will see that this weight is "off the chart." The weight for the *average* little girl of 50" who has not yet started puberty is 53 pounds. Mollie weighs 17 pounds more than the average girl her height: that's about 30 percent more. Mollie's weight is in the obese range.

If Mollie has not yet started puberty, increasing her daily exercise a lot and revamping the family's diet can help slow her weight gain. If Mollie can cut her weight gain to only 2½ pounds a year for the next year, by age 10 she'll weigh 75 pounds and be 54½" tall—just under the seventy-fifth percentile of weight for height, a much healthier place to be.

What about just letting Mollie slim down on her own, during the growth spurt of puberty? The problem is that the hormones of female puberty are designed to add more fat. (The average little girl going into puberty has 8 percent of her body weight as fat and by the end of puberty has 25 percent of her body weight as fat.) It is very unusual for a girl to slim down during puberty!

Skinny

If your child strikes you as very skinny—not just knees and vertebrae stick out, but also shoulder bones, elbows, and ankles, check it out on the weight-for-height chart.

Let's say that your 7-year-old, Scott, is 48" tall, average for his age, and weighs 40 pounds. If you plot these numbers on the weight-for-age chart, Scott's weight will be in the fifth percentile, a value most pediatricians accept without worry. But if you put Scott on the weight-for-height chart, you will see that he is way, way below—six little boxes below—the fifth percentile. This may be normal for Scott, but a visit to the pediatrician must determine that.

If your Kid is *above* the fifth percentile of weight for height, has been this skinny all along, and is maintaining his same old curve

for height growth, there's nothing to be concerned about. But if this is a change in body shape, or if your child is not in vibrant health or is not active and happy, a prompt visit to the pediatrician is very important.

PUBERTY ITSELF

(See also the discussion of sex in **Growth of the Soul,** beginning on page 102.)

Girls

Girls normally don't start puberty, with the first breast bud or pubic hair, before the age of eight. When a child younger than eight shows any sign of puberty, it's important to have it checked out promptly by your pediatrician. Most often, the start of puberty so early is "idiopathic," which means that the hormones in the part of the brain called the hypothalamus simply turn on unusually early.

However, it's important to rule out other causes, which range from problems with the adrenal or thyroid gland to growths in the brain. Your pediatrician will probably wish to order blood tests, x-rays of the hands to see what the "bone age" is (how mature the bones are compared to the child's chronological age), and even a scan—CT or MRI—of the brain. Many times a pediatric endocrinologist (a pediatrician with a specialty in studying hormones) is asked to consult.

If there is a medical reason for the early puberty, of course that must be addressed. If the cause is "idiopathic," many pediatricians and endocrinologists will discuss with parents and child the use of medication called Lupron to slow down and delay puberty. Early puberty can be very strenuous emotionally and also produces a decrease in final height. About a third of girls with precocious puberty wind up under 5 feet tall. Each family makes its own decision, of course, taking a number of considerations into account—not the least of which is the cost of treatment. It's expensive.

If puberty proceeds, it's very important that

the child be given special support and under-standing, and many, many opportunities to feel strong and successful.

When puberty starts at the age of eight in girls, it is considered not precocious, just early. However, puberty this early usually still is very difficult to handle socially and emotionally, and children and parents often need counseling and moral support. Some pediatricians will discuss the use of medication to slow puberty even in this normal situation. Most girls who start puberty this young will also start menstrual periods early—usually by age eleven—and also will stop growing sooner than they would have if puberty had occurred later.

Boys

Puberty in boys normally doesn't occur before the age of nine. If signs do appear, that indicates precocious puberty. This is much less common in boys than in girls, and always requires a similar prompt visit to the pediatrician to make sure that the cause is not a medical one that requires treatment. Such causes are more common in boys with precocious puberty than with girls.

How can you tell if a boy has started puberty? It's a lot trickier than with girls, because the early signs of puberty in boys are pretty subtle and very private: growth of the testicles and thinning of the skin of the scrotum. Acne may be the only "public" expression that parents notice. The growth spurt in boys usually occurs a year or so after puberty has begun, so it's not going to leap out at you.

Even if the cause of precocious puberty in a boy turns out to be not medical but "idiopathic," your pediatrician or the pediatric endocrinologist will want to discuss the use of medication to slow the pubertal development, especially in view of the decrease in adult height that occurs with such early puberty.

NUTRITION

Most Sevens and Eights still eat a good breakfast, a fair lunch, and not much dinner.

Many don't even eat a fair lunch; instead, they eat a couple of snacks. They're often erratic and finicky about foods. That's all normal.

A few Kids are voracious eaters. Some eat all day long and stay skinny; they generally have metabolisms that burn extra calories as waste. They also may be intrinsically active, bouncy, jittery children who burn a large number of calories just by existing. Some are very active in their daily lives and need calories for energy. And some are very tall and need them for growth.

Some, however, eat large helpings, love food, and tend to gain too much weight. A child this age with this pattern does need help, but that help should be primarily in the form of finding opportunities for sweaty, aerobic exercise (see discussion of chubbiness earlier in this section under **Growth**). Helping with nutrition means teaching about healthy choices, providing healthy food at home, and not nagging or bullying or harassing a child about eating—that will backfire. Exercise is the key.

All Kids this age can learn about making healthy food choices. Is it important to do so? Some experts think not. They feel, correctly, that it is unusual for middle-class children to become malnourished in America because so many foods are enriched with vitamins and because food is so plentiful and varied. They also feel that children demonstrate their autonomy by choosing freely among a wide variety of foods.

Well, yes. But to exercise real autonomy, Kids need information. They need to know that some foods are in fact healthier than others. They need to spot when advertisers are trying to lure them by implying that food is healthy when it is not—just as they need to know when advertisers try to lure them into thinking that beer and cigarettes are cool and safe and grown-up.

In fact, this is a great time for teaching about nutrition. Here are some suggestions.

KEEP THE ACCENT POSITIVE

Sevens and Eights are so aware of their bodies, they tend to be a bit hypochondriacal: they can take warnings too seriously. They don't understand terms like "probably" or "might" or "is likely to." It's better to avoid any such terms. Instead of saying, "Eating too much fat might cause heart problems or cancer later on" say "We want to keep our fat at a reasonable level because studies show that's healthier for our entire bodies."

TALK ABOUT THE GOOD THINGS FOODS CONTAIN, NOT THE BAD THINGS TO AVOID

"This orange juice contains lots of vitamin C to fight infection."

"This cereal has lots of fiber to make your intestine work the right way."

"These vegetables are high in iron."

Well, that's easy. Then try:

"This hot dog has hardly any vitamins or iron. It doesn't have anything that helps your body grow except protein and fat. But you get plenty of protein and fat from other foods. Hot dogs are special treats, not everyday food."
"Those french fries don't have any vitamins or iron or fiber or protein. I guess they're only for special treats, too."

WHAT YOU SERVE AT HOME IS MORE PERSUASIVE THAN ANY TALKING YOU DO

Sevens and Eights are old enough to help plan menus and shop. They can grasp the idea of a food budget. They can even learn to cook, with supervision. Sam's parents enlist each of their Kids, ages eight and ten, in planning and cooking one meal a month. They give the youngster $10.00 with which to make a meal for four people. Sam's brother Aaron routinely serves a rock-bottom meal: say, canned beans, home-made applesauce, iceberg lettuce and tomato salad, and milk; he pockets at least four bucks each time. Sam spends the whole amount. One day he carried home an entire half-watermelon all the way from the corner store: his stomach was so cold and red we had to apply a little cortisone cream.

Even if everybody in the family is thin and healthy, it's a good idea to try to stick to the American Heart Association's recommendation for total fat content—30 percent, no more, of the daily calories. When you can, it's a good idea to buy food that "remembers where it came from:" fresh fruit, vegetables, meat, fish. Rich desserts on a regular basis aren't necessary for anybody, child or adult, nor are high-fat sauces or fried foods.

POINT OUT ADVERTISING, BOTH HONEST AND MISLEADING, WHEN YOU'RE WITH SEVEN OR EIGHT

So often, ads flow right over kids, leaving a wash of impression as if it were Easter egg dye. Commenting on ads brings them right into the foreground and lets Kids see grown-ups trying to get away with something.

"That fruit juice ad says that it's wholesome and pure. Doesn't that make you think it's got lots of vitamins and minerals in it? And hardly any sugar?"

"Look at that big, dripping sandwich those teenagers are eating! They're having so much fun and they look so strong and thin and cute. Do you think that they got that way from eating those sandwiches a lot?"

"Look at the story the ad shows of how that little skinny boy grew up to be so full of muscles, just from drinking lots of milk. What do you think about that? Do you think they're hoping that kids your age will drink lots of milk?"

Or:

"That milk ad shows a dancer who doesn't want the fat in whole milk, but she still likes the calcium in the nonfat milk. Does that ad make you want to drink nonfat milk?"

"My, those strawberries look great! And the ad says they've even got vitamin C in them."

"I guess the egg farmers want us to know that eggs don't have as much cholesterol as we thought they did."

Health and Illness

HEALTH

A yearly checkup by the pediatrician when your Kid is eight and nine is a good investment for the future. It's not likely that the pediatrician will find anything wrong, but that yearly checkup serves to cement the relationship between doctor and child. In a year or two or three, the youngster may well be starting puberty or at least thinking of himself or herself as a potentially sexual being. At that point, disrobing for an examination will seem like a whole different ball game. Best to keep a yearly reminder that this is an expected, normal, important, nonsexual, nonthreatening, and completely friendly ritual.

At the moment, no immunizations are scheduled for this age. This could change at any time, though.

ILLNESS

Seven and eight are usually pretty healthy years medically, but you wouldn't know it by the number of complaints Kids can have at this age: stomachaches, headaches, "growing pains" in the legs, and weird symptoms: "There's a bump on my foot." (Yes, there is; it's a bone. There's a normal bump on the other foot, too.) "Sometimes my arm hurts when I have to push a revolving door." "My teeth itch." "My neck clicks."

One of the big questions facing a loving adult who hears these weird complaints is, Should we make an appointment with the pediatrician? Is

GROWING AND EATING

- The average boy or girl age seven is 48" tall, but the range is from 44" to 51".
- The average boy or girl age eight is 50" tall, but the range is from 46" to 53".
- Kids this age normally look lean and strong. Their ribs don't stick out, but their knees and elbows tend to do so. When they sit down, their bellies do not bulge over and rest on their thighs.
- Many still eat a good breakfast, a fair lunch, and hardly any dinner. Many take as much as 30 percent of their daily calories as snacks.
- Ideally, children this age should be taking 30 percent of their daily calories as fat. This usually means nonfat or 1-percent milk and cheese, avoiding frequent meals containing fatty foods, and watching snacks: cold cuts and cheese are often high in fat.
- If a child is of normal or slender weight, there need be no other restriction on calories. However, a chubby child needs help. Mostly, this help consists of increased exercise; but parents also need to provide food at home that doesn't tempt chubby kids to eat or drink high-calorie items.

this just one of Seven's odd items or Eight's hypochondriacal mysteries, or is it the very first symptom of some horrible thing?

Here are some suggestions for how to go about determining if you should call for an appointment. But first, let me say that no pediatrician is going to be exasperated at you or laugh or think you are an inadequate parent because you make an appointment for something of this nature. I remember as a sobering example the Eight who complained of an itchy right nostril and who turned out to be harboring an entire 3" eucalyptus leaf in there. Of course, how it got there Eight couldn't quite recall.

ARE THERE ANY OBJECTIVE SIGNS OR JUST A SUBJECTIVE COMPLAINT?

If Seven/Eight complains that his tongue is too big but has no trouble eating, talking, licking an ice cream cone and has no signs such as fatigue, irritability, fever, and is behaving normally in all other ways, it is unlikely that he has a thyroid problem (a cause for tongue enlargement), glossitis (infection of the tongue), a tumor of the tongue (so exceedingly rare, I can't tell you), or any other true tongue problem.

IF THERE ARE OBJECTIVE SIGNS, DO THEY SEEM TO HAVE ANYTHING AT ALL TO DO WITH THE COMPLAINT?

A Seven/Eight with a cough and a funny pain in his foot when he wears sandals but not shoes is unlikely to be harboring some awful syndrome. But if Seven/Eight with the odd foot pain has fever or limps or awakens at night complaining of foot pain; or if you look at the foot and see redness, swelling, or a streak; or if you press on the spot and the child shrieks and cries, take it seriously.

DOES SEVEN/EIGHT COMPLAIN SPONTANEOUSLY DAY AFTER DAY FOR MORE THAN A WEEK?

If you keep asking Seven/Eight if her teeth still itch, she is likely to answer yes. If you have ever had itchy teeth due to nerves, you will be aware that they tend to itch whenever you remember to notice it. This is quite different from Seven/Eight coming up to you with a worried face, unable to play, because her teeth itch.

A yes to any of these questions means that the pediatrician will regard your appointment as very appropriate.

Unlike Fives and Sixes, Sevens and Eights are much more receptive to explanations about how bodies work. They like to know facts: how many bones are in the human body, what different organs do, and so on. They also like to know how to stay healthy and what the medicine does. It is quite amazing how sophisticated Seven and Eight can be. Kids seven and older can understand, for instance, what asthma is and why the medicine helps and can participate in their own treatments. Kids seven and older with diabetes can give themselves their own injections of insulin.

Missing school because of illness is more serious at this age. A Seven/Eight who is out of school for a week may be able to catch up on the reading material, but it's a very good idea to check closely on the math. "She had strep the two days they started talking about measuring volumes and she never caught up." If Seven/Eight has illnesses so frequently that school absence is a problem, this is not typical: a pediatric consultation—an appointment to discuss this specific concern—is a good idea. Trying to sort out what's happening at the time of an appointment for an acute illness usually doesn't work; things are too rushed and the child is physically uncomfortable. It's best to make a separate appointment.

When Sevens and Eights do stay home sick, it's easy for recuperation to be prolonged. It's as if once Seven/Eight gets a taste of home, the whole work of returning to the challenge of school seems exhausting. If this seems to be a problem, the fastest way to help is to invite over a classmate to play as soon as it's safe, from the point of view of exhaustion and contagiousness. Of course, this should be only one classmate (three Kids this age tend to compete and fight) and a compatible one at that.

Seven and Eight can seem so competent that it's easy to be tempted to leave them home by themselves during a mild illness. This is a dangerous temptation. Sevens and Eights still have very little experience of the world. "I'm home by myself," they tell strangers cheerfully over the phone. "But it's okay: I know my mom's phone number at work." "The parakeet started vomiting so she called 911. And they found her at home alone and called Child Protective Services." "He found his father's stash of old copies of *Penthouse.*"

Most Sevens and Eights can learn to take their own medicine, whether it be liquid, chewables, pills to swallow, nose spray, eyedrops, or inhaled medications. Whether this is the best way to ensure the medicine gets taken depends on the child. Some very independent Kids do very well with a chart, and a sticker or gold star to be placed for each dose (monitored by a parent). Others regard being sick as a special state requiring cosseting and need adult help every time.

• Most liquid medicines can be given with food. If Seven/Eight doesn't like the taste of the medication, try matching it with a stronger but similar tasting food: often your pediatrician or the pharmacist will have a suggestion. Bland, oily medications that feel rather than taste yucky can often be given in chocolate or maple syrup. Another good ploy is to have Seven/Eight suck on an ice cube, which numbs the taste buds, before taking the medication straight; and then to give a strong-flavored drink or food to get rid of the aftertaste.

• If Seven/Eight is taking chewable tablets, make sure that they don't all get ground into the molars and then become stuck on and discarded with a subsequent piece of chewing gum.

• To teach a Seven/Eight to swallow pills, practice with a bag of M&M's or other pill-shaped candy. This overcomes the fear of not swallowing right away and tasting something awful. Have the child place the "pill" in the middle of the tongue and take a swallow of water. If many tries fail and the M&M disintegrates, use a new one. Five tries should be sufficient. After the M&M is swallowed, make sure Seven/Eight gets in the habit of drinking the rest of the glass of water to wash it down thoroughly. A real pill stuck in the esophagus can cause major problems.

• Nasal sprays can sting the nostrils: try coating the inside of the nose with a little petroleum jelly first. They also can smell bad. Try having a half lemon on hand: the child takes a sniff before and after the nose spray.

• Inhalant sprays for asthma are very useful at this age. The only problem is that Seven and Eight may not coordinate the deep inhale with the squirt of the inhaler, with the result that they swallow, rather than breathe in, the medication. This can be reduced or prevented by using a spacer that keeps the liquid from pooling. It's particularly important to use a spacer (available by prescription) when a youngster is taking medication with cortisone in it: orally taken, cortisone gets absorbed into the blood stream and over a long time can cause side effects, such as diminished growth, eye problems, and weakened immunity.

• Eyedrops: Seven and Eight can cooperate if they're sure the drops won't sting. The way to reassure them is to let them wash their hands, put a drop of the medication on a finger, and have them touch it to the eye. When you go to put in the drops, have them stand with their mouths open, focusing on something high up. This relaxes the eyelids (it is, after all, the usual eye-makeup-applying stance). Pull the lower lid down and drop the drops into the flipped-out lower lid.

HYGIENE

"I've been giving Kids baths for 15 mother-years." Anne Marie has seven-and-a-half-year-old twins. "Don't I get to stop pretty soon?"

No. You don't.

You'd think that Kids who are as self-preoccupied as Sevens and Eights would pay attention to hygiene, but they don't. (See the discussion of self-care in **Responsibility, Discipline, and Life at Home,** earlier in this chapter.) They generally require close parental supervision in a number of areas. When you correct Seven/Eight in public, it must be very tactful indeed. For instance, if Seven/Eight tends to sneeze in people's faces, remind him or her before going out. Then be alertly there with a Kleenex and when you see that sneeze coming, thrust the tissue into the child's hand and say "Gesundheit!" loudly.

Why are Sevens and Eights such confirmed nose-pickers?

Easy. It's a tension reliever, of course, but it's also another exploration of that philosophical question: Who is me? When I pick my nose, am I the agent committing the action or the object of the action? Hmmmm.

At any rate, they pick their noses and then consume the findings. The whole procedure is disgusting, but it's the picking part that can cause medical problems. First, it's an invitation to recurrent nosebleeds. Second, it's one of the most surefire ways to catch viruses, such as cold viruses. Third, it's also a good way to catch pinworms: The microscopic eggs get on fingers when Kids touch other children who are infested or touch contaminated objects; the eggs then get into the nose; then they go down the back of the throat and get swallowed. It is nose-picking that causes pinworms, not the other way around. Fourth, it's a good way to give oneself strep infections of the skin, such as impetigo or vaginal or anal strep: you pick your nose and get the germs on your fingers and then you—er—scratch or whatever.

To discourage nose-picking, minimize the gratification. Have the child coat the inside of the nostrils with a little petroleum jelly so that they don't get dry and itch, and so that the searching fingernail finds little reward. If recurrent strep is a problem, your pediatrician may recommend a prescription medicated ointment that both coats the nostrils and inhibits bacteria. Manicure the fingernails short so that it's harder to scrape around in there.

When you see Seven/Eight on a nose-mining expedition, present tissues and if you're in private firmly say,

> "Picking your nose can give you infections. If you need to blow, blow. If you're just bored, let's find something else to do."

You may need to do this only 500 or 600 times before it begins to have effect. If you're in public, present tissues and give the child that look.

Why can't they cover their mouths when they cough or sneeze?

Even Kids who used to do so when younger stop now. I think it is because they have so much to think about in terms of their effects on other people: paying back favors, keeping track of who did what to whom, watching what the group is doing so they can keep up. They're so preoccupied that they don't even realize that they're coughing in someone's face: a cough comes unpremeditated, so they can't think about it. My strategy is to stand at a safe distance from or in back of a Seven/Eight with a cold. Parents, however, need to try to alert Sevens and Eights to their behavior:

> "Lucy can catch your cold if you sneeze on her. She wouldn't like that."

Toileting

Female Sevens and Eights need to be reminded to wipe correctly, from front to back, so as not to bring rectal germs forward to the vagina and urethra where they can start surface and bladder infections. Some Sevens and even Eights of both sexes request that a parent finish the wiping for them after a poop.

Preventing catching what your friend has

• This is a big age for catching lice. Kids should be reminded every now and then not to trade hats or hair decorations or share brushes and combs. I wouldn't make a fetish of it, though, unless your Seven/Eight has long or easily tangled or very thick hair that makes de-licing a terrible chore and predisposes him or her to recurrent lice.

• Make a rule that pierced earrings do not get traded. No case of blood-borne disease trans-mission has been reported by this route, but why take chances on catching hepatitis B or C or even HIV from such a casual incident.

For a discussion of masturbation and sex education, see the section in Chapter 1. For a discussion of sex play at this age, see the sec-tion earlier in this chapter.

INJURIES

Sevens and Eights get injured away from home more often than younger children do. When they sustain an injury, they often panic and think that it is worse than it really is: their bodies at this age seem to them mysterious and therefore fragile. At the same time, they are very aware of how upset parents can get about injuries and may try to protect them. I am put in mind of my nephew Phil, who at this age got hit by a swing—the latest in a series of traumatic events—and called his mother from the nurse's office. "Hello Mom?" he said in his most reassuring voice. "Remem-ber my head?"

Some things may help and certainly won't hurt.

• Prevent injuries not by curtailing activities but by providing proper equipment and rea-sonable safety guidelines (see Appendix B for specific sports).

• If your child has an underlying medical con-dition, an allergy to medication or to food, takes medication regularly, or has other special requirements (including any religious dictates on medical matters, such as receiving blood) make sure he or she wears a MedicAlert bracelet or dogtag.

• Consider having your child wear an ID bracelet or necklace that carries relevant phone numbers, not just an address.

• Know your insurance plan. When the neigh-bor, coach, school nurse, or pediatric office calls, know:

Which emergency room, lab, and x-ray lab accepts your plan;

Whether you must stay in the plan or be responsible for the whole bill or whether you can go out of the plan and pay only a penalty

What your deductible is for emer-gency care. Sometimes a plan that does not have a deductible for office visits does have one for emergency care. If so, you may want to try hard to have a problem that doesn't affect life or limb treated in the doctor's office, even if it means a delay and a trip there.

• Teach Seven/Eight some basic first aid: apply direct pressure to anything that bleeds; try to get an ice pack or something cold on a soft tissue injury; flush a burn or a foreign body in the eye with lots of plain water. This will help him or her feel in control and may keep a complication from occurring. There may be a course for Kids available, or your Scout troop or other organization may come up with one if you nudge a little.

• Make sure Seven/Eight knows all relevant phone numbers: parents' work numbers, who to call if they cannot be reached, the pediatri-cian's phone number, and of course 911.

• Keep a note on file in your child's chart that your pediatrician or group has permission to treat the child for nonlife-threatening problems in your absence and without your previous consent. If you wish them to be able to perform x-rays, lab tests, and injections, add that to the note.

Behavior Problems

Every Kid will behave at times in ways that upset parents. This section looks at problem behaviors that are upsetting beyond what is ordinary. Either they are minor but annoying, like thumbsucking and bedwetting, or they are scary or angrymaking, like aggression. I have not included in this section hard and fast guidelines about when to seek professional help because there aren't any such guidelines. It is true that there are formal guidelines that list the behaviors that constitute a psychiatric diagnosis, such as "conduct disorder" or "oppositional disorder." However, these guidelines are used only to assist mental health professionals in recordkeeping and billing. To use such lists as a guide for "when to really worry" is inappropriate. Pediatricians are usually able to help parents to decide at what point they need professional assistance for a troubled Kid.

One kind of behavior that worries parents is not included in this section. That is behavior that suggests a Kid is unhappy with his or her sexual identity. Such feelings on the part of a Kid do not, in my opinion, constitute a behavior problem, but rather a condition of the spirit that we as a society don't understand or handle very well. It is more like a difficult situation than a behavior problem. So I've placed discussion of this conundrum in the **What If?** section of this chapter.

CONDUCT PROBLEMS

AGGRESSION

Younger children feel freer to act out their angry wishes to hurt. They are still learning how to see another person's point of view; they don't have the experience to realize that their acts will have consequences in how others treat them.

Sevens and Eights are engaged in all these enterprises. Unless they are chronically, deeply angry, they should be less aggressive at seven than they were at six; less aggressive at eight than they were at seven.

There should be much less in the way of hitting, punching, kicking, and such physical aggression should never be addressed to parents (although it could be turned on parents if they themselves are abusive). Angry or hurtful outbursts should be on the decline, as Seven and Eight learn other strategies for protest and persuasion. Destructive outbursts should be exceedingly rare. Sevens and Eights feel embarrassed afterward in a way that younger children don't, which serves as a deterrent.

Lying can be a form of aggression. Lying is aggressive when it bespeaks an angry attitude that doesn't take another person's feeling into account and that says, "I don't care if you trust me or not." Sevens and Eights should be lying less than they did at ages five and six, and the lies should rarely be ones that deny responsibility or that place blame on someone else. Lies that exaggerate Seven and Eight's own prowess in any regard still are lies, and if these are frequent, they count as a kind of masked aggression and anger. Sevens and Eights who lie aggressively to get others into trouble or to hurt people's feelings need help with their anger.

Stealing, too, can be aggressive. Every time Seven/Eight steals, he or she needs to balance his or her desire (for the object, for what it will get in terms of other people's praise or jealousy) against the distress of the owner. An aggressive Seven/Eight steals in part to cause such distress. Stealing at this age should be infrequent, highly motivated by desire, and accompanied by a guilty conscience. In any event, episodes of stealing should be decreasing in frequency.

It's important to address aggressive behavior now. Aggression reflects anger, even bitterness, and when it is on the increase at this age it tends to become a vicious, ever increasing cycle right into the teenage and adult years. Sooner or later, unchecked aggression spreads from the homefront to other areas of life, where the penalties—at school, in sports, with friends—tend to be greater. Kids who do not grow out of aggression in their prepubertal years are at high risk for antisocial, even criminal behavior as adults.

TEMPER TANTRUMS

These should be a minor problem. By minor, I mean that they are:
• Infrequent. You're surprised that a day contains one, rather than surprised when a day does not.
• Private. Rather than have a tantrum in public, Seven/Eight usually buttons the lip, glares, covertly kicks or punches something that doesn't break or hurt or make a noise. At home, Seven/Eight will storm into his or her room and slam the door, rather than throw a tantrum in the nonprivate areas.
• Engaged in without expectation that the tantrum will get the Kid what he or she wants. Seven and older should know that this strategy never ever works.

If tantrums don't fit this description, help is needed. Either there is something seriously amiss in the Kid's life that is causing enormous unhappiness and frustration or the tantrums are somehow being rewarded by other people's reactions.

OBEDIENCE

In general, Sevens and Eights should be complying more and more with parents' requests and demands rather than less. Of course, this depends on parenting skills. If a Kid is constantly being hounded, if he or she isn't rewarded by praise and attention for complying, if no reasons are given for requests and demands, just orders: well, I'd be surprised if such a Kid were much fun to live with. When parenting skills are appropriate, Kids should be complying with at least 70 percent of requests and all real demands, and the request score ought to be creeping up all the time.

BEHAVIOR AND MOOD

TICS AND TOURETTE SYNDROME

Many Sevens and Eights have a nervous twitch now and then—a habit like eye-blinking, lip-licking, or hair-twiddling that may last for several weeks. In this day and age, a parent's first thought often is Tourette Syndrome and the first feeling is dread. It's true that six through nine is the age at which this syndrome is often diagnosed in those who have it. However, the feeling of dread should certainly be modified.

Here are some things to know about tics and Tourette Syndrome (T.S.).
• The cause of Tourette Syndrome is still pretty mysterious. It certainly seems to be inherited, but that inheritance is very complicated, and environmental factors play a role. Boys with T.S. outnumber girls with T.S. by four to one.
• Symptoms can be mild or severe, and always wax and wane.
• Ordinary tics are very common in Sevens and Eights. Tourette Syndrome is uncommon—estimated to occur in fewer than one in one thousand people.
• When a person does have Tourette Syndrome, the tics often improve with age. In one study, they disappeared by young adulthood in 26 percent of patients and diminished considerably in another 46 percent.
• There is effective treatment not just for the tics associated with Tourette, but also for many of the associated problems such as obsessive/compulsive behaviors, attentional problems, and learning disorders.

Here is what it takes to diagnose Tourette Syndrome.
• Multiple bodily tics, such as eye-blinking and head-jerking; touching things, people, or one's own body parts compulsively; jumping uncontrollably or making faces; involuntarily grimacing.
• One or more voice tics: grunting, barking, throat clearing, or saying things uncontrollably—

syllables, words, phrases; repeating words just said; swearing or uttering obscenities.

• These tics wax and wane, but are present more or less for longer than a year.

Of course, to qualify as T.S., these tics must not be due to another medical condition (certain neurological problems or the rare side effect of rheumatic fever called Syndenham's Chorea).

If your child has persistent or increasing tics that may be symptomatic of Tourette Syndrome, see your pediatrician. Don't wait for a year to pass! There are other causes for tics besides Tourette and in any event both child and parents need information and counseling in how to manage the tics, whatever their cause. For more information:

Tourette Syndrome Association
42-40 Bell Boulevard
Bayside, NY 11361
(718) 224–2999

DEPRESSION

Deep sadness is sometimes the only human response to events: the death or loss of a beloved person or pet; an illness or injury that was lengthy or painful or that robbed Seven/Eight of the ability to control his or her world; family disintegration; disaster; or disharmony. (See the **What If?** section at the end of this chapter for a discussion of these major events in a child's life and how parents can deal with them.) This section concerns Kids who are sad without such disasters as the apparent cause or whose sadness is so overwhelming or prolonged that it interferes with normal growth or development.

"I hate myself. I wish I were dead." Yes, it's terrible to hear. But it's not unusual at seven and eight and it's usually not serious.

• Kenny mutters that he hates himself and wishes he were dead, stomps outside, and kicks the garage a few times. In the middle of the fifth kick, he pauses, jerks upright, dashes back in, commandeers the phone, and yells to his best friend, "How you do it is, you put the glue on a little stick! Don't do the blue thing yet!"

• Isabelle screeches that she'd rather be dead and shoots a bitter look at her sister and mother, who are used to it. This is a twice-a-week performance. Isabelle flings herself into her room, slams the door, and weeps rather noisily for twenty minutes. She comes out snuffling and morose. It takes dinner, watching the latest installment of "Full House," and a game of gin rummy with her dad—which she wins—but by bedtime she's humming a tune and demanding a bubble bath.

• For several days now, Brian has been coming home from school with a sad face. He slumps over and won't talk about what's bothering him. He brightens up a little at dinner and watches his favorite TV program afterward with a small, distant smile. He seems preoccupied and it's hard to get through to him when you need him to do something. "What's wrong?" his dad has asked five or six times. "Nothing," says Brian.

• Dorian quietly makes the statement that he'd rather be dead to his mother as she sets the table. He doesn't look or sound angry, just sad, depleted of energy. He is not interested in his Legos, his model train village, nor his new computer game. He isn't even interested in the dessert for dinner; in fact he hasn't been eating much for days. What he does do is sleep, sleep, and sleep.

Deciding whether Seven is in a temporary fit of gloom, whether Eight is suffering prepubertal mood swings, or whether a Kid this age is truly, worryingly depressed is not usually tricky.

For one thing, depression in a child—like depression in an adult—is catching. After spending time with Dorian, both children and adults feel a weight on their shoulders, a sense of hopelessness and despair. Kenny and Isabelle arouse quite other feelings, from sympathy to irritation to amusement. Brian arouses concern, but his sadness isn't really catching.

For another, a Kid who is depressed doesn't bounce out of it. The sad, depressed mood, the absence of interest and pleasure in the world, is there every day, for at least two weeks. Every now and again it lightens, but even then the child is still very low in energy and is clearly making an effort to climb out of some deep emotional pit.

Kids who are truly depressed may show physical signs—losing or gaining weight, or sleeping too much or too little. They may move draggingly, as if they were underwater; they may lose their usual fidgety habits—it's too much effort even to pick or scratch. "I'm just no good," they say angrily or bitterly or just announcing the fact. "Everything I do is wrong. Nobody likes me." They often have trouble concentrating or making even simple choices. "I found him staring at his sock drawer," Dorian's frightened mother tells me. "He couldn't decide which ones to put on. And they're all the same brand and color!"

Depression—this kind of depression; the kind that lasts for at least two weeks and is there like a black cloud every day—is and should be scary. It's not rare, either; somewhere between 2 percent and 13 percent of Sevens and Eights are diagnosed with serious depression. Suicide attempts are very, very rare but not unheard of in this age group. Even without such a catastrophic threat, the damage to the child and family is high. And the time the child loses in academic, physical, and social learning is a severe problem.

When a child is truly depressed, showing daily signs of the behavior just described, and when that depression lasts for longer than ten days, it's time to get help. Help, in this case, begins with the pediatrician, to exclude any medical causes and to obtain a referral for counseling. A counselor with a Master's degree, a licensed clinical social worker, a psychologist, or a psychiatrist could each perform the counseling. However, it's crucial that the therapist be trained, experienced, and eager to treat a child with depression.

More and more, children who are seriously depressed are prescribed medications—antidepressants—just as adults are. If this is recommended, careful discussion of pros and cons and side effects are necessary. If you and the therapist decide on medication, this does not mean stopping therapy! Very often, the family as a whole needs to be in counseling to figure out how to help Seven/Eight from sinking into depression again.

But what if you've got a Kenny, an Isabelle, a Brian? What do you do about a sad Kid, a disgruntled Kid, a Kid with the blues?

• Kids in a sad mood need to know that their parents realize they're unhappy and want to help. Ignoring the mood isn't usually helpful. Joining the Kid in the mood is even worse. Stay calm, reliable, quietly cheerful. If the Kid has only been in the mood for a couple of hours, it's appropriate to give the Kid a dignified offer of aid: "I can see you're feeling blue. If you'd like to talk, I'm here. Or if you'd like to just get out of the house, or play a game, or do something fun, we could do one of those things together."

• If the mood persists through to the next day or if it recurs within a day or two, make time alone with your Kid. Try to find out what's the matter. Most often, it will be a transient and, to an adult, a minor problem: the defection of a friend, a comment by an otherwise approving teacher, a failure at a test or game. The parent's role is to listen, to assist the Kid in coming to terms with the situation, and to provide a pleasant interval to take away the emotional taste.

• If the mood persists, try to find the cause. Possibilities: family disharmony, disarray, disintegration—or the worry, from something overheard, that a family disaster is afoot; learning problems at school; persistent trouble making or keeping friends; being excluded by a clique; being made to feel worthless on the playground or in sports and games; feeling as if a sibling is favored; the child feeling as if he or she is not in control of most of the important parts of his or her existence—as if things happen to her rather than that she controls her part of the universe.

• Try to fix the problem. This may mean getting marital therapy, talking with the teacher, finding a tutor or a coach, or helping Seven/Eight make friends. (See **Growth of the Soul,** earlier in this chapter.) Find ways for Seven/Eight to feel more in control of his or her world: able to make meaningful choices and to feel self-confident and up to taking on challenges.

Pediatricians are trained at helping families figure out blue moods and depression. Be sure, when you make the appointment, that you let the receptionist know you will need more time than usual. Moods are more complicated than viruses, usually.

Window of Opportunity

TRAVEL

If you are traveling out of the country, check with your pediatrician about the immunization for Hepatitis A and check travel advisories or with the Center for Disease Control (404–332–4555) about other travel precautions. Make sure you have any medications you need. Do not pack injectable insulin in checked-through baggage! It will freeze and lose its potency.

Sevens and Eights can be wonderful travel companions once you get beyond their suspicion of novelty. Here are some suggestions.

DON'T ASSUME THAT KIDS KNOW ANYTHING ABOUT WHERE YOU ARE GOING OR WHY IT SHOULD BE FUN

Surely, you say, everybody knows about the Eiffel Tower, the Golden Gate Bridge, Niagara Falls. Uh uh. Seven/Eight may have heard the name and formed his or her own opinion. "Where," asked Sara, after a tour of the British Museum, "are the marbles?"

SELECT HIGH POINTS AND PREPARE SEVEN/EIGHT TO EXPERIENCE THEM ACTIVELY

"We're going to climb all the way up the Eiffel Tower."

"We're counting on you to get a great picture of the Golden Gate bridge silhouetted against the sunset."

"We'll take a boat that goes right under the gigantic gorgeous thundering waterfall! And wear raincoats and get wet!"

PREPARE SEVEN/EIGHT FOR DIFFERENT CUSTOMS, AGAIN SELECTIVELY

If Sevens and Eights suddenly encounter a feature that violates all their previous experience, they tend to become angry; they take it personally, as if the whole other culture had ganged up against them.

"Pee! In a hole! In the Floor! That's mean!"

"Why is that lady wearing a black thing over her nose! She's trying to scare me!"

"I can't eat anything with those. They are trying to starve me. I want to go home!"

TACKLE MUSEUMS, MONUMENTS, AND SIGHTS WITH TACT

If you are planning to visit a museum that contains just a few things you are determined to see, prepare Seven/Eight ahead of time. Sometimes this means showing pictures of what you'll be viewing, plus telling Seven/Eight why looking at it in person is better than looking at the picture in terms he or she can understand.

> "Here is a picture of the painting called the Mona Lisa. They say that she watches you no matter where you stand to look at the painting. And nobody knows what she's smiling at. I bet if we see it, we'll figure out some guesses."

If you are just browsing through a museum, have a few techniques up your sleeve.

> "I'm going to go into this room and turn slowly until something catches my eye. Then I'm going to see if that something tells me a story."

> "I'm going to look at this picture and memorize everything that's in it. Then I'm going to close my eyes and see how many things I can remember. I'll bet I can remember more than you can."

If you're visiting an historical site, have a few stories for Seven/Eight that are about individual people—men *and* women; ideally, about a child, too—that aren't just about who won and who killed whom. Even if it's not historically accurate, tell historical stories with women as the character if your child is a girl. (After all, can you be positive that only men jousted and so on?) If there's an architectural feature involving war, that's often a good bet:

> "Those spiral stairs go in this direction because the owner had to defend the castle with her sword. Most women are right-handed. So if the stairs curve this way, the person coming down the stairs had an advantage. Here, you pretend you're attacking me, and we'll see what happens."

RETREAT WHEN NECESSARY

As with Kids six and younger, if you are in a very "foreign" place and your Kid seems about to detonate from tension, anxiety, and homesickness, regress. Spend a half-day playing a dumb old card game or eating comfort food, if you can find it, or playing catch in the park.

LEARN COMPUTER SKILLS

Sevens and Eights generally regard computers as toys and count work with them as play. This is the best attitude for learning, and taking advantage of it now reaps dividends later. To use a computer in a sophisticated adult way, you need to have good fine-motor skills and the ability to read comfortably and automatically. (This means you can learn keyboarding skills—what used to be known as touch typing.) Some Eights will have both skills—plus the play attitude—and can learn with joy all about spread sheets, graphics, writing their own programs, and so on. Those who aren't up to keyboarding yet can still manipulate their way around with glee. See **Window of Opportunity** in Chapter 3 for suggestions on how to enhance Kids' computer skills.

FIND A PASSIONATE INTEREST

This is a great age for introducing Kids to a variety of learning opportunities. Suggestions: computer skills, music lessons, art lessons with lots of different media and a teacher who talks about design and color, dance of all kinds, karate, juggling, swimming. It's also a good age for hobbies and collecting: stamps, coins, baseball cards, whatever.

BECOME BILINGUAL

A second language started now, ideally through ordinary conversation and play, not only can be learned without accent but also facilitates learning additional languages later.

LEARN PHYSICAL FEATS

Anything involving balance is likely to be learned more easily at ages seven and eight. Coordination is usually up to the task, and the child isn't growing so rapidly that his or her body feels a bit out of control. If a Kid learns to ride a two-wheeler, roller-skate/ice-skate, do tricks on the bars, ski, and so on now, it will be easy to keep up the skill later at the onset of rapid growth.

CONSOLIDATE BASIC ACADEMIC SKILLS

Seven and Eight need to be thoroughly comfortable with reading skills (reading for meaning and for learning new information) and math skills before going on to succeed in fourth grade. If you or the teacher have any doubts about the child's grasp of these skills, insist on formal testing. Fourth grade takes these skills for granted, and a Kid who is still having to think about them rather than using them automatically can get into a lot of trouble.

TALK ABOUT AND LISTEN TO INFORMATION ABOUT SEX AND OTHER DELICATE TOPICS

Before puberty begins (for your Kid's friends and classmates, if not for your Kid) it's a good idea to establish yourself as an askable and tellable parent. That means imparting information in as comfortable and casual a way as possible. Girls should be told about puberty and menstruation; both sexes should know how babies get started, where the fetus develops, and how the baby exits. Boys may be frightened or appalled at the idea of menstruation at this age unless they've already learned about it earlier, in which case they take it for granted. At any rate, both sexes need a review course at age nine.

This is also a good time to talk about dangers that Kids face as teenagers: tobacco, alcohol, drugs, gangs, reckless sex, and reckless driving. Sevens and Eights take such conversations seriously and aren't yet likely to regard them as intrusions into their peer-related lives.

For parents of Sevens and Eights:

BE ROLE MODELS

Ever more competent Sevens and Eights are very alert to what their parents value enough to spend their time and energy on. If your Kid sees you enjoying reading, honoring your work, helping other people, supporting important causes, and spending time having fun with and paying attention to your children, you've made an impression that's lifelong.

NURTURE INDEPENDENCE

Many Sevens are ready to go for an overnight at a friend's house; many Eights are ready for a week of overnight camp. Daycamp is a good introduction to camp.

What If?

Events that disrupt the tranquility of everyday life happen to every child. Sevens/Eights are in the power years of childhood, and this helps to determine how they react to life's surprises. They are starting to feel in control of their own small worlds, and any interruption in control feels like a personal threat. Too, they are aware for the first time that body and soul are in some ways independent, and this makes them regard insults to the body with new anxiety. Finally, they are beginning to have an idea of themselves as people with a public self and a reputation to establish and uphold.

MOVING

Sevens and Eights regard moving as a public event. They are much less upset than younger children about changing houses and bedrooms and yards. They're much more concerned with losing the old familiar world in which they felt in control: the world of school, friends, after-school activities. Here are some ways to help.

NO MATTER HOW YOU FEEL PERSONALLY ABOUT MOVING, FIND POSITIVE THINGS TO SAY ABOUT IT

• But whatever you say, don't put down or treat lightly the place you are leaving. Your words and feelings will be repeated unerringly to the very people you don't wish to know about them.

KEEP COMMUNICATING

• Let Seven/Eight participate in premove conversations, unless these are fraught with adult anxiety. As soon as you know for sure where the new home, neighborhood, and school will be, talk about them. (Uncertainty or a change once a decision seems to have been made tend to produce green-around-the-gills anxiety in Seven and Eight.) Make sure Seven/Eight knows you are taking everything into consideration: what he or she will do after school; the continuation of lessons, sports, activities; the preservation of hobbies or collections; where the bike or skates will be used.

LEAVE WITH CEREMONY

• Have the child's friends over to say good-bye. A nice thought: trade with each one a few stamped, addressed envelopes for notes, pictures, artifacts. Take pictures and send photos back to them. Say good-bye to important people—don't forget the pediatrician and office staff!

PREPARE YOUR KID'S WELCOME

Second and third grade can be very cliquey. A good ploy: talk or write to the new teacher before the move. Teachers may welcome the suggestion that they treat the arrival of a new child in the classroom as a class project, having the class write notes of welcome, with a photo and a few sentences about themselves. "I am glad you are moving here because there are only four girls in this class and three of them are stuck up. I like red likorish and horses and my dog is named Trouble. Love, Marcie." The Kid who's moving in can send a photo and letter, too. It's a good idea for the letter not to brag ("I am the best soccer player on my team") but to note interests that others are likely to share ("I like basketball and SuperMario III") and to hint at benefits to be had from friendship ("My Dad makes doublechocolate brownies and my Mom loves animals and we go to the zoo a lot").

CASE THE JOINT

• Make sure that your Kid has some expertise in whatever all the Kids there are doing. If you lived in a neighborhood where bicycling was dangerous but all the Kids in the new place ride 12-gears, try at least to get some biking tutorials in before you leave: even if you can't afford a bike when you get there, your Kid can borrow one from a new-made friend.

• See what the other Kids are wearing, and try to have at least one outfit that fits in for the first day or two of school.

• If this is going to be a big culture shock in any way, try to find an activity for your Kid to join right off the bat that is likely to make him or her comfortable. Explore religious institutions, the Y, scouting.

BE CAREFUL ON MOVING DAY

Seven/Eight will be pale with excitement, absent-minded, distractable, impulsive. Try to have a dignity-maintaining supervisor for the Kid: an uninvolved friend, relative, or hire a friendly teenager. Kids this age may get into dangerous trouble unsupervised: they try to move things that are heavy, breakable, unstable; they lose things and become distraught; they climb into large boxes or crawl off somewhere to think and cry, or accidently stow away in the moving van.

GIVE SEVEN/EIGHT A BACKPACK FOR PERSONAL TREASURES AND THEN KEEP YOUR EYE ON IT

Write yourself a note that you'll see last thing before leaving: "Check Kid's treasure pack!"

EXPECT ADJUSTMENT TO TAKE TIME

It may take Seven/Eight two or three months to adjust to the new home, neighborhood, school. It's also not uncommon to see a sea-change: a Kid who had a zillion friends in the old classroom now has only one or two, or vice versa. Often this merely reflects a change that was in the making anyway. If Seven/Eight eagerly greets the day and feels good about his or her accomplishments, not to worry.

TRAVEL

When travel isn't recreational but required and perhaps tense, even for adults, Sevens and Eights can lose their cool in a big way. There are a few strategies that can help.

• Be clear about where you are going and why. Sevens and Eights aren't very good with flat maps, but are somehow reassured by finding spots on a globe of the world. Sevens and Eights like to have a specific goal in mind.

> "We are going to Grandma's to help her move to the nursing home." "We are looking for a good school for Peter, where people will take care of him and help him be happy."

• Prepare them for what lies in store. If the Kid is going to be expected to take care of himself or herself and not get in the way, explain this.

> "All the grown-ups are going to be very upset. I'm afraid that nobody will feel like playing, not even Uncle Rusty."

• Let the Kid know that you count on him or her to come through in a pinch.

> "I remember how kind you were when Luanne was sick. I know you can do that again."

Make a plan for keeping busy.

> "They have a TV, but no video games. What do you think you'd like to do? Let's look over your stuff. What about books or crafts, or maybe you'd like to start a collection of bugs? There are lots of weird bugs in Grandma's yard."

• Promise a time each day to touch base and debrief.

> "No matter what happens, you and I will sit down every night before bed and talk. If you're having a tough time, we'll figure out what we can do about it."

• Vow not to turn Seven/Eight into a pseudo-confidante. Kids need to know what is going on, but they also need to know that adults are in charge.

• Recognize mature behavior as it occurs.

> "You brought me a glass of lemonade right when I really needed it. You are growing up right before my eyes. I am so impressed. Thank you."

• Have a reward when you get home. It could be a special meal with a toast to the Kid, a toy or treat, or just a special hug with a recounting of all the specific things the Kid did that were beyond the call of duty. Slip-ups on the part of the Kid may go unnoticed. However, if the Kid refers to them, they can be assessed fairly and set to rest. If the Kid was asked to perform at too high a standard, this mistake should be placed firmly on the shoulders of an adult: "Grandma should never have asked you to feed those chickens. You never did it before and nobody showed you how. I would have made exactly the same decision about the corn. It wasn't your mistake, it was Grandma's."

NEW SIBLING

When all goes well, Seven/Eight regards a new sibling with tolerant pleasure and falls into a role that is half sibling, half parent. There will be moments of insecurity and envy, but in general it's all much smoother now than when the big Kid was younger.

Here's what will facilitate this delightful course of events.

INCLUDE SEVEN/EIGHT IN AS MUCH OF THE PREGNANCY AND PREPARATION AS THE KID SEEMS TO ENJOY

Seeing the fetal ultrasounds, listening to the heartbeat, feeling the baby kick, helping to decorate the nursery—these are all terrific treats for most Sevens/Eights. I suggest drawing the line at having them join you for childbirth preparation classes or the birth itself, however. Sevens and Eights regard the body as a vulnerable new mystery, since they are newly aware that soul and body are not quite the same. Many will be very upset and resentful if they are exposed to adult pain, private parts, and bodily fluids.

PROTECT THE MEMORIES OF SEVEN/EIGHT'S OWN BABYHOOD

It's great to watch the videos and go over the baby book. But just because your older child is so big, it's not a good idea to usurp the trappings of his or her infancy without asking permission. This goes for baby clothes and linens, baby furniture, toys, feeding apparatus, and even family heirlooms. "That is *my* dress, for *my* being baptized. I think the new baby should have his *own* dress." Oh. Absolutely. Yes. You can negotiate if you want, but I'd just give right in.

PROTECT SEVEN/EIGHT'S PLACE IN YOUR ARMS AND HEART

It's a well-known phenomenon of pregnancy: as the new baby becomes a closer reality, the older child seems a whole lot older. Sevens and Eights still need hugs, cuddling, tucking in, reading to. And when the new baby arrives, their first glimpse of him or her should NOT be a sight of the babe in the arms of—oh, horrors!—Seven/Eight's very own mother or father. Having attended at least three zillion births, I cannot tell you how often I have had a parent to whom I have given this advice confess: "You know, I still remember seeing my baby brother in my mother's arms after he was born. It just broke my heart. I remember it like it was yesterday."

MAKE TIME FOR YOUR BIG KID

Seven and Eight are so capable and independent, it's easy to let them rely on their own resources. But the first few weeks with a new baby sibling strike Seven/Eight as making a huge change in life: the older child may start thinking of himself or herself as "practically grown-up." This isn't good. It means a bigger, more sudden distancing than anybody is really prepared for. Try to keep the old habits, rituals, and gestures of affection intact. A half-hour or even fifteen minutes of fully attentive, one-to-one time with Seven/Eight on a daily basis repays parents a thousand-fold.

KEEP LIFE NORMAL

Even though a Kid is big enough to be a great help, it's not fair or wise to press him or her into service. If the birth of a new sibling means having to do extra housework and forfeit play, sports, friends, the relationship is not likely to be happy. At the other extreme, parents of a cherished only child with a new sibling may be tempted to allow huge deviations from civilized behavior—out of guilt. Seven/Eight will be very upset if this occurs: it's as if his or her worst suspicions have been confirmed:—yes, Mom and Dad do love the new baby more, much more, and they feel so bad about it they are letting me get away with murder.

IF THERE'S A COMPLICATION, DON'T UNDERESTIMATE THE EFFECT ON SEVEN/EIGHT

There are three fairly frequent complications.

A stepsibling

The Seven/Eight who becomes a stepsibling with the birth of a new baby has a big cultural load to carry. This is particularly true of a Kid who was previously an only child. Parents who try to pretend that the arrival of the new child is not an event of major proportions are in for trouble. The smoothest courses require a lucky constellation of circumstance:

• Most crucially, amicable relations between the birth parents, and between the Kid and each birth parent.

• A tactful stepparent who doesn't rush the relationship and who has sane ideas and behavior when it comes to parenting.

• A Kid who feels like a success at home, at school, and with friends.

• Lack of disturbing financial or medical worries.

• Lack of social violence in the home and neighborhood: no drugs, gangs, or violence.Even then, expect some brooding and turmoil. What helps: the same things that help when it's NOT a stepsibling, but even more faithfully applied.

A premature or sick new sibling

When the new sibling does not come home from the hospital as scheduled, Seven/Eight is in a quandary: "Did mom and dad decide that I was really enough? Are we supposed to just forget about the new baby?" "Did I make the baby sick because I had bad thoughts about the baby?" "Being born is just terrible. They have to come out that teeny place. I bet practically everybody gets hurt being born." "If that new baby is sick, maybe I'll catch the sickness and die, or maybe Mom is really sick too and nobody wants to tell me."

It is difficult, when parents are distraught about the newborn, to reassure Seven/Eight. Yet it is vital for everyone's future happiness, no matter what happens, that Seven/Eight feel secure and reassured. This is a time when parents should call in all their chips: friends, relatives, neighbors, religious helpers, pediatrician—and ask everybody to make an effort to keep Seven/Eight's life as normal, scheduled, and in control as possible. They should be explicit in what they tell Seven/Eight.

Name the problem and say what is being done to help.

> "Baby Lee was born much too early. That's called being premature. Parts of her body aren't ready to work yet. The doctors are doing that work for her until she's older." "Baby Kirk has a problem with his lungs. He has a disease called pneumonia. The doctors are working hard to help him breathe. They give him special air and feed him through a special tube so that he doesn't have to try to eat and breathe at the same time."

Reassure Seven/Eight that the baby's condition is no one's fault.

> "Babies get born early pretty often. Nobody knows why. Sometimes doctors can give medicine that keeps that from happening, but sometimes the medicine doesn't work."

> "Brand new babies are more likely to get infections than older children. Their bodies just don't work in a grown-up way. The baby didn't get an infection because people didn't wash their hands or anything like that."

"You know, when I was a Kid, I worried that if I had even one bad thought about a person, it could make them sick or even die. But that's not so."

Don't keep secrets. If Seven/Eight hears you whispering, he or she will *know* that you're talking about him or her. Speak up. Even if it is technical, pretend that Seven/Eight can understand the words—and then define them. This way, Seven/Eight will know that the words he or she overheard are not code words.

"Baby Kirk had to have an endotracheal tube. That means that the doctors had to put a special tube down through his mouth to his lungs, so that a machine can help him breathe."

CROSS-GENDER BEHAVIOR

Please see the section about cross-gender behavior under **What If?** in Chapter 1, page 89, especially the general discussion at the beginning, which is an introduction to this topic.

This is a very tough age for Kids with cross-sex preferences. It's the age when a given class or group of Kids seems to decide what is acceptable behavior and what isn't, and then proceed to Out anybody who isn't acceptable.

There's a huge spectrum here of what (influenced by parents and the culture at large and their own mysterious whims) a given group of Kids decides upon. I know a second grade where no little girl had better show up in anything but a dress and where she is "supposed" to spend her free time with dolls and jewelry; and a third grade where anything "girly" is reviled and scorned, the uniform is overalls, the sport is street hockey, and woe to the little girl who confesses to owning a dollhouse. I know a third grade where three of the best-liked boys take ballet and a second grade where a best-friendship between a boy and a girl was dissolved due to teasing.

Some Kids of Seven and Eight who prefer the playthings and companions of the opposite sex are able to stand up against the will of the group. These are Kids who feel good about themselves and strong in their preferences. They take on their enemies with vigor, mostly, and occasional bouts of tears and rage. Most often, they are blessed with parents and other loving adults who are on their side without ambivalence. Most often, too, they do not shun the dress, play, and companions of the same sex; they just see them as too confining. It seems clear that the rules governing "acceptable" behavior are too rigid, and rebels are recognized as valuable. Very often, these Kids become leaders. They gain a great deal of strength from their experience.

Parents whose Kids are in this predicament often feel much better after talking about the problem with someone outside the situation. Pediatricians familiar with the standards of the community and with each school can often give a nonpartisan assessment that helps parents help their Kids through this cliquey, exclusionary age.

So I don't regard these Kids as having a problem with cross-gender behavior. But there are Kids who do. The Kids who do have a problem show any or all of the following behaviors:

• They display persistent mannerisms or styles of speech that are so exaggeratedly of the opposite sex that even a "macho boy" or a "feminine girl" would not be expected to engage in them. A little girl will swagger, stomp, spit, and growl. A little boy will "swish" his wrists, wiggle his hips, bat his eyelashes.

• They not only prefer other-sex play and companions; they seem almost "allergic" to those of the same sex, showing tears, physical symptoms like stomachaches, and very withdrawn behavior when with Kids of their own gender.

• They can't find friends of the same sex in any area of life, not in the neighborhood, not at school, not in outside activities.

• Their cross-sexual behavior is the first thing

that parents or other adults would list if making out a description of the Kid.

A Kid who shows any one or any combination of these signs at Seven or Eight is a child at high risk for depression and other serious mood or conduct disorders. After all, this is the age when Kids first confront the mystery of their own unique human identity. Before this, a Kid who is being beaten on usually blames the people doing the beating. Now, when inner feelings are at odds with what is socially acceptable, the Kid is more likely to blame those inner feelings—that is, to start to hate himself or herself.

A Kid in this situation is filled with fear and self-doubt and needs help. Unfortunately, at the same time parents begin to feel heat themselves. They often start to register that other adults—grandparents, teachers, coaches, even pediatricians—are blaming them for their Kid's atypical stance. This can make parents, in turn, angry at their Kids—making their Kid feel even worse, which usually exacerbates all the distressing behavior.

Here are some things that can help the situation.

• Every family in which this is a problem needs to have as a resource a professional person who can put things in perspective and help parents to help their child. This should be someone whose religious and moral attitude permits him or her to counsel without blaming. The job of this professional person is to help the family create a situation in which the Kid can continue to mature, rather than to get stuck in a fearful, self-hating mode. This usually means helping parents not to be angry at themselves or each other.

• Parents can make gentle, positive efforts to help their Kid find a niche in the world. This may not be the niche the parents had in mind. It may be that their Kid will be happier as an outcast at school with a rich life at home, church, or temple and in selected lessons and activities.

• Parents can help their Kid find a best friend. A best friend validates a Kid's whole self. A best friend makes it better when cliques and bullies are mean, and stands up with you to confront them—or runs away and hides with you. No best friend is perfect, and parents may need to put up with a child whom they would not have chosen themselves.

• Parents can try not to let the gender-identification issue overwhelm all other developmental issues. Kids need to develop character, perform chores, get good grades at school, take risks, and so on and so on. Such an attitude actually gives hope to a Kid who isn't sure whether or not he or she is "okay". It says, "We expect a lot from you. We wouldn't do that if you weren't okay. So shape up."

It's still crucial for a Kid not to be labeled as homosexual, but it may be helpful for a Kid whose feelings and behavior are causing him or her a great deal of pain simply to know that there are adults who have the same feelings and behavior and who have grown up to be happy, proud, and accepted. Parents may wish to discuss this aspect with a religious leader and with their pediatrician.

SERIOUS ILLNESS IN A LOVED ONE

Sevens and Eights are in a very tough spot. They are still very much like Fives and Sixes: they overhear everything but are so inexperienced that they can't organize the information. They are still highly egocentric and think that somehow or another anything that happens must have been because of something they themselves said, did, or didn't do.

On top of all that, they are just beginning to discover that they have a consciousness that is somehow separate from their bodies. This is a scary thought. It makes them newly aware of when people "don't act like themselves" because of illness, fatigue, or other influences such as mental illness or drugs. They count on parents and loved ones to be stable, dependable. They think of pets the way they think of people: as souls with a body.

When Seven/Eight's life is disrupted by serious illness of a beloved person or pet, he or she needs many of the same assists and will have many of the same responses that Fives and Sixes do (see **What If?**, Chapter 1).

What's different about Seven and Eight is that they worry about a loved one dying. They may become literally sick with worry and persist in this worry even after the illness has passed. They may develop nervous habits and separation anxiety. This separation anxiety is different from school phobia: not only does the child not want to leave the parent, the child feels strongly that the parent shouldn't leave, either. "But do you *have* to go play bridge?" the child says, in tears no less.

The best solace for a child in this situation is a very regular schedule, time, and distraction. It's not a bad idea to splurge, if possible, on an entirely new and enticing pastime. Knowing that this fear of a loved one dying is normal and pretty much inevitable helps adults to put up with Seven/Eight's excessive worry.

DEATH OF A BELOVED PERSON OR A PET

When a beloved person or pet dies, the grief of Seven and Eight is more complicated than that of younger children, and their fears are more complex as well. Like Five/Six, Seven/Eight may worry that he or she somehow caused the death—by not being good, by having angry thoughts, by arguing or fighting. Religious children may worry that they did not remember the lost person in their prayers or that they did something bad and that God is punishing them. And like younger children, Sevens and Eights fear for themselves: if a parent has died, what will happen to them? Who will take care of them? If someone so close to me has died, will I die too?

So far, the same comforts that helped Five/Six will help Seven/Eight (see **What If?**, Chapter 1). But there is another factor in the grief of

Seven/Eight. A beloved person or animal is part of the calming, approving "inner audience" that plays such a role in Seven and Eight's confidence in facing the world. When that voice dies, it feels like a little inner death.

So Seven/Eight may be shaken to the core. It's not unusual for families to see a personality change, with persistent sadness, loss of joy, and physical symptoms like decreased appetite and abnormal sleep. Seven/Eight may cling to a remaining parent, grandparent, or sibling, refusing to go to school or even to the bathroom without that person.

A kind, patient loving adult who is not distraught over the death can be an enormous help. The role of that person is not only to reassure Seven/Eight that the death was nobody's fault, that the person who died was not angry at or tired of the child, that Seven/Eight will be well cared for and protected. It is also to assume some of the role of the person who died—that of "being there," a patient, listening, attentive, calm audience that Seven/Eight needs at this stage.

If no friend or family member can successfully "be there" for Seven/Eight, or if the intensity of the child's need is very great, counseling sessions with a sensitive person are almost literally lifesavers. A child who goes from grief to depression can become quite ill.

FUNERAL/MEMORIAL SERVICE

Seven/Eights should be given the choice of whether or not to attend, but it is almost always better that they do: the ceremony helps to make the death real and distinct in their minds; and the community of mourners helps to validate the child's grief and to give him or her support.

Given that the person who died was a very close and beloved one, some consideration should be given to the child's reaction when the service is planned, if at all possible. An open casket, the lowering of the casket into the grave, discussion of ashes if cremation has occurred—these are all puzzling, upsetting features and to the child, at least, unnecessary. The child should be protected from any mourners who are likely to become truly distraught or to vent anger or other frightening emotions. Never underestimate what a Seven/Eight understands from adult comments.

Seven/Eight should sit next to a calm, kind adult, close to an unobtrusive exit and be assured that it is okay to leave at any point during the service.

DEATH OF A PET

Sevens and Eights usually want and need a homemade service, even for goldfish and turtles and lizards. It's not a good idea to replace the departed pet with a new one right away, even if the child insists that he or she wants one. Such insistence often masks either a denial that the pet has gone and a need to skip over sad emotions that can surface later in other, unhealthy, forms or an attempt on the part of the child to protect other family members from sadness. Children this age are often threatened by adult tears.

MOURNING

Sevens and Eights who have lost either a person or a pet take a long time to recover: a year is not unusual. They often have physical symptoms, such as appetite or sleep change, even when they are not acting very sad or depressed. For some reason, frequent urination (without any medical cause and appearing only in the daytime) is a common reaction—it is called pollakiuria (see Glossary). Many also will have an "anniversary reaction" of sadness, separation anxiety, and physical symptoms like pollakiuria in following years around the date of the death.

It's very important for Sevens and Eights to talk about the departed person and to hear others doing so; going over photo albums and videos is a kind and sensitive move.

HOSPITALIZATION

A parent or other guardian should try to be with a hospitalized child at all times, unless the hospitalization is very prolonged and this becomes completely impractical. There is no reason for any hospital to exclude parents from a child's bedside, though it may be necessary for parents to wait outside during certain procedures.

Not only does the presence of a parent or guardian calm and reassure the child: such an adult also can keep an eye on medical procedures and intervene in the case of a mistake. We like to think that mistakes in hospitals are rare; they are not, though usually there aren't any serious repercussions.

If you're with your child at all times, you can make sure that the pain medication is given promptly, that the infiltrated IV is noted and changed before there's a lot of swelling, and that the oxygen or the monitor that is turned off for a test is indeed switched on again. Be there and be alert.

Yet you do not want the staff to consider you an enemy or a spy. Your child's stay will be much more pleasant if you can find time to thank people, to write a note to the nursing supervisor or hospital administrator in praise of any special (or even ordinary) kindness or competence, to bring in a treat to eat.

For Sevens and Eights, as for younger children, the worst part of hospitalization remains separation from parents; lack of control over what happens; pain; and exposure to strangers of the private parts of the body.

The main differences between Sevens/Eights and younger children are:

first, that Seven/Eight also has to contend with living up to his or her own standards of dignity and courage;
second, that hospitalization means

being absent from school for a significant time, during which the class not only continues to learn academically, but during which the social structure of the class can also shift dramatically;

All the things that helped Five and Six will help Seven and Eight (see **What If?**, Chapter 1), but these special differences also need to be addressed.

DIGNITY AND COURAGE

Sevens and Eights are newly able to use their own minds to control their reactions of fear, pain, and anxiety. But they need help: they haven't yet had so much experience that it occurs to them: "Gee, if I can just get my mind on something else, maybe I can relax."

In fact, it's possible to teach Seven and Eight a variety of techniques, from relaxation to redirecting attention to visualization. These are not "self-hypnosis" or wild new-age fads; they are normal ways to redirect feelings and behavior that mature people use all the time.

Parents can help reinforce dignity and courage a great deal by serving as the child's protector in the hospital. They can make sure that procedures are explained and that the child is able to make an effort to prepare himself or herself. They can make sure that modesty is respected, with the private parts of the body covered unless they're being examined. They can explain and reassure about what the child may hear or see elsewhere on the ward. They can make sure that everyone who examines or performs a procedure on the child identifies himself or herself and makes a connection with the child.

MISSING SCHOOL

In the anxiety and household chaos of a hospital stay, how much school the child is missing may be furthest from one's mind. But keeping in touch with the classroom will help to speed convalescence.

Enlist the help of the teacher. Here are some things to ask.
• What new topics will the class be learning? What kind of review is scheduled? He or she may be able to give you a copy of each day's lesson plans. Be especially alert to any new math topics: missing out on one step in basic math can make the succeeding steps incomprehensible.
• What are the homework assignments? They are likely to indicate topics the teacher believes the class needs review in.
• Is there a way, say via computer, that your child can participate from home?
• How long must a child be out of school to qualify for a home tutor? Who are the tutors?
• Is there a classmate who could start coming to your home daily to help Seven/Eight keep up with the class? Sometimes a dear friend can do this; sometimes a dear friend is not the best person— even dear friends can have trouble with reading or math.
• What is the best way to tell the class about the hospitalization? If the indication for the hospitalization is something benign and common, would he or she consider making it a teaching unit? Or at least reading out loud about it? Big Bird gets his tonsils out; Madeline her appendix.

A teacher who goes out of his or her way to help, certainly deserves a note (from Seven/Eight, as well as from you), a small homemade gift, and a letter of commendation to the principal with a copy to the superintendent of schools.

DIVORCE

Sevens and Eights are dazed and bewildered by divorce in much the same way younger children are: they believe their homelife to be normal, even when parents fight bitterly, and can't understand why a parent must leave. They, too, tend to believe that they themselves must be the cause of the divorce: "Because of when I screwed up Dad's computer" "Because of how I whine too much" "Because of me and Jerry fighting all the time."

So all the things that are true about Five and Six in the face of divorce are also true for Seven and Eight (see **What If?**, Chapter 1).

The main difference between Sevens/Eights and younger children is that Sevens/Eights are much more likely to be placed in the role of a surrogate spouse or, if there are younger children at home, a surrogate other parent.

Sevens and Eights are competent, they can read and write—directions on a can of soup, a shopping list, a note to the plumber. It's not rare for Sevens and Eights to be asked to watch a younger child for hours, to prepare dinner, to clean the house. This shift of responsibilities onto Seven/Eight tends to occur gradually and just builds as the parent becomes more and more overwhelmed by the stresses and bitterness of the divorce.

This is highly destructive and unfair to the child. When a child takes over the normal responsibilities of a parent, the child's boundaries become blurred. He or she starts thinking of the parent as an equal. Kids of this age can start worrying about a parent to the degree that a complete role reversal takes place: "Mom, you didn't eat your breakfast! That's not good for you!" "Dad, I don't want to see you going to work with that sweater. It's got a spot on the sleeve." "You shouldn't be going out with that man. He's taking advantage of you."

Exacerbating this role reversal is the fact that many girls and some boys have started to make close friends by age Eight and have learned how to have a close, intimate conversation with a friend. They then may fall into being a single parent's friend and confidante as well, listening sympathetically to problems about child support and sexual incompatibility and worrying about dating and aging.

Rarely, tragically, a Seven or Eight is asked to fill the sexual needs of one or the other parent. Unhappily, this may seem to the child to be a perfectly natural, though dreadful, state of affairs and go unreported.

When this tendency to regard Seven/Eight as an adult goes unchecked, the prognosis for the preteen and adolescent years is grim. Some Kids rebel completely, abandoning with gleeful anger their chores and their now-dependent parent. Some take on the role of pseudo-spouse and pseudo-parent and demote the parent to the role of troublesome child. Some take out their anger and deprivation in a destructive way, turning to sex, alcohol, and drugs. Most have trouble succeeding in school and in other areas.

Parents who find themselves tempted in this way are strongly advised to seek counseling both for self and for child. One of the functions of such a counselor is to monitor the parent-child relationship and flag signs that it is becoming distorted.

SEXUAL MOLESTATION

Sevens and Eights are more likely to keep sexual molestation a secret, especially—as is usually the case—when the molester is an adult or teenager they know or have reason to respect and obey. Partly this is because they feel that they "brought it on themselves." Children this age are both egocentric—they feel that they are the cause of whatever happens—and incresingly aware that their actions affect others. A child who struts or shows off or flirts with an adult, who then engages the child in sexual acts, may feel very responsible and guilty.

This means that parents have three jobs.

• They need to protect their children from any adult friends or relatives who they have reason to suspect aren't entirely reliable. For instance, the uncle who strokes and pats Mom is likely to do the same or more to Seven/Eight and thus shouldn't have the opportunity to do so.

• They need to let Kids know that they, the parents, are askable and tellable parents. Parents who are authoritarian, who give frequent rigid demands and punish a child physically, are not likely to be seen as parents who would accept such a "confession." Parents who are permissive and who let any behavior go unchecked, may not be seen as parents who would reliably and effectively intervene. Parents who are unable to talk about sex—or other difficult topics—at all are likely to be seen as parents who need to be protected from the harsh truth.

• They need to tell Kids explicitly, every now and then, that it is not allowed for teenagers or adults to play with them in a secret or sexual manner, even if the older person tells the Kid that what they are doing is normal and allowed; even if the older person pays the Kid to let him or her do it; even if the older person has a position of power over the Kid's parents; even if the older person makes threats: "This would kill your mother if she knew about it."

Since Kids shouldn't be constantly worried about or even thinking about such possibilities, telling them about sexual molestation is best done when there is some kind of cue rather than right out of the blue, briefly and without too much emotion rather than with fear and tears, and within the context of every day life: while driving to pick up a friend, or when the subject comes up during carpool, or over a snack, rather than making a special Sit Down I Want To Talk With You session.

In a divorce situation, it is particularly important to fulfill all three roles, rather than just the last one. The accusation of sexually molesting a child is a hot, powerful one that either divorcing parent can make. When it is a false accusation, the emotional fallout is as great as when the suspicion is justified. A parent who suspects that the other parent or a friend of the other parent has the potential to sexually abuse the child needs to consult both a counselor and legal assistance before the occasion for accusation arises.

3

●■▲■●

NINE, TEN, AND ELEVEN
THE LAND OF THE ROLLING EYEBALLS

Overview of the Age

Crash goes the bookbag into the back seat. Slam goes the door. Down goes the window. Up goes the radio volume. The seatback goes up and down and the seat slides backward and forward. Click goes the seat belt. Various odors emanate: sweat, deodorant, peanut butter, zoo, and—What's that? A whiff of Dayla's mother's own Liz Claiborne cologne.

"Where did you come from!" Dayla's mother yells over the radio and punches the off button. "I was worried! You weren't on the school bus. I thought they'd left you at the zoo."

"And there was this warthog with the most enormous you know what." Dayla pops in a wad of bubble gum and snaps it vigorously. "And Ben and Matthew thought it was just so cute to make warthog noises in their Slurpees, so nobody could hear the guide and Mrs. Donaldson made the guy stop the tram so we had to get out and walk all the way back, I am *so exhausted*." Snap.

"But how did you get back to school? Why weren't you on the bus?"

"And then we were in the john talking about bras and little did we know Ben and Matthew were right outside, and that time Mrs. Donaldson made Ben walk with her and Matthew walk with Patty up front, but then Carmen threw up and Mrs. Donaldson had to take her to the ladies room and Ben got away and bothered the llama and this time it was the ultimate last straw so we had to get in the buses and go home."

"Poor Mrs. Donaldson. So who drove you back?"

"Nobody! I told you, I was in the school bus."

A dark thought occurs to Dayla's mother. "Were you embarrassed because I got on the bus and tried to find you?"

"'Dayla! Are you back there, sweetie honey lovie? Yoo-hoo, chickadee.'" Dayla rolls her eyes in exasperation.

"I didn't. You know I didn't. I said in a dignified, official voice, 'Excuse me. Is Dayla in here? We have to get to an appointment.'"

"Mumble mumble mumble sunglasses." Dayla's hair is over her face, her chin on her chest, and the gum seems to fill her mouth.

"What *about* my sunglasses?" Dayla's mother takes a quick look in the rear view mirror. "What *about* them?"

"Carmen says." The inflection makes it sound like a complete sentence.

"Says what? Carmen says what?"

"That they make you look a little bit, just a little teeny tiny bit, like, sort of, an insect of some kind."

There is a pause. "So Carmen threw up at the zoo, did she? How very distressing."

"Oh, Mom, she didn't mean it in a bad way. She just thought those sunglasses make you look a little teeny tiny bit— buggy."

"So you disowned me! You probably said we weren't even related!" Dayla's mother pretends to be massively insulted. She twitches her nose and makes antennae come out of her forehead with the fingers of one hand.

"Yo, bogitating!" Dayla dissolves in giggles. "I did not! I said, that's a friend of my aunt's boss."

What a great age, the age of older Kids. They are big and getting bigger, noisy and getting noisier, smart and funny and getting smarter and funnier—and they know it. It feels as if Seven and Eight was spent gathering in steam, and now it's all spouting forth.

THOSE ROLLING EYEBALLS

Things shift between parents and children during these years. For one thing, parents can feel extraneous. Not just extraneous; unwanted. In the land of the rolling eyeballs, children seem to think that their parents' mission in life is to embarrass them. "Why can't you be *inconspicuous*?" hisses Marcie, appalled that her father has actually applauded at the end of a movie when nobody else has.

This can actually be dangerous. A sensitive parent who repeatedly gets the message that he or she is unwanted may retreat, rejected and angry, at the very time a Kid needs parenting the most. Avoiding rejection and anger means understanding what Kids are going through and vowing not to take behavior personally. It means being willing, on issues of right and wrong, to shift your stance. Kids this age need parents who no longer are ultimate moral authorities, but who are patient listeners who help them to clarify their own ideas.

Older Kids are intensely caught up in their public life. You have to keep your eyes open, watch your words and actions, see who's doing what with or to whom. What did she mean when she said that? Does he like me or was he being mean? What are they whispering about? Can I sit at that lunch table or will they ignore me or make me leave? Am I as smart as he is? Am I as cute as those Kids? Is this the right shirt? Do they think I'm wearing a bra? Every day, a thousand tiny interactions and perceptions get logged in.

It's urgent work, because all those minute data are like colored dots that form a picture of who is me. Up to about nine, children think of themselves in terms of physical characteristics only. Now it's much more complicated. Me is defined as a composite of feelings, skills, interests, and how-other-people-act-toward-me.

When Seven yearns to be just like her best friend, she wants to have brown curly hair and furry arms, taps on her shoes, and a holster with a cap gun. She describes herself as short, blond, with painted fingernails and new shoes. When Ten yearns to be just like the most popular Kid in the class, he wants the other children to cluster around him, laugh at his jokes, choose him first on the team, and invite him to all their parties. Ten describes himself as smart in math, shy at first, a collector of miniature soldiers, terrific at shooting baskets, and medium popular—more popular than Gary, Phil, George, and Mark, anyway.

It's taken Ten lots of time and energy to establish these solid foundations of an identity. He has to compare himself against other Kids, gauge their reactions to him, and assign a value to each characteristic, and he has to do it over and over again, adjusting or reinforcing or refurbishing his version of himself.

Clearly, the nature of the group is as important as the characteristics of the child. If he had a different peer group, the same Ten might describe himself as really tall, bad at science, shy but funny, a collector of miniature soldiers, and least popular next to Brad.

At any rate, when you are so engrossed in building a public self, the presence of parents or other family can interfere. Merely by being there, they remind you that you already have a private, home self. This is the last thing you need! You don't need to be reminded of that self! It's composed of data that is either irrelevant or in conflict with your public self!

Here you are, confirming that you are, say, not shy with girls. Now here come your family, and all of a sudden, like a colored lens over your mental eyes, you see yourself as your private self: hates to meet new people, always spilling things, kind to little brother, in love with the dog! Who, pray tell, is this character

and how does this jibe with not shy with girls? How are you supposed to put all that together?

To say nothing of the fact that parents evoke the unwelcome attention of the other Kids. Insult is a prime method of communication in this age group, even between best friends. This is an age-related type of insult, in which perfectly normal attributes are named in an insolent tone of voice. "His mother was there, driving a *Chevy van!* Can you believe it! And she had on one of those *big, red sweaters.* OH MY GOD! You should have seen her!"

Why do Kids fear so much the exposure of their parents to the judgment of their peers? Perhaps it's because the whole group is so bent on establishing public personae that the presence of anybody's parents acts as a threat. Perhaps it's just because this is an easy way to find something to insult.

Also, of course, family acts as an audience. When you are in the act of constructing a public self, the mere awareness of an audience can give you performance anxiety. To say nothing of the fact that this may be a noisy, interfering audience. "Hey, look!" yells little brother. "Mom! He's over there with a bunch of *girls!*"

The main point is that this is a developmental stage. The behavior is normal though not admirable. It does seem to have a purpose, and above all *don't take it personally.* You look fine in your red sweater, and I like your Chevy van a lot.

So where do parents fit in? Do Kids this age need parents? You bet.

PARENTS NEED TO GIVE FEEDBACK

It's easy for parents to fall into the role of being mere facilitators or enforcers. They coach the team, provide refreshments for the slumber party, chauffeur, pay bills. They set limits, make sure chores and homework get done, warn about dangers, and squelch bad habits. And then they get out of the way.

These are crucial roles, no question about it.

But Kids this age need more from their parents. They need parents to help them make moral judgments and to act on them. They need to feel comfortable talking about moral dilemmas with parents.

If parents can take on this role with Nine, Ten, and Eleven, they can reasonably look forward to being a moral force in their children's lives in the teenage years and beyond. But this role requires a gigantic shift in how parents regard themselves. Starting now, they need to help children clarify their own moral judgment, rather than impose parental judgments on their children.

This is a key aspect to this age. When parents in our culture are unable to do this, encounters about moral issues become so painful and argumentative that children and parents often begin to avoid—even to hate—each other. Waiting until Kids enter adolescence to assume this role is too late. By then, the gap between parents and Kids is wide and deep and, worst of all, has come by both parties to seem inevitable.

Children aren't just creating a public image of themselves. They are forming their characters. By age nine, Kids have figured out that their actions produce predictable reactions from other people. They can plot their actions ahead of time.

Over the next few years, they learn the subtleties. For instance, you can feel one way and act as if you were feeling something else. You can experience two similar or contradictory emotions simultaneously and act on just one of them. You can be deceived by someone else's expression of feeling: a person can be angry and you think it's at you but it's really at somebody else.

All these discoveries can be put to use when you're establishing a public self. They are just as important when you are developing character. If you have an ideal image of the self that you're trying to attain, you can stretch your abilities to try to bridge the gap between "who I am" and "who I want to be." That means that you're not just creating a public self; you're developing character.

Character is how one reacts when things get out of control, and during these years things get out of control constantly. Character involves moral courage. Can you spot the right thing to do? Even if nobody else does? Can you do it, even if you'll be teased or shamed or worse? Character also involves style. Do you have a sense of humor? Are you generous or mean-spirited? Are you responsible, loyal, kind?

When parents help Kids develop character, they are nurturing what many experts believe are the four most important facets of high self-esteem.

The first is Significance. A child feels significant when he or she feels valued and loved and approved of by people he or she feels are important. It's much easier to feel oneself valued, loved, and approved by parents when they honor your experience as important enough to deserve careful attention. A child whose daily life and dilemmas go unremarked has a hard time feeling significant.

The second is Competence. Children need to feel that they can do some things well, and that this is appreciated. When parents recognize that a child can perform a demanding moral task, they're sending a message about being competent as human beings. This is much more fundamental than more fragile, context-dependent competence, such as ability with academics, sports, music, and so on.

The third is Virtue. Children need to feel that they are good. Children this age are maturing in their ideas of goodness and justice. Good no longer equals "that which parents approve." They need to feel instead that being good means doing what is right in their own view. Parents who keep the lines of communication open help bridge the gap between good and right.

The fourth is Power. Children need to feel that what happens to them comes about largely by their own efforts. They're not helpless, passive, or dependent. Children need parents who help them feel empowered, who let them know that what they do matters and that they will be rewarded with approval or held accountable for their actions.

During these years, Kids hone their characters on their peers just as they create a public self. They "catch" values and mannerisms from close friends. They find out whether they can stand up to cliques and bullies. But if this is all that they find out, they develop in a moral vacuum.

Kids need a great deal of feedback about how their characters are developing. This feedback needs to come in large part from loving adults, most importantly from parents. The feedback a child gets from other children is too unsophisticated, too variable, too shaped by secondary considerations like popularity, ulterior motives, and the need of the moment.

Helpful feedback doesn't mean giving a lecture. Lectures flow over children at nine, ten, and eleven leaving no mark except a residue of resentment. Helpful feedback means listening carefully, eliciting information, and guiding the child to finding his or her own insights, judgments, and decisions of how to behave. (See the section called **Growth of the Soul** later in this chapter.)

PARENTS ARE FACILITATORS

Is there life after carpool? It's easy to be fed up, frazzled, and bored doing things for busy Kids this age. They aren't good at showing appreciation—even well-brought-up friends of your well-brought-up child. They take you for granted and may not even talk to you when you're the only other one in the car. They're only aware of you—and then acutely and devastatingly—when you get out of your assigned place as adult.

But, of course, one of the important parental roles at this stage is that of facilitator.

HELPING YOUR CHILD FIND AN AREA IN WHICH HE OR SHE FEELS COMPETENT

Kids this age need to discover things that they are good at and then do them. Competence is one of the main supports of self-esteem, and self-esteem is what helps most in getting through adolescence into adulthood with all systems intact. It helps ward off disasters ranging from pregnancy to drugs, eating disorders to dropping out of school.

Moreover, when teenagers feel competent in an area, this makes living with them much happier. It's a neutral territory where parents and youngsters can interact without conflict. Competence in adolescence has its roots in experience that starts at nine, ten, and eleven.

Feeling competent doesn't mean you have to win. It means that you love what you're doing, understand how to improve your skills, and can feel yourself getting better at it.

Finding such an area of competence may be easy. If you're lucky, it's something like soccer, and there's a team at school. Many children, though, have hidden talents and unawakened interests. A Kid who could be a whiz in chess will never know until he or she has a chance to learn the game. A youngster who would devote his or her soul to ice skating needs ice and skates, at the very minimum. Your youngster may find a true love in an enterprise that is off the beaten track: acting out civil war battles with miniature soldiers, designing and sewing doll clothes, or Irish dancing.

It's worth making it a high priority for your child to find that enterprise and commit to it.

HELPING YOUR CHILD FIND A BEST FRIEND

A best friend isn't just somebody to play with. A best friend helps you grow up.

Parents and family let you know that you are loved unconditionally, without being compared to other people. The world of your peers shape your idea of how you compare in the public world. A best friend bridges the gap. A best friend is there when that unconditional love from your family slips. A best friend is also there when how you compare to others is given a big thumbs down.

During the years of puberty, how one's body changes can be too embarrassing to discuss with either parents or peers. It's a best friend who shares horror stories about erections in math class or starting your period during a tennis lesson; who reassures you that one breast doesn't look a whole lot bigger than the other or that it's normal for hair to grow on your toes.

A best friend can keep a secret that you can't even talk about with your family, maybe because your family *is* the secret. A best friend can reassure you that other Kids are mean or stupid and help bolster your idea of yourself in the face of unpopularity and put-downs.

How anybody gets through this period without a best friend is a good question. For more on best friends, see the section called **Growth of the Soul** later in this chapter.

LOOKING OUT FOR AND ADDRESSING AREAS OF WEAKNESS

Children who seemed to be rolling along without difficulty in any area can suddenly encounter problems at ages nine, ten, and eleven.

Learning problems can surface now that school work takes for granted the basic skills and relies on more complicated processing of material. Social problems can surface when children seek out intimate friendships based on sharing their private selves and when children may be pressured into precocious social forms, such as dating. Physical problems can surface when the skills required for sports become more demanding or when the hormones of puberty may contribute to acne or to overweight in girls, causing a feeling of cosmetic failure, as it were.

Children may find these experiences of sudden failure not just devastating to their self-esteem, but too painful to bring up to parents. They are more likely to try to hide the difficulty, at least for awhile. The child with difficulty learning may hide homework assignments or act up in class in order to be sent out of the room or coerce a friend into sharing work. The friendless child may pretend enormous popularity, constructing intricate stories of parties and play dates.

Parents who are tuned in sympathetically often can suspect these difficulties early on, when they're easier to assist.

MAKING SURE KIDS HAVE ACCESS TO INFORMATION

There's so much information poured into children these days from school, films, TV, computers, and other children. Yet it's amazing how little a well-informed child can know. The problem is that children, like adults, don't know when they don't know.

"I'm so GLAD I got my period and I'm only eleven." Tammy just glows.

"Why Tammy, I'm delighted! And congratulations."

"Yep! Now it's over and I won't have to worry any more. Boy, I'm glad that's over. I'd hate to have it when I'm like thirteen."

Or my young friend M., who was in a car accident—not seriously hurt, as it turned out, but the paramedics called lifeflight. When she heard about the helicopter, M., who had been remarkably brave, dissolved in hysterics. "I thought it was going to be like the animals during the flood [in the midwest]. I thought they were going to put me in a harness and I would dangle from that long rope." My heart broke for M.

Some misconceptions must go undiagnosed, but parents can make sure that Kids have information on at least three crucial topics. See

Health and Illness for a discussion of each.
- Puberty. Children need to know about changes in their own bodies and as much as they can assimilate about physical changes in the opposite sex.
- Sexuality. Children need to know the positive aspects of sexuality and its role in contributing to adult happiness. If parents feel that this has not been taught by example, they owe it to children to provide reading and viewing materials that counteract the bad stuff.
- Health. Children need to understand the importance of good nutrition, exercise, sleep, and making healthy choices with regard to alcohol, smoking, drugs, guns, and sex.

PARENTS ARE ENFORCERS

Just because your child is taller than you and wears bigger shoes, can program the VCR, and seems to wish you wouldn't impinge on his or her private life, doesn't mean that he or she is fully formed and ready to take on the world. Kids need their parents as never before to keep them safe and responsible.

For one thing, it's a dangerous world out there, and your child may be subjected to enormous pressures to take risks. A child who believes parents have given up enforcing rules can feel that parents have given up being parents and that they don't care about his or her safety, well-being, and success in life. This is a damaging feeling and one that pretty much squelches self-esteem.

On the other hand, the methods of discipline that seemed to work earlier are not likely to work now. Spanking, nagging, screaming, and so on no longer cut any ice (if they ever did). For one thing, many children this age are too big to be intimidated. Also, they've seen too many TV shows in which parents tried these tactics unsuccessfully. For another, Kids this age are focused on creating their own ideas of right and wrong and no longer see parents as the fount from which judgment springs.

This is Nature's way of telling parents to find another, more effective way of communicating with children. They need to get across two crucial things: First, that there is a boundary between parents and child, and that parents are still ultimately adults in charge. Second, that rules can be negotiated, but that responsibilities must be fulfilled and dangerous risks foresworn—and that the child will be held accountable.

SETTING LIMITS

Kids this age are most likely to respect parental decisions when parents have earned the right, in the Kid's eyes, to lay down the law. Earning this right requires that parents show the Kid that they are authoritative, not permissive nor tyrannical.

Authoritative parents establish the habit of approaching each case before them with an open mind. They listen and pay attention to the Kid's point of view, consider each decision on its own merits, and may be swayed by an argument. But once they render a judgment, they mean what they say and are prepared to follow through on their decision.

On the other hand, if Kids have learned that parents have a knee-jerk reaction to conflicts— "You heard me! I said no and I mean no! Why? Here's why: because I say so!"—they're likely to dig in their heels and produce major rebellion. If they have learned that parents are inconsistent and wishy-washy, they show this by smart-alecky behavior, lying, sneaking, and in general by demonstrating that they don't take parents' opinions—much less their demands—seriously.

For parents to earn Kids' respect, they need to have a rock-stable core of beliefs that won't be shaken. They also, however, need to recognize that many areas of life aren't bound by these beliefs and are negotiable. They need to know which is which.

For instance: the core belief is that Kids must tell the truth about important subjects. However,

Kids may keep secrets, have a private life, and tell white lies. Another example: the core belief is that Kids must follow important rules of safety. They must let parents know where they will be, what they will be doing, and with whom at all times. However, curfews, permissions to attend parties and sleepovers, and what types of activities are allowed are negotiable. A third example: the core belief is that Kids must not engage in aggressive behavior—behavior whose point is to harm someone else. However, Kids may fight to defend themselves or others, be assertive in getting what they want, and show anger—even indulge in temper tantrums that don't injure others emotionally or physically.

For parents to earn the respect and obedience of Kids this age, they need to demonstrate not just their ability to set and enforce a limit, but to debate issues that are negotiable. In the first example, such negotiable issues might include: the privacy of a Kid's room, a Kid's style of dress or haircut, the use of the telephone, choice of friends. In the second example, negotiable items might include what kinds of parties, movies, music, sports a Kid might engage in. In the third, matters for debate might be what kind of langage a Kid may use in anger, what kind of behavior he or she may exhibit in a temper tantrum, what kind of physical fighting defines roughhousing as opposed to aggression or bullying.

Parents get points every time they listen to the Kid's point of view, every time they nod and say "I see your point" or "You've made a case for that, all right" or "Well. You've changed my mind about that."

You might think it would work the other way around, that the more parents allow debate—the more they allow themselves to be swayed—the more power they give away. Not so.

It's as if Kids say to themselves: "Most of the time, Mom and Dad really try to see where I'm coming from. They pay attention to how important this stuff is to me. They are on my side, and

they change their minds whenever they can. They are rational beings and treat me like a rational being. So when they say Absolutely No or You Absolutely Have To, I know they've stretched themselves to the limit and that's it. I know that they respect me. In return, I'll accept their ultimatums. I am pleased and relieved that they care enough about me and about their standards to say No now and then. I may grumble and cast exasperated looks and sigh exasperated sighs or even slam the door and throw myself on the bed and scream, but I'll respect their decision and live with it."

If this style of discipline evolves during these years, adolescence is much, much more rewarding. Face it: you can't force adolescents to obey. They have too strong an urge towards self-definition and too many opportunities to escape parental control. Your only hope for adolescence lies in having the Kid *want* your trust, respect, and affection.

Here's a typical issue. Taylor (either sex) wants to go to a boy-girl party. From what you have overheard, you suspect that this is not an ordinary boy-girl party with rowdiness, kissing games, athletic dancing, and lots of food. This is more likely to feature older kids, serious necking, forbidden music, R-rated videos. There might even be smoking, alcohol, and who knows what else.

If Taylor and you have a backlog of negotiated requests, in which you have listened to Taylor's point of view and given in on a number of items such as hair style, clothing, the state of Taylor's bedroom, and so on, you are in a strong position to say no to this party.

Here is what works:
• Even though you have already firmly made up your mind, listen to Tayor's case. Give the request the same careful consideration you have given all the others. Ask questions. The more discussion before you render a decision, the better. You might say you need time to think the matter over thoroughly. Don't ridicule

or become angry at Taylor for making such an outrageous request in the first place.

- When you give your decision, make your statement brief, firm, and to the point. "I am sorry to disappoint you, but the answer is No. This party sounds as if it is going to violate all the standards I believe in." Period. Don't make preemptive statements: "If you try to sneak out of the house..." Don't assume you can read Taylor's mind: "I know you're going to have a fit about this, but..." Don't go on and on: "The music...The kids who will be there...Maybe even drugs..."
- Allow Taylor to be furious. Maintain a quiet, firm aura of certainty. Nothing shakes you. If a tantrum ensues, that's the breaks. Of course, it needs to stay within whatever rules have been set for tantrums—for instance, no cursing, no breaking things.
- After it is over, let Taylor come to terms with how friends are informed and what alternative plans should be made. Don't apologize, beg for forgiveness, prostrate yourself with guilt and sympathy, or go out of your way to produce an activity to compensate for the loss of the party.
- Whatever you do, don't weaken or change your mind.
- Don't bring it up again unless Taylor does. Don't let Taylor overhear you discussing the episode. Don't tell anyone about it who is going to tell Taylor you are obsessing over it.

BUT IS IT EVER ANY FUN?

You bet.

I hear it every day. "This is the very best time I've had being a parent." "I just love this age." "The neatest thing is, I keep getting flashbacks of how I was at that age and how my parents drove me nuts. I have to say, I think I'm doing it better." "He's just hilarious. Cal, do your imitation of that Bud Lite ad." "So I taught the whole crew the hand-jive to 'Gonna get along without you now.' It brought me right back to fifth grade gym class and those horrid little

green suits." "We talk about anything. I tell you, you're going to be voting for him—or against him—in about fifteen years."

The key to having fun is to allow change, relish it. Spread around any burdens: call in your friends to serve as listeners and mentors; your pediatrician to advise on weird episodes, physical symptoms, and atypical social behaviors; your religious mentors to help with questions about morals and ethics. Share all of it with the other parent and your spouse, whether or not that's one and the same person. Get to really know the parents of your Kids' friends. Take your Kid's teacher a gift of homemade brownies in exchange for an informal five minutes of his or her take on how your Kid is doing.

Use everything in your armory as a parent to keep your child attached by a wing or a prayer to home base: family celebrations, rituals, vacations. Keep up the hugs, the pats, the neck rubs—but not in public. Try not to terminally embarrass your child by using intimate language in public (including both compliments and put-downs), looking "weird"—whatever that means for his or her group, or horning in on the children's business unasked.

Here is a law of nature. No parent is able to do everything just right for a child this age. You are supposed to make a number of mistakes. This is really crucial for your child's development: one of the main things children this age are supposed to learn is that being an adult doesn't mean you have to be perfect.

If it did, who'd ever want to grow up?

Growth of the Soul

As noted in **Overview of the Age** at the beginning of this chapter, the land of the rolling eyeballs is dangerous territory for parents and Kids nine, ten, and eleven.

For instance, if Dayla's mother's mood had been grim rather than jolly, she might well have winced as Dayla commandeered her car. Her cute little girl has been replaced by this large, odorous, loud, critical person who sneaks her cologne and says she looks like a bug. With a shudder, she can just envision the day at the zoo, and her heart goes out to Mrs. Donaldson.

In a truly grim mood, Dayla's mother might confess that at that particular moment she can't stand her daughter, can't stand her daughter's friends, and would dearly love to throw up her hands—or just throw up—and not interact at all. If those moments add up, Dayla and her mom are in trouble.

Isn't this conflict between Kids and parents supposed to happen later, in adolescence? In fact, the ages of nine, ten, and eleven are crucial for what *will* happen during adolescence. During the years just following this period, many Kids truly grow apart from their families. They even seem to lose a part of their own authentic selves.

Mary Pipher, a psychologist who is the author of *Reviving Ophelia: Saving the Selves of Adolescent Girls* (Putnam, 1994) has noted that many girls change dramatically from about eleven to thirteen; they become subdued and lose their self-assurance. At the same time, many of these girls become angry at their mothers. They pick fights with them, push them away, and ignore them. Perhaps most worrisome to loving parents, they reject their family's moral values. Being an adult, in the eyes of these girls, is what the media says it is: adults have sex, smoke, drink, and party.

Pipher believes that the problem is cultural: that the mean halls of junior high lack civilized qualities and that the media have taken over children's minds. She believes that girls are angry at their mothers for having deceived them: for having raised them with values that are disregarded and mocked as the girls grow into adolescence. Puberty and entering junior high, with its highly sexualized teenage culture, makes for too steep a learning curve, she believes. Girls need a respite from it all and skills to handle their maturing selves.

However, by the time most girls enter Junior High, they are well into puberty. Many of them will have reached adult height and will have begun menstrual periods, some as early as Fourth Grade. While most boys are only starting puberty by Sixth Grade, they too have been affected by the maturing of their female classmates. Mood swings, increased ability to reason and argue, grown-up bodies, the influence of peers: The change in how Kids relate to parents starts now, not in middle school.

From watching so many children grow up, I am convinced that this cruel kind of divorce between youngster and parents can be prevented when parents are sensitive to how children change in these years from nine to twelve. Parents can prepare their Kids and themselves for the rigors of the adolescent years. When they do, they ensure, as much as possible, a mutually respectful and even enjoyable relationship with their children in the teenage years and beyond. The bottom line is that this is the only way parents in our culture can continue to be a moral force in the lives of their children when the Kids are growing up and grown-up (see box, **Looking Ahead to Adolescence,** page 159).

One of the most subtle but crucial parts of this growing and changing is learning a different stance when talking with older children about moral issues that occur outside the family, i.e., in their peer groups. The change in the parental role is an enormous one. In order to retain their moral influence, they must discard intrusive moral judgment and focus instead on helping their Kids reach moral clarity.

Up until Kids reach this age, parents have been the ultimate source for children's ideas of what is good and bad, right and wrong, appropriate and inappropriate. Younger Kids recognize parental authority. They don't question the source of the authority; they just question how it is used. "That's not fair. You make me do all the work" or "You like Kevin more than you

LOOKING AHEAD TO ADOLESCENCE

What To Do Now That Will Help Later
• Talk and listen in a way that's increasingly more grown-up, more the way you'd talk with an adult friend. Watch out for tendencies to tune out, interrupt, or jump in with criticism, unasked for praise, or solutions.
• Share impersonal areas of interest, so that your youngster doesn't think that you are constantly "on my case" and does think that you regard him or her as having an opinion worth soliciting.
• Let your child know that you think he or she is cute, attractive, funny. Pat the shoulder, ruffle the hair, give quick hugs, look at him or her with love and pride. Laugh at his jokes or at least react in some way—wince, clutch your forehead, pretend to throw up.
• Help your youngster find a best friend.
• Help your youngster to find and become accomplished at something that he or she will be able to pursue right through adolescence: a passionate interest, a hobby, a sport, a skill—music, art, dance.

like me. You let him get away with everything."

Older Kids reject your very right to exert authority. They don't argue like younger children. They say things like: "That's none of your business." "I don't care. I'm going to do it my way." "You can't make me." If they're polite, they may just say, "Oh honestly, Dad. You just don't understand."

There is a kernel of truth in every one of these statements. The world of peers *is* a separate place from the adult world. Children in that separate world *do* have to make their own decisions and act on them. Parents have very little say in what Kids do in that world, and they often don't understand the relationships, reputations, code of behavior, and all the subtleties that go into a child's decision.

Kids want their parents to help them make sense of moral dilemmas. Kids who suspect that their parents don't care how they behave in their world of peers feel unparented. Parents who do care, and who care enough to take on this new role, are saying to their Kids: "I can help you examine this problem so that you can come to a decision that makes you think well of yourself. That's my job. After all, I'm a grown up."

All parents want to be heroes to their Kids. They do this not so much by what they achieve

in the big world, but by helping their children to feel like heroes to themselves: people who can see what is right, can find it in themselves to do it, and can feel as if they did it on their own—not because their parents or anyone else was calling the shots.

The land of the rolling eyeballs is full of moral dilemmas. When Kids feel comfortable talking about them, they do so constantly, though often that talk is camouflaged as bragging, recounting anecdotes, or asking permission.

"I can't stand that Judith. She is such a snob. I can't wait not to ask her to my birthday party. I'm going to pass out invitations at recess and she won't get one. Neener neener."

"I don't get why Ben thought it was so neat to tease the llama. I think it's so mean, he threw ice cubes at him and the llama got frantic and spitted and danced around. And everybody laughed. Ben said that it was okay because it didn't really hurt and besides it was hot and the llama needed to cool off. I hate Ben."

"Jason's dad says everybody should have a gun. He's got a whole big collection. Jason got a beebee gun for his birthday and we're going to go and shoot at targets, okay? With his dad? His dad hunts deer and stuff. He says the deer would starve anyway. Shooting deer isn't like shooting people, is it?"

"Every single year the whole class just gangs up against Georgianne. Ever since first grade. They'd tag her and then run after you and wipe their hand on you and say, 'Yuck! You've got Georgianne on you!' So today Miss Hughes had to go to the office and so Jenna poured water on Georgianne's seat while she was at the resource booth. So she came back and sat in it and then the Kids said she wet her pants. I thought it was so mean. She looked awful, but I didn't know what to do."

The rush to soothe, judge, advise, command, and otherwise lift the moral burden from the child's shoulders can be intense. The hardest thing in the world is just to sit there and listen and ask questions, but it is what children in this situation need. It's the process of helping your child come to moral clarity, not the conclusion, that's key.

Conversing with older Kids about right and wrong requires sensitivity, caution, and courage, just like dancing with wolves. Pediatricians are like camera crews: we get to witness on a daily basis how parents give helpful feedback to youngsters this age—supporting their good instincts, causing them to think again about poor ones, stretching them morally and intellectually, having fun with them. We also get to record how things go wrong.

Lots of things can derail this important parental function.

• Kids may not talk, and it's very difficult to give feedback to a stone wall.
• Giving feedback means just that: not hovering and interfering, not lecturing or admonishing or preaching, not accusing or criticizing. It means feeding back to the youngster the worry you sense in his or her account of the situation—clarifying it, defining it, fleshing it out. This is never easy.
• Kids this age are very sensitive to interruptions, unsuccessful attempts at humor, and other conversational glitches.
• Parents and children sometimes mean different things by the words they use. For instance, children this age do not accurately understand probability terms such as likely to, might, certainly, probably, possibly, perhaps.
• The parent may have a different way of reasoning about the issue than a child. The difference may be individual or related to whether parent and child are of the same sex or not.
• When what is right goes against what the group says, does, or thinks, deciding how to behave becomes an issue of moral courage. If the question is one of safety, parents have no choice but to issue an ultimatum if the youngster cannot come to the right decision about how to act. But if the issue is one of justice, kindness, and decency, parents can only help clarify the issue and trust the child's ability to decide what to do. If the youngster takes the unpopular stand, that youngster needs support and reassurance. If he or she ducks out, parents need to find a way to show they understand the temptation to do so without condoning the decision.

GETTING KIDS TO TALK

For all the talking Kids do, they can give away remarkably little about their inner lives.

MAKING IT SAFE TO TALK

Children often keep mum about the important issues for the following reasons.

If a child thinks that the parent's identity is shaky

Children can be very sensitive. They will hold off "bothering" a parent who has just been divorced, lost a job, or suffered a similar blow to ego and integrity.

If a child suspects that the parent has blended parent-child identities

> "Julie's such a gorgeous child, the essence of grace. I just delight in her beauty every minute of the day."

> "Jason's a natural athlete. It makes me feel terrific to watch him play—it kind of makes up for my klutzy youth."

Perhaps the discovery that Julie is not popular will devastate Mom. Perhaps the discovery that Jason is being bullied will devastate Dad.

If a child believes that the problem is one that reflects ill on the parent

If your mother or father has always given you to understand that it's your job to be happy and that if you are unhappy, that means that parents have failed, you are unlikely to confide your misery about anything. If your mother or father is unable to help you look, dress, do things the way your friends do, you are not likely to berate them for their failure. Did Georgianne tell her parents of her pilloried existence? I doubt it.

If a child believes that parent and child have switched roles

A single parent, especially, may fall into the trap of turning a child this age into a pseudo-spouse, pseudo-co-parent, or even pseudo-lover. When this happens, the youngster may not feel entitled to assume his or her true, childhood identity. If a child seems to be listening a lot and offering sympathy and advice, it may be that roles have become confused.

If there's a family secret

When there's trouble at home like alcoholism, incest, drugs, mental illness, children may well feel that their small problems don't deserve parental time and attention.

Timing

Good timing means not instigating a delicate conversation when parent or child is ravenous, exhausted, in such a bad mood that he or she can barely make eye contact, rushed, or feeling brain dead. If a conversation derails because of any of these or other conditions, it's the parent's job to save the situation. "Abort! Abort! This is mission control. This conversation will have to continue at another time due to technical difficulties."

For instance, right after picking a Kid up from friends is often a hard time to initiate a serious talk; he or she is likely to stay in a performing mode for a while. It generally takes time for a Kid to switch gears. If Dayla's mother had tried to bring up the subject of what the girls in the john were saying about bras, for instance, she would have gotten—you guessed it: the exasperated sigh and the rolling eyeballs.

When it's not the parent but the child who instigates the conversation, however, that timing usually needs to be honored. Once a Kid gets up the courage to spill the beans about a troubling issue, parents do well to slow down and listen, laying aside personal discomfort or urgencies. Children this age don't do well being put on hold.

Radar

> "I feel like scum because I didn't step in to help Georgianne."

> "I was terribly mean on purpose to Jerry and made him cry."

> "Mr. Hamilton put his hand on my breast during my music lesson."

You are not likely to hear any of these sentences issue from a Kid's mouth. Instead, you might get:

"I felt so bad for Georgianne, but I didn't know what to do."

"That Jerry is such a whuzz. He's a gutless wonder."

"I can't stand that Mr. Hamilton. I don't want to take piano anymore."

You need radar and a secret decoder ring, which unfortunately you cannot get by sending in boxtops. Kids who have a guilty, sad, scary, or otherwise upsetting story to tell tend to reveal this in body language. They tear up, flush, fight, fidget, spend a lot of time in their rooms. Their tone changes when they come to the important part. There's more emotion in their voices that their words appear to warrant.

When they do say something, they expect parents to know exactly what they are trying to say and to respond with precisely the right combination of sympathy, attention, and support. This expectation, which generally goes unrealized, can lead to a fight.

A safe response, generally, is a look of expectant interest, featuring eye contact and some indication that you are going to slow down your present activity in the interests of paying attention. Actually stopping what you're doing may be too threatening. Pull over to the right-hand lane, put down the cookbook and just stir the stew, turn the TV down but not off, leave the buzz saw alone and do a little sanding.

Listening

When Kids talk with their very best friends, they don't often hurt each others' feelings. Parents aren't and shouldn't be best friends, but they can learn from the way best friends tend to listen to each other.

Act interested

Dayla's mother listens intently to the story of the trip to the zoo, making appropriate comments like "Poor Mrs. Donaldson!" and "So Carmen threw up. How distressing." Dayla reg-isters her mother's attentive stance with relief and gratitude.

In this first rendition of her afternoon, Dayla represents herself as the innocent bystander, one of many victimized by the actions of Ben and Matthew. In reality, Dayla herself laughed at Ben's harassment of the llama. Her excuse at the time was that: a) her friends were watching; and b) she "likes" Matthew and wanted him to be jealous of her attentions to Ben.

She would dearly like the relief of confession. Her heart breaks for the llama. Her mother's interest makes it easier for her to bring up the subject again later, when she's ready to face her feelings.

Interrupt sparingly and keep the focus on the child

You can interrupt an Eight without any effect at all. Eight stops, listens to you with mouth open, and then goes right on where he or she had left off. Older children take interruptions personally. They tend to assume that you are interrupting because you are bored or because you want to make a point of your own. Either way, this annoys them and makes them surly and uncommunicative.

Adults are allowed to interrupt "briefly." The interruption ought to register sympathy and support. If the conversation is an emotional one about sibling sins, for instance, far better to say something like, "I used to get furious at your Uncle Will for exactly the same reason" than to go into a detailed story of that time at the community pool when Uncle Will put on your swim top with tennis balls in the cups.

On the other hand, sometimes youngsters almost ask to be interrupted. They'll be talking along, then come to a point where they hesitate, swallow, rush, or stumble over a phrase or sentence, then march on again. That's often a signal to a parent that this particular part of the narrative is, to the youngster, the point of the whole thing. A good way to check this out is to wait for a stopping place, and then say, "You seemed uncomfortable when you mentioned [whatever it was]."

Giving feedback

The goal of giving feedback is to have the Kid reflect on his or her own interpretation of what happened. This means asking questions for information, not to place blame. "So nobody tried to make Jenna stop?" instead of "You mean you just stood there and *watched*? You didn't do a *thing*? You let her keep tormenting that poor child?"

Suppose Marcie says, "It's Georgianne's own fault. She acts like everybody's going to be mean. That's why everybody acts mean to her." That needs countering.

> "How do you think you might act if Kids ran around wiping their hands on you and yelling, 'I've got Marcie on me! Yuck!' or played jokes about wetting your pants? Don't you think you might get the feeling that everybody's likely to be mean to you?"

Suppose Marcie changes the subject right away. "Mom, don't you think we should make some brownies for dinner? We haven't had any in a long time." You can steer her back to the painful subject at the same time that you recognize her need for a treat.

> "Sweetie, I haven't seen you so upset in a long time. Sure we'll make brownies. But let's talk about Georgianne for a little bit."

Suppose Marcie can see only two courses of action, each of which is dreadful: befriending Georgianne all by herself, with its heavy social costs, or doing nothing, with its heavy moral costs. She needs to realize that there's no need for such draconian measures.

> "Marcie, if you're this upset, don't you think that Ginger is too? She's such a

good friend. Why don't we call her and ask? Maybe the two of you could get a group together to help Georgianne."

> "I'll bet your teacher doesn't even know this is going on. How about if we go together and talk with Miss Hayes about it? She's supposed to be one of the kindest and most experienced fifth grade teachers in the district."

Speak the same language

Speaking the same language doesn't mean that parents should imitate, like, you know, the way the Kid, you know, speaks.

In fact, most children respond well to a polite request to remember that they are talking to a member of a different generation. For one thing, it makes them feel rather superior.

> "It hurts my feelings when you put something down with the adjective 'old.' I feel all my grey hairs stand right up on end."

One particular glitch can cause more than conversational bumpiness. Children right through the teenage years tend to misconstrue words of chance. For example, when an adult says, "She'll probably get caught one of these days" the adult generally means "the chances are about eight out of ten that she'll get caught." A child might construe "probably" as "about four or five out of ten."

The same thing holds for all those words: might, possibly, likely, certain to, and so on. If an adult wants to make an important point, a warning, a serious prediction, it's better to avoid using these terms.

Give support

Suppose Marcie decides that she is too afraid of Jenna, too put off by Georgianne herself, and too untrusting of the class as a whole, to act in any way on Georgianne's behalf. Should you show your disappointment? Your relief?

What is most likely to help Marcie grow in this situation is to help her to frame her own decision, pointing out the reasons that she has decided not to act. "What would have to happen for any of these things to change?" Marcie may not be able to answer that right away, but the chances are good that the question will keep popping into her mind, perhaps paving the way to allowing her to assert her convictions.

Suppose Marcie does decide to confront Jenna's terrorism. Should you dissuade her? Point out that getting at least one ally is more likely to succeed? Get her to consider the possible outcomes?

It's hard to know how much to protect a child. However, when the issue is the child's moral courage, parents do well to consider the benefits of giving the child a proud smile, a pat on the back, and a forceful "Good for you! You've got guts! I'm with you every step of the way!" This means standing by Marcie with pride and support and even counseling, if necessary, as she confronts evil in fifth grade.

There may not be a happy ending, at least not right away. Marcie may buckle under. Jenna may become even more tyrannical. Even if Marcie succeeds beyond her wildest dreams and rescues Georgianne and lifts her to newfound popularity, Georgianne may herself turn terrorist and attack her savior. It's been known to happen.

If all this sounds exhausting, take heart. This is what you will look back on, with pride and self-congratulation, in a decade or two.

Make moral discussions seem adult

When you're engaging in such discussion with an older Kid, you're paving the way to a more grown-up relationship in the adolescent years. That's when parents and children need as much neutral territory on which to interact as possible. Neutral territory is turf where neither parent nor child is being judged, but

both parties can talk about issues of right and wrong.

When every moral conversation is focused on Kids' dilemmas, youngsters may well sense an atmosphere of condescension and begin to back off such discussions. Some older Kids will detect their parents' technique of giving them feedback, catch them at it, and rebel. "You sound like a shrink!" an Eleven I know rebuked his father. "Be real!"

What helps to counter such acute perceptions in older Kids is to make such conversations seem part of normal adult life.

Initiate and welcome talk about impersonal topics

Nines, Tens, and Elevens can talk about just about anything. Bringing up political, scientific, theological, and cultural topics honors them with the belief that their opinions are worth soliciting. This can make them more likely to offer their own observations:

> "Jury trials can't tell what the truth is. They just tell who argued better, the defense or the prosecution."

> "I don't get why every year there's a new car model. Why can't they make it perfect the first time? It's not as if they really change anything basic. Just how it looks and stuff."

> "Why is it white people think black people aren't as good but white people are always trying to get a suntan, even though that gives people cancer?"

When talking about impersonal topics, the rules for conversing with Kids can be a lot looser. In the heat of a good argument, interrupting, making firm opinionated statements, and disagreeing with force don't quench a Kid's enthusiasm but fire it. The only caveat: disagreeing with opinions is allowed, but accusing the other person of stupidity or other mental or emotional flaws is not.

Humor: Use it don't abuse it

This is no doubt the age that gave "Kidding" its name. For the first time, children "get" adult humor. No longer does a sense of humor necessarily mean acting silly, telling jokes, or even laughing. If you had the time and the incentive, you could chart Kids as they discover the ingredients: incongruity, surprise, irony. Of course, they can't get the hang of it earlier. If you don't know what's normal, how can you spot incongruity. If you haven't experienced enough of the predictable, how can you be surprised. If you don't understand that somebody's motives can be at odds with their actions, how can you appreciate irony.

Being funny can rescue a million dicey situations. You can get your mother to behave herself in front of your peers by joking that somebody thinks she looks like a bug in her high-fashion sunglasses. You can pretend to think it's perfectly normal when your father discovers a moldy Halloween pumpkin under your bed in April; and the humor of your underreaction saves you a scolding. When your choleric grandfather is about to explode at a rude driver, you can pick up the garage-door opener and zap the guy, saving Grandpa from at least a near stroke.

You can talk about puberty if you figure out how to be funny. Nanette's doctor told her and her mother that puberty often starts with a breast bud, a lump under one nipple "the size of a jelly bean." Now Nanette and her mother break up at any reference to jelly beans. Since this was under the reign of President Reagan, they had giggles galore.

Sarcasm ain't humor, at least not in the view of children this age. Sarcasm cuts right into a Kid's self-esteem. It can make an enemy, sometimes for a long, long time.

Recognize philosophical differences

One of the most valuable lessons Kids this age can learn is that well-meaning people can approach a dilemma from at least two equally honorable but opposite points of view.

For instance, boys and men—as a group, not as individuals—tend to see more situations as impersonal than do girls and women. When they judge a situation, they tend to do so by the guidelines of law and order. Girls and women tend to see those same situations as involving individuals, people who are connected and bonded to each other. They tend to make judgments that take all the factors into account and search for an answer that may bypass law and order (see box, **Different Voices**, page 184).

Marcie's mother hears about Georgianne, and thinks: Georgianne—isn't she that thin little girl who's always smiling and trying to fade into the scenery? What a horror! Call the teacher? The principal? Children's Protective Services? Who is this Jenna? That girl who dressed up as a hooker at Halloween? Her family must take some kind of award for dysfunction. Maybe she's even abused.

What on earth should I advise Marcie to do? Adopt Georgianne and be saddled with a child who needs much more than a 10-year-old can give? And most likely be shunned by her friends—whispered about, hair pulled, not sat with at lunch or on the school bus? Then there's that dreadful Jenna. Sounds maddened with power. Liable to do anything. But I certainly can't tell Marcie just to stand by and let this persecution continue. Should I call Jenna's mother? Or Georgianne's?

Marcie's father hears and thinks: What a bunch of little monsters. Boy, I can remember at that age. Somebody had better knock some sense of fairness into them. What's the teacher's name again? Miss Hayes. She ought to call a class meeting. I bet there's some kind of school code about this stuff. They should suspend the Kids who can't behave. How do they expect Kids to grow up into decent citizens if the schools don't take a stand on this kind of terrorism. Thank God Marcie knows what's right and wrong, but it isn't fair

DIFFERENT VOICES

How Kids Decide Right and Wrong

How children come to moral conclusions is a fairly new area of research started by the famous developmentalist Piaget, who began investigating this question in the mid-sixties. Most of the studies have focused on how children think and behave in a laboratory setting when either answering questions or reacting to a posed situation. Of course, it's hard to catch children in the wild, so to speak. You'd have to dress up as a 10-year-old or bug the school bathrooms or something.

Based on the studies, it appears that children go through developmental stages in moral thinking, just as they do intellectually and physically. Moral ideas start out primitive and become more sophisticated as children learn more about the world, think more about justice and equality, and experience the conflict between compassion and self-interest.

For several decades, many experts accepted a model that showed that boys tend to advance to the highest stage of moral development and girls tend to stay stranded on the lowest rung. This model came out of the work of psychologist Lawrence Kohlberg and his colleagues. According to Kohlberg and company, the most primitive ("preconceptual") level is thinking about right and wrong in terms of the (mostly) physical consequences to yourself. "Don't steal your sister's diary. She'll get mad and scream at you and slap your hand."

At the next level ("conventional"), an action is judged by whether it's good for society or not. The golden rule applies at this stage. "Don't steal your sister's diary. After all, you wouldn't want anybody to steal your stuff." Law and order is a consequence of applying the golden rule. "It's against the law to steal."

The highest level ("postconventional") means that the golden rule is modified by a concern for individual rights and justice. At the postconventional level, a law may be seen as wrong in a particular situation if a higher moral principle is at stake. "Steal your sister's diary to show to your parents. You need to convince them that she is very depressed and thinking of committing suicide." At this level, justice is omniscient and takes into account anything that makes circumstances unequal.

Then, in 1982, psychologist Carol Gilligan published *In a Different Voice*, describing a theory of female morality that is based on the work of psychologist Nancy Chodorow. Gilligan suggested that girls are not primitive in their ideas of morality; they just have a different way of thinking. It's so different, Gilligan says, that when you give a girl and a boy the same moral dilemma with a set of solutions to choose from, the girl's sophisticated reasoning may give the same solution as the boy's very primitive reasoning.

Gilligan's theory is that female morality is based on reasoning that places the highest value on interconnectedness and caring. There are three stages in this morality, as well.

• In the first stage, the caring applies only to oneself: don't get into trouble with somebody else. It's like the first stage of the Kohlberg theory. "Don't steal your sister's diary. She'll get mad at you and scream and slap your hand."

• In the second stage, caring focuses on other people only: self-sacrifice is the watchword of this stage. "Steal your sister's diary to show to your parents. So what if you destroy your relationship and you feel terrible about it. You need to convince them that she is very depressed and considering suicide."

• The third stage includes everybody, including oneself, in the caring. "Don't steal your sister's diary. She'll get mad at you and scream and slap your hand and she won't trust you any more.

There's a better way. Talk to her and convince her to get help for her depression."

So when you ask a morally *immature* boy and a morally *mature* girl whether or not to steal a sister's diary in order to get her psychiatric help, you may get the same answer unless you are very careful how you phrase your question.

The idea that these are competing male and female notions of morality appealed to many people for lots of different reasons, as you might imagine. Further research, however, makes it seem likely that there isn't any real gender difference in morality. Boys and men can reason morally using caring and interrelatedness as a standard, and girls and women can reason morally using justice and equality before the law as a standard. However, it may be that girls and women see interrelatedness in situations in which men don't. At any rate, these are both valid ways of approaching moral dilemmas.

for her to have to take on this mess on her own. The problem's with the institution.

No wonder that Marcie's conversation with her mother is likely to bear little similarity to her talk with her dad. If all three talked together, the adults could point out that each is coming from a different, valid point of view. Marcie could see both sides and start the adult work of balancing, choosing, and integrating them.

EMOTIONAL AND SOCIAL DEVELOPMENT

Feeling good about oneself during these years can be pretty tricky. Too many things tend to be out of control.

First, of course, there's puberty. Most girls and some boys will begin puberty at nine, ten, and eleven, so it's safe to say that at this age either you're starting puberty, in the midst of it, or watching other people experience it. No matter what your condition, there's something to wonder, worry, feel self-conscious, and be ambivalent about. People may think you are either much older or much younger than you really are. Some days you don't even know what age you "really" are, yourself.

Second, there's the world of peers. In that world, you have a reputation: you're popular or you're accepted or you're ignored or you're rejected. How your peers think of you can be confusing, exhilarating, worrying, and heart-breaking. If you aren't popular, it rarely occurs to you that there is something wrong with the other Kids; you assume that there must be something wrong with *you*. Even if you change your behavior in a way that *ought* to bring you more friends, your reputation may get in the way.

Third, there's the withdrawal from parents and family. Part of you wants to stay a child, part of you wants to grow up. Your parents, too, often seem to want to keep you a child and to have you grow up simultaneously. The problem is, your parents want you to stay a child in the very areas in which you want to grow up (like shaving your legs or roller-blading to school); and they want you to grow up in the very areas you want to remain a child (like not being given so many chores).

The job Kids expect their parents to perform is extremely challenging. Parents are supposed to stay the same toward you—find you cute, protect you, guide you, keep you in line. At the same time, they are supposed to change dramatically: give you more freedom, let you take risks, support your autonomy, allow you to make your own decisions.

It can be done. However, no parent can or should do this perfectly. For a child to have some sensation of growth, there has to be some conflict, pain, and hurt feelings for everybody.

Worries

The first job of parents is to make sure that children know what to expect of their bodies. (See **Growth,** page 224.) No matter how much a child knows from conversation or from books, all Kids this age still worry:

> "I know you said that one breast bud starts first. But when does the other one start? I got this one on December 11 and it's February 8 and nothing is happening."

> "When are you supposed to start wearing a bra and how come? Is it to keep you from sagging, or jiggling, or what?"

> "I am the shortest boy in the entire fifth grade. Actually, I am the shortest boy in the entire fourth and fifth grades put together. I suspect that I might be a pituitary dwarf. I looked it up on the CD-ROM encyclopedia."

> "Dr. Nathanson! Dr. Nathanson! Help! There's hair growing on my toes!"

These are just the questions that unusually self-confident, trusting children are able to utter. Many other questions go unspoken: they are too scary to ask.

Parents should be honored if their 9- through 11-year-olds ask them such questions, but shouldn't feel shut out and dishonored if they don't. Many children are exceedingly private on these matters. That privacy has many, many roots other than embarrassment and worry, including a sense of wonder and of ownership. There is also superstition—if I worry out loud that I'll never get breasts, I'll make it come true. There's even a particular kind of concentration that is sort of like body English—If I focus really hard on growing, I'll make six feet.

If a question does pop out, the most important thing is to let the child know that the question itself is perfectly normal. This is much more important than knowing the correct answer. Even if the question is very scary, it helps a child immensely if a parent stays calm and in control. The same is true if parents observe something that worries or scares them.

> "She hasn't even started having breast development, but she already is bleeding. Can it be a period? Or could she have a tumor or something?" (It's quite likely to be normal, but needs checking out.)

> "He's got one side of the testicles hanging down lower than the other." (The right side almost always is lower.)

> "She's got things hanging down between her legs, they just don't look right! What could it be!" (Probably, normal labia minora—the inner lips or labia of the vagina sometimes respond to estrogen before anything else does.)

Children in this kind of situation have two fears: of being found abnormal and of having someone look at their body. Therefore, the parental reaction that scares them most is a worried look or expression followed by the dreaded words, "We'd better have the pediatrician take a look at that."

Of course, that is the natural parental response. But there is often an alternative. A parent could also say, "You know, puberty is so individual. Everybody does it differently. I'll just give the pediatrician a ring and run it by him/her." To which, bet on it, your youngster will say: "Well, okay, but don't tell the doctor that you're talking about *me*." To which you answer, "No! Of course not!"

Most often, your pediatrician will want to see the child. Persuading Nine, Ten, and Eleven to come in for any puberty-related issue, even for the routine checkup, can be a job and a half. Sometimes it helps to bring along a best friend. Sometimes it helps for the doctor to speak to the child over the phone before the appointment.

If you are visiting for a puberty-related problem, I suggest you prepare a couple of notes. The first is for the office staff:

> "Jessica is here for a problem related to puberty. She's very embarrassed. Please don't ask why she's here or make any reference to it. If possible, please don't ask her to put on a paper gown."

Kids this age tend to hate paper gowns. They feel like sick people in them, and the gowns are always too small, or tear, or gape. So suggest that your youngster wear loose, easily removed or lifted clothing.

The second is for the doctor.

> "Jessica is here because of [whatever it is. Be specific. Even if you spoke with the doctor on the phone beforehand]. She's very embarrassed. If you think it is something abnormal, please tell her with me in the room or talk with me first. Even if it's not serious."

An astute, understanding pediatrician—who has enough time booked for the office visit—can give a lot of comfort simply by examining and naming what's going on.

> "Your breasts are developing perfectly normally. Many women have hair that grows around the nipple, the way you do; in a locker room in high school,

you'd see maybe one out of four girls are just the same."

> "It's perfectly normal for a boy to have an erection when he's anxious or when his penis gets touched, even by a doctor, even by a man doctor. It doesn't have anything to do at all with being sexually aroused."

> "I don't see any sign of puberty starting yet, and I wouldn't expect to. When I look at your parents' height, your mother's menstrual history, and your own growth chart and examination, I can predict you'll probably be about 5'9" as an adult. You'll probably start menstrual periods at about fourteen, and you'll probably start to develop breasts when you're about twelve."

If there is a deviation from normal, your pediatrician should give a full explanation, including a plan of action. Don't hesitate to ask questions. If your youngster is too tongue-tied to ask his or her own questions, ask them yourself. Remember that your child's great need is to find out whether he or she is normal. "Am I normal? If this is not normal, will I ever *be* normal?" So if he or she doesn't ask, *you* ask.

> "When you say that it's normal to have some vaginal discharge, do you really mean this much? So that she has to wear a pad in her panties?"

> "I guess you're saying that boys usually don't reach this stage of puberty until they're older, so we've got to check out this pubic hair and so on. What usually causes it? Is there any treatment for these conditions? If we didn't look into it, what could happen?"

Feelings

Since girls start puberty on the average a year or more earlier than boys, their parents are more likely to see moods increase in intensity and change rapidly. This may make some parents who have a boy and girl close in age jump to the conclusion that girls go bonkers during puberty and boys do not. Not so. Boys do it later and differently. They have mood swings, too. They may have more aggressive outbursts rather than fits of weeping. Not all hormonally influenced moods are negative, of course. Wild enthusiasm and euphoria are the flip side.

When a pubertal youngster is in the grip of hormones, he or she finds it very hard not to assign an external reason for the mood. It just seems so much more likely and dignified this way than to assign overwhelming emotion to hormones.

"I hate Miss Bosc! She always makes me sing alto in front of everybody!"

"Liver for dinner! Oh no! This terrible day! Everything is just awful!"

Slam!

When you're in the grip of that kind of thing, you depend on your parents not only to stand firm in the face of your outburst and not take it personally, but to behave in such a way that when you recover you don't have to be embarrassed.

Parents can facilitate the getting over of a mood.

Provide privacy

Ideally, of course, a mood requires a door to slam and a bed to fall upon, in a room that nobody else inhabits. A person in a mood needs to be able to pretend that either everybody hears him or her venting and feels sorry, or that nobody hears a thing, or both of the above simultaneously. If such a room, door, and bed do not exist, it's a great kindness to set aside some area of the home as a private place for your Kid. It can be called a work area or a private space or whatever, but should be inviolable. No siblings or adults should be allowed in without explicit permission.

Provide some dignity

Laughing at somebody in a mood is heartless on the part of a parent and could be dangerous. On the other hand, it's frightening if your family seems to take your moods too seriously. Certainly, a sibling shouldn't be punished for making nonhurtful but exasperated comments: "The time bomb's going off again." "Did you buy that stock in Kleenex, Dad?" But a parent? No.

Usually don't pry

If you've just had a fit of crying and pounding the walls and you can't really come up with a better reason than another page of math homework or a broken violin string or your frustrating magic trick, you just really don't want to go into it.

Far better to come out sniffing and red eyed and say, "I don't want to talk about it." That's your story and you're sticking to it. How nice when you don't have the feeling that everybody's been sitting around listening to your little fit and talking about you. How nice when your parents interrupt what they're doing only to give a friendly smile, a wink, a pat, and then steer the conversation to something else.

But pry when appropriate

Of course, there are some few occasions when you do want your parents to pry. If you are in real trouble or your friend is or you are frightened, you need your parents' guidance and support.

A youngster who is not in a hormonal mood but who has a real problem will almost always show it in between outburst behavior: withdrawing from activities, looking sad or angry most of the time, eating a lot more from apparent compulsion or a lot less, sleeping much more or much less, showing fears or phobias, having trouble with grades at school.

If you're in serious trouble, you need a parent who will find a time to take you aside and say something like,

> "I am worried that you seem so unhappy lately. I am sure that something is troubling you deeply. I need you to tell me what it is, so we can tackle it together. If you can't tell me, for any reason, I want you to think of whom you do want to talk to."

Once in awhile, the problem is not circumstances but a true biochemical mood disturbance, such as depression. If that's the case, a child is being accurate when he or she says, "Nothing's the matter." When a Kid is depressed—abnormal behavior lasts for more than two weeks without improvement—professional help is needed.

Sex

Children who have puberty early generally do not act out their sexual impulses with other people unless their culture encourages them to do so. The trick for parents is to make sure that Kids are not forced into sexual relationships that they are nowhere near ready to handle. There are several ways to help.

Just don't rush things

A Ten who is midway through puberty, as tall as her teacher and almost as developed, may still be attached to her dolls, stuffed animals, and model horses. She should be given all the time in the world, free of teasing or astonished or sarcastic comments, to grow into her body.

Rarely, parents actually seem to encourage or force children into a sexual culture. It's not a good idea to take youngsters to R-rated movies, to buy them make-up unasked, or to encourage anything that sounds like dating. A ten who "needs" a bra, but clearly believes her body "ought" not to could wear a sporty Kids' jogging top.

Once in a great while, a single parent may be tempted to regard a grown-up looking older Kid as having adult sexual impulses. This doesn't necessarily mean incestuous behavior! But it can mean assuming that the child is ready and able to hear about and even advise on a parent's own sexual interests. It may even mean thinking it is cute to double-date with the child and a friend of the opposite sex. This is highly confusing to children: it blurs boundaries and robs the youngster of parental authority. It's impossible to deal with a child as a sexual equal on the one hand and as a person upon whom you set limits and make demands, on the other.

Keep them busy

This good, old-fashioned advice for redirecting sexual energy still works.

For boys, male hormones increase the need to use one's body in a vigorous and even violent way. This isn't the same thing as aggression, which is acting with the desire to do harm. Boys with body-active mood swings are grateful to have activities that harness this energy for peaceful purposes. Active chores; aerobic activities like soccer, bike riding, skateboarding, roller-blading; strength-building activities like swimming; concentrated activities like karate; body contact activities like wrestling (not boxing) or roughhousing without real aggression—all help a boy this age cope with hormonal moods.

For girls, such unisex activities are equally welcome. They not only help temper mood swings, but help a girl to feel a sense of power and accomplishment. Traditionally feminine activities like dance can do the same thing.

Intellectual, artistic, and musical involvement can provide not just a focus that competes with hormonal impulses, but an arena for achievement and something to talk about on neutral turf with parents.

If your religion permits it, condone masturbation

From talking with many parents, worry about masturbation in pubertal children seems to focus on the idea that Kids might be using it to "practice" having sex with another person. Most often that's absolutely not the case. Most are simply continuing a long-term habit: Left to their own devices, children of all ages masturbate, even older infants and toddlers. A youngster who is tied in knots from a hormonal storm may find considerable comfort in masturbation and may seek that comfort almost absentmindedly, without even a fantasy of acting out sexual impulses with another person.

Expect crushes

Ah, the crush. Girls have crushes on girls. And on boys. Boys have crushes on boys. And on girls. Both have crushes on: teachers, coaches, dance teachers, music teachers, popular singers and musicians, movie actresses and actors, and on older Kids. A person in the grip of a crush is a lovely and pathetic sight.

Rarely is a crush acted on. Most crushes are not, or are only barely, requited. That's fine. The purpose of a crush is to expend a lot of energy safely. Group crushes do this most efficiently.

Expect dirty jokes

When a Kid this age tells a "dirty" joke, it's often just for the thrill of saying words or concepts out loud. It's not uncommon for the youngster not to get the point of the joke at all. In fact, many of these jokes are invented by the Kids themselves and actually have no point. They're just fooling around with words. A parent is expected to show mild exasperation and no shock at all.

Demeaning or cruel dirty jokes always deserve a parental put-down.

> "That's just ugly. It's not even remotely funny. You must have found it cluttering up your brain and needed to get rid of it. If you've got any more like that, I'll get a barf bag and the air spray."

Or, more seriously:

> "When people tell jokes like that, they get a reputation for being bigoted and racist (or sexist or whatever). I don't think you deserve that kind of reputation."

Encourage recreational reading

What, pray tell, does the Baby Sitter's Club or the Hardy Boys series have to do with sex? Not much! That's one of the reasons why the BSC and the HBS are so popular. If you're a Ten who's being buffeted about by hormonal winds, you can lose yourself in one after another novel in which the world is magically made innocent. It's a little vacation from puberty. Even comic books can serve this purpose. If you're desperate, the back of a cereal box will do. Reading works better than TV, because you can space out more easily, paying attention and daydreaming as it suits you.

NO PUBERTY YET

Most boys and a few girls won't start puberty until they're twelve or older. However, unless they fortuitously or on purpose are segregated from pubertal children, they too will be at least somewhat preoccupied with sexual issues. When you're a Kid who's still a child and some of your friends already are starting to look like teenagers, you can have any of several reactions—sequentially or simultaneously.

"Hurray! I'll never grow up!"

If the youngsters around you seem to be having a tough time with shooting up and developing, you may very well thank your lucky stars that you're "still little and don't have to think about sex," as one Nine told me.

For the vast majority of youngsters who wait until they're twelve and older to start puberty, this is a happy time, especially if they have plenty of activity and interests to involve them.

Boys who haven't started puberty may be

particularly girl-avoidant and regard the flirting of their classmates with undisguised hilarity and disgust. Girls may find the contrast with their developing peers rather scary and seek to differentiate themselves by accenting their lack of physical maturity. They may insist on unfashionable clothing, discover a new interest in traditionally boyish activities, and make fun of their developed classmates.

Once in awhile, a girl with a childlike appearance will become the mascot of more developed girls. This is often a symbiotic relationship, in which everyone uses the contrast to feel superior. This is all unworrying, for the most part. The role of parents is mostly to play along.

Rejecting puberty

If the world of teenagers and adults seems more threatening than welcoming, you may indulge in a wish/belief that you can bypass it altogether. This thought probably occurs to everybody this age at some point. It's a more forceful wish when a youngster truly feels ill-equipped to take on the future. The denial may come from a feeling of incompetence, lack of power, and poor self-esteem; it may stem from a specific problem such as a learning disability; or it may result from a family problem, in which the child believes that the stability of the family depends on him or her "staying little."

If a parent senses that a child has invested too much in the wish to remain childlike, it's important to get help. Signs would be: seeking out younger children; regressing in behavior; failing at school; demonstrating behavioral problems, such as aggression and oppositional behavior; and avoiding age-appropriate activities.

Rarely, the disorder anorexia nervosa can begin at this age, perhaps as an attempt to prevent or stop the earliest signs of puberty. A child who loses weight or fails to gain the expected normal amount, who seems to be obsessed with food but who eats little, who exercises compulsively, or who considers normal or slender weight as "too fat" needs prompt pediatric and psychological evaluation.

PEERS

Fourth, fifth and sixth grades are a complex and subtle social world. Brave adults (developmental psychologists) who have gone into this world as anthropologists have come up with interesting findings, most of which parents can support with their own observations.

These years are different from Kids' earlier years for a number of reasons. Reputation means more. At this age, alas, a Kid's unfortunate reputation may follow him or her like a giant shadow, overwhelming his or her present, improved social skills. Sometimes a Kid really does need a change of classroom or even school for an opportunity to start over.

Also, there's more of a distinction in everybody's mind at this age between being popular and having friends. Popularity and friendship are two different things, as they always have been. Popularity means that you are liked or accepted by a majority of your peers. Friendship means that you have an intimate, affectionate relationship with an individual.

At an earlier age, some children who were very popular weren't ready to have close friends. They were still attached enough to their families that they did not need to have an intimate friendship as a bridge or buffer between their private lives and their public ones. But at nine, ten, and eleven, children really do need such a chum. Studies show that having an intimate friend at this age is one of the factors that can help Kids do well through adolescence and into adulthood. A child who is popular (most people like to play with him or her and are pleased to be a partner for any kind of project) but has no close friends may need more assistance than one who is not popular but who has at least one good, close buddy.

Finally, these years are rife with cliques. Cliques aren't really friendships. They're groups with identities. They exist not to foster closeness among members with mutual affections and interests, but to exclude others. In almost every class, unless adult intervention outlaws clique behavior, there will be cliques and there will be outsiders.

There are popular cliques and unpopular cliques. Children with social aspirations yearn to be in the popular clique. The popular clique can decide whether an unpopular child is just ignored or picked on, whether the new Kid is a hit or a flop, whether the substitute teacher is greeted with cheers or gets a truly hard time. Believe it or not, these are not merely one pediatrician's observations: they're supported by research. Honest.

POPULARITY

Most parents want their children to be happy, and that means they want them to be liked, to be popular. Doesn't it? Sometimes. Sometimes not.

There are some children who seem to be effortlessly popular. Studies show that such children tend to be friendly, helpful, considerate, athletic, and good-looking. The very popular Kids tend to have friends of both sexes, even though the other children, popular or not, don't.

Yet there are plenty of friendly, helpful, considerate, athletic, good-looking children who do not consider themselves popular because they do not belong to the clique of popular Kids. Should parents worry about them? Is there something wrong?

And what about the unpopular children? In most fourth, fifth and sixth grades, there are a few Kids in every class who are either neglected or who are controversial—loved by some, hated by others. And there may be one or two who are downright attacked, like Georgianne.

Not in the popular clique

When you're not exactly unpopular but you aren't in the most popular clique, you *may* feel fine about it. You're happy with your friends,

interested in your activities, at peace with yourself. You may look at the most popular clique with a bit of envy, or with disdain, or with no particular feeling at all.

Why doesn't a given child, who seems just as attractive and just as much fun as another, "make" the most popular clique? There could be a million reasons. The most obvious one can be a difference in the timing of puberty. Another could be snobbery or racism. Or perhaps this clique formed way back in third grade, and your Kid joined the school in fourth. Maybe your child used to wet his pants at school and then cry about it, but hasn't since first grade. The reputation may have persisted, carefully preserved and handed down over the years. Most of the time, the reasons are invisible, mysterious, and trivial.

If your child is not accepted by the popular clique, parents have but one responsibility: never to say or do anything that would make their child suspect that parents are disappointed or that he or she has flunked the popularity stakes.

Unfortunately, the popular clique may be so powerful, or the child may be so focused on being liked, that he or she may yearn to be accepted. Kids in this situation feel as if the reason for their being excluded has everything to do with their own worth and nothing to do with group dynamics.

Kids in this plight often believe that the way to be in the popular clique is to act like the popular Kids: dress like them, talk like them, make fun of the people and things they make fun of. They also may believe that the way to be popular is to get the friendship of popular Kids by agreeing with them, doing things for them, giving things to them.

Parents can help by not feeding into this attitude. The last thing such a child needs is the feeling that he or she is not only a failure in his or her own eyes, but in the eyes of parents, as well. It does no good at all to try to help your

Kid "get into" the popular group. Throwing a party for that clique, trying to become friends with their parents, abetting your child's effort to purchase their good will—that kind of effort is very likely to backfire miserably.

Nor does it help to denigrate the highly popular children. Children see through that keenly. Worse, this makes them think that parents themselves place a very high priority on being in the most popular clique: after all, they care enough to take a "sour grapes" attitude.

Happily for their Kids, parents can help a great deal in this situation. It's particularly helpful if parents demonstrate that they enjoy, even relish, the friends the child does have. If they can have social ties with those children's parents, all the better. Making sure that their Kid feels good about accomplishments and feels powerful and in control of his or her own life is crucial.

Perhaps the thing that parents can do most to help is to foster more intimate, one on one friendships (see the following).

Kids who don't fit into a clique

There's no rule that says you have to be in a clique. Many children who are not included in any little group are quite happy that way, and it would be a pity to force them into something that doesn't fit. Once in awhile, though, being a "loner" does indicate a problem.

Happy to be me instead of us

Happy children who aren't popular are children who aren't especially liked or especially disliked by the others in their class. Such children just aren't very outgoing. You could call them unsociable, if you didn't attach any opprobrium to the term. They don't put much effort into going with the group; they'd just as soon watch. Other children don't seek them out to play with. When they are in a position to play with another Kid, it takes them some time to warm up or to get into the spirit of things. But once they warm up enough to start playing, these Kids have a good time.

These children who are contented, though not popular, have at least one good friend, a friend to share their fantasies, worries, and secrets with. It may have taken them weeks to cement that friendship, but there it is. They have areas of life in which they feel competent and powerful. They have interests, and often they have passions. They think of themselves as good, successful people, beloved by their parents.

Children with this profile are happy, contented, and well-adjusted. The biggest favor their parents can do for them is to be happy and contented, as well, and to foster their strengths: their capacity to have intimate friends and to meet challenges successfully.

Controversial Kids: feisty not nasty

Controversial children get mixed reviews from the Kids in their vicinity: the Kids either say thumbs way up or thumbs way down, whereas nobody says "take it or leave it." These are almost always high-energy Kids with hot tempers. They act out their feelings physically and get into fights.

What makes them attractive is that they also have social skills. They can think up good stuff to do, and when they see somebody else doing good stuff, they know how to join in and be one of the group. They get into trouble, and they may get their friends in trouble, but they apologize afterward. They are mostly happy, not angry or hostile, in their high-energy state. They are not aggressive. They fight because they're upset, not in order to do someone harm. They don't go out of their way to pick fights; they fight in self-defense.

In the heat of the fight, they may shriek, "I'm gonna kill you!" And sure, they can be mean. But they're equal-opportunity meanies: they don't hate you just because of mean-spiritedness, they wait until you do something they consider unspeakable. Once their tempers are aroused, they really go at it. If you get on the wrong side of such a Kid, you are in for it. Hence, the thumbs down.

But controversial Kids don't bully other children as a means to an end, extorting money or obedience. They don't round up their friends to attack a defenseless Kid who hasn't done anything bad to them. They don't delight in picking on Kids who are weak, rubbing others' noses in their failures. They're not cruel to animals. If there are a few such children in a class (Bless the teacher!), they often form a clique of their own, which nobody else tries to join.

Controversial children do not think of themselves as unpopular, and their parents shouldn't, either. These children might be able to use some help in reigning in their hot tempers, but they're not on the road to social pathology.

Rejected children

When *nobody* likes a child or wants to play with him or her, something is wrong. Such children aren't just excluded from the most popular clique or even from all the cliques: they're excluded by everybody. They don't have a best friend or friends.

"Different" children

Once in a while, a child is rejected because of being just too different for the rest of the class to tolerate. A child of a racial, ethnic, or religious minority; a child with a disability or a cosmetic deformity that has not been well-presented to the class. All of these children can be cruelly rejected.

Such children often have enormous potential for being liked. They often have courage, kindness, and interesting interests—if you know what I mean. The problem here is not with the child, but with the way the child's difference has been presented to the class. The parents of a child who has major differences often need to educate and befriend the teacher, the other Kids, and the parents of the other Kids before their child may be accepted.

The effort to do this is well worth it, and not because of popularity. Being accepted into a clique is not crucial; having a friend, at least one good friend, is. Studies show that at this age (and adults familiar with the age group can attest to it) a rejected child can have a terribly hard time making such a close friend, no matter what the reason for the group's rejection.

Children who invite rejection

Most children who are rejected share one overwhelming trait: they don't have social skills. They don't know how to approach a group so that they'll be accepted into it. If they're thrust into a group, they don't seem to be able to see how their behavior alienates the other Kids or what to do about it. They may not even be able to tell how somebody else is feeling from how that person looks and behaves. They may well not be able to tell the difference between someone who is angry and someone who is surprised or frightened. Moreover, they themselves may not give clues to others as to how they feel.

There are a number of styles that such a rejected child might display.

Aggressive: Aggressive children without social skills are bullies. They pick fights, usually with the same Kids each time, and when they've beaten a Kid to the point of submission, they don't stop. They disrupt things, they don't listen to other people, they don't cooperate.

Such children may not be anxious or insecure. They may think quite well of themselves. They may truly not understand why nobody seems to like them. Kids like these need help.

Submissive: These Kids have very diminished self-esteem. They knuckle under to bullying behavior, often with an apologetic smile. Other Kids say that they "were asking for it."

Georgianne appears to be this type of submissive child. Why would a youngster have such a defeated, pathetic, tragic opinion of himself or herself? Many have been abused, physically, emotionally, or sexually. Maybe they all have been. The jury is out on this one. They need help.

Avoidant or withdrawing: An avoidant child reminds you of a shadow, of a whisper.

These youngsters try so hard not to be there—wherever "there" is. They hide behind things or animals or people, clinging, avoiding eye contact. They cringe when you approach: a touch equals a slap. Have they been abused? No. What's up with them?

Avoidant, withdrawing children apparently start out with an inherited temperament (conclusions based on studies of identical twins have shown). With such a temperament, a normal, wholesome family and caring environment doesn't suffice to teach them how to reach out and enjoy other children. They are comfortable with close family and family friends, and that's it. The rest of the world is so absolutely other that they can't deal with it. It takes special intervention to help them cope with the outside world.

Such a temperament seems to be (surprise, surprise!) inherited. Parents who share such a temperament may or may not see it as a problem. Even if they do, they may need a bit of a push to find assistance for their child, because they themselves share the tendency to withdraw and avoid.

However, studies show that withdrawn children who don't get some help may indeed find themselves in difficulties later on, so isolated that they can't find pleasure in career or other interests. This is a good age to obtain help for such children. A best friend— not popularity; not a clique; just a friend— can help a withdrawn child find pleasure in contact that isn't completely intimate. Such a friend is a bridge from the world of family to the larger world, with all its choices and challenges.

Pseudo-adults: Sometimes a Kid will remind you of a middle-aged person in a child's body. Children who are pseudo-adults are sober, organized, intelligent individuals. They may very much like to play, but their play is focused, goal-oriented, and often intellectual. They are comfortable with adults, but adults tend to be nonplussed or amused or just generally uncomfortable with them.

A youngster with this social style may seem perfectly happy in his or her isolation. Such a Kid may find unlikely companions: somebody on the internet; a retired neighbor; the science-fiction librarian. Do these acquaintances count as intimate friends? Is such a child truly perfectly happy? Not usually. They know that they're different, they don't know what to do about it, and they're lonely.

Pseudo-adults have so much going on in their heads, so much thinking and wondering and conjecturing and worrying! Every time they encounter any kind of problem, whether it be emotional, physical, financial; whether it be small-scale, like a defective computer program, or large-scale, like parental divorce—they intellectualize it. Every time something pleases or delights them or amuses them— even if they find it hysterically funny—they intellectualize it.

Like the style of withdrawn children, pseudo-adults' style seems to be in large part genetic. And like the parents of withdrawn children, those of pseudo-adults may be cast in the same mold and not take any special steps to intervene in what they have every right to think is a normal way of being.

Children who are pseudo-adults in behavior may well find that they come into their own after adolescence. However, there's a risk. The storms of adolescence may be so stressful that isolation becomes terrifying. Such children usually have not developed even the bulwark of humor to see them through life's small crises.

Parents can help enormously by making sure that their Kid is not truly isolated. Sometimes two Kids with this temperament can become such close friends that even geographical separation doesn't affect the friendship. Sometimes a Kid can become part of a larger network of friends that functions as a kind of extended family with a common interest—chess, computers, fantasy games, science fiction, art, music. If a Kid seems to be unable to connect with anybody, however, parents would do well to seek professional help, starting with a consultation with the pediatrician.

BEST FRIENDS

Nines through Elevens demand a lot from their best friends. A best friend has to make you think well of yourself, bounce back from fights, stand up for you in your absence, laugh at your jokes, protect you from ridicule, and listen and listen and listen. It's not surprising that best friendships can be extremely intense and time-consuming. Amazingly enough, about two-thirds of friendships in this age group last at least a year, if the friends are close enough geographically.

Parents who enable a Kid to keep a best friend make an investment in the future. Having a best friend is good insurance for being socially comfortable in adulthood. It's as if the ability to trust another as much as you trust yourself develops most easily at this time: if it happens now, it's there for life.

So what should one do if one's Kid doesn't have a best friend? First, do a feasibility study. Perhaps your Kid is a little unusual: quieter; smarter; more mature or less mature; different because of a cosmetic or medical problem; possessed of unusual experiences, traumatic or otherwise; passionately interested in one aspect of life, such as computers or art or music. Your child needs a friend to match his or her unusualness. When you look at the profiles of the available potential friends, you may understand quite well why nobody qualifies. My strong suggestion: make it a priority to find a larger pool from which to choose. Get your Kid into activities where he or she is inclined to meet likely candidates. When adolescence hits, you will be very glad you did.

Second, assess your Kid's social skills. Has he or she had problems with group activities in the past? Have adults—teachers, coaches, other parents—said or hinted that there are problems in his or her behavior that keep other children at a distance? If so, this is the time to get professional advice. A child who feels left out and friendless at nine to twelve is likely to be in some deep trouble by sixteen.

Third, assess other barriers to friendship. Is your child in a religious, cultural, or racial minority? Have you been so concerned about exposure to others' values that you have restricted contact with other children? If so, consider that a child who is isolated because of his very identity may grow into adolescence angry at that identity. Make it a high priority to facilitate friendships, whether it means relaxing your standards or going outside the community for potential companions.

Fourth, could your child be avoiding intimate friendships because he or she is carrying a secret burden: a family secret, such as sexual abuse, incest, alcoholism or drugs? Could your child be clinically depressed? Or feel not entitled to take part in the activities of childhood because he or she is being asked to function as a pseudo-spouse or pseudo-parent? The problem here of course extends far beyond not having a best friend. Help is needed promptly.

Finally, some of the traits that make for intimate friendships and social ease seem to be inherited, according to studies of identical twins raised separately. If your child is temperamentally disinclined to seek out a best friend, it's possible that this is simply his or her nature. Such a child has had a long unchanged history of being perfectly contented with solitary play, despite opportunity and encouragement to join others.

What if it's the wrong best friend?

With luck, a best friend is somebody parents like and approve of. If not, the usual advice is to not interfere, to let the friendship run its course unless the best friend is frightening in some way—a true bully, who fights and extorts; a tragically precocious and troubled child who is involved in gangs or sex or smoking or alcohol or drugs; a youngster whose parents are truly frightening: guns all over the house, drug dealers, neglectful, abusive.

In these events, no question—parents need to step in and rescue their child and family, forbidding further contact, while carefully explaining the reason. It's a good idea to tell your Kid,

> "I know that this may make Theo seem even more exciting to have as a friend. I want you to be very grown-up about this. Being friends with Theo is dangerous. It isn't Theo's fault, I know, but I know you don't want to put your whole family in such a bad spot."

This "letting it run its course" can be very hard on parents, however. Often it helps to sit down and really analyze what the problem is that you have with the friend and what, if anything, can be done to make you more comfortable.

The best friend will change how my child feels about our family

A parent may feel that if a child's best friend has a much different socioeconomic, cultural, or religious background, it can throw one's own existence into an unflattering light. However, this is an adult perspective and may very well be skewed by adult preconceptions. Children take their own and each others' families for granted as normal. At this age, their primary concern is simply that they not be embarrassed. For the rest, the rule is I am I and you are you and this is just the way things are.

The fact that a best friend's family has a great deal more money than yours, for instance, is likely to simply be taken by your child as the way things are. The two buddies are far more likely to share such excruciating mutual concerns as the way their parents dress at Open House or the dreadful fact that a sibling plays the trombone or whatever.

In the same way, a best friend who is disadvantaged doesn't mean that your child feels like the oppressor. "He doesn't have an extra shirt to wear, so we washed his and I put it in the dryer on permanent press." "I don't want to go to camp if Myra can't come too. Maybe we could have a lemonade stand and earn money." Rather than assume that your child is seeing you in a different, inferior, or unethical light, check out your impressions.

The best friend has contagious and undesirable habits

> Lucy ducks her head, rolls her eyes back in her head till the whites show, shrugs, and whines in a high voice, "I don' know." Clearly she is possessed, and the evil spirit is her best friend Monica.

> "He started biting his fingernails after he got to be friends with Scott. I don't think there's a thing on his mind. It's just that he caught it, like a virus."

> "Tolly tells so many lies. He can't seem to tell anything straight. And now Pete's started doing it! He told me that his teacher's pregnant, and so of course I asked her when she's due and nearly died of embarrassment! I could wring both their little necks."

Here is a sad truth. Every best friend—every single one—will have some bad habit or annoying trait that your child will most likely adopt. It will be for a time like having a ghost twin in the house. Most of the time, with appropriate parental exasperation and firmness, this will pass. Take a look, a good close look, at the other potential buddies. You may wind up very glad that your Kid made the choice he or she did.

Responsibility, Discipline, and Life at Home

"Now just watch the light." I am performing a routine neurological check on Amy, watching her eyes as they swivel right, left, up, down. She starts looking a trifle spacey. "While you're hypnotizing her, tell her to clean up her room!" Amy's mother says. "If it works, you could open a drive-through window and retire in about three days."

It didn't work.

Kids this age demand a lot from parents in their homelives. For one thing, they seem to take up a lot more space. They leave their possessions about as if they were marking their territory. They make more noise. When they need things, they need them right away and exclusively: the phone, the bathroom, your attention. All this tends to be exaggerated if the particular Kid is in the throes of puberty.

But what makes the most difference in homelife is the way children this age start to think of their competence to run their own lives. "I have been making all my own decisions," a Ten writes with pride in her school journal, "since I was eight."

This is the age when Kids focus on crucial questions:
• Does my family consider me to be a competent and trustworthy person?
• Do my parents really want me to grow up?
• Can we be friends?

How Kids answer these questions will determine to a large extent what life will be like during adolescence. Parents whose youngster feels able to make decisions and take on challenges, and to be held accountable for the results, have a big head start.

But getting there isn't always easy. Children can change so rapidly now that it can seem as if they're always one step ahead of you. Old habits are hard to break.

RESPONSIBILITIES

Kids this age have the potential to think about responsibilities in a more sophisticated way than when they were younger. For children under about nine, doing your chores is a way to demonstrate your obedience to parents, and not doing them is a way to demonstrate your rebellion or opposition.

Older Kids need to learn that this attitude has to be outgrown. They need to discover that carrying out responsibilities (or not carrying them out) gives them a reputation with their parents. When parents consider a child trustworthy and competent, it's different from considering the youngster obedient. Obedience is something that you have to demonstrate from one parental order to the next. Being trustworthy and competent is part of your character. Establishing a reputation, forming a character, is a big step in growing up.

When parents don't grow out of thinking in terms of obedience and rebellion, Kids don't either. When faced with a choice between obedience and rebellion, Kids at nine, ten, and eleven are increasingly likely to choose rebellion. It makes them feel more grown-up than does obedience. Of course, the more Kids rebel, the more fed up parents get. So the more they crack down on the Kid.

To the Kid, the parental crackdown looks like an escalated invitation to rebel—to which the parents respond with even greater outrage. This is a truly vicious cycle. If Kids and parents stay stuck at this level throughout these years, there's likely to be trouble ahead.

Parents can do several things to help their Kid change his or her attitude.
• They can communicate to the youngster that he or she is now considered a mature and competent person who doesn't need reminding, coaxing, or scolding to perform tasks at home.

coaxing, or scolding to perform tasks at home.
• They can make clear to their Kid that family duties are as serious and important as the challenges they face in the larger world. Chores at home don't deserve to be ditched because of homework, showing up for practice or rehearsal, or completing paid-for jobs. Everyone in the family is responsible for keeping homelife running smoothly.
• They can allow the youngster the dignity of a private life at home, a life into which parents, siblings, and grandparents may not intrude.

Changing gears doesn't come naturally. Helping Kids grow into their new roles takes thought and intervention.

TEACHING KIDS THAT OBEDIENCE IS NO LONGER THE NAME OF THE GAME

"He doesn't listen. Do you suppose he has a hearing problem?" How long do you suppose insurance plans will continue to fund audiology exams on Nines, Tens, and Elevens who seem impervious to parental commands? Rarely, my friends, is this a hearing problem. The only ENT condition needing treatment is the voice of the parent, hoarse from telling the Kid to set the table, walk the dog, fold the laundry. In fact, the Kid *is* listening. It's just that the Kid is listening to a voice in his or her own little head, a voice that drowns out the parent's voice, a voice saying it's okay not to set the table. It may even be telling the Kid that it is *wrong* to set the table.

"Grown-ups are supposed to do all the chores. It's not fair for them to ask me, a Kid, to do their work."

"The object is to see who can get somebody else to do the work. I'm real good at it."

"Setting the table is a job for dorks. I must not think of myself as a dork.

Whatever I'm doing, it's more important than setting the table."

"I am the person who gets to tell me what to do when. That's more important than anything in the whole world. Period."

You can't silence that voice in a child's head. All you can do is change its tune. The trick is to teach the voice that's inside the Kid's own head to say: "It is time to set the table. That's my job, nobody else's, and if I don't do it, somebody else will have to, and that's not fair. It will make me not think well of myself."

The first task is to redefine chores and the status of people who perform them.

When only one person in the family performs or seems to perform most of the chores, that fact is a very important one to a child this age. What does it mean? Dad or Mom stays home, bakes bread, does the cleaning and laundry, and nags other people to "help" with the chores. Grandma does everything and seems to have no outside interest. The live-in or weekly or daily helper does everything, and nobody has a real relationship with her.

When everybody except the choremaster avoids doing household tasks, this demeans both chores and choremaster. The choremaster starts to be seen almost as a sibling—the sibling who knuckles under and gets stuck with the undesirable work. When a child comes to think of an adult in this way it's bad for the choremaster, but even worse for the youngster.

For one thing, if the choremaster is demeaned, a Kid this age can turn rude and nasty to that person. This is one way the youngster can distance himself or herself from the demeaned work. Kids at this age are hotly conscious of social pecking orders. Of course, this can turn into a racist, sexist, ageist, or otherwise prejudiced frame of mind. Such an attitude can easily become a serious problem both for the Kid and for society.

For another, such a misconception encourages a Kid to think that the boundary between child and adult has become blurred. It's easy to start to feel that a demeaned adult, demoted to sibling status, can be treated in a demeaning fashion in other ways. Well, if *that* adult can be treated in such disrespectful fashion, then so can *all* adults. Including one's parents.

Redefining all this means getting the youngster to grasp the notion that chores are shared responsibilities, albeit low on most people's list of favorite stuff. It also means learning that the choremaster is a three-dimensional, competent, fully grown-up adult. Parents set the tone by how they refer to and treat the choremaster both directly and in his or her absence.

The choremaster needs to become, in the eyes of the Kid, a person who performs necessary tasks in order to do something more important. That important task might be to nurture a family, keep a sense of order in the home, earn money to support other people, or pursue other interests. The important thing is that the youngster thinks of that person as someone on the adult side of the child/adult boundary.

Changing a Kid's attitude from rebellious nonhelper to reluctant but resigned co-worker also means getting a different handle on the chores themselves.

RATHER THAN ASSIGN CHORES, SHARE THEM OUT. NEGOTIATE.

One way to do this is to sit down as a family and list all the chores, starting with the chores that parents do that children are as yet unable to manage. These might include driving family members, making out a budget, shopping, cooking elaborate meals, paying bills, arranging or performing household repairs, and dangerous tasks like running a power mower or leaf blower.

When the family chores are thus shared out, Kids are faced with the fact that adults already are performing a baseline of chores that can't be shared. The remaining tasks, those that can be done by children or adults, then are up for division.

The danger here is that parents may be tempted to fall into the role of martyr. "See how much I do in this family! And all we're asking you to do is set the measly table!" Whoops! That takes you right back into putting the Kid into the "helper" mode. It's crucial to try to keep this from happening. Instead:

> "When you're sixteen and get your driver's license, I bet you'll want to trade in your laundry jobs for driving Cathy to the orthodontist."

> "You know, I'll bet you're old enough to help do the bills. We'll try that next month. Once you understand how a checkbook works, maybe we can get you your own, and I can be your bank. You could write checks on your next week's allowance."

> "You can start by planning and cooking one meal a month. I can start out supervising, and then you can gradually take over. You can learn to cook that sea bass thing you like so much."

GIVE TASKS DIGNITY

> "I don't see why we have to set the table every night. Why can't we just each grab our own plate and silverware?"

> "Why do we have to make the beds? We just mess them up the next night."

> "I don't care if the laundry gets folded. I like how stuff looks when it's wrinkled."

I know that many households don't set the table, make the beds every day, or fold the laundry. I have myself lived in such households without any problem whatsover. The above-mentioned tasks are just examples. The point is that each household's selection of chores is in many respects arbitrary. Rather than get into an argument about the virtue or necessity of, say, dusting the Fabergé eggs once a month, it often wins Kids over to stand on tradition. "This is the way we do it in our house. It's our tradition. It's part of how we define ourselves as a family. Period. The question is not 'What is going to get done?' The question is 'Who is going to do it?'"

HAVE KIDS DESIGN CHORE-TIME INTO THE SCHEDULE AT THE SAME TIME CHORES ARE ASSIGNED

If there's not a set time for making a bed, it won't get made. And so on. Children this age often like to have this presented to them as a problem. "Set the table during commercials," Rhonda says tersely. "That can be my job."

LET KIDS TRY OUT THEIR CHORE-DOING THEORIES

"I think we should each emerge carefully from our beds like a letter out of an envelope," intones Jacques. "Then it takes about two seconds to make it look made." "I can wear my Walkman when I vacuum."

"Put a library book box in the hall, and if you don't put your books in on time you have to pay the fine yourself."

MAKE REMINDERS AUTOMATIC AND IMPERSONAL. RITUALS ARE HELPFUL.

"'Roseanne' is on. Time for the table to get set."

"The toilet and bathtub and sink get scrubbed right before Saturday soccer practice."

"Jesse and I wash the car every Monday night while Mom and Boo watch football. Then Mom and Boo clean out the garage every Saturday morning while Jesse and I go to her ballet lesson."

MAKE THE CONSEQUENCES OF NOT DOING THE TASK AUTOMATIC AND IMPERSONAL, TOO

"We can't eat dinner until the table is set. So I'm afraid the hamburgers are going to be very, very well done."

"We can't leave for soccer practice until the bathroom stuff gets done."

"We didn't get the car washed Monday, Jesse, so we'll have to do it Saturday instead of ballet."

BE FLEXIBLE BUT NOT A PUSHOVER

Trade a task, don't do it for a Kid or "help" with the task. If Jesse's ballet was a recital, not a class, and Monday was spent rehearsing or throwing up from nerves, the car can be washed another day. This reinforces the idea that the family works as a team, and that parents are not adversaries to be outwitted, conned, or stalemated.

FIND WAYS TO PRAISE THE WAY THE TASK WAS DONE, RATHER THAN THE FACT THAT IT WAS PERFORMED AT ALL

"Clever old you, you looked up in Heloise's Hints how to get the jelly donut off the ceiling. And here I was trying to figure out how to tie a mop to the vacuum-cleaner extender!"

instead of

"I'm so thrilled! You actually thought to clean up after your slumber party!"

DON'T PRAISE ROUTINE CHORES

That would be like praising a Kid for eating breakfast or taking a bath. When praise is given, it means that one did something more than the expected.

DO PRAISE THE QUALITIES OF COMPETENCE AND TRUSTWORTHINESS

Not just when chores are the issue:

"You found my glasses! I looked everywhere—but of course I couldn't see anything because I didn't have my glasses on. I am so grateful. I can count on you."

"When I called and told you the chancellor was coming over for a drink, I prayed you'd get the message and tidy up. WOW! You really, really did it!"

THE BEDROOM DILEMMA

It is the nightly custom of every good mother after her children are asleep to rummage in their minds and put things straight for next morning.... When you wake in the morning, the naughtiness and evil passions with which you went to bed have been folded up small and placed at the bottom of your mind; and on the top, beautifully aired, are spread out your prettier thoughts, ready for you to put on.

Peter Pan, by J.M. Barrie

Maybe. But the Darling children, like Peter himself, were all prepubertal.

Whether you are nine or fourteen when puberty hits, you require some privacy. Even if puberty is not an issue, this is a big age for day-dreaming, trying out faces and voices and ways of moving, looking in the mirror, masturbating, and expressing feelings that you want everybody to pretend they don't hear. Most older Kids intensely want a private space.

The idea of one's child needing a private space can be disconcerting. What is he going to do in there? Is it healthy for her to need to be alone like that? Should a child have a secret life? Shouldn't parents be guardians over their child's inner life?

Allowing a private space reassures a youngster that parents respect boundaries. Parents who allow privacy are saying that they aren't confused about who's who. They don't take over a youngster's achievements or struggles, robbing the child of autonomy and accountability. A child who's allowed privacy is much more likely to seek out family company.

Lucky the Nine, Ten, or Eleven whose space is an entire bedroom. Most Kids won't have this luxury, however. Whether they do or don't, questions arise from both parents and children. What are the rules for one's own domain? How private is private? Here are some considerations.

• If space is tight, the private area can be one of time rather than of space. Perhaps the child could know that for two hours every afternoon or evening, one bedroom will belong to him or her alone.

• If both space and time are tight, and no real area can be created, at least privacy can be symbolic. Parents can protect a youngster who's involved with a project, homework, or day-dreaming from intrusion by the rest of the family. They can be firm about not reading private papers, such as a diary.

• Privacy never should require that a door be

locked from the inside. If a youngster became ill or distraught, adults must be able to enter. A sign on the firmly closed door should make the room off-limits to everybody except for an emergency.

When a youngster this age does have a room of his or her own, the question of standards arises. Why are so many children's rooms at this age and older so extremely messy? "What kind of flooring do you have in your room?" I ask Nancy, who has tumbled from the top bunk. "I don't know," she says. "I can't see it."

Are Kids just marking their territory, like dogs? No. It's more complicated than that. To have a neat room, one must put everything in its place, where it belongs. For growing-up Kids, this becomes impossible.

WHERE AN ITEM BELONGS OFTEN INVOLVES MAGIC AND SUPERSTITION

Here is my dollie Christina. Does she belong in my bed, like when I was little? Well, no, I'm not a little Kid any more. Does she belong on the shelf where I put all my not-played-with toys? No! That would hurt her feelings. Sitting on my bedside table? No, I don't want her staring at me in reproach. What about leaving her on the floor? Sure. Kind of a way station.

WHERE AN ITEM BELONGS OFTEN INVOLVES MAKING MULTIPLE JUDGMENTS. AFTER ALL THE JUDGMENTS ARE MADE, THERE ISN'T ANY PLACE LEFT FOR THE ITEM TO GO.

Is this shirt clean? No, it's been worn twice. It shouldn't be hung up. Is it dirty? No, it's just a little wrinkled and smelly. It shouldn't go in the hamper. Folded on the chair? No, I never really liked that shirt and I don't want to wear it anymore. In the charity box? No, Kookie said I looked good in it. What about dropping it on the floor? Sure. Kind of a way station.

WHERE AN ITEM BELONGS MAY NEVER HAVE BEEN DEFINED. IT MAY BELONG TO A CATEGORY THAT'S SO SMALL THAT IT DOESN'T REALLY HAVE A PLACE TO GO.

I've finished this library book. Should it go in the library book box in the hall? No, I want to go back and read that part again where they cut off his head. Should it go on my book shelf? No, because I'll forget to take it to the library. What about under my bed? Sure. Kind of a way station.

WHERE AN ITEM BELONGS MAY BE ALL TOO OBVIOUS AND YOU CAN'T BEAR IT

This sweater is my favorite but Kookie says it shows my boobs. Should it go into the charity box in the hall? NONONONONO! I bet that one of these days it'll look good again. Should it go in the drawer? No, because I might forget and wear it to school and get teased. Folded neatly on the chair? No, because I don't want to have to see it and deal with it. What about here on the floor? Sure. Kind of a way station.

A few days or weeks of this kind of decision-making and you've got the potential for an archeological dig. The reason that children this age get so upset if you try to clean their rooms for them is that although you see a mess, they see the outward expression of all their inner dilemmas and ambivalent feelings about growing up. You hear only the sound of mold growing and mice nibbling. They hear each item calling to them: "Love me! Don't discard me! Grow into me! Grow out of me! Don't forget me! Pay attention to me!" When you stomp in and clean it all up, what you've done is get everything out of whack so that they have to deal with it all over again.

Do parents feel a strong need to tidy up their Kids' rooms because the chaos is symbolic for them, too? Does the presence of all that stuff—every item in a state of flux, every item emotionally charged—harrow a parent's mind? Is this why a youngster's bedroom can seem as dangerous as a fox's lair—a hint of freshly killed prey, old bones, and maybe a nest of sharp-toothed pups over there? No wonder negotiations break down.

Maybe, parents think, we can just keep the door firmly shut and I won't have to think about it. Nope. It's there, lurking in one's consciousness, a no man's land in one's mental image of a safe and cozy home. Maybe the youngster can just abide by one or two simple rules: no food in there, ever; no living or explosive science projects; nothing on the floor; a thorough cleaning once a month. Is that too hard, too much to ask? Yes. It appears so.

Maybe the parents will just go in once a week and clean things up. They promise not to read the diary or the notes passed in class or the graffiti on the notebooks or the "slam" book with comments on everybody in the fifth grade. Isn't that a generous offer? No. It's intolerable. Parents will contaminate every item by imposing order on it.

There is no cure for the messy room. Parents will make rules or not make them. Children will object or acquiesce to one degree or another. And still, under the bed, sandwiches will mummify; cultures of mold will flourish in ancient glasses of milk; retainers and glasses and library books will become lost. The main thing is to regard the whole issue as a complicated developmental phenomenon, not just as a messy room, and respect it.

DISCIPLINE

"Earth to Jasper! Earth to Jasper! What **are** you so engrossed in?" Jasper blinks and takes his finger out of his nose. "Oh," he says, "I was figuring out a way to take the blame off me."

Authoritative parents recognize all along that children commit different kind of errors, and modify their responses accordingly. At ages nine, ten, and eleven Kids start to discriminate when they judge their own behavior: Does this thing that I've done really mean that I've acted like a bad person? How harsh on myself should I be? Some foibles are real breaches in moral behavior, actions for which one should be ashamed. Others are side effects of life and occur regardless of your intent to be good. The kind of atonement one makes depends on the kind of error, not just on what happened because of it.

Maybe the most frequent kind of error occurs because your skills weren't up to the task at hand. Not your fault. All that has to happen is a little bad luck, and doggone it, you've scratched your new glasses or left your spelling book on the bus.

Another kind of error happens because you thought one thing would happen but it turned out that another did. Morality doesn't have anything to do with it; it was just a mistake, no matter how distressing the results. "But I was sure I'd be able to get home before dark!" "I didn't think the birds would need to have their water changed that soon."

Some errors can be mistakes in the eyes of one person but not from the viewpoint of another. They are deviations from the expectations of a particular parent or family. That doesn't mean that you committed a moral mistake.

"I don't want to take piano lessons anymore."

"I want to go to Teddie's sleepover instead of Nana and Papa's on Friday."

"I don't want to eat family dinner. I want to read in my room."

"I got my ears pierced at the mall!"

"Jennie's mom didn't care that it was rated R, so why should you?"

Some errors really do involve a slip from an ideal of goodness.

> "All right, so I lied about wearing my helmet. I didn't get hurt, did I?"

> "So I ripped up all her homework. She deserved it. She used up all the rest of my bubble bath."

> "So I told the bus driver she's a big fat slob. Well, she is. And she's mean, too."

> "I had to cheat on the test so that I wouldn't have to go to summer school and we can go to the island after all."

Younger children make excuses for themselves too, but it's different. When younger Kids make excuses, they are asking the parent to overlook the error. Older Kids aren't merely making excuses. They are exercising their new ability to see complexity in moral issues. Even more critically, when they make excuses they aren't just trying to get parents to forgive and forget. They are addressing their excuses to themselves, as well.

Younger Kids have a simple way of judging actions. If you do something bad to me, the right thing is for me to do something back to you. If I do something bad to you, I fully expect you to do something bad to me. They don't take into account the other person's intention or special circumstances, such as the other person's age and maturity.

There's another wrinkle to this. By the time they're eight, most Kids realize that the other person has a point of view and they can see something from the other person's perspective. "Mom was really mad when I didn't come home by dark. She had to keep dinner waiting."

Older children can identify with someone else's feelings or thoughts.

> "Mom was really mad when I didn't come home by dark. She probably thought that if I was just late I would have called. I bet she thought I'd had an accident or had been kidnapped."

No wonder that, like Jasper, they make considerable efforts to take the blame off themselves. Parents of older children may be tempted to cut through all this complexity and switch to or return to or stay in an authoritarian mode. "Do what I say because I say it."

This would be a mistake. Kids this age are learning to think in the mode parents do: the what if? mode. What if I don't wear my helmet and I get hurt? What if I try to ride home before dark and don't make it? What if I rip up Ellie's homework and she flunks Latin? Is it worth it? Will I think well of myself?

They also have to look to themselves for judgment and repercussions.

> "Next time I'd better wear the dorky thing."

> "I didn't call and made you worry. Of course, you were dumb to worry because you know I never get hurt, but I see your point. I hate being grounded for the weekend and I'm sore as a boil about it, but I see why."

> "I should have put jello in her shoes instead."

They don't make these statements, but they process the thoughts.

Parents can help this maturing process a lot.

STATE RULES RATHER THAN DEMANDS

> "It's wrong to hurt old people's feelings, just because they're not very exciting to visit."

instead of

"I want you to come with us to Nana and Papa's every single Sunday. No excuses!"

Kids feed specific rules into their ideas of right and wrong. They'll work out permutations and combinations, they'll mull on it. Sometimes they'll come out with a surprising insight.

"Old people need younger people to keep their hearts working. If you didn't visit them, their hearts might stop earlier and they'd die."

Sometimes they'll come up with a possible solution:

"Maybe I could teach Papa how to play Mario Brothers. It's pretty easy."

Sometimes they draw a moral to the story.

"When I get old, I'm not going to be boring."

If they hear demands instead of rules, they'll shut down their newfound skills and regress back to the old obedience/rebellion mode.

LISTEN WITH AN OPEN MIND

A Kid has often devoted a lot of thought to the issue at hand. If the child has a point of view that does "take the blame off me," it's worth listening to. Sometimes it will turn out that he or she is correct.

"I didn't realize that the eye doctor told you the glasses were scratch-resistant."

Or at least that he or she has a point.

"So you forgot that we'd turned the clocks back last weekend, and you thought you had an extra hour of daylight."

Or even that something you thought was a minor infraction was really a flagrant breaking of rules:

"You mean that was the same R-rated movie I told you explicitly was utterly out of the question?"

REASON

Parents and child need to agree on what kind of error was made.

"Your judgment was off. You thought it was more important not to catch Jerry's lice than to protect your skull. I can see how you could feel that way, but your skull is more important than your scalp."

"Destroying Ellie's hard work was mean. You actually meant to do her serious harm. She didn't want to harm you when she took the bubble bath; she just wanted the bubble bath."

"How well you roller-blade isn't the issue. The problem is you knew I'd worry if you were late, and you didn't call, just because you didn't want Jerry to think you were a baby. You let your embarrassment be more important than your mother's sanity."

"When you don't join us at Nana and Papa's, it hurts their feelings and makes the family incomplete. Older people need to look forward to visits they can depend on. You won't understand that until you're old, so you'll have to take it on faith."

ASK THE CHILD TO PARTICIPATE IN DECIDING WHAT ATONEMENT, IF ANY, IS CALLED FOR

"I guess scratch-resistant doesn't mean scratch-**proof.** Not your fault. What do you think we should do about these scratched glasses?"

"Now I'll worry whenever you go out of the neighborhood. It makes me want you not to go out of the neighborhood at all. How do you think the damage in my trust can be fixed up?"

"Ellen is going to have to do all that homework over again. It's going to take her about two hours. What do you think your response to that ought to be?"

IF A TRUE MORAL OFFENSE WAS COMMITTED, CONDEMN THE BEHAVIOR BUT SHOW FAITH IN THE CHILD

A Kid who is new to thinking about moral issues in this complicated way can be much harder on his soul than any judgmental parent. Such a youngster can come to regard himself or herself as damaged goods, unredeemable. One terrible possible outcome is that Kids who give themselves reputations as sheer trouble live up to them. Another is that the child who can't tolerate the severity of his or her own conscience may pretend that no harm was done at all. This can become a destructive habit. Parents can help the forming conscience become a wise one.

"Something must have been going on in your life that made you feel really nasty. I've never known you to act in a mean way. That's just not you."

"When you're embarrassed, it's hard to think straight. I'll bet that next time you won't let Jerry's cool act keep you from doing the right thing."

PROVIDE A WAY TO REPAIR DAMAGES AND/OR TO ATONE

Even if the mistake wasn't a moral one, damage can still be done. Kids need to know that even innocent errors need to be fixed.

"How can you try to get your book back? Sure, you could ask the bus driver. Or put up a 'LOST' sign at school."

If the error was a moral one, something more is needed.

"Ellie is really upset about the homework. I know you're going to write a note to the teacher telling her that you destroyed it, so Ellie won't be blamed. That will help. But she feels as if you attacked her, not just her work. How can you let her know how sorry you are? Maybe you could bake her some brownies or offer to clean and polish her bike or take over her chores for a week."

LIFE AT HOME

Puberty! Grown-up moral judgments! Adult sense of humor! Demands for privacy!

Life at home definitely takes on a new flavor when you've got an older Kid. No wonder that many of its dilemmas have to do with sex. Dirty jokes; nudity at home; what to allow on television; how to monitor the talk and behavior of the Kid's friends; what kind of topics are allowed in family conversation or teasing—menstruation? masturbation? involuntary erections? wet dreams? marital sex? menopause? infertility? abortion? If they are allowed, who gets to talk about them? Who gets to listen? Who gets to tease whom? Who gets to see what or whom? Who gets to be seen by whom?

Sex permeates life with an older child whether or not puberty has begun. Even if you haven't started puberty, your classmates have—nearly all the girls by the end of this period and a whole bunch of the boys.

To say nothing of the fact that everywhere you go, you see and hear sexual material aimed at your age group, from Calvin Klein ads to popular music to graffiti to Joe Camel. ("Dr. Nathanson! Guess what Joe looks like!" Giggle giggle giggle giggle.) to movies rated PG. And that's just what you're *expected* to encounter. There's also: news on TV, radio, and in the paper; videos rated PG–13 and R and NC–17 at your home or elsewhere; and daytime talk shows featuring every variation on the theme.

Your friends, enemies, and classmates talk about sex a lot, too. On the school bus, in the carpool ("Dr. Nathanson, what's nymphomania?" asks a voice from the crowded back seat. "Just a second, Kiddo, let me get past this idiot in the 18-wheeler.") They tell dirty jokes you may or may not understand. ("But my kitty has a bloody nose! Get it? Get it?" Giggle giggle giggle giggle.)

For Kids this age, the big issue about sex is what it does to boundaries. After all, the great distinguishing function of sex is that it breaks down boundaries between individuals. Romance, courtship, seduction, sexual harassment, rape: that's what they're all about—the voluntary lowering or the forcible overthrow of boundaries.

Breaking down barriers is what makes romantic or experimental sex so exciting, forbidden, titillating, and dangerous. It's what makes harassment so distressing and rape so terrible. It's also what can make sexual bonds between adults strong, tender, and long-lasting. In order

for sex to have any significance at all—whether sex of the thrilling moment or sex of the committed bond or even sex used as a weapon—the boundaries have to be there in the first place.

The great overwhelming avalanche of sexuality in our culture floods boundaries. Parents hope and pray that maybe Kids this age don't notice that. That they don't notice that Joe Camel looks like a face full of male genitalia fitted out in the clothing of a reliable-looking Dad person. That they don't notice how young those Calvin Klein models are or that the seductive voice sounds like Coach; or understand the lyrics of popular music, or "get" R-rated movies or what's really going on with those talk-show guests or what happens on MTV.

Fortunately, many children who could easily "get" all this somehow realize that they need to protect themselves from this flooding of the barriers. Hence the giggle giggle giggle giggle. Welcome those giggles. They're music to my ears.

The giggle says, I'm a bystander, still. I may be on the cusp of the action, but I still have the luxury of finding the whole thing ludicrous as well as titillating. To giggle is to erect and maintain a barrier. YES!

Kids can't maintain this healthy status of onlooker if parents don't help them. What helps Kids the most is when parents put thought and effort into helping Kids maintain boundaries at home. Kids need to know that powerful as sex seems to be, it can't overwhelm trusting, important relationships.

They also need to know that as they go through the hormonal storms of puberty, their intense feelings don't really change the world. Their emotions aren't going to flood any important boundaries. Their changed bodies aren't going to arouse scary feelings in the people close to them. They need to be allowed to experience and come to terms with their new sexuality without having to be actors on a grown-up stage.

Finally, Kids realize more than the culture does. They know that puberty and adolescence are states of transition. Kids want to feel themselves growing and changing, and they want to know that there is an adult state—different from theirs right now—that's worth metamophosing into. Otherwise, why not just stop here in childhood, where it's at least safe?

Parents can do children a big favor by helping to keep this sense of boundaries straight at home. This isn't about nudity per se. Communities in which nudism is a cultural norm preserve boundaries at least as well as clothed ones. Nor is it about physical privacy. Ann Frank had a strong perception of boundaries living in a cramped hidden set of rooms with her own and another family.

Boundaries mean that a Kid feels strongly individual. He or she feels like a person who can select a choice, make a decision, act on it, judge it, and be accountable for the outcome.

They also mean that a Kid doesn't feel as if his or her personal life really belongs to somebody else. Parents don't take over the child's accomplishments or decide every detail of his or her life. They don't overprotect him or her from risk or challenge or the results of misbehavior. Parents who respect boundaries don't try to turn a child into a surrogate spouse or co-parent, no matter how great the stress in their lives.

This means that unless parents can think of a good reason to the contrary, they would be wise to heed the following guidelines.

NUDITY AT HOME SHOULD BE INFREQUENT, ASEXUAL, AND ACCIDENTAL. IT SHOULDN'T BE THE NORM, OR SEDUCTIVE, OR ENGAGED IN ON PURPOSE.

Unless you are part of a nudist culture, in which case nudity is the norm and you'd better watch out what signals you send when you wear clothes, nudity at home is not advisable. When postpubertal family members of either sex and any relationship take to undressing *on purpose* in front of pubertal Kids, this sends a message. Alas, the message that the naked person is sending is probably not the message that the child is receiving. (Getting waylaid by your Kid on the way to or in the bath or shower is a whole different kettle of fish. [I considered several metaphors before settling on this one.])

Adults believe that the message is: "Look. Nudity is natural and not necessarily sexual. This is how an adult looks naked. It's OK." The child receiving the message may think: "Oh no, here comes Mom or Dad (or whoever) in the altogether. What on earth are they trying to tell me? Maybe I'm supposed to say how young they look. Or maybe they want me to see how big they are up there or down there. Or maybe they want ME to undress so they can see me! What does that mean? This is scary. I think I'll see if I can stay over at Taylor's house."

What about when siblings of the opposite sex go about naked at home? This truly is playing with fire. Siblings always have strong feelings about each other, whether positive or negative or merely competitive. Here's something to think about: when a crime is committed, what detectives look for in finding the perp is means, motive, and opportunity. Siblings always have a motive in trying to break down boundaries. The motive is a mixture of love, pride, jealousy, dominance, competitiveness, and attraction based on similar genetic and environmental characteristics. Sexual maturity gives Kids the means by which to break down boundaries. Parents should protect them from having the opportunity.

WHEN IT COMES TO SEXUAL TOPICS, PARENTS STAY IN THEIR ROLE AS PARENTS

Yes, that does mean restraining your appreciation of dirty jokes. Whenever a child this age truly feels as if parents are treating him or her as an equal, the boundary is breached.

It also means that parents don't count on the

culture at large, on schools, or on peer groups to educate children about sex. They make the time and find the privacy to talk to children, they get books or videos, they make an appointment with the pediatrician to clarify any concerns. (See **Health and Illness,** later in this chapter, for what every Kid needs to know and some suggestions on how to enlighten him or her.)

This doesn't mean that you have to have a sit-down session—or the Talk, as it is sometimes known. Nor does it mean that you can't make kind, adult-type jokes about the topic. And it certainly doesn't mean that parents should conduct a sober, worried discussion about birth control, AIDS, unplanned pregnancies, abortion. Please, don't. Save those topics to introduce briefly, but seriously, when something in the news calls attention to them. You won't have to wait long.

Talking to this age group about sex in a way that helps them grow up means instilling confidence. Kids need to know that you think that they are and will be attractive. They need to know that you have every confidence that they will find a large number of people who think they are attractive, too. A Kid needs to know that you believe that out of this large number of people, the Kid will find at least one where the magic clicks. Defining "magic" and defining "click"—that's up to one's own ideas and culture.

IF YOUR COMMUNITY ENCOURAGES PRECOCIOUS SEXUAL BEHAVIOR, RESIST

"Bonnie's dad and his fiancée are taking Bonnie and Peter to Elton John! They're double dating!"

"Can I wear eye shadow? When can I get my belly button pierced?"

"But everybody's already seen *Fatal Attraction.* Nobody takes it seriously. I already saw part of it at Kylie's slumber party. Pleeeease? They'll think I'm a dork!"

It's not easy to dig in one's heels. When parents resist following the neighborhood or community flow, other parents can feel as if they are being criticized. They may respond in ways that are upsetting to everybody. And right when Kids are exquisitely sensitive to the stigma of being different.

Nearly always, in this kind of situation, more than one Kid's parents have serious qualms about what is considered normal, desirable behavior. So joining forces is one option. Another: introduce activities that can compete with the upsetting ones. Because sexually precocious activities seem so glamorous at this age, however, you're up against serious competition.

The key is to find a full menu of activities to keep the at-risk Kid busy, busy, busy. Forget concerns about no time to daydream or just veg out. If your child is veering into a peer group that espouses necking, R-rated videos, body-piercing, or other hair-raising activities, take action.

If you meet resistance, consider a counterattack, one designed to lure the Kid's friends back into the normal interests of this age group. Once you have led the group in a couple of activities and bonded with the Kids, you are likely to find yourself their designated adult.

There are several categories that fairly reliably fill the bill in keeping kids occupied. They are:

A. Food. A gathering that helps to cook and then eat the product is almost guaranteed to be a success, especially if the menu includes pizza and something chocolate.
B. Magic, juggling, circus stuff. Preteens are enthralled by mind-boggling tricks.
C. Animals. The zoo, animal parks, and marine exhibits are all good bets.
D. Scary rides. If you can find some that go

upside down with everybody's legs dangling into space, you've got it made.

E. Computers

F. Karate

G. Dance

MAKE A POINT OF ENJOYING UNPRESSURED ACTIVITIES THAT AREN'T ASSOCIATED WITH ANY ONE AGE GROUP WITH YOUR YOUNGSTER

Kids this age are under a lot of pressure to compete, achieve, and grow up. As the wonderful book *How to Talk So Kids Will Listen & Listen So Kids Will Talk** advises, parents are custodians of their Kids' childhoods. When your parents seek you out for a game of Concentration, Gin Rummy, or Clue, when you go out for miniature golf, bowling, or just to toss the old ball around or throw baskets—that's very reassuring. It says, "Here we are. You and me. Same old us. We did this when you were five; we'll do it when you're twenty. Boundaries intact. Everybody fine."

School

In second and third grades, children consolidate their basic reading and math skills. Starting in fourth grade, they put them to increasing use. They read to gain new facts, organize those facts into a logical sequence, and write reports. They reason out word problems and use their math skills to find the answer. If their school is lucky enough to sport up-to-date computers, they start learning to create spreadsheets, produce graphics of their own design, and write their own programs. They design science projects, from the simple to the complex, and carry them out—usually in their rooms—with a certain degree of odor, noise, or mess.

*How to Talk So Kids Will Listen & Listen So Kids Will Talk, by Adele Faber and Elaine Mazlish (Avon Books 1982).

You'd think that all the knowledge Kids are gaining would make life challenging enough. Not so. There are plenty of other things going on behind those classroom doors. Some of them can interfere with all those important intellectual challenges.

YOUR RELATIONSHIP WITH YOUR TEACHER IS MORE COMPLICATED

If you're a Nine through Eleven Kid, your relationship with the teacher is more complicated than before. How you feel about the teacher can make a big difference in how you learn.

It's not just that you can see the teacher's point of view. You've been able to do that for quite awhile. But, at this age, you realize that the teacher ought to be able to see your point of view, also! Before, if the teacher seemed cold and uncaring, you were unhappy and didn't want to go to school. Now, you aren't just unhappy—you're mad. You believe that if the teacher wanted to, he or she would be able to step into your shoes and see what your life is like.

He or she ought to understand that you hate to be embarrassed by being called to the board, that you don't want to sit next to Barry who makes faces at you, and that you just don't have time to do so much homework.

When your teacher is insensitive or clearly disregards your needs, it makes you mad. It feels like a personal insult. When your teacher does understand you, it feels like—well, like a crush.

Sometimes the whole class is mad at the teacher and sometimes the whole class suffers from a crush. More often, the temperature of the Kids' feelings is like a swimming pool in the sun, with hot spots and freezing ones.

If you feel that the teacher is your friend, you feel that you can take risks and even if you fail, he or she will still like you. If you feel that the teacher refuses to see life from your point of view, you may dig in your heels. Why should you learn anything. Why should you make his or her life easy.

Gender can make a big difference

Studies show that teachers have a tendency to call on boys more often, to give boys more chances to answer correctly, and to reward them for making a stab at the right answer. Girls tend to be rewarded for niceness and sweetness.

When you're faced with a classroom of thirty or more children, it's very hard not to fall into this mode, however. The boys tend to be very loud and active in demanding attention, insistent upon guessing until they get the right answer, and dramatically indignant when they are passed over. However, when teachers make an effort to reverse their automatic instincts, they may start discriminating against the boys!

HOW YOUR PEERS SEE YOU FEELS CRUCIAL

Every Kid has a reputation and a place in a complicated social structure. You have to watch your step all the time.

When Kylie goes to the blackboard, she carries with her her reputation as one of the popular Kids. When she gets stuck and the teacher asks for a volunteer to go and help her, only two Kids raise their hands: Kylie's best friend (unanimous approval) and Paul, the rejected Kid with no social skills.

Nobody else in their senses would dare to help a popular Kid. His or her clique could make life miserable. Only Paul, who has no idea of such things, innocently volunteers. The class moans a little, but doesn't give him a hard time: they all know that Paul is likely to do such things.

When Toby gives his book report, everybody is supposed to crack up—even if it's a dull report on a serious book—because Toby is the class clown. If you don't laugh at Toby, you're weird. Toby could burst into tears and recount a heart-rending story, and the class

would be torn, at first, about whether or not to laugh. They might wait to see what the popular Kids do, first.

Doing well in class may be a social handicap

This can happen in at least three situations.

• If the Kids in the powerful and popular clique aren't also the ones who do well in class, they may turn the class sentiment against anybody who seems to be "a brain."

• If sentiments toward the teacher are generally cold, doing well in class may be seen as a despicable way of "getting in good" with him or her.

• If the community in general regards academic learning as weak, pretentious, or dangerous, a Kid who does well is likely to be shunned.

THERE MAY BE A GREATER RANGE OF LEARNING STYLES

Some Kids in the class are able to think in a much more sophisticated way than others

It's not just because they're smarter, either. It's because of puberty. Before puberty, you can think very effectively, but you mostly think in concrete terms. You get an idea and test it and then see what happened. Somehow or another, the hormones of puberty seem to mature the mind. Kids who are into puberty start to be able to think up a theory and test it mentally, working out ahead of time what might happen. At this age, this means that girls may seem smarter than boys.

Lots of things become possible after you've gotten the knack of working things out in your head. Some of them are fairly trivial. For instance, suppose you have a word problem in math, in which you have to split $57.00 equally among three people. Suppose you make a silly mistake, and divide 57 by 3 and get 29 instead of 19. If your hormones are working, you are likely to think, Wait! That means that two people's total amount will be almost $60! So it can't be right! A prepubertal classmate might only come to that realization if he or she has the foresight to check his or her results by multiplying

29 times 3 and discovering that it doesn't come out right.

By the way, this increased mental sophistication of puberty can make negotiations with parents much more complicated too.

Being able to work things out in your mind can help you in every subject and in your social life, too. But it can also lead to more intense, anxious, distracting daydreams.

Learning disabilities can surface for the first time

Some perfectly bright youngsters will be having trouble keeping up with the regular schoolwork. For some of them, it's because they are placed a grade too high. They'd be perfectly fine back in third grade, and by the time they got to fourth grade, would be able to take on the work with aplomb.

For others, a learning disability may cause problems for the first time at ages nine, ten, or eleven. It may not have earlier because the work in the lower grades didn't demand the skills called for in the later grades. For a few, it may be because a subtle hearing problem now makes it too hard to follow instructions that are getting more and more complicated. Or because anxiety is getting in the way of their learning anything at all.

Often a learning disability is inherited. If a parent began falling behind in school at about this age, it's a good idea to keep an eye on the child. Behavior is often as good an indicator as test scores. The youngster who suddenly wants to stay home from school, who seems anxious or dejected, who forgets to bring home work or teachers' reports may be struggling academically.

The child who can't keep up with the class during these years needs careful testing and special help. Most of all, he or she needs the tactful support of parents and teachers, and real success in another area of life.

THE QUESTION OF HOMEWORK

In Fourth, Fifth, and Sixth grade there are two kinds of homework: drudgery and fun. Kids need to memorize things, from spelling words to multiplication tables to state capitals: that can be drudgery. They also need to use their imaginations and logical skills in book reports, science projects, math problems, poetry and literature, history, geography, and sociology: that can be fun.

Everybody knows that parents are supposed to provide a time, place, and equipment for the Kid to do homework. Ideally, this includes a place for books, a surface on which to work, good lighting, and paper, pencils, pens, and so on. Maybe it includes a computer plus or minus a printer. The time should be regular and protected, without distractions. But remember Abe Lincoln, scratching away on a slate by the dim light of the fireside. Don't be fooled: you can't guarantee academic success just by setting up the props, and you won't doom your child to failure if you can't provide them all.

What a Kid this age really needs are parents who take his or her homework seriously. Giving homework high priority doesn't mean saying, "You can't go outside/watch TV/call your friend until you finish your homework." It means taking a genuine interest in what the Kid is learning. That means respecting the subject matter and marking the progress the Kid is making. "I never realized that some penguins mate for life. How on earth can they tell each other apart?" "You're up to the sevens table already? You're going fast."

Parents can help Kids with the drudgery tasks. They can teach Kids how to make up mnemonic devices ("To remember the capital of Ohio, I always think of Columbus sailing his boats across all those cornfields.") They can chant the multiplication tables with the Kid. If the Kid has special trouble with a particular times table, parents can insert spot quizzes into odd moments of daily life ("White meat or dark? What's seven times eight?")

Parents can show Kids that they respect the tasks that require thought and imagination.

"You mean," they say with stunned faces, "you can tell me the difference between viruses and bacteria?" "Are you SURE that's Uganda?" "The pharaoh Ramses had HOW MANY sons?" Kids can overhear parents talking with other adults about how impressed they are with the Kid's abilities. "She wrote this essay on voting you would not believe." "Just look at these problems. Did we ever have stuff like this? But he figures it out like *that*..."

They can help a Kid learn how to approach a lesson in an organized fashion. They can point out that every paragraph has a topic sentence, and that if you write each of those sentences out so they're strung together you'll have a nice summary of the text. They can help the Kid make sure that the finished homework product is one to be proud of: a report in which each sentence makes sense, the words are spelled correctly, each paragraph has a topic, and the handwriting is neat. (Remember the Calvin and Hobbes cartoon in which Calvin feels he deserves an A because his one-sentence science report—"Bats are big ugly bugs"—is bound in a clear plastic binder?)

So yes, parents can help a lot with homework.

Sometimes a Kid will ask for help with homework for reasons that have nothing to do with difficulty completing assignments. Maybe, thinks the Kid, if they help me with my homework it will keep Mom and Dad from arguing or from paying so much attention to another sibling. Maybe it will keep them focused on me. If homework sessions seem to be getting prolonged, with the Kid seeming to purposefully drag his or her feet, this may be the reason. The cure is to give one-on-one focused attention to the Kid at other times as well. Other reactions, such as doing homework for him or her or abandoning the enterprise altogether, won't work.

With all this input into the homework situation, it's easy for parents to feel as if they are the ones responsible for the work getting done and handed in to the teacher. This almost always backfires. One of the most important things for a Kid to learn is that the homework belongs to him or her, not to parents. If the homework doesn't get done, the Kid is accountable to the teacher. Parents can help most by sitting down with the Kid and asking him or her to plan a solution. This works better than trying to impose one.

If the Kid consistently defaults on homework, consider the possibility that something is up. Perhaps the Kid is distracted by social or family stress, or has an underlying medical problem like constipation, or is encountering difficulty due to a vision or hearing problem or a learning disability. Make sure the Kid is not depressed or experimenting with alcohol, drugs, or inhalants. Discuss the problem with both the teacher and the pediatrician.

Finally, one of the best ways for parents to help with homework is to take the role of student and let the kid be the teacher. In medical schools, procedures like starting IV's aren't considered learned until the student sees one, does one, and teaches one. Teaching someone else is the best way for a Kid to consolidate knowledge, discover any gaps, and get a good feeling about his or her mental skills. And you might learn something. Ramses had fifty-two sons. Honest.

THE SCHOOL'S QUALITY

Surveys show that parents think that American schools are not doing a good job, but that they think their Kid's particular school is an exception.

How to explain this? The people who analyze polls give several reasons. Parents like to regard their Kids as successful, and by extension they regard the school as successful. Parents bond to individual parts of the school: the teacher who likes the child, the good report card, the fact that their child seems happy to go to class each day. Parents don't realize how their child's particular school compares with other schools or how American education compares with the education in other countries.

Once children have the basic tools for learning, they can be taught in a huge variety of ways how to use them. A child who would soar in one school may feel trapped in another. This can happen in the inner cities, but also in suburbia. Even in wealthy suburbia.

Some schools nurture classrooms where learning is honored and students are respected. It's not fair when a Kid feels uncomfortable showing how smart he or she is.

Some schools extoll teachers, paying them well and giving them the supplies they need. It's not fair when an overworked teacher burns out and makes a class, or part of a class, miserable.

Some schools individualize learning and fit the teaching to the child's learning style. It's not fair when a child is asked to do work that he truly cannot understand and gets punished for failing.

Some schools are simply richer, and can purchase and use high-tech equipment that makes all of these goals easier to attain. For instance, language learning is easiest before puberty: a language learned in the first few grades can be spoken practically accent-free. Some elementary schools have language labs, in which only the foreign language is spoken and read.

Some schools have up-to-date, high-capability computers with printers, modems, and CD-ROMs. Many more schools have older computers, which function as fancy typewriters. In fact, 80 percent of the computers in public schools are old models that won't even take a CD-ROM or get you onto the internet. Even that's a luxury, though. More than half of the public schools in this country don't even have the wiring in the classrooms to allow Kids to work with computers. The wiring itself can cost from $20,000 to $50,000.

Computers not only enrich school life, in general. They also are invaluable for children with even subtle learning disabilities, who may have trouble with sequencing, handwriting, or computing. They also help Kids who suffer from performance anxiety. It's much friendlier to have the computer say, "Let's try again" than it is to give the wrong answer in class to the displeasure of your teacher and to the always-eager-to-pounce reactions of your classmates (see box, **How Computers Help Kids Learn,** page 218).

HOW PARENTS CAN HELP

HELP YOUR KID TO FEEL GOOD ABOUT LEARNING

A Kid who feels uncomfortable at school displaying a vivid interest in learning or showing what he or she has accomplished is at a disadvantage. Parents can feel pretty ineffective in dealing with the result of classroom group dynamics. After all, you can't change the classroom ambience by sheer force of will. You can, however, let your child know that your values are very different.

• Show an interest in the work. Help the child to go a little or a lot further than the assignment. Praise accomplishment, not just good grades. "I learned a lot from your report about Egypt. I had no idea that the Sphinx is supposed to be so much older than the pyramids."

• Let your child know you value education highly. Let him or her see you learning actively: taking a course, reading, talking about topics that aren't limited to daily life. Talk admiringly about people who have achieved great things intellectually.

• Play down popularity. A Kid who thinks parents worry about his or her social status is likely to be much more intimidated by peers into not achieving (see **Growth of the Soul,** earlier in this chapter).

GET TO KNOW THE SCHOOL STAFF

It's hard for busy parents to find time for school functions, but attending Open Houses and parents' days and so on sends a signal to the teacher and the principal that you care, that you're an involved parent.

If you have a special request to make, put yourself in the teacher's (or principal's) shoes. Try to praise everything that you can praise. Bring the teacher a treat. Your Kid may be able to give you a hint: "She keeps pistachio nuts in her desk drawer."

Try to make the request specific and phrase it so that it is neither bragging nor a criticism of the staff.

> "Tremayne flashes through his math quizzes so fast that he gets done before everybody else. In fourth grade, he was always getting into trouble, trying to talk to people who were still working. Do you think he could bring a book from home to read?"

instead of

> "The class work is too easy for Tremayne. I should think there'd be some provision for the bright children."

If the teacher comes through, write a note to the principal, with a copy to the superintendent, praising him or her. Sneak in a word of praise for *their* astuteness in hiring and nurturing such good teachers. Send a blind copy to the teacher, along with a note of thanks.

Writing letters of complaint is not nearly as effective.

MAKE SURE YOUR CHILD GETS ANY EXTRA HELP NEEDED TO KEEP UP WITH THE CLASS

If your child is floundering, make an appointment with the teacher. Request that an Individual Educational Placement evaluation be made. Such an evaluation must, by law, make recommendations for helping the child, and those recommendations must be carried out by the school. If you disagree with the IEP, you have the right to appeal it.

Sometimes a child isn't really floundering, but shows a decrease in achievement from one grade to the next. A conversation with the teacher may not result in anything specific being pinpointed. In this case, consider hiring a tutor. Make sure the tutor is a good one who starts at the child's current level and challenges just a little more at each step, giving praise rather than criticism.

HELP YOUR KID BECOME AT LEAST COMPUTER LITERATE IF NOT EXPERT. IT'S WORTH CONSIDERABLE SACRIFICE IN MONEY AND TIME

Being a computer literate Kid means that you can touch-type on a keyboard, access programs and select functions, locate the internet or another information highway, and print. Being a computer expert Kid means that you can do spread sheets, graphs, tables, and original graphics; that you can troubleshoot and fix problems, and that you can help your parents when they get stuck.

A Kid who hands in a spell-checked, printed, graphics-enhanced report doesn't just tend to get a better grade than one who hands in a laboriously hand-written, slightly scruffy one. He or she builds on a reputation for competence. In the teacher's mind, this Kid can't help but seem clear-headed, alert, organized, self-starting. He or she is more likely to seek this youngster out for special projects, challenges, and praise. It's not fair, but that's the way it is. When a Kid gets that kind of recognition, the youngster starts to see himself or herself the way the teacher does and to expect such treatment. That's good.

Most American families can't afford a computer. A study done in 1994 by Children's Partnership, a research and policy group, found that nearly half of families with an income of $50,000 or more have computers, while only 7 percent of families with an income of $20,000 or less do. That's not surprising.

If you *can* afford a computer, that's terrific. When choosing the kind to get, here are the things that you might want to ask:

• How user-friendly is the computer? If you want to buy software, like Windows, to make it more user-friendly does it have the power for that software?

• Is it compatible with the computers at your child's schools—not just the one he or she is attending now, but those in the middle school too?

• If you aren't buying a CD-ROM or a modem when you purchase the computer, will the computer be compatible with them in the future when you can afford them?

• If you can afford a printer now, compare the quality of the printouts carefully. If you can't afford one that gives fairly rapid and clear work, consider sharing a printer or using a public one.

• If you can't afford a printer right away, is this computer compatible with the printer you'll be using at the child's school, the library, a neighbor's, or somewhere else?

• What kind of troubleshooting software should you get? The kind you need may be less expensive if you don't plan on using software borrowed from other people or downloaded from computer bulletin boards.

Instructing the Kid in how to use the computer also needs thought. This is the appropriate age for Kids to learn how to touch-type, since they're able to read automatically and comfortably.

The hunt and peck method can become a habit, and it's just not as fast and foolproof as touch-typing. Most Kids will need a touch-typing class, though there is good software out there that makes touch-typing a game. Your own Kid may know the program that is currently most popular. He or she may even be able to borrow this software from a classmate or parents may go in on the software together.

If you can't afford a computer, consider some less expensive alternatives:

• Many public libraries and regional high schools have homework centers, complete with computer equipment, software, and instruction.

• There are several franchises of computer schools, such as FutureKids (1–800–PRO–KIDS). Huge numbers of boutique computer schools have also sprung up. It's perfectly appropriate to ask the school to put you in touch with satisfied patrons.

• A local high school math or science teacher may be able to put you in touch with a student tutor.

ACTIVITIES AND LESSONS: THE AGE OF COMPETENCE

Kids at nine, ten, and eleven get a lot from structured activities and lessons. One of the most important things they gain is a sense of continuously increasing competence. This seems obvious, but to Kids in this age group this sense of growing mastery is relatively new.

When little Kids show off, it's pretty clear that they don't rate competence very high. "Look what I can do!" Clarissa shouts, flapping her arms. Yep, folks, that's it: arm flapping. When they're a bit older, they get pleasure from achievements—when they hit a golf ball, take off the training wheels, learn to tie their shoes. At seven and eight, they find out whether they have interest or talent in an endeavor—T-ball, piano, drawing.

Once they reach nine, ten, and eleven, they discover that working at something can make you better at it. This naturally leads to the question, "Yes, but how do you get them to practice?" One way is to look at what makes Kids want to practice. For example, take Little

Computers will never replace great teachers, but they do have a role. Kids who need extra incentive, nonjudgmental corrections, and help with getting organized or being neat often regard computers as their friends.

TRADITIONAL BOOK REPORT

Read the book, write a brief summary of the plot and say whether you liked the book and would recommend it to others. Might be jazzed up by having the Kid pretend to be a literary agent or someone who wants to make the book into a major motion film. Handwriting and neatness count.

Computer-Assisted Book Report

Read the book. Look up the subject or author on your CD-ROM. If the book was about horses, you can watch the evolution of the horse or listen to cowboys reciting poetry or learn about human-horse relationships or find out how to buy your own wild mustang cheap. Type either a report of the plot, a biography of the author, an essay on the setting, or some other aspect of the story. Use the spell-checker and the grammar-checker. Decorate the report with your graphics program. Print it out.

TRADITIONAL SPELLING LIST

Look at the words. Memorize them. Write each one over three or four times. Have somebody read them to you and you spell them back. Take a test Friday.

Computer-Assisted Spelling List

The words are highlighted in a story on your computer. When you come to a highlighted word, flash on it with the mouse. You then get some choices: hear the word pronounced, defined, and spelled by one of the characters. Or see the word taken apart so that you can see where each part came from ("co: with; oper: work; ation: the act of. Cooperation: the act of working with or together.") Take a test Friday.

TRADITIONAL MATH HOMEWORK SHEET

Read the problem. Write down the math. Do the adding, subtracting, multiplying, dividing. Check it. If you don't understand something, ask your mom or dad or grandparent or somebody. Bring it in to be graded.

Computer-Assisted Math Homework

See the problem as an animated cartoon. Select the parts that you need to solve the problem. If you select the wrong parts, the computer will say, "Let's go back and look at the problem." Then the computer will ask you a question to help you figure out what part to select. If you can't get that right, the computer will say again, "Let's go back and look at the problem" and ask you an easier question. Once you have the right "take" on the problem, ask the computer to set up the tasks of multiplying, subtracting, and so on. Do the calculations by following the guidance of the computer: type in your solutions. If your arithmetic is wrong, the computer will say, "Seven times six is not fifty four. Try again." When you have the answer, the animated cartoon goes ahead with the plot so you can see your answer have a happy ending. Print out your results and bring to class.

TRADITIONAL SCIENCE PROJECT

Think of a possible experiment. Last year, somebody did a really fun one: they read that most of what we think is taste really is smell. So they made everybody plug their noses and taste apples and onions, and nobody could tell which was which! Think of something like that.

Computer-Assisted Science Project

Think of a category you're interested in. Say, caves. Look up caves on your CD-ROM encyclopedia. See the movie about how stalactites and stalagmites form and how you can create the

NINE, TEN, AND ELEVEN

same chemical reaction with things most likely available in your pantry. Make a diorama of a cave with your own stalactites and stalagmites being formed by drips.

TRADITIONAL SOCIAL STUDIES ESSAY

Read about the principal products of Latin American countries. Write them all down. Cut out pictures from a magazine and paste them on your report.

Computer-Assisted Social Studies Project

Find Mexico on your CD-ROM. Watch a film of an open market. Look at all the wild birds—parrots and Toucan-like things. Press the button that shows those birds in the wild and how they get caught. Type up a story about a bird that gets hunted down and taken to market and sold to a dealer and then is bought by a Kid just like you.

League baseball. Here's what makes daily practice and weekly performances so appealing.

• You already know the rules. You don't have to spend time figuring out what you're supposed to do. All you work on is doing each part of the action well. If you do, then you know that you'll play a good game.

• You have an idea of what "well" means. It means hitting the ball so it's hard to catch and catching it if it's hit into your area. It means running to the base faster than the fielder can throw, and throwing the ball faster than the base-runner can run. And so on.

• Your teammates appreciate it when you do something well. They don't like it when you don't.

• At the end of a session you know whether you did well.

• Over time, you can tell whether you are getting better at the game. You can see that you hit the ball farther. You make more bases without getting tagged. You catch harder balls. Besides, other people tell you. In fact, people are always judging whether players are getting better or not.

• Your coach values you. It's important to the coach that you do well.

• The audience (whether it's just your teammates at practice or people in the stands at a game) cares a lot. They watch your every move. If you make a good catch, they'll holler. If you

fumble, they'll moan. Each individual play in the game is a new chance to do it well.

Now compare the motivation to well at baseball with, say, piano lessons.

• You are still and forever learning the rules. Just when you think you know them all, there's more. First it was just white keys and the key of C major. Then sharps and flats. Then playing in the key of G or B or whatever. First it was $\frac{1}{4}$ time, then $\frac{2}{2}$, then $\frac{3}{8}$, and so on. Nobody tells you when you will finally have learned all the rules and can concentrate on the game—er, the performance.

• What does doing each action well mean? There's no action to compare your own with to know if you're getting better at it. All you have is an idea of what the piece should sound like if you didn't make any mistakes. Getting there from where you are now can seem impossible.

• It's solitary. Just you and the piano and the sheet of music.

• At the end of a practice session, you can tell whether you've hit more wrong keys than you did the last time. If you've hit fewer wrong notes, you know that it doesn't mean that you're necessarily getting better at playing the piano. It just means you've gotten a little better at playing this piece.

• Over time, you can feel yourself getting better at playing a piece. You make fewer mistakes on that piece. But after the piece will come a harder one, and you'll start off all fumbly just the way you did with the previous one.

• Your teacher wants you to practice more. When he or she praises you, it's almost never because you did something exactly right. You despair of ever really pleasing your teacher.

• You have an audience that's there by accident because they happen to be around when you are supposed to practice. Or sometimes your parents ask you to show off or you give a recital. You can't imagine why they'd want to hear you practice. You just keep playing the same little bit over and over, trying to get it right.

Learning to play piano is pretty bleak in comparison to learning baseball. A Kid who is used to loving baseball practice is going to have to learn a whole different approach when it comes to something like music lessons.

You can't make piano lessons like baseball games. But you can make it possible for a Kid this age to value the differences. Here are some suggestions.

• Prepare the youngster for the differences. Kids this age like to know what the challenge is and how you're supposed to behave. Making the differences explicit is very helpful. Let the child know that because of the differences, you are going to ask for a commitment of six months. Make an informal agreement or sign a contract.

• Match child and teacher, and monitor how they get along. Youngsters this age are very sensitive to whether or not the teacher likes them. When they don't feel liked, they tend to get angry rather than sad. If they do feel liked, they will strive to please the person who likes them.

• A teacher needs to give the Kid the sensation that progress is being made and that it is practicing that makes it happen. If a teacher makes every lesson equal, whether you've practiced well or not, that's boring and confusing.

• Strongly consider group practice and lessons. Work in a little healthy competition.

• Be an audience. If a Kid is playing and you

are within hearing distance, you're an audience. Give feedback.

> "That sounded a good bit more confident." "I can hear the beat now with your left hand."

If this seems to make your Kid nervous or irritated, disappear so that he or she doesn't have the sensation of being overheard.

Exercise and Sports

These years see the parting of the ways when it comes to exercise. I don't mean a division in terms of gender, with girls devoting their energies to quiet activities and boys leaping around the great outdoors. That can happen, even in this day and age, but what I'm talking about crosses gender lines.

This is the time when a little change in the balance of a Kid's world can send him or her down the road to inactivity. A child whose temperament is more thoughtful than vigorous or whose family life subtly or directly discourages exercise or who undergoes temporary slacking off in daily activities often gets turned off for good, or at least for a good long time.

The truth is that for most children today in America, there must be a purposeful effort to involve them in physical activities if they're going to participate at all. The lifestyle is designed (Who designed it? Got me. I didn't.) to promote inactivity. Kids get bused or carpooled to school. Only 36 percent of American public schools have daily P.E., and there's no counting on them to provide exercise: the E in P.E. stands for education, not exercise. In the fourth, fifth, and sixth grades, that can mean learning rules or standing around watching demonstrations.

During recess and lunch, it's easy for Kids to be engrossed in totally inactive enterprises: gossiping, insulting, sharing secrets and worries; trading stuff; doing clique things, like singing or whispering or giggling in a group. You can sit around with your Gameboy, either alone or companionably with your friends. You can play intricate fantasy games. My, how time flies when you're having fun.

After school, you may be obliged to stay inside because your parents aren't home yet and they want to know where you are and what you're doing. Or you might have lessons to go to or tutoring or you might need to get back to the fantasy games you were working on at lunch. Oh yes, you also have homework. In the winter, it's too dark and cold to go out anyhow. You get the idea. The bottom line: it's not at all out of the ordinary for a Kid this age to get practically no exercise.

How come some Kids escape this route and spend these years running around, playing sports, outdoors every chance they get?

• These Kids generally have passed the novice stage of physical skills. They take for granted their abilities to throw, catch, bat, hit, and so on. By the time they reach this age they are ready to use those skills to play real games. They can feel their competence increasing, an enormous reward.

• Their parents go out of their way to resist the cultural impulses toward inactivity. They help Kids find time and space for play and practice. They carpool to games, stay and cheer, raise money for uniforms, coach. They don't allow long hours of TV or computerizing. They don't just say "turn it off," they make sure the Kid has something else to do—something active.

• They live in a community where year-round sports are available conveniently and at low cost, either because of the weather or because adults give athletics a high priority, providing opportunities, coaching, and transportation.

If a youngster seems to be heading down the path of inactivity, is this a problem? What will he or she miss out on? If the loss seems significant, how can you get the child to be more active? If the youngster is one of the active ones, what kinds of concerns surface at this time? What about healthy versus unhealthy competition, risk-taking, independence, safety?

ACTIVITY-AVERSE KIDS

They are not couch potatoes. They don't just lie in front of the TV and veg out. If you assessed their interests, friendships, ambitions, loyalties, and character, you'd be impressed. They are cute, funny, smart, and full of personality.

Here's what they miss by not exercising or participating in sports:

ONE OF THE BIG ADVANTAGES OF PHYSICAL SKILLS IS THAT YOU GET CONSTANT, INSTANT FEEDBACK ABOUT YOUR COMPETENCE

Feeling competent is one of the main ingredients in self-esteem. If you climb to the top of the bars or swing all the way across or hit a single to right field—or do just about any physical act—you can see and feel success.

Nonphysical activities are more dicey sources of feelings of competence. This is true even for extremely worthwhile activities. For instance, reading books may carry you away from bad feelings temporarily, but completing a book doesn't give a lasting feeling of "I did that. Myself. I did it well and I can do it again, too." Traditional girls' activities are often unsatisfactory, because either there's no real end point for them, (playing with dolls or model horses) or because their success depends on subjective judgments (making clothes or jewelry, cooking, art projects).

Computer games offer a feeling of competence, of course. The problem is that this feeling of competence is very specific; it doesn't carry over very well to anything else. It's hard to build a self-image on this type of achievement.

GAMES AND PHYSICAL ACTIVITIES CONSTANTLY BRING UP MATTERS THAT HAVE TO BE DECIDED BY THE GROUP PLAYING

This is important practice in developing a mature moral sense (see **Growth of the Soul,** earlier in this chapter).

IT'S VERY HARD FOR MANY CHILDREN WITH NORMAL METABOLISMS TO AVOID GAINING TOO MUCH WEIGHT IF THEY DON'T EXERCISE

See **Growth and Nutrition,** later in this chapter.

IF KIDS DON'T DEVELOP A SENSE OF PHYSICAL COMPETENCE AT THIS AGE, IT'S HARDER AND HARDER TO DO SO LATER ON

Take it from somebody who had to learn to ski at the age of thirty-five on a community rope tow. "Look! Dr. Nathanson's down again! Ooooh, she's *really* stuck now!" the little children, my pediatric patients, would cry as they hurtled by competently.

So how do you get a youngster this age back in action? Here are some suggestions.

• Find an activity in which it's normal to be a novice at this age. That way, a lack of skills doesn't set the Kid apart. Such enterprises include karate and related activities; ethnic dance groups; and relatively unusual sports such as archery, juggling, and snowshoeing.

• Have the child do the activity with a buddy. The buddy could be a friend or a parent, even.

• Arrange for the Kid to have help in working on basic skills. A parent can find a tactfully private time and place for the Kid to learn what everybody else learned years ago: throwing, catching, batting, whatever. If the parent can't, a nice, sane high school student could.

• If the Kid is hooked on a pastime that is inactive, let him or her earn time or equipment for that pastime by exercising. Half an hour of jump rope earns a new Baby Sitter's Club book.

An hour of walk-run earns an hour of video games.

• Try to design daily life to include activity. Have a walkpool rather than a carpool, in which the driving parent lets the Kids out a safe four or five blocks away from school and picks them up at the same point. If it's safe to get around the community, don't drive to the store: have it be the Kid's job to walk, run, bike, or skate there.

• Consider a one-on-one or small-group tutorial if the youngster feels way behind in skills. An inactive Kid's buddies may be in the same boat and parents might band together to hire— yes, hire—a high school student or other proficient person to instruct them all.

THE SPORTS-LOVING KID

Competence, competition, confidence.

"So this is your third year of ice hockey. Are you good at it?"

"Yeah."

That "yeah" rings with meaning. Often enough, when a youngster this age is asked, "What are you good at?" what you get is a shrug. Self-deprecating. Wistful. Honest, not modest. It is a joy to hear that calm, self-assured, matter-of-fact "yeah."

These are the years for getting really good at what you can already do well and feeling great about it. The main focus for parents is to make sure that getting good at something happens. Kids need parents to encourage bravery but not recklessness; competition that fosters sportsmanship and self-confidence; and balance, both in terms of the variety of sports and between sports and the rest of life.

STEERING A COURSE THAT ENCOURAGES APPROPRIATE RISK-TAKING BUT NOT UNNECESSARY ACCIDENTS

It can be very tricky controlling parental anxiety, fostering courage, and taking reasonable precautions, all at the same time. However, Kids this age need to feel as if parents provide an envelope for them to test, an envelope whose borders mark the place where challenge becomes unacceptable risk. The edges of the envelope are a little bit flexible, but when they stand firm, they stand firm.

Where each family's "envelope" borders lie will vary considerably, but it's a good idea to examine the concept every so often and update it. For instance, one family may decide that skiing is fine but snowboards are too risky. Another may decide that snowboards are fine, but that the Kid must wear helmet and goggles. A third may decide that snowboards aren't any more dangerous than a Flexible Flier sled and impose no guidelines at all.

Pediatricians as a professional group (The American Academy of Pediatrics), have constructed a kind of envelope. Some activities are just too risky: trampoline gymnastics or scuba diving under age twelve, for instance. Others are risky but less risky with proper equipment: skateboarding, in-line skating, skiing, and snowboarding. But there are controversial issues, even within the Academy. Some pediatricians regard some popular sports as unacceptably dangerous: boxing, jumping on horseback, tackle football. Some regard what many people see as very low-risk sports as dangerous enough to require special gear: baseball, for instance.

So parents need to follow their own best instincts. If their particular "risk envelope" seems either much more restricted or much more expansive than the community standards, a good move is to discuss this with the pediatrician. Even if your own pediatrician has extreme views, the discussion will be worthwhile.

Parents whose envelopes are at either extreme send a distinct message to the child, but it may be a surprising message. A youngster who is forbidden or discouraged or warned when trying new, mildly risky activities may become fearful and avoidant. Or he or she may take those risks, delightfully shocking the old folks, and feel like a hero. A youngster who is given no restrictions may be the daredevil of the neighborhood. Or he or she may impose limits sensibly on himself or herself. Or the Kid may feel as if parents regard him or her as dispensable and replaceable and develop behavior problems in areas having nothing much to do with athletics.

For safety concerns regarding specific sports, see Appendix B.

ENCOURAGE THE KIND OF COMPETITION THAT ENLIVENS, RATHER THAN EMBITTERS

Some communities are so engrossed in Kids' athletics that the hierarchy of teams becomes absolutely arcane.

> "I'm in Double-A soccer, but I'm in senior hockey, so next year I'm going to drop soccer unless I get into pre-premium. But if I get into pre-premium soccer, I won't have time for senior hockey but by next year I'll probably be up to ultra-varsity hockey, so I'll have to decide then. What do you think?" Ummm. Open your mouth and stick out your tongue.

Competition, competence, and self-confidence all ideally ought to go together. For Kids who progress step by step up a hierarchy, that generally does happen. But what of the Kids who don't or the Kids who see a friend or enemy or sibling always, always one step ahead?

Kids need parents to have their radar out, making sure that sports are helping a child to grow. If a Nine through Eleven is good at something, able to make plays, keep up with teammates, and satisfy the coach, he or she ought to be able to answer "Yeah!" to the question, "Are you good at that?" If the answer is always "Yeah, but—" or "Kind of" or, heaven forbid, just a shrug, that particular sport may not be doing its job for that particular Kid.

PROVIDE BALANCE IN THE CHILD'S LIFE, BOTH IN THE VARIETY OF ATHLETICS AND BETWEEN ATHLETICS AND OTHER ACTIVITIES

Kids need a balance in physical activity to avoid burnout and overuse injuries. They need a balance between athletics and other activities to avoid burnout, develop social skills, expand intellectual and artistic horizons, and keep their options open for the future.

ONE SPORT OR MORE?

Some Kids are appropriately one-sport athletes. Sometimes the sport demands it, if one is a serious contender. To be able to compete in a solo or performance sport like figure skating, gymnastics, tennis, or swimming means hours of practice. Serious contenders don't run the risk of overuse injuries because they are coached to prevent them.

However, when a Nine through Eleven is not a serious contender or is engaged in seasonal team sports, there's a lot to be said for balance among activities. The more devoted and skillful the player, the more likely it is that the sport inspires specialization. This can lead to overuse injuries: the elbows of pitchers and the knees of catchers and goalies can show distressing wear and tear.

Good coaches watch this carefully and abide by guidelines to limit this risk. But a Kid who pitches a season of Little League baseball and then spends the rest of the year perfecting his curve ball with his or her mom or dad may wind up on the disabled list. Good insurance: an off-season sport that concentrates on running, not throwing.

Burnout from overspecialization can have a number of causes. Simple repetition and boredom is one. Feeling too much pressure to perform is another. Sometimes, too, a Kid who is overspecialized doesn't get the sensation of becoming better and better: it's just the same

old thing, like a job. Finally, sometimes the youngster feels as if his or her competence is being co-opted by parents or coaches and doesn't belong to the Kid any longer.

BE A JOCK?

Being committed to sports usually means staying at the appropriate weight. Since excess weight brings on puberty early, most athletes in this age group will start puberty at the average age or later. This means that their growing spurt is likely to occur right at the time they're becoming most competent in a sport.

When your body grows and changes dramatically, you may discover that the sport becomes either a lot easier or a lot harder. Also, when you're growing rapidly, you need more sleep and you get tired faster. And this can happen right at the time that you enter middle school/junior high school, when there is a marked increase in competition. The combination may make you feel as if you aren't accelerating in skills, the way you assumed you would. This can be pretty distressing. If your sports life is the only bright, interesting area of your life that gives you a sense of competence, it can be devastating.

Looking ahead to that possibility doesn't mean sounding warnings of doom, but it does mean that it's sensible to keep open other avenues for adventure, challenge, and achievement. Parents can help a Kid this age by balancing their own investment in the youngster's sports success with eagerness to have him or her explore other areas of life. When a Kid is successful and proud, that can be hard to do, but that's what parents are for. Parents do the tough stuff.

Growth and Nutrition

GROWTH

Many boys and a few girls ages nine, ten, and eleven will continue growing at the same rate and will maintain the same shapes they had in earlier years. Most of these Kids will grow about 2½" and gain about 7 pounds a year. The others will start puberty. This means that there really isn't an average size Kid at this age. Everybody's different.

Most girls will be well into puberty by the age of twelve. Most boys will just be starting. These two sentences cannot possibly convey the drama of this situation. It's not just that many of the girls will be taller and heavier than many of the boys. The drama is that in a mixed-sex group of children, the boys spend some time being onlookers of the process and the girls spend some time being the looked upon. This governs a lot of the behavior typical of this period and maybe long after.

Puberty means that a child's internal clock has gone from childhood mode to growing-into-a-mature-sexual-being mode. The timing of puberty is complicated.

• There's a cultural influence on puberty that includes nutrition and exercise and maybe other things as well. This influence has caused the average age at which American children start puberty to become younger and younger, over the last century.

• There's an inherited effect: most children start puberty at about the same time that their same-sex parent did.

• There's the effect of individual health and lifestyle: a chronic illness or weight-loss can delay puberty; so can extreme exercise; so can extreme thinness. Excess chubbiness tends to accelerate puberty and also to cause a decrease in adult height.

Both sexes need lots of information and moral support from parents, and parents usually need information and moral support from pediatricians. In fact, the information needs here are complicated: what girls need to know about girls, what boys need to know about boys, what girls need to know about boys, what boys need to know about girls, what both need to know about sexual relationships, and what parents need to know about all of that.

There are many excellent books that cover all the aspects of puberty very thoroughly (see box, **Some Good Books on Puberty**, page 228).

It's a good idea to browse and to find a book that fits your Kid's personality.

The following is a description of the events of puberty for boys and for girls. It doesn't include the basics (eggs, sperm, conception). It is devoid of diagrams about glands (hypothalamus-pituitary axis, ovaries, adrenals, testes), and the mechanics of ovulation, ejaculation, intercourse, and conception. ("That frowning moose thing," Elevens call the drawing of uterus and fallopian tubes.) Instead, it summarizes answers to the most common questions I hear from Kids and parents.

GIRLS

Puberty means that your body is getting ready for you to be able to have sex and to have babies. That means you get breasts and hair growing under your arms and around your crotch, and sooner or later you get periods.

You'd think that this was pretty early to have puberty start, since you're probably not planning to have sex or a baby for years and years. But nature doesn't take that into account. Puberty starts when it wants to start. In fact, maybe it's a good idea to get used to a grown-up body long before you have sex or babies, so you know what it's like to be an adult first.

At any rate, as you look at all the things that happen during puberty, they may not sound like fun. They may sound like a lot of bother or as if stuff is happening that you can't control, and that's embarrassing. It's very hard to get across that puberty really is fun, almost always, and that any bother and embarrassment is worth it. You will just have to take it on trust.

Every girl has her own normal timetable. You could start noticing the first signs of puberty as young as eight or as old as fourteen. If you are younger than nine when you start puberty, your pediatrician might want to talk with you and your parents about possibly slowing down puberty until you are a little older. The average age to start puberty is about ten-and-a-half. You're likely to start at around the same age your mother did. You could ask her. You'd think everyone would remember something crucial like that, but some people don't.

As a rule, the earlier you start puberty, the sooner you stop growing. Most girls who start puberty at a very young age are taller than everybody else for a few years, but then they stop growing and can be shorter than average as adults. So a girl who is much shorter than everybody else for a few years, maybe right through sophomore year at high school, can grow so much that she's taller than everybody else.

The first things you're likely to notice vary from one girl to the next. Sometimes a girl thinks that because her body has changed, she's started puberty, but it may be a false alarm. (Well, not an alarm, really, but not an accurate signal.)

Most often, the first thing is a little lump under one nipple, about the size of a jelly bean. (No, it doesn't come in flavors.) It tingles and might hurt if it is bumped or squeezed. This is called a breast bud. Sometimes if a girl doesn't know that puberty starts this young or begins with a breast bud on just one side, she can get scared that the lump is cancer. Let your friends know that breast buds are normal, so that they're not scared.

Sometimes what you'll notice first isn't a breast bud but the fact that you smell different when you sweat—more like an adult—and have a few fine, soft hairs growing around the vagina. This isn't really puberty; puberty starts when the breast bud starts.

Usually, girls start having menstrual periods about two years after the first breast bud appears.

If you see *lots* of hair growing around the vagina, but no breast bud yet, it's a good idea to see your doctor. Sometimes a part of the body called the adrenal gland gets impatient and starts before everything else, and your doctor might want to help that gland to slow down.

After you notice the first breast bud, it can take a short or a long while for the other one to pop up. In the meantime, you notice that you're growing taller faster than you used to and that your hands and feet are growing faster, too. If you didn't have any before now, you'll probably notice at this point that there is some fine, soft hair growing around the area of the vagina.

Your vagina is changing, too: the inside lips may get large, and even sort of hang down. That's okay. You'll notice that you smell different when you sweat. You might get some acne pimples or zits on your face or chest or back. Once in awhile, there are lots of pimples. Nobody should have to have a bad case of acne that scars. Your pediatrician can help acne a lot (see box, **Zits,** page 231).

Pretty soon you're likely to notice some goopy stuff called discharge from the vagina. That's normal. It's to help the inside of the vagina be smooth. Some girls have a lot of discharge and prefer to wear a little pad in their underpants. The discharge shouldn't smell bad and it shouldn't have blood in it. If it does, your doctor will want to see you. (When the doctor looks at a girl's vagina, usually he or she doesn't need to put anything inside. If it's important to look inside or to put anything inside, your doctor will explain everything and be very gentle and let you have your mother, or father, or friend, or a nurse in the room with you.)

At the same time all these changes in your body are going on, you're likely to notice a bunch of new feelings, as well. You might feel

KEEPING CLEAN, SMELLING GOOD, AND SO ON

- It's okay to use a deodorant at any age for body odor. Antiperspirants are different from deodorants. They contain aluminum salts. If there are any open sores on the skin, an antiperspirant can irritate them. There's also some concern that aluminum salts could be absorbed into the body. There's no evidence that this is harmful, but it's certainly not recommended, either. If you have a major problem with sweating that these remedies don't help, talk with your pediatrician.
- Once you shave your arms or legs, it's really hard to stop, because the hair grows back really stiff and bristly. So don't start unless you're going to keep doing it. There are other things you could do, including nothing. Or you could use a bleach from the pharmacy. If you are going to shave your legs, you don't want to irritate the bases of the little hairs. They'll get bumpy and infected if you do.
- Soak the area in warm water for three minutes. That's long enough to soften the little hairs, but if you soak longer they'll lie down flat and be hard to shave.
- Apply a good shaving cream.
- Use a sharp razor. Keep your mind on what you are doing; it's very easy to cut yourself. (Don't read or daydream.)
- After you're done, rinse the area well. Wait at least ten minutes before applying any lotion or powder, so that the irritation from shaving has calmed down a little bit. Don't use alcohol or preparations with alcohol: they'll sting, and the stinging doesn't mean "something is working." It means "something is irritating."
- Don't shave your eyebrows! They may not grow back. If you pluck them, be careful and get some advice first. The plucked hairs may not grow back either. (Usually the ones you don't want to grow back do grow back, and the ones you do want to grow back don't.)
- Bubble bath and oil in the bathtub smell and feel good, but they can make a girl's vagina be very irritated. If you do use them once in awhile, make sure you rinse your vagina with clear water afterward.
- You may notice your hair is more oily and that it may be getting a lot curlier or darker or thicker or all of those together. That's normal. It's a good idea to get a shampoo and conditioner that are special for oily hair. Here is a warning: if you do your hair in very elaborate, tight braids and so on, and use lotions on it, the oils and lotions can build up. This can make a fungus grow. If you have that kind of hairdo and notice that you have spots where hair is falling out or your scalp is itchy, see your pediatrician.
- Piercing your earlobes is different and safer than piercing other parts of the body. First, your earlobe is just soft skin, and it's out in the open. If you pierce your earlobe and it gets infected, it's easy to see what's going on and easy to treat. (The infection won't go away, though, unless you take out the ring or stud.) But the firm part of your ear, and the nostrils, are made out of cartilage. If you pierce the cartilage and it gets infected, this can be a very serious infection that could even destroy the cartilage and leave a big hole. Not a good idea. That hole is not easy to fix and looks terrible.

sexy a lot, and think about other people in a sexy way. It's normal to think about both girls and boys in that way. It doesn't mean a girl is homosexual or gay or lesbian to think about other girls or women in a sexy way.

You might find that you want to touch yourself in a sexy way, and that's normal too. Touching yourself won't make you sick or crazy or make your body do anything weird. Some families and religions think that touching yourself in a sexy way is bad or a sin. How you feel about that will depend on what you have been taught.

You also might find that you feel really wild sometimes for no reason: excited or mad or happy or whatever. Of course, when you feel wild, it's natural to try to figure out why. But when it's hormones making you feel wild, you might not find any reason at all.

Sometimes it feels as if you have to make up a reason for how your feelings make you behave. This can get a person in trouble. For instance, if you are feeling really angry and awful, you could yell at somebody, "I hate you!" even though that's not the reason why you feel that way and even though you really don't hate that person. It's probably a better idea just to yell, "I don't know why I'm so mad! Just go away and let me BE mad!" until the mood passes.

The next thing that happens usually is that you get more hair around the vagina, and that hair is coarser and curlier. That hair eventually grows in front, too, all over the mound at the bottom of your belly that's called the vulva. Then it starts growing around the hole where the poop comes out: the anus. Also, hair starts growing under your arms, and the hair on your arms and legs gets darker and thicker, too.

While all this happens, you're still growing tall really fast, and you also start to gain weight faster. You're supposed to be really hungry. It's not a good time to go on a diet that limits portions or that cuts out fat or any other kind of food entirely. You could get really sick. If you are worried about your weight, try to get lots of

SOME GOOD BOOKS ON PUBERTY

There are lots of good books about puberty. These are some the Kids I see like.

Changes in You and Me
> (boys' version and girls' version),
> by Paulette Bourgeois and Martin Wolfish, M.D., Somerville House Books Limited, 1994.

A very straightforward, complete, emotionally restrained treatment of all aspects of puberty and sex. May be a little complicated for this age group, but they'll probably get a lot out of it. This is a picture book for teenagers: the illustrations with transparent overlays "help lift the mystery of puberty."

It's Perfectly Normal
> (unisex volume—only one version),
> by Robie H. Harris, illustrated by Michael Emberley, Candlewick Press, 1994.

An entertaining picture book account of all the same aspects, with a markedly politically correct attitude. The illustrations are very cute, but may be offensive to this age group—especially the pictures of naked adults. The illustrations include demonstrations of affection and sex and do not discriminate in terms of age, sexual preference, or race.

What's Happening to My Body?
> (two volumes, one for boys, one for girls),
> by Lynda Madaras, Newmarket Press, 1991.

A very complete, thick paperback (do not confuse with the picture book that has a similar title!) that will probably answer any questions Kids or parents have. Clearly written without gimmicks.

exercise that leaves you out of breath and sweaty.

Your breasts get bigger, and there's often a dark ring around the nipples, called the areola. Lots of girls will have a few long hairs that grow around the nipple. It's not a good idea to pluck these hairs because that's an easy way to get the base of the hair infected. Since many girls have hairs and anybody who sees them will know that, you could just leave them alone. You could shave them, but that's very tricky. Be careful.

At about this time, most girls start having menstrual periods. (It's okay to start earlier, but most girls start at this stage of puberty.) Periods are when bloody material comes out of the vagina. This bloody stuff lines the uterus, or womb, to make it ready for when a baby gets started there. When you have a period, it doesn't really mean that you are bleeding, the way you would if you cut yourself and open a blood vessel. It means that your body realizes that a baby hasn't gotten started this month, so it's time to get rid of the lining of the uterus.

Most periods last about three to seven days and happen about a month apart, because an egg gets released about once a month. When you are first starting out, periods are likely to be very, very irregular for about two years. That's because at first girls have "practice" periods for a while. They build up and lose the lining of the uterus without releasing eggs. Most girls don't have any cramps with those periods, because their ovaries haven't started to put out eggs yet. When the ovaries start to produce eggs, they make hormones that can cause cramps.

Periods often start about two years after you notice the first breast bud, but some girls get them much sooner—right with the first breast bud—or much later. Sometimes you might notice that you feel tired or crabby or have a stomachache beforehand, but usually there's no particular sign. The blood does not come gush-ing out like a fountain. It's not likely to get on your clothes and be noticed before you dis-cover it yourself when you go to the bathroom. But if you feel that your underpants are getting a little damp, you probably will want to check and see. The blood is bright red. It isn't dirty. It doesn't have any poop or anything in it. It's just plain old blood like when you skin your knees.

When you have your period, blood could get all over your clothes if you didn't wear something. You could wear a pad that goes into your underpants. When you change the pad, the pad with the blood on it needs to be wrapped up in toilet paper or put into a little bag and thrown away. Don't try to put it in the toilet, or it will plug it up and cause a flood.

You could also put a kind of plug into the vagina, a plug called a tampon. This plug is made out of special material that absorbs the bloody stuff.

When the tampon is inside, you can't feel it. It has a string attached that hangs down out of the vagina between your legs, so that you can pull the tampon out when you need to change it. That string will get wet when you pee, but that's OK. Also, it's a real short string and nobody will see it, even if you wear a bathing suit. Well, most bathing suits. The string doesn't mean that the tampon could get lost up inside. It can't get anywhere from the vagina. The string just makes it easier to take out.

Wash your hands before you put a tampon in so that you don't get germs inside the vagina and after you take one out. You won't get germs from your own vagina, but you might have some of the blood on your hands. Sometimes you can flush a tampon down the toilet, but it's safer on the plumbing to wrap it up in toilet paper and put it in the trash.

Wearing a tampon won't make you not a vir-gin. A virgin is somebody who has never had sex. It used to be that one of the signs that a girl was a virgin was that the opening to the vagina, the hymen, was real tight. Even if that were still true, you could get a tampon in through a tight opening. But most girls today have a stretchier opening to the vagina because they do more exercise.

It can be very tricky putting in the tampon. Be sure to start with a small size one. You might want to feel where to put it by putting your own finger in first. Wash your hands and cut the nail short and put some goop, like Vaseline or KY jelly, on your finger. Your vagina is the opening that's just in back of the place where the pee comes out. It's the only opening down there besides the poop-place that your finger will fit inside. When you find the right place, you'll know where to put the tampon. If you have trouble getting the tampon in, and you don't want to ask someone you know well to help, your pediatrician can help you.

It's important to know that there is a very rare disease called Toxic Shock Syndrome (TSS) that can happen when you wear a tampon. If you get sick while you have a tampon in take it out right away. If you have a fever, diarrhea, a red rash on your skin, or you feel really lousy, be sure and tell your parents right away. Make sure they know that you think you possibly could have TSS and need to see the doctor right away.

Well, that's puberty. You probably have lots of questions. I've put the most frequent questions in some boxes in this section of the book. You'll probably have more. Your parents or your pediatrician can give you the answers. There are also some excellent books about puberty (see box, **Some Good Books on Puberty,** page 228).

BOYS

Puberty is when the clock in your body starts you growing into an adult man who can have sex and make babies. Every boy has his own timetable. Some boys will start as young as nine, and some won't start until they are fourteen. The average age is about eleven-and-a-half. When you start depends on a lot of things, but mostly on how old your father was when he started puberty. He may not remember, but you could ask him when he grew fastest. That growth spurt starts about a year after puberty does.

As a rule, the earlier you start puberty, the sooner you stop growing. Most boys who start puberty at a very young age are taller than everybody else for a few years, but then they stop growing and can be shorter than average as adults. So a boy who is much shorter than everybody else for a few years, maybe right through sophomore year at high school, can grow so much that he's taller than everybody else. Most boys take about four-and-a-half years to get through puberty.

You'd think that the first thing puberty would do would be to make you grow fast. Not so. Most boys have signs of puberty for at least a year before they start shooting up.

I put that in dark letters because so many boys worry that they haven't started to grow really fast even though they've noticed changes in their bodies that go along with puberty.

The first sign of puberty is that your testicles (balls) get bigger. Nothing much happens for a while after that. Then after about six months, you're likely to see some fine, soft hair called pubic hair growing on your scrotum. A few boys will get hair on their face and under their arms before they get hair growing on the scrotum. About a year after your testicles start getting bigger, you notice your penis getting longer.

Then, about a year or so after you notice your penis getting longer, you start growing in height. The taller you get, the faster you grow and the more you need to eat. You can get so hungry you start to shake or get really angry and cranky or want to cry. That's normal. Go eat something. Carry food with you.

At the same time you start growing really fast, you notice more hair: on your upper lip,

ZITS (ACNE)

Acne is pimples on the face, chest, and back that start at puberty. Each pimple starts as a perfectly innocent hair follicle—the birthplace of an individual hair.

The little gland in each follicle is supposed to make a gooey substance called sebum. The hormones of puberty speeds up that production, and the sebum gets trapped down inside the base of the hair follicle. A bacteria called *P. acnes* flourishes down there and makes chemicals that irritate the whole area. Voilà! A pimple.

Sometimes acne is caused as a side effect of medication, too: anti-TB medicines, seizure medicines, antidepressants, and anything with cortisone in it can cause acne or make it worse.

Getting oils on your skin can do the same thing. Beware oily sunscreen: get the kind that says "non-comedogenic" (acne-free). Beware heavy makeup and hair oils. If you get grease or oil on your hands, from working with machines or from cooking or even eating, and then touch your face, that can make acne worse.

Eating chocolate, masturbating, or thinking sexy thoughts doesn't give you acne. Washing with soap and water won't usually keep acne at bay, though it will help if you've got oil on your skin. But do wash gently. Scrubbing with a washcloth or granules is more likely to make everything flare up than it is to help.

The medications that work for acne include creams and lotions that contain retin A or benzoyl peroxide or antibiotics. They work by releasing the trapped sebum and killing the bacteria *P. acnes*. Benzoyl peroxide is the only one that is available without a prescription. But the over-the-counter forms of acne medications are unreliable, because the active ingredient is often sensitive to the other ingredients in the cream, which makes it decompose.

Your pediatrician can prescribe effective medicines for significant acne (and any acne that worries a Kid or a parent is significant). Dermatologists can prescribe for really severe cases.

under your arms, even on the backs of your toes and fingers. How much hair you have depends on the kind of pattern you inherited. Some boys grow lots of hair on their bodies and others hardly any. How much hair you have has nothing to do with how male you are or how strong you are or whether you are homosexual (gay) or very "macho." You can't make hair grow or not grow by eating special foods or using lotions or shaving.

About a year after your penis begins to grow, and right before you start growing real fast, you start having ejaculations. That means that your penis gets big and hard and fluid comes shooting out. This can happen when you masturbate (jack off, play with yourself).

This can happen at night when you're asleep. When it does, it's called a wet dream. If you have a talk with your mother or father about puberty, it's a good idea to ask what to do about the sheets and pajamas when you have a wet dream. Wet dreams don't happen because you are masturbating (touching yourself, playing with yourself, jacking off) in your sleep. They happen because nature makes the nerves that run the penis get activated in the deep stage of sleep.

This is also the time when your voice is likely to start to change. It's normal not to know what voice is going to come out, the high one or the low one.

Right from the beginning, you're likely to notice a lot of sexy feelings. It's normal to feel sexy: that's what nature designed the whole thing for. Boys can have sexy feelings about girls, older women, boys, and men. Having sexy feelings about boys and men doesn't mean that you are homosexual or gay. The sexy feelings don't have to have any point to them at all: pretty often, they just happen.

Most boys masturbate a lot during puberty. Some boys have been taught that this is wrong or sinful. As far as nature goes, you won't get sick or crazy or do weird things to your body (like having hair grow on your palms) if you masturbate.

Sometimes sexy feelings occur at the most inconvenient times, and you get an erection. Believe it or not, most people won't notice, even if you think everybody is staring. You also might find that you feel really wild sometimes for no reason: excited or mad or happy or whatever. Of course, when you feel wild it's natural to try to figure out why. But when it's hormones making you feel wild, you might not find any reason at all.

Sometimes it feels as if you have to make up a reason for how your feelings make you behave. This can get a person in trouble. For instance, if you are feeling really angry and awful, you could yell at somebody, "I hate you!" even though that's not the reason why you feel that way and even though you really don't hate that person. It's probably a better idea just to yell, "I don't know why I'm so mad! Just go away and let me BE mad!" until the mood passes.

Boys get a lot of muscle during puberty. But most of this muscle doesn't start growing until you've been having puberty, and growing taller, for several years. (I put that in dark letters for the same reason I put the part about growing fast in dark letters.) Since the hormones of puberty turn calories into muscle, a lot of boys who were chubby before puberty get a lot skinnier now. To make this work best, it's a good idea to get lots of exercise. Taking steroids to make muscles bigger is a terrible idea. The medication can make you really sick or even go crazy. If you share needles to take the medication, you can get AIDS and other diseases.

If you are chubby at the beginning of puberty, it's normal to have extra weight on your chest under the nipples. If this is embarrassing, your pediatrician will give you a note so that you can keep your shirt on in gym class or swimming.

Most boys will get a little bit of swelling under the nipples in the *middle or last* part of puberty. Usually it's only a little bit, about the size of a quarter or half dollar. If it's embarrassing, you could ask your doctor for a note, too, about keeping your shirt on. That swelling goes away in about a year or so. It doesn't mean that you're getting breasts or turning female or have cancer.

If you notice any breast-like swelling early, before you start puberty or in the early stages of puberty, that needs to be checked right away by your pediatrician. It doesn't mean that you've got cancer or that you are turning into a girl, but it does mean that there's a chance that your hormones got confused and turned one part on sooner than nature intended.

Most boys and girls will have zits (pimples, acne) during puberty. Nobody should have to have a bad case or scarring. Your pediatrician can help a lot (see box, **Zits**, page 231).

NUTRITION

There are three important aspects of nutrition for Kids this age.

• Kids of either sex who are starting or in the midst of puberty have enormous appetites. Even the chubbiest child can't go on a portion-restricted diet at this age healthfully. To attempt weight reduction is to court disaster: not just malnutrition, but a sense of failure and of being out of control that can lead to depression and eating disorders. What does help is to concentrate on exercise and a healthy family diet, which holds down the proportion of fat calories to less than 30 percent of the day's total.

• There is some evidence that girls from nine to twelve absorb calcium much more effectively than they did earlier or will again. This may help to prevent the bone-thinning disease osteoporosis later on. If a girl tolerates milk well, a daily 16 to 24 ounces of skim milk won't hurt and might help her in forty years or so. Carbonated soft drinks decrease calcium in the bones of girls, and shouldn't be a regular part of the diet.

• Kids this age are deluged with temptations and opportunities to eat high-fat, nutrition-impoverished foods. Some experts even advise that it's a good idea to provide a variety of snack foods at home that includes candy, sodas, baked goods, cold cuts, and rich cheeses. They state that this wide variety helps a Kid become autonomous and make his or her own decisions about eating.

This is a peculiar interpretation of autonomy. Autonomy means being able to choose, make a decision, and be accountable for the consequences. For many children, the decision to eat a fat-rich food rather than a piece of fruit is not a choice. It's succumbing to overwhelming impulse. To choose to eat a piece of fruit instead of cookies wouldn't be an example of autonomy, but of heroism.

If a youngster is eating a well-balanced diet and has a metabolism that tolerates fat-rich foods on top of that diet, that's fine (although this can start an eating pattern that the Kid should not sustain later on). For any Kid with a problem controlling weight, however, parents are kindest when they provide healthy, nonfat, nonsugary snacks.

Health and Illness

HEALTH

Starting at nine or so, a Kid's relationship with the pediatrician starts to change. Instead of asking for details from the accompanying parent, most pediatricians start asking the child for more and more input. If they don't know enough to do that, the child will set them right.

By the time the Kid is eleven, many pediatricians suggest that the parent be out of the exam room for part of the well-child visit, so that the patient and doctor can have a private conversation. Many Elevens and most Twelves want to have the exam performed with only the doctor and maybe a nurse or medical assistant in the room. It's not a true rite of passage, it doesn't pack the wallop of, say, a bar mitzvah, and of course, there's no food. But it's still a developmental milestone.

It's a good idea for youngsters this age to have a yearly checkup. It helps to reassure everybody about puberty, for one thing. And it keeps the doctor-patient relationship alive when there are very few sick visits to act as reminders. Once in a while, a significant discovery is made: Eleven is nearsighted; Nine has been cheerfully going about with a popcorn kernel in his ear (True! True! "How did it get there, Kevin?" "I don't know."); Ten has a moderate scoliosis (spinal curve).

Ask the pediatrician if your Kid needs a pre-puberty booster of the immunization for measles, mumps, and rubella. The rubella immunization protects the unborn fetus, so it's best given before that eventuality arises. Also, check on whether your Kid has received immunizations for Hepatitis B, the liver virus.

ILLNESS

Kids this age like to have things explained and lab tests gone over. They want to know the right name for whatever is wrong: "I have otitis externa again," they say, displaying their swimmer's ear. They fracture their clavicles, not their collar bones, and suffer reactive airway disease instead of asthma. I try to get them all to consider medical school. (But they all want to be vets. Except for Josh: "I'm going to be a neurosurgeon and make a lot of money and then open a surf shop.")

They're such a pleasure to see and treat that it's almost a pity that many of them hardly ever get sick anymore. They don't usually come up with the weird, imaginative complaints beloved by Sevens and Eights, either.

In fact, they tend more often to deny symptoms. "But Mo-om," they say, rolling their eyes, "my throat *doesn't* hurt anymore. That was this *morning*." "Well of course my head hurts. Right there, see? Feel that little bump? That's where Jamie kicked me yesterday when we were playing checkers." Don't ask.

Some Kids this age have an underlying problem like asthma, sinusitis, or attention deficit disorder that requires frequent, or at least regular, visits. When they do need to come in fairly often, it's good for Kids this age to take on the grown-up aspects of the visit. Bad enough that they need to come in: at least they can show that they're competent, in charge, and ready to be treated with dignity. They can recount how they're doing, ask questions, issue complaints, discuss changes in medication, consult on a follow-up appointment, and check the billing form.

But most Kids this age rarely have problems: their colds are infrequent and mild, they tolerate minor stomach upsets well, and they've already had most of the named virus illnesses. Most of the time, those illnesses run their course at home. When the Kids need to be seen, the most common problems tend to be relatively minor but annoying. However, once in awhile there's something more serious going on. Here are some of the most frequent complaints that bring Nines through Elevens into the office.

TONSILS AND ADENOIDS

Most of the time, tonsils and adenoids have shrunk down nicely by this age. If they haven't, sometimes they need to be removed. A Kid who has four or more documented cases of strep throat in a year might need to have the tonsils out just to cut down on the chance of contracting the complication of rheumatic fever. A Kid who mouth breathes in the daytime, talks as if there's peanut butter on the roof of the mouth, and snores like a banshee at night because the T and A's block the airway is at risk for sleep apnea, orthodontic problems, and cavities in the permanent teeth (they're supposed to be bathed with saliva, which protects them).

ACNE

Zits can attack at the dawning of puberty or even before. Ordinary hygiene won't make a dent in real acne (see the discussion on acne in **Growth and Nutrition,** earlier in this chapter). With the medications available these days, no child should have to suffer more than a few zits. Kids whose same-sex parent had severe acne are at special risk: get them in early. So are Kids whose pimples are closed over, large and smooth, rather than open whiteheads or blackheads.

WHITE SPOTS ON THE SKIN

When these splotches appear on a child with olive, tawny, or dark skin, the youngster and parent get upset. Almost always these turn out to be something called pityriasis alba. It's not really a disease; it's a cosmetic condition. It's not contagious and it can be treated. Once in a while, though, white blotches can mean that there's something else going on—a fungus or a thyroid deficiency, for instance.

SKIN BUMPS

Little teeny bumps on the cheeks, upper arms, and thighs: They don't itch and they're always there. Why do they flare up right when you are going to be in the limelight? These are almost always something called keratosis pilaris: little inflammations of the hair follicles. Moisturizer helps. Prescription lotions and creams help more effectively.

PEELING TOES

Is it athlete's foot? Maybe, even if the Kid is a nonjock. The fungus of athlete's foot seems to prefer adult sweat, but even prepubertal Kids can harbor it. Sometimes, though, those peeling toes are fungus-free, and the inflammation is just due to sweaty feet sealed into shoes. Hence the name, sneakeritis. Your pediatrician will be able to tell the difference and fix it up.

PAINFUL FEET AND LEGS

Their heels hurt, their whole feet hurt, their knees hurt when they walk downstairs; they have growing pains that wake them at night. Most leg and feet problems at this age come from overuse, running on hard surfaces, jumping. Most are not serious, but even the innocent ones need diagnosis and treatment—usually a combination of rest, stretching, and protection from hard surfaces.

Once in a great while, a youngster this age has a serious problem. A limp that keeps recurring, even without much pain, needs investigating, and so does pain without limp. A pain that keeps a child from playing or that awakens him at night is a call for prompt investigation, even if there's no swelling or redness or history of injury.

INJURIES

Most injuries in this age group are due to wearing improper gear for sports; to car accidents with the Kid as pedestrian, bike rider, or skater; and to careless use of potentially dangerous stuff like knives, BB guns, or firecrackers.

Some Kids this age are accident prone, constantly spraining, skinning, or bruising something. Usually this is merely the by-product of an active and full life. However, a youngster who wants more attention may be using accidents to get it. A child who is not well-coordinated may be showing mild signs of a problem that could use a little physical therapy. A Kid who is miserable at school may keep trying to find excuses not to go. A youngster who is becoming nearsighted (because of the changes of puberty) may not see where he or she is going.

It's worth running the problem by the pediatrician.

SAFETY

"Don't forget your galoshes!" Increasingly, at this age, this kind of parental injunction is not going to work. This is a pity because there are so many more things you'd like to yell at a Kid's retreating back: "Don't forget your snow goggles!" "Nobody's allowed to touch your private parts!" "Stay away from those Kids at the corner, they're trouble!" "Sunscreen!" "Don't sniff household products!"

Kids need to explore, adventure, take risks, be independent, and do things in groups. Increasingly, their sense of taking appropriate safety precautions has to come from inside their heads, not from parents' directives. As Kids grow up, nurturing independence and responsibility and autonomy is part of keeping them safe.

However, many children this age are not yet mature enough to think ahead, in the adult sense. To do that, you have to set up a situation in your mind and theorize what will happen if you act one way or another. The ability to do this occurs after puberty starts, but it's unclear just how long after puberty starts. In essence: the hormonal changes seem to mature the brain, but you can't count on it. Even when a youngster is able to think in a sophisticated manner when it comes to writing a report on Egypt, for instance, that ability may lie dormant when it comes to deciding whether to wear wrist pads or not. So Kids this age need a good deal of parental direction, supervision, and monitoring.

When a Kid this age is warned about something, there are several barriers that can get in the way, between the warning and the safe action. Here are some ways to evade them.

The child needs to listen to what you say

Anxiety, anger, boredom, preoccupation, excitement all can get in the way. Adults are best heard when they clear their own manner of upsetting emotions, place a hand on the youngster, and make sustained eye contact.

Kids don't understand words that have to do with possibilities

The parent may say, "Wear your goggles. It's likely to snow on the mountain this afternoon." The Kid hears "likely" and thinks, "Oh yeah, maybe one chance in seven or eight. Not worth taking gloves." Ditch such terms as likely, probably, maybe, might, there's a chance, almost certainly, probably, possibly, and so on. The Kid is very likely to misunderstand: I mean, there is an eight out of ten chance that you'll be misconstrued.

Kids listen, acquiesce, and remember when you tell them what TO do rather than what NOT to do and when you are specific rather than vague

If at all possible, phrase your warning or order positively. They do better with specifics than with generalities. So "Be home by five" works better than "Don't be later than five." In fact, "Leave Jarrod's house at four-thirty" is even better.

When there's a principle to convey, it's done more effectively by positive reinforcement than by criticizing

Suppose the principle is: If you're going to engage in risky activities, you've got to wear protective gear. So you say, "If I catch you not wearing your hard hat one more time, I'm not paying for any more riding lessons." The instantaneous translator inside a Kid's head immediately turns this into, "I'd better not let Dad catch me riding without my hard hat. That's so dumb. He always thinks I'm going to wind up in intensive care. Lady Fly takes care of me. I never get hurt."

Better: When Emily is wearing her hard hat, make forceful commendations, ones that make an impression from the child's point of view.

> "I'm so impressed to see you wearing your hard hat. If you had a fall without it and passed out, Lady Fly could

get tangled in the reins and break a leg."

If an injury due to carelessness is minor, but a principle is involved, underreaction works better than overreaction

Underreacting lets the child own the problem. A little humor puts Kid and adult on more of an equal footing—raising the level of the Kid.

> "You should have worn your knee pads! Now look at that scrape! What a dreadful abrasion. I'm sure it's going to scar terribly. You're just lucky you didn't break your kneecap. You know you're supposed to wear your pads."

This won't command respect. Instead:

> "What a nasty scrape. A knee without protection is so vulnerable. We'd better call the lost and found: 'Hello! Jeffrey seems to have left his kneecap in the library parking lot.'"

Behavior Problems

Every Kid will behave at times in ways that upset parents. This section looks at problem behaviors that are upsetting beyond what is ordinary. Either they are minor but annoying, like thumbsucking and bedwetting, or they are scary or angrymaking, like aggression. I have not included in this section hard and fast guidelines about when to seek professional help because there aren't any such guidelines. It is true that there are formal guidelines that list the behaviors that constitute a psychiatric diagnosis, such as "conduct disorder" or "oppositional disorder." However, these guidelines are used only to assist mental health professionals in record-keeping and billing. To use such lists as a guide for "when to really worry" is inappropriate.

Pediatricians are usually able to help parents to decide at what point they need professional assistance for a troubled Kid.

One kind of behavior that worries parents is not included in this section. That is behavior that suggests a Kid is unhappy with his or her sexual identity. Such feelings on the part of a Kid do not, in my opinion, constitute a behavior problem, but rather a condition of the spirit that we as a society don't understand or handle very well. It is more like a difficult situation than a behavior problem. So I've placed discussion of this conundrum in the **What If?** section of each chapter.

When a youngster this age has behavioral problems, parents face two challenges. First, they need to know how serious the problem is and whether professional help is needed. Second, they need to know how to talk with the youngster about the problem. Kids this age can't stand it when they think parents are worrying and brooding about them in secret. On the other hand, they may clam up or stomp out or worse when you try to talk with them.

LEARNING

Problems learning are the most prevalent difficulty. Starting in fourth grade, Kids need more specialized and complicated skills to keep up in school. Children who have trooped right along up until this age can start having problems.

Sometimes the learning problems arise because the basic skills have not really been assimilated. In large busy classrooms, a child can fool other people and himself or herself into believing that reading and math skills are coming along just fine. Suddenly, it's clear that Nine is still sounding out words or missing the meaning of the print, or that Eleven really never got through the multiplication tables.

This could be because the youngster has been going through school placed a year ahead of his or her developmental level, because he or she has missed a significant number of school days (either physically absent or mentally/emotionally absent), or because the child has a true learning disability.

Physical problems can also pop up at this stage. Vision problems requiring glasses often develop at puberty: a child whose parents got their glasses in, say, the fifth grade needs at least a yearly eye exam and prompt assessment if blurred vision occurs. Fatigue is a major complaint in children having a growth spurt—mostly girls, at this age. Kids seem to do their growing at night, and when they don't get enough sleep, they're truly exhausted. Most Kids this age could really use ten hours sleep a night, and they rarely get it.

Emotional problems from anxiety to true depression can keep a child from learning. Kids who are rejected by the rest of the class, whether ignored or made fun of, may be too unhappy to learn.

Whatever the cause of learning difficulties, once a fourth through sixth grader falls behind in the work, things rapidly can get out of hand. The more lost you are, the more lost you get.

Nines through Elevens who are struggling academically usually have more than a learning problem. They feel bad about themselves and take measures to compensate. Sometimes these are comparatively benign, like becoming the class clown. Sometimes they are dangerous: frightening physical stunts, excursions into truancy or delinquency, risk-taking and status-seeking behavior such as sniffing glue, drinking alcohol, smoking tobacco or marijuana, taking drugs. A youngster who feels inadequate as an individual is likely to be more drawn to gangs or, at least, to dismaying peer groups than one who feels rock solid.

Parents alerted to learning problems need to take action promptly. The two first stops are the pediatrician's office, with child in tow, and the school, to see the teacher. Both the doctor and the teacher may want additional testing: medical lab work or diagnostic learning tests.

They may counsel that the child receive special assistance, such as tutoring or a neurological consultation. Make sure you are clear with the person who makes the appointment for the doctor that this is a visit for a complicated problem, not a brief exam for a simple infection.

It's best to bring a brief outline with you for the pediatrician to read *before* the appointment. Here is the kind of information to include in the outline.

• Is the child on any medication? Which one(s)? For what condition? How long has she or he been taking the medication.

• Has the child been evaluated by anyone else for this learning problem? Who? What tests were done? What was the diagnosis and treatment?

• Is the problem isolated to one subject— math, for instance? Or does it extend to several or all subjects?

• When do you believe the problem started? During this school year? Or has it been gradually worsening for a long time?

• Is the child acting sick in any way—tired, losing or gaining too much weight, sleeping a lot more or a lot less than usual?

• Is the child behaving in a way that scares you? Do you suspect that he or she is acting out dangerously, is depressed, or may have an eating disorder?

• What do you suspect is going on and why? What have you already done? What have you told the child?

Sometimes, based on your answers, the physician may order testing or even a referral to a specialist before the office appointment.

What to tell the child? The truth. But without blame or recrimination or labeling. Usually a brief statement does the job. Kids who feel as if they're a problem tend to "hate it when you go on and on."

"I know that you're having a lot of trouble at school. I don't know exactly what the problem is. Sometimes bright Kids run into learning problems because they have a physical problem. So we're going to have the pediatrician take a look at you. And I'm going to ask the teacher to help us figure out what's going on. Then we'll work on it together. We'll do whatever it takes."

MOODS

Puberty entitles Kids to be somewhat moody, but you've got to draw the line somewhere. If a youngster no matter how flamboyantly pubertal persists in a negative mood for two weeks, it's time to get help. The first step should be a visit to the pediatrician. Again, make an appointment that allows time for a complex evaluation and get an outline to the doctor to read ahead of time. Here is a brief list of what to include in the outline.

• Has something traumatic happened that explains the mood?

• Is the child on any medication? Which one(s)? For what condition? How long has she or he been taking the medication?

• Has the child been evaluated by anyone else for this problem? Who? What tests were done? What was the diagnosis and treatment?

• How long has the child been moody? Is the mood constant or does it lift?

• How intense is the mood at the worst? Has the child hurt, or tried to hurt, himself/herself or someone else, destroyed property, been cruel to an animal?

• Do you suspect any serious risk-taking behavior: truancy, drugs or alcohol, sex?

• Is there any family or life event or circumstance that triggered the mood? If there is a family secret, it must be revealed in this situation.

• Is there a family history of emotional illness, such as depression or panic attacks?

• Do you suspect sexual molestation or incest?

A child with a mood disorder such as depression may be very resistant to being touched or queried. Parents need to be firm. It's usually best to tell the child shortly before the appointment.

"I don't know what is making you so unhappy (angry, and so forth) and I know that you're unable to tell me what it is. This distress has lasted long enough that it isn't normal. We need help to figure out how to get to the bottom of it and fix it. I have made an appointment for us to see the doctor this afternoon. I've explained the problem to him/her."

PLUMMETING SELF-ESTEEM

A youngster who can't find enough self-esteem may not appear depressed. Such a child may simply give the impression of not having any substance: "There's no there there." When you ask a question, she smiles nicely, looks vacant, and says "I don't know." He makes no plans, takes no initiative, shows no excitement. She does what she is told, and then—stops. She sits there, doing nothing. He doesn't make any noise or demands or comments.

This isn't normal. At some point, a Kid who "doesn't have any there there" may start complaining of it: "I feel as if I'm not real." Or may start proving that he or she is real by pathological means: dieting to starvation, for instance. Parents who suspect this problem need to get medical and psychiatric help for their youngster. The problem isn't likely to go away on its own and can lead to danger.

Kids with this vacant sensation may be grateful for help and reassurance. Or they may resist, worried that "I'm going crazy."

Here's a way to broach the subject of the doctor's appointment:

"There are lots of reasons that people your age can feel kind of empty inside their souls. I've talked with the pediatrician and he/she says that this isn't uncommon, and that there are ways to find out what's going on and fix it. We have an appointment for tomorrow."

AGGRESSION

Aggression means attacking with intent to harm. Kids this age certainly do fight physically and insult each other. Heavens, even best friends— especially best friends—insult each other. But not with intent to harm. A youngster who is out to hurt people is a youngster in trouble.

Bullying behavior is frequent (an average of two Kids in each classroom are victims) and dangerous for both bully and victim: the former have a high risk of growing up into violent criminals; the latter, for depression and poor self-esteem. Kids can't deal with the behavior on their own. I urge parents and teachers to send for and establish the program Bully-Proofing Your School. Write to Sopris West Publishing at 1140 Boston Avenue, Longmont, CO 80501, or call 800-547-6747.

The child this age who picks physical fights, strikes (nonabusive) parents, tortures animals, or destroys property valued by others is not acting normally and needs help. Since an underlying medical condition might play a contributing role, a visit to the pediatrician is warranted. But the real assessment belongs to a psychiatrist. Such a youngster needs psychotherapy, a behavioral modification program, medication: any of the above, a combination of them, or all of them.

The youngster whose mode of aggression is emotional may not get the same degree of attention and worry, but his or her need is as great. If a child's primary mode of getting along with others is hurtful teasing, whining, or verbal bullying, that's not normal and the child needs help.

A Kid whose language is laced with obscenity, or racist or sexist epithets, is not behaving normally: that's a form of aggression, also.

An aggressive youngster may act out violently when told that he or she needs help and that the appointment has been made. It may be necessary to make clear exactly what will happen if the child acts, or threatens to act, with intent to harm physically.

> "I am very worried about how angry you have been. It shows me that you are in a lot of pain. I can't allow this to continue. I am scared that you will hurt yourself or somebody else really badly. We have a doctor's appointment in an hour. The doctor is a psychiatrist. He/she wants to hear what's going on and help us get to the bottom of it. Whatever is making you feel so terrible we can make better. We'll do whatever it takes. I am on your side completely. In fact, I am so worried about you that even if you fight me I'm going to get you help. If you try to hurt yourself, or me, or anyone else, I will find a way to keep you from doing it, even if it means giving you medicine against your will."

There isn't much time before the social forces of adolescence provide an apparent haven for troubled teenagers. That haven, which may look inviting to a disturbed teenager, could be drugs, sexual promiscuity, gangs, running away, or even suicide. These years just before adolescence are the time to recognize trouble and to get help.

Window of Opportunity

TRAVEL

Recreational and nonrecreational travel with a Kid who has not yet started puberty, or with one for whom puberty appears to have made little difference in behavior, is very much like traveling with Seven and Eight: See **Window of Opportunity,** in Chapter 2. For traveling with Kids preoccupied with puberty, see **What If?,** later in this chapter.

ONE-TO-ONE TIME, PARENT AND KID

You'd think they might have outgrown the need for time alone with a parent or rejected the whole idea. Not so. They just have a lot on their minds, and they find it hard to switch gears from the peer mode to the parental one.

When you make it a regular habit to enjoy (emphasis on enjoy) time alone with Nine through Eleven, you're setting a foundation for adolescence. That's when you'll really want to keep tabs on how things are going. If you have a recent history of having a good time alone with the Kid, you have a good chance of being let in on some, at least, of what's going on at thirteen and fifteen and later.

If you don't, it's easy to feel like awkward strangers with each other once the Kid reaches adolescence. Between nine, ten, and eleven and adolescence, so many things change: the kinds of jokes you can share, what you call each other ("Please call me Miranda, Mom! The Kids give me a hard time about Randy"), who are best friends and who are bosom enemies.

Just to return to the key word: enjoy. The one-to-one times often go best when you're actually doing something together, something that encourages conversation. Cooking, bowling, playing miniature or regular golf, gardening, driving the cat to the vet, going to the library—the enterprise supplies a neutral topic of conversation, and it's quiet enough to hear each other. (Well, maybe not with the cat.) The neutral topic of conversation helps to pass the time while the Kid switches gears.

SOMETHING TO BE REALLY GOOD AT

A Kid who gets really good at an art, a musical instrument, singing, a sport, a craft, or a hobby has a big head start on self-confidence. Self-confidence is a cornerstone of self-esteem, and self-esteem is what gets teenagers through adolescence without self-destructive behavior.

Parents who provide the opportunities and wherewithal for becoming good at something do everybody a huge favor, even if it means sacrifices of money and time.

Being good at schoolwork and getting straight A's doesn't really do the job. Getting good grades means meeting somebody else's approval, rather than your own standards. If an A is the sole basis of self-confidence, you might choose not to risk a class in a tougher subject, or you might convince yourself that it's okay to cheat just this once so as not to have your grade slip or you might be devastated by a B+.

THE SENSATION OF GROWING UP

At twelve or thirteen, some Kids do have a rite of passage, such as moving into middle school or junior high, or being confirmed or bar or bat mitzvahed.

But there's a lot of growing up going on between nine and thirteen. If you haven't had puberty yet and you're growing along slowly, it can feel as if you're not making much progress. People tend to treat you as though you're younger than you really are.

If you're in the throes of puberty, you know you're growing, but what does it mean? Your body is becoming strangely adult: are your mind and your soul pulling their weight?

Kids this age love enterprises where progress is acknowledged. They'll read thirty books for the library contest, progress through the colors of karate, and get their computer-camp passports stamped with glee.

Parents can help Kids pause and mark private and family rituals of growing up. Many Kids are embarrassed when the milestone is a physical/sexual one, like menstruation. But every parent can usually sense if this is the case: a special dinner or a lunch out for the girl (boy milestones are vaguer) might be just the thing. Milestones of

achievement, increased freedom or responsibility, or a spurt in intellectual sophistication are pretty safe reasons to celebrate.

The moment can be brief.

> "What an absolutely outrageous pun! Joan, did you and I give birth to this sophisticate? Wait until I tell the back office!"

> "Yes, I think you're responsible enough now to do daytime babysitting with the parent close by. And yes, I certainly think your services are worth paying for."

> "I'd like to propose a toast to Peter, for earning his sixth grade camp money washing cars. To our young adult."

Of course, it's possible to celebrate some milestones by weeping and murmuring, "My little baby is growing up." This is fine from the point of view of the eyeball-rolling Kid, as long as the occasion is really important and meaningful and as long as nobody sees or hears you except other adults.

STEADY GROWTH

Kids are not supposed to get fat right before, or at the beginning of, their growth spurts. This myth arose because sometimes boys do gain weight and then the hormones of puberty often help them get rid of it, turning the extra into muscle.

Girls who gain right before puberty will not lose the extra weight without a big battle: they'll gain more as the hormones of puberty take over. A Kid of either sex who gains chubbiness needs extra exercise in his or her life and a homelife that provides a low-fat, healthy diet. (See **Growth and Nutrition**, earlier in this chapter.) Restricting portions leaves a Kid hungry and at the mercy of terrible moods: it's very much a bad idea. Focusing on the weight as an issue is an even worse idea, unless the Kid states a concern. Instead, the motive for extra exercise and low-fat eating is health and fitness. And that's the honest truth.

FEELING CUTE

It can be easy to feel cute when you've got braces on your teeth, glasses on your nose, a few pimples, and feet bigger than your parents'. All you need are parents who look at you with love and a twinkle, who give you hugs and pats (in private, away from peers and the public; and never in a way that hints of seduction), and who tell you again and again that you look so much like your peer group that they can't stand it.

> "Here comes the Kid, looking terrific if you like plaid."

> "I looked at you with your friends today and I thought, What a good-looking bunch. Who's that really cute one in the middle? Why, I said, that's Josh! You were so much taller compared to Frankie that I didn't even recognize you!"

A caution: Feeling cute to Nine through Eleven doesn't mean looking gorgeous or fashionable or a knockout or even like a rock or movie star. For girls going through puberty, it can feel very threatening for a parent of either sex to comment on one's figure—no matter what one's figure might be. Much safer to stick with good old Mom and Dad comments:

> "That blue brings out your eyes just brilliantly. Makes me even tolerate that shirt."

MODERN TECHNOLOGY

The reason this age is such a good one for learning about computers, machines, and gadgets is that Kids usually have the reasoning and fine-motor skills to really play with them. Waiting until the teen years to introduce these skills— from keyboard typing to exploring graphics and spreadsheets to tinkering with engines—may risk having the Kids lose the spirit of play. By the time they're teenagers, the whole business becomes serious, competitive, and school-related. Play always facilitates learning. Far better to learn keyboard skills with Mario, and share the software with a friend, than to sit in class and do drills.

Of course, a supervising adult needs to be somewhere in the vicinity, preventing disasters whether technical or physical. Computers can crash, engines can injure.

SEVERE BEHAVIOR PROBLEMS

Why would behavior problems be a window of opportunity? Because ages nine to twelve is a golden time in which to attack such problems. Kids this age have near-adult ability to reason and to gain control of problems, yet they are still protected to some extent from the social and sexual pressures of adolescence. A problem left unaddressed after this age is very difficult to take care of.

Severe behavior problems are those that disrupt school life, make homelife a burden, or make people worry about the youngster's ability to cope with the normal life of his or her peers. These include a long, long list of behaviors, but the most common are

School problems: unable to do the work of the class, constantly in trouble with the teacher, truancy

Social interaction: aggression, withdrawal, precocious sexual behavior, history of molestation or sexual abuse without any acting-out symptoms, gang involvement, cruelty to animals, fire-setting, use of drugs, use of alcohol, or inhaling glue or other chemicals

Mood: depression lasting for two weeks or longer, panic attacks that keep the child from normal activities, extreme obsessive-compulsive behavior, extreme anger at parents or inability to tolerate divorce or custody arrangements

Eating disorders: dieting obsessively, weight loss in a thin youngster or lack of expected weight gain, vomiting, taking laxatives without being constipated, binge eating followed by self-starvation or vomiting

Disturbed self-image: Complaining of feeling "not real" or "not there," unable to take the initiative or to show pleasure in activities, feeling "as if I'm somebody else"

If a youngster at this age has any of these problems, this is the time to make it a top priority to get expert help. Parents should not count on any of these problems to go away by themselves, but rather should expect them to worsen during adolescence without professional help. Great progress can be made in most of these problems at nine, ten, and eleven, however.

What If?

MOVING

Moving takes you away from your best friend, your peer group, your classroom and teacher, your teams and activities, and your neighborhood. From Nine, Ten, and Eleven's point of view, moving can be either a godsend or a disaster of enormous magnitude, depending on your premove satisfaction with all those things.

What Nines to Twelves make of a move, of course, depends in large part on their resiliency, social skills, and good nature. Parents can do only so much to help. Here's what they can do.

They can treat the Kid's emotions seriously, but without guilt or pity.

> "A move is necessary; we took your needs into consideration; we couldn't find a way to let you stay here. No, staying here with your friend's family is not an option. Period."

If the move can coincide with the beginning of a school year, that may be easiest. If so, it often helps to arrive ahead of time and get the Kid enrolled in an activity likely to bring him or her into contact with classmates of the same sex. The more that activity encourages real social interaction and comradery, the better. A sport in which the Kids play and then all disappear off the field afterward may not do the trick.

The more parents can facilitate any burgeoning friendships, the better. Just one caveat. A disoriented youngster who has just moved may cling to the first offer of friendship he or she detects. If the relationship seems very one-sided, weird, or manipulative, parents may do well to encourage a wider variety of companions.

When a Kid who has moved has to enter class in the middle of the year, it's kind to help the Kid appear the first day with a certain cachet that says, "I'm a regular Kid, desirable to know, somebody to make overtures to." Most of this has to do with clothes and accessories. You would not believe how important it is to carry your lunch (the RIGHT lunch) in the cool container or to have a backpack rather than a bookbag or vice versa. Parents can find out ahead of time by simple observation (without the Kid in tow) or by asking the class parent.

TRAVEL

Suggestions for recreational travel with a Nine to Twelve who has not yet embarked on puberty is very much like such travel with Sevens and Eights (see **What If?**, in the previous chapter).

Travel with a Nine to Twelve who has already begun puberty may have a different tinge. Do not be surprised if the Kid is preoccupied, self-conscious, and more interested in being looked at than in looking. The very presence of the family group may cause a Kid to be uncomfortable and to behave morosely. Some girls this age will be supposed by strangers to be much older and romantically or sexually available. What can a parent do, short of hanging a sign on the Kid that says, "I'm really only eleven!" There are some strategies that help when planning a vacation.

• Activities that are nonsexual and absorbing help dissipate self-consciousness. A resort or cruise that advertises special activities for different age ranges should be viewed with suspicion. Pubertal Kids may not be comfortable with either teenagers or prepubertal youngsters unless the activities are very appealing and directed by charismatic people. Sometimes these groups are just a step away from babysitting, featuring everyday types of crafts and skits and spur-of-the-moment games. A better bet: Kid groups devoted to learning a specific desired skill such as skiing, circus acts, water sports.

• Think carefully before taking along the child's friends. Some friends pull a Kid out of self-absorption; others create an ambience featuring constant giggling and squeals. If one of the points of the vacation is to widen horizons and encourage family bonds, it might be better to make another choice.

• Consider a physically demanding vacation. Aerobic exercise is a wonderful antidote to moodiness.

• Provide a camera. A Kid who is focused on taking, rather than being in, pictures is much more likely to participate, order people around, and generally forget to be self-conscious. Better yet: get the photos developed as you go, and have a scrapbook handy.

NEW SIBLING

Nines to Twelves have complicated responses to a new sibling. They are a mixture of delight, pride, worry, embarrassment, jealousy, and self-pity. Would you want it any different? Of course not. Bringing a new person into the world is a complicated act. Most often, Kids this age will be wonderful with a new sibling, boasting and cooing and helping. They don't feel as vulnerable as younger Kids to being dethroned and love sharing such an exciting event with their parents. Here is what will help make most of the reactions positive.

• If the new baby is the product of a remarriage and the baby and the Kid will be half-siblings, be prepared for some brooding and questions from the Kid. Ideally, the remarriage should be cemented and the new relationships going smoothly before a new baby is on the way.

• Tell the Kid(s) before you tell adult friends or family members, so that he or she feels like the most important recipient of the news.

• Go easy on the medical details until you see how your Kid reacts. Kids this age can be embarrassed on a number of levels: figuring out that parents must have had sex for Mom to get pregnant; thinking about adult, parental body parts; contemplating a visit to a doctor who examines those body parts. Sometimes a Kid will be enthralled and want to hear all about the ultrasounds and amniocentesis, but often the whole subject produces anxiety and moods.

• It's normal for couples who are expecting a baby to be self-absorbed, but this self-absorption can alienate a Kid this age. Often it's more productive to wait for the Kid to bring up the topic—for example, the name for the baby, how active the fetus is, the need for baby clothes and equipment—rather than to introduce it yourself. If parents can maintain an active interest in what the Kid's doing, listening attentively and following up on stories it goes a long way toward enabling the Kid to show interest in the pregnancy.

> "I think today was the day your buddy Kerry was going to the orthodontist, wasn't it? How did it go? Have you called her?"

• Maintain dignified clothing and demeanor when in public or with the Kid's friends and classmates. Your Kid is likely to be teased if you show up in a very short maternity dress, or a cute shirt with an arrow pointing to the fetus emblazoned with the words "Woman at Work."

• Gratefully receive all offered help and request the assistance you need, but keep clear the boundary between parent and Kid. When you are exhausted, feet swollen, back aching, it's easy to want to be cared for. But if your Kid feels as if he or she is being pressed into an adult caretaking role, there are likely to be emotional and behavioral costs.

• Try not to use the pregnancy as an excuse for not doing what you generally do.

• Make a point of recognizing and praising your Kid for deeds that have nothing to do with helping with the new baby—as well as with those that are related.

• Consider carefully whether your Kid should be at the delivery. Parents may feel that this is important family bonding time and Kids may feel that having seen so many births on TV, they deserve and are equipped to witness one in person.

In favor of having the Kid at the delivery:

• It demystifies birth, demonstrating that it is not a horrible ordeal.

• It's a spiritual and natural event.

• Being present at a birth and holding the brand new baby can be a very bonding experience.

Against attending the delivery:

• The timing is unpredictable. A Kid may expect a couple of hours of involved participation and wind up stalking the halls for hours, looking for something to do.

• A delivery is only a normal delivery in retrospect. Rarely, something can go scarily wrong. Kids may take a long time to recover from such a fright.

• There isn't much for a Kid to do except comfort the laboring mother. This is good experience up to a point, but it rarely teaches the Kid what parents hope it will do: self-control under duress, patience, courage. These are what the laboring mother is showing, but the self-

involved Kid is likely to be concentrating on his or her own virtues (putting up with boredom and worry, being nice to adults) instead.

• Despite the fact that, to the parents, the delivery is normal and uncomplicated and thus unworried, to the Kid the whole process may seem very upsetting. There's pain, loss of control, and mess; the professional staff of nurses, doctors, midwives take over at the crucial moment.

• The baby doesn't look like the babies on TV. He or she looks more like E.T.

• The baby immediately is handed to the mother and takes over that special, loving place in her arms. What! That place! Where the Kid belongs! The heart can sink.

But you know your own Kid. These are just a few points to consider.

• When introducing the Kid to the new baby, try NOT to have the new one in the mother's arms (see explanation in the previous paragraph), or in the father's or grandparent's arms, if the Kid is strongly and intimately bonded to that particular adult. I can't tell you how many parents I've talked with who tell me the shock and distress they felt when they were children on seeing that place occupied by the new stranger.

• Try not to let parental involvement with the new baby overwhelm interest and participation in the Kid's life and well-being.

"I WISH I WERE A GIRL." ### "I WISH I WERE A BOY."

Please see **What If?**, *in Chapter 1, for an introduction to this topic.*

As the hormonal temperature of the classroom and peer group rises during this period of childhood, every daily act can seem fraught with sexual innuendo. Conformity is crucial: the wrong boots mean you're a dyke; wearing green on Friday means you're a fairy. One false move seems to be able to destroy a Kid's chance of being accepted as normal, much less of being popular.

This is hard on everybody between nine and twelve (though some seem to thrive, I agree), but particularly on Kids whose boats flounder in the onrushing tide of pubertal sexuality. It's also hard on parents. Parents who suspect that their Kid has been troubled by cross-gender issues may start to panic. They worry that their Kid is at risk for a million terrible things: for being molested, seduced, bullied, beaten, or ostracized. Most parents, regardless of their religious or political attitudes, are terrified that their Kids might grow up to be homosexual. It's dangerous to be homosexual in America today.

No wonder parents can be tempted to try to exert total control over a Kid's actions and feelings. However, attempts at overcontrol can lead to serious problems in adolescence. The developmental task of Kids this age, no matter what their attitude about gender, is to take charge increasingly of their own decisions and to find the strength to live with the results. If they don't start this now, the learning curve of early adolescence is too steep to cope with.

However, parents can help Kids with gender-identity problems get through this crucial pubertal age and lay the foundation for a rewarding adolescence. The first step is to see what's going on in their Kids' hearts and minds.

NONCONFORMISTS

Some Kids this age are just cut out to row against the current. Girls may scorn anything "girlish" and make fun of their female classmates who are trying out makeup and flirting. They may ostentatiously shun feminine dress (including a necessary bra), mannerisms, and topics of interest. These girls may band together and spend their time in asexual or conventionally masculine pursuits.

Boys may look at the rowdy behavior of their male classmates as threatening or as immature and boring. The increasing emphasis on a macho stance may take the fun away from team sports and neighborhood games. These boys may group together, intensely occupied by other activities, such as elaborate constructions or computer fantasy games.

Kids of both sexes who are destined to have puberty late and who just can't see what everybody's so excited about may simply opt out. They spring to life outside of school, continuing their interests of yesteryear. A parent whose Kid falls into any of these categories may worry that the Kid seems to be developing atypically. But this isn't the case.

The key is that these Kids are genuinely pleased to be of their given gender. Even though they may have shown cross-sex preferences (in the way of dress, toys, activities, and companions) in earlier years, they have not rejected their own identity as a boy or as a girl. Girls may have fantasized superhero roles in their play, but have always preferred the role of mother when that issue was raised. Boys may have been entranced with fashion and dance, but rarely have fantasized that they were highly feminized, passive heroines like Cinderella. Both boys and girls have made friends of Kids of the same sex and have social skills which make other Kids seek them out.

It's just that these Kids haven't been thrilled with what most members of their particular gender have been up to for the most part. At this age, they are even less thrilled. They can't stand the restrictions and fuss that go along with the preteen culture. However, they find their own ways of handling this, ways that are seen as socially acceptable. They rarely get badly teased because they don't feel vulnerable or confused. Parents need not worry as long as the Kid who resists gender-specific stuff:

• Seems to feel good about himself or herself, proud of skills and achievements
• Seems comfortable with how life is going most of the time and shows no signs of depression or anxiety
• Has friends of the same sex

- Isn't ostracized, teased, or bullied; doesn't have school avoidance or separation anxiety
- Participates enthusiastically in activities with other Kids of the same age

Such Kids do need parental support. They need to be appreciated as individuals and admired for their strength of character. Parents help most when they stand up for their Kids when others are critical, when they do their best to keep listening to and talking with their Kids, and when they make sure their Kids know that parents think they are lovable.

In contrast, there are Kids who suspect or are sure that Nature gave them the wrong sexual assignment. There are several profiles for such Kids.

OUTSIDERS

This group of Kids who are set awash by the tide of puberty is similar to the nonconformists. But these Kids are unhappy.

These are Kids whose preferences for companions and activities of the opposite sex caused them trouble in early childhood. However, they haven't ever actually wished to *be* of the opposite sex. For instance, as young children they never insisted, "I'm really a boy" or "I'm really a girl." They chose their fantasies—being able to fly or to perform operations or to take care of a baby—for the activities rather than for sexual roles. When playing house, the girls wanted to be the Mommy and the boys wanted to be the Daddy.

Unlike the nonconformists, however, these Kids haven't found anything much appealing about the dress, activities, or representatives of the same sex. More importantly, they have not been able to find a niche in which their true preferences are accepted. Instead, they have had to keep them secret. When they engage in same-sex activities, their hearts just aren't in it; they are putting up a false front. Other Kids sense this and are puzzled but not put off by it. As a result, most of these Kids aren't teased or ostracized, but they have had trouble being a tight member of a group of Kids.

Over the years, this persistent awareness of difference has made outsiders feel like oddballs. They have not been able to feel themselves comfortably male or comfortably female. As a result, they may experiment with wishes of being of the opposite sex. So when the nine to twelve atmosphere begins to be sexualized, they are confused and worried. If the world around them is homophobic, they may be obsessed with the fear that they are really homosexual. Even when that anxiety is not paramount, a Kid in this situation may feel as if it is his or her destiny always to feel like an outsider.

Parents of this kind of Kid can help enormously.

- It often helps to be fairly explicit in talking with such a Kid, but it's important to pick your timing. The conversation should be private and supportive, and the parent must communicate an unambivalent liking of and support for the Kid.
- A Kid in this position needs a friend. Ideally, this friend should be of the same age and sex. That's what helps to validate a Kid's non-oddball status and helps him or her to feel complete. Parents can nurture best friendships enormously (see the discussion of best friends in **Growth of the Soul,** earlier in this chapter).
- The child also needs a support group. Such friends do not need to be of the same age or sex. Parents can look into Big Brother and Big Sisters organizations, religious groups, or interest groups like music or dramatics or chess. A summer camp that focuses on directed, noncompetitive activities, such as work projects or dramatic or musical production, might work. Computer friends and old-fashioned pen pals are likely candidates, though parents must take steps to confirm the identity and integrity of such anonymous friends. Kids need to be aware that they are never to go to meet such a friend

without parental approval and chaperonage. Neighbors, homes for the elderly, animal shelters, and volunteer organizations may all be sources of friends. A lucky Kid might find a friend in a grandparent, aunt, uncle, or other relative.

• Once in a while, a Kid in this group can become truly ostracized. If not actually teased or bullied, he or she can be aggressively ignored. Such a Kid never gets chosen as a field trip buddy or a team member; other Kids sigh and roll their eyes when he or she is assigned to their group. On barbaric occasions like passing out valentines or party invitations, he or she is conspicuously avoided. If this is happening to a degree that the Kid becomes depressed, it is sometimes necessary to take the dramatic step of changing schools, but only when other strategies have been shown not to work. Even when Kids receive special training in "prosocial skills" and learn to act just like the popular Kids, cliques at this age are unforgiving. Just transferring from one class to another usually doesn't work, because word gets around. If a Kid does transfer to another school, it's important to be sure there's not a Kid or Kids from the old school already there who can contaminate the atmosphere and make life miserable all over again in the same way.

SECRET-KEEPERS

A smaller number of Kids resemble outsiders in that they have had to keep their true preferences secret. They don't have a comfortable same-sex identity and have had to construct a role that doesn't really seem to them to fit.

However, these Kids have a deeper secret: a true wish to be of the opposite sex. Over the years, they have often become angry at this wish, which can't be fulfilled and which appears to be regarded by those they love as unnatural, disgusting, or evil. A Kid wants to obliterate that wish and can feel hopeless and powerless. As a result, such a Kid comes to hate that wish, which means hating a part of his or her identity. A Kid may not become aware of this until the increasingly sexualized atmosphere of puberty forces the issue.

So a Kid in this position may start acting unhappy with himself or herself during these years. In such cases, here's what parents may notice.

• A Kid stops being friends with his or her old buddies, especially a previous best friend, for no apparent reason and does not seem to seek replacements.

• A Kid whose early years were characterized by intense or frequent cross-sex dress or behavior—especially, by fantasizing or stating that he or she "really" was of the opposite sex—seems depressed, withdrawn, or preoccupied.

• A forced or artificial quality appears in the Kid's interactions with others, especially Kids the same age.

A Kid in this situation usually needs more help than parents can provide. Such a Kid benefits enormously from sessions with a sympathetic and experienced counselor, one who is able to tactfully approach the problem. Parents sometimes worry that such counseling will force the issue, "causing" a Kid to adopt a homosexual orientation. It's important to remember that homosexuality versus heterosexuality is not the problem here. The problem is that the Kid is starting to hate and is trying to disown a part of himself or herself. The goal is to help the Kid be equipped to deal with ambivalence and to develop a sense of selfhood and pride before engaging in the challenges of adolescence.

PARIAHS

Finally, a very small number of Kids are defined by themselves and others in terms of their sexual dilemma. Such Kids avoid members of their own sex and may become physically ill if forced to participate with them. They display speech and mannerisms that are exaggerated and unusual. By nine, they usually have been ostracized, teased, or bullied on a regular basis. However, they may yet cling to the fringes of social activity, accepted by this clique on the basis of being smart or by that one on the basis of being artistic or by another, alas, on the basis of flattery, bribery, or blackmail. ("If you won't be my lunch buddy, I'll tell everybody your Dad got fired because he was drunk!")

A Kid with this burden to bear is at terrible risk for a disastrous adolescence—not because he or she might grow up to have a homosexual orientation (which is possible, if not likely), but because for such a Kid life is miserable and the Kid is filled with hate for himself or herself and for others. Such a Kid is at risk for running away, drug abuse, sexual promiscuity (of either or both sexual orientations), delinquency, and suicide.

Such a Kid needs psychotherapy. Now. Let me be very clear: the goal of psychotherapy is not to change a Kid's innate sexual orientation. We don't know if that ever happens. The goal of therapy is to help the Kid survive the emotional and sometimes physical beating he or she suffers on a daily basis. The therapist must be clear that this is the goal and must be 100 percent on the side of the Kid, without a hint of condescension or disgust or fear. Such a therapist is worth any sacrifice of money, travel, or time.

Parents usually are aware that their Kid is in serious trouble, but once in a while they seem unable to see this. This can be true particularly if a parent is seriously stressed. Parents who are depressed themselves or who are overworked, exhausted, or who are in the grip of drug or alcohol problems may be unable or unwilling to perceive a Kid's pain. In this situation, a caring relative, teacher, physician, or neighbor has a duty to intervene. If the parents are truly unreachable, such a caring adult may be able to have a sympathetic conversation with the Kid himself or herself, and direct that child to professional help provided through the school or such organizations as the YMCA/YWCA or Jewish community centers.

THE MORAL OF THE STORY

Even Kids who don't fall into any of these categories still worry "Am I normal?" And why shouldn't they? Being normal is a bone that their classmates growl over and toss around all day long. So all Kids need to know:

• It's normal and expected for Kids this age to have crushes on people of the same sex. It doesn't mean that a person is homosexual.

• It's normal and expected for Kids this age to be preoccupied with the changes in their own and other people's bodies. It doesn't mean that a person is a sex maniac.

• There are lots of different attitudes toward homosexuality, depending on a person's religion, upbringing, and culture. Nobody knows exactly why some people grow up attracted to those of their own sex.

• Whatever a Kid needs to do to make a complete life, parents will suppport. They will love him or her no matter what. They want their Kid to find someone to love, loyal friends, satisfying work, and ways to play. They want to stay friends with their Kids even when everybody is old and grey.

SERIOUS ILLNESS IN A CLOSE FAMILY MEMBER

Kids at this age do better when they have a defined role to play and feel in control of some aspect of the situation. They need to know the name of the illness, what caused it, and that it is not contagious, if it's true that the illness can't be transmitted. If the illness is contagious, they need to know how it is passed on and what kind of prevention or treatment is planned for them. They need to know what is being done for the patient, but not in great detail. Kids don't need to know about intimate details of care—just what you would tell a kindly inquiring close acquaintance.

They need to know that everything appropriate is being done and that the adults have confidence in the providers of care. If the condition is serious, and if it is fairly common—if it is cancer or a heart attack or a life-threatening infection—it is appropriate to assume that the Kid knows a lot about the disease from TV and word of mouth. In that case, it's important to be quite specific, meeting the youngster at his or her own level of sophistication.

Just because a youngster this age appears to know a lot, it's not a good idea to assume that he or she knows the basics. A Nine to Twelve may know everything about cancer, except that it's not contagious; or everything about heart disease, except that people can recover completely.

A role for a Kid this age takes some thought. Kids nine, ten, and eleven know when they are really helping and when they are being passed off to meaningless busywork. An ideal role for a youngster this age is one that stretches him or her a bit, enough to make the Kid feel special, grown-up, and appreciated: for example, fixing a good breakfast for the caregiver who's been up all night; doing the routine laundry; reading aloud to the invalid.

But any role that is assigned to the Kid is welcomed, when the alternative is retiring to one's room and trying to not listen or think. Sometimes the kindest role an adult can give a Kid is that of continuing a normal life:

> "We need you to remind us that after a while things will seem normal again. Your job is to keep telling us that. And we'll keep you informed of what's going on on the home front."

This is not at all the same as,

> "We need you to keep out of the way. Just keep up with your normal stuff and don't worry."

If the person is not expected to live, children need to be told. Children this age need to

mourn just as adults do, and go through the same stages of grief. They also need to make peace with the dying person, whether by just sitting with the person, talking, writing letters, drawing pictures, or making video or audio tapes. Hospice services are often invaluable in this situation.

What helps the very most in this situation is the attentive presence of a loving, trusted adult who has the emotional energy to be with the child, listening and explaining and comforting.

DEATH OF A BELOVED PERSON OR PET

Kids this age understand death in much the same way adults do. They know that it is inevitable and permanent; they don't believe that the dead person goes on living in a different form.

If a beloved person or pet dies suddenly, a youngster needs to know what happened. This can be very difficult in some situations—when the death was someone's fault or when the circumstances were horrific. However, the youngster had much better hear it from a trusted adult—a little at a time, with plenty of pauses to allow him or her to react—than from a potentially cruel source like another Kid or the media.

When the death is not sudden, Kids, like adults, do some of the work of mourning ahead of time. They, too, can make their peace with the ill or injured person. They can start to reorder their lives.

Children in this age group often choose to attend the funeral or memorial service. They should be allowed to choose to attend, and they should be seated with an adult who can help them to leave if they wish. The presence of a child should not push adults to make the funeral or service an "upbeat" one. In fact, most children this age will be very confused, even angered, by the contrast between their grief and a service designed to cheer people up.

The time that grieving takes is individual,

but it generally lasts two years. That's the time it takes to reorder life without the vanished person—the time it takes not to use the death as a point of reference for every other event. Many children will have an anniversary reaction at the same time of year the death occurred. Sometimes this will reveal itself in some physical mode, such as fatigue or nervous tics. Frequent urination, called pollakiuria, is not unusual (but always needs to be evaluated for medical causes).

HOSPITALIZATION

Whether the youngster is undergoing puberty or not, children this age think about hospitalization the same way that Sevens and Eights do. The main difference is that they are even more modest and more receptive to using mental techniques to handle fear and pain.

Please see the discussion of hospitalization in **What If?**, in Chapter 2.

DIVORCE

No matter how upsetting homelife is, Kids believe their families to be normal. If there is fighting, alcoholism, even incest, most Kids in this age group cling to the idea that their family life is just like everyone else's except for—whatever. They take for granted that the bond between parents is fixed and immutable, even when it is clear to everyone else that this is not the case.

This can knock parents for a loop. "Surely she heard us screaming at each other! She can't really believe that we're going to patch this up!" "And all the times he'd fall asleep drunk in front of the TV and then wake up violent! How can he not see that this can't go on?" Nine to Twelve thinks "I wish they'd stop!" not "This can't go on."

Kids this age regard divorce, however justified, as abandonment. They also believe that they themselves could have prevented the divorce and that they themselves are one of the root causes of the divorce. They often overhear conversation that confirms this, if parents argue over a Kid's achievements, behavior, or appearance.

When custody decisions are made, most judges will ask for and take into account the preference of a youngster Nine or older. Many youngsters do well with this, but some are agonized by having to make a decision that rejects one or the other parent. There is no one custody arrangement that is always better than another. However, Kids this age do not deal well with frequent disruption of their sense of home. They need roots: a private area of their own, a predictable schedule, the same friends, school, and activities.

Children who have to split custody on a frequent basis may have trouble getting their homework done or keeping intimate friends, as they may not feel comfortable being away from home (one parent might complain to the other) or having the friend over, due to tension in the home atmosphere.

The biggest favor divorcing parents can do for a child of any age is to focus on the Kid's needs more than on their own. Too often, parents become so involved in their own war that they have no time, energy, or wits with which to keep in close touch with their children. Kids this age need both parents to help them through a crucial period of growth. If they don't get this help, adolescence is likely to be fraught with bitterness, hostility, and pain.

SEXUAL MOLESTATION

No matter how old you are, being molested is a disaster. But there's a difference in how Kids react at this age. They are verging on the age at which they expect themselves to be actors on the sexual stage of life. They are often ambivalent about the role that they have played in the molestation. They may have upsetting, confusing feelings—part flattered, part responsible, part degraded. A Kid who has been exposed to the glamorization of sex—even of prostitution—may be seduced into thinking himself or herself now a member of an adult elite and at the same time feel like a violated, angry, humiliated child.

Distressingly, it's important to remember that even after puberty begins in Kids, the person most likely to engage in sexual molestation is somebody known and trusted, to some degree, by the Kid and his or her family. This could be somebody as close as a parent, somebody as trusted as a medical staff person.

Ideally, we try to protect Kids. If this fails, at least they should be able to tell the truth, as soon as possible after the event.

Whatever happens, Kids need support. A Kid needs to know that what happened was not the Kid's fault, but the fault of the molester. A Kid needs to know that abuse almost never "ruins" a Kid physically—making normal sexual relations and childbearing impossible. The medical examination is supposed to reassure them of that and to gather evidence so that whoever betrayed them will be punished.

A Kid needs to know that no matter how long or how bad the abuse was, he or she is strong and brave and can overcome the humiliation, anger, self-loathing, and all the terrible feelings, and that adults will commit themselves to getting help for that to happen. Whatever our role, as parents or teachers or counselors or pediatricians, we want a Kid to know that we are 100 percent on his or her side, no matter who committed the molestation, no matter the reason it happened, and no matter what the outcome entails in broken relationships or financial difficulties.

A molested Kid must never feel that a parent feels martyred because the Kid was molested and disclosed that fact.

PROTECTION

• A Kid's best protection is feeling like the proud owner of his or her own body, entitled to decide what happens to it in most situations.

Lots of things promote this: a feeling of competence, of being cherished by at least one loving adult, of being normal. A Kid with a big difference (a birthmark, a disability, unusually tall/short/fat/thin/sexually mature/homely/beautiful) may feel as if his or her body belongs to somebody else: adults, onlookers, the medical profession, detractors, admirers. Every effort parents can take to counteract this impression is an effort toward protection.

• Kids who are exposed to a sexualized environment may feel that sex is expected of them. Of course, our public world today is pretty much a sexualized environment. Fortunately, it's what goes on in the home that determines to a great degree whether Kids this age see themselves as "supposed to be" sexually active. Kids need to be protected from adults who act out sexual behavior in front of Kids, or who tease or flirt with them in a sexual way. They also need to be protected from unusual exposure to sexual material in the media. Sneaking a look at MTV while home alone is one thing: having parents who regard R-rated films, MTV, and other sexualized materials or programming as wholesome family fare is another.

DISCLOSURE

• Kids need to know that in a parent's eyes, they come first. They need to know that when the chips are down, the Kid matters more to the loving parent than anybody else—more than a spouse, a friend, an authority figure.

• Kids need to know that parents are paying attention. Under the unique stress of molestation, a Kid can revert to the emotional age of five: he or she assumes that parents know what is going on. If parents don't pay attention, listen, and act, a Kid is likely to feel unbearably betrayed. Therefore, a Kid who tells a parent that "Uncle Glenn acts really weird" needs to be debriefed. So does one who says, "I'm not going to go to piano any more! I can't stand Mr. B!" So does one who begs, "Don't go out tonight! Stay here!"

• A Kid needs to know that parents won't disintegrate or explode on hearing about an incident that made the Kid uncomfortable, that crossed the line. Parents are felt to be most trustworthy when they have a track record of getting the facts, considering them, and taking action in an adult fashion. The parent who goes into hysterics or picks up a gun at every provocation is not going to get the truth from a Kid. Nor is one who looks to the Kid for consolation, advice, and protection.

• Kids need to know that parents care. The parent who sees an adult take advantage of a Kid in some weird way—kissing the Kid on the lips or pinching a breast or snapping a bra strap—and does nothing is unlikely to be trusted to do anything when something worse happens.

SUPPORT

• Support means being angry at the person who molested the Kid, with practically no other reaction showing. Any demonstration of sympathy, understanding, or regret for the perpetrator is likely to be taken by the Kid as a hint that he or she was the party responsible. However, anger can be colored by explanation:

> "He is a very sick man."

> "Nobody realized that he was so sick."

• Support means making sure that during any medical or legal investigations or confrontations the Kid is given the utmost consideration. This means that each professional:

> Provides a private and dignified place to conduct the business at hand.
> Introduces himself or herself, and explains his or her role.
> Tells the Kid what is going to happen.
> Listens and asks questions and pays attention.
> Allows the Kid the option of having either a trusted adult or a professional chaperone in the room during any examination that requires undressing. Someone else must be in the room beside the examiner and the Kid.
> Thanks the Kid and gives the Kid a word of praise for honesty and bravery.
> Avoids inappropriate comments—not just teasing or making light of the incident, but chat about topics irrelevant to the Kid.

• Support means safety. If the perpetrator remains in the home or is permitted to have access to the Kid, the Kid is in a constant state of anxiety or terror. This must not be permitted.

• Support means apology. Whoever had any responsibility in the molestation needs to apologize. Ideally, this means the perpetrator. But it also means the parent or other adult who allowed the relationship, a representative of the institution that employed the perpetrator, or a representative of the system of justice who knew of the perpetrator's predilections and did not protect the Kid.

• Support means psychotherapy, even if a Kid appears to have coped well and appears to be having no problems. Loving adults close to a Kid may not be the people suited to hear the Kid's real angers and fears. Every molested child needs to have psychotherapy with a professional. The duties of that professional are: to listen, rather than to plant memories that aren't real; to ask helpful questions; to allow discharge of feelings in a safe environment; and to help the child reframe the experience in a way that blames the perpetrator rather than the victim. Kids need to be able to remember such an experience as one in which they did the very best they could to cope with an overwhelming injury. They need to feel whole, normal, brave, and in charge.

• Support means no further unsupervised contact with the perpetrator and supervised contact only with the consent of the Kid.

Appendix A

●■▲■○

DECIPHERING THE
GROWTH CHARTS

Growth charts are parents' friends when used right.

THEY CAN TELL YOU IF YOUR KID IS GROWING IN HEIGHT AS EXPECTED

From age five to puberty, Kids almost always stay on the same growth curve. A deviation, especially a decrease in height growth from the expected, needs to be investigated. Also, when used in the context of a thorough pediatric visit, a growth chart can help to predict adult height.

USED RIGHT, THEY CAN TELL YOU IF YOUR KID IS GAINING TOO MUCH WEIGHT

About one in four Kids ages five to twelve is in the obese category, weighing 20 percent or more over the expected weight for height, sex, and body build. Used incorrectly, the charts can be very misleading in this regard and can delay the child's getting help. It's important to know early on if a Kid is getting too chubby. Intervening early may well allow a Kid to just slow the weight gain and grow into the extra weight—much more effective than having to lose weight as an adult.

THEY CAN TELL YOU IF YOUR KID IS NOT GAINING AS MUCH WEIGHT AS EXPECTED FOR HIS OR HER GROWTH IN HEIGHT, SEX, AND BODY BUILD

Not gaining enough weight, too, needs to be investigated.

THEY ARE NOT AS GOOD AT TELLING YOU IF YOUR KID IS TOO THIN

A Kid who has always been lean, who is growing as expected for height, who is healthy and developing normally, and who is gaining enough weight to stay on his lean weight curve, is almost never too thin, no matter what the chart shows.

HERE'S HOW TO "PUT YOUR KID ON THE GROWTH CURVE

HOW TALL IS MY KID COMPARED TO OTHER KIDS OF THE SAME AGE AND SEX?

Use the chart at the top of the page labeled Height for Age. This is the one that has the word "Stature" going down the left-hand side. Make sure you are using the chart for your Kid's sex.

• Find your Kid's age along the scale at the bottom of the chart. Make a dot there.

• Find your Kid's height along the scale that runs down the **left-hand** side of the chart. Make sure you pick the right scale: don't confuse inches with centimeters. Make a dot there.

• Draw a line straight up from the age dot on the bottom and a line straight across from the height dot on the side. The lines should be at 90° angles to each other. Find where they intersect. Make a dot there.

• That dot will fall somewhere in relation to the percentile lines. These are the lines that go up from left to right. They are labeled 5 percent, 10 percent, 25 percent, 50 percent, 75 percent, 90 percent, and 95 percent. The location of the dot with respect to these lines tells you how tall your Kid is in relation to other Kids of the same age and sex.

• If your Kid's dot is on the line marked 95 percent, he or she is taller than 95 percent of Kids of the same age and sex. If the dot is at the line marked 50 percent, your Kid is exactly average, taller than half the Kids of the same age and sex and shorter than half of them. If it is at the line marked 10 percent, your Kid is taller than 10 percent of Kids the same age and sex, and shorter than 90 percent. If the dot falls between the two percentile lines—say, between 25 percent and 50 percent, you can roughly figure out where your Kid falls.

IS MY KID GROWING OKAY ACCORDING TO WHAT IS PREDICTED FROM PAST MEASUREMENTS?

To find this out, plot previous heights at different ages on the chart just as you did the present one. If your Kid stays just about on the same percentile line, or on a line parallel to a percentile line, he or she is growing as expected. If the dots that you have plotted don't stay on such a line, there's a deviation. A deviation from one curve to another (from the 50 percent to the 25 percent, for instance) is significant

enough to warrant seeing the pediatrician. However, many such apparent deviations are due to inaccuracies in measuring the Kid.

IS MY KID GAINING WEIGHT AS EXPECTED FOR HIS OR HER HEIGHT AND SEX?

• DON'T USE THE CHART THAT IS JUST BELOW THE HEIGHT FOR AGE CHART. That chart tells you how much your Kid weighs according to age. You don't care how much your Kid weighs compared to other Kids the same age; some of those Kids are tall and are supposed to weigh more; others are short and are supposed to weigh less. The weight chart is often misunderstood. For instance, many parents (and some pediatricians) believe that if a Kid is in a given percentile of height for age, he or she ought to be in the same percentile of weight for age. This is not true. This misconception can falsely reassure parents that a Kid is not too chubby.

• Use the chart that has a scale for Stature along the bottom and Weight along the right-hand side.

• As you did above, plot your Kid's weight on the scale along the bottom, height along the scale on the side, and draw two lines from these points. Make a dot where they intersect.

• If your Kid's weight for height is at or below the 75 percent line, this is a good indication that your Kid is not too chubby. If your Kid's weight for height is above the 75 percent line but below the 90 percent line, your Kid is probably overweight. If your Kid's weight for height is above the 90 percent line, your Kid is almost certainly overweight. If your Kid's weight for height is above the 95 percent line, it is likely that your Kid is above the cutoff point for obesity.

IS MY KID IN DANGER OF BECOMING OBESE?

The way to tell is to plot previous measurements on this chart. If your Kid's weight for height had always been at or below the 50 percent line but now is at or above the 75 percent line, it is likely that your Kid is starting to gain too much weight. A visit to the pediatrician is indicated to verify this and to analyze why it has occurred.

IS MY KID TOO THIN?

Defining what is "too thin" is tricky. If a Kid is chronically ill or malnourished and thin, it's important to try to fix the underlying problem and restore normal weight gain. Most very lean Kids who are healthy and developing normally and who have always been lean aren't too thin at all. If your Kid has gone down on the percentile lines of weight for height or if your Kid's weight for height is at or below the 5 percent line, check with your pediatrician.

BOYS: 2 TO 18 YEARS
STATURE FOR AGE &
WEIGHT FOR AGE

NAME _____

RECORD # _____

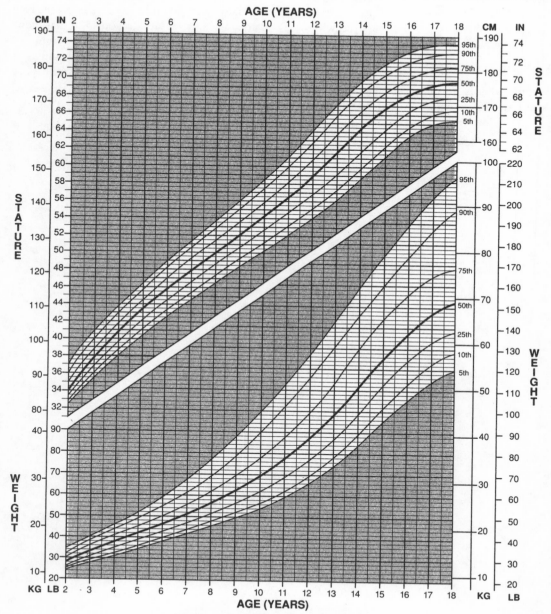

Department of Health, Education, and Welfare, Public Health Service
Health Resources Administration, National Center for Health Statistics, and Center for Disease Control

DECIPHERING THE GROWTH CHARTS

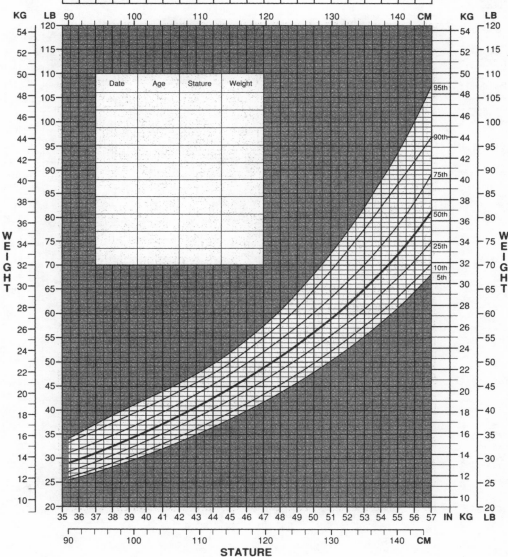

PRE-PUBERTAL BOYS: 2 TO 11½ YEARS

WEIGHT FOR STATURE   NAME_____   RECORD #_____

STATURE

Date	Age	Stature	Weight

Distributed by

Mead Johnson
NUTRITIONALS

Maker of:
Enfamil®, Lactofree®, ProSobee® and Nutramigen®
Formulas for Baby's First Year and Beyond
Pregestimil®, Infalyte®, Poly-Vi-Flor®, and Tri-Vi-Sol®

L-B50-11-94

DECIPHERING THE GROWTH CHARTS

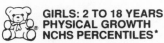 **GIRLS: 2 TO 18 YEARS**
PHYSICAL GROWTH
NCHS PERCENTILES*

Name_____ Record #_____

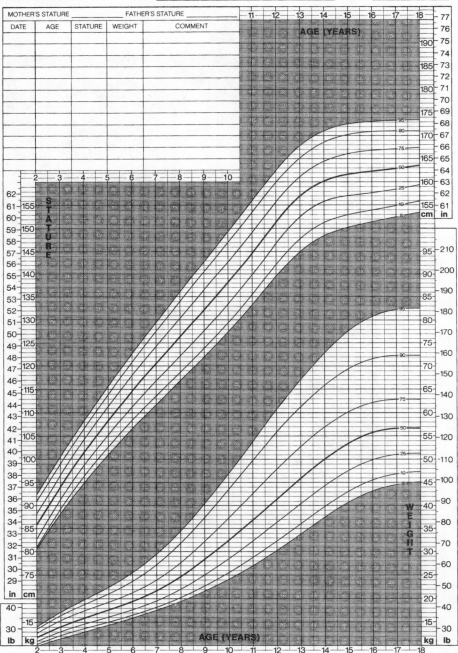

 ROSS
PEDIATRICS

PediaSure®
Complete Liquid Nutrition

The only complete
nutritional formula
designed for children
1 to 10 years old

Pedialyte®
Oral Electrolyte
Maintenance Solution

Quickly restores
fluids and minerals
lost in diarrhea
and vomiting

VI-DAYLIN®
Vitamins

Good-tasting vitamins
for infants and children

*Adapted from: Hamill PVV, Drizd TA, Johnson CL, Reed RB,
Roche AF, Moore WM: Physical growth: National Center for Health
Statistics percentiles. AM J CLIN NUTR 32:607-629, 1979. Data
from the National Center for Health Statistics (NCHS), Hyattsville,
Maryland.

© 1982 Ross Products Division, Abbott Laboratories

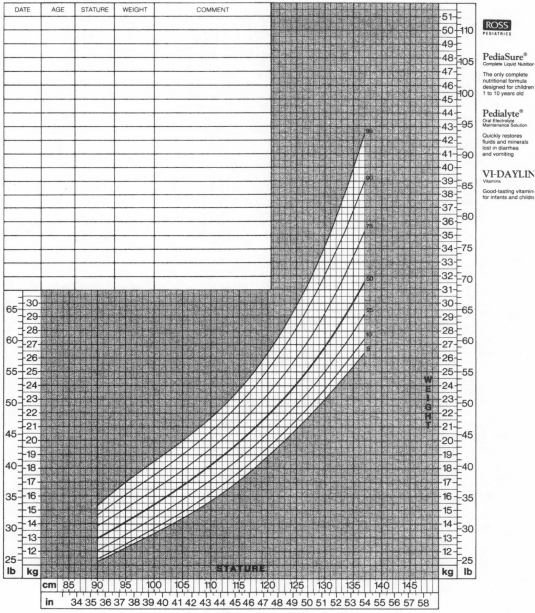

GIRLS: PREPUBESCENT PHYSICAL GROWTH NCHS PERCENTILES*

Name_____ Record #_____

DATE	AGE	STATURE	WEIGHT	COMMENT

ROSS
PEDIATRICS

PediaSure®
Complete Liquid Nutrition

The only complete
nutritional formula
designed for children
1 to 10 years old

Pedialyte®
Oral Electrolyte
Maintenance Solution

Quickly restores
fluids and minerals
lost in diarrhea
and vomiting

VI-DAYLIN
Vitamins

Good-tasting vitamin:
for infants and childr

51214 09893WB
(0.05)/JUNE 1994

ROSS ROSS PRODUCTS DIVISION
ABBOTT LABORATORIES
COLUMBUS, OHIO 43215-1724

LITHO IN USA

Appendix B
SAFETY

These are some considerations about safety that aren't obvious. By obvious, I mean such ordinary precautions as "Don't go bungie jumping."

Safety doesn't have to cramp a Kid's style. And it had better not: too many restrictions invite dangerous risk-taking. Ideally, safety becomes a nearly invisible aspect of an activity.

Some of the features that help keep fun safe can be built into equipment like bikes or skates. Other safety features, like helmets and pads, can become so habitual that they feel like necessary parts of the sports.

But the most important part is attitude. A lot of safety is sheer common sense, but common sense isn't inborn. It has to be learned. Kids know not to dive head first into the obviously shallow part of the pool; they have to be taught, though, not to dive head first into untested water that looks deep and clear.

Here is a look at some specific weather conditions, travel situations, activities, and sports from a safety perspective.

Weather Conditions

COLD

The smaller the Kid, the more vulnerable he or she is to cold injury (see hypothermia, frostbite, and chilblains in the **Glossary**). Kids need warm, layered clothing with special attention to socks, hats, and gloves. Keep an ear out for complaints about itchy fingertips, toes, ears, nose—the first sign of cold injury. Keep an eye out for whiteness of the same body parts: that can mean frostbite. Keep in mind that whiny, irritable behavior can be an early sign of hypothermia. Carry quick sources of sugar, like candy bars, and a folded survival blanket in your emergency-supply fanny pack.

SUN

Sun on the slopes and beaches is more dazzling than regular sun. It's best to avoid the most intense sunshine between the hours of 10 A.M. and 2 P.M. and to wear hats with brims. A blistering sunburn before adulthood doubles the risk of contracting malignant melanoma.

Kids need sun protection lotion (at least SPF 15). They also need to protect their eyes from the sun: Kids need to be educated never to look directly at the sun, even when wearing sunglasses. (This is true all the time, not just during an eclipse of the sun.) The ultraviolet (UV) rays can damage the eyes seriously. If the retina becomes damaged or if the sun produces cataracts on the lens, the damage to vision can be permanent. The more the exposure to the UV rays, the higher the risk.

If a Kid is in the sun long enough to get

sunburned or tanned or to need sun lotion, then sunglasses are needed, as well. The protection sunglasses give is created by adding a special, invisible chemical to the lenses. So you can't tell how good a pair of glasses is by how dark they are: the color is totally irrelevant. Dark sunglasses without UV protection can be particularly dangerous, because the darkness allows the pupil to dilate, letting in even more sun to the structures of the eye. Polarized glasses and mirrored glasses don't necessarily have UV protection, either. You have to go by the label. The label should stipulate one of the following:

UV absorption up to 400 nm

Maximum UV protection or blockage

99 percent UV protection or blockage

Special purpose

Meets ANSI UV requirements (ANSI is the American National Standards Institute).

The best sunglasses have large lenses that fit fairly close to the eyes. Good sunglasses needn't be expensive, but they aren't ridiculously cheap, either. They generally cost at least five or six dollars.

HEAT

Any Kid with an inherited condition that inhibits sweating is extremely vulnerable to overheating. It's rare for Kids this age who sweat normally actually to have heatstroke, but it can happen under extreme conditions. When heatstroke occurs, the body's temperature can rise to over 107°. In hot conditions, Kids need to have plenty of water to drink (you don't need special "sports" drinks; just water) and to splash on the body to help cool off. If a Kid becomes feverish in the sun, it may be from the external heat rather than from an infection. If that's the case, giving antifever medicines like acetaminophen or ibuprofen won't help. Instead, it's crucial to strip off the Kid's clothing and cool him or her down with cool water sponges in a cool room. This is considered an emergency, so simultaneously get the Kid to medical help.

Transportation

• Kids need to know that wearing a lap seat belt isn't enough. Many Kids will wiggle out of the shoulder harness because it chafes their necks. Get the gadget that prevents chafing or tell the Kid to put up with the minor discomfort. Serious spine, face, neck, abdominal, and hand injuries can result if only the lap belt is worn. The lap part of the belt should be worn low, below the belly button.

• Seat belts in school buses? The controversy keeps coming up. On one hand, most bus drivers feel that getting Kids out of the seat belts would be a problem if there were an accident. On the other hand, lives could be saved if a bus is involved in a bad accident. Certainly, seat belts must be worn in small school buses and vans. In fact, most accidents happen when the Kid is out of, but near, the school bus—picking up something he or she dropped and getting below the level of the rear view mirror or below the driver's sight in front of the bus; or dashing in front of a bus that's pulling away. Kids need to know that if they drop something, they should tell the driver before dashing to retrieve it.

• Front passenger seats with air bags have turned out to be dangerous places for Kids under the age of twelve. The air bags are designed for adults. A Kid in the seat when the air bag deploys is at risk for serious injury or death. Until this problem is solved, Kids are best off in the back seat.

• Car pools. Ah, a delicate topic. Some adults who drive car pools, alas, are not safe drivers. Kids need to be asked about this. Does the adult insist on seat belts? Drive responsibly? Avoid engaging in another activity at the same time as driving—talking on the car phone, drinking coffee, and so forth?

Guns

• Guns in the home are more likely to injure a family member or a friend than an intruder. In any home with a Kid under eighteen, guns should be locked up unloaded and ammunition should be locked up unloaded in another location.

• It's important to check out the gun policies the parents of your Kid's friends may have. Parents are very much within their rights to ask if there are guns in the home, and if so, what the parents' policies are about guns.

• Even the most responsible, well-taught Kid can have a tragic accident with a gun, including with BB guns and air rifles. Lost lives and eyes attest to this. Kids either shouldn't be shooting at all or should restrict their shooting to times when they are under extremely close, one-on-one supervision by a responsible adult.

• A Kid with a toy gun can resemble an intruder with a real one. Toy guns either should be avoided or should look much more like toys than like guns.

• Kids need to be reminded on regular occasions what to do if invited or dared to look at, play with, or otherwise have contact with a gun. YOUR Kid might be very responsible and sensible, but the other Kid might not be.

Activities

Activities deemed by the American Academy of Pediatrics to be too dangerous for Kids even with teaching and supervision: trampolines, cheerleading pyramids, bullet-shooting guns (they can be deafening as well as fatal to anyone in the way), and metal darts. Unsupervised use of air rifles and BB guns can be fatal or maiming. All-terrain vehicles have an unacceptably high rate of death, severe head and spinal cord injuries, and maiming of limbs. Riding in the back of a pick-up truck is an invitation for serious injury of all parts of the body; it's too easy to get thrown out.

BIKING (TWO-WHEELERS)

EQUIPMENT

The bike

A good first bike, for Kids under eight, is single speed bicycle with foot brakes and 16" wheels. At about eight, most Kids can graduate to one with multiple gears, hand brakes, and a 20" to 24" wheel. Girls should be able to stand flat on their feet while seated in the saddle, and boys should be able to stand flat while straddling the top tube. Tires shouldn't be too worn, and there should be reflectors on the wheels, a horn, and good brakes that are checked by an adult every few months.

The helmet

Wearing the right helmet reduces serious head injuries by 85 percent.

It's the responsibility of the salespeople to check helmet fit and of parents to check the salespeople. It's dangerous to get a helmet that's too big, thinking the Kid will grow into it. The helmet shouldn't be too tight nor should it wobble. It should cover the forehead but not the ears. Approved helmets have been tested for crash safety. They are labeled ANSI, ASTM, or Snell, either on the box or inside the helmet. A good helmet costs around $30.00.

Make sure that the helmet sports a three-strap arrangement. A single chin strap is dangerous: I shall always remember David, making funny noises in the back seat. His father looked around to find him strangling on the strap of the bike helmet that had slid back over his head.

COMMON SENSE

Kids don't have enough common sense to bike on or across streets with nonresidential traffic until they're ten. Before that, they need to ride one-on-one with an adult. Even at ten, they need to prove themselves before trusted out on their own. And a Ten who has excellent common sense as an individual can lose it completely when with a buddy or a group bent on adventure.

SKIING AND SNOWBOARDING

Kid-friendly ski areas sport learn-to-ski programs and special areas of the mountain set aside for Kids. While traveling to a ski area, don't be tempted to carry skis inside the car with passengers: they are extremely hazardous in even a minor accident. If your ski slopes are higher than 3500 feet, a Kid may have some adjustment to make; at 5000 feet or higher, there is likely to be some altitude sickness, with headache, lightheadedness, and shortness of breath. Rest, drinking lots of water, and a prescription for altitude sickness can help.

THE SLOPES

Collisions account for 75 percent of skiers' injuries. No wonder. The average skier travels at 30 to 45 miles per hour, and some go much faster. Kids can be terrific skiers, but they can also be impulsive, risk-taking, and oblivious to the threat of the faster skiers bearing down on them or to the stolid, slow-going novices in their paths. At the very least, Kids need to stay on the slopes commensurate with ability and venture into harder terrain only with adult supervision. Kids need to be supervised and to know ski etiquette.

Ski programs for Kids are offered at most major ski resorts and this is an excellent investment for fun and safety. Teaching Kids yourself is not a great idea. They are more likely to hear and internalize safety guidelines if there isn't a parent-Kid power struggle going on. Moreover, they actually learn differently (and quicker) than adults, and this just sets the scene for fights and impatience. They also may pick up some of a parent's bad habits—hard to kick, once established.

EQUIPMENT

Ski boots

The new binding technology that works so well for adults hasn't done quite so well for

Kids. Kids under the age of ten fracture their legs skiing six times more frequently than adults do. Most often (75 percent of the time) the problem is that the binding fails to release. Some of these failures aren't high-tech, but due to poor-fitting boots, dirt on the boot soles, or improper adjustment of the binding.

Helmets

Head injuries don't happen often (accounting for between 6 and 12 percent of ski/snowboard injuries), but they can be devastating. Kids' heads are relatively bigger and heavier when compared to their bodies than adults' are, so they're top-heavy. Helmets are so effective that in the Scandinavian countries, where they're required for Kids under twelve, serious head injuries on the slopes are almost unheard of. Make sure your Kid's is well-fitting, with a three-strap arrangement so that it can't fall back on his or her head and cause strangling.

Sungoggles

See sunglasses, mentioned earlier in this section under **Weather Conditions.**

INLINE SKATING

I myself gave inline skating a shot, but discovered a problem. "My husband is getting tired of being crashed into. Tell me. How are you supposed to slow down?" I asked the next Ten I saw. "Why," he asked, round-eyed, "would you want to?" Indeed.

EQUIPMENT

The skates

Skates need to fit very securely so that there's no ankle wobble. It is wisest to spring for well-known, brand-name skates. They're designed to fit and not break down, and they're balanced.

The pads

Inline skaters need full metal jacket padding: helmet, elbow pads, wrist pads, knee pads. In a report from the Mayo Clinic, 78 percent of all the in-line skating injuries were of the arms.

THE SKATER

It is possible to be a safe skater, padded up and filled with common sense, and still have a significant injury. Having said that, it's also true that far more injuries occur because the skater is *not* helmeted or padded. Skating on streets with traffic is more dangerous than biking, because the skater is often tempted to take even more chances. It's harder to wait for a traffic light as a skater than it is as a bicyclist, for instance. Skating outside of the neighborhood without adult supervision is risky behavior. Instruction for beginning skaters is very wise: learning how to brake, turn, and slow down is done most safely with a teacher rather than by trial and error.

SKATEBOARDING

The safety problems with skateboarding (and snakeboarding) arise from the fact that the board often is moving faster than the Kid can run, so when he or she needs to bail out, it's with a splat. Many Kids use the skateboard as a kind of extension of the feet as a normal means of transportation. They still need the same helmets, padding, and mature judgment as do in-line skaters.

SWIMMING, SAILING, AND WATER SPORTS

Kids are not born with common safety sense and need active teaching. "What should you do," I ask Kids from five up, "before you jump in the pool?" To a man and a woman, they say, "Hold your nose!" When I suggest meekly that it might be a good idea to check out the water for other people, they stare at me as if I came from the moon.

Formal classes and junior lifesaving courses for the older ones are ideal. Kids take classes seriously, much more seriously than just an old familiar parent nagging at them. If they are doing open water swimming, they need to know about holes in the surf, animal life like jelly fish, undertows ("It gets under your toes," Joey tells

me soberly, "and pulls you under") and strong currents.

Waiting for an hour after eating to avoid cramps is a myth. It takes longer than that for most meals to exit the stomach. Cramps happen most often in cold water, when a swimmer is fatigued. Every Kid needs adult supervision and a swimming buddy.

Kids—and adults—should be very careful not to swim in hot springs or warm, potentially polluted bodies of fresh water (including hot tubs.) An amoeba called *Naegleria fowleri* that lives in the water can be inhaled or perhaps enter through the skin. It causes a virulent form of meningitis/encephalitis that is nearly always fatal (only one survivor to date).

EQUIPMENT

The most important equipment is life jackets. Every Kid on a boat of any kind, every Kid in any body of water who isn't a swimmer, and any swimmer in dangerous seas needs a real life jacket, one that fits. Some are designed for adults. A small Kid in such a jacket may be thrown back so that his or her head is under water! Check it out by having the Kid put it on and get in the water, so you can see what would happen in a real emergency.

WILDERNESS CAMPING

Backpacking into the wilderness with Kids can be fabulous. For families who take this on in a serious way, I strongly recommend the article "Wilderness Medicine for Children" by Douglas A. Gentile, M.D. and Barbara C. Kennedy, M.D., *Pediatrics,* Vol. 88 No. 5 (November 1991): 967–981. It covers every contingency, with specific guidelines (for instance, how many miles a day to expect from Kids of different ages), specific recommendations for various contingencies such as getting lost, bit by a spider, or stuck in an avalanche, and referrals to excellent products from dressings of wounds to snakebite kits. It gives a complete medical kit rundown for the brave and hardy.

SAFETY

Team Sports

Someone who knows CPR should be present at every single game that involves balls, pucks, bats, or collisions. Yes, even baseball.

BASEBALL

Every year, more than 100,000 Kids visit an emergency room for treatment of a baseball injury. Fortunately, fatalities are rare; but eighty-six Kids died from baseball injuries between 1973 and 1994, usually after being hit in the head or chest by a ball. The Little League and the American Academy of Pediatrics (AAP) have formulated rules about equipment and procedures that will help prevent serious injuries.

EQUIPMENT

Helmets

Each Kid should have his or her own helmet that fits. If helmets are passed from player to player, they don't offer great protection and, moreover, can transmit lice. A helmet should have a face shield for batters and a face and throat shield for catchers. Every helmet should have ear-flaps and three-strap chin straps that work, so that the helmet doesn't fly off or drop down in back in such a way that the strap can strangle.

Eye protectors

Batters should wear goggles made out of polycarbonate and attached by a strap. If a Kid has a vision problem in one eye that can't be corrected by glasses, the good eye has to be protected: such a Kid should wear the goggles whether batting or playing another position.

Chest protectors

These aren't required by Little League (except for a ribbed chestguard for catchers) because there's not enough information to be sure they really make a statistical difference. However, since some of the deaths have occurred from being struck in the chest by a ball, they are worth considering.

The balls

Baseballs made with a polyurethane core may be softer than those with a core of yarn, but they are also heavier and may make a harder thump. It's a trade-off, and studies are still in progress as to which kind is safer.

THE GAME

Pitching

"Little league elbow" is caused by stressing the tendons in the elbow. Kid pitchers seem to be prone to the injury because they stay tense in the arm even after the ball leaves the hand. Limiting the total number of throws to 200 per week will help prevent it.

Sliding into base

Almost three-quarters of injuries happen when Kids slide into base, and the AAP advises that Kids under ten should not slide in head first. Moreover, the base itself should have a releasing mechanism, so that it's not like sliding into a brick wall. Breakaway bases reduce the risk of injury by a whopping 98 percent. The best bases use rubber grommets that break away under pressure. Other kinds of attachments can be interfered with by dirt or water.

Warming up

It's great to warm up, but a lot of Kids get accidentally walloped when they stroll too close to the batting on-deck circle. The American Academy of Pediatrics recommends eliminating this time-honored tradition.

ICE HOCKEY

Ice hockey is a great sport for Kids, but parents do well to assess the spirit of the enterprise. Some Kids' teams have gotten carried away. Players can be like armored knights in their black uniforms and helmets with face masks. Not only does the protective equipment prevent face and body injuries, but it's intimidating—something out of Star Wars by way of the Terminator. Unfortunately, the feeling of invulnerability and aggression fostered by this safety gear has led some of the "knights" to abandon not just

SAFETY

chivalry but sportsmanship. Because Kids feel immune to injury, they are freer with their sticks. As a result, there's been a dramatic increase in extremely serious neck and spine injuries.

The problem lies with the atmosphere of the game, which takes its cues from coaches and parents. One theory has it that Kids so garbed actually stop perceiving other players as human beings. When they attack with their sticks, they feel as if they're fending off inhuman invaders. Maybe it's all really like a video game.

Worse: Coaches and even parents may fall into the same trap the Kids do, thinking that the "armor" essentially protects Kid from injuries and that it permits much freer use of high-sticking. A push or a check from behind into the boards is the greatest cause of spinal-cord injuries, yet it's rare for coaches to discourage this. When the rule against checking is enforced, coaches may even tell players who are about to be checked to turn away to encourage checking in order to draw a higher penalty to the offending team! These adults may ignore foul after foul, calling a violation only when an injury has already occurred. Certainly, this happens in college and professional games, but it also occurs in games played by Kids.

The solution is to play the game right. Kids' teams need to be matched in terms of fitness and skills. Referees and coaches need to teach that opponents are people, no matter how garbed, and that illegal and dangerous stunts won't be tolerated, not even once, not even if calling a foul seems to "kill the game." The point needs to be made that it's not the referee who killed the game, but the player who committed the foul and who might have killed a teammate or opponent.

Parents with Kids who play hockey need to take a real stand on sportsmanship in the game. Neck and spinal cord injuries can kill or paralyze a Kid for life. And thinking of one's opponents as nonpeople can injure a Kid's soul just as devastatingly.

Horseback Riding

Horses are not as smart as they are beautiful. A horse who suspects that something is out to get him (a wheelbarrow, for example, or a mail box) will spook and buck and bolt even when a trusting Kid is in the saddle.

Kids who ride need hard hats, even when they are not jumping, and solid boots, even when they are dismounted. They need to have careful instruction not only in how to ride, but in how to fall safely. Yes, a horse will try to avoid stepping on something soft but not rolling on something soft. Kids should ride trails with an adult or sensible buddy, not alone. Kids who ride need to be up to date on tetanus immunizations.

Recommended Childhood Immunization Schedule
United States, January - June 1996

Vaccines are listed under the routinely recommended ages. [Bars] indicate range of acceptable ages for vaccination. [Shaded bars] indicate catch-up vaccination: at 11-12 years of age, hepatitis B vaccine should be administered to children not previously vaccinated, and Varicella Zoster Virus vaccine should be administered to children not previously vaccinated who lack a reliable history of chickenpox.

Age ▲ Vaccine ▼	Birth	1 mo	2 mos	4 mos	6 mos	12 mos	15 mos	18 mos	4-6 yrs	11-12 yrs	14-16 yrs
Hepatitis B [1,2]	Hep B-1		Hep B-2		Hep B-3					Hep B [2]	
Diphtheria, Tetanus, Pertussis [3]			DTP	DTP	DTP	DTP [3] (DTaP at 15+ m)		DTP or DTaP		Td	
H. influenzae type b [4]			Hib	Hib	Hib [4]	Hib [4]					
Polio [5]			OPV [5]	OPV	OPV				OPV		
Measles, Mumps, Rubella [6]						MMR			MMR [6] or MMR [6]	MMR [6]	
Varicella Zoster Virus Vaccine [7]						Var				Var [7]	

Approved by the Advisory Committee on Immunization Practices (ACIP), the American Academy of Pediatrics (AAP), and the American Academy of Family Physicians (AAFP).

SAFETY

Appendix C

●■▲■●

IMMUNIZATION SCHEDULE

If your Kid's immunizations do not conform with the chart, ask your pediatrician for help in getting them up to date.

Hepatitis B: A virus that causes an infection of the liver that can destroy it. The virus can be transmitted by contaminated needles, blood transfusion, or by sexual activity with an infected person, but 75 percent of the cases do not show a history of any risk factors.

Diptheria: A serious illness caused by a strain of bacteria. It can produce a membrane over the throat that can suffocate and a toxin or poison that can damage the heart.

Tetanus: A bacterial illness that produces "lockjaw" and convulsions, and which has a high mortality rate even if treated in the hospital.

Pertussis: The bacteria that causes whooping cough, which can be serious, even fatal, in babies. Immunization helps to keep older children from catching it and passing it on.

H. influenzae type b: The bacteria that causes many cases of meningitis and other serious diseases in young infants. The immunization isn't recommended for children Five and older.

Polio: a viral disease that can cause paralysis of the arms and legs as well as of the muscles that control breathing.

Measles: a viral disease featuring a rash, red eyes, and a runny nose that can be very serious; it causes blindness, deafness, mental retardation, and can even be fatal.

Mumps: A viral disease that can produce sterility in men and which causes swelling of the saliva-producing glands and of the pancreas in children. It can also produce an infection of the brain (encephalitis).

Rubella (three-day measles, German measles): A viral disease that can harm the fetus if the mother becomes infected. The immunization is to keep pregnant women from being exposed to the disease.

Varicella Zoster (Chicken pox): A viral disease that is usually not serious but that keeps a Kid (and often the Kid's parents) home sick for a week or so, and thus is a problem for school and work. Rarely, a case may be serious or even fatal, even in a previously healthy youngster. Scarring may also be a problem, though the spots don't usually give permanent scars.

GLOSSARY

●■▲■●

This is a list of selected medical terms, symptoms, and conditions that pop up often when caring for Kids ages five to twelve. It is not intended to replace consulting your own pediatrician.

Pronunciations below are given with a California accent. The emphasis on syllables is as follows: greatest emphasis on the syllable in capital letter; next greatest on the syllable in italics. As in: TELL-uh-*vizh*-un.

Throughout the definitions, I often use the word *innocent*. By innocent, I mean that the behavior or symptom or whatever is not seriously harmful and does not cause medical concern. An "innocent" heart murmer arises from normal causes and needs no treatment. An innocent rash is one that does not signify a serious underlying cause.

Abdominal pain—acute: From the point of view of parents, the most important question about Kids' sudden-onset belly aches is: Does this particular belly ache signify an emergency, like appendicitis? Most often, the answer is no. However, an urgent belly ache could mean that something, such as appendicitis or a blockage, is wrong with the intestines; or it could mean a problem with the pancreas, the liver, the kidneys, or even the lungs. Any of the following features mean that an urgent pediatric or emergency visit is necessary:

- The Kid is acting very sick—very lethargic and sleepy between spasms—and has poor color (pale, mottled, bluish) or is behaving bizarrely (confused, belligerent).
- There is shortness of breath.
- The pain is increasing to the point that the Kid is constantly preoccupied.
- The Kid cannot stand up straight because of pain.
- The Kid thrashes around to find a comfortable position or can't move at all without pain.
- The Kid vomits repeatedly, without relief from the pain, despite home treatment of the vomiting (see **Glossary** entry for Vomiting).
- The vomitus contains blood (more than a tiny streak) or is green or brown.
- There is blood in the stool or urine.
- The Kid's temperature is 104° or higher.

A Kid with a belly ache should be monitored over time for any of these signs. A Kid with a severe stomachache shouldn't be given anything by mouth until the cause is identified.

Abdominal pain—ordinary: Even a mild belly ache needs attention if it lasts without improvement for more than twelve hours or if it recurs frequently enough that the Kid complains of it. Such belly aches are often caused by relatively innocent problems such as chronic constipation or milk intolerance, but they can be an indication of more serious problems such as a chronic urinary tract infection, a kidney problem, liver disease, or a stomach ulcer. Sometimes the problem is more in the soul than in the body—anxiety, sadness, anger. When visiting the pediatrician for assessment, it's a good idea to make some notes first.

• How long has the belly ache lasted this time?

• If it recurs, when was the first episode? How often does the pain happen? How long does each episode last?

• Is there a pattern to the pain—a relationship to meals, dairy ingestion, emotional stress?

• Does the pain awaken the Kid?

• Is there nausea, vomiting, or burping?

• Is there any fever?

• What are the stools like? Any diarrhea, constipation, or blood in the stool or on the toilet paper?

• Does it hurt when the Kid pees, or is the Kid peeing unusually frequently?

• Where in the belly does the pain come? Is it always in the same place? If not, where?

• How severe is the pain? Does the Kid need to stop what he or she is doing? Lie down? Take medication? Does the Kid cry, wince, turn pale, sweat?

• Has the Kid been traveling anywhere unusual, been camping, been handling animals?

• Are there any other signs or symptoms, like fatigue, weight loss, rash, cough, headache?

• What do you think the pain is due to? What does the Kid think the pain is due to?

Acetaminophen (a-*seet*-ta-MEEN-ah-fen): The active ingredient in many medications (Tylenol, Tempra) that lowers fever and relieves pain. (It won't do a thing for a stuffy nose or cough.)

Acne: Zits are pimples that occur when hormones of puberty start flowing (see the section on acne in Chapter 3). With modern treatment, no Kid should have to endure disfiguring acne.

Acyclovir (ay-SIGH-klo-veer): An antiviral drug used against herpes infections and chicken pox (see **Glossary** entries for Herpes and Chicken pox). Brand name is Zovirax (ZOE-vir-acks).

Adenoids (AD-in-oyds): Lumps of lymph tissue, similar to tonsils, that sit up behind the nose. You can't see them just by looking down the throat. They are supposed to get bigger and bigger until around age seven, then gradually shrink down.

When they are very enlarged, they block breathing through the nose and contribute to middle ear infections. A Kid with enlarged adenoids sounds as if she were talking with a great wad of peanut butter stuck to the roof of her mouth. Very enlarged adenoids may need to be removed if they really obstruct breathing. Sometimes a Kid will have such large adenoids that she mouth breathes noisily, distorting not only mouth but nostrils and even pulling down the lower eyelids! That's called "gaping facies" (GAY-ping FAY-seez) and is a sign that jaw, chin, and teeth development may suffer. And sometimes a Kid will have such trouble breathing at night that she suffers from sleep apnea (see **Glossary** entry for Apnea).

AIDS (Acquired Immune Deficiency Syndrome): The disease caused by infection with the HIV virus. Children usually acquire this by transmission from the infected mother to the fetus or by transfusion of contaminated blood, rarely by sexual abuse. Children with AIDS cannot pass it on through casual contact or by hugging and kissing. They cannot pass it on from urine or stools. There has never been a report of a caretaker catching AIDS, or a household member catching AIDS, from an infected child.

Alice-in-Wonderland syndrome: Weird visual sensations (see **Glossary** entry for Infectious mononucleosis).

Allergen (AL-er-jen): Something that can give rise to symptoms of allergy. Dust, molds, dander, pollen, bee stings, and certain foods are all potential allergens.

Allergy (AL-er-jee): The outcome when the

immune system decides that something that is normal in the environment really is an enemy and is attacking it. Symptoms range from hay fever to asthma, from hives or eczema to anaphylaxis, from stomachaches to swollen, tingling lips. Finding out what the Kid is allergic to may mean a careful history taken by the pediatrician or allergist or it may mean blood tests or skin tests. Treating allergic symptoms involves first, getting away from the allergens, and second, taking medications. Prevention of allergic attacks consists of trying to avoid the allergens—which may mean avoiding a pet, dust, molds, pollen, or a food. It also may mean preventive medications. Finally, it may mean allergy shots (see **Glossary** entry for Allergy shots).

Allergy shots: These are injections of very tiny, diluted solutions of the substances a Kid is known to be allergic to. When the injections are given frequently, in increasing strength, they can persuade the immune system into realizing that the substance is normal and friendly, and does not require an immune response. It's crucial that allergy tests be given first, that the solutions be accurate and pure, that the staff giving the injections know what they're doing, and that the Kid getting the shot stay in the office for at least a half-hour after the shot. Once in a while, the injection itself can trigger a very severe allergic reaction.

Alopecia (*al*-oh-PEE-shyah): Absence of hair, baldness. This can happen for a number of reasons and always requires a medical evaluation. A Kid can have a bald spot from twiddling the hair and pulling it out. Or it could be because of a fungus: this is particularly likely to happen to Kids with elaborate, braided or knotted hairstyles, especially those that use hair oil or pomade or other oils or creams. Such a fungus needs diagnosis and treatment with medication taken by mouth, since the fungus gets into the hair follicles, beyond the reach of medicated creams. Once in a while, alopecia can be due to a thyroid or other hormonal problem, a vitamin deficiency, or an autoimmune problem in which a person makes antibodies to his or her own tissues. Of course, alopecia is a well-known side effect of chemotherapy or radiation treatments for cancer.

Amblyopia (*am*-blee-OH-pee-ah): Blindness in one eye, often preventable. It occurs when one eye has weaker vision than the other, and lets the other eye do all the work. Since the weak eye never sends impulses to the brain, the brain forgets how to make sense of images seen through that eye. If the weak eye can be made to work hard before the brain forgets, vision can be preserved. A clue to the threat of amblyopia is a "lazy" or "wandering" eye (see **Glossary** entry for Strabismus). Once in a while, a Kid will be found to have amblyopia that went undiagnosed because previous vision exams were normal. This is often because the child outwitted the patch that was supposed to block the vision of the stronger eye.

Anaphylaxis (*an*-a-fil-AX-is): A life-threatening allergic reaction, culminating in shock (loss of blood pressure). Fortunately, it's very rare. When it does occur, it is most often after exposure to a medication, a stinging insect, or food you already know you're sensitive to. Anyone with such a sensitivity should carry a prescription "beesting" kit containing adrenalin to give by injection. Benadryl or other oral medication in the kit won't do a thing for anaphylaxis. Early warning symptoms: tingly mouth, itching, pounding heart, trouble breathing. If in doubt, give the "shot" of adrenalin anyway. The only harm you can do is to wait too long. Then get emergency medical attention, even if the child feels fine.

Anemia (ah-NEE-mee-ah): Lower than normal red blood cell mass. This can mean either that there are too few red blood cells or that there is a normal number, but the red blood cells are too small. It can often mean "low iron," but not necessarily. A child can be anemic with normal iron (for instance, with sickle cell anemia) or have normal red cells but still have too little iron.

Animal bites: When a Kid is bit by an animal, there are five things to worry about. First: Is there any chance that the animal was carrying rabies? Second: Is there any chance that the bite is deeper and more dangerous than meets the eye? Third: Does it need stitches or surgical attention? Fourth: Is there likely to be a localized infection developing? Fifth: is the Kid up to date on Tetanus immunization? For the first worry, see the **Glossary** entry for Rabies. For the second: beware especially bites around the eye or on the face or scalp, especially if the animal has long sharp teeth—cats are notorious. A tooth can penetrate into eye tissue or even into the brain, with catastrophic results. For the third worry: if the bite is pretty minor and on a noncosmetic area of the body (I'm sure there is such an area, even in the nineties) it's usually wiser not to suture it. The chance of infection goes up with suturing. If the bite does need suturing, it's a good idea to inquire at least about having the most experienced person do the job, because usually the surrounding tissue needs to be cut away to get a clean, unbruised, uninfected result. For the fourth worry: cats, dogs, and other animals can carry a germ called Pasteurella multicida that can cause a red, swollen, draining infection. Some pediatricians treat significant bites preventively with an oral antibiotic. No matter what, an animal bite needs thorough washing with soap and water and flushing with water to try to get all the germs out. And, of course, Kids need to know safe behavior with animals: don't bother them when they're eating, don't annoy or tease them, and don't try to make friends with even the cutest strange animal. However, most bites are from pets in the child's own home. Sorry. But that's the way life is sometimes.

Anorexia nervosa (an-or-EX-ee-ah ner-VO-sa): A complicated eating disorder, in which Kids and adolescents have an abnormal relationship with food, control, and body image. They eat barely anything, are preoccupied with food, increase their exercise, and see themselves as too fat even when they are skeletally thin. The Kid's history, physical examination, and the absence of other reasons for weight loss are used to make the diagnosis. Treatment involves close medical monitoring, psychotherapy, nutritional counseling, and often hospitalization. The whole family must be involved in treatment, as certain family dynamics may trigger the disease. This is a serious, life-threatening disorder.

Antibiotic (An-tih-bye-OT-ic): Medication that either kills or prevents reproduction of bacteria. Antibiotics do not have any effect on virus illnesses, like colds. Each antibiotic is effective against certain bacteria and ineffective against others. For instance, tetracycline and sulfa medicines can't treat strep throat. More and more, bacteria are becoming resistant to antibiotics. It's very important to try to limit antibiotics to conditions that really need and benefit from their use, to try to slow this trend.

Antiviral drug: A medication that treats virus infections. These are not called antibiotics, because antibiotic means attacking a *living* enemy, and viruses aren't really living. They are bits of genetic material that have to harness the machinery of OUR cells to reproduce. There are only a few antiviral drugs—because it is tricky to get rid of the virus without harming the virus-infected cells.

Anus (AY-nus): The external opening through which poop exits from the rectum. A sore, red anus is often due to strep proctitis (see **Glossary** entry for Proctitis). If the soreness and redness happens more than once, suspect pinworms (see **Glossary** entry for Pinworms). Aren't we having fun!

Apnea (AP-nee-ah): The term used when someone stops breathing, temporarily or permanently. A nonbreathing person is said to be apneic. **Sleep Apnea** occurs in children whose upper airways become blocked during sleep, usually by tonsils and/or adenoids. These children are noisy, snoring, restless sleepers. If you listen to them snore, you may notice that they take two or more snores on one intake of breath, appear to hold their breath for a while, and then kind of lurch awake. During the daytime, they go around with their mouths gaping open, partly because they can't breathe through their noses and partly because they yawn a lot. Sleep apnea can put a strain on the heart and is a medically dangerous condition. If you suspect it, a visit to the pediatrician is mandatory. It may be helpful to bring a videotape of the child sleeping.

Aspiration (*as*-pur-AY-shun):

1. To inhale something foreign into the lungs. This often causes inflammation of lung tissue called aspiration pneumonia.

2. To suction or remove fluid from a body orifice or even from an internal part of the body.

Aspirin: Salycilic acid, a medication often used for pain and fever in adults. Aspirin in any form is not recommended for children under age sixteen, except under doctors' orders. Evidence suggests that aspirin taken during certain viral illnesses can bring on the serious, even fatal illness called Reye syndrome (see **Glossary** entry for Reye syndrome).

Asthma (AZ-mah): The tendency to have wheezing episodes triggered by something in the environment. The trigger could be allergy, emotion, an irritant like second-hand smoke, a change in the temperature, or dryness of the air (as opposed to wheezing because of a specific illness like bronchiolitis or because of an anatomic problem, such as a mass pressing on the breathing tubes.) Children with asthma have airways that react more sensitively than other people's to these stimuli. A Kid with asthma needs careful medical attention. Given that attention, nearly every asthmatic Kid can lead a perfectly normal life complete with friends, sports, and regular school attendance. But beware: a Kid who has asthma attacks that require frequent emergency visits can be building up to a life-threatening emergency. Also, using prescription inhalers too often, or without medical guidance, can be extremely dangerous.

Athlete's Foot: See the **Glossary** entry for toes that peel.

Atopy (AY-toe-pee): A condition in which the tendency toward allergy is inherited. The term is often used for children with a family tendency toward eczema, asthma, or hay fever. Such children are called atopic (ay-TOP-ic).

Bacteria: The plural form of bacterium. Bacteria are one-celled animals that cause infectious disease. Because they are independent and multiply on their own, they are more accessible to being killed or foiled by medications. These medications are called antibiotics (see **Glossary** entry for Antibiotics).

Bad breath: See the **Glossary** entry for Halitosis.

Baldness: See the **Glossary** entry for Alopecia.

Beesting: See the **Glossary** entry for Insect stings.

Bilirubin (BILL-ee-roo-bin): The yellow chemical that causes jaundice—yellowing of the whites of the eyes and skin (see **Glossary** entry for Jaundice).

Bladder infection: See **Glossary** entries for Cystitis and Urinary Tract Infection.

Breathing trouble: When a Kid has trouble breathing that isn't attributable to a stuffy nose, it's important to find out what's going on. Rapid breathing without effort occurs with fever, and the breathing becomes normal as the fever comes down. Wheezing (see **Glossary** entry for Wheezing) can be a sign of asthma, but also can result from an inhaled foreign body or an acute infection. Croup (see **Glossary** entry for Croup) is unusual in Kids this age, but can make it hard to inhale air: you might hear a deep or raspy sound with each intake of breath: that noise is called stridor. Pneumonia can make a Kid grunt with each breath. To tell if the trouble breathing is urgent, **watch** to see if the youngster is using extra muscles to breathe: the tummy under the breast bone, the muscles under and between the ribs or above the collarbone going in and out, the nostrils flaring: these are signs of significant distress. Watch also for paleness or a bluish tinge around the lips. These are signs of real trouble. **Listen** to his or her complaints and fears: Kids this age often know how much trouble they're in. As the child talks, see if the breathing allows the usual number of words to be uttered before he or she has to take another breath (see **Glossary** entries for Wheezing, Sighing).

Bronchitis (bron-KIE-tis): Inflammation of the large tubes of the lungs. It may be triggered by a sinus infection, go along with asthma, or be caused by an infection of the tubes themselves. Most often such an infection is caused by a virus, but sometimes the cause is bacterial and requires an antibiotic.

Bronchodilator (*bron*-co-DIE-later): A medication that opens up the tubes of the lung to make breathing easier. Used for asthma.

Burns: First- and second-degree burns hurt, often a lot. A **first-degree burn** displays redness without blistering. A **second-degree burn** has little or big blisters. A **third-degree burn** is often whitish and doesn't hurt because the nerves have been damaged. First aid for any burn:

• Make sure that you and the Kid aren't in further danger.

• If the burn was caused by liquid or food that has soaked through clothing, try to remove as much of the still-hot clothing as you can.

• Flush the burn with cold water for five minutes.

• Assess the damage.

Burns that must be seen by a physician: Second-degree burns on the face, hands, soles of the feet, or genitals; second-degree burns that cover an area as large as the child's hand elsewhere on the body; any third-degree burns. DON'T cover a second-degree burn with a cream, ointment, aloe, butter, or Vaseline. If the cold water and a dose of acetaminophen or ibuprofen don't stop the pain of a small, minor burn, call your pediatrician. Don't break blisters: they are an ideal sterile dressing. Cover the burn with a sterile non-stick pad. Make sure your Kid's tetanus vaccine is up to date.

Cataract: A clouding of the lens of the eye. It doesn't cloud the cornea: that's the clear covering over the iris. Rarely, a child can be born with a cataract, or can acquire one after eye trauma or long exposure to steroid medication.

Catheter (KATH-e-ter): A tube placed into any body opening or into a blood vessel, both for withdrawing fluids and for delivering fluids and medication.

Cat Scratch Disease (CSD): A (usually) young kitty gives a Kid a scratch or a bite-and-a-lick, and, lo and behold, a week or two later you notice a funny little round bump on the skin above the scratch. Then a week or two later you notice great big lumps: swollen lymph nodes (swollen glands) that are really scary. If the scratch was on a hand, the nodes are in the armpit. Sometimes there's fever and achiness. This is the classic form of CSD, a bacterial illness designed to scare parents. In rare cases, it can cause serious complications such as encephalitis or conjunctivitis (see **Glossary** entries for both these illnesses). But usually it's just a stubborn, low-grade infection that must be diagnosed and watched carefully. Diagnosis right now is by history and exam and sometimes by blood test, if there is any doubt. Safe skin tests for the disease are being developed: the old ones were based on actual pus from patients (Yuck!) and of course should not ever be used. If the child is really sick, antibiotics may be effective; but mostly the illness goes away by itself. In rare instances, the nodes are stubborn and need to be removed surgically.

Cerumen (ser-OO-min): Euphonious and dignified name for ear wax. The main thing to know about cerumen is that using swabs like Q-tips in the ears can push that wax right back so it just refuses to come out. This leads to pain, decreased hearing, and a visit to the pediatrician for scolding and treatment. (I am just kidding about the scolding.)

Cervical (SUR-vick-ul): Having to do with the neck, as in cervical spine or cervical collar—the brace used for injured necks.

Chicken pox: A childhood disease characterized by a rash caused by the virus *herpes zoster* (see **Glossary** entry for Varicella).

Chilblains: Red, itchy skin from exposure to the cold. Most often it's the top of the ears, the fingers, and the toes that get chilblains, but the condition can happen to any skin exposed to the cold. The immediate treatment is NOT to scratch or rub, which makes matters worse, but to rewarm the whole Kid. Treatment for the itching includes a cortisone cream to the affected area and dihydroxymine (Benadryl) by mouth. It may take a week or two for chilblains to subside, and the body parts may be more vulnerable to chilblains after one attack. Best to prevent them by dressing the Kid in warm clothing and using common sense.

Clitoris (KLIT-oh-ris): The sexually sensitive little hooded organ in front of the vagina and urethra.

Cold injury: The smaller the Kid, the more vulnerable he or she is to cold. How to protect, and what to watch for, are discussed in **Appendix B**, under Winter Sports (see also **Glossary** entries for Chilblains, Frostbite, and Hypothermia).

Colds: Some people call them upper respiratory infections. I call them colds. True colds are usually caused by any one of the over 100 strains of the virus called *rhinovirus*. They start out with a scratchy throat, followed in a day or two by a runny, stuffy nose, followed often by a cough. The symptoms go away in the order they came in, and a week after the start of the cold the only symptom left is the cough—which can hang on for another week or two. Kids with colds may have a fever under 102°. They don't have severe pain, shortness of breath, or severe body aches (suspect strep throat, pneumonia, or flu if these other symptoms are present). Kids over six often feel better when they take one of the over-the-counter cold medications. Sometimes a Kid will develop discolored green or yellowish discharge from the nose right when the cold is on the way out. If he or she is feeling better, this is probably a normal last hurrah of the cold, caused by the white cells in the mucous disintegrating and releasing colored granules. If the Kid is getting sicker when the discharge turns colored, it is more likely due to a bacterial infection that needs attention. Antibiotics don't do a thing for a cold, nor do they prevent pneumonia or complications like otitis media.

Concussion: A concussion is a bruise to the brain. It happens when the Kid's head hits something, usually in a fall or a collision of with another head or when the Kid's head collides with a pole or a wall. Since the brain is cushioned inside the head by fluid, this sudden bang makes the brain gently bounce forward and back and forward again. In a true concussion, there is always a time of being unconscious, though it may be very brief, and the Kid loses his or her memory of events surrounding the blow to the head. Anytime there is loss of consciousness, however brief, the Kid needs to be seen by the pediatrician or in the emergency room. Plain skull x-rays usually aren't useful, but a CT scan to look for bleeding in the brain may be required.

Congenital (con-JEN-i-tal): Born with the condition. This doesn't necessarily mean the condition is inherited. Nor does it necessarily mean that the condition was discovered at birth.

Conjunctivitis (kun-JUNK-tiv-IE-tis): Infection or inflammation of the white of the eye. Since it can be caused by viruses OR bacteria OR trauma OR a foreign body OR allergy, conjunctivitis as a term doesn't tell you much.

Constipation: Hard stools or *abnormally* infrequent stools. Most often, constipation is the result of a "vicious cycle" of painful stools and withholding pooping. Such constipation may be considered a minor problem, but left untreated, it can turn into chronic and major unpleasantness. Kids may even poop in or soil their pants (see **Glossary** entry for Encopresis). In certain rare instances, constipation may result from a thyroid problem or intestinal blockage.

Contagious: The tendency of an illness to pass from one person or animal to another, by any of several modes. Many infections are contagious; some are not. Those that are can be passed on by several different routes: feces-hands-mouth or nose-hands-eyes, for instance. Moods and behavior are also somewhat contagious.

Coxsackie (cock-SACK-ee): A family of viruses that can cause a number of disease syndromes, such as hand-foot-mouth and herpangina.

Cromolyn sodium (KRO-mo-lyn): A unique allergy medication. It stabilizes the membrane of the mast cell, so that it can't release its "allergy toxins" during an allergy attack. Thus, it is preventive, and must be taken regularly—as nasal spray or inhalation.

Croup (CROOP): This common illness features a cough that sounds like its name—like a seal barking or a goose honking. It also causes a hoarse voice and stridor—that is, trouble and noise inhaling. This is because the lining of the whole upper airway swells and the muscles encircling the trachea go into a spasm. Croup can be caused by any of several viruses or can be triggered by dry or dusty air. Croup in Kids

over age six may sometimes be due to a bacterial infection called mycoplasma, that responds to antibiotics of the erythromycin family.

Cuts (lacerations): Cuts require a visit to the doctor if stitches are needed to close a gaping wound, if there is trouble stopping the bleeding, if there is a possibility of a foreign body in the cut, or if the cut has injured an organ, nerves, or blood vessels. If a cut is only skin deep, and the edges can easily be brought together, it can often be treated at home. To do so: wash with plain ordinary soap and water and flush the cut well with plain water. Pat dry. Dry with a hair dryer if necessary. Apply "butterfly" bandages or "steristrips" so that the edges just meet. Keep the cut clean and dry until the bandages come off by themselves. Check on the child's tetanus immunizations. (See chart in Appendix C.) Once in a while, even a seemingly minor cut should get professional attention because of the cosmetic implications. A cut on the face that goes against the skin lines, for instance: the lines of the forehead and cheeks go side to side; a vertical cut can leave more of a scar than you'd think. Even more important: a cut that goes through a nostril or earlobe or, especially, through the border of the lip onto the skin. Such a cut can leave a very noticeable notch unless the edges are brought together exquisitely. **Cuts inside the mouth:** Most of these heal without sutures; the mouth is very forgiving and quick to heal. Cuts that need attention are: a cut that goes through the gum to the bone; a cut that won't stop bleeding; or a cut that goes through the border of the tongue. (If you drew a line drawing of the tongue, the cut would intersect the line.) An injury that happens very frequently is a cut to the frenulum, the little piece of tissue that holds the front of the upper lip to the gum: it almost never needs suturing (see **Glossary** entry for Teeth problems).

Cystic Fibrosis (CF) (SIS-tick-fie-BROH-sis): An inherited disease that causes a spectrum of lung, intestinal, and growth problems. Most often, the disease is suspected and diagnosed in infancy or toddlerhood in a child with chronic lung (and ear and sinus) infections and poor growth. Milder forms of the disease may not be diagnosed until later—sometimes not until adolescence.

There are treatments, but as yet no cure, for the disease. It is present in 1 in 1600 white babies and 1 in 17,000 African-American babies. It is very rare in Asian children. To inherit the disease, a child must receive a CF gene from each parent. If any family member has cystic fibrosis, parents may be able to be tested to see if either is a carrier. At this writing there are no tests for the disease that can be performed before the baby is born. If the disease is suspected in a child, the only test that is accurate is the sweat test.

Children with asthma are often tested for cystic fibrosis, even though most of these tests will be negative.

Cystitis (sis-TIE-tis): Cyst means bladder, and itis means infection or inflammation of. So cystitis usually means a bladder infection. It's not quite the same thing as a urinary tract infection (or UTI) because the term UTI could include infection in the kidneys, as well. Also, sometimes cystitis is due not to infection but to irritation (see **Glossary** entry for Urinary Tract Infection).

Dental caries (CARE-eez): Cavities in the teeth. Kids should receive fluoride in their water, or by tablet supplement, to strengthen the enamel and prevent cavities. Kids also should floss teeth (easy for me to say!). Many dentists urge sealants to protect Kids' teeth from cavities.

Depression: Depression in the medical sense can attack even young children, and it becomes more frequent as Kids get older. However, most children who act depressed are having a temporary response to a sad, upsetting life event. Such a response usually does not last longer than two weeks, unless the event was the loss of a beloved person or pet. If signs and symptoms of depression last for two weeks or more, a Kid needs help, no matter what the cause. Even if the depression is perfectly warranted and understandable, the Kid may have questions or worries that he or she is unwilling to confide to a parent or other close adult. Sometimes depression can be masked as aggression or hyperactivity or school phobia. Once in awhile, there's a physical problem causing or contributing to the depression. Your pediatrician may be able to help figure out what's going on or to refer you to someone who can. Most of the time, depression can be helped by analyzing the cause, if there is one, and helping the Kid to find new ways of coping. Sometimes, especially if there is a family history of serious depression or other emotional illness, medication is also needed.

Dextromethorphan (*dex*-tro-meth-OR-fan): An ingredient of many cough and cold medicines, it suppresses the cough reflex. Often abbreviated to "DM" on labels.

Diabetes (diabetes mellitus; type I diabetes; sugar diabetes; juvenile onset diabetes; insulin-dependent diabetes): Diabetes is a condition in which the sugar glucose can't enter cells, because there's not enough of the hormone insulin to open the tiny doorways to the cell. When this happens, it throws off the whole way the body uses energy, and the child becomes very sick. About 10 children in 100,000 have diabetes, with the peak age of diagnosis between eleven and fourteen years of age. The cause of diabetes is complicated, with both inheritance and some factor in the environment playing a role: for instance, if one identical twin has the disease, the chance of the other twin having it is only 50 percent. In children, the disease is rarely picked up as part of a routine screening. Rather, the Kids become sick. They are excessively thirsty, urinate very frequently, and lose weight; they may have a tummy ache, sore throat, vomiting, sighing-type breathing, and are sluggish or may even get to the point of losing consciousness. All Kids with early symptoms of diabetes need to be seen promptly. Diagnosis requires a urine and blood test. The only treatment for childhood diabetes is injected insulin. Most Kids with diabetes can lead normal lives if they regulate diet, exercise, and insulin. They need to feel in charge of their own care and to have a good grown-up relationship with parents and doctors. Most often, Kids need the services of a pediatrician, a pediatric endocrinologist, a nutritionist, and at times a psychotherapist.

Diarrhea: Loose or watery poop, often frequent, due to dietary excess, mild food poisoning, or virus infection. The three worries about diarrhea are: First, is the Kid becoming dehydrated? Signs include feeling miserable and lethargic, dry mouth and lips, dry sunken eyes, very decreased peeing—small amounts of strong, dark urine. Prevention and treatment consists of lots of fluids that won't make the diarrhea worse; this means no juices or milk. Many Kids wil drink the special hydrating fluid Pedialyte, which comes flavored. Diets otherwise needn't be very restricted, but should emphasize binding foods such as starches. Medication such as Lomotil, paregoric, or Pepto-Bismol can be dangerous and shouldn't be used without a doctor's OK. Second, is the cause of the diarrhea serious—a parasite, a serious infection, or an underlying disease such as colitis? Signs include blood or mucous in the stool, severe cramps, and weight loss. If diarrhea persists for ten days even without these symptoms, it needs checking. Third, how can you keep from catching it? The answer is handwashing after toileting, before touching your own face, and before preparing food.

Digit (DIDG-it): Medical term for a finger or a toe.

Ear pain: A painful ear can be caused by a middle ear infection (see **Glossary** entry for Otitis media) or by an external ear infection (see **Glossary** entry for External otitis). It can also be caused by pain referred from another region: a toothache or the pain of a sore jaw joint (see **Glossary** entry for TMJ).

Eczema (ECK-zima): An allergic skin condition. Kids with chronic eczema should be protected against chicken pox by the vaccine, since chicken pox can make the eczema much worse. If by chance they do catch chicken pox anyhow, it may be wise to give them the medication Zovirax to reduce the intensity of the illness.

Encephalitis (en-*sef*-ul-EYE-tis): An infection of the brain itself, not of its surrounding membranes (that's meningitis.) Encephalitis is most often caused by one of several viruses. The child with encephalitis has a headache and behavioral changes and sometimes, but not always, fever or vomiting. Encephalitis can be fairly mild or it can be deadly. The three viral diseases, measles, mumps, and rubella, which are covered by the MMR vaccine, used to be known for causing encephalitis. Chicken pox (herpes zoster) also can cause encephalitis. Herpes simplex can cause a very serious form of encephalitis, for which acyclovir may be used as treatment.

Encopresis (en-co-PREE-sis): Pooping in the pants or places other than the toilet after bowel control should have been established. Usually, it is a consequence of chronic constipation and results when little bits of poop finally escape the rectum. Children with encopresis always are emotionally troubled. Usually the emotional problems are due to the encopresis—rather than the other way around. Treatment of encopresis means making sure that stools are soft and regular. Often this means a period of "cleaning out" with enemas, followed by a long period of taking mineral oil or another stool softener. This all needs to be coupled with setting aside a regular time for the child to sit on the toilet. Many children will need lots of moral support (such as star charts) for having a daily poop. Some will benefit from psychotherapy. A child with encopresis always is upset by the condition, even if the youngster denies it.

Endoscopy (en-DAH-scop-ee): To look deep into a body orifice, such as the throat, airway, or rectum with a special instrument, usually a fiber optic light with a video camera attached.

Enuresis (en-yur-EE-sis): Bedwetting after daytime toilet skills are well established. See the discussion on bedwetting in **Behavior Problems,** in Chapter 1.

Epilepsy (EP-i-lep-see): A person with epilepsy has a tendency to have repeated convulsions or seizures. (Fever convulsions do not occur after age six.) Repeated seizures often can be prevented with medications. Epilepsy is not the same thing as mental retardation. Some children with epilepsy are retarded and some children who are retarded have seizures. But most people with epilepsy are perfectly normal. A number of Kids will have a very benign form called rolandic epilepsy, which often disappears in time.

Erythema (*air*-i-THEEM-ah): A reddening of the skin. Usually another word is tacked on.

Erythema infectiosum (in-fex-i-OH-sum): Better known as fifth disease or slaps. It's a common virus illness of childhood, featuring bright red cheeks and a lacey rash elsewhere on the body. It usually is more frequent in spring. It's caused by a virus called *parvovirus B19*. Once the rash appears, Kids are not contagious and may attend school—if you can persuade them that the rash is really very attractive and won't get them teased. Adults with *parvovirus B19* may have arthritis with no rash. If your Kid has had fifth disease and you come down with a swollen joint within two weeks, make sure you tell your own doctor. You may be able to avoid an expensive work-up.

Erythema multiforme (*mul*-ti-FOR-me): A particular rash featuring spots that look like bull's-eyes, donuts, or bagels, consisting of a ring with a different colored center. (They are called target lesions.) The rash can be caused by infections, allergy to drugs, or, in rare cases, foods. Most often the cause is not found. A rare, severe form called Stevens Johnsons syndrome afflicts the eyes and mouth, as well, and is often caused by allergy to medications.

Eustachian tube (you-STAY-chee-un): The tube that connects the back of the nose and throat to the middle ear, so that air can get into the middle ear, allowing the eardrum to vibrate. Not to be confused with the ear canal, where the wax is.

Excipient (ex-SIP-ee-ent): Fancy name for the inactive ingredients in medications, such as coloring, flavoring, sweeteners, and preservatives.

Expiratory (EX-pri-toe-ree): Having to do with breathing out (opposite of inspiratory). The high whistling noise made breathing out is called wheezing.

External otitis (oh-TIE-tis): Infection of the ear canal and outside of the ear, often known as swimmer's ear. You can suspect this infection if it hurts to wiggle the ear. Sometimes the outer ear will turn red and swollen. Swimmer's ear requires antibiotic ear drops and sometimes an antibiotic by mouth. Keeping the ear canal dry and slightly acid after swimming helps prevent swimmer's ear. A home prevention: make a solution of one part vinegar to one part rubbing alcohol and put three or four drops in each ear after a day in the water. DO NOT use these drops if there is a tube in the ear or a hole in the eardrum!

Fainting: See **Glossary** entry for Syncope.

Fatigue: There are so many causes of fatigue that you can become exhausted just thinking about them. They range from the common and innocent (at the top of the list: not enough sleep) to very serious, rare problems. When the cause of fatigue is not obvious, it needs to be investigated by the pediatrician. To get the most out of the visit to the doctor, take along some notes.

• How does the fatigue manifest itself? Does the child need much more sleep than usual, get out of breath easily, feel sad and withdraw from activities, or feel achy? Whatever the symptoms, be specific.

• When did it start? Was it sudden or gradual? Did anything happen or did anything in the Kid's life change at that time?

• Are there other symptoms: fever, rash, pain, swelling of the joints?

• Is the Kid taking any medication—over-the-counter or prescription? If so, bring it along to the visit.

• Is there any suspicion that the Kid could be drinking alcohol, taking drugs, or "sniffing" household products?

• What effect has the fatigue had on the Kid's life: school attendance, grades, social life, sports, behavior at home?

• Is there anything going on at home that could be worrying the Kid?

• Is there any chance that the Kid has a dark secret—sexual molestation, for instance? Is it possible that a sexually mature girl could be pregnant?

Fever: In Kids this age, the degree of fever isn't a good guide to the seriousness of the illness. Far more important are other symptoms, how sick the child feels and how long the fever persists. Any child with serious other symptoms such as shortness of breath, extreme paleness, blue lips, serious rash (see **Glossary** entry for Rash), persistent vomiting, severe pain, a limp, blood in urine or stool, or a change in behavior—very irritable, acting bizarre, or lethargic—needs prompt treatment regardless of the degree of fever. Kids who have moderate symptoms that point to a possibly significant cause also ought to be seen: moderate sore throat or pain with urination, for instance. Fevers that persist for longer than seven days, in the absence of serious symptoms or significant symptoms, also require a visit to make sure there is nothing of importance going on. Fever need not be treated unless it's making the Kid uncomfortable. Cold baths are not a good idea. Instead, use Acetominophen or Ibuprofen.

Fingers in the door: Most injuries don't result in fractures, amazingly. First aid: run cold water over the fingers. Don't use ice right on the skin; you don't want to produce a cold injury. Call or see the pediatrician: if there is a painful blood collection under the nail; if the finger is swollen and bruised or seems to be bent; if there is significant bleeding; if the child can't bend or straighten the finger.

Flea bites: Itchy bumps on legs and ankles, often in a line of two or three: that's because the flea bites and hops and bites and hops. Three bites equal breakfast, lunch, and dinner for the flea. For the itch, apply an ice cube, an anti-itch preparation, or cortisone cream to the area. For prevention: Get rid of the fleas—easy for me to say. Most fleas that bite humans need to have an animal available if they are to get the nutrients necessary to reproduce. Insect repellents will work for fleas, but shouldn't be used on a more than occasional basis. You could try the Avon product called Skin So Soft. Scratched flea bites often turn into impetigo (see **Glossary** entry for Impetigo).

Flu: Short for the word influenza, but a pretty meaningless term except when describing a particular epidemic caused by said virus. It is not useful to describe a set of symptoms as flu. To some, flu means high fever and aches; to others, vomiting and diarrhea; and to others, cold symptoms.

Frostbite: An injury to the deep tissues of the skin caused by cold. First the skin becomes red and itchy. If a cold Kid complains of itchy toes, fingers, or nose (sometimes called chilblains—see **Glossary** entry)—these are the most frequent body parts to be affected—this is an early warning sign: get the Kid inside and warm. (He or she may also be in the early stages of hypothermia—see **Glossary** entry.) If you see a Kid's nose or ears or fingers (or any other part, but these are the most frequent) turning white, much less blue, this is an emergency. **Don't massage the area or rub it, with or without snow or ice!** That makes matters worse. Placing the body part in warm, not hot, water is best. Test the water with the inside of your wrist: if it is slightly warm but comfortable, that's the right temperature. Get medical help as promptly as possible. And check the Kid for other signs of hypothermia.

Functional: A term used by medical personnel, meaning that the sign or symptom being discussed is real but normal and not a problem—such as: a "functional" heart murmur. The term can also mean that the symptom is real and abnormal, but is caused by behavior or emotion rather than an abnormality of the body per se: such as "functional" constipation.

Gastroenteritis (GAS-tro-En-ter-IE-tis): Diarrhea and vomiting, usually due to a virus infection. The main concerns with gastroenteritis are threefold. First: Could it be the sign of a serious underlying problem, not just a virus? (See **Glossary** entries for Abdominal pain, Diarrhea, and Vomiting.) Second: Could the Kid be getting dehydrated? Signs of dehydration are dry mouth, sunken eyes, and decreased urination, along with feeling worse and worse. Third: How do you keep from passing it around? Answer: Wash hands carefully and don't share food and drink.

German measles: See **Glossary** entry for rubella.

Giardia Lambia (JHAR-dee-ah LAM-bee-ah): A one-celled intestinal parasite, passed on through food, water, or dirty hands, that causes intestinal problems. Usually, this means diarrhea and cramping, alternating with constipation and pale-colored floating poops. Diagnosis involves stool samples and/or a blood test; treatment is oral medicine by prescription.

Gingivostomatitis (*jin*-ji-voe-sto-ma-TIE-tis): Gingivo means of the gums; stoma, of the mouth; itis, infection. This infection of the mouth and gums is usually due to childhood herpes virus.

Glands (as in "swollen glands"): Swollen glands aren't glands at all, really, but lymph nodes (see **Glossary** entry for Lymph nodes). True glands are organs that secrete a substance necessary for the body. The pancreas, thyroid, and adrenals are all glands.

Glaucoma: Increased pressure in the eye. It's rare in children, but can occur after an eye injury. Glaucoma shows up as a teary eye that looks enlarged and causes pain, especially when the child looks at a bright light. Any Kid who sustains a direct blow to the eye needs to be checked by the pediatrician. See **Glossary** entry for Hyphema.

Groin Pain: Groin pain can be caused by a sprain or an injury, but there are other causes. If it's persistent or if it is pain that spreads to include the front or middle part of the thigh, it's important to make sure that the source of the pain isn't a condition of the hip called slipped capital femoral epiphysis (ee-PIF-i-sis).

Growing Pains: Aching legs without any apparent cause are called growing pains. Whether they're caused by growing or by lots of jumping around nobody really knows. What is important is to be sure that the pain really is innocent. Growing pains are almost always innocent when they have the following characteristics:

- The pains are not constant or severe.
- They don't occur in just one leg, but affect both legs or first one and then the other.
- The pain isn't in just one specific spot, but all over, especially in the calves, shins, and thighs.
- The pain isn't in a joint, but along the bones and muscles.
- There is no fever, redness, or swelling.
- There is no limp.
- The child otherwise acts well.
- It feels good when the legs are rubbed; rubbing and touching doesn't hurt.

If the pains don't fit every single characteristic of this profile, there's a chance that these aren't growing pains after all, and a visit to the pediatrician is necessary.

Hair loss: See **Glossary** entry for alopecia.

Halitosis: Bad breath in Kids needs detective work. Sometimes it's due to tooth decay or food caught under braces. Sometimes it's from infected tonsils, sinuses, or adenoids. Sometimes it's because there's a foreign body in a nose or a vagina: this can make a smell you would not believe, and all the tooth brushing and gargling in the world won't get rid of it. Sometimes it's because the Kid sleeps with his or her mouth open, and the mucous on the back of the tongue traps bacteria there that makes an odor. Your pediatrician will be able to rule out many causes. The Kid could try brushing his or her tongue twice a day, too: not up front, but way in back, where it makes one gag.

Hand, foot, and mouth disease: A disease caused by the virus coxsackie that includes sores in the mouth and on the palms and soles. Not related to hoof and mouth (nor to putting one's foot in one's mouth and getting out of hand.)

Headaches: Innocent headaches are usually due to mild infections like viruses or to muscular tension, emotions, or hairdos that are too tight (Honest!). Headaches that need medical attention, but not urgently, can be due to strep throat or sinusitis; vision problems almost never cause headaches. Once in a blue moon, headaches herald something that needs **urgent** attention. Such a headache could have any one or more of the following characteristics:

• Pain so severe that the child is pale, frantic, immobilized by the pain, and frightened
• Abnormal behavior: lethargic, disoriented, bizarre behavior
• Repeated vomiting coupled with a worsening of the headache
• A rash that looks like bleeding points or bruises under the skin (see **Glossary** entry for Rash)
• Suspicion of a drug or poison ingestion
• A severe or increasing headache after a head injury
• One pupil looking much larger than the other, though this is usually a late sign of pressure in the brain

Sometimes headaches **recur** in a pattern that calls for prompt medical attention. Signs include: increasing severity and frequency of the headache; changes in behavior—irritability, sleepiness, worsening school performance; neurological signs such as blurry vision, stumbling, bumping into things; weight loss; excessive thirst or urination (a sign not only of diabetes, but of a problem with the pituitary gland; persistent nose bleeds; a previous history of kidney disease [not just bladder infections]).

Heart murmur: A noise made by turbulence of the blood as it whooshes from one place to another—through the chambers of the heart and from the heart into blood vessels. Most often, a heart murmur heard in childhood is perfectly normal, just due to enthusiastic whooshing. Next often, it is due to a small opening between two heart chambers or to an irregularity of a valve. Many of these causes require no special care at all. If care is needed, it often only consists of preventive antibiotics before dentist appointments. This is because any dental work (even cleaning and braces adjustments) gets bacteria into the blood stream, and they like to cling to valve irregularities and cause infection. A heart murmer may or may not require further investigation, such as a chest X ray or EKG.

Hematoma (*heem*-a-TOE-muh): Bleeding so as to cause a swelling. Sometimes used as a fancy name for an ordinary bruise, but also for more serious bleeding, such as bleeding occurring between the brain and the skull.

Hemophilus influenza (*h. flu*) (aitch-FLOO): A family of bacteria that has nothing, really, to do with the virus "influenza." The name arises because this was the infection that caused fatal pneumonia AFTER influenza, in the great epidemic early in this century. *H. flu* causes minor infections, like otitis media, and major ones, like meningitis and epiglottitis. The HIB vaccine gives excellent protection against the serious *h. flu* infections, but not against the minor ones.

Henoch-Schoenlein purpura (HSP) (just say aitch-ess-pee): An uncommon but not rare disorder in which tiny blood vessels become inflamed, causing a bruise-like rash on the legs. There can be complications in the kidneys, intestine, and other organs. The cause is not known. A Kid who has HSP needs close medical monitoring.

Hepatitis (*hep*-uh-TIE-tis): An infection or inflammation of the liver. Many viruses can cause this as a kind of side effect; "mono" is famous for doing so. The ones that primarily cause liver disease are called hepatitis, and named using capital letters: hepatitis A, B, and C. Symptoms of hepatitis include nausea, abdominal pain, and fatigue. The older the child, the more likely it is that there will also be jaundice: a yellowness of the whites of the eyes and skin. Kids with hepatitis need medical monitoring, plus rest and special diets. **Hepatitis A** is the most common. It is carried by contaminated food, is usually innocent, and often goes undiagnosed in childhood. A vaccination is available, but not given routinely. However, it is advised for travel to certain areas. Exposed people can get a gamma globulin shot to protect against disease. a**Hepatitis B** is also usually undiagnosed in childhood, but it is much more serious. The virus can linger lifelong and in young adulthood it can spring to life again and cause serious, even fatal liver disease. The earlier in childhood the disease is caught, the greater the chance of this happening. Immunization is recommended for all children, especially those under age five. **Hepatitis C** is also a dangerous hepatitis, often passed by blood transfusion. A vaccine for hepatitis C should be available shortly.

Hernia (HER-nee-ah): An opening in a body wall that shouldn't be there, allowing a bit of the body contents to protrude through, either into another body compartment or into the outside world. There are several varieties.

> **Diaphragmatic hernia** (*die*-uh-frag-MAT-ic): An opening in the diaphragm, the muscle that moves the lungs when we breathe, fails to close during fetal life and

a bit of intestine (in rare cases, a LOT of intestine) protrudes through into the chest. The rare, severe form can be life-threatening at birth, because it may keep the lungs from developing or from expanding well.

> **Inguinal hernia** (IN-guin-al): The most common hernia, in which a passage where the testicles descend during fetal life stays open, allowing a bit of intestine to protrude into the scrotum. This is the hernia that boys are checked for routinely. The doctor places a finger in the scrotum and asks the boy to cough or laugh. The ensuing increase of pressure in the abdomen forces down the bit of intestine if a hernia is present, allowing the doctor to feel it.

Herpangina (*herp*-an-GINE-uh): A virus syndrome often caused by coxsackie virus, in which there are painful sores in the back of the throat. Alas, antibiotics won't help. Pain medication, rest, and sweet fluids do.

Herpes (HER-peez): A virus that causes both common, innocent, and, in rare instances, serious disease in childhood. Fortunately, most children who come into contact with herpes acquire immunity to it without ever getting sick. There are two big categories of herpes, herpes simplex and herpes zoster, both of which can, if necessary, be treated with the antiviral drug acyclovir (Zovirax).

Herpes simplex (SIM-plex): Causes, among other things:

> **Herpes stomatitis** (*sto*-ma-TIE-tis): This is a common and usually innocent infection of the inside of the mouth, the gums, and the tongue. It is nonetheless very painful and upsetting.

> **Herpetic whitlow** (her-PET-ick WIT-loe): A painful herpes sore on fingers or hands, usually where a child sucks.

> **Canker sores:** These are painful sores that occasionally pop up inside the

mouth and on the lips. They are little outbursts caused by the herpes simplex virus. Once a Kid has herpes stomatitis, the virus stays in the nerve cells for life, and these little outbursts can be triggered by sun, stress, illness, maybe foods, or nothing in particular.

Herpes zoster: Causes the following: Chicken pox, also known as **varicella** (*vare*-i-SELL-uh): A usually innocent childhood disease that causes a rash. Many Kids have had chicken pox in early childhood. If not, parents may wish to talk with their pediatrician about immunization (see **Glossary** entry for Varicella).

Shingles: A painful skin rash, caused when the chicken pox virus, which stays dormant in the body lifelong, becomes aroused by stress, sun, or renewed exposure to chicken pox.

Ocular herpes (OCK-you-ler) or **keratoconjunctivitis** (CARE-at-oh-con-*junk*-ti-VIE-tis): Both herpes simplex and herpes zoster cause these uncommon but dangerous eye infections that need prompt diagnosis and treatment by an ophthalmologist.

Hip pain: Pain in the hip joint always needs to be checked by the pediatrician. Often it's just a mysterious, innocent pain that resolves by itself, but it's very important to make sure that the cause isn't something that needs fast treatment, such as an infection, or a problem with the circulation of blood to the bones in the joint called Legg Calve Perthes disease. In rare cases, too, there can be a stress fracture through the hip bone. If the pain persists and no source can be found, it may be necessary to examine the lower spine for the cause.

Hives or urticaria (oor-tick-AIR-ee-ah): Itchy welts or raised pink or red blotches on the skin can be caused by an allergic reaction to any of a number of allergens: foods, medications, insect stings, or even a virus or strep infection. These welts range from tiny to huge (by huge, I mean many inches in diameter). They come and go. Much of the time, the underlying cause isn't ever determined. Adrenalin by injection and antihistamines by mouth help. Sometimes steroids are needed.

Hoarse voice: A Kid with a sudden onset of hoarse voice usually has a virus. It's uncommon for strep throat or bacterial infections to cause hoarseness. If the voice stays hoarse for longer than two weeks, the Kid needs evaluation. Most often, the cause is vocal cord nodules: little benign tumors that are associated with voice overuse. Sometimes such a Kid just needs to be reminded to speak softly and not yell; sometimes speech therapy helps; in rare cases, the nodules must be removed surgically. There are other rare causes of hoarseness and certainly a Kid with trouble breathing plus a hoarse voice needs special, thorough, prompt evaluation. Cigarette smoking can also cause hoarseness in Kids—it's easy to smell out that cause.

Hydrocephalus (high-droh-SEF-oh-lus) :Increased pressure of the fluid that bathes the inside of the brain, often caused by an obstruction to its drainage. It is rare and found predominantly in very premature babies and in children who have spina bifida or brain tumors, or who have had bacterial meningitis. But once in a while a child with no underlying problem will have hydrocephalus. Hydrocephalus shows up in this age group as increasingly severe headaches, fatigue, blurred vision, and other neurological signs.

Hymen: The normal opening from the vagina to the outside world. It's easily stretched during normal masturbation and sports activity. A virginal hymen means only that there has been no sexual penetration. You can't tell from looking whether a girl is a virgin or not. (Of course, if there has been vaginal trauma, you will see signs—but usually only right after the trauma has occurred, unless it is chronic or severe). Girls can use tampons right from the beginning of menstrual periods without changing their status as virgins.

Hyper: Too much of something. Too much of a hormone (as in "hyperthyroid") or too much of a symptom (as in "hyperemesis"—too much vomiting) or too much of a good thing ("hyperimmune" from getting a tetanus shot with every booboo or hyperactive, as in attention deficit hyperactivity disorder).

Hyperventilation: A Kid in the grip of anxiety can over-breathe. He or she has a sensation of not being able to get enough air in, and may feel upset and panicky. Yet it's obvious that the child is able to breathe deeply without any obstruction at all. A Kid who takes too many rapid deep breaths blows off enough carbon dioxide to throw off body chemistry. The end result is to lower the ability of the calcium in the body to do its work. This can produce tingling of the hands and feet and even cramps. As Macbeth notes, "By the pricking of my thumbs, something wicked this way comes." It's that kind of feeling. The immediate treatment to relieve symptoms is to re-breathe one's own air by breathing into a paper bag (not plastic that could smother, of course!). The curative treatment is addressing the cause of anxiety.

Hyphema (high-FEE-muh): Bleeding into the front little chamber of the eye, which can happen after a direct blow or a piercing injury to the eye. If it's not diagnosed and treated, vision can be impaired or destroyed, which is one of several reasons why blows to the eye need to be looked at by the pediatrician, emergency room doctor, or ophthalmologist.

Hypo: Too little of something—hypothyroid or hypocalcemia or hypotension (low blood pressure).

Hypothermia: Dangerous lowering of the body temperature. This can happen from being too cold in the winter or from immersion in cold water any time at all. It's life-threatening. Early signs of hypothermia are behavioral changes: crankiness, irrational behavior, fatigue. Regard these as cold-induced, not as disciplinary problems, and get the Kid indoors and warm as soon as possible. While you're doing that and as he or she is warming up, try to get the Kid to take something with sugar in it—cocoa, candy, and honey are all good choices.

Ibuprofen (I-byu-PRO-fen): The active ingredient in such medications as Advil and Motrin, which reduces fever, pain, and swelling.

Idiopathic (*id*-ee-oh-PATH-ick): A word that describes a baffling symptom, disease, or condition when something is causing it, but we don't know what and all known causes have been excluded.

Immunoglobulins (im-myun-oh-GLOB-you-lins): Protein molecules made by the immune system as a response to "attackers" like viruses, bacteria, and allergens.

Impetigo (im-puh-TIE-go): Not "infantigo," though it is often young children who get this skin disease with its blisters, crusting, and oozing. Impetigo is usually caused by strep bacteria, sometimes with staph helping out. Treatment may be prescription ointment or antibiotics by mouth. Kids catch impetigo by getting the bacteria on their fingers and then scratching something, often an insect bite. Prevention means short fingernails, hand-washing, and discouraging nose-picking. Easy for me to say.

Incubation period (in-kew-BAY-shun): The amount of time from exposure to the germ that causes a disease to when signs or symptoms appear.

Infectious: Describes a disease caused by an infection rather than by a metabolic disturbance, ingestion, or some other agent. Infections can be caused by viruses, bacteria, fungi, algae, and yeast. Some infections are contagious and some are not.

Infectious mononucleosis: Also known as mono and the kissing disease, this illness is caused by the virus named Epstein-Barr (often called EB virus or EBV). Most Kids who catch the virus make immunity without ever getting very sick, but some will be diagnosed as having "mono." Kids with mono usually have very sore throats with pus on the tonsils; swollen lymph nodes in the neck, under the arms, and in the groin; and an enlarged spleen (see **Glossary** entry for Spleen). They are very tired and may have puffiness around the eyes. The diagnosis is confirmed by a blood test. Kids can be sick for several weeks and need rest and a nutritious diet. Since the spleen is a blood-filled organ, when it's swollen you don't want it traumatized by direct blows or falls or by lifting heavy items. Kids with mono can stay contagious for months and months after they're all well, so isolating them while they are sick is pointless. There is no specific medicine to get rid of the virus at this time and no immunization. In rare instances, a Kid with very, very swollen tonsils may need cortisone to shrink them down. Once in a while, a Kid with mono will have scary visual problems: things shrink or enlarge or look too close or far away. This is called the Alice-in-Wonderland syndrome and while it needs to be diagnosed, the main treatment is assuring everybody—especially the Kid—that he or she is not going crazy.

Influenza (*in*-floo-EN-za): A family of viruses that cause "flu" epidemics just about every year. Symptoms generally include aches, fever, cough, and sore throat. A new vaccine is needed every year. Such vaccines are only about 80 percent effective. That's because these viruses are so clever at changing their protection against immune defenses. Which Kids SHOULD get yearly vaccinations: those with HIV or other diseases of the immune system, those with chronic lung or heart problems, including asthma, those who have had regular medical care or hospitalization due to chronic diseases of any kind, those taking long-term aspirin therapy (which may be recommended for forms of arthritis), and those who live in the same house with people who are at high risk for getting complications of the flu. Kids should NOT be immu-

nized if they have severe allergic reactions to eggs. If a Kid has an acute, feverish illness, the immunization should be postponed until he or she is better. There are medications (amantadine and rimantadine) that can be given to prevent influenza after a known exposure. Amantadine also can make influenza A milder, but has no effect on influenza B. These medications are not used routinely—only in special cases.

Inhalants: Household and office chemicals that some Kids sniff to get high. Especially popular: white-out, glue, cleaning solutions. This is an extremely dangerous practice and can lead to sudden death. Parents need to educate and supervise their Kids.

Inhalation: The act of breathing in something. This could be medication in an aerosol or something toxic like second-hand smoke.

Insect stings: Stinging insects include bees, yellow jackets, wasps, and hornets. The difference among them: honey bees and bumble bees sting once, lose their stingers and then die. These bees generally only sting if stepped on, swatted, or swallowed. Yellow jackets, wasps, and hornets can sting multiple times without losing their stingers. They are more likely to attack and sting without provocation. Africanized ("killer") bees are not more poisonous than regular bees, but pursue their victims more aggressively and sting not as individuals but as hives.

Protecting against insect stings means, of course, not trapping or swatting or stepping on or swallowing them. Avoid loose floppy clothing. Don't walk barefoot in territory popular with bees. Teach Kids not to swat at bees. Beware the half-empty, open can of soft drink that could have a half-drowned bee inside. Protecting against the more aggressive insects means not wearing perfume or sweet-smelling lotions or looking like a colorful flower. It also means not leaving food out to attract them. Protecting against the Africanized bees means not poking around where their nests might be. Beware power mowers and weed-whackers that could stir up a nest.

First aid for a sting: scrape out the stinger with a dull edge like the edge of a credit card or the dull side of a knife. Squeezing the stinger with fingernails may release more venom. If you can remove the stinger within twenty seconds, you often can avoid a beesting reaction. Then apply ice or a paste of meat tenderizer mixed with water to try to inactivate the venom.

Keeping the body part elevated and applying cold will help. The over-the-counter antihistamine diphenhydramine (Benadryl) and acetaminophen or ibuprofen will help symptoms of itch and pain.

A Kid who has any symptoms other than pain and swelling at the site of the sting is having a systemic reaction and may need an injection of adrenalin quickly. If you have a bee sting kit, use it. Do not fool around with tourniquets or antihistamines like Benadryl. A Kid who has trouble breathing, swollen lips, drooling, hives, feeling faint, severe abdominal pain—that Kid needs a quick trip to the emergency room or to the pediatric office (call first to make sure that it's open and that a doctor is there).

Inspiratory (IN-spri-toe-ree): Occurring while breathing in rather than out. The opposite of expiratory. The noise made by breathing in is called stridor.

Intubate (IN-toob-ate): To place a tube into the airway either to suction, to deliver oxygen, or to enable the physician to take over the whole act of breathing by pumping air through the tube into the lungs.

Intussusception (in-tuh-suh-SEP-shun): An uncommon but not rare severe intestinal problem of infants aged three months to three years old. It's rare in older children. The intestine telescopes on itself, as if you wrinkled a sleeve. Symptoms are recurrent spasms of severe pain, with paleness and fatigue in between, plus bloody stool.

Itching: Generalized body itching is most often due to hives (see **Glossary** entry for Hives), very dry skin, eczema, body lice, or scabies. Some children with asthma will have bodily itching just before an attack. Itchy scalps often indicate head lice, very dry skin, or an allergy to a hair preparation. Of course, the best cure for itching is to find the cause and get rid of it. The worst cure for itching is scratching: it irritates the skin and makes it itch more. A Kid can get temporary relief of symptoms by taking over-the-counter diphenhydramine (Benadryl); however, this may make asthma worse by drying secretions. Baking soda or oatmeal preparations like Aveno in the bath water help, too.

Jaundice (JAWN-diss): The yellow color to skin and whites of eyes caused by too much of the substance bilirubin (see **Glossary** entry for Bilirubin). Although jaundice is usually normal in newborn babies, any Kid who has jaundice needs to be evaluated by the pediatrician. Jaundice can be caused by infections, such as infectious mono or hepatitis (see **Glossary** entry for Hepatitis) or, in rare cases, by other conditions.

Kawasaki disease or syndrome (cow-a-SOCK-ee): A serious disease that shows up as a blotchy rash, red cracked lips, redness of the whites of the eyes, and fever. Any Kid with this set of symptoms needs prompt diagnosis and care. Most patients with Kawasaki syndrome are under five, and it is very rare over the age of eight. The serious aspect is that the coronary arteries (the ones that supply the heart with blood) can become damaged afterward. Treatment can often prevent this serious complication. The cause isn't yet known for sure. (It used to be called mucocutaneous lymph node syndrome.)

Ketosis (kee-TOE-siss): What happens to the body chemistry of a child who has had vomiting and diarrhea, prolonged fever, or other metabolic stress. Acid substances build up that make the child feel worse and less inclined to take fluids. And that makes the ketosis worse. Children with diabetes can also get ketosis, but they will need medical help (and insulin) to get relief from the problem.

Kidneys: The paired organs in back under the ribs that purify the blood, returning the good stuff to the bloodstream and sending the rest out as urine.

Knee Pain: Knee pain in Kids most often has an innocent cause. However, if the pain causes a limp, persists for over a week, or comes and goes for over a month it is very important to have it checked. In rare instances, there may be a serious cause, such as a tumor. Kids with knee pain must always be checked to make sure the pain doesn't come from a problem in the hip, as pain there can refer down to the knee.

Labia (LAY-bee-ya): The folds surrounding the vagina. The inner folds are the labia minora (min-OR-ah) and the outer ones the labia majora (ma-JOR-ah).

Labial adhesions (LAY-bee-al ad-HEE-zhuns): When they get a bit irritated, the labia minora sometimes stick together and actually fuse, so that when you look at the child's vagina there seems to be no opening. This can be very alarming: it looks as if something were terribly wrong, but it's not. There IS an opening through which urine can exit; you just can't see it. Sometimes treatment is required, but usually adhesions eventually will go away on their own.

Lactose: Milk sugar, present in human milk, cow's milk, and goat's milk. It is really a complicated sugar in which each molecule is composed of two little sugars (glucose and galactose). Lactose can't be absorbed from the intestine until the enzyme lactase splits it apart. No lactase, no absorption: instead, diarrhea and gas. Some Kids lose their ability to digest lactose as they grow older. Since yogurt and many cheeses contain only a little lactose, most children in this boat can still eat them—and they are great sources of calcium.

Laryngitis (lare-in-JIE-tis): Hoarse voice. It can be caused by infection, usually viral but sometimes bacterial. It can also be caused by little benign growths on the vocal cords or, in rare cases, by other structures pressing on them.

Larynx (LARE-inks—not pronounced lare-nix or lare-ninx): Voice box.

Lazy eye: Seems to have two meanings, so be careful.

1. An eye that wanders and lets the other eye do all the focusing and seeing.

2. A droopy eyelid (see **Glossary** entry for Ptosis).

A Kid with a wandering eye usually has one strong and one weak eye, and the weak one wanders (see **Glossary** entry for Amblyopia). However, there are rare cases in which an injury or even a tumor can cause a wandering eye, so prompt evaluation is crucial.

Leukemia (lew-KEE-mee-ah): The nightmare of parents, a rare cancer of the bone marrow, attacking only 2.4 nonwhite and 4.2 white children out of 100,000. Leukemia is much more common in children younger than this age group, with a peak at age four. The two symptoms that parents worry about most—dark circles under the eyes and frequent upper respiratory illnesses—are not what herald leukemia. They are much more likely to result from allergy, second-hand smoke, and fatigue. Leukemia more often presents itself as paleness, fatigue, no appetite, and often a rash that looks like tiny red dots that do not blanch out when you press on them or one that looks like purple-black bruises. New treatments have made many cases of leukemia truly curable.

Lice: See **Glossary** entry for Pediculosis.

Limp: A limp that isn't the result of a perfectly obvious injury—like a blister or a sprained ankle—needs to be investigated, even if nothing hurts. There are a couple of sneaky hip conditions (Legg Calves Perthes disease and slipped capital femoral epiphyis) that cause intermittent limping. Any Kid with a limp needs, among other things, a careful hip exam, often with special X rays.

Liver: The organ underneath the right ribs. It gets rid of toxic products our own bodies make or that we imbibe or ingest, and produces helpful chemicals like cholesterol. (Cholesterol is NOT an enemy unless it's in excess. It's the basis for many delightful substances, like sex hormones.)

Lyme disease: A difficult-to-diagnose (at this time) disease caused by bacteria and spread by certain ticks in certain parts of the country. It often starts on the skin, with a spot that spreads to become a big, wobbly circle with a clear center, fever, and aches. Later on, joint swelling and even signs of meningitis and other neurological disorders can appear. It's a tricky disorder. First, it's hard to find the ticks, and a bite may go overlooked. The ticks that carry the disease are tiny, about the size of a pencil dot. You need to look for "moving freckles." Fortunately, the tick has to be attached for twenty-four hours before it can pass the disease, so a careful, hilarious tick search with magnifying glass and flash light every night should prevent problems. Do this, if you're hiking in lyme country (The borders change all the time. Ask.) A great preventive: a shower every twenty-four hours. Second, it's hard to diagnose: the skin rash may not be present, the symptoms may be nonspecific, and blood test results can be confusing. Fortunately, if suspected and treated early, the disease tends to be shorter and milder than if it's detected later. But treatment too soon can distort the blood tests! So it's tricky, tricky, tricky. If you live in Lyme disease territory, obtain guidance from your pediatrician.

Lymph nodes: These are the "glands" that get swollen when a child has "swollen glands." They're not really glands at all. Glands are organs like your thyroid or your pancreas, organs that work all the time, making specific substances needed for the body to thrive. Lymph nodes just sit there until an infection occurs and then jump in to arrest it. Many times, parents worry that enlarged nodes may mean something ominous, such as a malignancy. Such a diagnosis is most unlikely, because lymph nodes swell up with many innocent infections. However, since it's crucial to diagnose and treat serious diseases as early as possible, sometimes a bit of worry is warranted. Enlarged lymph nodes that persist without shrinking for a week after the child is well, that feel rubbery or matted, that are NOT associated with a clear-cut illness, or that are present in the area just above the collar bone or around the elbow, should be checked promptly by the pediatrician.

Mastoiditis (*mas*-toyd-EYE-tis): Infection of the bone behind the ear. It used to be a feared complication of chronic middle ear infections, but has become much less common (but not unheard of) since the development of antibiotics.

Measles (the fourteen-day or "red" kind): See **Glossary** entry for Rubeola.

Meningitis (*men*-in-JYE-tis): An infection of the membranes surrounding the spinal cord and brain. "Spinal meningitis" is a redundant term that doesn't convey any more information than the term "meningitis" by itself. The important distinction, usually, is what causes the meningitis. **Viral meningitis** very often is mild and doesn't usually produce problems like mental retardation, seizures, deafness, and so on. **Bacterial meningitis** can be very serious, even fatal, even if treated promptly. Early signs include a severe headache, stiff neck, and fever. The stiff neck of meningitis makes it painful to touch the chin to the chest: it's not the kind that makes it hurt to turn the head side to side. There may be a rash that looks like little bruises or like red dots that don't blanch out when you press on them. These are all urgent signs. If the rash is present, or the child seems to be falling into unconsciousness, this is even more urgent— demanding a 911 call, if available.

Metabolic (met-a-BALL-ic): Having to do with the body chemistry that allows us to turn food into energy, get rid of toxins, maintain a normal temperature, and grow. An inborn error of metabolism occurs when a child is born without the ability to perform one particular, specific part of a metabolic task. When this happens, the whole "chain" of metabolism, from the missing link on, becomes distorted. Diabetes (see **Glossary** entry for Diabetes) is the most common metabolic disease in childhood.

Molluscum contagiosum (moll-USS-cum con-*tage*-ee-OH-sum): With a name like that, you'd think it would be more than warts, but it simply refers to tiny, a bit shiny viral warts. Look closely and you'll see a tiny dimple in each. These warts are easy to treat when they're new and few, harder when they're older and bolder.

Mongolian spots: Bluish, blackish, or grayish flat spots present in many newborns (about 80 percent of Asian, Native American, and African-American babies; about 10 percent of others). They can be anywhere on the body. They aren't bruises, but can be mistaken for them; a newborn may be thought to have been battered during delivery. Most go away by late childhood.

MRI (magnetic resonance imaging): An imaging technique that doesn't use x-rays but does indeed involve magnets. It is sometimes used instead of or with a CT scan to examine soft tissues, like the brain and abdomen, and joints. Any part of the body can be examined by MRI. Young children usually need anesthesia, because they must hold very still, and be encased in a kind of tunnel for the procedure. Older Kids can do well with techniques like visualization and with moral support.

Mumps: The disease Kids used to get in droves, in which their faces were swollen and it hurt to even think about sour foods like lemons. The mumps virus infects the salivary glands, the pancreas, and often the testicles. It can also cause encephalitis. Most children are immunized when they received their MMR vaccine for measles, mumps, and rubella. If a Kid

hasn't been immunized, talk with your pediatrician about having it done now.

Mycoplasma (*mike*-oh-PLAZ-muh): A tiny bacterium that often causes "walking pneumonia," mycoplasma has some virus-like characteristics. It usually responds to erythromycin or tetracycline (which is not given to children) but not to other antibiotics. It is not related to mycobacteria. Mycoplasma in some rare cases can cause a croup-like syndrome in Kids, as well.

Nails that are grungy: Fingernails and toenails both can catch fungi that make them look thick and rough and even warty. A visit to the pediatrician or dermatologist is necessary to make sure that this is a fungus infection and not another condition (such as the inflammation called psoriasis). Oral medication is the treatment for fungus of the nails, because the growing part of the nail in the nail bed is infected, and putting cream on the outside won't reach that part.

Nasolacrimal duct (*naze*-oh-LACK-ri-mal): The tube or duct that carries tears (which are made in a gland under the upper eyelid) from the eye into the nose, where the lining absorbs the moisture.

Nauseated vs. nauseous: Nauseated means feeling as if you're going to vomit. Nauseous, believe it or not, means causing a nauseated feeling in somebody else. Most people use the word "nauseous" to mean "nauseated," and usually that's fine. But it is very disturbing to those who are fastidious or overfastidious about words. I don't know any nauseous children, myself, she said fastidiously.

Neck pain, stiff neck: See **Glossary** entry for Torticollis.

Nose bleeds: I sometimes think there are more theories about how to treat a nose bleed than there are noses. Here's what to do. First, if the nosebleed is from a blow to the nose, check the rest of the Kid first and make sure there's nothing worse going on. Then, have the Kid blow once to get rid of clots. Then have him or her sit up, leaning forward. Pinch the nostrils together firmly for five full minutes *without peeking.* (Here's what *not* to do: lean head back; put something under nose, or ice on the back of the neck.) Most nosebleeds, even recurrent ones, are caused by dry air, irritated nostrils, and nose-picking. If a Kid has any other signs of illness, a rash that looks like points of bleeding into the skin (see **Glossary** entry for Rash) or trouble clotting blood in general, or if there is a family history of a bleeding disorder, by all means have the pediatrician investigate promptly.

Obesity: Being 20 percent or more over one's ideal weight. For instance, the 7-year-old of average height and body build usually weighs 50 pounds. A weight of 60 pounds means that he or she is 10 pounds overweight or 20 percent overweight. That's obese.

Otitis media (oh-TIE-tis MEE-dee-yuh): Infection in the middle ear, the tiny chamber enclosed by the eardrum. In Kids, this often occurs as the complication of an ordinary cold, as a result of swimming with water coming up the nose and through the eustachian tube into the middle ear, or because of big pressure changes (as in flying) that cause the eustachian tube to glue itself shut. Many Kids over five with otitis media will not need an antibiotic, even though the cause is often bacterial; they have enough immunity to get rid of the infection on their own. A common exception: when there is a diagnosed sinus infection, the cause is often the bacteria *S. pneumoniae,* which frequently needs antibiotic treatment.

Pancreas (PAN-kree-us): The organ tucked away near the stomach that produces digestive enzymes and insulin. When the pancreas is inflamed, the condition is called pancreatitis. Common causes include trauma, the nephrotic syndrome (see **Glossary** entry for Nephrotic syndrome), and viruses.

Parasite: An animal that lives in and off of another animal—for example, you or your child. Some parasites are microscopic and one-celled, like giardia lambia. Others, like pinworms, are small but quite visible and others, like roundworms, are repellently obvious.

Parenteral (par-EN-ter-al): Given by needle into a muscle or vein.

Passing out, loss of consciousness: See **Glossary** entries for Seizure or Syncope (fainting). If passing out or loss of consciousness occurs after a head injury, it is very important to get medical attention— even if the loss of consciousness was brief.

P.A.T. (paroxysmal atrial tachycardia) (just say pee-ay-tee): The most common abnormal heart rhythm in childhood, P.A.T. doesn't occur very frequently. Abnormal rhythms happen when the heartbeat loses its "feedback" regulation from the body, so that it doesn't adjust its rate to what the body needs. In P.A.T., the heart rate climbs very fast very suddenly—too fast to count. The smaller the child, the more exhausting this is and the more dangerous.

Pathologic: A term used by medical personnel that means that something is abnormal or caused by a disease process. A bit stronger than "organic," pathologic is the opposite of "functional."

Pectus excavatum (PEK-tus ex-ca-VAH-tum): A scooped out breast-bone (or sternum) present from birth, probably caused by the baby's position in the womb. In rare instances, it may be severe enough to consider surgical reworking of the sternum: a major undertaking. Most often, pectus excavatum is a cosmetic annoyance.

Pediculosis (ped-ick-yozu-LOW-sis): Head or body lice. **Head lice** are very common in Kids and travel through a classroom or Scout troop or team like wildfire. Suspect lice if a Kid has an itchy scalp. You aren't likely to see the bugs themselves wandering around, but if you do, be prepared for a whitish, six-legged critter. More likely you'll find nits—tiny white eggs glued to the hair shaft. The most effective treatment for lice is the non-prescription rinse Nix, that contains 1 percent permethrin. It kills all the lice and 98 percent of the nits. To really get rid of lice, you have to remove all the nits in order to get rid of the 2 percent of still-living eggs. This means going over the scalp hair by hair and combing them out with a fine-tooth comb, or picking them off with your fingernails. This can be made easier by first rinsing the hair with vinegar (which stings, and you smell like a salad) or Step Two creme rinse (8 percent formic acid). To prevent lice from coming back, wash in hot water or boil anything you can in the way of clothing, bedding, combs and brushes, head gear including headbands and bows etc. If items can't be boiled or washed in hot water, put them in a tightly sealed trash bag for three days. NOW: take it from me, make sure your Kid isn't trading items such as hats, combs, headbands. Beware sports headgear! **Body lice** are very sneaky, and you won't see them or their eggs on the Kid, because they hide in clothing and linens. What you will see is your Kid itching and scratching. Body lice need medical diagnosis and prescription treatment.

Pee problems: Painful peeing can be caused in girls by vaginitis, in boys by irritation of the meatus of the penis—the little opening for the urine, and in both by urinary tract infections (see **Glossary** entry for Urinary tract infection). Frequent urination accompanied by increased thirst and fatigue can be an early sign of diabetes mellitis (see **Glossary** entry for Diabetes). Frequent peeing without other symptoms more often is due to anxiety: it's called pollakiuria. One hint that this is the cause is that the child has to pee very frequently in the daytime but doesn't wet the bed or have to get up to pee at night. Sometimes the anxiety is connected with an experience with death—even a movie or video or an anniversary reaction occurring around the same time of year as a previous

death.

Perineum (*pair*-in-EE-yum): The region known as "down there" by bashful adults everywhere. It includes the penis, scrotum, and anus in boys and the clitoris, the urethra and hymen, the labia, and the anus in girls.

Pertussis (per-TUSS-iss): The bacterial infection that causes whooping cough, against which all children should be immunized. The "P" in the "DPT" vaccine. Kids with whooping cough usually don't get nearly as sick as babies, infants, and toddlers. They may have a prolonged, persistent cough, however, and pass on whooping cough that way.

Petechiae (pet-EEK-ee-yi): Tiny red spots on the skin that don't blanche to skin color when you press on them. They can be innocent, but may be the sign of a serious infection or problem with the blood-forming system (bone marrow), so always must be checked out.

Pink eye (conjunctivitis): When the white of the eye is pink or red. This term doesn't tell you WHY the white of the eye is pink. The most likely cause is a viral infection. But other causes include a bacterial infection, a foreign body in the eye, a scratch on the surface of the eye, chemicals in the eye, allergy and, in unusual cases, potentially serious problems such as iritis (an inflammation of the colored part of the eye), herpes in the eye, or glaucoma (increased pressure in the eye.) Signs that a pink eye needs urgent attention: recent trauma around the eye like an animal bite or an encounter with a sharp object; chemicals in the eye; severe pain on trying to open the eye or on looking at a bright light; feeling very sick with a headache or stomachache or fever; redness and swelling of the eyelids. If a pink eye persists for longer than three days without getting better, even without symptoms, it needs attention.

Pinworms: These are tiny worms that look like ½", moving snips of white embroidery floss (I bet you can tell how old I am!) Their only virtue is that they are basically innocent, not invading the tissues of the body or causing other serious disease. A Kid catches them by getting the microscopic eggs on his or her fingers, then putting the fingers in the mouth or up the nose. Nose-picking is a cause, not an effect, of pinworms. The eggs hatch in the intestine, and the adult worms crawl out the rectum and lay their eggs on the skin of the perineum (see **Glossary** entry for Perineum). They irritate the skin and hurt and itch so the child scratches and gets eggs on the fingers, and contaminates friends, objects, and himself all over again. Diagnosis can be made by seeing the worms, but your doctor may want a lab exam to make sure that these are pinworms and not tiny segments of longer, more dangerous worms. Treatment is by prescription. It's a good idea to wash sheets and towels in hot water, but an orgy of housecleaning is neither required nor useful. What works better is keeping those little fingers washed, and away from nose and mouth. (You really can't monitor touching the perineum, nor should you.) Suggestion: do NOT tell a squeamish Kid he or she has worms! Do NOT shriek and jump onto a chair when you see them, no matter how disgusting they are! Your Kid will freak out.

Pityriasis alba (pit-ee-RYE-uh-sis AL-ba): The name given to those scaly white patches that tend to come and go. They're often most prominent in the summer in Kids with a suntan or naturally dark skin. The cause isn't known, and they respond to a moisturizing cream, a cortisone-containing cream, or simply to time and patience. It's a good idea to make sure that they're not caused by a fungus (tinea versicolor or tinea corporis) before you use cortisone on them. Also, cortisone on the face, or if overused, can cause its own irritation and rash, so be careful.

Pneumonia (noo-MONE-yuh): An infection or inflammation of the lung tissue—of the microscopic little air sacs, not of the tubes of the lung. It can be caused by viruses, bacteria, chemicals, or irritation (for example, from aspirated food or a foreign body.) Signs of pneumonia include a cough, but it may not be a major feature. More accurate signs: shortness of breath—trouble getting breath in and out, often with a grunt at each breath; fever; fatigue; a tummy ache that may be severe; chest pain. Diagnosis involves an examination and sometimes a chest x-ray and/or a blood test. Treatment always involves rest, and antibiotics for the nonviral forms of pneumonia. It is rare for a virus cold caused by rhinovirus (see **Glossary** entry for Colds) to "turn into" pneumonia. When that seems to have happened, what has most likely occurred is that the beginning of pneumonia looked a lot like cold symptoms.

Poison ivy, poison oak, poison sumac: The very first time a Kid touches these plants, there's no reaction. That initial contact sensitizes the skin, though, and the next encounter is likely to cause a blistery rash and swelling of the tissues. So the best way to deal with poison is to avoid the plant. (This means not getting any of it in your campfire, either, because inhaling the fumes can cause a severe reaction.) If you know that a Kid has touched the plant, here's first aid: Wash the entire child three times with ordinary soap and water, unless you are positive that the plant only touched one area and that the Kid didn't spread the oils from that one body part. If the Kid only touched the plant with a finger, you can wash that finger carefully with rubbing alcohol or an alcohol sponge to get the oils off. Remove all possibly contaminated clothing (wash it and clean the shoes). Once the rash appears, it can be treated by over-the-counter preparations: anti-itch lotions that contain pramoxine are safe; those that contain diphenhyramine (Benadryl) can cause problems because the medication can be absorbed through broken skin into the blood. It's possible to get an overdose this way. Antihistamines like oral diphenhydramine are also helpful. Topical cortisone cream can help, too. However, many cases of poison oak, in particular, are so violent that a Kid needs to be seen by the pediatrician. Oral steroids, often in high doses and for several weeks, may be needed. You can't catch poison oak, ivy, or sumac from another person unless you are contaminated with the oils on his or her skin or clothing.

Pooping in pants: See **Glossary** entry for Encopresis.

Port-wine stain: A birthmark, the color of dark wine, different from other birthmarks because: 1. It is present right at birth, and many "birthmarks" aren't; 2. It can signify problems beneath the skin, such as eye and brain abnormalities, so it is taken seriously; 3. It is permanent if left untreated, but can usually be nearly erased by laser therapy.

Proctitis (prock-TIE-tis): Infection of the rectal area, often caused by such nuisances such as strep and yeast. Pediatricians always consider the possibility of sexual abuse, but most cases are simple problems of hygiene and childhood.

Ptosis (TOE-siss): A droopy eyelid. There are many causes, from injury to nerve disease, so such a droop needs to be checked.

Purpura (PUR-pur-a): Multiple bruise-like spots that don't blanch when pressed. These are ALWAYS a sign of a problem, but some causes are highly urgent and others a bit less so. It is safest to treat purpura as an urgent problem, as it may herald an overwhelming and fatal infection.

Pyelonephritis (*pie*-lo-nef-RITE-is): Inflammation of the kidneys due to infection (see **Glossary** entry for Urinary tract infection).

Rabies: Rabies is a horrible disease with a 100 percent fatality rate. Once a person has symptoms of rabies, there is no hope for a cure. Rabies can be transmitted by the bite of an animal with rabies or by the rabid animal transmitting its blood or saliva in some other way to a person's mucous membrane or to an open wound like a scratch or cut. Since it is such a dire disease, it is appropriate to be paranoid about it. Kids should be taught to avoid stray,

wild, wounded, or odd-acting animals. They should be taught to report any unusual contact with an animal, even a bat flying into the bedroom. Bats, raccoons, and skunks are the biggest source of rabies in the wild (rabies affects only mammals). They can bite domestic animals and the domestic animals can bite Kids. Any time there is a suspected exposure, one of the urgent questions must be whether there is a possibility of rabies. Sometimes an animal must be observed for about two weeks; sometimes, with wild or sick animals, it's necessary to kill the animal and examine the brain. If there is any chance of exposure, the Kid must undergo the rabies immune globulin and vaccine series. The rabies vaccine has a very bad reputation because it used to be very painful and dangerous. Today, it's not. It's just rather expensive. If a Kid is going to be handling stray animals a lot, say in a Vet clinic or a pound, it's a good idea to get pre-exposure vaccination. The early symptoms of rabies, if you really want to know, are anxiety, panic, and aggression; trouble swallowing; convulsions; and sometimes paralysis.

Rash: Kids ages five to twelve often get comparatively innocent rashes, from hives to plant dermatitis (poison ivy or oak). In rare cases, it will be obvious that a rash is a feature of a serious illness (see **Glossary** entry for Meningitis). Some rashes, however, need prompt or even urgent medical attention, even if the youngster isn't acting very sick. Any rash that suggests bleeding into the skin falls into that category. Such a rash can look like tiny little red dots that don't blanche when you press hard and rub on them. Or it could look like bruises. These rashes indicate a problem with clotting the blood and can be signs of infection, a disorder of the bone marrow, or inflammation of blood vessels.

Reduce: A medical verb that can mean "to fix or correct." You can reduce a hernia by poking the protruding part back into the abdomen, you can reduce a fracture by aligning the bones straightly, you can reduce an intussusception by unwrinkling the intestine. I guess you just "reduce" the problem.

Reflux (REE-flux): When a fluid goes in the wrong direction in the body. Gastro-esophageal reflux is when stomach contents go back up the esophagus. Urinary reflux is when urine goes back up the ureters to the kidneys, rather than out the urethra into the outside world.

Renal (REE-nal): Having to do with the kidneys.

Retractions: Sucking-in of extra muscles to help breathing when it's difficult. These muscles include abdominal muscles, muscles between the ribs, and muscles over the collar bone. Retractions mean medical help is needed for the breathing problem.

Reye syndrome (rye, not ray): A rare disease of the liver and brain that, when it does occur, tends to happen after influenza or chicken pox, especially if a child has taken real aspirin (rather than acetaminophen or Ibuprofen) for fever and pain. Sleepiness, vomiting, headache, and bizarre behavior are key symptoms. Urgent care is needed.

Rheumatic Fever (rew-MAT-ick): An uncommon disease that causes swollen painful joints and often damage to a heart valve. It occurs weeks after a strep throat, as a complication of the way the immune system handles the strep bacteria. The best way to prevent rheumatic fever is to get rid of strep in the body fairly soon (within two weeks) after infection. It's not the same thing as scarlet fever at all. Symptoms of rheumatic fever are joint pain and swelling, fever, and abdominal pain. Sometimes a child, usually over the age of eight, will have involuntary jerking motions called chorea (the old name was St. Vitus's dance).

Rhinovirus (RINE-oh-vie-rus): See **Glossary** entry for Colds.

Ringworm: It's not a worm! It's a fungus. Ringworm of the scalp can cause hair loss, so that you see little black dots on the scalp where hair used to be. Ringworm of the skin gives a round, scaly patch that has a clear center. It can be easy to confuse it with the rash of Lyme disease (see **Glossary** entry). The border of the ring is raised and I guess it looks like a worm, but not really. Sometimes there's a whole bunch of such rings and, in rare cases, they can spread all over. If the diagnosis isn't clear by looking, a scraping can be cultured. Treatment of skin consists of over-the-counter metronidazole (Lotrimin AF) or any of several prescription creams. Ringworm of the scalp or nails requires medicine by mouth, because the growing parts of the hair or nails are infected.

Rubella (roo-BELL-a): Rubella (not rubeola) is three-day or German measles, a virus that is mild in most people, but potentially devastating to the unborn child whose mother gets a case. Immunization via the MMR vaccine has kept this tragedy under control over the last twenty-five years.

Rubeola (roo-bee-OH-la): True measles. A serious disease (see the death of little Johnny in Dickens' novel *Our Mutual Friend*). A blotchy rash, red watery eyes, and runny nose and cough are bad enough, but complications such as pneumonia and encephalitis can occur as well. There's not a cure, but there is a prevention: the MMR vaccine.

Scabies (SKA-bees): A common rash that's very itchy—especially at night—caused by tiny mites that burrow under the skin. It's often hard to diagnose because it can masquerade as nearly a dozen other conditions. Treatment is by prescription, usually with the lotion Elimite. Catching scabies does not mean you are dirty! Ordinary soap and water neither prevent nor cure it.

Scarlet fever: Strep throat with a rash. The rash, which is red and feels like sandpaper, can be all over or just in the groin area and/or the armpits. Of course, it's important to make sure that such a rash really is scarlet fever and that the underlying strep throat gets treated, but scarlet fever isn't any more contagious or dangerous than an ordinary strep throat.

Scope: A catch-all verb, used to describe looking into any body orifice, usually with a fiber-optic instrument. As a noun, it refers to the instrument itself.

Scrapes: If the scrape is just down to the deep layer of the skin, you can probably treat it at home, unless it's very dirty and extensive. This means soaking the scrape in lukewarm, soapy water. (Don't clean with hydrogen peroxide or zephiran or bleach, just warm soapy water. Use any kind of soap.) Then you need to scrub out all the dirt. If not, the new healing skin may seal in the grime and the child will be left with a "road tattoo" that is permanent. Rinse well, inspect under a magnifying glass for little grains of dirt, and pat dry. Apply an antibacterial ointment that does not contain neomycin (Polymyxin; Bacitracin) if the scrape is on the face or can't be bandaged. Otherwise, a dry, sterile, nonstick dressing (such as Telfa pads) is fine. See the pediatrician: if the scrape is on a significant cosmetic area, like the tip of the nose; if the scrape is deep enough so that you can see fatty tissue, muscle, or bone; if the scrape is very dirty or you think something is embedded in the abrasion; if you can't get the dirt out yourself. Make sure that the child is up to date on diphtheria and tetanus immunizations.

Scrotum (SKRO-tum): The sac that holds the testicles.

Sickle cell anemia (disease and trait): A hereditary disorder of red blood cells. This is a complex of conditions affecting many black people, though most go through life with no symptoms because they carry the trait but do not have the disease. If two people with the trait have children, however, there is a one in four chance that any given child will have the disease, which is a severe, chronic, and life-threatening one. One in 650 African Americans has this disease. In **sickle cell disease** or anemia, the hemoglobin in the red blood cells is abnormal, so that when the cells are deprived of oxygen they curl up into a "sickle" shape. When they do so, they clog blood vessels, caus-

ing severe pain in the belly, the limbs, the back, and elsewhere. Moreover, the spleen (which gets rid of old red blood cells) is damaged by all these abnormal cells and can't produce normal immunity. So children with sickle cell disease can get overwhelming infections. Treatment is very helpful, but there is no cure as yet; perhaps gene therapy will provide one eventually. In **sickle cell trait,** which affects about 8 percent of American blacks, there is enough normal hemoglobin that the sickling cells don't cause problems most of the time, except in conditions when oxygen pressure is low—at very high altitudes, for instance. Routine newborn screening for sickle cell disease is done in several states. It allows treatment for disease to start early; in fact, babies with the disease are started on daily penicillin at only three months of age. Screening also allows carriers of the trait to know about their status before planning a second child (or a trip to high altitudes.) While sickle cell is found mostly in African Americans, it can be found in people of any background, most frequently in people of Mediterranean, Middle Eastern, and Indian descent.

Seborrhea (*seb-or-REE-a*): Too much oil on the scalp and face. Seborrheic dermatitis is the red scaly rash that seborrhea helps cause.

Seizure (SEE-zhur): The medically preferred name for a convulsion or fit. Seizures are terrifying to watch, and yet it is rare that a seizure means that a Kid is dangerously ill or has a serious underlying disease. The most scary type of seizure to witness is one in which the Kid falls down and loses consciousness with eyes dilated and rolling back or to one side, rhythmic jerking of arms and legs, labored breathing, and change of color. The Kid may pee or poop during the seizure. Parents witnessing their Kid having such a seizure almost always think that their Kid is going to die. Knowing this, and that the seizure itself is not harming the Kid's brain, may help parents keep more calm if they should be in this position.

The best way to help a Kid who is having a seizure is to make sure that there's no danger from anything in the environment (such as an onrushing vehicle or incoming tide), loosen any tight clothing around the neck and chest, and turn the Kid on his or her side. That way, if there is vomiting (which is unusual), it's not likely to produce choking. If you can do so without leaving the Kid, contact 911. If not, stay with the Kid until the seizure is over. If that takes more than fifteen minutes, however, leave the Kid to get emergency help.

Even though it is likely that the seizure will be over by the time the paramedics arrive, there's a small chance that the Kid may need suction, oxygen, or other assistance from them. Rarely, too, the seizure may be due to a serious underlying cause, such as an injury to the brain, infection, or poisoning, or may be accompanied by an irregularity of the heart rhythm. So call 911.

Here's what not to do. Don't try to prevent the Kid from biting the tongue, either by holding it (nearly impossible, anyway) or by putting something between his or her teeth. Don't try to give the Kid medication or anything by mouth, or a cold bath or sponge bath. It's rare that a Kid over five has a "fever convulsion." Besides, cold water doesn't help those, either.

After the seizure is over, the Kid will fall into a deep sleep with heavy breathing and be very hard to rouse. This is normal.

Seizures are caused by various kinds of "electric storms" in the brain. There are several kinds of seizures besides that described above. Sometimes a Kid will have periods of blanking out for ten or twenty seconds at a time, and may say that he or she "feels funny" or "feels something crawling inside me." Sometimes a Kid will have episodes of odd behavior: smacking the lips, chewing, doing things with the hands like rubbing clothing, or even walking or running. While having these episodes, the Kid seems to be "not there." You can't get his or her

attention. Afterwards, the Kid doesn't remember the episodes.

Any such behavior that suggests or is clearly a seizure needs very prompt assessment, usually including blood tests, an EEG (brainwave test), and sometimes a CT scan or MRI of the brain. Most often, all these tests will show nothing particular except, perhaps, a tendency to have seizures. This tendency is called epilepsy. Epilepsy doesn't mean mental retardation. Most Kids with epilepsy have their seizures controlled with medication and lead normal lives. A number of Kids will only have one seizure in their whole lives, and many more who have epilepsy will actually outgrow the tendency to have seizures.

Sepsis (SEP-sis): An overwhelming and serious infection, usually bacterial, in the blood.

Sighing: A Kid who sighs a lot often does so from anxiety. In this case, the child otherwise seems healthy, though may show other signs of distress of the soul, such as withdrawing or clinging, a worried expression, and saying things that demonstrate his or her unhappiness. Sighing also can be a sign of medical illness, especially diabetes (see **Glossary** entry for Diabetes).

Sinuses: Sinuses are holes in the bones of the skull. Those holes aren't there at birth; they develop gradually over childhood. The holes are supposed to have just air in them. Many people think that the reason we have sinuses is that our heads would be too heavy to lift if we didn't. The sinuses get air in them through a drainage system that opens into the nose.

Sinusitis: Fluid and pus in the sinuses. Sinusitis can be a complication of colds or of allergy. Symptoms include thick, colored nasal discharge that lasts for more than ten days after cold symptoms began; a sore throat; a cough, day and night; and sometimes a headache. Once in a while, sinusitis starts like gangbusters with thick discharge, a fever, and pressure in the sinuses. A Kid with sinusitis is often not up to acting as his or her best self. Crabbiness, irritability, short temper, obnoxiousness all have been known to magically clear up when the sinuses do. Sinusitis also can trigger wheezing attacks in Kids who are prone to them (see **Glossary** entry for Asthma). Diagnosing a sinus infection requires a history, a physical examination, and sometimes an x-ray of the sinuses or even a CT scan of them. Kids who keep getting sinusitis may have allergy, a blockage of the sinus draining system, or, in rare instances, an underlying problem such as cystic fibrosis or a deficient immune system. Treatment usually includes an antibiotic and medications such as decongestants and prescription nose sprays to open up the drainage system. A sinus infection may need weeks of treatment, so it's important to make sure that this is what you're dealing with, not just hay fever or a bad cold.

Sniffing: The practice of sniffing household products to get high. Extremely dangerous (see **Glossary** entry for Inhalants).

Sore throat: Most sore throats are due to mild virus illnesses like colds, herpangina, or influenza. The causes of the others range from strep throat to infectious mono to sinusitis to allergy to rare serious problems like epiglottitis. A sore throat with severe symptoms, such as trouble breathing or swallowing saliva or inability to open the mouth wide, needs immediate attention. A sore throat that lasts for three days or longer without improving deserves a visit also. A scratchy throat that isn't sore but doesn't improve can wait for a week before the doctor looks at it.

Sphincter (SFINK-ter): Any muscle that squeezes shut, a bit like a drawstring purse. The bladder and the anus both have sphincters.

Spleen: The organ under and behind the left ribs that gets rid of old red blood cells and produces important immunity. Since it is blood-filled, the spleen can rupture when injured and it tends to become swollen with some virus diseases, like mono.

Sprains or strains: Kids with a sprained ankle or wrist or knee need the same first aid that adults do. Remember the word **RICE: R** means rest the poor, injured part; **I** means Ice or Cold, ideally about twenty-five minutes of it, followed by a two-hour rest and another twenty-five-minute session as often as possible for the first twenty-four hours; **C** means compression, as in a sensibly applied elastic bandage; and **E** means elevate. Keep that leg up on the sofa or bed or a chair. However, if the pain and swelling and bruising are significant, prompt pediatric attention is needed. For many Kids, the ligaments are actually stronger than the bones: it takes less force to fracture a bone than to sprain a limb. Moreover, it's important to make sure that the growing part of the bone, the growth plate, hasn't been injured. This may not show up on a regular x-ray. Suspect injury to the growth plate if the pain and swelling worsen or last longer than expected.

Staph (STAFF): A particular family of bacteria that tends to cause and complicate skin infections, though any site in the body can be infected.

Steroids (STARE-oids): Hormones put out by the adrenal gland or by medications that simulate them, such as Prednisone and Decadron. Steroids reduce inflammation and swelling, but when taken over long periods can have important side effects, such as mood changes, eye diseases, skin changes, suppressed growth, and suppression of the immune system.

Stomatitis (sto-ma-TIE-tis): Mouth infection (see **Glossary** entry for herpes).

Strabismus (stra-BIZ-mus): A wandering or lazy eye (not eyelid) that doesn't focus with the other. Usually, the vision in this eye is not as good as the one that doesn't focus, so it lets the "good eye" do all the work (see **Glossary** entry for Amblyopia).

Streptococcus (say "strep"): A family of bacteria that causes many childhood infections, most notably strep throat and strep vaginitis.

Strep throat: A sore throat caused by strep.

Most strep throats come on suddenly and bring with them not just a sore throat but fever, a headache, often a stomachache, and swollen tender lymph nodes in the neck. However, any sore throat that persists for longer than three days without getting better deserves to be looked at and maybe tested for strep. Most strep throats make the throat look beefy red. Pus may or may not be present: most sore throats with pus really are caused by viruses. Testing for strep can be done either with a rapid test, available the same day, that looks for "fingerprints" of the strep bacteria or by culturing germs from the throat and seeing if strep grows—this takes twenty-four to forty-eight hours. Either test relies on a really good, which means a necessarily rather unpleasant, swab of the throat. Strep throat needs to be treated because of the concern about rare complications, especially rheumatic fever (see **Glossary** entry for Rheumatic fever). It can be treated with a number of different antibiotics, though penicillin is traditional and reliable. Sulfa medicines (like Gantrisin, Septra, Bactrim) won't work; neither will tetracycline. Treatment needs to be started within seven to nine days to prevent rheumatic fever (see also Scarlet fever).

Stuttering, Stammering: Kids age seven and under frequently stammer when they are tense or excited or nervous. Most often, they outgrow this tendency, especially if people close to them are able to help. Help for a Kid who stutters means making it easy for him or her to be unself-conscious about the stuttering, avoiding frustration and tension. That means no criticizing, correcting, or indulging in upset looks or sighs. I means giving a reassuring pat or wink and maybe the comment, "everybody has trouble with a word or two now and then." Most of all, it means letting the Kid know you find him or her cute, fun, smart: you spend enjoyable time one on one together, paying undivided attention, laughing at the Kid's jokes, listening.

When Kids don't seem to be outgrowing the tendency to stutter, or when Kids or parents find the stuttering frustrating of annoying or worrying, then it's time to take a look at what's going on. We don't know exactly what causes stuttering, but there's good evidence that some Kids have an inborn tendency to stutter even though parents have made every effort to help them out. Such Kids need professional help.

Signs that a Kid needs such help include:

1. Very frequent repetitions of sounds, syllables, or short words, so that they happen just about every sentence, and even when the Kid isn't nervous or excited.

2. The Kid shows tension with these repetitions, making a face or closing the eyes or looking to one side. Or the voice gets higher in pitch with the stuttering.

3. The Kid stutters on vowels, not just consonants, so that a word takes a long time to be spoken: "Feeeeeeeature presentaaaaaaaaation."

4. Sometimes the stuttering occurs inside the child's head instead of vocally—all you hear is a long pause in the flow of speech as the child grimaces.

5. The Kid seems embarrassed or worried about the stuttering and avoids certain words or talking altogether on occasion.

Kids with this degree of stuttering need a visit to the pediatrician for referral to a speech therapist experienced in stuttering. Other good resources: The Stuttering Foundation of America, 1–800–992–9392, and the pamphlet "If Your Child Stutters: A Guide for Parents," from The Speech Foundation of America, P.O. Box 11749, Memphis, TN, 38111.

Sulfa drugs: Medicines used for urinary tract and middle ear infections, mostly, but also crucial for the "AIDS pneumonia," *pneumocystis carinii.* Includes such familiar names as Gantrisin, Bactrim, Septra. Allergic reactions and reactions from sun sensitivity are not uncommon, and parents need to watch out for rashes.

Suppository (su-PAHZ-i-tor-y): Medication placed into the rectum (and sometimes the vagina, but not in the age group covered in this book!) These are given either to the constipated to produce a poop or to administer medication when it can't be given (or won't be taken) by mouth. Absorption can be unreliable, which is why only a few pediatric medicines come in suppository form.

Sweat test: A laboratory test for the disease cystic fibrosis. It involves stimulating and then collecting and analyzing a little sweat, looking for too much chloride. Sweat tests are done routinely on Kids with wheezing, problems growing and gaining weight, diarrhea and foul stools, and a number of other symptoms. Most children who have sweat tests performed do not have cystic fibrosis. It's important to do the test because it's the only way to diagnose this condition, which has many symptoms and signs and a range of severity.

Swimmer's ear: See **Glossary** entry for External otitis.

Swollen joint(s): A swollen joint (or joints) in a Kid this age often has an innocent cause, such as fifth disease (see **Glossary** entry for Erythema infectiosum). However, such a symptom is presumed significant until proven benign. Once in a while, a joint can harbor a bacterial infection: this is an urgent situation that usually gets the urgent care it needs because the joint is very painful. Other causes of swollen joints include rheumatic fever and juvenile rheumatoid arthritis. In rare cases, a swollen joint may portend a tumor.

Syncope (SIN-co-pee): Fainting or passing out, losing consciousness without an injury or seizure. A Kid who faints after standing in one place for a long time probably has had something called a vasovagal attack, in which the blood just pools in the lower extremities. But a Kid who loses consciousness during or after activity needs to be assessed for a rhythm problem in the heart. Such a Kid needs prompt attention and usually an EKG, a record of the electric activity of the heart. First aid for faint-

ing: Elevate the legs. After the Kid revives, offer something with sugar in it. Have the Kid get up slowly. A fainting attack warrants at least a phone call to the pediatrician.

Tachycardia (tak-ee-CAR-dee-ah): Rapid heartbeat from any cause.

Teeth problems: A dingy, grey-colored tooth means that there's been an injury to the nerve; a dentist needs to be consulted. If an injury loosens a tooth, try not to stress the tooth and get a dental evaluation as soon as possible. If a tooth is knocked out, preserve it by placing it in milk or in the parent's mouth, tucked into the side of the cheek, and get dental help as soon as possible. Don't re-implant it into the Kid's mouth: the Kid could start to cry again and loosen the tooth and swallow it or even choke on it.

Testicles: The two "balls" in the scrotum that manufacture sperm. **Pain in the testicles:** Injury can cause this, of course, and if there's swelling or major pain, a visit to the pediatrician is mandatory. If testicles hurt or swell without injury, the cause could be a twisting of the testicle on its stalk. This causes a sudden onset of pain: the whole area is swollen and you can't touch it without the Kid screaming. Immediate treatment can save the testicle; waiting may cause the blood supply to be cut off for too long. In rare cases, a boy who has progressed into puberty may have an infection that causes pain in the scrotum. But in boys who haven't reached puberty, a red and painful testicle means torsion (twisting) until proven otherwise.

Thalassemia: An inherited group of conditions that can cause anemia. The anemia is due to abnormal hemoglobin, the molecule that makes a red blood cell a red blood cell. Many Americans carry a gene for one of the thalassemias, and if two people with such a gene have children, each child has a one in four chance of having a thalassemia disease. Such children are anemic and grow poorly. They need blood transfusions frequently and care from a pediatric hematologist. Most people with the trait, however, have no symptoms or only mild anemia, which often gets treated, inappropriately, with iron. A child with ancestors from Africa, the Mediterranean, the Mideast, or Southeast Asia who has anemia (a low hemoglobin or low hematocrit) may well be carrying the thalassemia trait. Diagnosis is made using a blood test called hemoglobin electrophoresis.

Thyroid: The gland in the neck that produces thyroid hormone, crucial for growth, intelligence, and sexual maturation. A Kid who doesn't have enough thyroid hormone tends to: stop growing in height; gain extra weight; have dry skin; be tired, sleepy, and pale; and lose energy and liveliness. He or she may be constipated and notice hair loss. A Kid with too much thyroid can be irritable, excitable, and have a trembling of the hands. He or she may lose weight or not gain weight, despite a huge appetite. Sometimes the Kid's eyes will start to look very prominent. In Kids with either too much or too little thyroid hormone, the thyroid gland itself can become enlarged and produce a bulge in the front of the neck.

Tic: A nervous habit, like blinking or throat-clearing. See sections on specific tics and on Tourette Syndrome in the text.

Tick: An insect that bites animals and people and sometimes carries disease (lyme disease, rocky mountain spotted fever, tick paralysis, tick fever). The tick injects the bacteria or toxin as it sucks blood from the victim. To remove a tick, do not fool around with putting petroleum jelly or alcohol or gasoline on it in hopes of anesthetizing it. It doesn't work. Worse: it may make the tick regurgitate contaminated blood back into the Kid. Also, don't use your fingernails. You could get contaminated, too. Get tweezers. Grasp the tick firmly as close to the skin as possible and pull upward steadily; then use a magnifying glass to make sure you got the jaw parts. (Sorry.) Then wash thoroughly with soap and water.

TMJ (Temperomandibular joint) (just say "tee-em-jay"): The jaw joint near the ear. If this joint is a little dislocated, it can cause pain that radiates to the ear that can be confused with an ear infection. One way to check: put your fingers in the Kid's ears, have him or her open the mouth wide and then shut it slowly. If the TMJ is out of whack, you will feel a distinct CLUNK. Often the pain responds to ibuprofen and to a very restricted chewing regimen: no gum, hard candies, or anything very chewy; nothing that you have to open up wide for, like a McWhopperburger or an ear of corn.

Toes that peel: The most common causes of peeling toes in Kids under puberty are:

"Sneakeritis": perspiration sealed in by nonbreathing footwear, like sneakers. Usually, this means that only the bottoms, not the sides of the toes, peel. They can peel a lot and even get red and infected. If they're infected, the pediatrician must evaluate and treat. Otherwise, the treatment is to go barefoot, keep feet clean and dry, and apply an over-the-counter cortisone cream.

Athlete's foot: There's peeling and itching between the toes caused by a fungus, and you don't need to be an athlete to catch it. However, the fungus seems to prefer the kind of sweat that Kids make after the hormones of puberty begin. Treatment can be an over-the-counter cream like metronidazole (Lotrimin AF) or any of several prescription creams. It also helps to keep feet clean and dry, and to prevent recurrences by not sharing footwear and by being careful not to wander around pools and locker rooms barefoot.

Tonsils: Lumps of lymph tissue found on each side of the throat. They increase in size up until about age seven or eight and then gradually shrink down. In older Kids, tonsils often feature pits, and sometimes there's a little white debris in one or two of those pits. Tonsils only have to come out if they are causing big trouble: if a Kid gets more than four or five documented strep throats in a year, for instance, or if the tonsils are so big that they are hard to breathe or swallow around.

Tonsillitis: Any infection or swelling of the tonsils, whether due to bacterial or viral causes. Pus on the tonsils does not automatically mean a bacterial infection; in fact, most of the time pus goes along with a viral sore throat.

Torticollis (*tor*-ti-COLL-is): A pain in the neck, literally, causing a stiff neck. Most often in Kids this is due to an ear or throat infection or to sleeping in a weird position. Rarely it can be due to trauma that jostles the neck bones or to serious causes like tumors. (This is really rare. Honest.) In the usual case, the Kid awakens in the morning with a neck that hurts when he or she turns the head in one or the other direction. If the Kid seems otherwise fine, it's okay to try first aid: a dose of ibuprofen and a **cold** massage, say with a bag of frozen peas. If there is any other sign of illness, a history of injury, or if this first aid doesn't help, then of course a visit to the pediatrician is in order.

Toxic: The appearance of a child who is very sick, possibly with sepsis (infection of the blood stream). Such a child typically is whimpering, very irritable, or limp and has poor color and is unable to pay attention or make much eye contact. These symptoms are usually but not necessarily combined with fever. Urgent medical attention is indicated.

Tuberculosis (TB): TB is a potentially very serious bacterial illness that used to be called "consumption." It most often causes lung disease—resulting in persistent cough, fever, and chest pain—but can infect any organ; it can even cause meningitis (see **Glossary** entry for Meningitis). TB is making a comeback, and there are even strains that are resistant to many

of the usual anti-TB antibiotics. The test for TB infection is a skin test, called the Mantoux test. It is given by syringe and makes a tiny bubble in the skin of the forearm. The site of the test should be checked after forty-eight to seventy-two hours by a medical staff member. If the test is positive, it doesn't mean that the child is sick, but does mean that there are probably TB germs in the body. A chest x-ray tells whether there is actual disease. How often a child should be tested for TB depends on whether he or she is in a high-risk group. Your pediatrician will determine whether this is the case.

Tympanic membrane (tim-PAN-ick): The eardrum, which vibrates to sound and conducts those vibrations to the necessary nerves.

Tympanogram: A reading of the eardrum's ability to vibrate, produced by a machine called a tympanometer. This doesn't hurt and is fast. It works by reflected sound and doesn't deliver any electricity or rays into the head or ear.

Ultrasound: An imaging technique that can look at soft tissues of the body without delivering radiation. Most of the time a child doesn't even need sedation: it doesn't hurt and it doesn't matter if the child wiggles a little. Many parts of the body can be viewed by ultrasound: brains and spinal cords in very young infants and for everybody, kidneys and abdomens. It's often abbreviated to UTZ.

Urethra (you-REETH-ra): The tube through which urine exits from the bladder to the outside world.

Ureters (YOUR-e-*tours*): The pair of tubes, each connecting a kidney to the bladder, that transport urine.

Urinary difficulties: See **Glossary** entry for Pee problems.

Urinary Tract Infection (UTI): An infection of the bladder and/or kidneys. The physician often uses this term when she or he isn't sure if the kidneys are involved as well as the bladder. The worry about any UTI is that the kidneys may be damaged, either by infection or by a condition called vesical-uretero reflux. Reflux occurs when urine goes the wrong way: when it goes back up the ureters to the kidneys, rather than out the urethra into the toilet. This can happen in some Kids when the bladder squeezes to empty itself. If it occurs, the kidneys may be damaged, either by the pressure of the refluxing urine or by bacteria in that urine. So after your Kid has a UTI, your pediatrician may advise studies to make sure that no damage has occurred. This might be an ultrasound (ultrasound) of the kidneys and/or an x-ray study called a VCUG (see **Glossary** entry for VCUG) or a kidney scan.

Uterus (YOU-ter-us): The hollow, muscular organ also known as the womb, a very small organ in girls before puberty.

Uvula (YOU'VE-you-la): The little thing that dangles down from the roof of the mouth. Usually it's single, but sometimes it's split like an upside-down Y. It assists with swallowing, and sometimes gets infected, often with strep.

Vagina (vuh-JINE-a): The pocket-like structure leading to the uterus and opening at the hymen (see **Glossary** entry for Hymen).

Vaginitis (*vaj*-in-I-tis): Irritation of the vagina with or without infection. In girls ages five to twelve, vaginitis is often caused by irritation from bubbles in the bath water: it's best to use bubble bath, bath oils, and other creations sparingly and to avoid sitting in water containing shampoo or water made soapy by a floating bar of soap. Girls should also know to wipe from front to back. Another common cause of vaginitis is strep, which gives a flaming red vaginal irritation with discharge. Yeast is very rarely the cause of vaginitis after the days of babyhood and before puberty. Diagnosis of vaginitis means a look at and sometimes a swab from the outside of the vagina for a culture and/or a look at the secretions under the microscope. Treatment means meticulous hygiene and, if there's an infection, antibiotics.

Varicella (vare-ih-SELL-uh): Chicken pox, the disease caused by herpes zoster.

Varicella immunization: The chicken pox vaccine, released in 1995, is a safe and effective vaccination. It is closely related to the vaccine that has been used and studied in Japan for 20 years. This is killed vaccine—it can't give anyone AIDS or other diseases. It almost completely prevents the rare, serious complications—like encephalitis or Reye syndrome (see **Glossary** entries for both these illnesses)—and fatalities. It probably also cuts down on cases of shingles (see **Glossary** entry for Herpes zoster). However, it is likely that Kids who are vaccinated will need a booster later in life. At this time, the vaccine is recommended but not required for school attendance. By the time you read this, it is likely that most insurance companies and Medicaid will be paying for the vaccine.

Vascular (VAS-kew-lur): Anything having to do with the blood vessels.

Vasculitis (vas-kew-LIE-tis): An inflammation of the blood vessels.

Ventricles (VEN-tri-cal): The two lower pumping chambers of the heart. The left one pumps red blood to the body. The right one pumps blue blood to the lungs.

Virus: An exceedingly tiny bit of DNA (genetic material) wrapped in a coat of protein that causes infectious diseases, from colds to measles and mumps to AIDS. Viruses take over the body's cells in order to replicate, so it is very hard to get rid of them without damaging the body itself. Antibiotics don't work on viruses.

Vital signs: Temperature, pulse, rate of breathing, and blood pressure.

Vitiligo (vit-uh-LYE-goh): Pale spots on the skin from lack of pigment. Vitiligo can occur after a skin infection or from hormone problems or other medical entities; but usually it is only a cosmetic bother. White patches on the skin also can be due to pityriasis alba (see **Glossary** entry for Pityriasis alba).

Vomiting: Vomiting is often caused by mild

viruses (see **Glossary** entry for Gastroenteritis) or food poisoning but, in rare cases, can be a sign of a serious problem. **A sudden onset of vomiting** can go along with appendicitis, diabetes, a drug or poison ingestion, or a blockage of the intestine (see **Glossary** entry for Abdominal pain). Vomiting after a head injury can indicate that there is bleeding into the brain (see **Glossary** entry for Concussion). A Kid who has none of these indications, but who continues to vomit after appropriate treatment (see **Glossary** entry for Gastroenteritis) needs to touch base with the pediatrician. **The treatment for simple, unworrisome vomiting:** Wait for an hour after the stomach has emptied with vomiting. Then start offering a debubbled soft drink with sugar in it in small amounts, about a measured tablespoon every ten minutes, for two hours. If the Kid is feeling much better, which is usually the case, fluids can be increased, and it's okay to gradually advance to the "invalid" diet of toast, bananas, and clear soups. **Vomiting that recurs** is another problem. Sometimes this is a sign of food allergy, temporary emotional distress—such as stage fright, or constipation; but it's a good idea to rule out more serious and less likely causes. Certainly if there is a change in the Kid's general health and activities, a prompt visit to the pediatrician is needed. Even if no changes in health and activities are apparent, vomiting that recurs for a month needs to be evaluated. Before taking the child to the doctor, make some notes—use the same questions outlined in the **Glossary** entry for abdominal pain, "ordinary," but substitute the word "vomiting" for "pain."

VCUG (Voiding cysto-urethrogram) (just say "vee-see-you-jee"): A study often performed on a Kid who has had a urinary tract infection or whose urinary stream seems weak or forced. The study shows if reflux is taking place. Reflux occurs when urine goes back up the ureters into the kidneys, rather than out the urethra into the outside world. In a VCUG a catheter is placed through the urethra into the bladder, dye is injected, then x-rays are taken as the child urinates. Placing the catheter may be briefly painful, but hardest on Kids is the idea of somebody seeing and handling their private parts, then of peeing in public while x-rays are taken. Kids this age deserve a thorough explanation appropriate to their understanding. I often show them how it's done using a doll and give parents a catheter so that the Kid can get used to the idea at home. The best tack for a parent is to project calm acceptance that this is an important but stressful test, that the people who order and perform it do this all the time and are kind to children, and that of course there will be a treat afterward. Too much worry and sympathy are likely to produce hysteria.

Warts: Warts are tiny skin tumors caused by a virus named *human papillomavirus* (HPV). Only people can catch this virus. You don't get warts by touching toads or frogs or animals; you only get them from other people. If you scratch a wart, you can spread the virus along the path of scratching. If you have warts on your fingers and then suck your fingers, you can get the warts on your lips. (So don't.) If you leave warts alone, they almost always will eventually go away by themselves. The key word here, though, is eventually. There are lots of treatments for warts. As usual, when there are lots of treatments, there's not a specific or dependable one. The most important thing about wart treatments is not to do more damage than the wart did. If you create a scar, the scar is there for life, whereas the wart may well go away by itself. Treatments include:
• Freezing the wart with liquid nitrogen. It hurts but is often very effective, and scars are uncommon
• Laser or electrodissection
• Acid therapy, with salicylic or lactic acid or Vitamin A acid (retin A), takes a long time but

doesn't hurt and is unlikely to scar
• Hypnosis, which may or may not work, but makes you feel as if you are doing something

Warts on the genital or anal areas may be innocent ones transferred there by plain old wart virus on the Kid's own hands. However, the worry must be set to rest that these could be true genital warts caused by a different brand of virus, transmitted by sexual molestation. Sometimes a dermatologist or gynecologist may have to be enlisted to be sure.

Wheeze: The sound made when the bronchial tubes of the lung clamp down. It's a high-pitched whistle made most noticeably while breathing out.

Wheezing (WEEZ-ing, not weezelling): Repeated wheezes while breathing; usually requires effort getting the air out. If the cause is not found to be a specific infection or anatomic problem and the wheezing occurs more than once, the child is said to have asthma (see **Glossary** entry for Asthma).

Whitlow: See **Glossary** entry for Herpetic whitlow.

Whooping cough: See **Glossary** entry for Pertussis.

Yeast: A microscopic organism that is ubiquitous. It equally doesn't cause an infection in the vagina until the hormones of puberty start to be secreted. Children with an impaired immune system may get very severe, stubborn yeast. There is no evidence that normal children, without an immune deficiency and without a catheter into a blood vessel, ever get "systemic" yeast.

Yellowness of the whites of the eyes: See **Glossary** entry for Jaundice.

Zovirax (ZOH-veer-ax): See **Glossary** entry for Acyclovir.

Partial Bibliography

These are some of the sources readers might be most curious about. I haven't included standard medical references.

Books and Articles for Parents

Ames, Louise Bates, Ph.D. and Carol Chase Huber. *Your One-Year-Old* through *Your Ten- to Fourteen-Year-Old*. The Gesell Institute of Human Development series. New York: Dell, 1976 to 1991. These small books give an overall portrait of a Kid's life and focus special attention on whether the age is one of high or low tension. Despite the fact that these books are apparently based on studies from the Gesell Institute, no description of the studies appear in the books, which is unfortunate given that readers may not know about the Institute and the writings of Dr. Gesell. These soothing books paint childhood in a somewhat traditional light. Girls play with girl things, boys with boy things, Mother stays at home (her presence is primary), and Father is reliable, kind, and there to help in a pinch, but rather distant. There is practically no mention of sex education and molestation is referred to only once, in the book on Eights.

Brown, Jeffrey, M.D. "Imagination Training: A Tool with Many Uses." *Contemporary Pedi-atrics* 12, no. 2 (February 1995):22–36. A description of several ways to help a child use imagination—reframing, visualization, relaxation, and other techniques—to cope with many different kinds of stresses.

Dobson, James, Ph.D. *The Strong-Willed Child*. Wheaton, Ill.:Tyndale, 1978. I fear that Dr. Dobson's advocacy of spanking is misguided. His main point is that parents must not tolerate bratty behavior—and boy is he right. However, I don't believe, as he does, that there is a special category of strong-willed children. I do believe that parents who are uncertain how to discipline can create children who are oppositional. I've never seen this difficulty resolved by spanking. Dr. Dobson's other suggestions on how to manage sibling rivalry, oppositional behavior, and other disciplinary problems are excellent.

Ekman, Paul, Ph.D. *Why Kids Lie: How Parents Can Encourage Truthfulness*. New York: Viking, 1989. This useful book by "a world-renowned expert on lying" contains many anecdotes that may be instructive and reassuring.

Elkind, David, Ph.D. *The Hurried Child*. Reading, MA: Addison Wesley, 1981. A plea to allow children a respite from the harried pace of modern society. The book presents an interesting perspective, but I don't know whether parents will find much specific help here. Dr. Elkind says that in his practice he doesn't see any spoiled children, just stressed ones.

Faber, Adele, and Elaine Mazlish. *How to Talk So Kids Will Listen & Listen So Kids Will Talk.* New York: Avon Books, 1982.

——————*Siblings Without Rivalry.* New York: Avon Books, 1988.

——————*Liberated Parents/Liberated Children.* New York: Avon Books, 1990.

——————*How to Talk So Kids Learn.* New York: Simon & Schuster, 1995.

All four of these books on communicating with Kids are useful and easy to read.

Healy, Jane M., Ph.D. *Your Child's Growing Mind: A Guide to Learning and Brain Development from Birth to Adolescence.* New York: Doubleday, 1989. A very interesting book on theories of learning that have been developed by neurophysiologists. A teacher, Dr. Healy relates these theories to helping Kids develop various skills. The book is organized according to topics rather than age groups, which can make it hard to pinpoint information specific to a child's current stage of development. But the author's practical suggestions are often very valuable and worth searching for.

Kleinman, Ronald, M.D., and Michael Jellinek, M.D. *Let Them Eat Cake! The Case Against Controlling What Your Children Eat.* New York: Villard, 1994. In an attempt to help parents relax about food questions, the authors advise parents to give Kids autonomy—which they interpret as giving Kids the freedom to indulge themselves or to satisfy an impulse. I

disagree that providing a Kid with rich or sweet snacks is a necessary prerequisite to nurturing autonomy. Second, the authors' take on Kids' weight problems differs from my own. Nowhere do they express concern about the growing number of obese Kids, and they tend to downplay chubbiness and its consequences. I found a few upsetting references to the one and only obese child in the authors' case histories as a "slug" and a "bowling ball."

Konner, Melvin, M.D., Ph.D. *Childhood.* Boston: Little, Brown, 1991. This is a companion to the public television series on how different aspects of childhood are manifested in different cultures.

Laliberte, Richard. "Baseball Danger: What Every Parent Needs to Know." *Parents* 70, no. 4, 1995:32–34. A very thorough article on Kids playing our national pastime.

Levinson, Harold, M.D. *Smart But Feeling Dumb: The Challenging New Research on Dyslexia—And How It May Help You.* New York: Warner Books, 1994. Dr. Levinson believes that dyslexia is caused by a disturbance of the inner ear and that a combination of medications, including "antimotion sickness medications, antihistamines, antidepressants, antipanic drugs, and vitamins" can help. Alas, he doesn't substantiate his theories with results from double-blinded studies (in which uninvolved professionals judge the results) or controlled studies (in which two groups are studied, one receiving medication and the other going untreated or receiving placebo medication—medication that looks like the real thing but is inactive). Nor does Dr. Levinson appear to have published articles or papers on his research in journals affiliated with academic institutions or academies. And he includes testimonials, rather than hard scientific data, as proof of success.

Nathanson, Laura, M.D. *Kidshapes: A Guide to Helping Your Children Control Their Weight.* New York: HarperCollins, 1995. My own take on controlling chubbiness differs from that of Kleinman and Jellinek (see **Partial Bibliography** under authors' names). Parents need to be alert to Kids' increasing chubbiness from toddlerhood on. They need to: realize that we have lost our sense of when a Kid of a given age is just the right weight or too chubby; understand why pediatricians often don't help parents to keep Kids the right weight; and approach the problem in a way that increases family harmony and a Kid's self esteem. Overweight Kids are lucky: if helped, they have an opportunity to slow down or stop weight gain, rather than have to lose it (a hard battle) the way overweight adults do.

Pipher, Mary, Ph.D. *Reviving Ophelia: Saving the Selves of Adolescent Girls.* New York: Ballantine, 1994. Dr. Pipher's well-written analysis of the problems girls in junior high/middle school face is compelling. However, since puberty begins for most girls and is complete in some of them before they enter seventh grade, parents need to start helping their daughters be strong and self-confident years before they approach adolescence. Parents do well to look at this book during the Kid years, before girls and boys are confronted with the pressures that characterize adolescence in America.

Rincover, Arnold, Ph.D. *The Parenting Challenge: Your Child's Behavior from 6 to 12.* New York: Pocket Books, 1991. The focus here is on behavior problems and conduct disorders, and the book dispenses firm and helpful advice about handling them. As with the Ekman book, however, the author seems to single out one of his Kids, his son Benjamin, in giving examples of behavior problems.

Silver, Larry B., M.D. *The Misunderstood Child: A Guide for Parents of Children with Learn-ing Disabilities.* Blue Ridge Summit, PA: TAB Books, 1992. A very clear and useful guide by a physician who speaks with both professional and personal authority.

Turecki, S., and L. Tonner. *The Difficult Child.* New York: Bantam, 1985. An indispensable book for parents and other loving adults whose Kid displays a temperament that's hard to live with.

Professional Literature

Carey, William B., M.D. "The Difficult Child." *Pediatrics in Review* 8, no. 2 (August 1986):39–45.

Chess, Stella, M.D. "Commentary on The Difficult Child." *Pediatrics in Review* 8, no. 2 (August 1986):35–37.

Christophersen, Edward, Ph.D., and Melvin D. Levine, M.D. "Development and Behavior: Older Children and Adolescents." *Pediatric Clinics of North America* 39, no. 3 (June 1992).

Damon, William, Ph.D. *The Moral Child.* London:Free Press, 1990.

Dixon, Suzanne D., M.D., and Martin T.Stein, M.D. *Encounters with Children: Pediatric Behavior and Development.* St. Louis: Mosby, 1992.

Dunn, Judy, and Shirley McGuire. "Sibling and Peer Relationships in Childhood." *J. Child Psychol. & Psychiat.* 33, no. 1 (1992):67–105.

Eisenberg, Nancy, Ph.D. *The Caring Child.* Cambridge, Mass.:Harvard University Press, 1992. An account of the research being done on ways to promote compassion and altruism in children.

Gentile, Douglas A., M.D., and Barbara C. Kennedy, M.D. "Wilderness Medicine for Children." *Pediatrics* 88, no. 5 (November 1991): 967–981.

Golombok, Susan, Ph.D., and Robyn Fivush, Ph.D. *Gender Development.* Cambridge: Cambridge University Press, 1994.

Harris, Paul, Ph.D. *Children and Emotion.* Oxford: Basil and Blackwell, 1989.

Levy, Daniel J., M.D., and James Buck, M.D. "Safety on the Slopes." *Contemporary Pediatrics* 11, no. 12 (December 1994):51–58.

Murray, T. M., and L. A. Livingston. "Hockey Helmets, Face Masks, and Injurious Behavior." *Pediatrics* 95, no. 3 (March 1995):419–421.

Sarrni, Carolyn, and Paul Harris, editors. *Children's Understanding of Emotion.* Cambridge: Cambridge University Press, 1989.

INDEX

Abdominal pain, 273–274

Absence seizures, 76

Accelerated school programs, 52

Acetaminophen, 274

Achievement, fostering, 38

Acne, 231, 234, 274

Acquired Immune Deficiency Syndrome, 274

Activities, structured, and feelings of competence, 217, 219–220

Acyclovir, 274

Adenoids, 68, 69, 234, 274

ADHD (attention deficit hyperactivity disorder), 37, 75–77
  diagnosis of, 75–76, 77

Adolescence, looking ahead to, 177

Adoption, explaining, 18

Advanced academic skills, in five/six-year-olds, 50–52

After-school lessons, 133–134

Aggression, 73, 194
  divorce of parents and, 95
  nine- to eleven-year-olds and, 239–240
  when disciplined, 24–25

AIDS, 274

Alcohol, 113

Alice-in-Wonderland syndrome, 274

Allergy, 274–275

allergens, 274

atopy, 277

as cause of attention problems, 76, 77

chronically stuffed nose as sign of, 69

reaction (anaphylaxis), 275

shots, 275

Allowances
  seven/eight-year-olds, 114–115

Alopecia, 275

Amblyopia, 275

American Academy of Pediatrics, position on dangerous activities, 57, 265

American Heart Association recommendations, 142

American National Standards Institute, 264

Amusement park rides, 73

Anaphylaxis, 275

And to Think that I Saw it on Mulberry Street (Seuss), 6

Anemia, 275–276

Animal bites, 276
  rabies and, 298

Anorexia nervosa, 276

Antibiotic, 276

Antiperspirants, 227

Anxiety, chronic, and attention problems, 37, 77, 78

Apnea, 68, 76, 276
Apple juice, 36
Arithmetic. *See* Math
Aspiration, 277
Aspirin, 277
Assertiveness, 15–16, 91
Asthma, 68, 145, 277
Athlete's foot, 305–306
Athletics. *See* Sports
Atopy, 277
Attention, ability to focus, 34–37, 38
Attention-getting behavior
    five/six-year-olds, 73–75
Avoidant children, 194

Bacteria, 277
Bad breath. *See* Halitosis
Baldness (alopecia), 275
Barrie, J. M., quoted, 202
Baseball, 268. *See also* Sports
Bathing, seven/eight-year-olds and, 116,
    145–146
Bathroom(s)
    safety, 72
    school, 43, 55
    traveling and, 84
Bedroom neatness, 202–204
Bedwetting, 68, 79–81, 110
Behavioral problems
    five/six-year-olds, 73–81
        aggression, 73
        bedwetting/soiling, 79–81
        bossiness, 73–75
        compulsions, 77–78
        hyperactivity-ADHD, 75–77
        thumb-sucking, 78–79
    nine- to eleven-year-olds, 236–237,
        242–243
    seven/eight-year-olds, 148–152
        aggression, 148–149
        lack of obedience, 149

    and mood, 149–152
        temper tantrums, 149
Best friend, 171–172, 196–197. *See also*
        Friendship
Bibliography, 311–314
Bicycle
    learning to ride, 57, 83
    safety, 71, 265–266
Bilingual schools, 46
Bilirubin, 277
Biofeedback techniques, 94
Bites, 276
Bladder
    catheterization, 117
    infection, 277
Book reports, and computers, 218
Boredom/nervous habits, compulsion and, 78
Bossy children. *See* Demanding children
Boys, puberty and, 141, 230–232
Breathing trouble, 277–278
Bribes, 29
Bronchitis, 278
Bronchodilator, 278
Brown, Jeffrey L., 94
Bullies, 55, 109–110, 194
Burns/burn hazards, 72, 278

Camping, 267
Camps, 154
Canker sores, 287–288
Car safety, 71
Cataract, 278
Catheter, 278
Cat Scratch Disease, 278–279
Centers for Disease Control, 84
Cerumen, 279
Changes in You and Me (Bourgeois and Wolfish),
        228
Character development, 170
Checkups
    kindergarten, 69–70

nine- to eleven-year-olds, 233
Chemical (household) hazards, 72
Chicken pox (Varicella), 271, 307
Chilblains, 279
Child Protective Services abuse hotline, 96
Chodorow, Nancy, 184
Chores
    five/six-year-olds, 22–23, 82
    nine- to eleven-year-olds, 199–204
    seven/eight-year-olds, 115–121
Cliques, 107–108, 191–193
Colds, 279
Compassion
    five/six-year-olds, 10–11
Competence, 170
    computer literacy and, 216–217
    helping children find area of, 171
    nine- to eleven-year-olds and, 217–220
    sports/exercise and, 218–219, 221–222
Compulsive behavior, 77–78
Computer
    help with learning and, 218
    literacy, 216–217
Concussion, 279
Congenital conditions, 279–280
Conjunctivitis, 280, 296
Consciousness of self, in seven/eight-year-olds,
        100–101
Constipation, 36, 68, 76, 81, 280
Contact lenses, 117
Controversial children, 193–194
Conversation, encouraging, 178–185
    feedback and, 181
    giving support, 181–182
    humor, 183
    impersonal topics, 182–183
    interruptions and, 180–181
    moral discussions, 182
    philosophical differences, recognizing, 183
Cosmetic deformities, 48–49, 194
Coxsackie, 280

Criticism
    disguised as praise, 28
    reaction to
        five/six-year-olds, 11
Cromolyn sodium, 280
Cross-sex behavior
    five/six-year-olds, 86–91
    nine- to eleven-year-olds, 246–247
    seven/eight-year-olds, 159–160
Croup, 280
Crushes, 190
Cultural differences, 47–48
Curling irons, 72
Curriculum objections, of parents, 52–54
Custody arrangements, 96
Cuts, 280
Cystic Fibrosis, 280–281
Cystitis, 281

Dancing, 83, 137
David Decides: No More Thumbsucking (Heitler),
        79
Death, of loved person or pet
    anxiety about, and media influence, 19
    five/six-year-olds and, 91–93
    nine- to eleven-year-olds and, 250–251
    seven/eight-year-olds and, 101, 161–162
Defecation in pants, 68, 81
Defiance, when disciplined, 24
Demanding children
    five/six-year-olds, 73–75
    seven/eight-year-olds, 121–122
Dental health/problems, 304
    brushing, 116
    cavities, 281
    thumbsucking and, 78–79
Deodorants, 227
Depression, 13, 150–152, 281
    chronic, 77, 151
    medication, 151
Dextroamphetamine, 77

Dextromethorphan, 281
Diabetes, 281, 282
  bedwetting and, 80
  insulin injections, 117
Diaphragmatic hernia, 287
Diarrhea, 282
Dignity, 188
Diphtheria, 271
Dirty jokes, 190
Discipline
  five/six-year-olds, 24–25, 29–33
  nine- to eleven-year-olds, 173, 204–207
  seven/eight-year-olds, 121–125
  spanking, 31–32
Discussion, with nine- to eleven-year-olds, 178
Divorce
  custody arrangements, 96
  five/six-year-olds and, 95–96
  nine- to eleven-year-olds and, 251
  seven/eight-year-olds and, 163–164
Double promotion, 51
Dressing, 116
Drug use, 113

Ear pain, 282
  infections, 68
    otitis media, 295
Ears, pierced, 117, 147, 227
Earwax, 279
Eating disorders, 243, 276
Eczema, 282
Education. See School
Electrocution hazards, 72
Emotional development
  five/six-year-olds, 11–13
    frustration and, 12–13
    patience, 11
    resilience, 11–12
  nine- to eleven-year-olds, 185–191
Emotional problems
  attention problems, 76, 77

bedwetting and, 80
  thumbsucking and, 79
Empowerment, nine- to eleven-year-olds and, 170
Encephalitis, 282
Encopresis, 68, 76, 282
Endoscopy, 282–283
Enuresis. See Bedwetting
Environmental problems, and attention disorders, 77
Epilepsy, 283
Erythema infectiosum, 283
Erythema multiforme, 283
Exaggeration, 5
Exercise, 134–137, 220–222
  bladder stretching or strengthening, 80
  equipment, safety and, 72
  virtues of, 58
  and weight, 64–65, 136
External otitis, 283
Extra-curricular activities, 133–135. See also Sports
Eyes
  diseases of
    conjunctivitis, 280, 296
    glaucoma, 285
    ocular herpes, 288
  eyedrops, 67, 145
  eye exercises, 40
  lazy eye, 292

Fainting. See Syncope
Fairness, concept of, 102–103
Family secrets, 49–50, 179
Fatigue, 283–284
  nervous habits/compulsions and, 78
Feedback, from parents, 169–171, 178, 181
Fever, 70, 284
Fifth disease. See Erythema infectiosum, 283
Fights, 122–123
Fingernail(s)

biting, 78
care of, 116
grungy, 294
Fingers in the door, 284
First aid, teaching, 147
First grade
  challenges, 38–43
    math, 40–42
    printing and writing, 42
    reading, 38–40
  readiness, 37–38
  troubles, 56
Flea bites, 284
Flu, 284
Flying, 73
Food, as reward, 28. *See also* Nutrition
Foreign languages, 82–83, 153
  bilingual schools and, 46
Friendship
  best friends, 171–172, 196–197
  casual friends, peers, cliques, 107–110,
    191–192
  facilitating, 14
  five/six-year-olds, 13–15, 56
  inappropriate, 106–107
  moving and, 84
  parental assistance in finding best friend,
    171–172
  seven/eight-year-olds, 103–109
Frostbite, 263, 284–285
Frustration, 12–13
Funerals and memorial services, 92–93,
    161–162. *See also* Death, of loved person
    or pet
FutureKids, 217

Games, 137
Gang recruitment, 103
Gastroenteritis, 285
Gender atypical behavior. *See* Cross-sex
  behavior

Genital warts, 309
Gentile, Douglas A., 267
German measles, 271
Germs, avoiding children's, 68
Giardia Lambia, 285
Gifted programs, 52
Gilligan, Carol, 184
Gingivostomatitis, 285
Girls
  puberty and, 140–141, 225–230
    acne, 226, 231
    breast development, 226
    menstruation, 226, 229
    personal hygiene and, 227
    physical changes, 226, 228–230
    sexuality, 226–228
  weight and, 64, 136, 260–261
Glaucoma, 285
Groin pain, 285
Growth, physical
  charts
    boys, 258–259
    deciphering, 255–257
    girls, 260–261
  five/six-year-olds, 61–65
    height, 46–47, 61
    weight, 61–65
  growing pains, 285
  nine- to eleven-year-olds, 224–233, 241–242
    nutrition, 232–233
    puberty, boys, 230–232
    puberty, girls, 225–230
  seven/eight-year-olds, 139–141, 143
    weight, 139–140
Growth, of the soul
  five/six-year-olds, 4–11
    compassion, 10–11
    encouraging honesty, 5–9
  nine- to eleven-year-olds, 175–185
  seven/eight-year-olds, 102–104
    moral and ethical dilemmas, 102–104

Guns, 71–72, 111, 265–266
  toy guns, 138

H. influenzae type b, 271
Hair care, 116
Halitosis, 285–286
Hand, foot, and mouth disease, 286
Hand skills
  of first graders, 42
  kindergarten readiness and, 36
Headaches, 286
Health
  see also Illness
  access to information about, 173
  five/six-year-olds, 66–70
    kindergarten checkup, 69–70
    medication, 67–68
    normal/abnormal signs, 68–69
  nine- to eleven-year-olds, 233
  seven/eight-year-olds, 143
Hearing
  diminished
    attention problems and, 76
    reading problems and, 39
Heart murmur, 286
Heatstroke, 264
Heaven, conversations about, 92. See also
      Death, of loved person or pet
Height, 46–47
  charts
    boys, 258–259
    deciphering, 255–257
    girls, 260–261
  five/six-year-olds, 61
  unusually short children, 47
Heitler, Susan, 79
Helmets, safety, 265, 268
Hematoma, 286
Hemophilus influenza, 286
Henoch-Schoenlein purpura, 286–287
Hepatitis, 84, 271, 287

Hernia, 287
Hero worship, 86
Herpangina, 287
Herpes, 287
Herpes simplex, 287–288
Hives, 288
Hoarseness, 69, 288
Hockey, 268–269
Homework, 131–133
Homosexuality, behavior/feelings perceived as,
      86–91, 227, 231, 245–246
Honesty, encouraging
  five/six-year-olds, 5–9
  seven/eight-year-olds, 105
  Why Kids Lie: How Parents Can Encourage
      Truthfulness, 311
Horseback riding, 269
Hospitalization, of child
  five/six-year-olds, 93–95
  nine- to eleven-year-olds, 251
  seven/eight-year-olds, 162–163
Hot springs, 267
Hot tub, hazards of, 72, 267
Hot water heater, 72
Household equipment, safety and, 72–73
Housework. See Chores
How to Talk So Kids Will Listen and Listen So Kids
      Will Talk (Faber and Mazlish), 211
Humor
  "dirty" jokes, 190
  use of in conversation, 183
Hydrocephalus, 288
Hygiene. See Personal hygiene
Hyperactivity, 75
  see also ADHD
Hyperventilation, 289
Hyphema, 289
Hypothermia, 263, 289

Ibuprofen, 289
Ice hockey, 268–269

INDEX

Idiopathic, 289
Illness, 70
    avoiding children's germs, 68
    fever, 70, 284
    five/six-year-olds, 70–71
Illness (cont.)
    medication, 67–68
    nine- to eleven-year-olds, 233–235
    serious, of loved one, 91, 160–161, 249–250
    seven/eight-year-olds, 143–145
    tonsils and adenoids, 68
Imagination Training: A Tool with Many Uses, 94,
    311
Immunization(s), 271
    distress over, 28
    schedule, 270
    travel outside of country and, 84
Immunoglobulins, 289
Impetigo, 289
In a Different Voice (Gilligan), 184
Inattentiveness, 75
    see also ADHD
    medical causes of, 76
Incentives, 28
Independence, nurturing, 154
Individual Educational Placement evaluation,
    216
Infectious mononucleosis, 289–290
Influenza, 290
Inguinal hernia, 287
Inhalants, 290
Inhalers, 67–68
Injuries, 70–73, 147, 235–236
    see also Safety; Sports
    cars and traffic, 71
    fingers in the door, 284
    guns, 71–72
    household, 72–73
    sprains or strains, 302
Inline skating, 57, 266–267
Insect stings, 290–291

Insulin injections, 117
Intussusception, 291
Itching, 291
It's Perfectly Normal (Harris), 228

Jaundice, 291
Jealousy
    new siblings and, 85–86
Judo, 57

Karate, 57, 137
Kawasaki disease or syndrome, 291
Kennedy, Barbara C., 267
Ketosis, 291–292
Kindergarten
    bathroom terror, 55
    checkup, 69–70
    readiness, 33–37
    repeating, 43–44
    trouble leaving home, 55
Kitchen safety, 72
Knee pain, 292
Kohlberg, Lawrence, 184

Labial adhesions, 292
Language study, 153
Laryngitis, 292
Lazy eye, 292
Lead poisoning
    attention problems and, 76
Learning
    disabilities, 76, 77, 213
    first-grade difficulties, 56
    nine- to eleven-year-olds and, 172, 237–238
Leukemia, 292
Lice (pediculosis), 147, 295–296
Life jackets, 267
Limits, setting
    for five/six-year-olds, 30
    for nine- to eleven-year-olds, 173–175
Limping, 292–293

Lying. *See* Honesty, encouraging
Lyme disease, 293
Lymph nodes, swollen, 293

Magnetic resonance imaging (MRI), 294
Magnet schools, 45–46, 51
Manipulation, 12, 25
Manners, 82
  shyness and, 14–15
Mastoiditis, 293
Masturbation, 19–20, 190, 231
  anxiety as cause of, 19–20
  boredom as cause of, 20
  defining, 18
  during puberty, 190, 231, 232
  as sign of sexual molestation, 20, 96
  vaginal irritation and, 20
Math
  computers and, 218
  first grade, 40–42
  second/third grade, 128–129, 130, 154
Meals. *See* Nutrition
Measles, 271
Medication, 145
  acne, 231
  antibiotic, 276
  antiviral drug, 276
  attention problems and, 76, 77
  bedwetting, 80–81
  bronchodilator, 278
  eyedrops, 67, 145
  ibuprofen, 289
  inhalers, 67–68, 145
  nebulizers, 68
  pills, 145
  nose spray, 67, 145
  sulfa drugs, 303–304
  suppository, 304
Memory builders, 131
Meningitis/encephalitis, 267, 293–294
Menstruation, 18, 154, 226, 229–230

Methylphenidate, 77
Molestation. *See* Sexual molestation
Molluscum contagiosum, 294
Mongolian spots, 294
Montessori schools, 51
Moodiness, in nine- to eleven-year-olds,
    238–239
Moral issues and judgments, nine- to eleven-
    year-olds and, 170, 176–178, 182, 184,
    207
  girl and boy differences, 184–185
Motorcycles, 71
Motor skills, and kindergarten readiness, 36
Mourning, 162. *See also* Death, of loved person
    or pet
Mouthwash, 72
Moving
  five/six-year-olds, 83–84
  nine- to eleven-year-olds, 243
  seven/eight-year-olds, 154–156
MRI, 294
Mumps, 271, 294
Museums, 153
Music lessons, 83, 219–220
Mycoplasma, 294

Nagging, 121–122
Nebulizers, 68
Negotiation, 174–175
  chores and, 200
Nervous habits, 77–78
Ness, Evaline, 105
Nonconformists, 246–247
Nosebleeds, 294–295
Nose picking, 146
Nose spray, 67–68
  cromolyn sodium, 280
Nutrition
  five/six-year-olds, 65–66
    constipation and, 36
    meals and snacks, 65–66

nine- to eleven-year-olds, 232–233
seven/eight-year-olds, 141–143

Obedience, 149, 199
Obesity. *See* Weight
Occupational therapy, 42
Ocular herpes, 288
Openness, with nine- to eleven-year-olds, 178–185
Orthodontist visits, 79
Ostracized children, 107–108, 194, 248–249
Otitis media, 295
Outsiders, 247–248
Over-conscientious kids, 11–12
Overheating, 264

Pain
    during hospitalization, 94
    in feet and legs, 235
    groin, 285
    growing, 285
    hip, 288
    knee, 292
    neck (torticollis), 306
    in testicles, 304
Parent
    attitude toward learning, 215–217
    as coach of team sport, 139
    death of, 91–93
    divorce of, 95–96
    limits set by, 173–175
    listening skills of, 206–207
    negotiations with, 174
    nine- to eleven-year-olds and, 167–171, 215–217
    reaction to child's starting kindergarten, 55
    as role models, 154
    separation from, while child is hospitalized, 93, 162
    serious illness of, 91
    sexual discussions and, 209–210

treating child as substitute mate or parent, 119, 164, 174
Parenting effectiveness
    five/six-year-olds, 25–26
Passing out. *See* Syncope
P.A.T. (paroxysmal atrial tachycardia), 295
Patience, 11
Paying attention
    kindergarten and, 34
Pectus excavatus, 295
Pediculosis, 147, 295–296
Pee problems, 296. *See also* Urinary tract infection
Perfectionism
    in six-year-olds, 12
    in seven/eight-year-olds, 133
Permissiveness, 29–30
Personal hygiene
    girls, 20, 227
    seven/eight-year-olds, 116, 145–147
Pertussis, 271, 296
Pet
    animal bites, 276
    Cat Scratch Disease, 278–279
    death of, 91–93, 162
Petechiae, 296
Peter Pan (Barrie), quoted, 202
Petit mal seizures, 76
Philosophical differences, 183
Physical aggression, 73
Physical differences
    five/six-year-olds, 46–50
        height, 46–47
        physical abilities, 48–49
        racial or cultural differences, 47–48
Physical skills
    first graders and, 43
Piaget, 184
Pierced body parts, 227
    ears, 117, 147, 227
Pink eye, 296

Pinworms, 276, 297
Pipher, Mary, 176
Pityriasis alba, 297
Pneumonia, 70, 297
Poison hazards, 72
Poison ivy, poison oak, poison sumac, 297–298
Polio, 271
Popularity, 192–196
Port-wine stain, 298
Praise, effectiveness of
    chores and, 201–202
    encouraging effort as well as achievement, 41
    five/six-year-olds, 26–29, 74
Prejudice, racial and cultural differences and,
        47–48, 103
Primary nocturnal enuresis, 68
Privacy
    in bathroom at school, 43
    in bedroom, 203–204
    during hospitalization, 94–95
    for nine- to eleven-year-olds, 188
Proctitis, 298
Prying, 188–189
Pseudo-adults, 195–196
Ptosis, 298
Puberty
    abnormally early signs of, 68, 140
    access to information about, 173
    books concerning, 228
    discussions with friends about, 172
    emotional development during, 185–190
    onset of, 139, 140–141
        boys, 141, 230–232
        girls, 140–141, 225–230
    late onset of, 190–191
    nutrition during, 232–233
    rejecting, 191
Public self, establishing
    nine- to eleven-year-olds, 170
    seven/eight-year-olds, 100
Punishment. See Discipline

Purpura, 298
Pyelonephritis, 298

Rabies, 298
Racial differences, 47–48, 194
Rash, 298
Reading
    disabilities, testing for, 44
    first grade, 38–40
    nine- to eleven-year-olds and, 190
    second/third grade, 125–128, 154
Regression
    lack of control and, 93
Rejected (by peers) children, 107–108, 194,
        248–249
Religion, 81–82
Religious schools, 109
Relocation. See Moving
Repeating a grade, 38
    because of difficulty in one subject, 42
Reputation, importance of, 191
Resilience, 11–12
Responsibility
    five/six-year-olds, 22–24
    nine- to eleven-year-olds, 198–204
    seven/eight-year-olds, 114–121
Reviving Ophelia: Saving the Selves of Adolescent
        Girls (Pipher), 176
Rewards, 29
Reye syndrome, 299
Rheumatic Fever, 299
Ringworm, 299
Ritalin, 77
Ritual, 81–82
Role reversal (treating child as substitute mate
        or parent), 119, 164
Roller skating, 57, 266–267
Rubella, 271, 299
Rubeola, 299
Rules, 205–206
Running, 137

Safety
  bicycling, 265–266
  cars and traffic, 71, 264
  in cold weather, 263
  guns, 71–72, 264–265
  horseback riding, 269
  household, 72–73
  maturity and, 235–236
  overheating, 264
  seatbelts, 264
  skateboarding, 267
  skating, 266–267
  skiing and snowboarding, 266
  in the sun, 263–64
  team sports, 268–269
  transportation, 264
  wilderness camping, 267
Sailing, 267
Sam, Bangs and Moonshine, 105
Scabies, 299
Scalding, 72
Scarlet fever, 299–300
School
  advanced students, 50–52
  bilingual, 46
  bullying behavior in, 55
  choice of, 45–46
    magnet schools, 45–46
    year-round school, 45
  computers and learning, 216–217, 218
  curriculum objections, of parents, 52–54
  first grade challenges, 38–43
  first grade readiness, 37–38
  girl vs. boy behavior, 130–131
  homework, 131–133, 213–214
  hospitalized children and, 163
  inappropriate placement in, 77
  kindergarten
    problems, 54–55
    readiness, 33–37
  nine- to eleven-year-olds

  change in learning styles, 212–213
  homework, 213–214
  learning problems in, 172, 213
  parental assistance, 215–217
  peer pressure in, 212
  relationship with teacher, 211–212
  quality, 214–215
  refusal to attend, 54–58
  repeating a grade, 38
  responsibility for schoolwork, 22
  seven/eight-year-olds, 125
  skipping a grade, 51
  teacher problems, 53
  writing skills, 128
School bus safety, 73
Science projects, and computers, 218
Scrapes, 300
Seat belts
  in airplanes, 73
  in cars, 71, 264
  in school buses, 264
Seborrhea, 300
Secrets, 248
  family, 49–50, 179
Security, feelings of
  travel and, 84
Seizure, 76, 300–301
Self-care skills, and kindergarten readiness,
    36
Self-centeredness, 25
Self-consciousness, 100–101
Self-criticism, 12–13
Self-esteem
  five/six-year-olds, 38, 74
  nine- to eleven-year-olds, 170, 239
Sepsis, 301
Sexual behavior/sexuality
  see also Cross-sex behavior
  access to information about, 173
  learning the facts of life, 16–19, 34
  nine- to eleven-year-olds, 207

nudity, at home, 209
  parental attitudes toward, 114
  precociously sexual behaviors, 90, 210
  redirecting, 189, 210–211
  sex play
    five/six-year-olds, 20–22
    seven/eight-year-olds, 111–113
  sexual topics, discussed with parents,
      209–210
  unhappiness with sexual identity, 73
Sexual molestation
  five/six-year-olds, 17, 90, 96–97, 112
  nine- to eleven-year-olds, 251–253
  seven/eight-year-olds, 164–165
Shampoo, 72
Sharing
  five/six-year-olds, 32–33
Shaving, girls and, 227
Shingles, 288
Showers, 72
Shyness, 13–14
Siblings
  death of, 91–93
  new babies, 85–86, 157–158, 244–245
    premature or sick, 158–159
  serious illness of, 91
  sharing with, 32–33
  seven/eight-year-olds and, 121
  stepsiblings, 158
Sickle cell anemia, 300
Sighing, 301
Significance, feelings of, 170
Sinusitis, 301–302
  attention problems and, 76
Skateboarding, 57, 267
Skating, 57, 266–267
Skiing and snowboarding, 57–58, 266
Skin
  acne, 231, 234, 274
  bumps on, 234
  eczema, 282

rash, 298
  white spots on, 234
Skipping a grade, 51
Sleep apnea, 68, 276–277
  attention problems and, 76
Sleep deprivation
  and restlessness in five-year-olds, 37
Sleepovers and slumber parties, 110–111
Smoking, 113–114
Snacks. See Nutrition
Sneakers, and peeling toes, 305
Snoring, 68
Soccer
  five/six-year-olds, 60
Social dangers, 113–114
Social development
  five/six-year-olds, 13–22
    assertiveness, 15–16
    friendship, 13–15
    sexual behavior, 16–22
  nine- to eleven-year-olds, 191–197
    best friends, 196–197
    peers, 191–192
    popularity, 192–196, 215
Social studies projects, and computers, 219
Sore throat, 302
Soul, conversations about the, 92. See also
      Growth, of the soul
Spanking, 31–32
Speech
  five/six-year-olds, 68–69
Spelling, computers and, 218
Sports, 56–58
  appropriate competition, 223
  balance of activities with, 224
  feelings of competence in, 218–219, 221
  non-athletic children, 58–59
  parent as coach, 139
  skills, 83
  team
    for five/six-year-olds, 59–61

for nine- to eleven-year-olds, 219
for seven/eight-year-olds, 138–139
Sprains or strains, 302
Stammering
  five/six-year-olds, 68–69
Stealing, 105
Steroids, 302
Stevens Johnsons syndrome. *See* Erythema
  multiforme
Stomatitis, 302
Strabismus, 302
Strep throat, 303
Stuffy nose, chronic, 69
Stuttering/stammering, 303
Submissive children, 194
Sun safety, 263–264
  sunglasses, 264
Sweat test, 304
Swimmer's ear. *See* External otitis
Swimming/swimming lessons, 57, 83, 267
Swollen joint(s), 304
Syncope, 295, 304

Tachycardia, 304
Talented programs, 52
Tampon use, 229–230
Tantrums, 74–75
  as reaction against new sibling, 86
Tattling, 123–125
"Teachable moment," 5
Team sports
  baseball, 268
  fives/sixes, 59–61
  horseback riding, 269
  ice hockey, 268–269
  safety in, 268–269
Teasing, 16, 30
Teeth
  care of, 116
  problems, 304
    cavities, 281

thumbsucking and, 78–79
Television, 125
  aggressive behavior and, 73
  discussions of, 82
  eating and, 65
Tetanus, 271
Thalassemia, 304–305
Thank-you notes, 82
Thermometers, 70
Three-day measles, 271
Thumb-sucking, 78–79
Thyroid problems, and attention problems,
  76
Tics, nervous, 77–78, 149–150, 305
Ticks, 305
TMJ, 305
Toes, peeling, 234–235, 305–306
Toileting, 146
Tonsils, 68, 234, 306
  tonsillitis, 306
Torticollis, 306
Tourette syndrome, 77, 78, 149–150
Toxic Shock Syndrome, 230
Toxic symptoms, 306
Toy guns, 138
Traffic safety, 71
Trampoline, 57, 265
Transitions, readiness to make
  five/six-year-olds, 37
Travel, 84–85, 152, 240–241, 243–244
  immunizations and, 84
  required, 156
Tuberculosis, 306
Tutors
  math, 41–42
  reading, 39
Tympanogram, 306

Ultrasound, 306
Untruthfulness, 25. *See also* Honesty, encouraging

Urinary tract infection, 68, 296, 306–307
  bedwetting and, 80
Urticaria. *See* Hives

Vacation travel. *See* Travel
Vaginal irritation, 227
Vaginitis, 307
Values, 81–82
Varicella, 307
Varicella Zoster, 271
Vasculitis, 307
VCUG, 308
Virtue, 170
Viruses, 307
  fevers and, 70
Vision
  diminished
    attention problems and, 36, 76
    reading problems and, 39
Vitiligo, 307
Voice quality, 69
Vomiting, 308

Warts, 308–309
Weakness, addressing areas of, 172
Weapons, 110
Weight
  see also Nutrition
Weight (*cont.*)
  charts
    boys, 258–259

deciphering, 255–257
girls, 260–261
and diet, 65
five/six-year-olds, 61–65
  boy-girl differences, 64
  exercise and, 64–65
  growth charts, 62–63
  overweight, 62–63, 82
obesity, 295
Wet dream, 231
Wetting, 68, 79–81
What's Happening to My Body? (Madaras),
  228
Wheezing, 309
"White lies," 7–8, 30
White patches on skin. *See* Pityriasis alba
Wilderness camping, 267
"Wilderness Medicine for Children," 267
Windows of opportunity
  manners, 82
  one-to-one time, parent and kid, 240
  specific skills, 82–83, 153–154, 240–241
  travel, 152, 240–241
  values, ritual, and religion, 81–82
  weight control, 82
Withdrawn children, 194–195

Year-round school, 45
Yellowness of whites of the eyes. *See* Jaundice

Zillions: Consumer Reports for Kids, 115